HERITAGE/REALITY/VISION
1908-1983

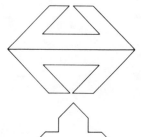

The two arrowheads represent a time line from Past to Future by which we consider our Past Heritage, our Present Strengths and our Future Vision.

Psalm 48:12-13

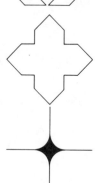

The cross at the center indicates a desire to seek God's will, and to draw from His power in our present reality.

Psalm 48:14a

The star at the center indicates our conviction that this vision is from Him.

Psalm 48:14b

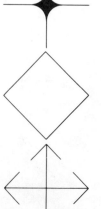

The diamond shape represents the Celebration of our 75th Anniversary.

Psalm 48:13c

The four smaller arrows represent our abiding dependence on God (vertical) and our ministry of equipping men and women for Christian service (horizontal).

TELL THE GENERATIONS FOLLOWING

A History of
Southwestern Baptist Theological Seminary
1908-1983

TELL THE GENERATIONS FOLLOWING

A History of Southwestern Baptist Theological Seminary
1908-1983

Robert A. Baker

BROADMAN PRESS
Nashville, Tennessee

Scriptures marked RSV are from the Revised Standard Version of the Bible, copyrighted 1946, 1952, © 1971, 1973.

Portraits on pages 363, 437, and 438 are by Gittings of Fort Worth, Texas.

The Campus Guide on page 528 is by Brad Price.

Dewey Decimal Classification: 286.09
Subject Heading: SOUTHWESTERN BAPTIST THEOLOGICAL SEMINARY—HISTORY
Library of Congress Catalog Card Number: 81-68737
Printed in the United States of America

Dedicated to
more than forty thousand students
who have enrolled in Southwestern
since 1908

Contents

Foreword 11

Preface 15

1. Roots of Southwestern Seminary 23

2. The Founder 53

3. Immediate Antecedents 111

4. Southwestern Seminary Founded 135

5. A Challenging Decade 197

6. Storm and Struggle 245

7. A Shining New Day 285

8. Five Golden Years 329

9. Unprecedented Growth 371

10. The Vision Will Not Tarry 445

Appendix 481

Foreword

Why another history of a Southern Baptist agency? As the Southern Baptist Convention approaches its 150th year, concern for our heritage is to be expected. Some might view this as an unnatural preoccupation with the past, reflecting the reluctance of a denomination to face the future and a desire to dwell instead on its supposed faded glories. Are all attempts to understand the past only meaningless exercises in nostalgia?

The writer of Hebrews thought not. "Remember your leaders," he wrote, "those who spoke to you the word of God; consider the outcome of their life, and imitate their faith" (Heb. 13:7, RSV). We cannot forget the leaders of our spiritual heritage, especially those of our own century. With that thought in mind, Robert Baker presents this history of Southwestern Baptist Theological Seminary.

Every day at Southwestern we are mindful that this great institution functions on a foundation built by many well-known and nameless individuals in the past. Some of the stones in that foundation are financial and administrative, providing the seminary with operating endowment income and a strong organization. Other stones in the foundation are theological, giving the seminary a widely accepted reputation for its mainstream doctrinal position. Still other stones in the foundation have to do with that indefinable spirit which is still expressed in the contemporary commitment of Southwestern to evangelism, missions, scholarship, and practical local church ministry.

Of course, the entire foundation is built upon the solid rock of our commitment to the lordship of Christ, recognizing that "other foundation can no man lay than that is laid" (1 Cor. 3:11).

It is singularly appropriate that *Tell the Generations Following* should be published now. This year marks the seventy-fifth anniversary of the founding of Southern Baptists' second oldest institution of theological education. The anniversary celebration committee has endeavored to fill the 1982-83 school year with significant events, and one of the earliest recommendations was to commission a history of the school. This committee was especially eager to employ the scholarship of Robert Baker, whose professional career in church history spans nearly forty years of the seminary's life and whose recent retirement from the lecture

11

hall allowed him the enormous investment of time needed for this task.

Except for a number of articles, no historical accounts of the seminary have appeared since L. R. Scarborough's *A Modern School of the Prophets* in 1939, and that also compels the publication of this book. *School of the Prophets* was essentially the remembrances of Scarborough up to 1937. The forty-five intervening years have seen radical changes on Seminary Hill, in the Convention, and across the nation—changes that demand to be chronicled. Professor Baker documents these and more, beginning with Southwestern's birth in the Baylor theological school in Waco, Texas.

Perhaps the most compelling reason for a new glimpse of Southwestern Seminary is a crisis of identity among Southern Baptists that becomes more apparent each year. The seventy-five years of Southwestern's existence have seen the transformation of Southern Baptists from a predominately rural, Southern, Christian sect to an enormous religious enterprise, the largest non-Catholic denomination in the United States, strongly rooted in every section of the nation.

As the Convention has stretched north and west encompassing those whose antecedents are not Southern and often not Baptist, an alarming, hazy understanding of Baptist tenets manifests itself. Who, in fact, are we? The answers come from all directions, too often phrased in shallow, theological aphorisms without historical dimension. The history of Southwestern's commitment to the faith and its response to change can be a reminder to new generations of this denomination's spiritual strength.

Finally, the sheer influence of this seminary has created an interest in its heritage. Every year Southwestern enrolls thousands of students, teaches them, prays with them, worships with them, and graduates them. These students go across the nation and around the world as witnesses to the gospel. At this writing, about 50 percent of Southern Baptists' three thousand missionaries studied on Seminary Hill. The executives of eleven of the denomination's agencies hold Southwestern degrees. The school's enrollment makes it the largest theological institution not only in the Southern Baptist Convention but in the world and probably at any time in Christian history. These are significant statistics, and the story should be told.

For those thousands of students who serve around the world, this book is a reminder of who they are. The history of Southwestern has left its imprint on all its graduates, and, in at least some sense, this spiritual heritage is more important than any familial roots. The history of this seminary is, in a way, the biography of us all.

As we observe the seventy-fifth anniversary of Southwestern, our heritage naturally points us to the reality of the present and the vision of the future. The largest student body ever assembled in a theological institution is a constant reminder to us of the present reality of opportunity which is ours. Every faculty member and staff person here at the seminary is humbled by the awesome dimensions of the present task which is ours. Coming as they do from every state of the Union and over thirty foreign countries and going out as they do around the world to minister in Christ's name, these students represent an incredible body of committed, growing witnesses. Our task then is not just educational but broadens quickly into the arena of spiritual growth and formation as well.

How else, then, could we look to the future other than with optimism and hope? Operating on a firm foundation and possessing so many present resources, the possibility of unlimited progress is encouraging— progress, that is, in quality, in greater efficiency of operation, in bold new dimensions of ministry training, and in seeing the seminary reach an even higher plateau as a staging center for a whole army of Christian workers committed to winning our world to the Lord Jesus. Heritage, reality, vision—measurements of an enterprise worthy of personal, sacrificial commitment.

Indeed, we cannot forget the past. We must return to it again and again to understand the present and discern the future. Like the Psalmist, we must remember to:

> Walk about Zion, go round about her,
>   number her towers,
> consider well her ramparts,
>   go through her citadels;
> that you may tell the next generation
>   that this is God,
> our God for ever and ever.
>   He will be our guide forever.
>   (Ps. 48:12-14, RSV)

Russell H. Dilday, Jr.
President
Southwestern Baptist Theological Seminary

Preface

In the fall of 1980, the committee charged with arranging to have a history written for the seminary's seventy-fifth anniversary on March 14, 1983, invited me to discuss this project with them. The committee consisted of James Leo Garrett as chairman, Jesse J. Northcutt from the School of Theology, Leon Marsh from the School of Religious Education, Jack Coldiron from the School of Church Music, and Wayne Evans from the administration. John Seelig later joined this committee. When Professor Garrett began his sabbatical leave in the spring of 1982, Professor Northcutt was elected as acting chairman of the committee.

At this 1980 meeting, the committee and the chief administrative officers who were present requested me to prepare the history. I was hesitant about accepting this commission for three reasons: the heart bypass surgery which I had undergone carried a prognosis of uncertainty about my longevity; my service at the seminary had bridged over half of the years of its history and rendered my objectivity questionable; and my fear that my plain writing style, adversely affected further by the short time left for research and writing before the manuscript was due on June 1, 1982, would not do justice to the significant and challenging story of the school that I love. Nevertheless, I agreed to attempt the project, and after my retirement from the faculty on July 31, 1981, I set myself promptly to the task.

The committee provided guidelines for me to follow: the book should be both readable and scholarly; it should be objective and balanced; it should emphasize the ideas that have shaped the seminary; it should magnify the faculty in a person-centered way; it should not neglect the context in which the seminary developed; and it should make use of oral history sources.

The principal sources for this story have been the trustee minutes, the personal papers of the several presidents, and the faculty minutes. The trustee minutes are complete and have been well written. The presidential papers have been helpful. Most of the early minutes of the three faculties of the seminary are missing. Many secondary works have been consulted, including books by or about the seminary presidents and faculty members, as well as other relevant titles: the *Southwestern News*, the seminary's paper (since 1943); the *Baptist Standard* of Texas and other state papers; and a few secular newspapers like the *Fort Worth Star-Telegram* and others which threw light upon some activity of the seminary. Wherever possible, oral history has been used.

Most of the resources for this study are housed at Southwestern. President Russell H. Dilday and his secretary, Nancy Morgan, made certain that every record of the seminary was made available for my research, including the restricted papers of previous presidents.

I am grateful for the generous assistance of all the administrative officers, and especially of vice-presidents Wayne Evans, John Seelig, and John Newport, as well as their secretaries, Mina Bickerstaff, Sandra Lovelace, and Evelyn R. Smith. W. Edwin Crawford, Philip Poole, Sara Stovall, Grace Wilson, Phillip Sims, Jean Bell, and Gary D. Skeen also helped me. The history committee members of the seminary interrupted their busy schedules to read each chapter as it was completed, and Professors Northcutt and Marsh prepared summaries and recollections that were valuable. Dean Jack Terry and Joe Davis Heacock, dean emeritus, also contributed recollections and evaluations.

Keith C. Wills and his staff in Fleming Library of Southwestern Seminary provided their customary excellent service. Archivist Ben Rogers was invaluable in making available the material in the Treasure Room of this seminary, and he graciously provided the lists of the trustees and the faculty found in the appendices of this book. Myrta Ann Garrett opened the resources of the Serials Division for my extensive use.

Walter Shurden and Clara McCart of The Southern Baptist Theological Seminary copied several items from the minutes of that school for me. Jess Bigbee and James C. Hill helped me obtain copies of the court records at Caldwell, Texas.

I am indebted to many persons who shared recollections of seminary history, including Bess Boone, Baker James Cauthen, Carl Clark, J. Kenneth Clark, Jerry L. Glisson, L. Jack Gray, Cal Guy, Travis Hart, Herschel H. Hobbs, Boyd Hunt, Evelyn Linebery, Albert McClellan, Kate Durham P. Morgan, Nannie Don Beaty Northcutt, and Tallie Williams.

My wife Fredona read all of the chapters and made excellent emendations that improved the story. Sue Rainey not only typed the manuscript but served as proofreader with her exceptional expertise. I am alone responsible, of course, for errors that remain.

I have tried to be accurate both in my interpretations of events and in the mechanics of documentation. Unfortunately, the hand is quicker than the eye in these areas also. I suppose that some mistakes are inevitable in collating events of another era and in the several transcriptions of hundreds of specific dates and numerous quotations. The quotations I have tried to reproduce as they appeared in the literature, occasionally inserting [sic] in the case of obvious slips. Financial statistics have been a problem because the seminary's fiscal year has differed from that of both the Baptist General Convention of Texas before 1925 and the Southern Baptist Convention since that time.

The scriptural theme chosen for the anniversary year was Psalm 48:13-14, which urges the readers to observe the bulwarks of Zion that they may tell the story to the generations following. The title of this book has been adapted from that text.

I hope that the readers of this story will share the inspiration and challenge that came to me as I watched the actors struggle to find and follow God's will. I admire them, every one, and marvel how God has used both their strengths and their weaknesses to bring this seminary to its present place of wide influence in the cause of Christ.

ROBERT A. BAKER

B. H. Carroll
Founder and President (1908-14)
English Bible (1908-14)

Trustee committee choosing site for the seminary

Fort Worth Hall
First building on campus

Charles T. Ball
Missions (1911-19)

William W. Barnes
Church History (1913-53)
Faculty Chairman (1926-48)

Walter T. Conner
Theology (1910-49)

J. W. Crowder
English Bible (1910-19)
Extension Study (1919-43)

James B. Gambrell
Ecclesiology (1912-14
and 1917-21)

Calvin Goodspeed
Theology (1908-10)

C. M. King
Business Manager (1913-51)

A. H. Newman
Church History (1908-13)
Dean (1908-13)

Jeff D. Ray
Homiletics (1908-44)

J. J. Reeve
Hebrew (1908-13)

J. B. Weatherspoon
Hebrew (1913-18)

Charles B. Williams
Greek (1908-19)
Dean (1913-19)

1

Roots of Southwestern Seminary

Founding the Southwestern Baptist Theological Seminary on March 14, 1908, demanded an audacious faith. Every indicator of the school's prospects warned of disaster. Not surprisingly, there was little sympathy for the enterprise from influential people in the political, economic, and social world who had been blistered by the scathing attacks of B. H. Carroll in the struggles for state prohibition, the sanctity of Sunday, and similar moral confrontations.

But there was also much opposition to the seminary within the ranks of Baptists both in Texas and across the South. Some were aghast at the wrenching of this department of instruction from Baylor University by what they considered political machinations. Some denied the need for another seminary as a rival to the revered Southern Baptist Theological Seminary at Louisville, Kentucky. Other Baptists noted the heavy burdens already being shouldered by Texas Baptists in their support of missions, Buckner Orphans Home, the new hospital at Dallas, and the continuing campaign for endowment by the Texas Baptist Education Commission. Still others pointed to the financial exhaustion of Texas Baptists from incessant efforts to raise money for other important causes, to the lack of any endowment for the seminary, and to the promises made to other Texas Baptist institutions that they would be given precedence in financial campaigns in Texas. The denomination was just recovering from one of the most vitriolic ecclesiastical confrontations Texas Baptists had yet known which had resulted in a schism by a portion of their number. The Whitsitt controversy, which will be discussed later, was still unsettling some, and older preachers shook their heads when they recalled the dismissal of Professor C. H. Toy of the Louisville seminary. It was also true that some Texas Baptists were not convinced that men called of God to preach would find it necessary to secure human book learning.

In some respects, it appeared that everything warred against this new seminary enterprise. The great financial depression of the previous decade still lingered; military alliances by the Great Powers of Europe ensured the outbreak of a world conflagration in the event of some relatively minor incident; philosophical and scientific pioneers were

23

laying the foundations for a newer and more radical type of antisupernaturalism; religious leaders in America were being polarized by the new
social gospel movement; and wrangling between labor and management
was causing mammoth economic, political, and social dilemmas.

Perhaps the most crucial immediate threat to the life of the new
Baptist seminary in Texas was the rapidly deteriorating health of the only
man who was capable of commanding support for the movement. B. H.
Carroll spent months in his bed during the 1890s due to illness, and at
the time of the chartering of the seminary, this "lonely deaf man," as he
called himself, had but six years of life remaining—the last two of which
found him almost constantly bedfast.

But none of these things deterred B. H. Carroll from pursuing his
convictions concerning the imperative need for a theological seminary in
Texas. Until the spring of 1905, he seemed to have been somewhat
ambivalent about what he should do. At that time he had a memorable
experience on a train speeding through western Texas. Later he pointed
to this hour as the time when God burned upon his soul the call to found
a theological seminary despite all opposition he might encounter. He
later described that overwhelming moment:

> I was passing through the Panhandle on a Fort Worth and Denver train on
> my way to Amarillo to meet my wife and baby. I had read all day and my
> eyes were exhausted. My deafness made it impracticable for me to sustain a
> conversation with people on the train. So I fell to musing. As I looked out
> over those plains over which in my youth I had chased the buffalo, there
> arose before me a vision of our Baptist situation in the Southwest. I saw
> multitudes of our preachers with very limited education, with few books
> and with small skill in using to the best advantage even the books they had.
> They are consecrated men, many of them vainly hungering for better
> training in the work to which God has called them and to which with
> singular self-sacrifice they have dedicated their lives. I saw here in the
> Southwest many institutions for the professional training of the young
> teacher, the young lawyer, the young doctor, the young nurse and the young
> farmer, but not a single institution dedicated to the specific training of the
> young Baptist preacher. It weighed upon my soul like the earth on the
> shoulders of Atlas. It was made clear to me on that memorable day that, for
> the highest usefulness of our Baptist people, such an institution was an
> imperious necessity. I seemed to hear the age-old question of God: "Whom
> shall I send and who will go for me?" I was ready to give Isaiah's answer:
> "Here am I; send me," but at once there arose before me what seemed
> insuperable obstacles. In the first place, I thought of the many struggling,
> half-equipped institutions of other important and necessary lines of our
> work and of the heavy burdens that these institutions had placed upon the
> shoulders of our pioneer people and wondered if it would be right to place
> upon this brave people yet another burden. I thought, too, of the fact that I
> am now an old man and could hardly hope to live long enough to

consummate such a gigantic enterprise. I thought, too, of my physical infirmity that would make leadership in such a movement exceedingly doubtful. It occurred to me, also, that much of my life had been given to promoting denominational enterprises and that I had hoped to give these last years to the quiet, unmolested companionship of my books and was about to dismiss the matter, feeling that I could not do it—when there came to me as clearly as if audibly spoken the assuring word of our Lord: "I am he that liveth, and was dead, and behold, I am alive for evermore." With this trumpet-tongued call and assurance of divine help resounding in every part of my being, I wrestled with the problem until at last I was irresistibly driven to say, "Lord, it is clearly thy will; what is impossible with man is possible with God; go thou with me and I will try." When I came to myself I was standing gripping the back of the seat in front of me. Becoming conscious that my fellow passengers were looking at me, some with amusement and some with amazement, I sat down, confused, embarrassed, and humiliated. But from that hour I knew as definitely as I ever knew anything, that God would plant a great school here in the Southwest for the training of our young Baptist preachers.[1]

Despite this inspirational experience which solidified the conviction of B. H. Carroll that God wanted him to spend his last years in the founding of a theological seminary in the Southwest, it would be a mistake to conclude that this movement was a root out of the dry ground. On the contrary, Carroll affirmed that ministerial education in Texas had deep roots and that he and other Texas Baptists were only agents of a God who had made preparation in history for this undertaking. In one of his last appeals to the Baptist General Convention of Texas for support of the seminary, he concluded:

At this juncture we are constrained by necessity to press our requests. If, however, you do not hear us, that does not mean that the Seminary will die. God who called it into being will not suffer it to perish. "Who knoweth whether ye are come to the Kingdom for such a time as this? But even if ye altogether hold your peace at this time, then will relief and deliverance arise from a higher source."[2]

Carroll's successor, L. R. Scarborough, reiterated that the Southwestern Baptist Theological Seminary was deeply planted in the will of God and that its roots were imbedded in the moving of the divine hand in earlier history.[3] It is clear that these historical roots not only laid the foundations for Southwestern Seminary but determined as well the character of the institution. It should not be surprising that this seminary has a passion for evangelism and missions, for it is the offspring of two sweeping historical movements which incarnated these biblical teachings. The First Great Awakening in the middle of the eighteenth century provided Baptists for Texas, while the Second Great Awakening in New England in the opening years of the nineteenth century initiated structural patterns for organized benevolent work, including ministerial education, that made it possible for autonomous Baptist churches to work together in missionary and educational enterprises.

Baptists for Texas

Before the First Great Awakening, Baptists in America had numbered only a handful scattered along the Eastern seaboard, despite more than a century of activity. In the South, for example, in 1740 there were only eight Baptist churches of record: four in South Carolina, two in Virginia, and two in North Carolina. The membership in these churches did not number over four hundred persons. But revival fires changed this. Baptists in the South were greatly advanced by the fiery preaching of George Whitefield, the Calvinistic Methodist, who for thirty years trumpeted the gospel message from New England to Savannah, Georgia, where he had founded his orphanage.[4] Not only did he inspire evangelistic and missionary activity by the eight older Regular Baptist churches, as they were called, but from two of his converts an entirely new Baptist group sprang forth, known as the Separate Baptists.

These two converts were New England middle-aged men named Shubal Stearns and Daniel Marshall.[5] Zealous, but ineffective at first, these men found their niche in God's plan in the formation of the Sandy Creek Baptist Church in central North Carolina where in 1755 they migrated with almost a dozen relatives and friends. Their program of evangelism and missions, combined with the increased activity of the older Baptists, transformed Baptists in the South.[6] By 1790, South Carolina Baptist churches had increased from 4 to 67; Virginia Baptist churches from 2 to 204; North Carolina Baptist churches from 2 to 94; and Maryland and Georgia Baptists, who had organized no Baptist churches before 1740, had formed 4 and 42, respectively. Baptists in the South had increased from 300-400 members in 1740 to 36,100 in 1790 and in addition had begun to storm the westward moving frontier.[7]

After the First Great Awakening, the trickle of Baptists moving to the West became a torrent. Virginia leaders like William Hickman and Thomas Tinsley preached to numerous Baptists in Kentucky in the spring of 1776. Half-a-dozen Virginia Baptist preachers, along with Tidence Lane of North Carolina, pushed into Tennessee by 1780. Baptist churches in these two frontier states numbered sixty by 1790. Richard Curtis of South Carolina established a Baptist foothold in Mississippi in

1798, Thomas R. Musick moved from Kentucky to eastern Missouri to form the Fee Fee church by 1807, and George Gill from South Carolina and Virginia entered Arkansas in 1814 to preach to Baptists there. These and scores of other Baptists, preachers and lay persons, carried the Baptist themes of evangelism and missions from the older seaboard states to the huge and mysterious province of Mexico known as Texas.[8]

This new land had been explored by Spanish adventurers as early as the mid-sixteenth century, but the hostility of the fierce Indian inhabitants discouraged colonization. Despite French claims based on exploration, Spain retained Texas under the Treaty of Paris in 1763 following the Seven Years' War. Even the purchase of the Louisiana Territory by the United States in 1803 did not affect Spanish claims, and by 1819 the United States formally renounced any claim on Texas. In 1821, however, Mexico successfully revolted against Spain, and it was from Mexico that Texas won her independence in 1836. Many Baptists were involved in this struggle.[9]

In the decade of Texas independence, Baptist preachers and leaders crossed into the new land from every side. Freeman Smalley forded the Red River to enter Pecan Gap in north Texas. Judge Richard Ellis, Thomas J. Pilgrim, and others penetrated the northeast gateway from Tennessee and Arkansas. Joseph Bays, Z. N. Morrell, and R. E. B. Baylor crossed the Sabine River from the east. Gail Borden and others debarked from the southern waters at Galveston.[10] The preaching of these Texas Baptists resembled that of the earlier children of the First Great Awakening: warmhearted, evangelistic, biblical, effective. Indeed, although Shubal Stearns was a small man and R. E. B. Baylor a huge one, there was little difference in their preaching. Descriptions of the sermons of the two men show them to have ministered with the same emotional earnestness and effectiveness.[11] Stearns would have rejoiced to know that his spiritual grandchildren were echoing his zealous, evangelistic preaching about a century later in a province a thousand miles to the West.

The first missionary Baptist church in Texas was formed with eight members at Washington-on-the-Brazos in early November, 1837, under the leadership of the colorful, limping Tennessee giant, Z. N. Morrell.[12] On November 7, immediately after organizing, the church addressed letters to the American Baptist Home Mission Society of New York and to the General Missionary Convention for foreign missions in Boston asking them to send missionaries to the Republic of Texas.[13] It was the response of the first of these societies which illustrates how Texas Baptists were provided a pattern for the development of ministerial education.

Pattern for Educational Activities

American Baptists struggled for more than a century to find some method by which independent Baptist churches could cooperate to promote missions, ministerial education, and similar benevolences without destroying the autonomy of the Baptist churches so involved.[14] As early as 1755, Oliver Hart, pastor of the First Baptist Church, Charleston, South Carolina, had organized the Baptist Religious Society in his church to provide support and supervision for the education of young ministers. His successor at Charleston, Richard Furman, continued this program through the Charleston Association, making it possible for many young ministers to secure an education. Furman's activity was continued after his death by the founding of the first Baptist college in the South, an institution which bore his name. Furman also won Silas Mercer of Georgia to the support of ministerial education, and Silas and his son Jesse Mercer provided Georgia Baptists the school which now bears their name.[15] Meanwhile, in 1764 New England Baptists formed Rhode Island College (now Brown University) at Warren, Rhode Island, the first Baptist school in the nation involved in the education of the Baptist ministry.

The development of structural patterns for all sorts of benevolent activity like missions, ministerial education, and Bible and tract distribution occurred in the opening years of the nineteenth century during what has been called the Second Great Awakening in New England. One of the unique results of this awakening was the unparalleled organization of structures for benevolent work by many denominations. Baptists were no exception. In 1802, Massachusetts Baptists formed a domestic mission society, as did Baptists in Maine in 1804, New York in 1806-1807, Connecticut in 1809, and New Jersey in 1811. The idea for these Baptist societies probably developed from the Baptist Missionary Society organized in 1792 in Great Britain, which initiated the modern foreign mission movement. All American Baptists joined in the formation of a national foreign mission society (called the General Missionary Convention) in 1814, a national tract society in 1824, and a national home mission society in 1832. It was to the first and last of these three national societies that the first missionary Baptist church in Texas sent her appeal for assistance in 1837.[16]

Although delayed, the response of the American Baptist Home Mission Society was the appointment to Texas of two outstanding missionaries. James Huckins, the first, a native of New Hampshire and a graduate of Brown University and Andover Theological Seminary, had been appointed as an agent to raise money in Georgia for the society and was very successful. His close friendship with Jesse Mercer likely turned his thoughts toward Texas, and he accepted an appointment to serve there. This talented man was described by R. E. B. Baylor as being "tall and slender with a quick black eye, one slightly dropped, dark hair, sallow complexion" and bold and prominent features, "particularly his nose."[17] He arrived at Galveston on January 24, 1840.

The other gifted man appointed by the Home Mission Society to Texas was William M. Tryon. Born in New York City in 1809 and orphaned at an early age, he moved to Georgia for his health in 1826. Having felt a call to preach, he entered Mercer Institute as a student in 1833. Probably through the influence of Jesse Mercer, who helped ordain him in 1837, Tryon was appointed as a missionary to Texas by the Baptist Home Mission Society in 1841. R. E. B. Baylor described him as being a little below medium height with a symmetrical figure. "His hair was dark flaxen or brown, hanging in profusion about his face; his eyes were grey and of mild expression; and his countenance, altogether intellectual, sedate, and sometimes tinged with sadness." He was an eloquent and effective preacher, sometimes "affected to tears" when addressing impenitent sinners.[18] Z. N. Morrell judged that "no preacher has ever lived in Texas who was his equal."

These two men, both well-educated and gifted, both befriended by Jesse Mercer of Georgia, both familiar with the missionary and educational structures developed during the Second Great Awakening in New England, and both sharing the missionary and educational zeal of that awakening, were joined by R. E. B. Baylor in laying the foundations for ministerial education in Texas.

R. E. B. Baylor, the third principal leader, was the grandson of the stalwart Virginia Baptist preacher Joseph Bledsoe, who had been imprisoned for preaching. Baylor was born in Kentucky in 1793. After serving in the War of 1812, he studied law and was admitted to the bar. Moving to Alabama in 1820, he served in the state legislature and later in the United States Congress. On the last Sunday of July, 1839, he was soundly converted in Talladega, Alabama, after years of avowed atheism. This church promptly licensed him to preach, and this handsome physical giant migrated to Texas to assist people struggling in "the great cause of humanity for religious and civil liberty." On January 7, 1841, the Congress of the Republic of Texas named him Judge of the Third Judicial District of Texas. The indefatigable Z. N. Morrell immediately enlisted Baylor to begin preaching, and for almost twenty-five years this devout and noble man held court during the day and preached at some Baptist church on many nights and Sundays.[19]

Thus, by 1840 the impetus of the First Great Awakening had provided a steady stream of Baptist people assaulting the western frontier, establishing churches along the route from the James and Ashley rivers to the Sabine, and finally moving into Texas both before and after the war that brought independence from Mexico.[20] Huckins and Tryon were carriers of the missionary zeal and the experience in organizational structures for supporting missions and education that developed in the Second Great Awakening in New England in the opening years of the nineteenth century.

However, this brief description of the settling of Baptists in Texas has not called attention to the great diversity in doctrine and ecclesiology among those who came. Many of them were in the tradition of the older Regular Baptists who were primarily Calvinistic in theology. Some had come from the Separate Baptist background, spiritual children of Stearns and Marshall, and were mildly Calvinistic. Fortunately, by the time Texas was being settled, these two groups were practically united and working together in benevolent causes. However, at this very time other divisive and growing parties in Baptist life were also represented among the early settlers in Texas. One important party came to be known by the various names of Primitive Baptists, Hardshell Baptists, Anti-Effort Baptists, or Old Line Baptists. This group so interpreted God's sole sovereignty that they denied any place for man's activity or service. They asserted that before the world was created God had predestined some to be saved and some to be lost, and that human efforts to win people to Christ, educate ministers, and send missionaries were not only useless but actually blasphemous in that such activities were endeavoring to take God's own work out of his own hands. They opposed missions, Sunday schools, theological education, tract distribution, and Bible societies.[21]

One of the strong antimission leaders was Daniel Parker, who was born in Virginia in 1781, reared in extreme poverty in Georgia, and converted there in 1802. Despite the lack of any formal education, he was licensed to preach and after his removal to Tennessee was ordained as a Baptist minister. After a remarkably influential ministry in Tennessee and Illinois, he organized the Pilgrim Predestinarian Regular Baptist Church in 1833 in Illinois and moved the church as a body to Texas in that year.[22] His was the first organized Baptist church of record in Texas, and he strongly advocated his antimissionary views until his death in 1844.

A Critical Confrontation

It became evident that the radical disagreement between the antieffort parties in Texas and the party of missions and education would bring conflict. In June 1840, probably through the initiative of R. E. B. Baylor and Z. N. Morrell, an attempt was made to form a Baptist association as a means of strengthening the witness of the few small Baptist churches in the Republic. About twenty-five Baptists (including four preachers) met at Independence in that month to discuss the matter. Two antimissionary preachers attended—Abner Smith and Asael Dancer. Another Baptist preacher in attendance was T. W. Cox, who had migrated to Texas from Alabama. Cox was a follower of Alexander Campbell, who had joined Baptist ranks in 1812 but by the 1830s had been declined Baptist fellowship because of his non-Baptist beliefs. Curiously, although Campbell was Arminian in theology, he was opposed at this time to any extrachurch body that might threaten the autonomy of a local church. For this reason, he and his followers rejected missionary societies and other denominational bodies.

The difficulty of forming a Baptist association to unify Texas Baptists was compounded because Cox was bitterly opposed to the two Hardshell preachers—Smith and Dancer—yet was adamant in holding his Camp-bellite ideas against the missionary views of Baylor, Morrell, Huckins, and Tryon. The critical nature of the problem was magnified because Cox was pastor of the three most important churches in the area—at Independence, Travis, and La Grange.

At the first meeting, in an effort to secure Abner Smith's cooperation, R. E. B. Baylor urged the election of Smith as moderator. At first this conciliatory policy seemed to promise success. This hope was destroyed, however. After several days of discussion, reported Baylor, "through the prayers and tears of myself and others, the stern old Calvinistic brother Smith softened down a little and drew up a platform of principles to which we all assented except Elder Cox. . . ." A shouting match between Smith and Cox dissolved the meeting without any action being taken.[23]

On October 8, 1840, another attempt was made to form an associational body without the presence of Smith and Dancer. Only three churches with a total of forty-five members sent messengers: three attended from Independence, three from Travis, and four from La Grange. Since Cox was pastor of these churches, it is not surprising that he was chosen moderator. Z. N. Morrell and James Huckins were not present, the former being ill and the latter having gone to New York to confer with members of the Home Mission Society.

These ten messengers organized the first Baptist association in Texas on October 9, 1840, naming it Union in the hope that it might draw together the scattered Baptist constituency in Texas. The influence of the Campbellite views of Cox can be seen in an interesting "Bill of Inalienable Rights" which was adopted. This magnified the sole authority of the local body and asserted that each member of a church should forever have the right to exercise his own discretion as to whether or not he should contribute to the support of missions and other benevolences.[24] Cox's influence may also be glimpsed in the sixth article of faith, which was Arminian in its wording.

The critical clash between the missionary and antimissionary parties occurred in the second meeting of the Union Association at the La Grange church on October 7, 1841. In March of that year, William M. Tryon, who was associated with Cox as pastor of the Independence church, found that Cox was openly following the teachings of Alexander Campbell. Tryon endeavored to counter these. Meanwhile, Baylor, who had become associate pastor with Cox at the La Grange church, had learned that Cox had been dismissed from the Talladega church in Alabama for financial fraud. When the Union Association gathered at La Grange for the second annual meeting, Cox preached two sermons which contained, according to Morrell, Huckins, and Tryon, "the errors embraced in the system commonly known as Campbellism."[25] Morrell publicly protested against these views, resulting in a church trial of Cox at La Grange. As a result, Cox was excluded from the La Grange church.

The friends of missions and education promptly took advantage of this victory. Through the influence of Tryon, Baylor, and Huckins, two societies were formed after the pattern of those developed in the Second Great Awakening: a home mission society for cultivating the Texas field and the Texas Baptist Education Society "for establishing an academical and theological institution."

Beginnings of Ministerial Education in Texas

Early leaders of Texas Baptists have marveled that a handful of Baptists on the extreme western frontier would even consider the founding of a college at this early stage in their development. Many Baptists, particularly those on the frontier, had the attitude that education could often "spoil" preachers. Most Baptist preachers not only were unpaid and forced to spend most of their time making a living for their families but even gloried in their lack of compensation and education as evidence that God had called and equipped them for ministry without "man-made" institutions. It is impossible to read the accounts of many Baptist pioneers of this period without detecting a note of hostility toward a "hireling" clergy that viewed ministry in a professional sense and counted education as a tool of self-advancement. But Baptist attitudes were changing at this very time. Since Baptist preachers received their pastoral calls from congregations composed of lay members, the rapid increase in general education reminded the Baptist minister that he must be adequately prepared to lead his flock which now was composed of educated people. Texas Baptists were fortunate that their early leadership contained many well-trained lay people and ministers, and prejudice against ministerial training was minimal from the very beginning of Texas Baptist history. The prompt interest in ministerial education on the Texas frontier is explained by the background of men like Tryon, Huckins, Baylor, and others.

The victory of promissionary, proeducation, and proeffort leaders over the antieffort forces in 1841 was critical for the missionary and educational advance of Texas Baptists from that day to the present. These early pioneers preserved the evangelistic and missionary thrust of the First Great Awakening and utilized the structural patterns of the Second Great Awakening in New England for the early organization of missionary and educational societies. This story must deal primarily with the educational aspect of Texas Baptist history, for the roots of Southwestern Seminary are found in this activity.

Various writers have named different men as being responsible for the earliest educational efforts among Texas Baptists. Frederick Eby pointed to Huckins;[26] Lois Smith Murray magnified the leadership of Baylor;[27] Baylor himself said that Tryon suggested the idea.[28] There is enough glory for all of these and for the hundreds of other men and women who gave sacrificial support to the educational movement during its early struggles. Some of these are not even mentioned in many of the accounts. The original Education Society elected Baylor as president, S. P. Andrews as recording secretary, William M. Tryon as corresponding secretary, and J. L. Farquhar as treasurer. The first board of managers included Stephen Williams, a layman, and four ministers—Hosea Garrett, N. T. Byars, Richard Ellis, and Z. N. Morrell.[29]

At the suggestion of Tryon, Baylor applied to the Texas Congress for a charter for a school on December 28, 1844. The title of the institution had not been discussed until it became necessary to affix a name in the charter. Against Baylor's protests, Tryon insisted that the school be named Baylor University in the charter signed on February 1, 1845. It is the only school of the fifteen chartered by the Republic of Texas to survive to the present.[30]

There has been some confusion about the purpose of the school. Although ministerial education was certainly in the minds of the founders of Baylor University, the school was not simply a place for the training of the ministry. The charter called for "an institution of learning," and in 1844 Huckins wrote:

> It was resolved to found a Baptist university in Texas upon a plan so broad that the requirements of existing conditions would be fully met, and that would be susceptible of enlargement and development to meet the needs of all the ages to come.[31]

The founding of a literary school to lay the foundations for the training of ministers was the normal method of ministerial education at this time. In this way, young ministers were given a good classical background and were provided lectures in certain aspects of theological training when the situation permitted. The skills of the pastoral ministry were usually acquired by a program of internship. Young preachers were permitted to move into the home of an older minister and accompany him to funerals, weddings, revivals, worship services, and to participate in the performance of other pastoral duties. The neophyte also was allowed to use the minister's library and to receive personal instruction in such important items as the preparation and delivery of sermons, how to make pastoral visits, ministerial ethics, and the like. This intern-type method of educating young ministers continued into the twentieth century in many parts of the country.[32] When it was not convenient for the young minister to live in the home of the older man, he would follow the other procedures in a more informal fashion.

As a matter of fact, it would have been totally impracticable to have established a school solely for theological training in Texas at this time. There simply were not enough young ministerial students to maintain such a school. As late as 1851, for example, Baylor University reported only two ministerial students, and the first ministerial student to graduate received his diploma in 1856.[33] There is no question that Baylor at Independence emphasized the education of the ministry. Each of its five presidents was a Baptist minister, as were many of its longtime trustees and fund raisers, boards of visitors, and university lecturers. Even in the awarding of honorary degrees, Baptist ministers were the principal recipients.[34]

The charter of Baylor University was typical of those secured in the founding of other schools by educational societies. All authority over the

school was vested in a board of trustees, whose members and replace-
ments were named by the Texas Baptist Education Society. After
receiving bids from several interested communities, the trustees chose
Independence as the site of the school. This was a happy choice in many
respects. Independence was situated in the beautiful, undulating valley
of the Yagua Creek in Washington County and already was becoming a
denominational center for the increasing band of missionary Baptist
people. The church there was strong and would be closely related to the
new Baptist school. Four of the five Baylor presidents would also serve as
pastor of the Independence church, and the students found themselves
in a laboratory of Baptist life as they attended the services and
denominational meetings at the church. How awed they must have been,
for example, when President Rufus C. Burleson prostrated himself on
the floor of the church and prayed that he might be forgiven if he had
spoken offensive and unchristian language about a brother in the
church.[35]

The first president of Baylor University was Henry Lee Graves, termed
by J. M. Carroll as "a princely gentleman, a ripe scholar, a strong and
dignified convention presiding officer, and a splendid school man."[36]
Graves was born in North Carolina and graduated from the University of
North Carolina. Converted as a student at this school in 1831, he taught
mathematics briefly at Wake Forest College. Then in 1837, after being
ordained to the ministry and teaching briefly in a Baptist high school in
Georgia, he attended Hamilton Literary and Theological Institute at
Hamilton, New York, from 1840 to 1842. He was teaching at Covington,
Georgia, when the invitation to become president of Baylor University
came in 1846.[37] The cause of ministerial education in Texas suffered a
great loss in the year after President Graves arrived, when William M.
Tryon died in the yellow fever epidemic at Houston.

A significant action took place in 1848. The Union Baptist Association, meeting at Houston in 1847, had passed a resolution urging the
formation of a state body. On September 8, 1848, fifty-five messengers
from twenty-one churches gathered at Anderson in Grimes County and
organized the Texas Baptist State Convention. At this meeting, a
Committee on Education consisting of James Huckins, Richard Ellis,
and A. C. Horton reported on the importance of education and resolved:

> That we regard the efforts of the trustees of Baylor university to build up,
> and so to endow and furnish that institution, as that it shall be able to give a
> thorough and polished education, as a subject deeply interesting to every
> Baptist, and that we commend that institution to their prayers, their
> affections, and to their liberal support.

The resolution continued by asserting that the demand "for a holy and learned ministry in this country" calls for "our ministers and brethren generally" to take up at least one yearly contribution "for the purpose of aiding those young men in procuring a suitable education, who shall give evidence of being called of God to preach the gospel."[38] Doubtless this action caused the Texas Baptist Education Society, whose trustees were struggling to keep the young school solvent, to authorize J. W. D. Creath to present a communication to the State Convention in the following year asking that Creath, A. G. Haynes, and J. L. Farquhar (all representing the Texas Baptist Education Society) be authorized to confer with a committee from the state body

> relative to the propriety of obtaining from the Legislature an alteration in the charter of Baylor University, giving the power to fill all vacancies in the Board of Trustees, into the hands of the convention.[39]

J. M. Maxcy of Huntsville responded with a resolution to appoint a committee of five to confer with the committee from the Education Society. At the last session of the State Convention in 1849, Creath as chairman of the Education Society's committee and Maxcy as chairman of the convention's committee recommended that the state legislature should be petitioned to amend the charter of Baylor to permit the convention to fill vacancies in the Board of Trustees of Baylor University. The State Convention approved this action.

At the next meeting of the convention in Huntsville in 1850, Maxcy reported that the legislature had complied with the request of the Education Society and the convention and had amended the charter of Baylor University to show that the convention would hereafter name the board of trustees for the school.[40]

This action was much more significant than might appear at first glance. At this very time, two methods of supporting denominational benevolent activities were competing for acceptance among Baptists. Beginning about 1755, home mission work was included by Baptist associations as a part of their regular denominational program. In England in 1791, when the Northampton Association refused to adopt William Carey's plan for carrying the gospel to the South Sea Islands, he turned to an alternative method which has become known as the society plan. Under this plan, the individuals interested in carrying out some benevolence simply pooled their financial resources and provided active support for that benevolence without recourse to any structured denominational body like an association, state convention, or even national convention. Most of the benevolent activity which developed as a result of the impact of the Second Great Awakening utilized this society method. This became the accepted method of carrying on benevolent work of almost every kind among Baptists in the North. Baptists who formed the Southern Baptist Convention in 1845, on the other hand, deliberately chose to foster their benevolences through a strictly denominational body after the associational pattern.[41]

The critical weakness of the society plan, especially relative to benevolences such as Christian education, was that under this method the denomination might lose the ownership of an institution. A small educational society or self-perpetuating board of trustees acting as an educational society could become so financially dependent upon generous givers who were not Baptists that they would relinquish denominational control in order to preserve the life of the institution. This is how Baptists lost Brown University, Providence, Rhode Island, their first school, as well as Columbian College, now George Washington University in Washington, D.C. When the trustees of a school or some other institution are elected by a general denominational body, however, it becomes impossible for the denomination to lose the institution since any untoward action by the trustees could result in the election of new trustees by the denominational body.

Whether these considerations induced the Texas Baptist Education Society to offer Baylor University to the State Convention or not cannot be determined, due to the lack of records of the society. The action of the Education Society could have been prompted by the hope of additional support for the struggling school without reference to denominational strategy. It should be noted, however, that just three years earlier the Southern Baptist Convention had been organized with the denominational type of structure which deliberately turned away from the society plan; also, Brown University, organized on the society plan, was being lost to the Baptist denomination during this very period.

However, the only observable result during the next several decades was the polarization of Texas Baptists when additional territorial denominational bodies developed. By 1885, there were five of these territorial denominational bodies in Texas, and when any one of them fostered a school (as several did), this action promptly alienated constituents of the other territorial conventions from any institutions fostered by competing bodies. Perhaps the alienation between the several conventions in Texas was not as marked or as deep as J. M. Carroll suggested in his story of Texas Baptists, but it was evident that many Baptists in Texas turned away from Baylor because of the rivalry involved between competing Baptist territorial conventions.[42]

When President Graves resigned in 1851, after five years of service, only two ministerial students were then enrolled in Baylor. Graves's successor was Rufus C. Burleson, who became a dominant figure in Texas Baptist and Texas public educational activities for the next generation.[43] Burleson was an Alabamian, precocious as a child, who was converted in 1839 in his sixteenth year. He forsook his plans to become a lawyer and began preparing for the ministry. After teaching five years in Mississippi, he was ordained in 1845 and in the following year entered the ill-fated Western Baptist Theological Institute at Covington, Kentucky, which was soon destroyed because of the slavery-abolitionist controversy.[44] During his study there he became interested in Texas and upon his graduation was reported to have lifted his arms towards the West and cried, "This day I consecrate my life to Texas." One Texas historian, in noting the short life of the Covington school, remarked that if the institute had done nothing more than graduate Rufus C. Burleson, it had well repaid all of the investments, prayers, and efforts made to establish it.

Burleson was appointed to Texas by the Home Mission Board of the Southern Baptist Convention and arrived in January, 1848, to become mission pastor of the First Baptist Church, Houston, to replace the lamented William Tryon. On January 3, 1852, shortly after accepting the Baylor post, Burleson married the daughter of James R. Jenkins, one of the charter members of the first missionary Baptist church in Texas at Washington. Jenkins became a well-to-do lawyer, plantation owner, and congressman and was counted in the inner circle of early Texas Baptist leaders.

Impressive in appearance and gifted as a speaker and scholar, Burleson worked tirelessly for the success of the young school at Independence. Probably his outstanding achievement at the school was the broadening and liberalizing of the classical curriculum.[45] The first catalogue included a course in "Evidences of Christianity" as a part of the curriculum, although only one ministerial student (D. B. Morrill) was identified. A ministerial student was also allowed to take Hebrew instead of a modern foreign language.

Evidently the new president seriously considered taking a large step in ministerial education. Reference was made in the November, 1851, meeting of the Baylor board of trustees to a large committee which had been appointed to consider the organization of a theological department at Baylor. At the December 13 meeting, this committee reported that it was not expedient at that time to do so. It was suggested that instead of initiating this major effort President Burleson should

arrange such young men in a Theological class and give them whatever
instruction he may be able, also that Brother Baines be requested to deliver
to said class lectures on Pastoral Theology.[46]

Perhaps one of the reasons Burleson broached the question of a
theological department for Baylor at this time was the imminent demise
of his alma mater, the Western Baptist Theological Institute at Covington,
Kentucky. Because of Northern-Southern friction over slavery, this
institution, located near the Ohio border and staffed with a divided
faculty (half were proslavery and half were proabolition), had only one
student in 1849. The sectional animosities of the next few years
destroyed the school.[47] Meanwhile, the controversy over the Covington
school caused Baptists in the South to consider establishing a theological
school of their own. This subject was agitated in Southern Baptist
Convention meetings from 1847 until 1859 when The Southern Baptist
Theological Seminary was opened at Greenville, South Carolina.[48] It is
interesting to notice that President Burleson of Baylor was named by the
Texas Baptist State Convention in 1858 to be a messenger to the Southern
Baptist Convention at which the developments in ministerial education
leading to the opening of the seminary at Greenville were being
discussed on every hand.[49] Perhaps it was familiarity with these
Southwide developments and the annual cry by the Committee on
Ministerial Education for additional ministers that led the State Convention at its 1859 meeting to adopt a resolution presented by the Committee
on Ministerial Education (chaired by Horace Clark) as follows:

> That we deeply feel the necessity of ministerial and theological
> education, and recommend to the Board of Trustees of Baylor University to
> inquire into the propriety of establishing a Theological Department as early
> as in their wisdom they deem it can be permanently done; and that
> arrangements be made for courses of theological lectures to be delivered for
> one or two months in each year, to which all of the ministers of this
> Convention shall be invited.[50]

Baylor's trustees promptly discussed this resolution. I. A. Fortune,
W. W. Harris, Pressley O'Kief, H. F. Pahl, J. Pruett, C. H. Schmeltzer,
M. M. Vanderhurst, and D. N. Wheat had been enrolled as ministerial
students during this year. Burleson had been giving them instruction as
best he could, although his long absences for raising funds and enlisting
students made this training rather haphazard.

> The plan which was most acceptable to the friends of ministerial
> education and training, was to secure the services of two learned and pious
> Theologians, to spend three months in the University during the sessions,
> and deliver courses of lectures on Systematic and Pastoral Theology,
> Homiletics, Biblical Interpretation and Church History. The sessions of the

Theological Department were expected to embrace the winter months,
when the least work was done by the preachers of that day owing to the
scattered condition of the churches, and their consequent inacessibility
during bad weather. This would enable young pastors and missionaries to
attend the lectures.[51]

Burleson made it plain, however, that he was not trying to establish a
rival to the newly-opened seminary at Greenville, South Carolina. He
was thinking of a Department of Theology such as the one at Union
University in Tennessee, where ministers who "from age or other causes
are prevented from pursuing a more extended course" studied. Only
young ministers who had been licensed by their churches to preach the
gospel would be allowed to attend these lectures.

Unfortunately, when this plan was begun in December, 1860, two
factors destroyed its effectiveness: civil war was just beginning, and a
long smoldering feud between President Burleson and Principal Horace
Clark of the Female Department brought a shattering explosion. This
feud probably had its roots in a controversy that took place over the
question of state aid to Baylor at almost the very time Burleson accepted
the Baylor presidency.[52] The antagonism accelerated during the following
decade, and on April 29, 1861, Burleson gave notice that he would
resign the presidency of Baylor on June 27 to accept the presidency of
the Waco Classical School. Most of Baylor's faculty and the seven
members of the senior class also accompanied Burleson to Waco.[53] The
antecedents of ministerial education in Texas through Baylor University
thereafter assumed a dual form: the continued efforts of Baylor at the old
Independence center and the activities in this direction by the new
university and rival of Baylor located at Waco. The remaining years of
ministerial education at Independence will be discussed first, then a
word will be added relative to such training in Waco University.

Baylor University at Independence

The removal of Burleson and the faculty to Waco brought a crisis to the
Independence school. The prospects for all educational institutions were
harmed greatly by the outbreak of the Civil War. After bitter debate,
Texas seceded from the Union and became a part of the Confederacy.
Some of the students and faculty promptly enlisted in the Confederate
army.

At the July meeting of the trustees in 1861, George W. Baines was
named president of Baylor. The choice was a good one. This fifty-two-

year-old North Carolinian had come to Texas by way of Georgia, Alabama, Arkansas, and Louisiana, having engaged in a rich ministry as teacher, preacher, and editor. He was known to the trustees through his service as pastor of the Independence church in 1851-52 and as a member of the board until 1859. At the end of his one year of service as president of Baylor, Baines declined reelection, mentioning principally the state of his health.[54]

No president was found for the 1862-63 session of Baylor, and the school limped along with as much help as trustees G. W. Graves and B. S. Fitzgerald could provide. Finally, on August 16, 1863, after months of negotiation, the board elected William Carey Crane as the new president of the school. He was the oldest son of the outstanding Baptist deacon William Crane of Virginia and Maryland. He had been thoroughly trained in classical and theological disciplines at Richmond College, Columbian College, and Colgate University. After his ordination in 1838 at Baltimore, he had served as pastor in Alabama and Mississippi and had been president of several colleges in Mississippi and Louisiana.[55] J. M. Carroll termed Crane "the best equipped college man that had ever been in Texas." His dedicated service from 1863 until his death in 1885 can be documented from his revealing diary preserved in the Texas Collection of Baylor University. Crane had good reason for his oft-criticized moodiness: he sacrificed the years of his mature scholarship, his personal funds, and his health in his strenuous efforts to keep Baylor alive.

He could not have been pleased with the action of the State Convention which met at Independence in 1863 shortly after his election as Baylor's president. It is true that Baylor was named first in the discussion of ministerial education, but equal time was given to praising Baylor's rival, Waco University, as well as the Baptist college at Tyler. Crane constantly resisted Burleson's efforts to bring Waco University into the same relationship to the convention that Baylor enjoyed, although it must be said that the advantages of this relationship appeared to be of rather dubious value during most of Crane's presidency. The school lived from crisis to crisis because of the lack of financial support and of students. Between 1863 and 1867, the convention reports mentioned the claims of Waco University and other schools, as well as the work at Baylor.

Nothing had been done about the Theological Department for Baylor which had been discussed before civil war had come. In 1863 the State Convention passed a resolution requesting that the trustees "make, as soon as practicable, arrangements for theological instruction to such young ministers as may repair to that Institution for that purpose, . . ."[56] In the following year, the trustees reported that they had established a theological chair and appointed President Crane as the professor of theology, urging upon the convention "the great importance of initiating measures for the endowment of said Chair."[57] In response, the state body passed a resolution requesting the trustees "to employ, as soon as the condition of the country will allow it, an agent to secure endowment for the Theological Chair, and to increase the endowment of the Chair." To the chagrin of Crane, the resolution continued by urging the support of other Baptist educational institutions in the state, none of which was under the patronage of the State Convention.[58] A brief word in the 1865 minutes of the convention urged that "at an early day" the theological professorship at Baylor be endowed. Little was said at the convention about the claims of Baylor in 1866, but in 1867 an event occurred which favored the sole allegiance of this convention to Baylor. The Baptist Convention of Eastern Texas, which had broken away from the State Convention in 1853, had reorganized as the Texas Baptist General Association in 1867 and received the support of the Waco Baptist Association, which was fostering Waco University. Consequently, the minutes of the State Convention in 1868 expressed approval for Baylor University only.[59]

A significant movement occurred in 1868. R. E. B. Baylor introduced a resolution at the meeting of the State Convention to reorganize the old Texas Baptist Education Society. In the following year, it was recommended that this be done. A setback for the school came in 1871, however, when some messengers felt that the claims of Baylor were being too strongly pressed upon them. After the report of the school, a resolution was passed asserting that anything in Baylor's report "calculated to convey the idea that any past, present, or future action of this Convention, can impose upon Baptists any moral obligation" in the support of Baylor was denied.[60] Later the same day, this resolution was softened by another which affirmed that there was no intention "to disparage the claims of the Institution to the sympathies and prayers of the Baptist denomination of the State of Texas."

Bringing encouragement to Baylor in its ministerial education, however, was the reorganization of the old Texas Baptist Education Society. The original society had turned over the operation of the school to the new State Convention in 1848, as described heretofore. Thereafter the society promoted ministerial education in Baylor as a principal item, although complete records of its activity have been lost. Z. N. Morrell spoke of the meeting of the society in 1858, when the treasurer, J. W.

Barnes, reported almost seven hundred dollars on hand for ministerial education. In 1860, the society had $211.74 in the treasury for that purpose.[61] The war evidently suspended the operations of this society and displaced its records.

Z. N. Morrell wrote his reminiscences praising the work and bewailing the loss of the earlier Education Society in 1872, just before it was resuscitated. In support of his assertion that the society would provide excellent support for ministerial education among Baptists if it were still in existence, Morrell told the story of James H. Stribling, the first ministerial student to be assisted by the old society. Morrell recalled that in 1845 he had been asked to preach at the Dove Baptist Church in Burleson County, and in order to provide young Stribling an opportunity for pastoral experience, he had invited him to go along. Morrell continued:

> For nearly nine years I had, with others, been praying the Lord of the harvest to raise up young men in Texas to preach the glorious gospel of the blessed God. Nearly all our ministers then at work had been borrowed from the old States. The few that had been ordained in Texas, so far as I then knew, had been converted elsewhere. Here was a youth converted in Texas, and impressed to enter upon the ministry,—the first case of this kind we met. At the Saturday meeting the young brother was put forward to open the services, notwithstanding all his objections and great timidity. We went to Caldwell expecting to stay two days, but continued a meeting of great interest for about six. The young brother was put forward at every service, and required to work. He would frequently falter, and sometimes stand with his finger pointing upwards for nearly a minute, without uttering a word. . . . During the meeting, old brother Pruitt, who will receive notice at the proper time, and I covenanted to pray to the Lord to loose the young brother's tongue. Just as we were about to close this meeting and return to our homes, brother Stribling rose, in the midst of a weeping congregation, and asked permission to speak. God loosed his tongue on that spot, beyond all question, for about five minutes, and he has not been tongue-tied since.[62]

It is quite likely that Morrell's praise of the work of the original Education Society in his book that was published about 1872, along with the resolution of R. E. B. Baylor, led directly to the reorganization of the old body.

On October 4, 1872, at a mass meeting in Independence, a committee was named to make recommendations about the possibility of re-forming the old society. That committee brought the following resolution:

> Whereas, the Baptist Educational Society of Texas, organized in the year 1841 in the days of the Republic, has been reposing since the late war; and
> Whereas, during its active existence its efficiency was patent in

educating young men called of God to preach the everlasting gospel of the Son of God, and fostering our literary institutions; and

Whereas, the hearts of many young men are now burning with love to God and the souls of the human family, and asking aid at our hands to educate them in the ministry, and,

Whereas, the constitutions and other papers of the society have been lost, therefore,

Resolved, that we now reorganize the said Society and adopt the following constitution, which embodies the original, with certain emendations.

The reorganization was accomplished, naming as its officers Henry L. Graves, president; J. W. D. Creath, R. C. Burleson, and F. M. Law, vice-presidents; William Carey Crane, corresponding secretary; J. T. Zealy, recording secretary; Charles R. Breedlove, treasurer; and J. H. Stribling, James E. Harrison, and James M. Williams, executive committee.[63] About fifty signed as members, including most of the old guard and several women.

The reorganization of this society made an immediate impact upon the life of one young man. James M. Carroll was twenty years old and married. He desperately wanted to enter school in preparation for the ministry but had no funds. He thought about entering Waco University, located in the same town where his older brother B. H. Carroll had just become pastor at the First Baptist Church, but his brother, who had been present at the reorganization of the society, advised him to seek assistance from the new society and attend Baylor at Independence.[64] In the first year after the reorganization of the society, the following young ministers were helped by its gifts: Charles B. Hollis, M. M. Haggard, A. F. Ross, M. F. Miller, James M. Carroll, James R. Horne, Julian K. Pace, and George W. Baines, Jr. Three other young ministers were enrolled at Baylor also.

Most of the emphasis upon ministerial education at Baylor University thereafter until 1885 originated with this society. Its minutes were generally published along with those of the State Convention. It offered a resolution in 1876 urging that each pastor aid an agent of the society in raising funds for young Baylor ministerial candidates and another resolution in 1877 calling for the completion of the building at Baylor which had been commenced before the war intervened.[65] A cyclone on February 27, 1882, severely damaged most of the buildings of the school at Independence, but President Crane personally led in the collection of funds to repair the campus.

During the twenty-two years of Crane's presidency, the program of ministerial education at Independence continued in about the same fashion as before. There was little change in the curriculum for ministerial students, for Crane was a firm believer that the basic classical course was the best preparation for a minister. Perhaps he was influenced in this also by the fact that The Southern Baptist Theological Seminary (initially located at Greenville, South Carolina, in 1859 and moved to Louisville, Kentucky, in 1877) was now looked upon as the proper place to complete the training of a minister who had taken the classical course in a university.

President Crane fought valiantly to forward Baylor's cause. He watched closely for any movement to help the school. The efforts begun in 1870 to concentrate Baptist support in a single new university crept wearily through an entire decade, but the desired unity did not come.[66] The hopes raised by the formation of the General Baptist Education Convention in 1870 were dashed.[67] The agitation in 1871 for a Texas university system composed of Texas denominational colleges bore no fruit for Baylor.[68]

It is an interesting note that in 1873 the ministerial students formed the Richard Fuller Theological Society at Baylor, named after the eloquent preacher of Baltimore who had been a longtime advocate of ministerial education. After 1873, some distinguished minister would deliver a baccalaureate sermon before this society as a part of the commencement program. A missionary sermon was also preached at this time each year. The number of ministerial students between 1872 (when the Education Society was reorganized) and 1885 (when President Crane ended his service) averaged about ten each year, a marked increase over the number attending Baylor before the society began rendering assistance. In 1883, in his report on ministerial education, George W. Baines said that not less than eighty men had been trained for the ministry at Baylor; F. M. Law had estimated the year before that about one hundred had been aided. J. M. Carroll's figures suggested that probably the latter figure was accurate by 1885.[69] The kind of help given involved cash, livestock, provisions, and the like. An announcement on August 1, 1884, remarked that students for the ministry "can mess in Creath Hall by clubbing to purchase room furnishings and provisions."[70]

Before describing ministerial training at Waco University after Rufus C. Burleson moved there in 1861, a word should be said about the contributions to ministerial education made by Baylor University at Independence. Each of the five presidents was uniquely equipped to serve the institution; each struggled sacrificially to keep the school solvent; and each was totally committed to the education of the ministry.

Z. N. Morrell never tired of praising the sons of Baylor at Independence in the ministry. Typical are his encomiums of early graduates of the school. Reference has been made to the tentative and backward attempts by J. H. Stribling to preach when he began his ministry and enrolled in Baylor. After his tongue was loosed, Stribling became one of the most fruitful Baptist leaders of his generation. From his first pastorate at Gonzales beginning in January, 1851, until his death on August 13, 1892, at the home of Major W. E. Penn, the great Texas evangelist, Stribling won great multitudes to Christ by his ministry and blessed his school and denomination by his effective service. J. M. Carroll judged that he was "probably the most universally loved pastor in all the several thousand preachers of our Texas Baptist ministry."[71]

A similar example was Stribling's close friend, David B. Morrill. James Huckins discovered Morrill in a successful and profitable enterprise as part owner of a stage line between Galveston and Matagorda. That Morrill possessed excellent business acumen was evidenced by his having purchased valuable Galveston property for investment purposes. When Huckins noticed that Morrill carried a Bible and often studied it on the stage, he boldly challenged the young man to leave his worldly prospects and become a ministerial student at Baylor. Morrill did so and became a close friend of Stribling. They studied hard together during the weekdays, and on Sundays the two preached in all of the surrounding neighborhoods. Their revival on New Year's Creek, where over seventy-five were converted, was one of the outstanding revivals of those early years.[72]

Were one to multiply a life like that of Stribling or Morrill by about one hundred, he might gain an accurate impression of the value of the Independence venture in ministerial education.[73]

Also, the importance of the church at Independence must not be overlooked, as she complemented the efforts of the school in the training of ministers. Here served such outstanding lay people as O. H. P. Garrett, A. G. Haynes, John McKnight, D. B. Madden, B. S. Fitzgerald, General Sam Houston, George W. and Charles R. Breedlove, Willett Holmes, J. M. and W. L. Williams, John Stribling, W. H. Cleveland, George B. and Fannie B. Davis, T. J. Hairston, Henry Haynes, and many more. Before the pulpit of this church had knelt for ordination such preachers as Stribling and Morrill, H. C. Renfro, Horace Clark, F. Kiefer, Pickney and W. W. Harris (who baptized B. H. Carroll), J. M. Carroll, J. K. Pace, J. A. Bell, J. R. Horne, F. S. Rountree, Z. C. Taylor (the dedicated missionary), Bennett Hatcher, J. W. Anderson, W. G. Wood, and many other effective preachers of God.[74] More of the meetings of the old Baptist State Convention were held at this church than had assembled at any other three places in these early years, and most of the Executive Board meetings also met here. Strong foundations were laid at Independence for the large growth made by Texas Baptists, and the thrust for ministerial education here changed the history of the Baptist denomination.

Waco University

It will be recalled that Rufus C. Burleson moved from Baylor University at Independence to become president of Waco University in 1861. The Waco school was begun as a male school by the Trinity River Association, which had been organized in 1848 and within a few years included McLennan County as a part of its territory. This association had planned to open a female school also, but that project did not materialize. The Waco school was opened in 1856 as the Trinity River Male High School, with S. G. O'Bryan as its first president. Classes were conducted initially in the building of the First Baptist Church, Waco.

On February 2, 1860, the school was chartered under the name of the Waco Classical School. In November of that year, the Waco Association was formed and became the sponsor of the school. John C. West, the principal of the school, resigned on January 1, 1861. Word had come to the trustees of the school that Burleson might be available, along with his faculty. In September, 1861, J. W. Speight, president of the trustees, reported to the association that on September 2 the school had secured R. C. Burleson as president and the faculty of the Male Department of the Independence school as teachers. This action was approved by the association.[75] Evidently at the suggestion of Burleson, the name of the school had been changed by charter amendment on August 28, 1861, to Waco University.[76]

The work of Burleson at Waco began under difficult circumstances. Civil war had erupted in the spring of 1861, and many teachers and students of the school enlisted in the army. Even Burleson himself served as chaplain of the Fifteenth Texas Regiment for about a year before the trustees of the school requested his return. Despite the problems involved in the war, the reports of the school were optimistic. Ministerial education continued. In 1864, for example, the school reported that two of the school's young preachers had become chaplains in the army and another was still in school. In 1866, reference was made to the "successful operation" of the theological department where two young men were preparing for the ministry. Evidently "lectures and instructions

in theology" formed the basis of the theological department.[77] W. C.
Buck, the former Kentuckian and outstanding minister, was secured as a
teacher for this department.[78] In 1871, B. H. Carroll reported that the
school had "educated and otherwise assisted" fifteen young ministers,
besides gratuitous instruction to preachers' children.[79]

Meanwhile, the significant development of 1867, already mentioned,
gave new direction to the school. Because of disagreements about the
opening of a female school at Tyler during the meeting of the Baptist
State Convention in 1852, many of the Baptists in eastern Texas had met
in November, 1853, at Larissa and organized the Texas Baptist General
Association as a rival to the State Convention. This took the name of the
Baptist Convention of Eastern Texas in 1855, but in 1867 it was
reorganized as the Baptist General Association. In that year, the Waco
Association passed resolutions endorsing the new body and sent
messengers to assist in its formation. After this time, the General
Association became an advocate of Waco University. In 1873, the
Ministerial Education Board of the General Association was placed in
Waco, and in that year pledges taken at the Waco Association for young
ministers at the Waco school totaled $240, two hundred pounds of pork,
and fifty bushels of corn.[80] More important, in 1881 the Waco Association
passed a resolution to the effect that "at the request of said University,"
the supervision of Waco University as heretofore exercised by Waco
Association under the provision of the charter of that institution, "be,
and the same is hereby transferred to the Baptist General Association of
Texas."[81] Evidently this transfer was not completed until 1883, shortly
before consolidation took place.

The Movement for Consolidation

As J. M. Carroll has pointed out, the rivalry between Baylor at
Independence and Waco University was such that only the death of
President Crane of Baylor or of President Burleson of Waco could have
brought about a consolidation of the two schools.[82] There had been
efforts earlier to remove Baylor to some habitat other than Independence, and the "central Baptist university" movement of the 1870s
involved the possible removal of Baylor. However, supporters of the old
school refused to move or consolidate it as long as William Carey Crane
was alive. Nevertheless, as will be later related, in a surprisingly short
time and with an unusually fine spirit, consolidation of Baylor at
Independence and Waco University was achieved on December 9, 1885,

during the brief presidency of Reddin Andrews, with the relocation of Baylor Female College delayed until shortly thereafter.[83] The consolidation of the Baptist State Convention and the Baptist General Association insured a united sponsoring body for the new school. The Independence property was returned to the Union Association, while the new school at Waco was named Baylor. Friction between two conventions and two schools was eliminated, but the rivalry between the two principal Baptist papers, which will be discussed briefly hereafter, continued to accelerate.

This story, sketched only briefly, has attempted to identify the genetic factors that prepared the way for the founding of Southwestern Seminary and the earliest efforts in Texas to provide Baptist ministerial education. Texas Baptist literary schools other than Baylor at Independence and Waco University helped in the training of young ministers before 1886 (when the Independence and Waco schools were consolidated), but the immediate precursor of the seminary was Baylor University at Waco. By 1886, a new giant had come upon the ministerial scene in Texas. His name was Benajah Harvey Carroll. According to Frederick Eby, it was Carroll who was chiefly responsible in 1886 for the successful consolidation of Baylor at Independence (which Carroll had attended as a youth) and Waco University and who was the man whom God led to establish a new Baptist seminary in the Southwest.[84] In the following chapter, this story will be continued with the introduction of B. H. Carroll and his preparation for the task which God had given him to complete in his last years.

Notes

1. Jeff D. Ray, *B. H. Carroll* (Nashville: Baptist Sunday School Board, 1927), pp. 136-38.

2. *Proceedings of the Baptist General Convention of Texas* for 1910, p. 81 (hereafter cited as *Proceedings*, BGCT).

3. Lee R. Scarborough, *A Modern School of the Prophets* (Nashville: Broadman Press, 1939), pp. 17 ff.

4. For a good account of George Whitefield's ministry see L. Tyerman, *Rev. George Whitefield*, 2 vols. (New York: Anson D. F. Randolph & Company, 1877).

5. Robert A. Baker, *A Baptist Source Book* (Nashville: Broadman Press, 1966), pp. 16 ff.

6. The best story of the Separate Baptist movement is William L. Lumpkin, *Baptist Foundations in the South* (Nashville: Broadman Press, 1961).

7. Robert A. Baker, *The Southern Baptist Convention and Its People 1607-1972* (Nashville: Broadman Press, 1974), pp. 75 ff.

8. Ibid., pp. 86-93, 118-43.

9. For this story see Robert A. Baker, *The Blossoming Desert* (Waco: Word Books, 1970), pp. 13 ff.

10. Ibid., pp. 24 ff.

11. See Baker, *Source Book*, p. 17, for a description of Stearns's preaching, and compare Baker, *The Blossoming Desert*, p. 50, for Baylor's warmth and emotion.

12. Baker, *The Blossoming Desert*, pp. 28-30.

13. Ibid., pp. 37-38.

14. For this development see Baker, *Southern Baptist Convention*, pp. 94-101.

15. See Norman W. Cox, ed., *Encyclopedia of Southern Baptists*, 2 vols. (Nashville: Broadman Press, 1958), I:849-52. A third volume was published in 1971 by the same press with Davis C. Woolley, ed. All volumes will be hereafter cited as *Encyclopedia*.

16. Baker, *Southern Baptist Convention*, pp. 104-17.

17. R. E. B. Baylor to J. H. Stribling, 13 April 1871, from Holly Oak, Texas, the Texas Collection, Baylor University Library, Waco, Texas.

18. Letter of R. E. B. Baylor to unknown addressee, 1 March 1859, from Holly Oak, Texas, the Texas Collection. See also Z. N. Morrell, *Flowers and Fruits in the Wilderness*, 4th rev. ed. (Dallas: n.p., 1886), pp. 134-35. For Tryon's life see *Encyclopedia*, II:1431.

19. Baker, *The Blossoming Desert*, pp. 41-44.

20. Ibid., pp. 17-52, for a detailed account.

21. For a description of one of these groups see Baker, *Source Book*, pp. 78 ff and also Baker, *Southern Baptist Convention*, pp. 150-53.

22. For Parker's life see *Encyclopedia*, II:1071.

23. Baker, *The Blossoming Desert*, p. 75.

24. J. M. Carroll, *A History of Texas Baptists* (Dallas: Baptist Standard Publishing Co., 1923), p. 175.

25. Baker, *The Blossoming Desert*, p. 79.

26. L. R. Elliott, ed., *Centennial Story of Texas Baptists* (Dallas: Baptist General Convention of Texas, 1936), p. 129.

27. Lois Smith Murray, *Baylor at Independence* (Waco: Baylor University Press, 1972), pp. 21-24.

28. Ibid.

29. Ibid., pp. 21-22.

30. Ibid., p. 25.

31. Ibid., p. 23.

32. See Baker, *Southern Baptist Convention*, p. 84. See also letter dated 18 May 1911 from E. C. Routh, Lockhart, Texas, involving this type of internship, File 180, B. H. Carroll Papers, Fleming Library, Southwestern Baptist Theological Seminary, Fort Worth, Texas.

33. J. M. Carroll, p. 233, and Murray, p. 384.

34. Murray, pp. 361 ff.

35. Ibid., pp. 186-87.

36. J. M. Carroll, p. 233.

37. Murray, pp. 75-76.

38. *Organization and Proceedings of the Baptist State Convention of Texas* (Huntsville: Banner Printers, 1848), p. 10 (hereafter cited as *Proceedings*, State Convention).

39. Ibid., 1849, p. 3.

40. Ibid., 1850, p. 7.

41. See W. W. Barnes, *The Southern Baptist Convention* (Nashville: Broadman Press, 1954), pp. 3-10.

42. J. M. Carroll, p. 423.

43. For Burleson's life see Georgia J. Burleson, comp., *The Life and Writings of Rufus C. Burleson* (Waco: By the Author, 1901).

44. W. C. James, comp., *History of the Western Baptist Theological Institute* (Louisville: Baptist World Publishing Co., 1910).

45. See J. D. Bragg, "Baylor University 1851-1861," *The Southwestern Historical Quarterly* 49 (July 1945):52-53.

46. Murray, p. 110.

47. See *Encyclopedia*, II:1486.

48. For this story see Barnes, pp. 125-33.

49. *Proceedings*, State Convention, 1858, p. 25.

50. Ibid., 1859, p. 14.

51. Burleson, p. 184.

52. Murray, pp. 102-104.

53. Ibid., pp. 175-96. See also *Proceedings*, State Convention, 1861, p. 11.

54. Murray, p. 210.

55. See *Encyclopedia*, I:328, for Crane's life.

56. *Proceedings*, State Convention, 1863, p. 2.

57. Ibid., 1864, p. 9.

58. Ibid., p. 5.

59. Ibid., 1868, p. 15.

60. Ibid., 1871, p. 8.

61. Morrell, pp. 216-17.

62. Ibid., pp. 218-219.

63. J. M. Carroll, p. 375.

64. Ibid., p. 376.

65. *Proceedings*, State Convention, 1876, p. 9, and 1877, p. 10.

66. Murray, pp. 259-62.

67. Ibid., p. 262.

68. Ibid., p. 269.

69. J. M. Carroll, p. 523.

70. Murray, p. 292.

71. J. M. Carroll, p. 720.

72. J. B. Link, *Texas Historical and Biographical Magazine*, 2 vols. (Austin: n.p., 1891-92), 2:656.

73. For other outstanding leaders see J. M. Carroll, p. 234.

74. Ibid., p. 136.

75. Ibid., pp. 405-7.

76. Burleson, p. 426.

77. J. M. Carroll, p. 409.

78. Ibid.

79. Ibid., p. 412.

80. J. L. Walker and C. P. Lumpkin, *History of the Waco Baptist Association of Texas* (Waco: Byrne-Hill Printing House, 1897), p. 63.

81. J. M. Carroll, p. 543.

82. Ibid., p. 525.

83. Ibid., pp. 639 ff.

84. Elliott, p. 158.

2
The Founder

Jeff D. Ray never forgot the first time he saw B. H. Carroll. Ray had just completed study at the University of Pennsylvania, and in January, 1880, he entered Waco University at the age of twenty—both as a student and part-time teacher. He could not help comparing the splendid buildings and modern equipment of the Pennsylvania school with the "small, dilapidated, inadequate buildings and the utter absence of laboratory, library, or other equipment" which he found at Waco. Even the student body and faculty seemed "raw and ragged" compared with the Eastern people. The building of the First Baptist Church in Waco had burned in the previous year, and at this time the church was worshiping in a "dingy little, unplastered, crudely furnished room called the college chapel." Dejectedly, Ray drifted into the Sunday morning service.

> The whole atmosphere intensified my cynicism and I was conscious of a wicked sense of scorn for the whole procedure. The song finished, a man arose on the platform. He stood for a moment without uttering a word. What a striking figure! As handsome as Adonis—as preeminent in physique as King Saul!—as vibrant with personal magnetism as Absalom! At once my youthful soul began to uncover in his presence. When he spoke his voice was as full of melody and witchery as Kreisler's violin. The first words that he uttered were these: "If I were an infidel, as I once was . . . ." I remember nothing else he said that day, but having myself just emerged from a nightmare of skepticism, my soul by a telepathic instinct knew that it had found a brother. When the service ended I asked a man who the preacher was. He looked at me with evident surprise, and said, "That is B. H. Carroll." I had never heard of him before, but from that hour I have sustained for him an uninterrupted period of extravagant admiration and passionate devotion.[1]

B. H. Carroll was the man whom God was preparing to found the Southwestern Baptist Theological Seminary. He had a distinguished appearance. He towered six feet four inches and wore a full brown beard which, like his hair, would turn silver within another decade. His deep gray eyes seemed to dance as he affably conversed with friends, but in a high moment of preaching they were piercing in their intensity.

Any single sermon of B. H. Carroll revealed his remarkable gifts as a preacher. Straightforward and relevant in his style, he enhanced his sentences by pertinent allusions to the ancient classical writers and to the history of many nations. His retentive memory seemed to gather up every important reference in Scripture and literature bearing upon the subject of his message. With effortless skill, he quoted long poetic passages illustrating some point he was making. His preaching moved the congregation and convinced doubters. Though not yet forty years of age, he was already recognized as one of the oustanding pulpit orators of the Southern Baptist Convention.

When one first studies a person like B. H. Carroll, one must always wonder what factors in the man's background and training could produce a leader of this quality. In the case of Carroll, the story has some unusual aspects.

Carroll's Early Years

B. H. Carroll was an infidel for the first twenty-one years of his life. He sketched these years in perhaps his most famous sermon, entitled "My Infidelity and What Became of It."[2] His father was a self-educated Baptist minister, preaching—mainly without compensation—to village and country churches. His mother was "a devoted Christian of deep and humble piety." The boy was born on December 27, 1843, on a farm near Carrollton, Mississippi, one of twelve children of Benajah and Mary Eliza Carroll. This godly couple also adopted twelve additional orphans to rear. To support this huge family the father engaged in farming, but to fulfill his calling he preached whenever he had the opportunity. The large family moved to Drew County, Arkansas, probably in 1850, and in the fall of 1858 they loaded their goods into an ox wagon, a horse wagon, a hack, and a buggy and set out for Texas. Not knowing exactly where they were going, they settled finally near Caldwell in Burleson County. The boy Harvey rode a mule most of the distance, usually far ahead of the caravan and engrossed in a book, which explains why he occasionally was separated from the remainder of the family.

Some of the characteristics of the father were reproduced in his sons—their huge bodies, high spirits, love for books and reading, and their "concentrated energy."[3] From his mother, B. H. Carroll surely gained his unselfish disposition and generous nature.[4] This lad, however, displayed some attitudes and endowments that differed from those of his family during these early years.

For one thing, the mix of his inheritance, environment, and disposition produced in him an insatiable hunger to learn everything about his world and to feed that appetite by digesting thoroughly every book that he could find. He developed a remarkable memory from this constant study, and even as a boy in Arkansas he had been able to make a good showing in debates with his friends. On this trip to Texas, he spent the evenings reading by the camp fire and the days consuming more books as he perched on the bony mule. His brother J. M. Carroll, also a good scholar, recalled:

> Even in the days of his early boyhood twenty hours consecutive reading was nothing unusual, and very often the whole twenty-four hours of the day. . . . To read all night was a common thing.

This may account for the hints that are found in recollections by B. H. Carroll's family that the preacher often suffered from insomnia during his mature years.

> He read history, all history, ancient, mediaeval, modern, civil, political and religious; biography and autobiography he absolutely devoured. He read all science, all romance, all poetry. For at least sixty of his seventy-one years, he averaged reading 300 pages a day. . . . Only a little while before his death he was known to average 1,000 pages a day for ten consecutive days.

His younger brother also recalled the exceptionally retentive memory. To illustrate how B. H. Carroll's mind recorded even the details involved in his reading, his brother wrote:

> On one occasion I went to Waco to see him. Without knocking, I walked into his study. He was writing an article for some paper. He raised his head, saw who I was (I had not seen him for months) and simply remarked, "Hello, Jimmie; wait awhile; I will talk to you directly; I am nearly through this article." He did not stop to even shake hands with me, but continued his writing, and in a moment he raised his head and said to me, "Jimmie, you can help me a little and I will get through quicker. I want a book. It is in a certain room" (which he designated as there were books in all the halls and in every room on the place). He continued his writing, but told me how to find and recognize the book. It was in a certain case on the third shelf from the top about sixteen inches from the left-hand of the shelf. I found the book instantly, just where he said, and carried it to him. He did not lift his head. He kept writing and simply said, "You can find what I want;" (I had never read the book). "I want only to refresh my memory on a story." He hesitated for one brief moment from his writing, and then said, "Look— on page—about 143—about one-third of the way down the page and you will find the story." I looked and it was there. I then asked him, "How long since you read this book?" He answered, "At least fifteen years." "Have you looked at it since?" "Not once." His memory in many other things was just as striking and remarkable as his memory of books.[5]

This sort of story might cause some raising of eyebrows were it not for the fact that many other men and women have displayed, perhaps to a lesser degree, this same ability. Similar stories about Carroll were told by too many trustworthy witnesses to make this an apocryphal account.

It is not surprising to learn, then, that by the time he was sixteen years old Carroll had a library "very nearly, if not quite as large, as the one he had at his death. He spent all that he made for books."[6] He had attended school briefly in Arkansas before moving to Texas. Arriving at Caldwell when not quite fifteen years of age, this young giant standing over six feet tall enrolled in the school of T. K. Crittenden which was located about two miles from his home. After his first school year, the teacher, capable of teaching college students, said to the boy, "Harvey, I can't teach you any further; you know more now than I do." Harvey then began gathering the younger children in the home to teach them elementary subjects.

In addition to his hunger for learning, young Carroll displayed an unusual attitude for the Carroll family: Amid a family of devout Christians and preachers, he was an avowed infidel. It seems strange that this lad, born and reared in a fine Christian home and faced every day with a dedicated preacher-father and loving Christian mother, developed an anti-religious attitude at a very young age. In his autobiographical sermon, Carroll said that he had become an infidel even before he knew what infidelity meant.

> There were no infidel books in our home library, nor in any other accessible to me. My teachers were Christians, generally preachers. There were no infidels of my acquaintance, and no public sentiment in favor of them. My infidelity was never from without, but always from within.

When no more than thirteen years old, he said, he had already become skeptical of the truth of Christianity and had eagerly sought out books dealing with infidelity. He later analyzed the character of his skepticism of those early years. He said:

> By a careful retrospect and analysis of such of them as memory preserves, I now know that I never doubted the being, personality, and government of God. I was never an atheist or pantheist. I never doubted the existence and ministry of angels—pure spirits never embodied; I could never have been a Sadducee. I never doubted the essential distinction between spirit and matter: I could never have been a materialist.
>
> And as to the origin of things, the philosophy of Democritus, developed by Epicurus, more developed by Lucretius, and gone to seed in the unverified hypothesis of modern evolutionists—such a godless, materialistic anti-climax of philosophy never had the slightest attraction or temptation for me. The intuitions of humanity preserved me from any ambition to be descended from either beast or protoplasm. The serious reception of such a speculative philosophy was not merely a mental but mainly a moral impossibility. I never doubted the immortality of the soul and conscious future existence. . . .

> But my infidelity related to the Bible and its manifest doctrines. I
> doubted that it was God's book; that it was an inspired revelation of his will
> to man. I doubted miracles. I doubted the divinity of Jesus of Nazareth. But
> more than all, I doubted his vicarious expiation for the sins of men. I
> doubted any real power and vitality in the Christian religion.

During a protracted revival meeting in Arkansas when he was
thirteen, young Carroll mechanically answered questions by zealous
church workers about desiring to be saved, and without experiencing any
inner change, was baptized and voted into a Baptist church. This
experience only deepened his infidelity.

> My answers had been educational. I did not believe that the Bible was
> God's revelation. I did not believe its miracles and doctrines. I did not
> believe, in any true sense, in the divinity or vicarious sufferings of Jesus. I
> had no confidence in professed conversion and regeneration. I had not felt
> lost nor did I feel saved. There was no perceptible, radical change in my
> disposition or affections. What I once loved, I still loved; what I once
> hated, I still hated.

So young Carroll asked the church to withdraw fellowship from him on
the ground that he was not converted. They asked him, instead, to read
the Bible and pray. He read the Bible repeatedly, but, in a reflection of
his unregenerate state, spent most of his energy seeking for "contradic-
tions and fallacies, as they seemed to me, from Genesis to Revelation."

In the fall of 1859, young Carroll applied for admission to Baylor
University at Independence, about twenty miles from his home; and
President Rufus C. Burleson, after examining him, enrolled him in the
junior class. Burleson was particularly impressed with Carroll's gifts as a
speaker and debater. He had doubtless been informed of the young man's
prowess. One of the favorite stories around Caldwell related how Carroll
took the affirmative side of the question of whether the followers of
Alexander Campbell were right in their doctrines. He won the debate.
He then promptly took the negative side and won that also. This suggests
the precocity of the sixteen-year-old boy who was not at that time
religiously inclined.

Upon entering Baylor, Carroll was soon recognized as the best debater
in school. This may not sound impressive in the context of present-day
extracurricular activities, but at that time the school debates were the
equivalent of today's football, baseball, basketball, track, tennis, and
golf competitions combined. During his two years at Baylor, Carroll
debated twice each week and was greatly feared as an adversary.[7] He
continued to read everything that he could find whether it was Christian
or skeptical.

What a multitude of them of both kinds! Hume, Paine, Volney,
Bolingbroke, Rousseau, Voltaire, Taylor, Gibbon, et al, over against
Watson, Nelson, Horn, Calvin, Walker, and a host of others. In the
meantime I was in college, devouring the Greek, Roman and oriental
philosophies.[8]

When Carroll entered Baylor in 1859, he discovered that among the
student body of 275 were 8 young men studying for the ministry. Of
course the official records could not report how much young Carroll
enjoyed debating with them and many times vanquishing them. Among
these young preachers were two brothers, Pinckney and W. W. Harris,
both of whom were ordained at the Independence church in 1860. The
latter was already renowned for his eloquent and zealous preaching and
received the nickname "Spurgeon," after the outstanding London Baptist
minister. Doubtless Carroll and "Spurgeon" Harris had little in common
during their Baylor days as they studied and debated, but the day would
come when they would embrace in a baptismal pool.

With the outbreak of the Civil War in the spring of 1861, "worn out in
body and mind," Carroll volunteered to serve in McCullough's Texas
Rangers, the first regiment mustered into the Confederate service. On
April 10, 1861, along with his brother Andrew Fuller and a dozen young
volunteers, he began the ride from Caldwell to the San Antonio frontier,
about two hundred miles distant. It is rather curious that he joined the
Rangers and was mustered into Confederate service, because in his
debating at Baylor he had consistently argued (as did Sam Houston) in
favor of remaining within the United States instead of seceding.

In his autobiographical sermon, Carroll then described a tragic
incident in his life which became a very sensitive point during the
remainder of his days. He said:

> But now came another event. I shall not name it. It came from no sin on my
> part, but it blasted every hope and left me in Egyptian darkness. The battle
> of life was lost. In seeking the field of war I sought death. By peremptory
> demand I had my church connection dissolved, and turned utterly away
> from every semblance of Bible belief. In the hour of my darkness I turned
> unreservedly to infidelity. This time I brought it a broken heart and a
> disappointed life.

These cryptic words have caused much curiosity on the part of many
about what took place at this time. His brother J. M. Carroll made no
reference to the event in his account of B. H. Carroll's life, nor did J. B.
Cranfill. Jeff D. Ray simply remarked:

> Then came his life's great tragedy. I shall not describe it, nor even discuss it
> further than to say that I lived four years in the community where it
> occurred and I know that everybody there acquitted him of blame in the

tragic transaction, and there was no spot on earth where he was more honored and trusted than in that community.[9]

Some have conjectured that he accidently killed a friend, as did George W. Truett in later years; others have surmised some unspeakable sin. The truth can be found in the Carroll papers.[10] The two Carroll boys, Andrew Fuller and Benajah Harvey, returned from the frontier on a furlough on November 8, 1861. Their father had been severely hurt in an accident at the farm, and it was believed that he would soon die. On this furlough, the teenage infidel boy fell deeply in love with a young lady of the community (who is named in the material), and they were married on December 13, 1861. It did not take long for everyone to realize that this immature lad's heart had led him to mistake the young woman's character. Her actions demanded that the marriage be dissolved because of fornication, and this was done. Devastated by this experience and the death of his father not long thereafter, young Carroll transferred from the Ranger service to the regular army, and he was assigned to the Seventeenth Regiment of Texas Infantry. In his bitterness and infidelity during his service in the army, he became the dread of the preachers who attempted to minister among the troops. His brother noted:

> It was not an unusual thing for him, while in the army, to mount a stump or log and reply to the preachers who preached to the soldiers. More especially was this true if the preacher happened to have any vagaries. He thoroughly knew orthodoxy. He was always a dreaded antagonist. His knowledge of all subjects, his wit, his sarcasm, his logic, his eloquence, made him almost irresistible in debate. Every soldier would stop and listen when he arose to speak. He would speak on any subject and on any occasion. He was a born debater and loved it from his youth up. No wonder all preachers dreaded him.[11]

Young Carroll showed himself to be a good soldier. His colonel praised him as a gallant man who was always on the firing line and behaved with marked courage. He participated in the battles of Perkins Landing on April 30, 1863, Milliken's Bend on June 7, 1863, and Mansfield on April 8, 1864. At Milliken's Bend he led the charge on the enemy's breastworks through a half mile of open field, miraculously escaping death. He and his two brothers, Andrew Fuller and Laban, fought side by side during the four years of battle. James M., another brother, remarked that during these four years Harvey's infidelity and bitterness had full sway and the lad seemed to care little for his life. "He sought the most dangerous duties and volunteered for all the most hazardous enterprises." He was not to escape unscathed. At the battle of Mansfield on April 8, 1864, his thigh was pierced by the enormous ball of the "Minnie rifle."

The bullet passed between the bone and the femoral artery, grazing both. In those days of crude surgery, a hair's breadth variation either way would have meant certain death. His brother Laban, a Samson in strength, 6 feet 4½ inches in height and weighing 200 pounds, found him, picked him up and carried him two miles off the battlefield.[12]

Many years later a monument was placed on the battlefield at Mansfield, Louisiana, honoring the heroic Confederate General Polignac, and a gavel made of wood from a tree under which Carroll and others were first treated was presented to Southwestern Seminary in honor of B. H. Carroll.

After a partial recuperation in a little cottage near the field of battle, B. H. Carroll and John West, a young comrade, returned to Caldwell. Both were hobbling on crude crutches, which they were forced to use for several months. Young Carroll's wounds finally healed, but he suffered from the effects of this severe physical injury during the remainder of his life.

This was a desperate period for B. H. Carroll. Cynical and resentful, he faced a difficult hour. The war had maimed him, and along the way he had picked up the tobacco habit which he never abandoned. The debts of his family were overwhelming, and remunerative work was scarce. He courageously assumed the obligations of his widowed mother and set out to provide a living for the younger children and orphans in the home. He soon opened a school in the community known as Yellow Prairie, about five miles from his home, attracting a number of children; after about a year he moved it to Caldwell. During this spring of 1865 he learned about the surrender of General Lee at Appomattox and the fall of the Confederacy. Another war, one within himself, would also soon end.

In his sermon Carroll revealed that his great trials in the wounding of his heart and his body seemed to have driven him to seek for a healing truth. He said:

> Happy people whose lives are not blasted may affect infidelity, may appeal to its oracles from a curious speculative interest, and may minister to their intellectual pride by seeming to be odd. It was not so with me. With all the earnestness of a soul between which and happiness the bridges were burned, I brought a broken and bleeding, but honest heart to every reputed oracle of infidelity. I did not ask life or fame or pleasure. I merely asked light to shine on the path of right. Once more I viewed the anti-Christian philosophies, no longer to admire them in what they destroyed, but to inquire what they built up, what they offered to a hungry heart and a blasted life. There now came to me a revelation as awful as when Mokanna, in Moore's "Lalla Rookh," lifted his veil for Zelica.
>
> Why had I never seen it before? How could I have been blind to it? These philosophies, one and all, were mere negations. They were

destructive, but not constructive. They overturned and overturned and overturned; but, as my soul liveth, they built up nothing under the whole heaven in the place of what they destroyed. I say nothing; I mean nothing. To the unstricken, curious soul, they are as beautiful as the aurora borealis on arctic icebergs. But to me they warmed nothing and melted nothing. No flowers bloomed and no fruit ripened under their cheerless beams. They looked down on my bleeding heart as the cold, distant, pitiless stars have ever looked down on all human suffering. Whoever in his hour of real need, makes abstract philosophy his pillow, makes cold, hard granite his pillow. Whoever looks trustingly into any of its false faces looks into the face of a Medusa, and is turned to stone. They are all wells without water, and clouds without rain.

I have witnessed a drouth in Texas. The earth was iron and the heavens brass. Dust clouded the thoroughfares and choked the travelers. Water courses ran dry, grass scorched and crackled, corn leaves twisted and wilted, stock died around the last water holes, the ground cracked in fissures, and the song of birds died out in parched throats. Men despaired. The whole earth prayed: "Rain, rain, rain! O heavens, send rain!" Suddenly a cloud arises above the horizon and floats into vision like an angel of hope. It spreads a cool shade over the burning and glowing earth. Expectation gives life to desire. The lowing herds look up. The shriveled flowers open their tiny cups. The corn leaves untwist and rustle with gladness. And just when all suffering, trusting life opens her confiding heart to the promise of relief, the cloud, the cheating cloud, like a heartless coquette, gathers her drapery about her and floats scornfully away, leaving the angry sun free to dart his fires of death into the open heart of all suffering life. Such a cloud without rain is any form of infidelity to the soul in its hour of need.

Who then can conjure by the name of Voltaire? Of what avail in that hour is Epicurus or Zeno, Huxley or Darwin? Here now was my case: I had turned my back on Christianity, and had found nothing in infidelity; happiness was gone, and death would not come. The Civil War had left me a wounded cripple on crutches, utterly poverty stricken and loaded with debt. The internal war of infidelity, after making me roll hopelessly the ever-falling stone of Sisyphus, vainly climb the revolving wheel of Ixion, and stoop like Tantalus to drink waters that ever receded, or reach out for fruit that could not be grasped, now left me bound like Prometheus on the cold rock, while vultures tore with beak and talons a life that could suffer but could not die.

In this condition young Carroll approached his twenty-second year. He had vowed never to put his foot into another church house. His mother, however, persuaded him to attend a Methodist camp meeting at Caldwell in the fall of 1865. The preacher's sermon left him unmoved. But at the close of the service, the unnamed vessel of God asked some questions of the audience, and at a venture his gospel arrow smote the young, scornful infidel. "You that stand aloof from Christianity and scorn us simple folks, what have you got?" he inquired. "Have you found anything worth having where you are?" "Are you willing to try it now; to make a practical, experimental test, you to be the judge of the result?" The preacher then quoted a different translation of an old Scripture, saying, "Whosoever willeth to do the will of God, he shall know of the doctrine whether it be of God." This struck young Carroll because it emphasized that "the knowledge as to whether the doctrine was of God depended not upon external action and not upon exact conformity with God's will, but upon the internal disposition."

For a second time in his life Carroll made his way to the front of a church, but quickly arrested the excitement of those who knew him by saying that his heart was as cold as ice and that he was only agreeing to make an experimental test of the truth and power of the Christian religion.

> The meeting closed without any change upon my part. The last sermon had been preached, the benediction pronounced, and the congregation was dispersing. A few ladies only remained, seated near the pulpit and engaged in singing. Feeling that the experiment was ended and the solution not found, I remained to hear them sing. As their last song, they sang:
> "O land of rest, for thee I sigh,
>   When will the moment come
> When I shall lay my armor by
>   And dwell in peace at home?"
> The singing made a wonderful impression upon me. Its tones were as soft as the rustling of angel's wings. Suddenly there flashed upon my mind, like a light from heaven, this scripture: "Come unto me all ye that labor and are heavy laden, and I will give you rest." I did not see Jesus with my eye, but I seemed to see him standing before me, looking reproachfully and tenderly and pleadingly, seeming to rebuke me for having gone to all other sources for rest but the right one, and now inviting me to come to him. In a moment I went, once and forever, casting myself unreservedly and for all time at Christ's feet, and in a moment the rest came, indescribable and unspeakable, and it has remained from that day until now.

At that time Carroll made no public expression of the change that had come to him, but spent the night wondering if he would feel the same way when the morning came.

> When I reached home, I said nothing about the experience through which I had passed, hiding the righteousness of God in my own heart; but it could not be hidden. As I was walking across the floor on my crutches, an orphan boy whom my mother had raised noticed and called attention to the fact that I was both whistling and crying. I knew that my mother heard him, and to avoid observation, I went at once to my room, lay down on the bed, and covered my face with my hands. I heard her coming. She pulled my hands away from my face and gazed long and steadfastly upon me without a

word. A light came over her face that made it seem to me as the shining on the face of Stephen; and then, with trembling lips, she said, "My son, you have found the Lord." Her happiness was indescribable. I don't think she slept that night. She seemed to fear that with sleep she might dream and wake to find that the glorious fact was but a vision of the night. I spent the night at her bedside reading Bunyan's "Pilgrim's Progress." I read it all that night, and when I came with the pilgrims to the Beulah Land, from which Doubting Castle could be seen no more forever, and which was in sight of the heavenly city and within sound of the heavenly music, my soul was filled with such a rapture and such an ecstasy of joy as I had never before experienced. I knew then as well as I know now that I would preach; that it would be my lifework; that I would have no other work. [13]

A few days after this conversion experience, a dramatic scene occurred. W. W. "Spurgeon" Harris, Carroll's schoolmate at Baylor in 1859-60, came to Caldwell for a preaching service. The records do not show whether Carroll sent for him or if Harris had heard of Carroll's conversion and had come to rejoice. When they had last met in Baylor University at Independence, Harris was the eloquent preacher, Carroll the gifted infidel, and each recognized this adversary relationship. Now, six years later, the two tall young men clasped hands in a new fellowship. In nearby Davidson Creek, Harris immersed B. H. Carroll while repeating the words of the baptismal service. Despite a shortened ministry by reason of an early death, Harris became a part of the vast stream of blessings that flowed from the life of the man he baptized that day.

The records of the Caldwell church showed that on the fourth Sunday (27th) of May, 1866, B. H. Carroll was licensed to preach. He was appointed as a messenger to the Sunday School Convention at Plantersville on the fourth Sunday of June (24th), and in the following month he was shown as the moderator of the church conference. The next church record was dated November 15, 1866, at which time a presbytery composed of M. Cole, a Brother Gage, W. T. Allbright, and J. S. Allen set him apart for ministry by ordination with the laying on of hands. [14]

J. M. Carroll, who knew his older brother as well as almost anyone could, aptly commented about him:

The early Christian life of the young convert, even though his conversion was nearly as bright as that of Paul, was no smoothly running thing. The devil did not let go without a struggle. Many hard battles had to be fought. B. H. Carroll was naturally a proud Lucifer and fearfully quick tempered. Even to question his honor meant war.

But then he added. "Grace did more for Harvey Carroll than for any other man I have ever known. Never was a life more thoroughly made over."[15]

The Effective Pastor

All of the gifts that B. H. Carroll had developed to oppose the gospel of Jesus Christ were now utilized in its defense and proclamation. Within a few weeks after his baptism, Carroll preached his first sermon at Caldwell. Shortly thereafter a revival meeting was held in Caldwell. Although Carroll was not the preacher for the services, he was called upon to add a word of exhortation before the service closed. His brother attended one of these services and remembered with deep emotion the appeal made by the young preacher.

> One night there sat in the audience many of the soldiers recently returned from the war—most of them from the Second Texas Regiment. None of these had yet been moved during the meeting. Things were moving slowly that night. The young preacher had not preached, but near the close of the service he arose and made an appeal, such as it seemed then to me I had never heard. It appeared to my young mind almost enough to raise the dead. He closed with words something like these: "Where are the old Second Texas boys? There are not many of them left. Most of their comrades sleep their last sleep on the hard-fought battle-fields of Shiloh, Corinth and others. But God spared a few of them to return to their destitute homes. Some of them are here tonight. Will they not tonight come and seek the salvation of their souls which God in great mercy kept for them through so many dangers? Won't they come now?" They came—all of them came. Oh, what a night that was![16]

Although B. H. Carroll had now found peace in his heart, he still faced the old struggle with debts and poverty. One of the few bright hours of that first winter after his conversion was his marriage. The Bell family had moved from Mississippi to Caldwell after Appomattox, and lovely Ellen Bell soon won the heart of the young preacher. Young Carroll rode horseback nearly ninety miles to Waco to ask his old college president and friend, Rufus C. Burleson, to officiate at the wedding. In a borrowed coat and with a noticeable limp from his war wound, Carroll was married on December 28, 1866, at the Caldwell church. The new home was begun with nothing in hand and poor prospects. "But having each other they counted themselves rich and faced the future with a smile."[17] During one of his first revival meetings at Caldwell, his new wife made a profession of faith under his preaching. Said his brother:

> I can shut my eyes now and see in my memory one of the happiest scenes

ever imprinted there. It was not at church, but at home. Sister Ellen (that is
what I always called her) had been under deep conviction for several days.
Suddenly the light had burst into her heart. It shone out gloriously upon her
face. She and Harvey were locked in each other's arms and the dear, sweet,
ever-believing mother was trying to hug them both at once.[18]

The end of the Civil War brought the collapse of the older Southern
culture and the outbreak of lawlessness in Texas. Governor Pendleton
Murrah was unable to maintain order during the closing days of the war,
and after Lee's surrender at Appomattox, the governor and other state
officials fled to Mexico.[19] A military government was named, and Texas
experienced the corruptions and confusion of Reconstruction until the
election of Richard Coke as governor in 1874.

The limping young preacher struggled to support his wife, as well as
his mother and other younger children in the family, and pay on the debts
that he had assumed. For three difficult years he taught school during the
week and preached on Saturdays and Sundays at churches in Burleson
County. When the school and churches that he served could not pay him,
he tried farming along with his other tasks. But continuing heavy rains
thwarted his strenuous efforts to raise a good crop. "He did not gather a
grain of corn or a lock of cotton." Spiritually, however, he reaped a
bountiful harvest. In revivals at his small churches, young Carroll
baptized his oldest brother (nearly fifty years of age) and his youngest
(then seventeen). Later in the year, his brother James was converted at
the Post Creek Baptist Church and was baptized by Harvey.

The first published word written by Carroll as a preacher was found in
the January 16, 1867, edition of the *Texas Baptist Herald*. Signed
"Harvey Carroll," the letter reported the results of a revival.

> The brethren had waited so long for prosperity in Zion that "hope
> deferred made their hearts sick." But our Lord has shown that "He is not
> the God of the dead, but the living." Seventeen professions and baptisms
> evidence the passing of new-born souls from death into life . . . . Even the
> world seems to be convinced the good feeling yet abides. Christmas day,
> which is accustomed to be ushered in by bon-fires and booming guns and
> celebrated by parties and bacchanal jubilees, was devoted as becomes the
> anniversary of the birth of our Lord and Savior, Jesus Christ, to worshiping
> the true and living God.[20]

Another letter from Harvey Carroll was published in the August 2,
1868, edition of the *Herald*. This described a revival held by Carroll at
Spring Hill, about ten miles southeast of Waco, in which twenty-six were
baptized on profession of faith and a new church was constituted with
about eighteen presenting their letters or coming by statement. A house
of worship was planned, and eight hundred dollars were raised in cash

and subscriptions. This was the New Hope church, of which Carroll later became the pastor.[21]

In the late spring of 1869, still preaching with little compensation to several churches in Burleson County, Carroll received an invitation to deliver the commencement address at Waco University, doubtless through the initiative of his friend President Rufus C. Burleson. At the same time, he had been invited to preach to a church beyond Waco with the possibility of becoming her pastor. He planned to deliver the Waco address and then visit the church on the same trip. A strange providence altered his plans and his life. Enroute to Waco he spent the night at Masterville, where a thief stole all the money that he had—a twenty-dollar gold piece. This made the trip to the prospective church impossible, so he planned to return to Caldwell after the commencement address.

The impressive message of this twenty-five-year-old preacher at the commencement service on July 17, 1869, stirred every hearer. He chose the text in Matthew 27:36 which reads, "Sitting down they watched him there." With appealing eloquence, Carroll described the several classes of people watching Christ on the cross, and then, revealing his insight and maturity, he applied the text to the students and others at the commencement service.[22] Some of the members of the church at New Hope, which Carroll had helped organize about a year earlier, attended the service and requested young Carroll to spend a week with them to discuss becoming their pastor. President Burleson had been preaching for this church, but the people needed a pastor and promptly called Carroll at a salary of five hundred dollars a year. Unlike the several churches in Burleson County which Carroll was then serving, the New Hope church would actually pay what she had promised.

Moving to the new field meant breaking old ties and arranging for later payments on old debts. The young preacher sold almost all of his possessions, even giving away some of his beloved books to make room for necessities on the journey. Loading the remainder on a neighbor's wagon, the Carroll family began the three-day journey to New Hope. Harvey and Ellen had buried an infant child in the cemetery near Caldwell, and they wept as they drove past the spot. Their second child, B. H., Jr., accompanied them in the wagon. Upon their arrival at the New Hope community, they were taken to the plantation home of General James Harrison, where they boarded while serving this church. For the first time since their marriage, the Carrolls enjoyed a comfortable home and an adequate place to live.

But Carroll's pastorate at New Hope was a brief one. The church at

Waco became pastorless in 1869 when Martin B. Hardin resigned, and the congregation had turned again to Rufus C. Burleson, who had twice before been their preacher. Burleson was mightily engaged at this time in his efforts to keep Waco University afloat. He told the church that he was willing to preach on two Sundays a month and suggested that they might consider securing the brilliant young New Hope preacher for the other two Sundays. Carroll agreed to this, and for the year 1870 the Waco church was served by both men while Carroll continued to preach half-time at the New Hope church. At the close of the year, the church at Waco called Carroll as full-time pastor, and he accepted. For the next twenty-eight years, he stood in this pulpit.

From the standpoint of his personal preparation for the task of founding Southwestern Seminary, these years as pastor were significant. For one thing, they brought his sparkling personality to full maturity. From the very depths of cynicism and antagonism against spiritual things which had characterized his preconversion years, Carroll was molded into a loving and caring person whose natural gifts were now fully utilized in calling people to the Christian faith and seeking their spiritual growth. During his years as pastor in Waco, Carroll constantly received letters of love and appreciation both from his own church members and from strangers who were acquainted with him only from his platform appearances and writings. A. J. Barton, who later became pastor of the Waco church and of Carroll, remarked that an important part of the greatness of Carroll was his total personality. He wrote:

> Across the intervening years, now nearly a third of a century, I see as vividly as if it were yesterday, or even today, the towering figure, the giant intellect, the gentle heart, the beaming face, the laughing eyes, the lifting and helping hands of our Kingdom Hero, and I am forced to exclaim from a heart of deep admiration and great joy, "There stands the greatest achievement of the life of B. H. Carroll."[23]

The Carroll papers are filled with illustrations of the change in B. H. Carroll from the antagonistic and sometimes violent skeptic of his unregenerate days to a sensitive and loving minister of the gospel. He constantly boarded needy young preachers in his home, sometimes without remuneration—men like George W. Truett, Jeff D. Ray, and George W. McDaniel. His door was always open for counsel and comfort. F. M. McConnell wrote:

> Imagine such a young preacher going timidly to the home of the pastor of the greatest church in the state, knocking at the door, being ushered into the library and finding there a big, kind-hearted brother, a true, unwavering friend, and you have what occurred almost daily at B. H. Carroll's home

in Waco for over thirty years. The story of doubts and fears were told with much more ease and in much more detail than the young preacher anticipated.[24]

Carroll was a friend to all preachers. Brother Hurt, an old and uneducated missionary on the Texas frontier, counted Carroll's home as his own.

> He used to drive up to the gate in his rickety old buggy, and coming, unannounced, into the house, would receive a welcome as hearty as if he had been the highest dignitary in the land. I recall once when this same old missionary had spent the night in the home, I walked out on the back porch early in the morning and Dr. Carroll was carefully polishing the old man's rusty boots, while their owner slept. I said, "What are you doing, Doctor?" With that twinkle in his eye that none who know him will ever forget, he said, "I am washing the saint's feet."[25]

Jeff D. Ray, without mentioning his own name, shared a tender recollection of Carroll's love. He wrote:

> An orphan boy who had no real claim on him fell sick in his home and for weeks hung between life and death with typhoid fever. The boy does not remember what took place during the delirium of the fever, although he had been told that during all that time this great busy man would take his place by the bedside and minister to the friendless orphan as tenderly as if he had been his own son. But the boy does remember that when he was convalescent, but unable to stand on his feet, this princely man would drag a portable bath tub into the room, bathe him from head to foot, rub him down and put him back in bed as gently as a mother. Do you wonder that for the intervening forty years that boy has loved him with all the passion of an ardent nature?[26]

The impact of his personality became one of Carroll's greatest assets as in later years he made personal appeals to other preachers to raise funds to finance the seminary.

Another noticeable carry-over from his pastorate to the work of the seminary was B. H. Carroll's emphasis on evangelism and missions. Rarely a year passed that the associational minutes did not take notice of a good revival at Waco. On two occasions, the church experienced unusual results. On April 30, 1876, Major William Penn, a lawyer of Jefferson, Texas, began a revival meeting at Carroll's church. Just one year earlier, Penn, a Baptist deacon, had decided to leave his legal practice and give himself to singing and preaching in Baptist revival meetings. Some have called him the first Texas full-time evangelist. Penn later described some of the unusual experiences of that Waco revival in extraordinary terms.

> God's grace rested on us in power like as on the day of Pentecost, and the

whole congregation seemed to be filled with the Holy Spirit. I think I can truly say that it was the most heavenly meeting I ever witnessed.[27]

The revival lasted eighty-one days, and Penn preached 184 different sermons. The *Texas Baptist Herald* reported that

> There have been about 370 conversions. There have been 152 baptized, five await baptism, eight have been restored, 34 received by letter, and seven are under watch care until letters are secured. . . . The meeting had to contend with court sessions, Fourth of July celebration, school examinations and commencement, the heat of the summer, the disadvantages of insufficient room to accommodate the people, and a spirit of opposition from some other denominations. The work has been most searching as well as extensive. Some of the most hardened sinners have been brought in, and backsliders reclaimed. Some of the bitterest quarrels have been settled and most inveterate enemies have been reconciled. All the denominations, perhaps, except the Episcopalians and Catholics, have started meetings in their places of worship. The work extended to the colored Baptist church, and some 200 have been converted there. This wonderful work of grace has been extended to the country round about and revivals are in progress there.[28]

The other notable revival meeting of the church began on September 13, 1893, and continued for eight weeks. Although hundreds were converted and joined the First Baptist Church, the biographer of the church felt that the greatest results of the revival were seen in the influence of this meeting in every church in the city. Carroll preached two sermons a day (except for three days when he was ill, and George W. Truett, who was a member of the church, did the preaching). The pastor, in addition, used the opportunity to meet personally with many of the prominent people of the city "whom he alone could reach and influence most effectively." Describing this as the greatest revival of religion in the history of the church, Judge W. H. Jenkins, the church clerk, wrote:

> One of the main features of this revival was the fact that it was carried out without the aid of an evangelist. Dr. Carroll, himself, preached two sermons a day throughout the meeting, except for three days when he was ill. During his absence George W. Truett, one of the elders of the church, did the preaching.
>
> Though hundreds were converted and one hundred and seventy-three additions were made to the church during the revival of 1893, these were not the greatest results. The influence of the meeting was felt in every church in the city. People talked about the revival on the streets, in stores, in the slums, in the surrounding country, in distant parts of the state, and even in other states. Letters came from other cities and other states asking for special prayer. No case was too hard or too far off for the faith of this church, for they were a "willing people."[29]

The missionary thrust of the church was also remarkable. The pastor led in the founding of mission stations and chapels all around Waco, a number of which grew into churches. For twenty-five years, his church paid one-half of the salaries of the missionaries of the Waco Association. His church regularly led the state in gifts to state missions, and the State Mission Board of the General Association made Waco its headquarters because of Carroll's leadership in that work. "Under the leadership of Dr. Carroll at this time his Waco church was contributing one-third of all the home, foreign, and state mission money that was being given by Baptist churches in Texas." From his church came many volunteers for the foreign fields.[30]

These years as pastor in Waco also developed in B. H. Carroll the excellent organizational skills that later proved to be of such value in launching the seminary venture. Jeff D. Ray briefly summarized this aspect of Carroll's skills.

> In a day when organization in a church was rarely thought of and more rarely undertaken, and usually greatly feared, he was for himself working out in Waco the problem of an organized church. In that day the word "organize" was regarded with such suspicion that when a church was started you must not say you had "organized a church." You must say you had "constituted a church." And when denominational activities began to be referred to as our "organized work" there was high prejudice against the term, so much so that the newspaper articles gave it the belittling parody— "the agonized work." But in that day when church conferences were mostly disciplinary wrangles and associations and conventions were conclaves for the defense of the faith once for all delivered—even in that day B. H. Carroll worked out and put into operation an organization in the Waco Church and Waco Association that put them at the forefront and made them easily the leaders in Texas in every phase of denominational activity. In doing it he demonstrated the fact that effective organization and soundness in the faith were not inconsistent, for his church and association were more intelligently grounded in Baptist faith than any similar organization in the state.[31]

In a Founder's Day address in 1918, F. M. McConnell, one of Carroll's successors in the First Baptist Church, Waco, asserted that Carroll "showed the students of Baylor University how to carry on the real business of a church by giving them every month an actual demonstration."[32] While Carroll was pastor at Waco, the church formed her first choir, adopted the budget plan for church finances (anticipating by a generation such a pattern among Baptist churches generally), thoroughly organized her Sunday School, developed a church library, and utilized the periodical literature being published by the Sunday School Board.[33]

A critical test of the pastor's organizational gifts occurred in 1883 when the Southern Baptist Convention accepted Carroll's invitation to meet in the new building of the First Baptist Church. At this period in Southern Baptist history, those attending the Convention were considered to be guests of the people in the city where the meeting was held. Hotels and restaurants were not important items, for the messengers were housed and fed in the homes of the people in the convention city. First Baptist Church, Waco, had been told to expect about a thousand people, but instead this became the largest Southern Baptist Convention on record up to that time. The minutes of the church stated:

> On the 9th instant, the Southern Baptist Convention, according to agreement, met with our church. We had expected originally 1,000 delegates and visitors, which was nearly 400 more than any other church had ever entertained. And we were somewhat doubtful of our ability to entertain this number when it became certain that there would be that many. And when the ever-increasing list went up to 1,500 we were alarmed and began at once to notify our Texas brethren that we could not entertain them. But when that list had grown to 2,500 we were appalled. But with dogged perseverance we worked away both night and day in despair, hoping little, praying much, working more, fearing most. And now that the agony is over, it is but justice to our Heavenly Father to whom be all the glory, that we make this record, though it may cause us to blush for our little faith. Instead of one thousand, fifteen hundred, or twenty-five hundred delegates, the committees have assigned to homes delegates and visitors to the number of three thousand or possibly thirty-five hundred. And yet during the five days we have always had an abundance of places unoccupied, the committee being actually annoyed by our people calling and begging for more delegates. It is the miracle of the widow's cruse of oil over again, only there has been a much larger bill of fare.[34]

Furthermore, the long and active pastorate at Waco also trained B. H. Carroll to carry heavy leadership burdens similar to those he would later shoulder in fostering Southwestern Seminary. Many illustrations of his leadership skills are available, but only some typical instances from his pastorate may be mentioned.

On Sunday, February 22, 1877, the beautiful City Market Opera House, located near the church in Waco, was burned to the ground. The fire spread to a private residence and then to the church, totally consuming both. Although the church had not a single wealthy member at this time, the resolutions prepared by the pastor and adopted by the church on February 25 reflected the bold optimism and inspiring leadership of the pastor. The first resolution accepted "with cheerfulness and unqualified submission" the severe loss sustained. The second stated that "we have long needed a more convenient and commodious house" and listed deficiencies of the old one. The sixth resolution affirmed that this was an occasion to unify the church more thoroughly by "furnishing us something to do, commensurate with our numbers, capacities, and resources" and by providing the opportunity to "enlist more heartily our sympathies and engage more earnestly our prayers." In the remaining resolutions, the pastor proposed that the church plan to pay for the new building as it was being erected so that there would be no indebtedness when the work was completed. For this reason, the entire new structure was not completed until 1883. The ground floor was ready in 1880, and the congregation moved into that section for the Sunday School and preaching services. Until that time the church had worshiped in the chapel of Waco University, in the courthouse, and in the men's dormitory for a season. There is a note of wonder in the language of the church's historian when he wrote:

> During the period when the church was carrying this heavy building load, the pastor's salary was increased, contributions to home and foreign missions and other denominational causes were maintained, the poor were remembered, and the congregation assisted other struggling churches over the state in building houses of worship. Under the leadership of Dr. Carroll at this time his Waco church was contributing one-third of all the home, foreign, and state mission money that was being given by the Baptist churches of Texas, the records reveal.[35]

In the Waco pastorate, Carroll's leadership also included spearheading many battles for civic righteousness. As early as 1873, he led his church to adopt a strong article into the church covenant by which all members pledged "to abstain from the use of or traffic in intoxicating liquor as a beverage." In a day when many preachers, as well as church members, practiced moderation but not prohibition in this matter, this action stirred a widespread discussion in Texas and beyond.[36] Because of his conviction that the use and sale of intoxicating beverages were matters of moral and civic concern, Carroll was called upon often to assume leadership in campaigns for prohibition. In 1886, McLennan County called a local option election, for which Carroll provided the leadership, and in the following year Carroll became chairman of the dry forces of the state in a prohibition referendum. All biographies of the preacher enjoy describing his debates with United States Senator Roger Q. Mills, Governor L. S. Ross, and United States Senator Richard Coke in these prohibition campaigns. Senator Coke (whose wife was a loyal member of Carroll's church) cried out during the heat of the debate, "If your parsons go into politics, scourge them back by stopping their rations!" One of Carroll's preacher friends, hearing this statement, remarked to a large gathering, "That man [Carroll] would live on corn cobs and stump water the rest his life rather than to turn Texas over to the whiskey whelps."[37] Senator Coke later apologized for his statement, and Carroll, just as generously, defended Coke later as an outstanding political leader.

Similarly, in the stormy controversy of 1894 over the opening of the Cotton Palace in Waco on Sundays, Carroll spoke out plainly in opposition and was told that he would destroy his usefulness if he did not cease. George W. McDaniel remarked many years later in a Founder's Day address that he could still hear Carroll's voice ringing out:

> If I knew the fate of Laocoon awaited me and my family, if I saw even now the pythons of vengeance emerging from the sea of popular wrath, and gliding toward me in noiseless slime, uncoiling their glittering length, revealing in supple sinuosities their deadly power of constriction, and freezing my heart with their cold, green, unwinking, basilisk eyes, yet would I, for Christ's sake, smite the hollow, treacherous side of this huge horse, and cry out: "There are Greeks in it." Woe to the city that makes a breach in the walls of religion and morality to give entrance to an enemy's gift, designedly too wide for passage through her regular gates.[38]

Carroll championed every other movement for personal and civic righteousness. His tract on dancing was in wide demand by pastors, and his aversion to impure speech and smutty stories was known well by all his acquaintances.[39]

Finally, these twenty-eight years of B. H. Carroll's pastoral service provided him the opportunity of developing his natural and spiritual gifts for communication to their highest power. All of his early and continued reading and study were made captive to his chief delight of preaching the gospel. His spacious mind learned well how to marshall all of his knowledge in his discussion of any subject, and his forceful logic and an impressive preaching style drove home the demands of the gospel to his hearers in sermon after sermon, year after year. His personal appearance, of course, added to the impact of his preaching. He towered above his fellows in height, and in the words of A. J. Barton, unlike some tall persons "he never slouched." In his early life, he had grown a beard that became totally white before he completed his Waco pastorate. His face and eyes were expressive, and his regular features and white hair made him an attractive figure.

It is difficult to judge how much influence the powerful preaching of Carroll had on his hearers during these twenty-eight years of pulpit proclamation. An entire generation of Baylor students, many of them young ministers, sat under his preaching. S. P. Brooks remarked:

> Whatever may be said of his versatility, in my judgment his greatest influence over the students of Baylor was from the pulpit. Sunday after Sunday his sermons grew on me. . . .

In the course of the nearly thirty years he preached in Waco thousands of
students were gripped and held in the same way. It was during my student
days that he preached some of his greatest sermons. At that time he was
about forty-five years of age. His physical and mental possibilities seemed
boundless. One never forgets his illustrations taken from great movements.
When Edwin Markham's "The Man With the Hoe" appeared Dr. Carroll
made an address that swept the gamut of human feelings and showed that
the toiling masses had restful sympathy in his heart.[40]

Carroll loved to preach, counting it the principal function of his
pastoral work. Through preaching he witnessed effectively and led his
congregation to grow in all of the graces of Christ. A letter from the
chairman of his board of deacons at the church on the occasion of the
twenty-fifth anniversary of his coming to the pastorate at Waco reflected
this. Judge W. H. Jenkins wrote:

Much of the little growth I have made as a Christian I gratefully confess to
have resulted from your wise, tender and loving ministration . . . . On the
first day of this year, remembering my past failures, I, in the fear of God
and earnestly begging His help, promised amongst other things to be more
helpful to my pastor this year than ever before in my life.[41]

It would be impossible, of course, in a work of this kind, to quote
extensively from the outstanding sermons of B. H. Carroll to show how
well he had mastered the art of effective preaching. J. W. Crowder, who
collected most of Carroll's sermons, listed the impressive number of
published materials that came from the pulpit and pen of the preacher.
Included were seventeen volumes of an exegetical nature entitled *The
Interpretation of the English Bible,* eighteen volumes of sermons, five
volumes of popular addresses, three volumes of debates and other joint
discussions, one volume of questions and answers, one volume of
discussions on the church and the Articles of Faith, and four volumes of
miscellaneous writings.[42] Perhaps one brief quotation from his sermon on
the text "I magnify mine office" (Rom. 11:13) will suggest the depth of
Carroll's conviction about the centrality of preaching. He concluded the
message with these words:

I magnify my office, O my God, as I get nearer home. I can say more
truthfully every year, "I thank God that He put me in this office;" I thank
Him that He would not let me have any other; that He shut me up to this
glorious work; and when I get home among the blessed on the bank of the
everlasting deliverance and look back toward time and all of its clouds and
sorrows, and pains, and privations, I expect to stand up and shout for joy
that down there in the fog and mists, down there in the dust and struggle,
God let me be a preacher. I magnify my office in life; I magnify it in death; I
magnify it in heaven; I magnify it, whether poor, or rich, whether sick or
well, whether strong or weak, anywhere, everywhere, among all people, in

any crowd. Lord God, I am glad that I am a preacher, that I am a preacher of the glorious gospel of Jesus Christ.[43]

S. P. Brooks sat in the congregation when Carroll preached this sermon. He later wrote:

> The preacher's office was held aloft, not the big preacher's alone, but the little preacher as well. The dignity of the work he showed not to be limited to the city pastors alone, but extended to the humble country workers as well. He exalted the work of the ministry to such a point that it presented the one single time in my life that I wished I were in its service. Up to the time I heard Dr. Carroll preach on this great theme I had in spirit resented all my life the hardships incident to the life of my own father who, as a country preacher, had labored on the farm and in the schoolroom for a living while he literally gave his life for others in unremunerative toil. I grew up in rebellion that my mother, a cultured, educated woman, should endure the toils incident to the home of the country pastor and missionary. I honestly felt that somehow they did not get a square deal. Then came Dr. Carroll's sermon. He exalted the preacher and crushed my arrogant pride. He spoke a language that my father and mother had long known well, and he spoke it in such terms that I began to see a meaning in pastoral ministrations to which I had been a stranger theretofore. I left the house with a broken spirit. My heart was crushed. I went to bed that night with sleepless eyes. I cried the live long night. I could not get away from the picture Dr. Carroll had drawn. Morning came. With it, a joy that had not been mine before. I was glad that my father was a preacher, and a little one at that, as the world counts greatness. I felt a new kinship and spoke a new language. I had been born again as to appreciation of what constitutes a really noble purpose in life.[44]

To evaluate Carroll's life-changing and mind-elevating pulpit ministry, one needs only envision the effect this kind of preaching would have on his many hearers over a full generation. The statistics show that the public response to this preaching in the First Baptist Church, Waco, was impressive. The additions to the church from the time it was organized on May 31, 1851, to the coming of Carroll in 1871 were 224 by baptism and 327 by letter. Under Carroll's ministry, the church baptized 793 and received 1,532 by letter, making it one of the largest churches in the state at that time.[45] Added to this, of course, was his impact upon thousands of hearers and multiplied thousands of readers of his published sermons.

The Denominational Stalwart

The numerous and important activities of this busy pastor, of which only a brief sketch could be given, were matched by an unbelievable participation in every denominational interest of the Waco Association, the state convention in Texas, and the Southern Baptist Convention. Beyond this, he took an active part in the sectional disagreements between the Southern Baptist Convention and the northern benevolent societies; he lashed out at theological liberalism that accelerated after the Darwinian hypothesis of 1859; and finally, as a prelude to his climactic achievement in the establishment of Southwestern Baptist Theological Seminary, he nurtured and guided Baylor University, which became the golden thread linking the earlier efforts for ministerial education in Texas to the founding of the seminary. These activities will be discussed briefly, but it must be remembered that these events were not unrelated historically to his busy pastorate nor did they occur as chronologically consecutive events; rather, they developed in the context of an active pastorate. Sometimes they were overlapping and concurrent, bringing increased pressures and strains in critical days. The tumultuous times and the nature of Carroll himself aroused in him a sense of moral obligation to enter into any struggle, however unpopular it might be, as a defender of truth and righteousness. For this reason there was hardly an advance or controversy among Baptists during his generation that did not include him as a principal participant. He never shrank from taking sides. George W. McDaniel compared him to the brave Scottish martyr, James Guthrie.

> When persecution was rife in Scotland, Mr. Rollock once said to that martyr, James Guthrie, "We have a Scottish proverb, 'Jauk that the wave may go o'er you;' will you jauk a little, Mr. Guthrie?" "Mr. Rollock," replied Guthrie gravely, "There is no jauking in the cause of Christ." B. H. Carroll never ducked![46]

Waco Association

B. H. Carroll's name first appeared in the minutes of this association in 1870. Within the next few years, his influence in the work of the association multiplied geometrically. He dominated the work in this body for two decades. Rarely a year passed that he did not preach the introductory or doctrinal sermon. He was president of the important Mission Board of the association from 1874, when it was established, until 1888 and again from 1889 to 1892.

The burdens of this task were many. The minutes of 1874 remarked that a part of the duties of the president of this board included the visiting of each church in the association during each year, the holding of mass meetings in the interest of missions, and the instructing of the churches about their missionary duties.[47] Carroll performed these arduous duties with enthusiasm and excellent results.[48] A brief glimpse of Carroll's faithfulness in matters of personal stewardship appeared in the minutes of 1887. The clerk mentioned that the crops of that year failed everywhere because of the driest year in the history of central Texas, but that the liberality of B. H. Carroll and his wife, among others, had made possible a good report on missions for that year.[49]

The minutes of the association showed that Carroll served as chairman of many important committees and boards, preached more than any other person at different sessions of the association, initiated organizational and constitutional improvements,[50] and was the first messenger of the association to the Southern Baptist Convention in 1888 when the constitution of that body was changed to provide for associational representation.[51]

One of the skirmishes involving the association developed in Carroll's own church. M. T. Martin, an ordained minister and a trained mathematician and logician, became enamored with the necessity of proving Christian doctrines in the same fashion that he demonstrated mathematical truth. This error, old in Christian history, led him to extreme positions on several basic doctrines of Baptists, especially on the need for absolute assurance of salvation from the time of one's conversion. He was a member of the First Baptist Church, Waco, and unsettled many lay people and preachers alike with his aberrant views about regeneration, sanctification, faith, assurance, and the like. Many of the preachers and deacons of the church, along with his pastor, labored with him to show him the critical nature of his errors. When he refused to hear, the church in conference on July 11, 1889, instructed the deacons to prepare charges against him for heretical doctrine. This was done, and Martin's credentials as a preacher were withdrawn, although he was granted a letter as a lay member to join elsewhere. Soon Martin placed his letter in the Marlin church, which promptly invested him with credentials to preach. This violated the Baptist practice of fellowship under which a Baptist church would not reverse the action of a sister church in the matter of ordination. At the meeting of the Waco Assocation in 1890, the Marlin church was declared out of fellowship with the association.[52] The association later again condemned the views of Martin,[53] although it restored the Marlin church to fellowship in 1891 after a gracious response which admitted justification for the action.

Baptist General Association

The minutes of this body after 1871 are filled with references to the participation of Carroll. This sectional convention had developed by the withdrawal of a large party in eastern Texas in 1853 who were dissatisfied with the policy of the State Convention in educational matters. After several reorganizations, this group took the name of the Baptist General Association of Texas in 1868.[54] The economic and political convulsions following the Civil War disrupted most of the work of this body.

B. H. Carroll first appeared in the minutes of this General Association in 1871 as chairman of the Committee for Schools and Education.[55] He startled the convention by pressing for a campaign to raise thirty thousand dollars for the endowment of Waco University, as well as urging support for the Texas Baptist Educational Union just being organized. This union was an effort to unify Texas Baptists in the support of "one great central Baptist university," and Waco University followers hoped, of course, that Waco would be the site for it. The union was formed in 1872, but in the words of J. M. Carroll, it was a "light that failed."[56] The rivalry between Baylor at Independence and Waco University was too great to allow either school to claim single support from all Texas Baptists. However, in some respects it laid the foundation for unification that would come in the following decade.

After about 1874, B. H. Carroll was the dominant figure in this general body, just as he was in the Waco Association. R. C. Burleson was elected president regularly for most of the years between 1871 and 1885, while Carroll was named vice-president. Carroll served in almost every other capacity for the General Association until its dissolution in 1885. As in the Waco Association, Carroll helped restructure the General Association and initiated constitutional changes.[57] He aided in the establishment of Buckner Orphans Home;[58] was the recognized leader in the tense discussion over choosing from two sets of messengers sent by the First Baptist Church, Dallas, in 1880, a situation which involved a principle later magnified in the Hayden controversy;[59] and was active in every part of the program of the state body.

Carroll was one of the leaders in bringing about the unification of Texas Baptists. This could have been anticipated since he had been a student at old Baylor and was also well acquainted with many of the leaders of the State Convention. The two principal rival general bodies were the State Convention and the General Association. The General Association took the initial step in 1883 when a special committee was named to discuss relations with other Baptist general bodies.[60] As chairman of this committee, Carroll showed his favorable attitude toward unification. His report recommended that the General Association send fraternal greetings to all general bodies in the state, requesting the appointment of a committee of five from each to discuss unification.[61] The first response was not encouraging.[62] In the following year this move to unify the general bodies was joined by an effort to unite the schools at Independence and Waco. The General Association appointed committees to discuss the unifying of both Baptist schools and the general bodies. The death of President William Carey Crane of Baylor on February 27, 1885, along with the increasing isolation of Independence as a center of Texas Baptist life, evidently brought the State Convention to the decision that many of its constituents had long favored: namely, that a removal of Baylor from Independence to a new location would be wise. As a result, committees were able to work out the consolidation of the two general bodies and the two schools as well. The unification of Baylor and Waco University will be discussed later. When the two general bodies united in 1886, they took portions of the two older names and titled the new unified body the Baptist General Convention of Texas.[63]

Baptist General Convention of Texas

As one of the principal leaders of the unified state body, B. H. Carroll bore the brunt of two severe attacks against the missionary methods and leadership of Texas Baptists: the Gospel Mission movement and the Hayden controversy. Both of these were offshoots of the system known as Landmarkism, developed by J. R. Graves of Tennessee.[64] Graves was a native of Vermont, a convert from Congregationalism, who had joined R. B. C. Howell of Nashville, Tennessee, in 1846 as assistant editor of the Baptist paper, known as the *Tennessee Baptist*, and assistant to Howell in the First Baptist Church. When Howell accepted a pastorate in Virginia in 1850, Graves became the editor of the paper and leader in the church. Upon returning to the church as pastor in 1857, Howell found that Graves had launched a movement known as Landmarkism. This eclectic theological system emphasized the authority of the local church, identified the Kingdom of Christ with the aggregate of true local churches of Christ, and asserted that true churches must possess all the doctrinal and ecclesiastical characteristics of the New Testament churches if they were to be members of this unbroken Kingdom of Christ. Churches not possessing these characteristics should not be called "churches" but "religious societies" which did not possess the scriptural authority of true churches. Graves identified Baptist churches as "true churches" and declined to associate ministerially with any but Baptist churches.

Because of his emphasis on the authority of local churches, Graves became antagonistic to the assumption of any ecclesiastical powers by the boards of general bodies. In February, 1859, just a few months before the meeting of the Southern Baptist Convention at Richmond, Virginia, Graves warned the readers of his paper that the Foreign Mission Board of the Southern Baptist Convention was trying to take over some of the authority of the churches affiliating with it and that this might well bring "the disruption of the relation of the Convention and the Foreign Mission Board to the body of the Southern Baptists." He wrote:

> There are schemes of consolidation and centralization now urged by certain brethren who exercise a controlling influence in the Biennial Convention which, if they succeed in consummating, will as certainly destroy the present union of Southern Baptists in Foreign Missions as the Convention meets in May next. And there is a determination on the part of some, moved more by partizan than missionary zeal, to make the next Biennial Convention an ecclesiastical Court and to force its decision into antagonism with Churches and Associations.[65]

When the Convention met in May, 1859, however, Graves was able to work out an agreement with the Foreign Mission Board about safeguarding the authority of the churches. He did not fare so well in some of his other attempts to secure control of the Convention.

Four months later, J. R. Graves attended the session of the Baptist State Convention meeting in Waco. He was heartily welcomed and asked to preach for the convention on the next morning (Sunday). Few recognized what this first contact would mean to Texas Baptists. The minutes record that he

> delivered an able, eloquent and lengthy discourse to a large and attentive audience, defining the ancient landmarks, proved up the disputed title to the kingdom by producing the original deeds, defining the meets and bounds, also giving the laws and regulations of the settlers of the kingdom.[66]

So delighted were the hearers that by motion Graves was asked to speak again when the Sunday School report was made, and he did so.

Texas Baptists were never quite the same again. Graves visited Texas on many occasions, spoke both at the State Convention and the General Association meetings, and had almost as many subscribers to his Tennessee paper as the Texas Baptist papers enjoyed.

It is not known exactly when B. H. Carroll first met J. R. Graves.

When the Southern Baptist Convention met at the First Baptist Church in Waco in 1883, Graves was one of the convention preachers. Not long before his death, Graves visited the Baptist General Convention and was greeted with great affection.

It is interesting that many Baptist writers classify Carroll as a Landmarker. This probably stemmed from two facts. First, Carroll magnified the authority of the local church, publishing in 1903 a lecture titled *Ecclesia—The Church* in which he concluded that this word, sometimes used abstractly or generically, always refers "to a particular assembly."[67] This view of the church exactly coincided with the basic view of Graves. The other reason for calling Carroll a Landmarker was his opposition to William H. Whitsitt, the church historian, who wrote articles and books asserting that Baptists did not immerse for baptism until the seventeenth century. This controverted the Landmark view that Baptists could be traced historically from the days of the New Testament to the present. The Whitsitt story will be told later in connection with Carroll's activities in the Southern Baptist Convention.

The Landmark movement was badly crippled by the events of the Civil War and was quiescent during the 1870s and 1880s. In Texas, it erupted in several forms in the 1890s. Carroll could not have been a true Landmarker, since he was the implacable opponent of each of the offshoots of Landmarkism in Texas. Doubtless he was influenced by the personality of Graves and the many followers of Landmarkism among Texas Baptists; but he did not emphasize the need for Baptist succession, was completely loyal to the board system of denominational work (so distasteful to Landmarkers), and was the enemy of Landmarkers who attacked associations, state conventions, and the Southern Baptist Convention.

Several controversies arose in Texas over the principles of Graves in the Landmark movement. The earliest of these was called Gospel Missionism and developed from the missionary views of T. P. Crawford. Crawford, a veteran Southern Baptist missionary in China, had become increasingly cynical over the methods employed by the Foreign Mission Board in conducting mission work in China. He had been able to attain a measure of financial security from investments in China, which made it easier for him to display his hostility to the Foreign Mission Board. Finally, after making some radical demands upon the board to change its methods in mission work, in 1892 he published a fourteen-page booklet entitled "Churches to the Front!" In blistering language he called for a return to the authority of the New Testament churches in mission matters, very similar to the challenge of J. R. Graves at Richmond in

1859. In fact, it is likely that Crawford heard the message of Graves at the Richmond Convention. As a result of this frontal attack on the Convention, Crawford was relieved of his missionary duties in 1892. He then initiated the Gospel Mission Movement and sought support in the United States.[68]

B. H. Carroll became involved in this movement about the time Crawford left the Foreign Mission Board. Jeff D. Ray summarized the immediate response of Carroll.

> Along in the early nineties there sprang up as if by magic a widespread cult called the Gospel Mission Movement. Their plan was to have no Mission Boards. If a man felt moved of the Holy Spirit to go to a given field, let him pick up and go, and the Holy Spirit, who impressed him to go, would impress somebody to send directly to him the money to support him. It was surprising how many people were more or less inoculated with the idea. . . . One of the best missionaries in China became impregnated with it, resigned as a missionary of the Board, came home and toured the states in the interest of the iridescent dream. It had a perceptibly depressing effect upon the receipts, not merely of the Foreign Mission Board, but of all mission boards. Seeing the disintegrating tendency, Dr. Carroll, in 1894 asked a summer's furlough from his church that he might combat this vagary and raise a threatened deficit on the Texas Board. He succeeded in both. The Convention met that fall without a debt and the Gospel Mission cult never got anywhere in Texas. It gained considerable sporadic following in some of the other states, but he so thoroughly exposed its impracticability that it never made any headway in Texas.[69]

Another aspect of Landmarkism that confronted Texas Baptists brought the most virulent quarrel Texas Baptists had yet known. Its roots were complex, including personality clashes, rivalry between editors of Baptist papers, resentment at the increasing amount of structured denominational machinery, financial deficits by the state mission board, and other tensions held in solution in Texas Baptist life. Its principal base was Landmark ecclesiology.

The conflict began on April 2, 1894, when S. A. Hayden, owner and editor of the *Texas Baptist and Herald,* circulated a letter charging that the expenses of the state mission board were excessive, that the board would show a deficit when the convention met in November, and that the mission work was deteriorating rapidly under the board system of organization.[70] Replies and countercharges brought increasing hostility. B. H. Carroll determined that there would be no deficit in November; so, with the aid of George W. Truett, the young assistant whom Carroll had enlisted to help pay the debts of Baylor University, the Waco pastor took time from his church to campaign for mission gifts. In the files of Carroll may be found a letter sent to him by Truett "in confidence" and "to you only," describing Truett's efforts to secure mission offerings and support of the mission board in Fannin and Grayson associations of north Texas. Truett began the letter, "Dear, Dear Dr. Carroll" and closed with "warmest, most grateful affection to you & Mrs. Carroll" from Josephine (Mrs. Truett) and himself. Truett reported great success both in raising money and in rallying support for the board.

Despite the elimination of any deficit in the board's work, Hayden continued to attack it and its supporters. By 1896, Hayden's verbal abuse had become almost unbearable as with sarcasm and rapier-like pen he used his paper to flog his opponents. B. H. Carroll was his chief antagonist, and the correspondence of these years bears witness to the intensity of the struggle. In 1897, Hayden was finally denied a seat at the state convention for his incessant attacks on that body. He appealed this action on the Landmark grounds that the state convention was made up of authoritative churches whose elected delegates must be seated by the convention. The ruling by President R. C. Buckner that general bodies are not subject to the authority of churches but are made up of messengers, not delegates bringing authority from the churches, laid the groundwork for the schism that came.[71]

One of the unfortunate aspects of this controversy was the decision by Rufus C. Burleson, longtime friend of B. H. Carroll, to support Hayden and his movement. This, along with the events involved in the leadership of Baylor University at this time, caused a considerable strain on the friendship between Carroll and Burleson, although Jeff D. Ray said that they remained friends until death separated them.[72] Although Hayden was not in favor of forming a rival organization in Texas, his followers did so on July 6, 1900, calling it the Baptist Missionary Association. Hayden affiliated with this body and remained a constituent of it until his death in 1918. He filed civil suits against the convention leadership for unseating him, but these were finally settled out of court.[73]

Although this brief summary of the Hayden controversy simply sketches the developments in broad strokes, the minutes of the state body, Carroll's correspondence, and many eyewitness accounts reveal how very much of the time and energy of the busy Waco pastor was expended in defending the work and methods of the state mission board.

The Southern Baptist Convention

B. H. Carroll attended his first Southern Baptist Convention when it met at Jefferson, Texas, in 1874. Between the 1877 session at New Orleans and the 1908 session at Hot Springs, Arkansas, he was a "conspicuous figure" at twenty-two sessions of the Convention.[74] Lansing Burrows wrote later that he had met Carroll in Waco at the 1883 convention "when for the first time I could say that I knew him, winning my reverence and affection with the impression that I was in the presence of my superior, although of the same age."[75]

Burrows had served as secretary of the Southern Baptist Convention from 1882 until 1913 and had heard from the platform during that long period all of the eloquent Baptist preachers in the South. He noted that Carroll, at the age of thirty-five, had preached the Convention sermon in 1878 when the Convention met in Nashville and said that Carroll "was appointed to preach at every session, unless important reasons existed." Burrows counted as most impressive the messages of Carroll at mass meetings in 1888 at Richmond; in 1892 at Atlanta; in 1895 at Washington; and later, after the close of this period, at Hot Springs in 1900; Chattanooga in 1906; and again at Hot Springs in 1908.[76]

Burrows felt that the committee work of Carroll for the Southern Baptist Convention was of great significance. "There were a few occasions when there were topics which occasioned a suppressed excitement among the brethren, and in each instance Dr. Carroll was upon the committee that we looked to for the solution of vexing problems." He served on the committee to discuss the scriptural base for a proposed union with the Disciples of Christ; and both at Chattanooga in 1896 and in the "tense hour" at Wilmington in 1897, in connection with the Whitsitt affair, Carroll's influence in the committee was great.[77]

B. H. Carroll not only served the Convention itself but made a valuable contribution to that body by his unswerving loyalty to it when the very life of the Convention was at stake. Severe ideological and geographical tensions developed between Northern and Southern Baptists in the critical days following the Civil War. The principal crises involved the sectional rivalry between the Northern Home Mission Society and the Southern Home Mission Board relative to territorial jurisdiction in the appointment of missionaries, the efforts of the Southern Baptist Convention to establish a Sunday School Board, and the promotion of young people's work in the South.[78]

The first of these sectional disagreements developed during and after the Civil War when the American Baptist Home Mission Society of New York asserted its right to appoint missionaries anywhere in North America by reason of its original charter and motto and pursuant thereto sent missionary ministers and teachers in large numbers into the South where the Southern Baptist Convention was at work.[79] Jeff D. Ray summarized Carroll's leadership in Texas at this point.

> Back in the early eighties there was an effort made to commit Texas
> Baptists to a policy of joint cooperation with the Home Mission Society of
> New York and the Home Mission Board of the Southern Baptist Conven-
> tion. There were two arguments: (1) There were many Northern people in
> Texas and their wishes ought to be regarded. (2) Texas, in her pioneer
> struggles very much needed the money the Home Mission Society was so
> able and so willing to give. For these two reasons, but more particularly the
> latter, many brethren felt that it ought to be done. In fact, it was tried out
> for a short while in the old State Convention. Dr. Carroll's keen eye saw that
> such a policy would bring endless confusion and complications, and
> probably strife in the Texas work. Altogether apart from partisan or
> sectional ground, and solely on the ground of solidarity of our Texas work
> he threw himself into the fight against such a policy. Because Texas Mission
> work was in such desperate need of the money the New York Board could
> give, and for other reasons, some of the brethren were hard to convince.
> But he fought it out on principle and at last succeeded in committing Texas
> Baptists to the permanent policy of undivided cooperation with the
> Southern Board. In a marvelously short time after he won the fight the
> brethren came to see he was right, and now everybody sees how
> impracticable, and ultimately disastrous the other plan would have been.[80]

But Carroll was also a pivotal figure in this debate beyond his home
state. The Home Mission Board almost perished in the sectional
struggles of the 1880s. Part of its problem was caused when Southern
state mission boards judged that missions in their own states were more
important than the Southwide challenge, in a sense reflecting the same
type of inner sectionalism which had divided Baptists North and South
in 1845. However, the principal threat to the life of the board came from
the militant challenge of the Home Mission Society of New York. This
society had entered into mission work in the South after the Civil War
and despite the protests of Southern Baptist leaders, had flooded the
Southern states with missionary preachers and teachers. In 1887, the
Northern society published in its *Journal* an article which approvingly
observed that "some influential Southern Baptists are openly asserting
that the Home Mission Board of the Southern Baptist Convention is a
superfluity and ought to be dispensed with entirely."[81] In the following
year, at the request of I. T. Tichenor, corresponding secretary of the
Home Mission Board, Carroll addressed the Southern Baptist Convention at Richmond, Virginia, on the necessity for home missions. Ray
summarized the effect of this outstanding message.

> Men who had come to make speeches and motions against the Home
> Board's continued existence were most of them converted to the side of the
> Board. Those that were not converted, realizing that their guns had been

spiked, went home with a consciousness of defeat. From that day few, if
any, really thoughtful men have doubted the value and what is more the
necessity of the Home Mission Board.[82]

The second of the sectional disagreements in which B. H. Carroll
played an important part was the struggle between the Southern leaders
who desired to establish a Sunday School Board in 1891 and the leaders
of the American Baptist Publication Society of Philadelphia. Carroll had
been friendly with the Philadelphia society, which had published some
of his books and had supplied much of the Sunday School material for
the South after the demise of the first Sunday School Board in 1872.

Carroll had always been a strong advocate of the Sunday School
movement, helping with the organization of a strong school in his own
church and encouraging teachers and other preachers by publishing
expositions of Sunday School lessons in state periodicals and by
speaking at Sunday School conventions. Jeff D. Ray remarked about
Carroll that "one of the greatest sermons he ever preached was on the
thirteenth chapter of 1 Corinthians before a State Sunday-school convention at Houston."

When the Southern Baptist Convention appointed a committee in 1890
to consider the wisdom of establishing the second Sunday School Board,
Carroll was a member of it. Ray remarked:

> Nobody who knows the inside history of that Board is ignorant of the vital
> part he played in its founding. Nobody familiar with the facts doubts that
> J. M. Frost would have found it exceedingly difficult, if not absolutely
> impossible, to carry through the Convention his proposition for the
> establishment of this Board, when the matter was fought out in Fort Worth
> in 1890, had it not been for the influence and golden-mouthed advocacy of
> B. H. Carroll. . . . His speech had much to do with the adoption of the
> majority report. It was just a short while till all the men who fought him
> hardest in that memorable contest came to see that he was right.[83]

After the Southern Baptist Convention had approved the formation of
the second Sunday School Board in May, 1891, Carroll introduced a
resolution at the next meeting of the Baptist General Convention of
Texas, which read:

> *Resolved*, That we heartily approve of the creation by the Southern
> Baptist Convention of a Sunday School Board, and pledge our sympathies,
> prayers and contributions in furtherance of the objects for which said Board
> was created.

He then commended to the churches the series of Sunday School
publications by the new board as being "in every way worthy of their
patronage and support." This was adopted, although there was strong

opposition to this action by many friends of the American Baptist Publication Society of Philadelphia.[84]

The third sectional tension between Northern and Southern Baptists involved the beginning of organized structures for promoting work among Baptist young people. Northern Baptists had taken the first step in 1891 with the organization of the Baptist Young People's Union of America. Southern Baptist young people were included as one department of this national body, and it was the purpose of this union (formed on the society philosophy) to break down geographical boundaries and unite all Baptist young people in the nation in a single body.

In 1893, many leaders of the Southern Baptist Convention officially spoke out against this plan, which they had discussed privately, noting that the allegiance of Baptist young people in the South might be endangered under this type of structure. After two years of sometimes heated debate, on November 21, 1895, a consultative meeting was held at Atlanta, Georgia, resulting in the formation of the Baptist Young People's Union, Auxiliary to the Southern Baptist Convention. This action was approved in the following year by the Convention.

B. H. Carroll's correspondence showed that he was a participant in these discussions and concurred that there was a possibility of alienating Southern young people in the Northern program. As a matter of fact, Carroll seems to have been a part of every concern of Southern Baptists during his entire ministry, whether on the associational, the state, or the Southwide level. His correspondence with Southern leaders showed his interest in every aspect of Baptist life, whether with T. T. Eaton about the first comity meeting between Northern and Southern Baptists at Fortress Monroe, Virginia, in 1894 or with Illinois Baptists about unorthodox writings by Chicago professors. As a trustee of The Southern Baptist Theological Seminary, Louisville, Kentucky, from 1894 to 1911, Carroll gained much familiarity with the inner workings of a seminary and made the acquaintance of many Baptist leaders of the South. He was invited to deliver the commencement address for May, 1895, and the Julius Brown Gay Lectures in the following year.[85] He preached the baccalaureate sermon at the commencement in 1905.

The Whitsitt Controversy

As a member of the Board of Trustees of The Southern Baptist Theological Seminary, B. H. Carroll became intimately involved in the unfortunate controversy among Southern Baptists which centered around William H. Whitsitt, the senior professor at the seminary, who had been elected to the chair of church history in 1872 and, following the death of John A. Broadus, was named president of the school in 1895. He was probably the best technical scholar among Southern Baptists at the time the controversy erupted and personified the new historical-scientific methodology of the modern period.[86] From a later perspective, it appears that a conflict between the older method of "historical assumption" and the newer method of "exact documentation" was inevitable at some point. As is often true in such ideological and methodological conflicts, good men are irretrievably hurt and the participants involved are often misunderstood.

Evidently Whitsitt was accepted as orthodox before he adopted the modern scientific methods of history. He was questioned at his ordination by none other than J. R. Graves, the founder of Landmarkism, and as late as April 19, 1883, replied to a query from Texas about historical succession by saying that "I have never affirmed the impossibility of a succession of Baptist churches, but I have admitted my inability to demonstrate the existence of a succession from the historical material at my command."[87] Texas Baptists applauded his election as president of the seminary in 1895, doubtless reflecting the opinion of Carroll, although some Texas Baptists had not been pleased with Whitsitt's background of European study.[88] Whitsitt himself debated in 1874 whether or not he could remain within the Baptist denomination, recognizing the tension between his historical-scientific methodology and the views of many Southern Baptists.[89]

In the summer of 1880, Whitsitt spent several months in the libraries of Great Britain and concluded from his study that Baptists in England and America had baptized by sprinkling or pouring before 1641, when they adopted immersion. On September 2 and 9, 1880, he published two anonymous editorials in a Congregationalist weekly of New York asserting this position. In 1895, he wrote an article on Baptists in *Johnson's Universal Cyclopaedia* over his own name setting out these same views and at this time admitted authorship of the anonymous editorials in the paedobaptist weekly in 1880. His principal challenger initially was T. T. Eaton, pastor of the Walnut Street Baptist Church in Louisville, editor of the *Western Recorder* of Kentucky, and a trustee of the seminary. Curiously, Eaton had been reared in an anti-Landmark home and atmosphere but now opposed Whitsitt's views from a Landmark perspective. He published J. H. Spencer's first violent attack on Whitsitt on April 23, 1895.[90] Professor A. T. Robertson of the seminary promptly answered Spencer in an article defending Whitsitt as orthodox and noting that Baptists were not in the business of manufacturing or distorting whatever history showed to be true and that history was no test of orthodoxy.[91] The following week John T. Christian, pastor of the East Baptist Church of Louisville and a student of church history, challenged the truth of Whitsitt's new synthesis and complained that it had been published as fact in the most permanent type of publication—an encyclopedia.[92]

During the remainder of the summer of 1896, the various Baptist newspapers in the South began to take sides. Generally speaking, the states along the Eastern seaboard supported Whitsitt, while those farther west, which had come under the influence of J. R. Graves, condemned Whitsitt both for his views and for the furtive method used in publishing the material in a paedobaptist journal anonymously.

The controversy reached Texas promptly. Whitsitt was well known there, having spoken in behalf of Southern Seminary in 1891 when the state convention met in B. H. Carroll's church at Waco and having received a substantial offering for the seminary. Both sides wooed Carroll. Among Carroll's papers are letters from Eaton; from A. T. Robertson, the distinguished New Testament professor of the seminary; from John R. Sampey, then professor of Old Testament but later to become president of the school; from Professor F. H. Kerfoot of the seminary; and from many other leaders on both sides.

On July 14, 1896, Eaton wrote Carroll asking for suggestions about how to be fair to Whitsitt and at the same time be faithful "to the truth and to the denomination."[93] Robertson wrote Carroll in July, 1896, to say that he had reviewed the documentation of Whitsitt's findings and felt "sure he has a very strong case that ought to be given a hearing." He closed:

> I am sick and tired of all this fuss and feathers, tempest in a teapot. Dr. Whitsitt is a gentleman, a Christian, and a Baptist and merits courteous treatment. Is there anything you can do to help quiet all this furor?[94]

Professor Sampey's letter on August 24, 1896, advised Carroll that Whitsitt's book, *A Question in Baptist History,* would be published by September. He said:

> It occurs to me to say to you that the eyes of many thousands of our people will be fastened on you pretty soon after the appearance of this little book, and they will look with interest to see what you think of the argument. Don't forget the responsibility resting on you to speak the truth in love. Your opinion will be final with thousands of people who are not in the habit of doing their own thinking, while at the same time powerfully influencing the most thoughtful of our brethren [sic]. I trust the Lord will give you the right word to speak. I will say to your face what I have many times said behind

your back, that you are now—since Broadus is gone—our natural leader in
the Southern Convention.[95]

Professor Kerfoot wrote several long, emotional letters to Carroll, as will
be mentioned shortly.

Evidently these men felt that at this time Carroll had not taken an
anti-Whitsitt position. He had written a letter to the *Baptist Standard* on
May 7, 1896, urging that Whitsitt should not be judged until all the facts
were clear. He said:

> I love the seminary. I love it much. I don't want to hurt that. And I do
> deeply love Dr. Whitsitt. Let us keep cool, brethren, and get before us all
> the facts. The foundation of God standeth sure. Hear Davy Crockett: "Be
> sure you are right—then go ahead."

He had also written an article for the same paper on July 2, 1896. In this
he spoke in high terms of the seminary and Whitsitt, again expressing
the wish that the people be calm and wait for all the facts before judging
Whitsitt. Carroll did not appear upset so much over the facts presented
by Whitsitt as the manner in which he presented them in paedobaptist
publications.[96]

It is interesting that Carroll pointed out that Whitsitt was dealing with
events that happened in England and in Rhode Island many centuries
after Christ and for that reason did not impugn his orthodoxy. Carroll
said that he had no interest in Roger Williams's succession. These are
strange words for one accused of being a successionist after the Graves's
pattern.

A curious development may be glimpsed in one reaction to the
Whitsitt controversy in Texas. The two Texas Baptist papers—the *Texas
Baptist and Herald*, published by S. A. Hayden in Dallas, and the
Baptist Standard, published by J. B. Cranfill in Waco—had been
engaged in a bitter war with one another. Hayden had been attacking the
work of the Texas Baptist state body from a Landmark position. One
would expect him to rage against Whitsitt, and he did.[97] However,
Cranfill forgot about his battle with Hayden and was just as antagonistic
to Whitsitt as was Hayden.[98] In the June 25, 1896, issue of his paper,
Cranfill urged all Baptist associations and conventions to express
themselves on the Whitsitt matter. They did so promptly. Resolutions
against Whitsitt were passed in practically every association in Texas,
incuding Salado, Fannin, Hill, Central, Enon, Bryan, Dallas, and many
others.

Texas Baptists fell into several categories, practically all opposing

Whitsitt. Some wanted to withdraw all support from the seminary; some
wanted the entire faculty to resign; some wanted to support the seminary
only after Whitsitt had resigned. A moderate voice like that of Carroll in
his article on May 7, 1896, did not suit the temper of most of the
constituency.[99] More fuel was added to the fire when it was learned that
Whitsitt's sister had been reared as a Baptist but had married a
Presbyterian and that Whitsitt had given his approval to his sister's
leaving Baptist life and becoming a Presbyterian with her husband.[100]

In 1896, Carroll was named on a committee of the Southern Baptist
Convention to report on the relation between the Convention and the
seminary. With keen insight, he showed that the seminary was structured
on the society basis and that the relationship to the Convention was
slight and tenuous.[101]

At the annual meeting of the Baptist General Convention of Texas
on October 9-13, 1896, the desire to condemn Whitsitt's views was
everywhere expressed, but through the personal influence of B. H.
Carroll a moderate motion was adopted which noted the views of Whitsitt
and concluded:

> Whereas, Our people are not satisfied with the case as it now stands, and
> are willing to get before them all facts ascertainable within a reasonable
> time, before reaching a final judgment, therefore,
>
> Resolved, That we respectfully and lovingly, but very earnestly, refer this
> whole matter to the trustees of the Seminary having jurisdiction over the
> case, as worthy of their most serious consideration, and do earnestly
> request from them, assembled in annual session at Wilmington, NC, next
> May, a clear-cut deliverance on the merits of the whole case, according to
> all the facts. And that this deliverance be submitted to the Southern Baptist
> Convention, then and there in session, for such action as may be lawful and
> right.
>
> In the meantime, loving as we do the Seminary as a precious institution,
> devised to us by those who founded and cherished it, and whose memories
> are precious, therefore,
>
> Resolved, That with the exception of the aforementioned teachings on
> Baptist history, we commend it most heartily to the esteem and patronage of
> our people.[102]

When the trustees of the seminary met on May 6, 1897, at Wilmington, North Carolina, just preceding the session of the Southern Baptist
Convention, Carroll offered a resolution which was intended to accomplish the request of the Texas convention in the previous fall. His
resolution urged that the trustees pronounce upon Whitsitt's teachings
and publications "according to our best judgment of the facts and merits
of the case" and report to the Convention "our feelings and recommenda-

tions for such action on their part as may be deemed expedient or lawful."[103] W. J. Northen promptly offered a substitute motion, which was adopted, as follows:

> The Trustees of the Southern Baptist Theological Seminary, assembled in their annual meeting in Wilmington, N.C. May 6, 1897, desire to submit to the Baptists of the South the following statement in regard to the institution whose interests have been committed to their care and management.
>
> 1) That we account this a fitting occasion to reaffirm our cordial and thorough adherence to the Fundamental Articles adopted at a time when the seminary was established and to assure those in whose behalf we hold in trust and administer the affairs of this institution that it is our steadfast purpose to require in the future as in the past that the Fundamental Laws and scriptural doctrines embodied in these articles shall be faithfully upheld by those who occupy chairs as teachers.
>
> 2) That we cannot undertake to sit in judgment upon questions of Baptist history which do not imperil any of these principles concerning which all Baptists are agreed, but concerning which serious, conscientious, and scholarly students are not agreed. We can, however, leave to continued research and free discussion the satisfactory solution of these.
>
> 3) That, believing the Seminary to hold an important (position) relative to the prosperity and usefulness of Southern Baptists, we consider it our duty, while demanding of those in charge of its department of instruction, the utmost patience in research and the greatest discretion in utterance, to foster, rather than repress the spirit of earnest and reverent investigation.
>
> 4) That, having fully assured that the tender affection which we cherish for this institution founded by our fathers and bequeathed by them to us, is shared by the Baptists of the South, we can safely trust them, as we ask them to trust us, to guard its honor, promote its usefulness, and pray for its prosperity.[104]

By invitation of the board, Whitsitt appeared on the next morning and on his own initiative made the following statement to the board:

> Dear Brethren:
> I beg leave to return sincerest and heartiest thanks for the noble and generous treatment that you have bestowed upon me. I have only words of affection for every member of the Board. After consulting with the committee I have the following to say:
> 1. That in regard to the articles written as editorials for the *Independent*, I have long felt that it was a mistake and the generous action of the Board of Trustees renders it easy for me to make this statement. What I wrote was from a Pedobaptist standpoint with a view to stimulating historic research with no thought to disparage Baptist doctrine or practices.
> 2. That the article in *Johnson's Encyclopedia* has probably passed beyond my control, but it will be very pleasing to me if I can honorably procure the elimination from it of whatever is offensive to any of my brethren.
> 3. Regarding the charge that I expressed a conviction that a kinswoman of mine ought to follow her husband into a Pedobaptist church, that it was

never my intention to indicate a belief that the family outranked the Church of God. I believe that obedience to God's commands is above every other human duty, and that people in every relation of life ought to obey God rather than men.

4. That on the historical questions involved in the discussion I find myself out of agreement with some honored historians; but what I have written is the outcome of patient and honest research and I can do no otherwise than to reaffirm my convictions and maintain my position. But if in the future it shall ever be made to appear that I have erred in my conclusions I would promptly and cheerfully say so. I am a searcher after truth and will gladly hail every helper in my work.

5. That I cannot more strongly assure the brethren that I am a Baptist than by what I have recently declared with regard to the Abstract of Principles set forth in the Fundamental Laws of the Seminary. I am heartily in accord with my Baptist brethren in every distinctive principle that they hold. My heart and life are bound up with the Baptists and I have no higher thought on earth than to spend my days in their fellowship and service, in the name of the Lord Jesus Christ.[105]

On the following day the statement of the board and the letter of Whitsitt were read to the messengers of the Southern Baptist Convention, and Whitsitt received a warm ovation from the body.

Without any question, Carroll was disturbed by the action of the trustees on May 6. Upon his return to Texas after the meeting of the Convention, he was besieged by questions about why the trustees had not acted on the question as requested by the Texas state body and many other groups, why he had not brought a minority report to the Convention if he had not acquiesced in the decision of the trustees, why the Convention did not take some action, and so on. In response, Carroll wrote an article on May 20 describing exactly what had taken place at the trustee meeting and followed his discussion of it by answering some of the specific questions that had been put to him.

Over and over, Carroll came back in this explanation to one basic fact: that the trustees had asserted that "we cannot undertake to sit in judgment." His logical mind protested that the trustees were the only group who could sit in judgment on any professor, since the seminary was formed on the society plan. He pointed out that the report to the Southern Baptist Convention was simply for information only, not for action. The resolution of the trustees had made plain what Carroll knew: that they alone had supervision and authority over the seminary by reason of its charter, which provided for what amounted to a self-perpetuating board of trustees clearly not under the authority of any convention or other structured body of Baptists. Carroll said that he made no minority report to the Convention since that body had no power to change anything in the seminary.

At the conclusion of his article, Carroll said that if the trustees declined to sit in judgment, then the whole matter must return to the arena of public discussion. He wrote, "The trustee statement relegates what remains of the controverted matter back to the realm of that discussion which a short time ago was so much deprecated."[106] He then prepared an article for the *Baptist Standard* entitled "Back to the Realm of Discussion," in which he emphasized the widespread reverberations all over the world of the Whitsitt affair.[107] This was reproduced in the *Western Recorder* of Kentucky and elsewhere. In response William E. Hatcher, Richmond pastor and seminary trustee, published an article in the *Religious Herald* of Virginia remonstrating against reopening the discussion. Carroll viewed some of Hatcher's statements as a personal attack upon his character but was unable to secure a response from Hatcher.[108] A definite hardening of Carroll's position in opposition to Whitsitt can be observed after this time.

On August 5, 1897, Carroll published an article in the *Baptist Standard* entitled "The Real Issue in the Whitsitt Case." Carroll said,

> As I expect to stand before the judgment bar and answer to my Lord for my conduct and stewardship on earth, I do solemnly aver and avow that the main question in this case is not Eaton vs. Whitsitt, is not a mere question of English Baptist history, is not "shall Landmarkism be arbitrarily forced on the Seminary for dogmatic teaching," is not this or that theory of organic church succession, is not traditionalism versus the Scriptures. . . .

The real issue, Carroll indicated, was "the breaking up of Southern unity, and the quite possible dismemberment of the convention." For the first time he openly stated, "You cannot hold Southern Baptists in alignment for the Seminary with Dr. Whitsitt as president," and he reiterated that "the Convention was worth more than the Seminary." He took occasion to answer the arguments of W. E. Hatcher to which he had taken issue in his correspondence with the editor of the *Religious Herald*. It is interesting that in this article Carroll expressed his inability to prove historical succession in almost precisely the same language Whitsitt used in 1894, as mentioned heretofore. He denied that his chief aim was "to force on the Seminary the bending and warping of historic facts to support any particular view of church succession" and said that he had "never been able to trace it [the church] historically, link by link, to my own satisfaction."[109]

The action of the trustees on May 6, 1897, could not end such a widespread controversy. Professor Robertson wrote Professor Sampey in the Holy Land on May 21, 1897, stating that T. T. Eaton was talking much "privately and publicly." The trustees continued to receive an avalanche of protests from associations and state conventions calling for the resignation of Whitsitt.[110] Professor F. H. Kerfoot was also undermining Whitsitt by writing letters to Carroll and others in an effort to succeed to the presidency of the seminary.[111]

The situation became critical in August of 1897 when J. W. Bailey, editor of the *Biblical Recorder* of North Carolina and later United States Senator from that state, informed Carroll that he and other North Carolina leaders were forsaking their support of Whitsitt.[112] Less than a week later, Carroll received a similar letter from Joe E. White, secretary of the Board of Missions and Sunday School of the North Carolina state body.

Perhaps the most serious blow, however, was the rapid deterioration of financial support for the seminary, particularly from the Southwestern states where the influence of J. R. Graves lingered. In the last analysis, the person who ultimately brought the resignation of W. H. Whitsitt on July 13, 1898, had been lowered into a grave five years before; for J. R. Graves's disciples made it impossible for the brilliant and dedicated scholar to practice freedom of research and expression when his findings cut across the basic teachings of the founder of Landmarkism.

In the following year (1898), Carroll gave notice at the Southern Baptist Convention that he intended to present a resolution at the session of 1899 which would sever the seminary from its slight relationship to the Convention. By this action, Carroll was not renewing the attack nor acting on caprice. His correspondence (especially letters from F. H. Kerfoot of the seminary) indicated that many were fearful that the division over Whitsitt would split the Southern Baptist Convention, thus destroying the agency of Southern Baptists for missions and other benevolences. Under Carroll's proposed resolution the seminary would "stand on its own merits, and be managed by its own trustees."[113] This action was not taken as intended in the following year (1899) because of the resignation of Whitsitt. It is interesting to observe in perspective that the longtime secretary of the Convention, Lansing Burrows, later looked back to Carroll's service in this controversy and praised him for his "strong, guiding hand," adding that possibly "Dr. Carroll never did a more valuable work than in those days."[114]

The Christian Apologist

Beyond his participation in the organized work of Baptists through churches, associations, state bodies, and the Southern Baptist Convention, Carroll was widely known for his conservative biblical theology. Every week he received letters from Baptists in Texas and beyond, asking about a scriptural interpretation of some kind or his judgment on some movement that looked toward liberalism. His answers were always to the point and reflected what he preached. A brief review of his many volumes of sermons and lectures on the Scriptures reveals the complete abandonment of his youthful skepticism and infidelity. He accepted the total inspiration of the Scriptures and measured all religious movements in terms of how they compared with this revelation.

He constantly expressed his deepest admiration for two men who had greatly influenced his theological mind-set and who, in the theological struggles in which they had engaged, stood firm on the basic doctrines of the Scriptures. One of these men was John A. Broadus of The Southern Baptist Theological Seminary. When Broadus died on March 16, 1895, Carroll wrote in the Texas *Baptist Standard*:

> For the last ten years Doctor Broadus has exercised a greater influence over my own life than all other men put together. My first introduction to him made an epoch on my ministerial life. It was at a meeting of the Southern Baptist Convention, in Jefferson, Texas, in 1874. In one respect that Convention was a disillusion to me; the great men of whom I had read falling so short of my expectations when I met and heard them. Only one man came up to and surpassed my expectations. That man was Doctor Broadus.[115]

Carroll digested thoroughly the life story of Broadus by A. T. Robertson and Broadus's biography of James P. Boyce, and more than once he expressed his approval of Broadus's dismissal of C. H. Toy in 1871 for Toy's liberal views on the inspiration of the Scriptures. Toy was a brilliant young scholar who had joined the faculty of the seminary in 1869. He had volunteered to go to Japan as a missionary of the Southern Baptist Convention, but civil war forced a change in these plans. Instead, he studied in Europe in the field of Old Testament at a time when German scholarship was enamored with Higher Criticism. Upon Toy's return, it was evident that he had become a pronounced evolutionist, even presenting a popular lecture in Greenville advocating Darwin's views of the origin of man. Broadus asserted that the acceptance of these views seriously compromised the doctrine of the inspiration of the Scriptures held by most Baptists and that it was necessary for Toy to realize "that such teaching was quite out of the question in this institution."[116] Carroll had studied Darwin's hypothesis at great length and applauded the action of Boyce and Broadus in dismissing Toy.

The other object of Carroll's admiration was Charles H. Spurgeon, who had confronted theological liberalism in Great Britain in the 1880s in what was known as the Downgrade Controversy. After Spurgeon died on January 31, 1892, Carroll preached a memorial sermon in which he lavishly praised the conservative theology of the London pastor.[117] It will be observed shortly that Carroll evidently was influenced by the kind of theological institution Spurgeon had developed in his college in London and initially may have considered imitating some aspects of it in the seminary in Texas.

Carroll and Baylor University

The account of B. H. Carroll's constant labors in behalf of Baylor University at Waco after 1886 has been purposely saved until the end of this chapter, for in his mature years this interest overshadowed all others in his life. Carroll was God's final link between the earliest efforts by Baptists to foster ministerial education in Texas and the founding of Southwestern Seminary. In his summary of Baptist education and educators, Frederick Eby, a late contemporary of Carroll and a careful scholar in the area of education, pointed to Carroll as the dominant figure in the development of Baptist education in Texas from the time this young giant accepted the Waco church until he founded the seminary.[118]

Carroll's active part in promoting ministerial education at Waco University before 1886, when this school and Baylor University at Independence were united, has already been sketched. In 1886, J. W. Speight made his final report as president of the board of trustees of the united school.[119] In 1887, the convention was informed that a Texas charter had been granted to Baylor University at Waco on August 7, 1886, and that B. H. Carroll had been elected president of the trustees.[120] He was reelected annually to this post until 1907, even after he had become a professor in the school. During most of this time, Rufus C. Burleson remained as president of the university. The united institution promptly erected two buildings—Old Main and Georgia Burleson Hall. Unfortunately, a depression was just beginning to grip the nation, and the debts incurred in this building activity became burdensome.

An interesting statement concerning the founding of a theological department was included in the report of Carroll for the trustees in 1890. He wrote:

> We have never claimed to have a theological department, nor do we issue diplomas to that effect. But we do furnish facilities for great improvement

in this direction by way of preparation for a regular theological seminary.
Regular lectures are delivered and courses of reading and study marked out
to those young ministers.[121]

Twenty-six young preachers and twenty children of worthy Baptist
pastors were receiving free tuition in that year. Some of the young
preachers were being helped with board and other expenses.

As early as 1886, Carroll had urged that a financial agent be put on
the field to raise funds for paying the building indebtedness of Baylor.
Several had been appointed and had served for short periods; but in 1891
Carroll reported that George W. Truett, a gifted young minister, had been
secured to help raise the money to pay off Baylor's debts. In that year,
Truett had labored for seven months, and Carroll had been in the field for
three months raising funds. They reported that $37,000 in cash, lands,
and pledges had been obtained.[122] In the following year, the state body
passed a long and adulatory resolution of appreciation for Carroll and
Truett. Carroll, the resolution said, had patiently and faithfully served
"as from city to city and from town to town he has gone, amid personal
discomfort by day and by night, teaching the masses what our Christian
fathers and brethren have done for the cause of education." Of Truett it
said that he had "with a self-sacrificing spirit, put away, for the present,
the completion of his own education that he might help lift Baylor
University from its peril."

In 1892 the convention was informed that $33,000 had been secured
by Truett and Carroll, leaving only about $20,000 yet to be paid on
Baylor's debts, and in 1893 the convention was advised that all debts of
Baylor had been paid on the new buildings and grounds.

With the retirement of these debts, immediate efforts were made to
enlarge the work of ministerial training. It was announced to the
convention in 1893 that a Bible Department had been formed as an
integral part of the university. Carroll was named to the chair of Exegesis
and Systematic Theology; R. C. Burleson, the "nestor of our commu-
nion," filled the chair of Pastoral Duties; and J. H. Luther, a graduate of
Brown University and Newton Theological Seminary, held the chair of
Homiletics. Seventy-five students had been enrolled in that year.[123]

The Bible Department was reorganized in the following year. George
W. Truett presented a strong report to the convention emphasizing that
the Bible Department at Baylor, while primarily for preachers, was open
to all and that under the direction of Carroll, "the *Bible*, pre-eminently
the preacher's book, is regularly studied in the classroom." A few
changes had been made in the curriculum. R. C. Burleson had begun
lecturing in church history, homiletics, and kindred subjects. Forty

students were enrolled in these classes, and Truett called for an *"increased emphasis"* on the proper education of the ministry.[124]

Carroll taught Bible classes for Baylor students for many years on a voluntary basis, receiving no remuneration of any kind. Jeff D. Ray recalled sitting in these classes in 1880 but was not sure how much earlier Carroll had been doing this teaching. George W. McDaniel highly praised Carroll as a teacher. He remarked:

> The lecture room was crowded with students to whom no credit was allowed for the work. The classes of '94–'98 went with him through the Pentateuch, the Gospels, and Acts. No one who ever sat in these classes would say he was not a great teacher. If teaching is causing others to know then he was *primus inter pares.*[125]

An unpleasant episode occurred in 1895 which, according to Carroll's report to the convention by the trustees, decreased the number of girls enrolling at Baylor that year. The report described how Antonio Texeira had been brought to Texas in January, 1892, from Brazil by Z. C. Taylor, a missionary there, as an attendant to his sick wife. When the girl was no longer needed for this purpose, Taylor hoped that she could attend Baylor since he disliked the idea of returning her to the unfavorable environment she had known in Brazil. The laws of Baylor would not permit her to live in Georgia Burleson Hall, where she would have been under the constant supervision of the school, so President and Mrs. Burleson agreed to permit the girl to board in their home and help with the housework for her keep. Unfortunately, the girl was found to be with child out of wedlock. Although the facts showed that the university and the Burleson family were not negligent in their efforts to watch over the girl, William C. Brann, the publisher of a monthly paper called the *Iconoclast,* sowed the state

> with papers and pamphlets making a most violent and scurrilous attack on Baylor University as a proper school for girls, and particularly on its president as unworthy to have charge of female education and commending instead the Convent schools under the direction of the Romish nuns.[126]

It is interesting that Carroll himself wrote and said little about this affair apart from his report of the trustees to the convention. In fact, a letter to him from a Baptist friend asked Carroll why he had not been more outspoken, especially after Brann continued his withering sarcastic attacks against Baylor, Burleson, the faculty, and everything related to the school. In this report of the trustees Carroll justified his silence by saying that he relied on the sanctified common sense of the Baptist people. He wrote:

As a rule the free press of the country is not disposed to wantonly injure public institutions. It is only when there is a manifest grudge—a desire to glut vengeance for some supposed offense, or where another axe is to be ground against the good name of the institution assailed, that such criticism becomes venomous and should be accordingly distrusted. And even when it is thus manifestly unfair in the grudge-motive which colors and distorts facts, it is far better to bear it with patient dignity and to avoid haste and heat by rushing into print. . . . In according with this policy, the trustees have refrained from any publication whatever in the secular press, reserving this brief and colorless statement of the facts for this report to this body which alone has jurisdiction over the management of Baylor University.[127]

Brann made many enemies with his caustic pen, and one of them later shot him to death.

In 1897, Carroll announced the creation of a chair of Hebrew and Greek and the naming of John S. Tanner to fill it. This was a significant move. Next to Carroll himself, Tanner probably was the most influential individual in laying the groundwork for the new seminary in the Southwest. Born October 9, 1869, on a farm near Comanche, Texas, Tanner was a student at Baylor from 1886 to 1890 to secure his B.A. and while studying for the M.A. degree, awarded in 1893, taught some classes at Baylor. Upon graduation, he matriculated in The Southern Baptist Theological Seminary at Louisville. In 1895, he wrote a long letter to Carroll which revealed the influence that Carroll had over him. The letter mentioned that he had expected to have a long conference with Carroll at Louisville, where the Texas trustee of the school was to bring an address near the close of the spring term. Since illness had kept Carroll from making the trip to Kentucky, Tanner decided to write instead. Incidentally, Carroll's correspondence has several letters from faculty members and others at Louisville expressing their regret that illness had kept Carroll from performing this service. President W. H. Whitsitt wrote that he had read the address Carroll was supposed to bring and called it a "work of genius, and very timely."

The letter of Tanner to Carroll was dated May 28, 1895, and read in part:

Your former interest in me has been to me a constant inspiration, and your counsel a guide in my course. And I have no other excuse for coming to you now again.

I have finished the full course and will receive the degree of Th. M. tomorrow night. The New Testament Tutorship I have held the last two of my three years in the Seminary. And, by the Lord's blessings I have had a good country pastorate since January of my first year. My success in the pastorate has been not only gratifying to me but surprising. I have become passionately fond of preaching and pastoral work, retaining, however, in full my former love for teaching. You remember that my desire and your advice agreed that completing the course here I should take a University course somewhere. Being invited by his exceeding kindness to do so, I laid the matter before Dr. Broadus nearly a year ago. Giving me reason to believe that he wanted me to work into a position in the Seminary he proposed for me, instead of leaving here, to pursue a course for Th. D. here and at the same time other studies in History, Classic Greek ec. under him. I was considering it when, alas! the stroke came that smote us all. Now, a new order of things is inaugurated. With all of it I am highly pleased so far as regards the Seminary to which I feel so much devoted; but as for my work it seems to me that I can do better elsewhere. Here is what I have done thus far in regard to the matter: I made application Apr. 1st for a Fellowship in the University of Chicago, sending specifications, testimonials, specimen of work ec. Somewhat to my pleasant surprise I was notified recently that I had been elected. It yields $300 and commands a small part of my time for teaching in the University. I trust that I can get preaching enough to complete a competency while in residence. It will take two years to go *Ph. D.* Being then twenty-seven, I should expect to enter upon my permanent work. Now two questions: (1) Shall I go to Chicago? Some of my most esteemed and most influential friends advise me in the negative, suggesting various and sundry other lines of procedure, none fearing, as they say, that I would take to the loose views reported to have a footing there, but rather, that I would be doing an injustice to the Seminary to go to its chief rival at this crisis, and running the risk of losing favor in the South. These and many other questions I have tried to consider, but am loath to make a mistake in this matter. (2) If I go to Chicago, what departments shall I emphasize?

I want your candid and impartial opinions on these matters for the sake of a young man who wants to do right and to make the most of himself for the Kingdom of Christ and the Master's service.

My plans have scarcely changed at all, but my motives largely. My former personal ambition I humbly trust has been supplanted with a consuming desire to be useful.

Then, I wanted to ask you about the present outlook for Baylor University and the developments of the past few years. While there is no commitment on either side, yet I have all along entertained the feeling that my work is in Texas in connection with Baylor. Your views on this subject, as freely given as you feel justified, would be appreciated. I can modestly say that it is not a question of getting a job, but of spending my life where God can use it to most effect.[128]

Tanner went on to Chicago for additional study and, upon returning in 1897 to Baylor, was named to teach linguistics. Philosophy was later added to his teaching duties. As though conscious that his gifted life might be cut short, John S. Tanner threw himself wholeheartedly into the work of the Bible Department and the ministry. W. T. Conner said of him, "He was the most inspiring teacher I ever knew." J. M. Dawson sat at Tanner's feet and wrote later:

> Convinced that the properties of a school should never lie idle, he organized in 1896 at Baylor the first summer school ever held in Texas. Aflame for the improvement of his brother ministers, he also organized the Baylor Summer Bible School.[129]

The brilliant young scholar also formed a Workers' Band for soul-winning and a Foreign Mission Band for young people in the field of missions.[130]

The Summer Bible School begun by John S. Tanner began to grow rapidly. The keen eye of B. H. Carroll saw the potentiality of the large number of Texas preachers who needed training. He was encouraged by others in this vision. J. B. Gambrell, who was just coming from Georgia to become missions secretary for the Baptist General Convention of Texas, wrote Carroll on July 13, 1896, to say:

> In studying your situation, it appeared to me that your great need is a Texas raised & Texas trained ministry. Your university has a rare opportunity. It ought to have 100 preachers there all the time in training for your home field. These ought to come directly under your personal training. Ten years of this would give Texas a solidarity not attainable by any other process. This is the biggest thing that can be done. If it should be necessary to send your mission work to another point to take up this other work, it seems to me it might be done.[131]

In addition, on July 17, 1897, Carroll received a letter from Oscar H. Cooper, who would become president of the university in 1899 succeeding R. C. Burleson. Cooper had read Carroll's lecture of June 13, 1897, at the Baylor Summer Bible School and commented:

> I have been specially interested in your presentation of the necessity of theological instruction in a complete university. The history of the development of universities from the time of their beginnings in Bologna and Paris in the twelfth century up to our own time confirms, it seems to me, your contention that a university which lacks the department of Theology lacks the department of learning which is the highest, the deepest, the most comprehensive, the most far-reaching of all.[132]

As one reviews the life of B. H. Carroll, he gets the impression that the death of Carroll's wife on November 6, 1897, was the first of several contributing human factors that turned him from his longtime pastorate at Waco into the area of ministerial education. His participation in the Hayden and Whitsitt controversies had been most exhausting, his own illnesses had constantly reminded him of his mortality, and now his beloved companion had been taken. This "lonely old man," as he termed himself, was challenged by his younger brother, James M. Carroll, to give his final years to ministerial education. J. M. Carroll had been named as financial manager of Baylor Female College at Belton, Texas, on August 1, 1895. He found there a debt of over $140,000 which, he said, was "more money than had been given altogether by the Baptist denomination, as such, to denominational schools since the founding of Baylor University in 1845, even including the amounts recently collected by Truett and Carroll." This statement did not include amounts given locally for school support.[133] As he began to seek funds to retire this huge debt on Baylor Female College, J. M. Carroll found that a large part of Texas was closed to raising money for Baylor College because other denominational schools claimed the financial support of areas situated around their own school. He discussed this problem with J. B. Gambrell, state mission secretary, who suggested that if all of the Baptist schools of Texas pooled their debts, it might be possible to have a statewide campaign for the payment of all the debts. Beginning with this idea, J. M. Carroll developed a plan in early 1897 for federating all Baptist schools in Texas and mounting a statewide campaign to pay all their debts and provide endowment for those schools which had few debts.[134] After consultation with several denominational leaders, J. M. Carroll called for an educational conference on September 15, 1897, at Fort Worth. Growing out of this, a mass meeting was held on November 8 in conjunction with the fall session of the Baptist General Convention of Texas at San Antonio in 1897, and a federated system of schools in Texas was approved. The matter was referred to a committee of thirteen, who subsequently became the Texas Baptist Education Commission. The principal goal of the commission was to pay the debts and provide needed equipment for all the federated schools, and since Baylor University was without debt, a campaign for $250,000 endowment would be included for that school.[135] J. M. Carroll was elected financial manager of the commission and began his work on January 28, 1898. When the state body met at Waco on October 7-11, 1898, he reported that approximately $53,200 had been pledged (including an initial sum of $25,000 by Colonel C. C. Slaughter of Dallas). At the end of the year, however, J. M. Carroll was greatly concerned because less than $5,000 had been collected in cash.

From the beginning he had believed that his gifted brother, B. H. Carroll, should be enlisted to lead this movement. However, the older brother's principal concern was for Baylor University, and he had not been involved in the earlier conferences on the Education Commission. J. M. Carroll determined to secure his brother's assistance in this movement.

> This was no easy task. He was devoted to his church and the church was devoted to him. They had been together some 28 years. These ties would have to be broken. It was a trying situation, but B. H. Carroll was finally tremendously impressed with this school movement. It would mean much to Baylor. It meant much to all our Texas Baptist affairs. This was the psychological hour in which to secure unity and active co-operation instead of friction between our schools. For the plan to fail meant the total loss of some of the schools, and a permanent and unpleasant rivalry among those that survived.[136]

When B. H. Carroll was finally convinced that he should turn his life into this new channel, he decided to put out the fleece one more time before making the move. He abhorred the thought that he would be raising his own salary as he began to collect funds for the commission. J. M. Carroll listened to this objection. Without his brother's knowledge, he sent a dozen night telegrams to special friends, asking each one to be responsible for one month of his brother's salary—$208.33. All promptly replied favorably. When B. H. Carroll learned of this, he said in amazement, "God must be in it! I accept."[137]

On the last night of 1898, the Waco pastor sat in his study until the early hours of Sunday morning, endeavoring to find the proper words to tell his church that he was resigning as her pastor. His handwritten message, interlined occasionally with words to clarify a sentence, was typical of all his writing: thorough, clear, and at times eloquent. He tenderly spoke of his twenty-eight years of service to the church, more than half of his life (he was then fifty-five years old); of his loved ones sleeping in the cemetery in Waco awaiting the resurrection; and of touching memories of ministering in joy and in sorrow to the congregation. He dwelt at length upon the reasons for which he was not resigning: in order to secure some additional benefit from the church through negotiation; because he thought the congregation wanted a change in pastors; because he had some grievance against the church; because the pastoral work did not now appeal to him; or because of a desire to leave the city of Waco. In strong terms, he declared that none of these would have influenced him at all. He finally said that he was taking this action because in his heart he could no longer deny the voices calling to him for help in the field of Christian education. "In the general cause of Christian education is involved the work of the Bible Department of

Baylor University, which more than any other agency possesses the Solution of the thousand ills which have heretofore afflicted and crippled us."[138]

With resolutions of love and appreciation for their longtime shepherd, the First Baptist Church of Waco sorrowfully released him. During the next several years, he preached for the church while she was pastorless and retained his membership there until he moved from the city in 1910.[139]

As one views these events from the perspective of later years, he is impressed with the magnificent faith displayed by B. H. Carroll. Almost completely deaf and often ill, he could have remained as the Waco pastor for his remaining years in relative comfort. For him to resign from this church and accept a position involving the raising of money for denominational schools appeared to be a poor exchange. There is no hint in his writings or correspondence that he was looking beyond the work of the Texas Baptist Education Commission to make plans for organizing a theological seminary; on the contrary, he specifically denied later that he had such an intention. Whether conscious of it or not, however, he was a large step closer to that golden period when he would inaugurate the greatest achievement of his eventful life.

Notes

1. Ray, pp. 149-50.
2. J. B. Cranfill, comp., *Sermons and Life Sketch of B. H. Carroll D. D.* (Philadelphia: American Baptist Publication Society, 1908), pp. 13-23.
3. J. W. Crowder, comp. and ed., *Dr. B. H. Carroll, The Colossus of Baptist History* (Fort Worth: By the Author, 1946), pp. 11-15.
4. Ibid., pp. 14-15.
5. Ibid., p. 25.
6. Ibid., pp. 28-29.
7. Ibid., p. 23.
8. Ibid., pp. 28-29.
9. Ray, p. 16.
10. See B. H. Carroll, Personal Memorandum Book, p. 1, File 158, Carroll Papers. Also see S. A. Hayden to B. H. Carroll, 5 July 1890, File 167, Carroll Papers, saying that he had never discussed "the misfortune of your first marriage." This material has been confirmed by a copy of the marriage license dated December 11, 1861, issued by the county court of Burleson County, which showed that the marriage service took place on December 13, 1861, and the return made on December 14, 1861. The service was probably conducted by the county judge, since the name of the officiating person is not shown. It is curious that the divorce was granted by a jury trial, which assessed all expenses to the defendant, who was the wife. The divorce records are dated November 9,

1863, and the wording seems to indicate that Carroll himself was not present. Probably Carroll was in the Confederate army fighting in Louisiana, although he could have returned to Caldwell for this trial. On April 4, 1864, about five months later, Carroll was wounded severely in the battle of Mansfield, Louisiana. The legal records for December 11, 1861, and November 9, 1863, are found in the office of the District Clerk, Burleson County, Caldwell, Texas (col. C, p. 277).

11. Crowder, p. 55.

12. Ibid., p. 48.

13. Cranfill, *Sermons*, pp. 13-23.

14. Crowder, p. 64.

15. Ibid., p. 67.

16. Ibid., pp. 67-68.

17. Ray, p. 41.

18. Crowder, p. 78.

19. For this story see Louis W. Newton and Herbert T. Gambrell, *A Social and Political History of Texas* (Dallas: n.p., 1935), pp. 301 ff.

20. Article in File 165, Carroll Papers.

21. Ibid.

22. Cranfill, *Sermons*, pp. 45-57.

23. A. J. Barton, Founder's Day Address, 31 January 1940, in Carroll Papers.

24. Ray, p. 109. See also the words of J. B. Gambrell in Crowder, p. 102.

25. Ray, pp. 151-52.

26. Ibid., pp. 153-54. This illness occurred after Ray entered Waco University. Although he was over twenty years old, he still referred to himself as an "orphan boy."

27. W. E. Penn, *The Life and Labors of Major W. E. Penn* (St. Louis: C. B. Woodward Printing & Book Mfg. Co., 1896), p. 110.

28. Frank E. Burkhalter, *A World-Visioned Church* (Nashville: Broadman Press, 1946), p. 88.

29. Ibid., pp. 127-31.

30. Ibid., pp. 95, 100.

31. Ray, p. 110.

32. Burkhalter, p. 97.

33. Ibid., pp. 97-100.

34. Ibid., pp. 105-106.

35. Ibid., pp. 95-96.

36. Ibid., pp. 80-84.

37. Ibid., p. 113.

38. Crowder, p. 160.

39. Ray, pp. 159-60, 164-65.

40. Ibid., p. 105.

41. W. H. Jenkins to B. H. Carroll, 16 January 1895, File 169, Carroll Papers.

42. Crowder, p. 174.

43. Ibid., p. 114.

44. Ray, pp. 64-65.

45. Burkhalter, pp. 190-91.

46. Crowder, p. 163.

47. Walker and Lumpkin, p. 67.

48. See ibid., p. 206, for a summary of Carroll's leadership.

49. Ibid., pp. 107-10.

50. Ibid., pp. 170 ff.

51. Ibid., p. 113.

52. See ibid., pp. 123-47, for an extended discussion of this controversy.

53. Ibid., pp. 195-96.

54. See Baker, *The Blossoming Desert*, pp. 105 ff, for this story.

55. *Proceedings of the Fourth Annual Session of the Baptist General Association of Texas*, 1871, p. 4 (hereafter cited as *Proceedings*, General Association).

56. J. M. Carroll, pp. 422-28.

57. *Proceedings*, General Association, 1875, pp. 6, 9; 1878, pp. 16-17; 1879, pp. 9, 26 ff.

58. Ibid., 1877, p. 35.

59. Ibid., Called Session of 1880, pp. 13 ff, 21 ff.

60. Ibid., 1883, pp. 18, 26-28.

61. Ibid.

62. Ibid., 1884, p. 25.

63. For this story see J. M. Carroll, pp. 639-51.

64. For this movement see Baker, *Southern Baptist Convention*, pp. 208-19.

65. *The Tennessee Baptist* (Nashville), 5 February 1859, p. 2.

66. *Proceedings*, State Convention, 1859, p. 4.

67. B. H. Carroll, *Ecclesia—The Church* (Louisville: Baptist Book Concern, 1903), p. 6.

68. Baker, *Southern Baptist Convention*, pp. 278-80.

69. Ray, pp. 101-2.

70. J. M. Carroll, pp. 708-16.

71. Baker, *The Blossoming Desert*, pp. 157-62, and Baker, *Southern Baptist Convention*, pp. 281-82.

72. Ray, p. 14.

73. J. B. Cranfill, *Dr. J. B. Cranfill's Chronicle* (New York: Fleming H. Revell Co., 1916), pp. 455-56.

74. Crowder, p. 130.

75. Ibid., p. 131.

76. Ibid., pp. 133-34.

77. Ibid., p. 132.

78. For this story see Baker, *Southern Baptist Convention*, pp. 256-84, 299-300.

79. For this story see Robert A. Baker, *Relations Between Northern and Southern Baptists* (Fort Worth: By the Author, 1948 and 1954), pp. 92-132.

80. Ray, pp. 97-98.

81. Baker, *Southern Baptist Convention*, p. 262.

82. Ray, pp. 98-99.

83. Ibid., p. 100. See Robert A. Baker, *History of the Sunday School Board* (Nashville: Convention Press, 1966), pp. 37-46 for this story.

84. *Proceedings*, BGCT, 1891, p. 45.

85. See letter of W. H. Whitsitt to B. H. Carroll, 7 June 1895, in which Whitsitt extravagantly praises Carroll's proposed message, File 171, Carroll Papers.

86. Barnes, pp. 137-38.

87. Ibid., p. 137.

88. *Texas Baptist Standard*, 25 May 1875, p. 1. Although this paper absorbed others and changed its location to Dallas, Texas, it became the sole denominational organ. Its name is unique in Texas, so it will hereafter be cited simply as the *Standard*.

89. W. O. Carver, "William Heth Whitsitt: The Seminary's Martyr," *Review and Expositor* (Louisville), October 1954, pp. 454 ff.

90. John H. Spencer, "Dr. Whitsitt on Baptist History," *Western Recorder*, (Louisville), 30 April 1896, p. 13.

91. A. T. Robertson, "Dr. Whitsitt and Early English Baptists," *Western Recorder*, 30 April 1896, p. 13.

92. John T. Christian, "Dr. Whitsitt and the Early English and American Baptists," *Western Recorder*, 7 May 1896, p. 2.

93. T. T. Eaton to B. H. Carroll, 14 July 1896, File 208-1, Carroll Papers.

94. A. T. Robertson to B. H. Carroll, 15 July 1896, from North Carolina, File 208-1, Carroll Papers.

95. John R. Sampey to B. H. Carroll, 24 August 1896, File 208-1, Carroll Papers.

96. For Carroll's letter see *Standard*, 7 May 1896, p. 13; for his article, "Dr. Whitsitt's Position," see *Standard*, 2 July 1896.

97. See his editorial in the *Texas Baptist and Herald* (Dallas), 9 July 1896, p. 8.

98. See, for example, his editorials in the *Standard*, 9 January 1896, p. 4; 30 April 1896, p. 4; and 21 May 1896, p. 4.

99. See, for example, the blistering article by W. A. Jarrell, a well-known successionist, "Dr. Kerfoot's Apology for Dr. Whitsitt," in the *Standard*, 4 June 1896, p. 3, after Professor F. H. Kerfoot had published an article urging moderation in the *Standard*, 14 May 1896.

100. See John H. Spencer, "Dr. Whitsitt on the Baptists," *Standard*, 7 May 1896, p. 1.

101. *Annual of the Southern Baptist Convention*, 1896, pp. 28-29 (hereafter cited as *Annual*, SBC).

102. *Proceedings*, BGCT, 1896, p. 68.

103. The Southern Baptist Theological Seminary (Louisville, Kentucky), Minutes of Meetings of the Board of Trustees, meeting of 6 May 1897, Items 18, 58.

104. Ibid., Item 23.

105. Ibid., 7 May 1897, pp. 223-24.

106. B. H. Carroll, "The Whitsitt Case at Wilmington," *Standard*, 20 May 1897, pp. 1-2.

107. B. H. Carroll, "Back to the Realm of Discussion," *Standard*, 27 May 1897.

108. See letters from R. H. Pitt, editor of the *Religious Herald* (Virginia), dated 24 and 26 June 1897, and Carroll's reply dated 30 June 1897, File 208-1, Carroll Papers.

109. B. H. Carroll, "The Real Issue in the Whitsitt Case," *Standard*, 5 August 1897.

110. William A. Mueller, *A History of Southern Baptist Theological Seminary* (Nashville: Broadman Press, 1959), p. 172.

111. See J. W. Bailey to B. H. Carroll, 18 August 1897, and F. H. Kerfoot to Carroll, 2 April 1898, File 208-1, Carroll Papers.

112. See J. W. Bailey to B. H. Carroll, 10 August 1897, File 208-1, Carroll Papers.

113. *Annual*, SBC, 1898, p. 23.

114. Crowder, p. 132.

115. A. T. Robertson, *The Life and Letters of John A. Broadus* (Philadelphia: American Baptist Publication Society, 1902), p. 444.

116. John A. Broadus, *Memoirs of James Petigru Boyce* (New York: A. C. Armstrong and Son, 1893) pp. 259-64.

117. For this sermon see Cranfill, *Sermons*, pp. 24-44.

118. Elliott, pp. 157-58.

119. *Proceedings*, BGCT, 1886, p. 25.

120. Ibid., pp. 21-25.

121. Ibid., 1890, p. 35.

122. Ibid., 1891, p. 27.

123. Ibid., 1893, pp. 81-82.

124. Ibid., 1894, pp. 60-61.

125. Ray, pp. 113-14. See also Crowder, pp. 153-54.

126. *Proceedings*, BGCT, 1895, p. 50. See Charles Carver, *Brann and the Iconoclast* (Austin: University of Texas Press, 1957), for Brann's side of the affair.

127. *Proceedings*, BGCT, 1895, p. 51.

128. John S. Tanner to B. H. Carroll, 28 May 1895, File 171, Carroll Papers.

129. File of John S. Tanner in Vertical File, Treasure Room of Fleming Library, Southwestern Baptist Theological Seminary, Fort Worth, Texas.

130. For additional information on Tanner see *Baylor Bulletin* (Waco), IV (1900-1901):103, in Texas Collection, Baylor University Library, Waco, Texas. Also see Dayton Kelley, ed., *Handbook of Waco and McLennan County, Texas* (Waco: Texian Press, 1972); *Baylor Bulletin*, the Memorial Edition, July 1901; the *Baylor Lariat* (Waco), 23 March 1901; the *Waco Times Herald*, 22 March 1901; and the oral memoirs of J. M. Dawson, Baylor University Library, 1972.

131. J. B. Gambrell to B. H. Carroll, 13 July 1896, File 172, Carroll Papers.

132. O. H. Cooper to B. H. Carroll, 17 July 1897, File 94, Carroll Papers.

133. J. M. Carroll, pp. 819-20.

134. Ibid., pp. 820 ff.

135. Ibid., pp. 825-28.

136. Ibid., p. 835.

137. Ibid.

138. Resignation of B. H. Carroll from First Baptist Church, Waco, Texas, File 14, Carroll Papers.

139. Burkhalter, pp. 136-41.

3

Immediate Antecedents

One step remained before B. H. Carroll would be completely free to concentrate his energies solely on ministerial education. His language as he resigned from his pastorate at Waco in 1899 did not reveal whether or not he was looking beyond the challenge of the Education Commission to a full-time ministry with Baylor. In their reminiscences, Jeff D. Ray, J. W. Crowder, and J. B. Cranfill seem to pass over this stint with the Education Commission, and they move directly from the pastoral ministry of Carroll to his teaching. J. M. Carroll interpreted his brother's resignation as pastor as motivated by the challenge of the Education Commission. Perhaps there is an element of truth in both: B. H. Carroll saw the imperative need to enlarge Baylor's program of ministerial education through additional funding; he viewed the Education Commission as the opportunity to secure that funding. It cannot be known whether he went a step further in his thinking and envisioned the enlarged program at Baylor as an opportunity for him to engage directly in that program. It seems quite certain that he did not have in mind organizing a theological seminary at this time.[1]

The Texas Baptist Education Commission

B. H. Carroll promptly entered actively into the campaign to achieve the goals of the Education Commission. He took office on January 1, 1899, with his brother as his assistant. Despite the increasing pressure of the Hayden controversy, he was able to make an excellent report to the Baptist General Convention which met at Dallas on November 14, 1899. Only $4,940.90 had been paid on the pledges made in the previous year, but in the current year the cash collections were $60,109.99, and unpaid subscriptions amounted to about $40,000, for a total sum of approximately $105,000 that had been pledged so far.[2] Carroll detailed how some of this money had been used to rescue Decatur and Howard Payne colleges and provide some necessary equipment for Baylor University.

It had been the plan of the two Carroll brothers to take a public offering at the convention after this good report, but the Hayden struggle left no

111

time for this. The convention simply adopted Carroll's report in silence. "One hour before that throng would have secured $50,000 without expense," commented B. H. Carroll.

In the following year at Waco, Carroll reported to the state body that an aggregate of $94,679.15 had been raised for the work of the Education Commission, and he made an accounting for all that had been done during the year 1899-1900. He reviewed the saving of school properties at Decatur, Brownwood, Burleson, Rusk, and Belton, as well as providing additions to the property of Baylor University at Waco. "Thus, the Education Commission has lifted up the despondent Baptist heart, restored confidence, revived hope and enthusiasm. Unquestionably we are getting our money's worth. . . . "[3]

During the year 1901 B. H. Carroll suffered a protracted illness, and it appeared that the goal of raising $100,000 to complete all of the task except the endowment campaign for Baylor University was unreachable. When the convention met at Fort Worth on November 8-11, 1901, the commission was $25,000 short of its $100,000 goal. Some of the remaining $75,000 had been pledged on the condition that the commission raise the whole $100,000 and complete the campaign. When B. H. Carroll scanned the Baptists present at the convention, he said to his younger brother, "Jimmie, we can't raise that $25,000 balance from this crowd." He began naming many strong friends who were absent from this meeting. J. M. Carroll replied that he would wire these friends for a pledge. He sent a dozen telegrams, explaining their plight and asking each one for $1,000 more. Not one of these friends refused to make a gift. Over $5,000 was obtained in this way, and the entire $25,000 was raised at the convention. J. M. Carroll later wrote:

> Up to that date it was the largest cash collection ever taken in the State by the Baptists. . . . The author can shut his eyes now and see the rain of checks and bills as they fell from the galleries. R. T. Hanks' spirit during the collection will never be forgotten. He was constantly crying out, "Go on, Carroll! We will get it!"

J. M. Carroll recorded his brother's address, which he termed, "eloquence on fire. It seemed almost enough to raise the dead."[4]

There was a tender word in the closing part of this message. J. M. Carroll had been called as pastor of the First Baptist Church, Waco, and his brother paid tribute to him in golden words.

> For thirteen years in succession he has served the denomination in the general field, for all this time homeless and apart from his family. His character is spotless, his spirit as gentle and conciliatory as ever animated a denominational leader. As financial secretary for Foreign Missions, as

superintendent of State Missions, as secretary of Baylor College, as secretary and assistant secretary of the Commission, he has traversed Texas, known all its heat and cold, been a mighty factor in all the denominational victories. He is weary. He is homesick. He longs to re-enter the pastoral work. . . . He has harmed no man. He bears malice against none. Covered with scars of many battles, all fought for you and for God, he bids the general work farewell.[5]

How revealing of the character of the speaker were these tender expressions!

B. H. Carroll served the commission during all of 1902, although he accepted a salary for only three months. J. M. Carroll was prevailed upon to return to the commission to assist in the endowment of Baylor University, and he reluctantly resigned from his church to do this. B. H. Carroll then tendered his resignation to the commission but agreed to "round up the unfinished work of the debt paying and equipment department." The report of 1903 showed that J. M. Carroll had been able to secure from John D. Rockefeller a provisional gift of $33,950, provided the convention would raise an additional $126,000 by January 1, 1904. He had already raised $22,000 of this amount.[6]

B. H. Carroll resigned from the Education Commission to enter "wholly into the theological work at Baylor." His brother and others had long been urging him to do this. But Baylor had no money to pay theological teachers. Again his younger brother responded. "Profoundly impressed that B. H. Carroll should give the closing years of his life to the teaching and training of young preachers," J. M. Carroll appealed to seven men to pay the salary of his brother for the remaining nine months of 1902. They too were convinced that B. H. Carroll's place was in the classroom, so the money came promptly: $1,000 from George W. Carroll (no relation), Beaumont; $500 from R. H. Hicks, Rockdale; $100 from J. B. Cranfill, Dallas; $100 from J. L. Smith, Amarillo; $100 from J. A. Walker, Brownwood; $100 from Herbert Kokernot, Alpine; and $50 from W. H. Cowden, Midland.[7] Did any investment ever pay greater dividends?

The Theological Department at Baylor

Ministerial education among Baptists in Texas made large strides between 1901 and 1908. During the previous half century, ministers had been trained in literary institutions with only peripheral formal instruction in theological disciplines. Students who desired additional academic training would generally attend The Southern Baptist Theological Seminary, located after 1877 at Louisville, Kentucky. The forming of the Bible Department at Baylor University in 1893 was an important step toward providing ministerial training, and the organizational skills of John S. Tanner helped formalize the curriculum after his coming to Baylor in 1895.

As his contemporaries have written, however, it was the personality and vision of B. H. Carroll that made possible the gigantic steps that were taken following the turn of the century. Here was a man who was both immensely gifted and thoroughly seasoned for the crowning work of his fruitful life. His personality and position made it possible for him to do the thing that no other individual in Texas Baptist life could have achieved in the founding of Southwestern Seminary. His twenty-eight years in the pastorate at the First Baptist Church, Waco, had honed his natural gifts of communication and persuasiveness; his integrity was recognized everywhere; his warm and selfless spirit caused many to love and revere him; and his powerful preaching to an entire generation of young preachers and other Baptist leaders at Baylor University gave him great personal influence among Texas Baptists. His shadow had been extended through ceaseless activity in associational, state, and Convention-wide bodies. His expertise in the educational field had been developed by close ties with Baylor University since 1886 and with Waco University since 1870. As a trustee of Southern Seminary at Louisville since 1894, he had become intimately familiar with the complete operation of a theological school, and his wide reading included much material on theological education. His image as a loyal Southern Baptist was enhanced by his leadership in sectional debates. His ability to raise large sums of money had been displayed in his campaigns for Baylor, the state mission board, and the Texas Baptist Education Commission.

In 1901, at the age of fifty-eight, he was an imposing figure. His advancing years had brought no slouching in his large frame, and his white hair and beard gave him a patriarchal appearance. Some of his addresses to large bodies of Baptists and others after 1901 revealed that he had lost none of his intellectual acumen and platform eloquence. Lansing Burrows later spoke of Carroll's stirring addresses before the Southern Baptist Convention meetings at Asheville in 1903, at Kansas City in 1905, at Chattanooga in 1906, and especially at Hot Springs in 1908 "in which he swayed the multitude."[8] He still retained much of the driving energy that had characterized his earlier years. Like Caleb, he felt capable of grappling with giants.

Carroll was fortunate in having an admiring friend as the new president of Baylor University. Oscar H. Cooper had succeeded Rufus C. Burleson in 1899 and had already committed himself to the idea of a theological department in Baylor University. With the full support of Cooper, Carroll announced in 1901 that ministerial instruction would now be known as the Theological Department of Baylor University.[9] He had already been at work to provide the faculty for the proposed new department. In 1900 he had engaged Albert Henry Newman of McMaster University, Toronto, Canada, to deliver the commencement address at Baylor University and lecture at the summer Bible school. Newman was awarded the honorary LL.D. degree at the spring graduation. He was one of the most distinguished church historians of that day and had even been seriously considered as a successor to W. H. Whitsitt in the presidency of the Southern Seminary. During Newman's visit to Waco, Carroll strongly urged him to join the faculty of the new theological department of Baylor. Newman was reluctant to leave the Canadian school, but Carroll continued in his efforts to persuade him during the remainder of the year.

In the midst of these negotiations, tragedy struck the Baylor campus with the unexpected death of thirty-two-year-old John S. Tanner on March 21, 1901. His dedicated scholarship and outstanding teaching gifts had been utilized in the instruction of young preachers at Baylor, and in the comparatively few years of his teaching he had become an inspiration to his students. One of them, standing by Tanner's grave at Oakwood Cemetery, wrote:

> What meaning more is in this mound of earth
> I stand beside, that I should feel the tears
> Scald my burning cheek, my heart to leap
> With voiceless prayer and make me fall with face
> Upturned to God? Great maker of the great,
> Why did'st thou seal his lips so soon, that moved
> With flaming truth; O Wise and Just, quench thou
> These dark rebellious thoughts! He died too soon!
> The world was in his heart; Eternity
> His vision, Truth his theme and Love his work.
> Peerless thinker, prophet, seer! Where is
> His like? The flush of youth was on his cheek
> His eyes were sparkling o'er the prospect of
> His plans, forever widening in their scope;
> His heart was tremulous for action strong;
> He knew no fear, for he was born to lead
> Men up to higher things, O Mighty God,
> I thank thee that he lived, though 'tis strange he died
> And thou, Infinite One, help me to walk,
> The paths he trod, and give to me His deathless name![10]

The death of John S. Tanner made it even more imperative that a person with the stature of A. H. Newman be brought to the theological faculty. After agonizing over the decision, Newman finally consented to come. With undisguised pleasure Carroll announced Newman's acceptance to the state convention in November, 1901, saying that "Doctor Newman's scholarship, intellectual power and character, make his coming to Baylor University a matter of national significance."[11] Mrs. Newman was placed in charge of Burleson Hall for young ladies. At the same time, Carroll announced that Robert N. Barrett, a close friend of Tanner, was leaving the church at Waxahachie to join the faculty as professor of biblical languages and missions. In his opening address to the department in September, Carroll said that its new name, by the action of the trustees, was the Theological Department of the university.[12]

What appeared to be a significant step in the direction of providing additional financial support for this new department of study was couched in a recommendation to the state body from the Committee on Ministerial Education in 1901. The recommendation urged that

> the matter of securing funds for ministerial education be referred to our Education Commission, and that all collections taken by them for this object be prorated among these institutions [Baylor's Theological Department, ministerial education in the correlated schools, and the seminary at Louisville] according to the number of theological students in each.[13]

Unfortunately, however, this plan was not successful in providing funds for Baylor's Theological Department, and it was discontinued.[14]

The appointment of the two new professors and the formal inauguration of the Theological Department at Baylor did not escape the attention of Southern Baptist leaders in the East. J. W. Bailey, editor of the *Biblical Recorder* of North Carolina, editorialized on July 10, 1901:

> It is understood that the removal of Rev. Dr. A. H. Newman from McMaster College, Toronto, Canada, to Baylor University, Texas, has regard to the establishment of a theological school in connection with that university. With such a host of Baptists as Texas counts, it is not unreasonable that it be made the home of a theological school which shall hold the young men thus educated to their own section of the country. Heretofore it has been difficult to get them back again when once they got as far away as Louisville.

Adding substance to this speculation, Professor R. N. Barrett, writing in behalf of President Cooper, announced in the Texas *Baptist Standard* of August 29, 1901:

> For some time there has been a demand and expectation that a full department of theology be announced, but as the Education Commission

does not make a final report till November, it is not yet known whether all debts will be paid, so that endowment can be claimed. For that reason the trustees prudently refrain from promising too much, but have authorized what is here outlined as the first year's work in a course leading to the degree of Bachelor of Theology. But next year it is confidently expected that there will be a large endowment, which will enable the institution to employ the best instructors, who will proceed with the full curriculum of a well-organized theological Seminary.

New resistance to the further expansion of the Theological Department developed when President O. H. Cooper of Baylor University was succeeded in 1902 by S. P. Brooks. Brooks had been teaching economics and history at Baylor after earning an A.B. degree from that school. In 1902, he was awarded the M.A. degree by Yale University, where he had studied on a leave of absence. He was an excellent teacher and educator and led Baylor University to a new era in its history. He was not pleased with the unique administrative structure which had existed for several years at the Waco school. B. H. Carroll was regularly elected as president of the board of trustees and in this capacity exercised a considerable amount of authority over the president of the school. This situation was not critical during the time Carroll was pastor of the Waco church, but when he came to the faculty of Baylor to teach Bible, it produced a remarkable administrative structure in which the president of the university found himself under the authority of one of his faculty. Conscious of this paradox, Brooks moved to assert the prerogatives of his position. No longer did Carroll report to the state convention as chairman of the trustees, but from the time Brooks came in 1902 it was he who made these reports as president. He, like R. C. Burleson, believed that a preacher needed first of all a strong literary education like any other student, after which the distinctive ministerial training could be added. He kept a careful watch on the new department.

The statistics for 1901 and 1902 have been garbled at times, but evidently there were 87 ministerial students in 1901 and 80 in 1902.[15] In 1903, they numbered 87 again[16] and 101 in 1904.[17]

Editor J. W. Bailey of North Carolina touched a sensitive spot when he wrote early in 1903 that "Baylor University has been bidding for a place as a rival of the Louisville Seminary with the Whitsitt controversy as a basis." Carroll indignantly replied:

> This, however unintentionally, does great injustice to Baylor University in two particulars: (1) The Institution here has not been bidding as a rival of the Louisville Seminary. (2) The Whitsitt controversy is not a basis of anything done here.
> Whenever I regard Baylor University's theological department as a rival

of the Seminary, then I will resign as Seminary trustee and quit influencing Texas preachers to attend the Seminary. The Seminary sustains a peculiar relation to the whole Southern Baptist Convention which, so far as I know, no theological department in any Southern Baptist college or university seeks to share.

Entirely apart from this fact the theological work here is a necessity for the thousands of the Texas ministers of whom under the most favorable conditions a very small number comparatively will ever be able to attend the Seminary.

While there are doubtless some things taught in the Seminary from which some Texas brethren may dissent, the spirit here is one of good will toward and co-operation with it.

Moreover, we are delighted here with most of the work done in the Seminary and hold it in high honor as a Baptist institution. Whenever we can, we get its scholarly professors to aid us in our work here and even now are looking forward with pleasure to Dr. Mullins' promised visit and co-operation in the forthcoming dedication of the new Carroll buildings.

We see no good to anybody, but only evil to all concerned in the creation of a jealous or hostile sentiment between the Seminary and Southern colleges and universities.[18]

President S. P. Brooks was not unmindful of this discussion when, in reporting to the state convention of Baptists in November, 1903, he wrote concerning the Summer Bible School:

For several years, instruction has been given in Bible study to the preachers who could not go to the Seminary at Louisville. . . . It must be understood that the Summer Bible School, and even the Theological School of Baylor University in no sense is, or expects to be, a rival to our own Seminary at Louisville. Our object is to help train the men of the Southwest contiguous to us, whom the Seminary may never reach. . . . So long as the Seminary can offer, as it clearly does now, more advanced Theological training than Baylor, we shall encourage our students to go there for the so-called completion of their studies.[19]

In this same report in 1903 Brooks mourned the death of Robert N. Barrett "who had wrought so well whatever he undertook along the lines of ministerial education and the promotion of the spiritual welfare of the student body."[20] B. H. Dement, a scholarly pastor from Louisville, was elected to replace Barrett but resigned after one year to accept the pastorate of the Waco church. L. W. Doolan was then named professor of Hebrew and cognate languages and homiletics. Doolan was an honor graduate of Southern Seminary, with additional training at the Rochester Theological Seminary, and had been a successful pastor.

It is interesting to notice that although President Brooks began making the report for Baylor University in 1902, B. H. Carroll did not allow himself to be cut off from his communication with the state convention.

He began to make the annual reports on ministerial education, and in 1904 his twelve-page report (compared to Brooks's eight-page report for the entire university) developed his ideas about ministerial education at Baylor University. He argued convincingly that ministerial education was vital. With humor he said that

> it is not a violation of Divine prerogative, nor wrong per se, to teach a God-called man how to spell association, or how to make his verbs agree with their nominatives, or how to preserve and promote his health, or how to train his voice or mind, or how to study the Bible and oversee the Church. And since God himself has embodied the subject matter of preaching in at least two earth languages it can not be against his duty of exegesis to know somewhat of the laws of the language whose words he undertakes to interpret.

Carroll estimated that the cost of sustaining the Theological Department at Baylor for the next year would amount to about six thousand dollars.[21] It was this sort of background that enabled him later to make specific plans for financing this department of study.

Baylor Theological Seminary

The stage was set for the momentous events of 1905. Just before the close of the spring quarter, Carroll began the campaign. Using a sentence from an article by J. B. Gambrell which stated that the most important work being done at Baylor University was the training of preachers, Carroll prepared an eloquent article for the *Baptist Standard* of May 4, 1905, calling for greater efforts in this work.

> About one-fifteenth of the Baptists in the world are here in Texas. As the Great Northern Lakes are the nesting place of all migratory fowls, so is Texas the breeding place of preachers. From the timbered sections of East Texas; from the prairies and plains of the West; from red lands, black lands, and white lands; from wheat fields, corn fields, rice fields, cane fields, cotton patches, and ranches they hear and heed the moaning prayer of a destitute world: "Laborers, more laborers, Lord." They hear the Master's inquiry: "Whom shall I send" and they respond, each for himself, "Lord, send me." They ask no question of the thither. Anywhere in the world where needed. The missionary nestling prepares for migratory flight to any destitute field in the wide world. They go flight by flight. First to some country church; thence to a town pastorate; thence over the Texas border to some city pastorate in the older states; thence, by a longer flight, they light on foreign shores, Mexico, Cuba, Brazil, Europe, Africa, Asia, the islands of the sea. In the meantime, as they swarm they fill a thousand mission fields and three thousand pastorates in Texas.[22]

Carroll went on to say that these preachers were molding the world, but that they first needed training. "Their axes and scythes are dull, their forks blunt, their plows not pointed."

A week later, in the *Baptist Standard* for May 11, Carroll reported to the people that he, Newman, and Doolan were able to offer the Bachelor of Theology degree only but that his greatest concern was not for training technical scholars but for preparing a great multitude of pastors, evangelists, missionaries, and Sunday School teachers who had no training whatsoever for their tasks. "The graduates this year from all the theological seminaries of the world would not suffice in number to supply the Baptist churches of Texas, if all were Baptists and acceptable." He noted that the Theological Department had enrolled 138 students in 1905, of whom 118 were preachers, 11 were laymen, and 7 were young women. This number did not include many who would attend the Summer Bible School and many who were taught in the institutes conducted by the faculty in various parts of Texas during the year. The work was vitally important, he emphasized.

> It is leavening Texas. It is awakening the dormant. It is kindling fires in the valleys and lighting beacons on the hilltops. Evangelism acknowledges its stimulation, missionaries diffuse its spirit, churches are trained in the things of peace, led into brotherhood and cooperation, discipline acknowledges its power, covetousness dies in its light, and liberality blooms in its track.

How difficult it was to withstand a man with such overwhelming enthusiasm and vision!

Then, as Carroll traveled by train in the Panhandle of Texas, as described in the first chapter, he had that mystical experience in which he felt that the risen Christ was commissioning him to found a theological seminary in the Southwest. Before returning to Waco, he had begun his effort to raise $30,000 which, because of his prior experience with the expenses of the Theological Department, he felt would provide for salaries and expenses of a seminary staff for three years. He made a list of one hundred friends, then wrote each a personal letter asking for one hundred dollars a year as an emergency fund for the proposed seminary. He spelled out the great need for a seminary which would "teach all the courses and confer all the degrees common to a regular and first-class theological seminary."[23] Before the end of the summer, he had pledges and cash in the amount of $22,000. He had not yet asked the trustees, the president of Baylor, nor the Baptist General Convention of Texas if he would be allowed to wrench one of the departments of Baylor from the university and make it a separate institution. Knowing the sometimes capricious nature of Baptists, their boards, and conventions, he must have had an audacious faith to step out ahead of all of these. Not only could no other man in Texas have done this; none of them would have tried it.

Carroll's next moves would be difficult. He had to communicate to the president of the university, the trustees, and the state convention his unique vision and convince them that they also must acknowledge its demands. The curious administrative situation at Baylor helped him. Not only was Carroll president of the trustees of Baylor (and could thus institute action without the sanction of the university's president), but S. P. Brooks happened to be in Europe during the summer and had not yet returned to Waco. These two factors provided a milieu that had never before existed nor would ever occur again.

The minutes of the trustees of Baylor show that on August 31, 1905, the following were in attendance: Carroll, E. R. Nash, Pat M. Neff, M. H. Standifer, Homer Wells, W. H. Jenkins, and two new members, J. F. Rowe and H. H. Crouch. The minutes said:

> Dr. Carroll offered the following resolution: Resolved, that Baylor University now make the Theological Department a complete School of Divinity— teaching all the courses and conferring all the degrees of a regular first class theological seminary, provided that no debt on the university is contracted in prosecuting this work—the resolution was adopted.
>
> The following resolution was also adopted to wit. Moved: That B. H. Carroll be authorized to raise, without cost to Baylor University, funds with which to pay the salaries of the teachers employed in the Theological Department of Baylor University for the three scholastic years 1905-6, 1906-7, 1907-8. Said funds, as raised, to be deposited with the Treasurer of Baylor University and to be known as the "Theological Teachers Salary Fund" and to be so entered on his book. This fund to be used exclusively and to be the only authorized fund, for the payment of salaries of said teachers for the three scholastic years designated.[24]

For a few moments after Carroll made this proposal, said Jeff D. Ray, there was "a silence as still as death." Finally, Judge W. H. Jenkins, the venerable secretary of the body, rose to his feet, trembling with emotion, and said:

> None of us is prepared for this. Humanly speaking, it seems a rash step to take. But evidently our noble brother has had a vision from God. I move that his request be granted and immediate steps be taken to launch the enterprise.[25]

S. P. Brooks returned from Europe to learn that without his acquiescence one of his departments had become a separate institution.

The fall quarter of 1905 opened at Baylor University about a week later. Carroll delivered an opening address to the Theological Department stating that "what is undertaken is an expression of the sublime audacity of faith." He described his vision on the train and announced that the Theological Department was now officially the Baylor Theological Seminary, in accordance with the authorization of the trustees. He outlined the great need for a seminary in Texas, noting that in the South, where over half of the Baptists of the world lived, there was but one seminary, and it could not possibly train even the 3,000 preachers of Texas whose numbers were increasing annually by 250 to 500. When about twenty of these preachers "go abroad" for training each year, he said, few return to serve in Texas. In addition, new preachers were immigrating into Texas each year, some of them with "loose doctrines"; and there had also been developing

> a more menacing invasion of theological literature assailing the very foundations of the faith. . . . Like the plague of frogs in Egypt, these evil communications swarm in our streets, hop into every house, nestle in every bed, and spawn in the bread-trays of every college—secular or religious. In this way all popular religious thinking is being gradually leavened with hurtful teachings, as we regard them, on fundamental and vital doctrines, thus preparing the way for much confusion and trouble to the churches in the future.

Furthermore, said Carroll, "many of our home preachers" are badly in need of training for ministerial service. Finally, the western area of the country was developing so rapidly that a new seminary was necessary to keep up with the economic, intellectual, and religious growth of this section.[26]

Carroll did not minimize the problems that this large step would create. In this opening message, he reported having raised $22,000 of the $30,000 needed to operate the new seminary for the three following years, after which "a smaller number of different persons or a like number for smaller amounts, will be secured to carry on the work two or three years longer if that much additional time is needed to complete endowment." He emphasized that this enlargement of the work was not in rivalry with the Southern Seminary, "but is based upon our deep conviction that no one seminary can train all the preachers of the South and the Southwest." It also was not a disparagement of the work of other schools, especially the Baptist literary schools offering Bible study and partial ministerial training. "When all is done, that all of us are doing, we will fall short of meeting the necessities of the case."

Two additional faculty members were added in the fall of 1905. To supplement the teaching of Carroll, A. H. Newman, and L. W. Doolan,

Charles B. Williams and Calvin Goodspeed were brought to Baylor Seminary. Williams was a graduate of Wake Forest and Crozer Theological Seminary and had done additional work in the Greek New Testament at the University of Chicago. He had also been a successful pastor. In the curriculum, he was assigned to biblical Greek, New Testament theology, biblical introduction, and pastoral theology. Goodspeed came from a fifteen-year professorship in McMaster University, Toronto, Canada. He was a graduate of the University of New Brunswick and Newton Theological Seminary and, in addition, had studied at the University of Leipzig. He was also an experienced pastor and writer. At the Baylor Seminary, he taught systematic theology, apologetics, polemics, ecclesiology, and "Biblical Introduction, with special reference to recent destructive criticism of the Old Testament."

Three degrees were offered in 1905-1906: the Bachelor of Theology, the Master of Theology, and the Doctor of Theology. The requirements for degrees reflected the curricula of other seminaries. During the first year, the student carried seventeen quarter hours for each of three quarters covering English New Testament (fifteen quarter hours), systematic theology (twelve quarter hours), church history (twelve quarter hours), biblical introduction (four quarter hours), apologetics (four quarter hours), and missions (four quarter hours). In the second year, the student carried approximately the same load: twelve quarter hours of New Testament Greek, twelve quarter hours of Hebrew, eight quarter hours in homiletics, fifteen quarter hours in the English Old Testament, and four quarter hours in ecclesiology. In the third year, the load was about the same: eight quarter hours in Old and New Testament theology, eight quarter hours in Hebrew, eight quarter hours in New Testament Greek, four quarter hours in church history, four quarter hours in pastoral duties, four quarter hours in polemics, four quarter hours in religious pedagogy, and four quarter hours in history of preaching.

The Th.B. degree was awarded after the completion of the second year of study, while the third year of study was required for the Th.M. It is interesting that a doctorate in theology was offered this early. Carroll was careful to emphasize the rigid requirements for the Doctor of Theology program. The candidate must have the B.A. or B.Ph. from a standard university, and a good working knowledge of German and French was recommended.

> Such a course will ordinarily embrace a major study in one department and two minors in other departments, and will consist largely in research work, carried on under the direction of members of the faculty, and the production of an elaborate thesis in which a high standard of originality,

scholarship and literary finish will be required. Only such men as, in the opinion of the faculty, are likely to do the work required in a highly creditable way will be encouraged to enter upon work for this degree and only those who devote themselves with all diligence to the tasks assigned can hope to succeed.[27]

This format for the Th.D. degree was continued with little change for many years.

The address by Carroll at the opening of the new seminary in 1905 was published in the *Baptist Standard* of Texas and caused widespread comment across the South. J. W. Bailey of the North Carolina *Biblical Recorder* could not refrain from remarking editorially on September 27, 1905, "Once upon a time we pointed out that another theological seminary was rising in Baylor University, Texas; and promptly did we receive most weighty denials from the men in charge." Carroll made no reply. The Southern Baptist Theological Seminary at Louisville was gracious in its general response to the development of a new Baptist seminary in Texas. John R. Sampey, who later became president of the school, was at this time a young professor at Louisville. He wrote many years later:

During the closing years of the life of Doctor Broadus, especially after the death of Doctor Basil Manly in January, 1892, he frequently invited me to join him in his afternoon walks. On one of these he said to me, "It will not be long before another theological seminary will be founded among Southern Baptists, and it will probably be in Texas." He then added to his young colleague one significant remark, "When the new seminary comes, it ought to be with the good will of the Southern Seminary."[28]

In 1906, Carroll made his first report to the Baptist General Convention of Texas as dean of the new seminary. In his usual candid style, he shared the many burdens that this new venture had brought to him. It was his responsibility, he wrote, both to obtain funds for supporting the faculty and to help sustain the ministerial students in school. He noted that for ten months of the year he had lectured to large classes in the English Old and New Testament (requiring much more preparation than a pastor needed to make for preaching) and that his heavy correspondence required daily attention. He had no organization across the state to assist in raising funds for the seminary, and the convention had specifically designated 1905 for a campaign in behalf of the correlated schools, making it necessary for him to do his fund raising by individual appeals. He called attention to the fact that "some good and honest brethren" were still openly questioning the wisdom of beginning seminary education in Texas at this time.[29] Carroll did not mention among his tasks a heavy schedule of speaking in behalf of various benevolences before many groups, including the Southern Baptist Convention.

Despite these problems, the seminary reported a very successful year. A total of $18,702.64 had been given for ministerial education, which had met the expenses of both faculty support and the students' beneficiary fund.

> By the grace of God and through the loving cooperation of tried friends the Dean has never been embarrassed. His body, soul and spirit are given to the work—a whole burnt offering. But sweeter to him than the notes from a wind-swept aeolian harp—sweeter than the smell of violets—sweeter than the chimes from cathedral towers are the loving letters and cheering words which accompany the money sent.[30]

The attendance of 1905-1906 was encouraging. In addition to 140 preachers, more than a score of gifted young men and women were enrolled in preparation for denominational service of various kinds.

> No other Seminary on the Western Continent ever had so large and prosperous a beginning. . . . No other Seminary has a higher grade of theological study and in some respects our curriculum requirements are higher than any other. No other Seminary provides a four year's course in the English Bible.[31]

Allowing for the enthusiasm of a participant, it is doubtless true that the faculty of Carroll, Newman, Goodspeed, Williams, and Doolan, complemented by distinguished and scholarly special lecturers, provided an excellent group of teachers in the young school. From the faculty of Baylor University, Frederick Eby, professor of philosophy and education, also taught a course in Christian pedagogy for the seminary.

One significant part of the report of Carroll in 1906 was a strong appeal for a chair of evangelism in the seminary. Doubtless he was reflecting the large part he had played at the Southern Baptist Convention in 1906 when he called for the Convention to approve the policy on evangelism by the Home Mission Board. There he had said:

> If I were the secretary of this [Home] board, I would come before this body in humility and tears and say: "Brethren, give me evangelists. Deny not fins to things that swim against the tide, nor wings to things that must fly against the wind."[32]

In this first mention of a chair of evangelism for the seminary, Carroll wrote:

> There is great need to create and endow a chair of evangelism. Revivals are not only the hope of a lost world but the hope of the churches. If a

seminary have not the mind of the Lord it is none of His. If the Spirit of the
Lord do not indwell it, it is a vacant house. The mind and spirit of Jesus
appear in His life. His school of the prophets was intensely practical. The
wisdom he inculcated was the winning of souls.[33]

His report outlined what such a department should teach and how it
should be organized. One of the young ministers listening to him with
rapt attention was the pastor of the First Baptist Church, Abilene, Texas,
named L. R. Scarborough. He would later fill the first Chair of
Evangelism in this or any other seminary.

At the meeting of the state body in 1906, George W. Truett reported on
ministerial education in his typical impressive language. After naming
the Louisville seminary as richly deserving "our cordial appreciation and
co-operation," he wrote:

> We have also the Baylor Theological Seminary, which is now a vital part
> of our work, bone of our bone, the child of our prayers and labors. It has as
> its Dean a man whom all our great land delights to honor—for his works'
> sake—a man who is easily, in any field, first among equals as a preacher
> and teacher of God's Word. To this incomparable work he has consecrated
> his noble life. His ripe scholarship, his varied learning, his large
> experience, his splendid manhood, his unswerving devotion to the Master,
> and his simple, abiding, unconquerable faith in the old Book as it is
> written, all conspire preeminently to fit our beloved brother Carroll for the
> arduous responsibilities of the position that he now occupies.[34]

High praise for the new seminary also came from the pen of J. B.
Gambrell, the state mission secretary of Texas. This wise, plainspoken
leader called attention to the great need in Texas for the seminary.

> We have come, in our missionary department in many places in Texas, to a
> dead standstill from the lack of trained leaders for the churches. No church
> is likely to go beyond its pastor, and no pastor can go beyond his
> conceptions and training. It is fundamental to everything we are doing in
> Texas, to train our ministers in large numbers—in ever-increasing num-
> bers. The Seminary is needed now, sorely, but its need will increase with
> the years. . . . There is no greater nerve center in all of the denomination
> than the Baylor Theological Seminary. Dr. Carroll has taken on himself a
> herculean task in the founding and exploiting of the Seminary. We must
> make it possible for him to do his best. It will be poor economy for him to
> use up his strength on outside and subsidiary matters. . . . Let us stand by
> Dr. Carroll and make the Seminary an abounding blessing to our people.[35]

But the vision of B. H. Carroll was larger than simply providing a
seminary as an adjunct to a great university. Early in 1907, he called a
meeting of the trustees of Baylor University and requested that a
committee be appointed to consider the proper relations between the
seminary and the university and to recommend some definite plan to the

trustees. Carroll was named chairman of this committee. Shortly after the completion of his spring quarter lectures, Carroll prepared his report. In the introductory paragraph he stated:

> While it is my profound conviction that a Theological Seminary, west of the Mississippi River, to attain its full legitimate life, must *ultimately* be placed on its own distinct *habitat* and under a distinct charter and management, separate from any other institution, I am quite sure it is premature to consider that matter just now.

He continued that while the seminary was a part of Baylor University, "there is and must be sufficient distinctness of life to gain for it recognition and honor among other Theological Seminaries. Otherwise it would never fulfill the term 'first class' in your establishing resolution." He then named nine things which he called "indispensable" as a minimum. These looked principally toward establishing the autonomy of the seminary and its faculty.[36]

On June 26, 1907, President Brooks responded to the report of Carroll to the trustees. He was then in Shreveport, Louisiana, and his letter was cool and crisp. He said in part:

> I regret to dissent from the conclusions reached in that communication, as to the various points, and will submit my reasons therefore either to the Committee or to the Board in session as you may suggest.[37]

Evidently Carroll and others had already discussed the possibility of a new habitat for the seminary, for in a private letter of August 16, 1906, R. C. Buckner suggested Dallas as a possible site for the school.[38]

It is hardly surprising that President Brooks should respond unfavorably to the methodical steps being taken by Carroll, for it was clear that Carroll's goal was the complete separation and removal to another city of what had been the Theological Department of the university. Brooks had not concealed his opposition to these steps. Professor Doolan resigned from the seminary faculty in 1907 and later on, in a letter to Carroll, remarked: "I believed at the time of laying down my share of the task and still believe, the tender vine can never find a favorable soil on the campus of a University whose administration is opposed to its existence." He seemed to suggest that this was one reason for his leaving the faculty to accept a pastorate in Louisville.

Between June 26 and September 19, 1907, President Brooks totally reversed himself. He later wrote:

> In all my life I have never had so complete a reversal of judgment as in this idea of separation and removal of the Seminary from the University. About the time the Seminary came into well-defined existence suggestions began to be made about removal from Waco. I promptly tabooed the whole

of it. In fact I never dreamed that anybody could really be serious about its going. . . . I promptly said it was impossible and unthinkable, that if need be I would oppose it as an individual Baptist, and also as President of the University. I thought I should oppose it in the papers and on the platform, in the Convention or wherever it might arise.

In discussing the matter with J. B. Gambrell, however, he was amazed when Gambrell "delicately but plainly told me that those who advocated complete separation and removal were far sighted and that I as President would come to see it." Later, as he reflected on the situation, he began to see that young preachers were not simply young students but were already zealous ministers who were losing sight of their work as simply students and were looking longingly to their future as preachers.

His Seminary teachers admonished him that he should not try to fly till his wings grew, but how could he help it in the face of attractive cultured teachers whose courses pertained to his life work? How could he hold himself down to the so-called hum-drum of Greek grammar or the hair-splitting theories of Philosophy and Mathematics in the face of a course of Missions wherein he learned of a lost world? Who would blame a preacher boy for taking kindly to a discussion of the great doctrines of the Bible? . . .

It gradually dawned on me that the work of a Theological Seminary was not the work of merely giving instruction to college preacher boys and men. . . . I found it distinctively a graduate school. When I saw it thus I began to understand what the experienced wisdom of our great Mission Secretary sought to make plain to me.

At once, said Brooks, "I abandoned my former position." He became an earnest convert of separation; and when he looked at separation, he could see nothing short of removal also. He then gave many logical reasons for separation and a new habitat for the seminary.[39]

Thus, on September 19, 1907, he wrote to Carroll and said:

Before the meeting of the Committee to which was referred the consideration of the question of the Baylor Theological Seminary to the University I submit to you the following suggestions:

In view of the facts (a) that you do not think that the Seminary can reach its highest usefulness as now situated, and (b) that it is your "profound conviction that a Theological Seminary west of the Mississippi River, to attain its full legitimate life, must *ultimately* be placed in its own distinct *habitat* and under a distinct charter and management, separate from any other institution."

(1) I believe now that the Seminary should be (a) under a distinct charter, (b) with separate trustees, (c) with separate name, (d) located in a different city (preferably Fort Worth), (e) with a temporary home in the Baylor buildings, at least for a year or two, pending a legitimate effort at establishing the new location.

(2) I believe if you the Dean, and I the President, backed by a request

from the trustees, will go before the State Convention, a practically unanimous vote can be had to the above suggestion.

(3) By such a course of action we remove any possible local future friction and in my judgment will help both the Seminary and the University.

(4) If the Theological ideals are so radically different from that of the college ideals as set forth by you to the Trustees, then our differences are not personal but professional. For either of us to yield what we believe to be fundamental to get temporary relief from friction is not settling the matter wisely since our successors in office would meet the same difficulties. Then surely the friction should be permanently removed at once.

(5) If I understand the public mind at all it is no secret that the Seminary may move. This fact has grown since the Convention at Dallas, 1905. It is true the people do not agree as to whether it should remain in Waco or go elsewhere. It is also true that very many who primarily like myself believed that the Seminary ought to have grown up as a part of the University, now in the light of circumstances think it ought to be set up elsewhere. There are very many who do not believe it ought to have been enlarged two years ago, but now that it is enlarged, believe it ought not to be neglected, but can grow best under its own habitat and management.

(6) You do not believe it should remain as now. Your paper submitted to the Trustees practically separates and remains in Baylor. Bro. Ray's suggestions mean actual separation and yet location in Baylor.

I do not believe it should separate and *remain in Baylor or in Waco.* I believe it would mean endless conflict of student bodies and of the faculties, that the very fraternity that should exist, and that you and I want so much to develop, would fail utterly.

In very fact you and I believe in absolute and complete separation. Let us work together to attain it. But to guard against mistakes let us, you and I, officially invite at once a group of denominational leaders, pastors and laymen to come to Waco or elsewhere in a short time, to consider the Seminary and the University, to advise with us and help us to arrive at what is right and most far-reaching for Christian Education in Texas, preacher and laymen alike all for the glory of God.

If such a group of men, and we, agree, then there is no probability of the coming Convention being hurt by hasty or unwise resolutions from anybody.

I believe that such a body of men would meet with us. They would have no power or rights to force us, and though our judgment might remain the same after the conference as it is now, surely no harm but good only would come of it.

I write this letter with the prayer that the Seminary and the University may come to live in harmony here in Baylor or to live in harmony apart, each helping the other.[40]

As intimated in Brooks's letter, there was considerable public talk about the proposed separation of the university from the seminary. In the *Baptist Standard* for October 17, 1907, some weeks before any action was taken by the state convention, W. K. Penrod, pastor of the First Baptist Church, Cleburne, Texas, wrote a long article which reflected

precisely the views of B. H. Carroll. It set out the great need for a Baptist
seminary in Texas and urged that the Baylor Seminary be separated from
the university and moved from Waco. Penrod used the suggested name
"Southwestern Baptist Seminary." He gave the standard reasons for
separation of the seminary, although he agreed that it must remain for a
year or two at Waco. He said that he felt profoundly impressed to do
something at the state convention in the following month about establishing a "great Southwestern Baptist Seminary."

> One great reason for the necessity of beginning this enterprise now is that
> one of the assets, and a very large one, too, in Texas' ability to accomplish
> this work, is that matchless leader, Dr. B. H. Carroll. He can do more in
> Texas, and out of Texas, for this enterprise than any dozen other men. He is
> unquestionably the man for the hour—the man to lead us in this
> movement. Only a few years remain for this work. If we should neglect to
> begin this work while we have the benefit of his experience, ability, and
> influence, it would be a most egregious blunder. With Dr. Carroll as our
> leader and our soul on fire as it is for the accomplishment of this great
> work, I feel sure the Baptists of the Southwest would respond in such a
> manner as to make it a success. Dr. Carroll can raise endowment, enlist
> other states, and secure a sufficient bonus from some Texas city, I am sure.
> If we delay, if we neglect the opportunity we have while the few years of Dr.
> Carroll's life remain to us, it might be years before such another opportunity
> would be ours.

Backed by this kind of public sentiment and the strong letter from
President Brooks, Carroll went to the trustees to enlist their aid in
winning the approval of this important step by the Baptist General
Convention of Texas, which was scheduled to meet at San Antonio on
November 7-11, 1907. The trustees responded by appointing a committee
on September 30, 1907, to study the matter and then adopted their
report, which read as follows:

> Your committee appointed to suggest a plan to harmonize differences
> between the literary and theological departments of the University, report
> as follows:
> 1st.—We recommend that the Board of Trustees request the Convention
> to immediately incorporate the Seminary with its domicile at Waco until, if
> ever, it seemed most to the interest of the Redeemer's Kingdom to remove it
> elsewhere.
> 2nd.—That till its charter is obtained the Seminary be conducted under
> the same plan and arrangements as now in operation.
> 3rd.—That the charter name of the Seminary shall be such as to clearly
> differentiate it from Baylor University at Waco, Texas.
> 4th.—That in case our request is granted by the Convention, the
> University will continue to furnish teaching quarters to the Seminary,
> temporarily, till suitable accommodations can be provided for it.[41]

This report was signed by the committee of the trustees composed of B. H. Carroll, Jeff D. Ray, W. H. Jenkins, and S. P. Brooks.

It was arranged that Jeff D. Ray, one of the committee, would present this to the convention when it met at San Antonio on November 7-11, 1907. On the evening of Wednesday, November 6, Carroll went to the room of his pastor, A. J. Barton, who had attained a reputation already as a knowledgeable parliamentarian. Until midnight the two talked about the recommendation, and Carroll urged Barton to make a motion that the trustees' report be adopted at once. Barton felt, however, that there was a great deal of opposition from some leading pastors and suggested that his motion should look, rather, toward referring the matter to a committee for study and report. At midnight, Barton recalled, Carroll agreed. On the following afternoon, through the cooperation of George W. Truett, chairman of the committee on order of business, the recommendation of Baylor's trustees was considered at the very beginning of the business sessions. Ray read the recommendation, and Barton promptly moved that it be referred to a committee of fifteen to be appointed by the chair. It is interesting to notice that when reading the recommendation, Ray could not mention "a plan to harmonize differences" without stopping to point out that these differences were in no sense personal between the president of the university and the dean of the seminary, nor any other persons connected with the administration, but that both the president of the university and the dean of the seminary heartily approved this explanation and wanted it made.[42]

The committee named by President R. C. Buckner of the convention consisted of J. B. Gambrell, George W. Baines, W. B. Kendall, John Holland, W. C. Lattimore, W. B. Denson, D. I. Smyth, C. W. Daniel, W. M. Harris, J. H. Taylor, J. L. Gross, J. M. Carroll, N. A. Seale, J. W. Brice, and J. P. Boone, Jr. This was by no means a "rubber stamp" committee, for it included some strong voices on each side of the question. Their report came two days later from J. B. Gambrell, the chairman. It recommended:

1. That the Convention grant the request of the Board of Trustees of Baylor University for separation as desired.

2. That a committee of five be appointed by the chair to nominate a Board of Trustees for the Seminary, who shall be charged with the duty of securing a charter and as soon as practicable a habitat for said Seminary; and to do such other things as shall be necessary, permanently to establish said institution.

3. That a provision be made in said charter for other advisory boards, large enough to conserve the highest ideals of sound orthodoxy and solid business management.

4. That it be and is hereby understood and expressly stated that in taking this step Baylor University is not to do less work for the literary training of young preachers, but that hereafter as heretofore, the University will continue to furnish such training in the academic and collegiate branches and may also furnish such instruction in English Bible as the authorities may think proper and their resources justify.[43]

A. J. Barton described how he sat next to Carroll and repeated into the old veteran's hearing horn the full discussion that followed this recommendation; and after a unanimous vote had approved this action, Carroll agreed that it had been wise to refer this to a committee so that the utmost harmony would prevail.[44]

One significant aspect of this recommendation should be noted. In the recommendation of the Baylor board of trustees to the convention, nothing was said about whether Baylor University would offer any instruction in the Bible at all after the seminary was separated from the university. It appeared that Carroll had in mind that all of this type of instruction would move with the seminary. However, the fourth article of the convention's committee specifically asserted that Baylor University would continue to provide literary training for young preachers and also "furnish such instruction in English Bible as the authorities may think proper and their resources justify." This insured the continuation of some ministerial training in the university.

Immediately after the convention's approval of the separation, two significant reports were made. The first by J. M. Dawson on ministerial education recommended The Southern Baptist Theological Seminary at Louisville "to your affection, prayers and active support," and praised the work of the several Baptist schools in Texas who were providing ministerial training. But a special plea was made for Baylor Theological Seminary, "under whatever name it may be called and in whatever place it is located" for the training of preachers.

B. H. Carroll followed this with the report of the Baylor Seminary. He traced the steps that led to the present situation. He then reported that in "a quiet endowment canvass," one which did not obstruct any other denominational activity, he had obtained in cash and interest-bearing notes during the last summer a total of over $49,000 and 400 acres of land worth about $5,000. Since that time he had raised $4,000 more endowment and, through the work of I. E. Gates, $2,500 more, making a total endowment of $61,011.16. Meanwhile, he and Gates had collected an additional $5,000 for the emergency fund. He continued:

Brethren, the success of a quiet summer campaign for endowment conducted by one lonely deaf man, does it not lend to the conviction that

> four men for two years could round up the endowment of a quarter of a
> million dollars and entire grounds, buildings and equipments for present
> needs?

Carroll noted that the new seminary had enrolled 153 preachers
during the year 1906-1907, many of these from other states and several
foreign countries. He followed this with extensive review of the history of
Southern Seminary at Louisville and the contributions of Charles
Haddon Spurgeon, Francis Wayland, James P. Boyce, and John A.
Broadus. In view of later developments, it is interesting that he
specifically called attention to the curriculum of Spurgeon's College,
evidently thinking of his own plans.

> Spurgeon found on his hands as the fruit of his own ministry a host of God-
> called men with scanty educations and was driven by Divine providence to
> establish his pastoral college which gave both biblical instruction and such
> literary instruction as bore most directly on their life work.[45]

He closed his report with a long apologetic for the establishment of more
than one seminary among Southern Baptists.

At this convention, Carroll requested that he not again be made a
trustee of Baylor University. He had been elected each year as a trustee
since 1886, and the board had regularly named him as chairman since
that time. Because of this place of influence, he had been able to
communicate his "audacious faith" to the trustees, the president of the
university, and the leadership of Texas Baptists. He now threw himself
into the new challenge of ministerial education in the Southwest with an
old physical body but a youthful spirit.

Notes

1. See J. W. Bailey, ed., *The Biblical Recorder* (North Carolina), 10 July 1901.
2. J. M. Carroll, pp. 837-38.
3. *Proceedings*, BGCT, 1900, pp. 63-70.
4. J. M. Carroll, pp. 846-51.
5. Ibid., p. 851.
6. *Proceedings*, BGCT, 1902, pp. 32-37.
7. J. M. Carroll, pp. 851-52.
8. Crowder, pp. 133-34.
9. B. H. Carroll, *Standard*, 16 November 1905, p. 2.
10. J. M. Dawson, *A Thousand Months to Remember* (Waco: Baylor University Press, 1964), p. 59.
11. *Proceedings*, BGCT, 1901, p. 41.

12. J. M. Carroll, p. 981.

13. *Proceedings*, BGCT, 1901, p. 35.

14. Ibid., 1903, pp. 17-18.

15. Ibid., 1902, p. 59.

16. Ibid., 1905, p. 36.

17. Ibid., 1906, p. 28.

18. J. W. Bailey ed., *The Biblical Recorder,* 25 March 1903.

19. *Proceedings*, BGCT, 1903, pp. 43-44.

20. Ibid., p. 40.

21. Ibid., 1904, pp. 38-50.

22. See also Scarborough, pp. 21-22.

23. Evidently the letter quoted by Scarborough, pp. 103-105, dated 26 August 1905, is the one sent by Carroll.

24. Baylor University (Waco, Texas), Minutes of Meetings of the Board of Trustees, meeting of 31 August 1905.

25. Ray, p. 139.

26. B. H. Carroll, "Opening Address before the Theological Department, Baylor University," *Standard,* 14 September 1905, pp. 1 ff.

27. B. H. Carroll, "The Theological Seminary Affiliated with Baylor University, History," *Standard,* 16 November 1905, p. 2.

28. Barnes, p. 202.

29. *Proceedings*, BGCT, 1906, p. 42.

30. Ibid., p. 44.

31. Ibid.

32. See tract containing this address, File 22, Carroll Papers.

33. *Proceedings*, BGCT, 1906, pp. 45-46.

34. Ibid., p. 27.

35. J. B. Gambrell, "Baylor University as an Educational Force," *Standard,* 2 November 1905, pp. 1 ff.

36. See this report in File 177, Carroll Papers.

37. S. P. Brooks to B. H. Carroll, 26 June 1907, File 177, Carroll Papers.

38. R. C. Buckner to B. H. Carroll, 16 August 1906, File 177, Carroll Papers.

39. S. P. Brooks, "Baylor University and the Seminary," *Standard,* 23 January 1908, p. 3.

40. S. P. Brooks to B. H. Carroll, 19 September 1907. See also *Encyclopedia,* II:1278.

41. *Proceedings*, BGCT, 1907, p. 13.

42. Ibid.

43. Ibid., pp. 45-46.

44. A. J. Barton, Founder's Day Address, 31 January 1940, File 142, Carroll Papers.

45. *Proceedings*, BGCT, 1907, p. 51.

4

Southwestern Seminary Founded

With a light step, an elated B. H. Carroll returned to his hotel in San Antonio on Saturday, November 9, 1907, after the Baptist General Convention of Texas had unanimously approved the founding of the seminary with its own charter and board of trustees. It had been only two years since his vision, and miracles had already occurred. He realized that now the time had come to build but was uncertain how many years remained to complete clearing the ground and assembling workers and tools for the task.

Southwestern Seminary at Waco

Before leaving San Antonio, the board of trustees for the new school held their first session. On November 11, 1907, J. B. Gambrell, J. M. Carroll, C. W. Daniel, D. I. Smyth, A. E. Baten, George W. Truett, and A. J. Barton met at their hotel and elected Gambrell as president and Barton as recording secretary. By motion the two officers, along with D. I. Smyth, were constituted a committee to work with B. H. Carroll in securing a charter and preparing a constitution, bylaws, and articles of faith for the school.

The trustees soon met again, evidently on November 14, at Dallas. Their principal purpose was to correct a mistake made in the naming of the trustees by the convention. It had been thought erroneously that the laws of Texas permitted only thirteen trustees. Because of this small number, the convention had approved the formation of a larger board of directors or advisory board "to conserve the highest ideals of sound orthodoxy and solid business management."[1] B. H. Carroll reported to the trustees that he had consulted "good legal counsel" and had been advised that the laws of Texas permitted twenty-five trustees but distinctly forbade an additional board of directors or advisory board. Since it was necessary to resolve this matter before a charter could be obtained, the trustees agreed to elect twelve additional members and to disregard naming a board of directors. As a result, the first trustees of the new school (thirteen named at the convention and twelve named by these thirteen) were J. B. Gambrell,

135

George W. Truett, J. B. Cranfill, and C. C. Slaughter of Dallas; C. W. Daniel, W. D. Harris, and P. E. Burroughs of Fort Worth; J. M. Carroll and G. W. Baines of San Marcos; A. J. Barton of Waco; D. I. Smyth of Grandview; J. P. Crouch of McKinney; F. W. Johnson of Pecos; R. H. Hicks of Rockdale; A. E. Baten of Brownwood; W. A. Pool of Mansfield; J. B. Tidwell of Decatur; L. R. Millican of Allamore; W. K. Penrod of Cleburne; J. M. Cowden of Midland; G. Z. Means of Valentine; H. L. Kokernot of Alpine; T. D. Joiner of Sherman; W. H. Fuqua of Amarillo; and G. L. White of Brandon. Of this group, fourteen were ministers, and eleven were prominent laymen.[2]

On March 5, 1908, J. B. Gambrell, D. I. Smyth, and A. J. Barton, on behalf of the twenty-five trustees, applied to the state of Texas for a charter for the school. On March 14, 1908, the charter was officially filed with the secretary of state, marking the birth of the seminary. The charter name was shown as The Southwestern Baptist Theological Seminary, a private corporation.[3]

In March and April, 1908, B. H. Carroll wrote a series of four articles in the *Baptist Standard* concerning the charter of the seminary. In the second article, he discussed several parts of the document. His remarks about the second section, which set out the purpose of the seminary, introduced a provocative interpretation. This section said that the seminary was formed "to be mainly for the promotion of theological education, but to include the instruction of a Woman's Training School for special Christian service, and such other instruction as may be needful to equip preachers for their life's work." In his discussion of this article, Carroll quoted this last clause about "such other instruction" and asserted that the great majority of Texas preachers were married men with families, some near middle life, or had other circumstances which would prevent them from attending any school for more than a year or two. He argued that if they spent this time in a purely literary school they would be missing the more important theological study and, as well, they might be misled by some of the skeptical philosophical and scientific hypotheses which were often presented in universities. He concluded:

> The only ultimate solution is for the Seminary to go back to the Bible model of the School of the Prophets, and which was also for quite a while the historical model in post-Biblical times, namely, that the seminary teach the preacher on all lines of his education. I say we must ultimately come to that. And when we do, one part of the preacher's education will not forever war with another part.
> This charter looks in the right direction at least. It controls all the lines of education which it touches, whether theological strictly, the Woman's

Teaching School, or such other instruction as may be helpful to the preacher's life work.[4]

W. W. Barnes judged that Carroll had in mind to copy the model of Charles H. Spurgeon's Pastors' College in London by including in the Texas seminary some of the more important features of a literary curriculum.[5]

Some of Carroll's contemporaries were uneasy about this possibility, so when the trustees met on May 8, 1908, W. A. Pool offered the following motion, which was adopted unanimously:

Resolved that there is nothing in the Charter of the Seminary that allows the establishment of a literary college and that the Board has no purpose to establish such an institution.[6]

This action was deemed of sufficient importance that the editor of the *Baptist Standard* requested A. J. Barton, the secretary of the board, to prepare an explanation for publication. Barton wrote:

It had come to some members of the Board that some of the good brethren in Texas had come to have apprehensions as to the possible scope of the work which it was intended that the Seminary should do, questioning whether or not it was the purpose of the Board to establish an institution that would in any sense duplicate the work already being done by Baylor University, and other schools and colleges. This apprehension, as we were advised, was based on the last clause of Section 2 of the Charter, which reads: "and such other instruction as is needful to equip preachers for their life work." Possibly the apprehension of the brethren had been strengthened also by some personal views held and expressed by the president as to the type of institution best suited to the training of young ministers. The Board was very anxious that all apprehension on this point should be allayed at once, and that all brethren should understand that we are establishing not an academy nor a college, but a theological seminary. To accomplsh this desire the Board passed unanimously the following resolution: "Resolved that there is nothing in the charter that allows the establishment of a literary college, and that the Board has no purpose to establish such an institution." I doubt not that this will put all minds at rest on this important matter.[7]

With this interpretation, the trustees adopted the charter at the May 8 meeting, and the charter name of The Southwestern Baptist Theological Seminary was used thereafter in the minutes. The board was organized under the charter with the reelection of Gambrell as president and Barton as secretary. A committee on bylaws and order of business was named, and B. H. Carroll was elected president of the seminary.

The charter also named as a part of the purpose of the seminary "the

instruction of a Woman's Training School for special Christian service."
Young women, of course, had been trained in the Bible classes at Baylor
University and in the Baylor Theological Seminary, especially those who
had committed themselves to missionary service. When the new seminary was chartered on March 14, 1908, there was already a Woman's
Missionary Training School in Dallas. In the fall of 1904, R. C. Buckner
had discovered that four of the older girls in Buckner Orphans Home had
a desire to become missionaries. It was financially impossible for them to
go to the seminary at Louisville, Kentucky, so Buckner, while driving his
buggy from the home to the Dallas Pastors' Conference, conceived the
idea of forming a missionary training school on the campus of the home.
The Dallas pastors cordially approved the plan, and the Baptist Women
Mission Workers of Texas applauded the founding of the school. It
opened on September 15, 1906, and the pupils numbered from three to
eight during the year. They were taught by Baptist pastors and wives and
others who volunteered their services.[8]

Meanwhile, during the school year 1907-1908, the seminary at Waco
had enrolled twenty-six women as students. Anticipating the continuation of this program in the classes of the seminary, the charter contained
the clause concerning the training of women, even though an agreement
about this had not yet been reached with the home at Dallas.

President Carroll commented that the charter provided not only for the
degrees, diplomas, and certificates usually conferred by seminaries but
for "such other degrees as its curriculum may warrant." This meant, said
Carroll, that the seminary would confer certificates and diplomas
relative to instruction in the "Woman's Training School." Also, he
continued, the seminary would confer a special degree in English Bible.

> This is not the usual Seminary's one-year historical course in the English
> Bible looking to the degree of Bachelor of Theology. That one year's course
> may stand as in other Seminaries. It is the good outline or skeleton course
> looking mainly to a mastery of the Bible. The four years' course which
> secures the degree of the English Bible will be more profound and
> elaborate in its details, including exposition of the whole Bible, so that the
> preacher, though not a classical scholar, may as the man of one book, be
> able to teach all of God's word with power. If he be right in heart and life,
> truly called of God to preach, so equipped he will be a good and able
> minister of Jesus Christ, yea one of the earth's great men, though he possess
> no other school education whatever. And these are the men needed for the
> masses of mankind.[9]

Carroll went on to laud the curriculum for this degree designed, he
believed, to correct the mistakes of English and Northern Baptist
schools which had majored too much on producing literary scholars

rather than providing thorough English Bible study for the overwhelming majority of preachers who could never become technical scholars.

Finally, said Carroll, this charter provided under Article Nine a way by which the state bodies of Baptists in states other than Texas could cooperate in the support of this seminary and share in the appointment of trustees.

At the spring meeting of the trustees in May, 1908, the board approved the first graduating class since the charter was secured on March 14. In an interesting move, Carroll recommended to the trustees that at this graduation all previous graduates of Baylor Theological Seminary be awarded the same degrees that they had earned from that school and that they be recognized as alumni of Southwestern Seminary. This was voted unanimously.[10]

The first commencement of the new seminary was observed on June 24, 1908, in Carroll Chapel of Baylor University at Waco. Carroll addressed the graduates, as did J. B. Gambrell, president of the board of trustees. Degrees were then conferred upon all graduates of Baylor Theological Seminary and the Southwestern Seminary, totaling seven Master of Theology and fourteen Bachelor of Theology degrees. Some familiar names were included in this class: Walter T. Conner, who later became a teacher in the seminary, and several men who became outstanding pastors and leaders in Texas—F. M. Edwards, J. B. Holt, and Harlan J. Matthews.[11]

At the spring meeting of 1908, the trustees also agreed to the recommendation of President Carroll that the faculty be enlarged. The three members of the faculty of the previous year (A. H. Newman, Calvin Goodspeed, and Charles B. Williams) were reelected for the 1908-1909 school year. L. W. Doolan had resigned in the spring term of 1908 to accept a pastorate in Louisville, Kentucky, and the board approved efforts to find a replacement to teach Hebrew and cognate languages. In addition, two new faculty were elected: Lee R. Scarborough for evangelism and Jeff D. Ray for homiletics. This was the first chair of evangelism ever created in a seminary curriculum.

Lee Rutland Scarborough was the eighth of nine children born to a pioneer Baptist preacher who had come to Texas in 1874 when the boy was four years old. The father held many revival meetings in west Texas while operating a small "farm ranch." The boy had dreamed of becoming a lawyer. But God had other plans for him. Scarborough later recalled:

> When I left my father's country home in Jones County, Texas, January 7, 1888, my father had me promise him that I would hear Dr. Carroll preach every Sunday morning while a student in Baylor University, and in the

afternoon write him all I could remember about the text and the sermon.
Every Sunday, almost without exception, for four and one-half years I kept
this promise. At first the reports were meager, later more extended, and
later sometimes forty or fifty pages of letter. That was my course in
Systematic Theology, Bible Exposition, Homiletics, Evangelism, Missions,
and in denominational co-operancy,—a whole seminary course from the
pulpit of the First Baptist Church of Waco. God was indirectly preparing
me for his call and for my ministry later.[12]

In that first year at Baylor, Scarborough was converted, and Carroll
baptized him. He took his baccalaureate degree in 1892 and, looking
toward the study of law, declined an offer to teach at the university. He
took another baccalaureate degree at Yale University, where his excellent
scholarship brought him the coveted Phi Beta Kappa key. A conviction
that he should preach the gospel sent him back to Texas in 1896. In that
year, upon Carroll's recommendation, he was called as pastor of the
church at Cameron. He and Carroll were bound by a bond of deep love.
Carroll gave him a list of books he would need as a preacher and
endorsed his credit at the book store so that he could buy them.
Scarborough took one year (1899-1900) from his Cameron pastorate to
attend The Southern Baptist Theological Seminary, Louisville. He
married Neppie Warren in 1900 and in the following year accepted a call
to the First Baptist Church, Abilene, Texas.

Carroll had been watching this talented young preacher and coveted
him to teach evangelism, which he called the Chair of Fire. Scarborough
declined these offers, but Carroll would not desist. Jeff D. Ray recorded
Scarborough's account of his struggles to find God's will.

> Just before going to Pine Bluff, Arkansas, in early February, 1908, to
> hold a revival meeting with Pastor Ross Moore, I had another letter from Dr.
> Carroll. While preaching one afternoon to a great audience in the First
> Baptist Church of Pine Bluff, speaking on the will of God, mainly
> preaching to myself, my heart broke. I went to my room and fell across the
> bed and cried like a baby for a long time, and finally under the pressure of
> the call of God I accepted the call that Dr. Carroll had voiced, as I took it,
> from Heaven, and there offered my life to the Seminary. I immediately
> wrote Dr. Carroll of my decision. On returning to my home and to the
> church at Abilene, early Sunday morning my wife and I, as we had often
> done in prayer and loving consultation, agreed, she having the same
> impression that I had, and that morning, to a crowd that filled the church,
> with many turned away, I offered my resignation, telling them of my
> decision.[13]

This unexpected resignation caused most of the huge congregation at the
Abilene church to remain for an hour after the morning service. Leader
after leader publicly pressed Scarborough to withdraw his resignation,

but neither these entreaties nor conferences with the deacons and church members during the afternoon could shake Scarborough's conviction that he should join the ranks of the seminary faculty. After his election by the trustees on May 8, he began his service on June 1, 1908, as professor of evangelism.

The other man elected to the faculty on May 8, 1908, was Jefferson Davis Ray, a forty-eight-year-old seasoned pastor and denominational leader. Ray had been trained in journalism and elocution and, after completing Baylor, had served in several important Texas pastorates. From 1895 to 1897 he studied at The Southern Baptist Theological Seminary, Louisville, Kentucky, and at the time of his election to the faculty was pastor of the Seventh and James Baptist Church, Waco.[14]

The correspondence of President Carroll reveals that he and the faculty were taking prompt steps to secure a professor of Hebrew. On May 28, 1908, a letter addressed to Dean A. H. Newman from Editor S. M. Brown of the *Word and Way*, the Baptist paper of Missouri, highly recommended J. J. Reeve, at that time the professor of Hebrew at the Kansas City Baptist Theological Seminary, Kansas City, Kansas; but he closed with the plea, "I trust nothing will occur that will tempt him away from this new institution." Although additional correspondence with Newman is lacking, a letter to Carroll from the Kansas City Seminary dated July 13, 1908, said that Southwestern Seminary had taken "our excellent Dr. Reeve from us, and I am emboldened to ask you about Rev. P. E. Burroughs of Fort Worth, Texas. Would he make a teacher of Old Testament and Hebrew?"[15] Reeve was a scholarly and seasoned pastor and teacher. He had been pastor in Ontario for six years and for about three years had been professor of Hebrew at the Kansas City Seminary. Evidently he moved to Waco about June 1, 1908, to begin his work with Southwestern Seminary.[16]

The president and faculty were busy during the summer months of 1908. Carroll preached almost every Sunday and lectured on the New Testament from one to three times daily in Texas, New Mexico, Louisiana, Illinois, and Arkansas. His correspondence reveals that during all of these engagements he was constantly endeavoring to raise money to operate the seminary. A. H. Newman supplied for a number of churches in England on his way to the Baptist World Congress in Berlin, where he made an outstanding address on "Baptist Pioneers in Soul Liberty." C. B. Williams completed his study at the University of Chicago and received the Ph.D. degree. Jeff D. Ray used the summer to solicit funds for the seminary students, while L. R. Scarborough preached at revivals, encampments, and associational gatherings. Gifts of more than $32,000 in cash, notes, and pledges were received for the seminary during the year 1907-1908, despite the fact that President Carroll was injured in a fall at Eureka Springs during the summer.[17]

On October 1, 1908, the first formal opening of Southwestern Seminary took place in Carroll Chapel. The program consisted principally of the message by A. H. Newman which he had delivered at the Baptist World Congress in Berlin and "a captivating address" by J. J. Reeve, the new Hebrew professor. Matriculating during this year were 148 men and 33 women.[18] The curriculum was basically the same as it had been during the previous year, but it was divided into four sections: Exegetical Theology (biblical introduction, English Bible, Hebrew, Greek, and biblical theology); Historical Theology (church history, history of doctrines, and history of preaching); Theoretical Theology (systematic theology, apologetics, polemics, and ecclesiology); and Practical Theology (homiletics, missions, pastoral duties and hymnology, religious pedagogy, and evangelism).

The board of trustees met on November 12, 1908, between the sessions of the Baptist General Convention of Texas and heard President Carroll's report to the convention. I. E. Gates was elected field secretary; the employment of J. J. Reeve for Hebrew and cognate tongues was approved; President Carroll was given responsibility for the financial campaign of the seminary; and the faculty was authorized to confer "The Degree of the English Bible," the only one of its kind which had ever been offered.

In addition, upon the recommendation of Carroll, permanent laws and articles of faith were adopted for both trustees and faculty. These permanent laws provided that a trustee must be a member of a "regular Baptist church" in the state for which he was appointed. Any trustee absent from the meetings of the board for three years may not be reappointed in less than three years. Removal from the state from which a trustee was elected or exclusion from the church of which he was a member automatically vacated the office of a trustee. Two regular meetings of the board would be held—just before the Baptist General Convention sessions and at the time of seminary commencement. Perhaps the most significant item was the fourth article, which authorized the appointment of an executive committee of five, including the president, secretary, and treasurer of the board of trustees. This committee, with the president of the seminary, "shall have charge of the institution and the business of the board between sessions." Any action by this committee must be confirmed at the first regular meeting of the full board.

Relative to the faculty, the permanent laws were specific. A faculty member must be a member of a "regular Baptist church" and exclusion therefrom automatically vacated his professorship; he must subscribe to the New Hampshire confession of faith (with a slight alteration), and a departure from these doctrines in his teaching would be grounds for his removal. In further action, the trustees voted that the faculty may appoint tutors for special classes; the president of the seminary may appoint a registrar, with the approval of the Executive Committee; the president or dean shall regularly prepare the annual reports to the convention, subject to the approval of the trustees; and the faculty "shall have charge of the curriculum of the Seminary and all matters relating to order and discipline, and may enact rules and regulations conducive thereto, and shall confer all degrees." The trustees must approve these degrees.[19]

On November 14, President Carroll reported to the convention that in this first year the new school had matriculated 190 ministerial students, together with laymen and women preparing for special Christian service, for a total of 215. They had come from four foreign countries and eleven states and territories.[20] After this report was accepted, L. R. Scarborough took an offering of nearly $57,000 in notes and cash for the operation of the seminary.

President Carroll was slow in recovering from the severe fall he had suffered in the summer. As late as March 25, 1909, in replying to a letter from a friend of many years, Carroll spoke of his poor physical condition. For over three weeks he had not been able to go down the stairs of his home. He shared with this friend a personal note. In the spring of 1899, Carroll had married Hallie Harrison, whom he had known almost all of her life. After telling about the rest of his family, Carroll wrote: "Then I have a little boy, Francis Harrison Carroll about seven years old. He is sitting before me now writing in a book and all of his toys just back of him."[21]

Carroll was not idle while confined to his room by illness. His correspondence shows that he constantly sent personal and circular letters seeking funds to finance the seminary. He was the principal collector of pledges and interest on them.

Carroll's correspondence during this period also reveals the genesis of the Holland Foundation Lecture series. Lewis Holland of San Antonio, Texas, wrote Carroll on March 10, 1909, to inquire about endowing a lectureship at Southwestern Seminary. This series would begin in the spring of 1913 when George W. Truett delivered the first of the lectures.[22]

At this time Carroll was corresponding with J. W. Jent, pastor at

Hubbard, concerning the possibility of Jent's employment as registrar and private secretary to Carroll.[23] After Jent came, the correspondence of Carroll was typed rather than handwritten.

In some respects, the school year of 1908-1909 was disappointing for the Waco seminary. The enrollment decreased to 181 from the previous year's total of 215. The second commencement was observed in Carroll Chapel of Baylor University on May 28, 1909. Seven received the Th.B. degree; one, the Th.M.; and J. W. Crowder was awarded the degree of the English Bible (E.B.), the first in the history of seminary education. There were three addresses. Carroll delivered the baccalaureate first. The owner and editor of the *Baptist Standard,* thirty-two-year-old J. Frank Norris, brought the second message. Carroll was favorably impressed with him and soon recommended him to be pastor of the First Baptist Church, Fort Worth, and the church called him. The commencement sermon was delivered by George W. Truett.[24] As the three men sat on the platform together, none could have guessed that Norris would become the greatest adversary of the seminary during the first half of the twentieth century. The three worked together to locate the seminary in Fort Worth during this year and the next. That story will be told after the account of the seminary at Waco has been completed.

Promptly after the commencement, Carroll and his faculty began a summer of strenuous labor in behalf of the school. It was a time, said Carroll, that tested their faith and courage.

> There came a drouth which dried up our water courses, burned up our grain fields, cut off our cotton crop and parched our stock ranges until thousands of our cattle miserably perished. As it grew in intensity it extended from fields and cattle to the faith of men. In the case of thousands great faith became little faith and subscribers to benevolent funds began to "say before the angel our vow was an error." It withered emergency subscriptions behind us, it melted away present endowment pledges so that they lost the name of action; it sealed up once freely flowing fountains of benevolence ahead of us and even as we considered, behold! Israel was in a desert crying out for rock-smiters who would bring forth water.[25]

The first Doctor of Theology graduate of the seminary was approved by the trustees in the spring of 1910. He was William T. Rouse, who became a Texas Baptist leader. In addition, eleven other men were approved for diplomas and degrees.[26] Enrollment during the year 1909-10 increased from 181 in the previous year to 201, made up of 171 men and 30 women.

In their spring meeting, the trustees also elected the faculty for the following year. Carroll reported with deep regret that Calvin Goodspeed's health had forced him to resign from the faculty after the spring term, and said of him:

It is questionable if Systematic Theology and Apologetics ever had, anywhere, an abler and more judicious expounder and it is certain that history tells of no sweeter Christian spirit and courtesy than he invariably exhibited to all. . . .

We grieved sorely and still grieve over the loss of his services. He is a demonstration that scholarship may be high without conceit and pride of opinion and that clearness of vision and denominational soundness in doctrine need not be separated from the broadest charity, nor from the graces of a perfect gentleman.[27]

Upon the recommendation of Carroll, Walter Thomas Conner was elected by the trustees to teach the classes of Goodspeed in the fall of 1910. Conner became one of the outstanding teachers and authors of the seminary. From his inauspicious beginning as a replacement for Goodspeed, W. T. Conner would develop into one of the foremost theologians among Southern Baptists.[28]

Another faculty addition reommended by Carroll was Joseph Wade Crowder, who was named Carroll's assistant in English Bible. Crowder was the first graduate of Southwestern Seminary with the degree in English Bible in 1909.[29] He was a devoted disciple of Carroll, later furnishing the manuscripts for all but four of the thirty-five volumes of Carroll's published works.[30]

Finding a New Habitat

During the school years 1908 and 1909, President Carroll was greatly concerned about relocating the seminary. He felt, as did many others, that if the seminary remained at Waco it would either overshadow Baylor University or would be overshadowed by it.[31] Articles in the *Baptist Standard* during 1907 and 1908 had already mentioned the desires of Dallas and Fort Worth to have the seminary locate there.[32]

Carroll published an article in the *Baptist Standard* on April 2, 1908, asking any city in Texas to invite the seminary to come there. He emphasized the need for immediate action and expressed the hope that the seminary could be located in its own buildings by the fall session of 1909. He mentioned that he had stopped in Fort Worth on his way to Mineral Wells for a few days of rest in late March. L. R. Scarborough was conducting a revival meeting at the pastorless First Baptist Church in Fort Worth at this time. Doubtless this contact with Scarborough caused a group of Fort Worth pastors to call on Carroll at his hotel to present the desire of this city to obtain the seminary. They requested him to return on the following Sunday afternoon, April 5, to address a mass meeting at the First Baptist Church relative to the seminary.[33] He did so, "presenting the plans and ideals and prospects of the Southwestern Seminary." P. E. Burroughs, pastor of Broadway Baptist Church, described the meeting.

> It was an hour not to be forgotten. Dr. Carroll is greatly loved in this city, and as if in recognition and appreciation of this fact, he spoke in tender, almost confidential fashion of his heart's deep thinking and his soul's mighty desire to establish for the Baptists of Texas and surrounding states an institution which will meet their needs and be based upon the foundations of the Biblical theological schools.

Burroughs went on to say that Fort Worth earnestly desired the seminary. "She has been impatiently awaiting the opportune time to say as much, and now Dr. B. H. Carroll's statement in last week's Standard opens the way for her to unburden herself." Burroughs continued:

> Ft. Worth Baptists were swept by the vision as the need and possibilities of this vast section were set forth, and as step by step, were unfolded the thought and the ideals of the institution needed to meet the demands of such an empire. It is safe to say that no audience ever assembled in the old First Church was ever more mightily moved than was the audience which assembled there last Sunday afternoon.

When Carroll had finished his address, said Burroughs, W. D. Harris, mayor of Fort Worth and a deacon in the Broadway Baptist Church, offered a resolution which

> proposed to the Seminary faculty, its Board of Trustees, and to the Baptists of Texas, the city of Fort Worth as a suitable permanent location and pledged support both moral and financial to the effort to offer satisfactory inducements for its coming.

The resolution was signed by eight laymen who possessed some wealth and wide influence. After half-a-dozen leaders had spoken, the entire congregation stood and pledged themselves to the movement to bring the seminary to Fort Worth. They then agreed that the following Sunday (April 12) would be observed throughout the city and county as "Seminary Day" and the week following as "Seminary Week." Burroughs closed his article by outlining the program the Fort Worth leaders planned to follow in attempting to acquire the seminary for their city.[34]

The Tarrant County Baptist Association reflected the enthusiasm of Fort Worth Baptists about the possibility of acquiring the seminary. The first meeting of the association after the events in Fort Worth during the spring occurred on August 20-21, 1908. On Friday evening, August 21, J. N. Hunt offered a resolution saying that

> it is an earnest desire that the Seminary be located within the bounds of
> this Association, and that we here and now pledge our unfaltering loyalty
> and support of the institution by our prayers and with our money.

A committee was appointed "to make plans by which the interest of the
Seminary can be presented to every Baptist in the Association and see
that all is done to locate the Seminary at Fort Worth."[35] In an article in
the *Baptist Standard* two weeks later, Prince E. Burroughs, chairman of
this committee, wrote:

> Yes, the people in these parts are thinking and talking much about "our
> Seminary." The Association gave this institution right of way and the better
> part of two sittings were spent in the discussion. As an earnest of our
> interest the largest offering ever made by an Association was given for the
> students' fund, and the Seminary is invited to come to Fort Worth. Dr. L. R.
> Scarborough, emboldened by the consciousness that he was in the midst of
> his own and the Seminary's friends, made a most eloquent and powerful
> plea for the speedy and final establishment of the Seminary. It is to be
> doubted whether Tarrant County Baptists were ever more swept by any plea
> and it was resolved with much earnestness that they were unanimous in
> their desire and determination that the Seminary shall locate within their
> bounds.[36]

The key meeting that went far to determine the new habitat of the
seminary took place on a Sunday afternoon in August, 1909, when
President Carroll called the faculty to his home in Waco for a discussion
of the proposed sites for the school. Present were Professors Goodspeed,
Newman, Ray, Reeve, Scarborough, and Williams. The invitation of
Dallas was considered first, since that city was the denominational
center of Texas Baptists. The site offered by Dallas, however, was felt to
be inadequate for the needs of the seminary.

The invitations of other cities were discussed. In the correspondence
of Carroll may be found letters from leaders offering inducements for
locating the seminary at Handley (on the interurban railway between Fort
Worth and Dallas), McKinney, Denton, Cleburne, and elsewhere.[37]

The warm invitation of Fort Worth was taken up. Carroll suggested that
they test the people of that city to determine whether they really wanted
the seminary located there. As a result, a meeting was arranged for
Tuesday, September 7, 1909, in the office of Clarence N. Ousley, editor
of the *Fort Worth Record*. About twenty leading Baptists of Fort Worth
attended. R. E. Guy, one of the students of the seminary in 1910 when it
first moved to Fort Worth, recalled a story that he had heard while a
student. This tale recounted how at some time during these initial
meetings the leaders had offered to provide a small space downtown as a
site. When Carroll did not show up after a recess, they began to look for

him. He did not answer their knocking on his door at the hotel. They knew he could hear little without his horn, so they looked over the transom and saw the old man lying on the floor in prayer and heard him say: "Oh God, they don't have any idea about what needs to be done. Their dream is not big enough!"[38]

Evidently their dream grew. Plans were made to open every Baptist pulpit in Fort Worth to a representative of the seminary. On the following Monday, September 13, Carroll met with the pastors of the city at the First Baptist Church and presented his proposal. If Fort Worth would raise $100,000 as a bonus for building purposes and would provide an adequate and well-located site, he would recommend that this city be the home of the seminary. The pastors hesitated about guaranteeing such a large sum, so it was agreed that the pastors and some of the leading men and women of the churches would meet on that evening at the church.

About one hundred were in attendance that evening. Strong leaders like Clarence Ousley, editor; William Reeves and G. H. Connell, bankers; A. J. Long, ranchman; O. S. Lattimore and W. D. Harris, judges; Mrs. William Reeves, women's leader; and Mrs. O. S. Lattimore were there. Editor Ousley became excited, and his enthusiasm spread. The seminary proposition was accepted unanimously.[39]

In order to clothe this proposition with trustee authority, the Committee on Location named by the trustees was convened in Fort Worth on September 21. Present were D. I. Smyth, W. K. Penrod, P. E. Burroughs, and A. J. Barton, along with B. H. Carroll, L. R. Scarborough, and Jeff D. Ray. Some time was spent reviewing the whole situation in Fort Worth and pondering the procedure the committee should follow. W. K. Penrod informed the committee that a group from Cleburne was then in Fort Worth to propose that the seminary be located there, but it was agreed that this Committee on Location would first make a decision on the Fort Worth proposal before considering any other proposition.

On that afternoon, a subcommittee of Fort Worth citizens, consisting of W. D. Harris, G. H. Connell, G. E. Cowden, J. W. Spencer, A. J. Long, Clarence Ousley, and William Reeves, met with the Committee on Location. They were informed officially that if Fort Worth would raise $100,000 as a bonus to be paid one-third when contracts were let for buildings, one-third in one year from that date, and the remaining one-third in two years from that date and would furnish a site acceptable to a committee composed of Smyth, Carroll, Scarborough, and Ray, "we would recommend to the Board of Trustees that the Seminary be permanently located in Fort Worth."[40] In reply, Mayor Harris announced that they accepted the proposition so far as they had the right and authority as a subcommittee of the General Citizens Committee and that they would proceed to the task of raising the money and complying with the terms of the proposition.

Carroll then said:

> Most of our professors have classes and responsibilities on their hands at Waco. I am going to leave my boy, Lee Scarborough, here for thirty days, and if you will back him and give him and your people a chance and do not raise $100,000, we will pass to another place and look elsewhere for God's guidance, with no criticism on your city, trusting that God will reveal his will.[41]

Scarborough was overwhelmed by the assignment.

> The task of raising $100,000 was in those days titanic. Nothing like it had ever been done in Fort Worth for educational institution or benevolent enterprise. . . . It was a bone-breaking, heart-crushing undertaking. That night was a night of intercessory prayer and Jacob-like wrestling with God. Dr. Carroll was inspired by a heavenly vision to venture the launching of the Seminary by faith. So, in the late hours of the night God seemed to vitalize every spiritual energy of my soul. I was quickened and inspired by a divine touch. Jeremiah 33:3, "Call unto me and I will answer thee, and show thee great things, and difficult, which thou knowest not," and Daniel 11:32, "The people that know their God shall be strong, and do exploits," came into my soul like flaming swords and challenged me to trust God and to undertake the seemingly impossible. A clean and quiet restfulness and peacefulness filled my soul. I slept like a restful child the remainder of the night. Since that time I have never doubted that the Seminary was of God and that his will was that it should be located at Fort Worth.[42]

The raising of this large sum was made more difficult because the citizens of Fort Worth already had many calls upon their resources. Just a few years before, the city had raised a $100,000 bonus to bring two large meat processing firms to the city. At this very time, a campaign was underway to raise $150,000 to secure other manufacturing enterprises. The interurban train connecting the city with Dallas was requiring another $125,000, Polytechnic College was conducting a campaign for $75,000, and efforts were being made to raise $120,000 to rebuild churches which had been burned. Too, the cattlemen of the city had suffered heavy financial losses because of the drought and low prices, which also affected banks and other institutions.

Despite these many demands on its generosity, the city responded promptly to the challenge of obtaining the seminary. In view of later events, it is interesting to notice how J. Frank Norris praised the work of Jeff D. Ray, L. R. Scarborough, and other faculty leaders. He wrote:

> It was Seminary morning, noon and evening. Seminary for prayer-meeting. Seminary for Ladies' Aid Society. Seminary for B.Y.P.U., Seminary for

Sunday School, Seminary for saloon talk, so much so that a bartender said, "We will have preachers to burn." It is reported, how true I dare not say, that one hotel had a Seminary menu card.[43]

With the cooperation of the Baptist pastors and community leaders, Scarborough organized a team of canvassers. Within the thirty days, the $100,000 bonus was oversubscribed.[44]

On Monday, October 25, the Committee on Location met in the parlor of the Worth Hotel. Scarborough announced that the $100,000 bonus had been raised and that the committee members had been summoned to view the nine sites which were available. W. K. Penrod served as proxy on the committee for D. I. Smyth, who was out of the country at the time. From October 25 to 27, the committee visited the sites and listened to propositions about each one.

On October 30, this committee met to take action. Scarborough "spoke feelingly of the unanimity and enthusiasm of the Ft. Worth citizens in the accomplishment of this large and noble task." He then presented one by one the different sites and the propositions involved in each. It was then unanimously voted that Fort Worth be recommended to the board of trustees as the place for the seminary, provided a satisfactory site could be found.

Consequently, on November 2, 1909, the full board of trustees gathered in the parlors of the Worth Hotel in Fort Worth. J. B. Gambrell presided, and the secretary, A. J. Barton, listed the following in attendance: George W. Truett, W. K. Penrod, J. P. Crouch, W. D. Harris, D. I. Smyth, P. E. Burroughs, J. B. Cranfill, W. A. Pool, G. L. White, R. F. Jenkins (proxy for W. H. Fuqua), and O. S. Lattimore (proxy for L. R. Millican). Also attending were B. H. Carroll, Jeff D. Ray, and L. R. Scarborough.

Gambrell announced that this special meeting was called to receive the report of the Committee on Location. After approving what the committee had done, it was agreed to spend the afternoon visiting three of the proposed sites. At 2:00 PM, the board members were taken in the automobiles of Fort Worth citizens to the three sites under consideration. In the seminary archives is a picture taken of the group inspecting Seminary Hill, where the school was later located. That evening, after thorough consideration, W. D. Harris offered the following resolution, which was seconded by W. A. Pool and W. K. Penrod and unanimously passed by the group.

Whereas we have considered the different sites tendered for the location of the buildings of the Southwestern Baptist Theological Seminary and have concluded that the proposition made by J. K. Winston with its several accompanying offers from H. C. McCart, Matt S. Blanton, the heirs of J. T. Wright, G. E. Tandy, W. D. Reynolds, Edwards et al, presents and constitutes the most suitable and valuable offer made and that the same embraces a suitable site for said buildings, grounds, etc. and in every way meets the requirements of the case, therefore,

Resolved, that the Board accept the said Winston proposition with the accompanying sub-offers as above mentioned and that the buildings be erected on said grounds embraced in said Winston offer reserving the 60 day option to decide whether the Board will not elect to buy the Winston tract instead of taking the 30 acres and half interest in the remainder of said land. It is understood that in accepting the proposition it is the second or alternative proposition and not the first proposition of McCart that we accept.[45]

The exact description of the proposition involved in this resolution was then given.

A thirty-acre site and one-half interest in 194 acres of the Winston land; ten acres outright and a half interest in ninety-nine acres of land, owned by H. C. McCart; a tract of twenty acres owned by W. D. Reynolds; a ten-acre tract owned by Matt S. Blanton; a twenty-acre tract owned by the heirs of J. T. Wright; a thirty-acre tract owned by the owners of the S. J. Jennings survey and another tract of fourteen acres owned by G. E. Tandy. Other parties unconditionally give $4,000 cash and $3,000 additional upon certain conditions.

This done, George W. Truett offered a resolution, which was passed unanimously, expressing the appreciation of the trustees to the pastors and citizens of Fort Worth and giving special thanks to the Baptists, the *Fort Worth Record,* and the *Star Telegram* for their goodwill and generosity. L. R. Scarborough was authorized to obtain the deeds to the land involved in this proposition. He commented:

This site was about five miles south of the Courthouse and was divided nearly equally by the Santa Fe Railrod. It was nearly three miles from the city limits, had no city conveniences of street-car, lights, water, sewerage, and so forth. From its high point and from nearly all of its acreage a wide horizon including all of the city and beautiful country for miles around opened to view. It truly is a city set on a hill, with a rolling, woodless expanse of rich agricultural and pastoral land extending to the horizon on the east, south, north, and west, high and beautiful.[46]

J. Frank Norris, who had become the pastor of the First Baptist Church of Fort Worth in early November, was unrestrained in his lavish praise of the choice of Fort Worth for the seminary. In an article for the *Baptist Standard* on November 11, 1909, he wrote:

Form has become fact, promise has been converted into deed, and prospect turned into money—the Southwestern Baptist Theological Seminary has found its permanent home until Jesus comes again. In all it was a campaign of just forty days and nights, thirty days for the raising of more than $100,000 bonus, and ten days for securing a suitable location and other valuable property, conservatively estimated at $100,000. . . .

The Lawgiver Moses was forty days in the mountain receiving the Law; the Prophet Jonah preached the forty days repentance to Ninevah; the Saviour was forty days in the wilderness preparing for his ministry; and the Prophet Scarborough was forty days in Fort Worth loosening the purse-strings of the brethren to the amount of $200,000, or more. With deepest reverence, and true to fact, it can be said that the fourth forty days was as successful as the others, and it might be said to be even greater when considered in the light of Jesus' words, "Greater works than these shall ye do." Just forty years old, standing full fledged in the prime of his strong young manhood, Christly in his motive, world-wide in his vision, Pauline in his faith and doctrine, richly endowed with many natural gifts, abundantly endowed with supernatural power, Scarborough stands forth among his fellows like Saul among the brethren—a born leader of men. Words of personal praise are given for two purposes: Either to help and encourage the subject, or to help and encourage the brethren. In this case, it is the latter purpose. Our great men, sent and anointed of God, are our chiefest asset. When Israel had great leaders they were victorious.[47]

The Removal to Fort Worth

Thus, the decision was made on November 2, 1909, to locate the seminary in Fort Worth. The city had a colorful history. It had been founded in June, 1849, when crusty Major Ripley A. Arnold, a seasoned veteran of the Mexican War, established a small fort just below the bluffs on the northeast side of the present city. This was one of a line of forts ordered to be built just west of Dallas, Waco, Austin, and San Antonio by General William Jenkins Worth of Mexican War fame, as a defense for the Texas settlers against the marauding Indians to the west. Almost twenty small, whitewashed log buildings were erected near the abundant water supply in the beautiful Trinity River valley. However, it soon became necessary to rebuild the fort on the bluff above the valley to escape the regular flooding and the constant attacks of malaria in the valley. Major Arnold named the fort after General Worth, who died of cholera before learning that his name had been so used. The fort became unnecessary after about five years and was abandoned, but civilians had already occupied the area and continued the name of Fort Worth.

The town grew little before the Civil War, but thereafter several events accelerated its growth. It became the principal junction of cattle drivers who were taking their herds from Texas to Abilene, Kansas, where the early railroads could then transport the animals both east and north. The legendary Amanda Blake drove her herds of cattle through Fort Worth. By the 1880s it was not unusual for thousands of cattle to pass through Fort Worth each day. The drovers always stopped to spend their money, for this was the last regular station before entering Indian Territory on the way to Kansas. It is not surprising that the nickname "Cowtown" was soon affixed to the city. It was also dubbed "Panther City" because of the presence of roaming panthers.

Fort Worth gained notoriety as a rough and rowdy frontier town because of the antics of some of these cowboys but reaped many financial benefits from their trade. The untamed cowboys demanded entertainment; and numerous saloons, gambling parlors, and houses of prostitution could be found, especially in what was known as Hell's Half-Acre located on what is now Commerce Street. Contemporaries testified that the section earned the name. Wanted outlaws like Butch Cassidy (George Parker with several aliases) and the Sundance Kid (Harry Longbaugh) made the town their headquarters.

The population was only about one thousand by 1873, due partly to drought and depression, but the dramatic completion of the laying of rails of the Texas and Pacific Railroad to Fort Worth on July 19, 1876, changed the history of the area. The railroads finally ended the popularity of the Chisholm Trail leading north, since now the cattle could be shipped by rail from Fort Worth. The two new meat-packing plants brought hundreds of employees to the city.

With these events, the population of the city increased from about twenty-six thousand to approximately seventy-five thousand by 1910 when the seminary arrived. It had grown in the shape of a huge fan, the houses of the city extending from the courthouse about three miles equidistant to the east, south, and west. The original Main Street was laid out from the courthouse, principally to the south, flanked on the west by Houston Street and on the east by Commerce. From east to west the courthouse was framed by Belknap and Weatherford streets, but south of the latter the streets were numerically numbered from First Street. The original downtown streets were laid out at an angle that deviated slightly to the northwest and the southeast, but later additions corrected their streets to a north-south direction.

By the time the seminary arrived, the city had developed into an important business center. Wealthy cowmen and successful bankers were among the forward-looking citizens, and oil discoveries would soon open a new era of prosperity for the city.[48] Gone were most of the dilapidated wooden buildings of the earlier downtown years, and in their places were attractive brick buildings, many of them five to six stories high.

Baptists were not the strongest denomination in Fort Worth in 1910. There were fourteen Baptist churches, most of them small. The strongest ones were probably First Church, Broadway, Rosen Heights, College Avenue, and Worth Temple. An estimate of five thousand Baptists in the city may be fairly accurate.

The full board of trustees met in three sessions at Dallas for the regular semiannual meeting in connection with the state convention. On November 12, 1909, A. J. Barton resigned as secretary of the body, and P. E. Burroughs replaced him. Carroll was reelected president of the seminary, and upon his recommendation, the faculty and registrar were also reelected for another year. Carroll was asked to continue serving as the treasurer and financial manager of the school. On the following day, the trustees discussed lending seminary endowment funds to erect church buildings, deciding not to do so for the present. On November 15, the Executive Committee was named, consisting of G. H. Connell, W. D. Harris, and A. F. Crowley together with J. B. Gambrell, B. H. Carroll, and P. E. Burroughs as ex officio members.

By resolution, the Building Committee was created, consisting of L. R. Scarborough, P. E. Burroughs, J. F. Norris, G. W. McCall, G. H. Connell, W. D. Harris, J. K. Winston, and A. F. Crowley. This committee was empowered to make decisions in the erection of the first building of the seminary. A resolution was also adopted authorizing the Executive Committee to plat the tracts of land about the campus.[49]

At the state convention in session at this time, the seminary made two reports, one by J. Frank Norris and the other by B. H. Carroll. Norris was still pleased with the seminary and its leadership. In typical boisterous language, he began the report:

> Not since Peter preached on Pentecost and baptized three thousand converts had there been anything more glorious than the founding, endowing and locating of the Southwestern Baptist Theological Seminary. . . .
> This is to be the last year of the Seminary in temporary quarters. Even as Elisha, president of the oldest Baptist Theological Seminary, moved from his smaller quarters to larger ones on the banks of the Jordan, so does Dr. Carroll, President of the youngest Baptist Theological Seminary, and very similar to Elisha in faith, in physique, in vision, in prophetic power, move from temporary quarters kindly furnished by others to the banks of the Trinity. . . . Starting with nothing, except the faith of one man and the favor of God, it has discharged every obligation promptly, paid every salary without an hour's delay, met every bill when due and never has had an overdraft one time.[50]

In his report to the state convention, President Carroll rejoiced in the raising of the new endowment of $200,000 relative to the Fort Worth location, the $10,000 raised for the students' fund, and the addition of $20,000 to the interest-bearing bonds of the seminary. He described the campaign in Fort Worth in which he, Scarborough, Ray, and Williams had engaged. "They heard us in their city and county conferences, repeatedly in their churches, on the streets and in their offices by day and in their homes by night." He said that "what in the beginning seemed impossible except to prayer and faith was a unanimous verdict" with respect to the site.[51]

Building plans were hastened. The Executive Committee met on December 30, 1909, and voted to let the option lapse on the proposition to pay $55,000 for the second half of the Winston tract (the first half being granted to the seminary as a part of the site). Evidently the Committee on Sale of Lands was experiencing difficulty in selling lots adjacent to the seminary campus, and the Executive Committee authorized them "to make concessions on lots to induce rapid building of homes." Scarborough had moved to Fort Worth to supervise collection of the bonus pledges, employ architects, lay out the campus, and oversee the erection of the new building. Carroll said to his protégé, "Lee, prepare a place for us. The rest of us will carry on the Seminary at Waco until you get ready for us."

Scarborough worked strenuously with the architect, and the January 13, 1910, issue of the *Baptist Standard* carried a picture of the proposed building, known as Fort Worth Hall, from the architect's model. In the accompanying article, Scarborough proposed that this building would occupy the northwest corner of the campus, an administration building would be placed in the center of the campus, the Woman's Missionary Training School would be erected on the southeast corner of the campus, and a gymnasium would be placed on the southwest corner. It is interesting to look at the campus seventy years later and note that what Scarborough visualized has been almost precisely developed.

In laying out the streets, those running east and west immediately on the south and the north sides of the campus were named in honor of James P. Boyce and John A. Broadus, former presidents of The Southern Baptist Theological Seminary, Louisville, Kentucky. On December 29, 1909, President E. Y. Mullins of that school wrote to Scarborough and described his pleasure on learning of the naming of these streets, saying that this act would deepen the bond of friendship between the two schools.

Scarborough wrote Carroll every few days about the progress of the work on the building. Every sort of problem was discussed. Should Fort Worth Hall have a pyramid top or a flat top? Should the seminary erect store buildings around the campus with its endowment and lease these to merchants? Scarborough, faced with the shortage of cash flow, urged that the seminary sell lots to the people and let the individuals build their own structures. Other such matters were discussed by correspondence.

On January 18, the full board met to ratify all previous actions of the Building Committee and approve several legal actions relating to the land and contracts. The Executive Committee of the board was authorized to sign contracts on behalf of the seminary and to engage an attorney in connection with the erection of the building. Scarborough was finding it necessary to handle matters in Fort Worth that involved the expenditure of funds, so in order to expedite his work, the trustees voted to appoint a local treasurer to handle funds for the building in Fort Worth, while Carroll at Waco would continue to handle funds for the seminary's operation and endowment. Scarborough was also authorized to purchase an automobile for the seminary's business and to employ a stenographer. Expenses for his office and the operation of the automobile were to be paid upon his signature. The Executive Committee met on January 29, 1910, to elect W. D. Harris both as attorney for the seminary and as the local treasurer to handle funds, countersign checks, and perform similar duties.

On March 2, 1910, the contract was signed for the erection of Fort Worth Hall for the sum of $105,000, which did not include wiring, heating, or plumbing. The uneasiness of Scarborough about the financing may be seen in a provision of the contract that permitted the seminary to end the contract after the basement and first story were completed at a cost of about $85,000. Scarborough felt that the two other proposed floors of the building could be completed at a cost of about $9,000 each. The contractors said that the building would be ready for occupancy on October 1, 1910, and this date became the target for the opening of the school.[52]

The minutes of the board of trustees for June 1, 1910, reveal the severe financial struggles being experienced in the erection of Fort Worth Hall. The action of the Executive Committee in securing three loans was approved, as follows: one of $25,000 from the First State Bank and Trust Company of Fort Worth and the First State Bank of Caldwell, Texas; one of $25,000 from the State National Bank of Fort Worth; and one of $15,000 from the First National Bank and the Farmers and Mechanics National Bank of Fort Worth. The trustees approved a contract for installing the electric wiring of Fort Worth Hall and authorized the

Executive Committee to borrow money to pay for "the plumbing, heating and power plant and wells and necessary fixtures and appliances for finishing the Fort Worth Hall and grounds."[53]

It will be recalled that the Woman's Missionary Training School begun by R. C. Buckner in connection with the orphans home in Dallas had opened in 1906, while the seminary conducted its own women's training school in connection with classes in the seminary. During the spring of 1910, the leaders of the two institutions conferred at length and agreed that the seminary was the proper place for this training. At the quarterly meeting of the Executive Committee of the Baptist Women Mission Workers of Texas in June, 1910, L. R. Scarborough spoke to them about the challenge of missionary training for women and the plans of the seminary to erect a building on the campus at Fort Worth for a Woman's Missionary Training School. Enthusiastically, the committee voted to recommend to the next statewide meeting of the body in November that they "set about the splendid and glorious task of erecting a $50,000 building for the Woman's Missionary Training School of the Seminary."[54] Scarborough promptly published an article in the *Baptist Standard* calling attention to the need for the training of women for missionary and other Christian service, evidently intended to buttress the appeal for the new building by the Executive Committee of women at the next convention.[55]

The third annual catalogue of the seminary for the year 1909-10 included the first catalogue of the Woman's Missionary Training School. Instruction was provided by the seminary faculty, supplemented by lectures from various denominational leaders. The diploma, "Graduate in Missions," would be awarded for a two-year course, requiring about fifteen hours a week for six quarters. Most of the nonlanguage courses required for the Bachelor of Theology degree were included in the curriculum, as well as instruction in domestic science, kindergarten, child problems, nursing, medical care, and women in mission work.[56]

At the close of commencement in Waco in May, 1910, buoyed by the promise that Fort Worth Hall would be ready for use by October 1 of that year, President Carroll and his faculty made plans for moving to Seminary Hill, as the location in Fort Worth came to be called. All the faculty members borrowed money to build homes adjacent to the new campus. Scarborough recalled:

> If it had not been for Dr. Carroll's helpfulness and that of the finance committee in lending funds out of the endowment principal, some of the men could not have built their homes . . . . Some of the banks of the city, not knowing the future of the Seminary, cautiously loaned us money.[57]

Carroll seems to have built his home by correspondence. His files are replete with directions about it. Even details of the house were discussed extensively. For example, he was afraid that the windmill which pumped the water from his private well to his home might be so noisy that it would interfere with his study. The contractor solemnly assured Carroll that if he would oil the windmill as he would a buggy, it would give little trouble.

During the summer of 1910, in addition to planning their move to Fort Worth and endeavoring to find funds to build their homes there, the members of the faculty attended various conventions and institutes, raised funds to aid ministerial students, and preached in revival services. The immense task of picking up the young seminary from its home in Waco and transporting it to the partly-finished building at Fort Worth involved many problems. President Carroll wrote in November, 1910:

> My own house was to be ready by September 1. So I boxed and shipped all seminary records with my private library and household goods late in August and rented my Waco house. To this day all these goods, books, and papers are stored in Fort Worth. It may be yet a month before I can get at them. I expressed to a Fort Worth bank the files of the seminary pledges, notes and deeds, and carried only my cash book in my suitcase.[58]

The seminary in Fort Worth opened its doors on Monday, October 3, 1910. Editor Frank Norris of the *Baptist Standard* described it in his customary gaudy style, noting the large number of visitors at the occasion. J. B. Cranfill said that "it was the greatest event in Texas Baptist history and led by the greatest Baptist in the whole world." J. B. Gambrell "congratulated the student body on their brilliant prospects of a glorious hard time."[59] B. H. Carroll could not see much humor in the difficult situation. He wrote later about the opening.

> To secure ground enough for expansion, it was necessary to locate the institution one mile beyond the end of existing car-lines, and until the extension of these lines transportation over that mile by auto must be supplied.
> On account of the same difficulty of getting material on the ground at the right time, the homes of the faculty were not ready for occupancy. By a makeshift arrangement a part of a lower story was prepared for temporary use and heated by stoves. Yet the sound of a hammer, the buzz of the saw and the tread of the hod carrier were continuous.
> The wisdom of attempting an opening in such quarters and under such conditions was gravely questioned. A generous proposition by the First Church tendering the use of its building, with free light and heat, accompanied by a sufficiently cheap rent of a downtown hotel for the boarding quarters was soberly considered.

But after mature deliberation we decided to commence on scheduled time on our own grounds and in the necessarily cramped and inconvenient quarters our building afforded, with the few students who were willing to endure hardness as good soldiers.

We knew that the great majority of prospective students would defer entrance until there were better and more adequate preparations, and we did not blame them.

Seventy-nine students decided to matriculate and rough it out. The wonder is that there were so many.

They justly counted that the conditions would improve each week, the space enlarge, and indeed that all the difficulties were under constant process of removal and that by January 1, the roof would be on, the steam heat in operation, and two full stories ready for use. On account of these conditions it was decided to have no program of formal opening and send out no invitations abroad. . . . The occasion called for the cheerful, heroic spirit and it was manifested all around. One white-headed sage even ventured to say: "I am glad that you people are having a hard time at the start. It will do you good and work out great things for you in the long run." The First Church gave a grand reception with refreshments to the whole outfit. Anyhow, there we are. There stands the majestic building approaching completion, and scores of residences erected by faculty and students. After all, what is one year's privations in the life of an institution, which expects to be doing duty when the great trumpet of the judgment sounds, and to hear the cry: Behold the bridegroom! Go ye out to meet him!

Well, we plead no baby act and play no whining role. We have camped out before.[60]

Inspiring words were these from a man nearly deaf who had left his comfortable home after forty years and moved in his last days from the graveyard of loved ones in Waco to begin again where the vision from God had led. He had only four years left to complete his task. Two of these would find him almost bedfast. Fort Worth Hall was barely completed before his death.

The First Year

The faculty and 126 students who matriculated during the first year on the Fort Worth campus faced dismal prospects. The campus itself was hardly visible. Two square blocks totaling thirty acres had been separated from the surrounding fields by sparsely graveled roads. Little had been done to improve the campus. A few trees had been planted, but most of these did not survive. Professional nurserymen hinted darkly that it might take a little dynamite to get the trees some root space in the rocky ground. They were evidently attempting humor, not knowing that in later years this would actually be necessary for the successful planting of some of the trees. In 1913, W. W. Barnes came to the campus as a new professor. He arrived in early summer, and his wife was to join him in late August. He wrote:

> I had hoped that Seminary Hill might be fresh and green for her first sight of it. There had been a little rain in June. Other than that there had been no rain in Fort Worth for two years. The campus was a cross section of a Johnson grass farm. For one building at the northwest corner, Fort Worth Hall, driveways had been marked off in curves by the plough and the grading machine, but they had all grown up in Johnson grass again, and people drove across in wagons, buggies, and a few automobiles in whichever direction they chose. There were no trees or shrubbery of any sort on the campus. Around the campus on the side, trees had been planted when the seminary first came three years before. About three trees at the east entrance were living. The whole campus presented a most bedraggled and despondent appearance.[61]

On the northwest corner of this campus were the unfinished basement and first floor of Fort Worth Hall. Scarborough wrote:

> Some rooms were finished. The only roof we had on the building was the concrete floors above the first and second floors. We had no heating plant, no water system installed. We had to improvise our heat by putting stoves in the rooms and pipes out the windows. The story of sacrificing, doing without conveniences, waiting and working is a long, glorious one. Mrs. A. H. Newman was Superintendent of Fort Worth Hall. Her task was somewhat like Mrs. Noah's after the flood.[62]

Almost half-a-century later, C. M. Smith, a student at the seminary in 1910, recalled the wretched living conditions. He had sold his farm at Yoakum to follow a call to preach but affirmed that all of the hardships endured in the cold winters and hot summers were a small price for the excellent training he received from men like Carroll, Newman, Scarborough, and others.[63] Another one of the first-year pioneers was R. E. Guy from Scotsville, Kentucky. He fared better, however, for he was able to purchase a little house near the end of the city car line on Hemphill Street. He and his young wife walked a mile across Johnson-grass fields to attend classes each day.[64]

Since most faculty homes were not yet completed, it became necessary for some of the professors to share the lot of the students in the unfinished building. Mrs. Jeff D. Ray described the experience of her husband.

> Classrooms as well as bedrooms, as such, were scarcely a reality. The section originally intended for a library was much too large for the supply of books, and was mostly that year appropriated as living quarters for some

thirty single men and a certain young professor by the name of Jeff D. Ray. Describing that area of the living quarters, Mr. Ray confessed that he was a bit highbrow, for while the thirty students slept indiscriminately and quite uncomfortably on the floor, moving about to dodge the rain when it fell, and for other reasons, he had a modern American bedstead on which to rest his weary bones at night. . . .

For heating that winter the entire floor boasted the comfort (?) of two or three aging coal stoves, the pipes from which ran ludicrously each out through a convenient window—pipes intended to convey the smoke outside but which, alas, when the wind blew contrary acted in the opposite fashion.[65]

All of the accounts of this first year mention the problem of transportation. In those early days Seminary Hill had no stores or cafes to provide food, and the city had refused to extend its streetcar lines beyond what is now the location of the steel mills on Hemphill. Mrs. Ray continued her comments, saying:

The heart of the city of Fort Worth lay six miles away, and between that section and the seminary campus stretched a wide area of little more than pasture land. The city in reality offered a change of scene if one could find some way to get to the wide-awake center of commerce, but that was not easy to accomplish. It was a mile and a half to the nearest streetcar connection and to reach it you usually must walk the prairie. If it were during the rainy season (which must have lasted the year round in those days) you did so over rugged pasture land or at best on unpaved roads, risking your footing in the muddy, black-waxy land that lay between "Seminary Hill" and the nearest streetcar terminus at the "Bolt Works." This you must do unless you were fortunate enough to qualify as "desperately sick" and on your way to a hospital. The only alternative was to get a ride (and who ever did?) in the one old automobile the "Hill" could boast (useless in muddy weather)—or you might appropriate the one horse and buggy, property of a seminary professor, Dr. A. H. Newman. Do you wonder that along with the important, dignified items set out in the seminary catalogs in those days and for many years to come, was the unequivocal order, "Students MUST bring overshoes"? And this was to be the transportation system of the seminary constituency for the first two years, after which time a very poor, lame excuse for a connecting link between city streetcar and "Seminary Hill" was provided at seminary expense. This improved means of conveyance the students named appropriately "The Dinky," which when it ran reminded one of a lot of people, with much noise and rattle, but poor dependability. It was a common saying that "The Dinky" never ran when you wanted to ride and was constitutionally completely at rest on weekend days when it might have served a welcome purpose.

There was no sewage system for the first five years. Water came from an old ranch well on Broadus Street near the northeast corner of the campus. The gasoline pump that operated it was not dependable; at best, it slowly propelled the water through a one-inch pipe to Fort Worth Hall about five hundred feet distant.

The difficulties of carrying on classes under wretched living conditions were matched by the financial burdens on the administrators. President Carroll was constantly engaged in the task of soliciting funds to keep the school in operation, while L. R. Scarborough exhausted every means to finance the completion of Fort Worth Hall. In his usual fashion, by correspondence Carroll made individual appeals to pastors, men whom he had taught or had known in denominational service. One such letter written shortly after Carroll moved to Fort Worth contained the statement, "I am up a tree. Can you and your fine men help me?" Frank S. Groner, pastor of the First Baptist Church, Stamford, Texas, replied, "I'm in a hole. How can a man in a hole help a man up a tree?" Carroll replied, "When you come up the tree to help me down, you will be out of your hole."[66] With humor, eloquence, and importunity Carroll labored, even though he was a sick man already.

To L. R. Scarborough was given the task of completing the collection of the $100,000 bonus from the citizens of Fort Worth. It had been hoped that the pledges would all be paid and that this source would provide enough funds to erect Fort Worth Hall. Scarborough later remarked, however, that the final total of pledges collected on the bonus was $73,000 and that the total cost of finishing Fort Worth Hall in four years was about $175,000.[67] At a called meeting of the trustees on March 21, 1911, one of the items for discussion was an application by the Building Committee to the Mercantile Trust Company of Saint Louis, Missouri, for a loan of $60,000, to be secured by a mortgage on some seminary property. Scarborough gave some of the details of this transaction. The banks which had made one-year loans to the seminary in the previous year were pressing for payment. Scarborough called together the Building Committee, several of them substantial businessmen, but after several days they reported that no local bank would lend the money to repay the loans because the seminary was new and had no liquid assets. Scarborough described how he had prayed earnestly about the matter and how he could not sleep at night. His wife saw his anxiety and inquired about the cause. He said:

> The payment of $60,000 is pressing hard. The building committee has failed to make satisfactory arrangements for refinancing. The life of the Seminary is involved. We have no funds and our credit is already strained with what we owe. The banks must have their money, or at least they think so. I do not know where to turn.

After a pause, she replied, "Honey, you know God has never failed us; let's pray."

> And on our knees, with our arms about each other, we prostrated ourselves in prayer and she led the prayer—a prayer the like of which I have rarely heard in my life. My own faith was strengthened and my hopes were revitalized and I tried to pray—came struggling along in supplication after the lead of this faithful heroine. When we got up from our knees, she said: "God has answered and we will get the money."

Within three days, the Saint Louis bank granted the $60,000 loan. "The money was secured, the banks paid, credit was confirmed and established, and the Seminary went on."[68]

At the time when the site was given to the seminary, both Carroll and Scarborough had hoped that the sale of some of the lots around the campus might provide needed funds. As noted, however, these sales were very slow at first. Scarborough felt that the reason for the slowness in the sale of lots was the reaction in Fort Worth to the excessive number of suburban additions which had been developed so quickly that few people were interested in buying such lots. George Clark, a real estate agent, was employed to sell the lots around the seminary. The total income from all lot sales for the building fund finally reached $45,000. Thirty years later, the seminary still had over a thousand lots not yet sold.[69]

One of the basic needs of the seminary, of course, was an adequate library. It cannot be determined how many volumes were brought to Seminary Hill from Waco.[70] During the first year, the library was housed in one of the large rooms on the first floor of Fort Worth Hall. Professor Charles B. Williams was librarian in 1910-11, and the faculty voiced appreciation for the gift of books worth one thousand dollars by A. J. Harris. The catalogue of 1910-11, the first year of the school in Fort Worth, referred to "the splendid nucleus already secured, about 3,000 volumes" in the library. This statement was repeated in the catalogue of the following year. The original accession book of the library was begun on February 13, 1911, in the handwriting of Professor Williams. The first 3,511 books were labeled "gift," but the next one was shown as being purchased by the Library Fund.[71]

The faculty and curriculum of 1910-11 were almost the same as in the previous year. To provide more unity to the story, the curricular developments in music and religious education will be told more completely in the following chapter. In his report to the state convention in November, 1910, Carroll said that the seminary had eighteen employees, not counting four special lecturers and a keeper of the building during the summer. These included eight professors, two tutors, a teacher for the Woman's Training School, a teacher for music, an assistant librarian, a matron for the training school, the registrar, the office stenographer, the stenciler of lectures, and a financial secretary for nine months.[72] Mrs. J. S. Cheek was the matron of the boarding hall, and Mrs. Herbert Heywood taught "Choral Music, Vocal Expression and Reading."[73]

Although not teaching in the first year, Charles T. Ball was elected by the trustees as professor of missions and field secretary in the spring of 1911. He had been dean of the Bible Department at Simmons College from 1904 to 1911.[74] His service began in the summer of 1911 as field canvasser for funds.

Jeff D. Ray, the professor of homiletics, was forced to resign in the spring of 1911 because his wife had tuberculosis. Her doctor advised that she remove to the dry climate of west Texas. Ray accepted the pastorate of the First Baptist Church, El Paso. To replace him, the trustees elected E. C. Dargan, but he declined the position. President Carroll then refused to seek another teacher for homiletics, suggesting that the faculty divide the work among themselves with the hope that Ray would be able to return later.[75]

At the first commencement held in Fort Worth in the spring of 1911, the seminary conferred seventeen diplomas and degrees, including Thomas W. Talkington and Charles R. Taylor with the Doctor of Theology.[76]

This, then, completed the first year of the seminary in its new Fort Worth habitat. President Carroll reported to the Baptist General Convention of Texas in the fall of 1911 that during the year he and his helpers had collected $15,078.55 for the emergency fund. The endowment had been increased by interest-bearing promissory notes in the amount of about $30,000.[77] This good report heartened the messengers at the state convention, although it did not reflect the financial struggle taking place in the building of Fort Worth Hall. Like a plane catapulted from the deck of an aircraft carrier, the seminary at first seemed to hesitate precariously after departing its old home but soon found the surge of power that began to lift it up and away from the threat of a catastrophic crash.

It should be added here that the effect of the coming of the seminary to Fort Worth was soon evident. Within a year, the Tarrant County Association turned to the young preachers of the seminary to supply its churches, and the employment of associational missionaries was discontinued. During the next seven years, fourteen new Baptist churches came into affiliation with the association.[78]

Last Years of Carroll's Administration

B. H. Carroll and his small band of scholars waited tensely for the opening of the fall term in 1911. Would the students of the previous year return for another session despite the wretched conditions for living and studying? Had the excellence of the teaching compensated for the cold, drafty classrooms by day and the damp, hard floors for sleeping by night? Could they endure another year of the constant hammering and sawing that almost drowned out the voices of the professors? Prospective students had undoubtedly heard of these difficult conditions. Would they be willing to "camp out" in the unfinished building at Fort Worth with all of its inconveniences?

Indeed they came. The previous year's enrollment had included 89 ministers, 2 laymen, and 35 women, for a total of 126. This had been a decrease from the last year at Waco, when 201 had enrolled. To the joy of the faculty, the enrollment increased in the fall of 1911 to 104 ministers, 10 laymen, and 51 women, for a total of 165. In the remaining two years of Carroll's life, the enrollment increased to 187 in 1912-13 and 208 in 1913-14.

These last years of President Carroll brought him much suffering. His correspondence with friends constantly spoke of his impaired heart, causing a loss of strength and difficulty in breathing. One of the students, George Henry Boone, who had brought his wife and two daughters to Seminary Hill in 1910, learned that Carroll had great difficulty breathing when lying down, so the student prepared a large board and installed it over Carroll's bed. With small ropes this board could be pulled back and forth like a fan so that Carroll's body would be cooled and his breathing helped.[79] Another student, C. M. Smith, said that Carroll was so weak he could come but once a day to lecture in 1911-12. In that year and the next, he would dictate his lectures to a stenographer in his bedroom. These would be reproduced by mimeograph and distributed to the students. J. W. Crowder would review the class on these lectures and supervise the examinations.[80] His demand that the students reproduce the precise language of Carroll on the examinations made him rather unpopular.[81]

It is a rather curious quirk of history that this continued illness of Carroll brought the first serious internal contention in the faculty. Because of this illness, it became necessary for the faculty to assume many of the administrative decisions. The dean of the faculty was A. H. Newman, and it fell to him to provide faculty leadership during the period. The faculty minutes of January 2, 1912, recorded that Newman raised a question about students being unable to earn the required eight hours in Carroll's English Bible courses because of the absence of Carroll through illness. The decision by the faculty present (Professors Newman, Williams, Scarborough, Conner, Ball, Reeve, and Crowder) was that if a student could not complete his full eight hours in English Bible with Carroll in two years, he would be permitted to take courses in New Testament by Williams and Old Testament by Reeve and "thus complete the required 8 course [sic] for the English Diploma."[82]

This appeared to be a sensible solution at the time, and there was no suggestion that any of the faculty present objected to it. But the substitution of a course in the New Testament Department or the Old Testament Department for one in English Bible introduced a principle which President Carroll felt was subversive. The trend in this direction continued. At the faculty meeting on February 27, 1912, the recommendation was made to Carroll by the faculty that a course in Hebrew at another school be substituted for one of the courses in English Bible.

The faculty appointed Professors Williams and Reeve to a special committee on curriculum revision on April 4, 1912. On April 10, this committee reported. It recommended that the two-year requirement of evangelism for all students be lessened; but when Professor Scarborough protested, this requirement was restored. Another revision recommended by this committee noted that President Carroll was ill and unable to meet his classes in English Bible and suggested that the curriculum be revised to permit the English Old Testament to be taught in conjunction with Hebrew and Old Testament theology and that the English New Testament be taught by professors of Greek and New Testament theology. This, said the committee, was the way the teaching of the English Old and New Testaments was done in all standard seminaries, since it was felt that men trained in the original languages would be better equipped to interpret the English Bible than those who did not know the languages.

W. W. Barnes reported later what took place. President Carroll had been ill during most of 1912 and in the spring of 1913 had fallen into a coma. It was believed that he would not recover from this illness. However, he rallied unexpectedly and began gaining strength. When he learned that Dean A. H. Newman and Professor J. J. Reeve and others were looking toward dismantling his Department of English Bible and putting these studies into the Old and New Testament Departments, he promptly called Newman and Reeve to his home and asked for their resignations from the faculty. A cryptic sentence in the minutes of the trustees for May 29, 1913, simply announced, without explanation, that the resignations of Newman and Reeve had been accepted.

In a private letter written on June 8, 1913, Newman said to a friend that Mrs. Carroll had assured him that Carroll

> would not have interfered with me had it not been that in his illness the thought pressed itself upon him that if he left me in the Faculty and as Dean of the Faculty my influence might result in the destruction of the chair of English Bible (with the "Degree of English Bible" probably) and the division of the work between the Greek and Hebrew chairs; and that if he had continued in health he would not have taken the step he did.

Newman's gracious spirit was shown as he closed the letter by expressing his appreciation for Carroll and the faculty and saying that he had never questioned their motives. "For myself I lay no claim to infallibility or impeccability. It may be that the Seminary will get on better without me than it would have done with me."[83]

Involving both Carroll's persistent illness and the dismissal of Newman and Reeve was a letter from Carroll to the trustees on May 29, 1913. In this he said:

> I hereby request that you designate some suitable person as assistant to the President of the faculty—to hold such position for the ensuing year, or until time as my health and strength may admit of my doing all the work which belongs to the office of President. And that the duties of such assistant to be to aid the President in the details of his work, and in the name of the President, do all such work and perform all such acts incident to, or falling within the scope of the duties or [sic] the President as the President may by general or special request, direct such assistant to do and perform; and also in the absence or inability of the President, to do and perform all such work and duties as may be necessary to be done to keep the work of the President fully up to date, and that the said assistant be invested with full authority to issue all vouchers, checks, receipts, etc. as may be necessary under the conditions existing at the time, and to do all such other and further acts, for and in behalf of the President as may be necessary and proper; but that such acts on the part of such assistant to the President at all times be done in the name of the President, and under the supervision of the President, when he is able to supervise, and at such time (if there should be any such time) as the President may not be able to supervise, that the same be done by such assistant in line with the general plan, purpose and policy of the President as has heretofore been pursued. That said position of assistant to the President exist for and during the twelve months next ensuing, or until such time during the twelve months as the President may feel able and see fit to dispense with the help of said assistant.
>
> And in view of his thorough understanding of the work and duties of the President, and his intimate acquaintance with the details of the work of the

President as said work has heretofore been done, and his familiarity with
the books and records kept by the President, I recommend and request that
you name L. R. Scarborough as such assistant to the President.[84]

The trustees approved this action, and after this time L. R. Scarborough was the principal administrative officer of the seminary. The
faculty was notified, and thereafter Scarborough presided at their
meetings.[85]

Trustee and Faculty Activity

The giant stature of B. H. Carroll, even during the illness of his latter
years, can be glimpsed in the fact that he totally dominated the trustees
and faculty at the seminary, just as he had done in his relations with
Baylor University earlier. Every action taken by the seminary's trustees
and faculty reflected the enormous influence of Carroll. Even as
shocking an experience as the dismissal of Dean A. H. Newman and
Professor J. J. Reeve, two of the finest scholars of the faculty, over what
seemed to be no more than a small matter, was accepted without
comment. Many of the decisions of the faculty with Carroll presiding
seemed to usurp trustee prerogatives.

One reason for this, of course, was the impressive personality,
conspicuous gifts, and lengthy leadership of Carroll. Even strong
personalities like J. B. Gambrell, George W. Truett, J. Frank Norris,
Judge W. D. Harris, and Carter Helm Jones listened carefully when
Carroll spoke. Another reason was the rather rapid turnover in the
personnel of the trustees. By 1911, sixteen of the original twenty-five
trustees had either died or rotated off the board. By 1914, there were
eighteen new names. Under the provisions of Article Nine of the charter,
two trustees were elected from New Mexico in 1909. Between 1911 and
1914, trustees were being elected from Arkansas, Louisiana, New
Mexico, and Oklahoma, along with Texas.

The reports of the trustees to the Baptist General Convention of Texas
were made by President Carroll in 1911 and 1912. At the latter meeting,
Carroll made a strong appeal to the convention for approval to commence
a campaign for $500,000 in new endowment.[86] In 1913, due to the illness
of President Carroll, L. R. Scarborough made the report and summarized
the financial progress of the seminary from 1910 to that time, as follows:

The first month of our first year in Fort Worth three years ago we enrolled
seventy-nine students and had in financial assets $184,000.00 in endow-
ment notes. We had no other property or building when we went there. The
first month of the year three years later we opened with 184 students and

$400,000.00 endowment, $250,000.00 in buildings and grounds, $200,000.00 in land notes, street car, bonus pledges and $79,000.00 in cash and notes and pledges for the Training School Building, making a total of more than $800,000.00 after all liabilities are deducted. This represents a growth in three years of 150 percent in students and 450 percent in finances.[87]

In the following year (1913-14), the endowment was increased by $72,346, most of it from smaller or country churches, bringing the total endowment to $461,500.[88]

Despite these admirable gains, the seminary was in a precarious financial condition during the remaining years of Carroll. He continued to bear the responsibility of obtaining operating expenses, although after 1912 he was assisted greatly by Scarborough. Scarborough also was assigned the collecting of the bonus pledges for building Fort Worth Hall, the raising of funds for the development of the campus, supervising the sale of lots, developing the transportation system, and similar difficult duties. Professor Jeff D. Ray usually led in appeals to the churches, associations, and conventions for the student aid fund. Tarrant County Baptists became some of the most liberal supporters of this.[89] Between $5,000 and $10,000 a year was usually secured for student aid. In Carroll's final year, for example, almost $10,000 was allotted to sixty-eight students from this fund.[90] The faculty regularly made relatively substantial gifts to the operating fund.[91]

Because of the financial stringency, the development of the thirty-acre campus of the seminary was slow. Until almost the time of President Carroll's death in 1914, classes, chapel, offices, administration, and faculty were housed in an incomplete Fort Worth Hall. Dwellers in the dormitory became accustomed to rain seeping into their quarters. The heat of the early fall was oppressive, but it was preferable to the cold and chilly winds that came with the late winter and early spring. The campus resembled a field of Johnson grass at the time of Carroll's death, almost impassable in the wet season and unlovely in appearance. As early as November 23, 1911, the trustees authorized their Executive Committee to "finish up the third story of the Seminary building known as Fort Worth Hall, if the said committee can obtain the funds necessary to do the same." Nothing was done for six months, and on May 28, 1912, the faculty asked the trustees to complete the third floor during that summer if possible. Finally, on January 9, 1913, the trustees approved letting a contract for completing the third floor at a cost of $12,000 and authorized L. R. Scarborough to award a plumbing and heating contract for the third floor and install an elevator in the building. Scarborough reported to the state convention in November, 1913, that the third floor had been finished during the summer and that a water system with a sixty-foot steel tower and tank had been installed together with new water mains. The sidewalks and drives had also been completed during the summer at a cost of about $2,000.[92]

The second building on the campus was erected on the southeast corner. It will be recalled that at the quarterly meeting of the Executive Committee of the Baptist Women Mission Workers of Texas in Fort Worth in June, 1910, Professor Scarborough had addressed the group relative to the plans of the seminary to erect a building to house a Woman's Training School. At this time, the Executive Committee voted to recommend to the state meeting in November that the women sponsor this project. At the state meeting on November 8-9, 1910, in Houston, a special committee appointed by the Executive Committee, composed of Mrs. William Reeves of Fort Worth, Mrs. F. S. Davis of Dallas, and Mrs. J. W. Byars of Waco, presented the following resolution:

> Whereas, in the enlarging Kingdom of Jesus Christ, God is more and more using women as missionaries, as teachers in Sunday Schools and Mission Schools, and as soul winners and soul builders; and,
> Whereas, God is calling hundreds of our daughters in the Southwest to be workers in every department of this glorious service; and,
> Whereas, He has already blessed our land in the starting of the Woman's Missionary Training School as a department of the Southwestern Baptist Theological Seminary; and,
> Whereas, This school needs and must have a great and worthy building in which to house the scores and hundreds of women who are coming and will come to it for training in God's work and word; and,
> Whereas, This convention could lay its heart and hand to no nobler or more far-reaching task than to provide this building; therefore be it,
> Resolved, That the B. W. M. W. of Texas, in session at Houston, at once begin the glorious work of raising funds for the erection of a $50,000 building for this Training School, and that we continue by our prayers, sympathy and money, until this building is finished, furnished and dedicated as the Woman's Temple of Missions.[93]

After prayer by Mrs. Jeff D. Ray and a motion to adopt by Mrs. J. B. Gambrell, L. R. Scarborough was invited to speak. Then in a standing vote the resolution was adopted, and at the request of the body Scarborough was asked to take pledges for this work. By societies and associations the women pledged $42,210 within a short time. Scarborough was asked to collect these pledges.[94]

On May 29, 1913, the trustees of the seminary authorized their Executive Committee to work with the Baptist Women Mission Workers of Texas in arranging for the construction of this building. After conferences with all involved, Scarborough presented a proposal to the Executive Committee of the seminary on July 21, 1913, from a Fort Worth contractor to erect the building for $78,000. This contract was let. On September 23, 1913, the faculty approved a suggestion by the Advisory Committee of the women that the name of the building be the Baptist Woman's Missionary Training School of Southwestern Baptist Theological Seminary, and this was approved by the trustees. Scarborough reported to the state convention in November, 1913, that the building was under construction, and a year later he said that the building was complete on the outside only at a cost of $63,000.[95] The catalogue of 1913-14 announced that the seminary hoped to occupy this building by October, 1914, for the accommodation of 112 students, but it was still unfinished when B. H. Carroll died.

Thus, by the fall of 1914 there were two buildings on the thirty-acre campus of the seminary. Sidewalks and driveways provided assistance in traversing the campus. Evidently some landscaping was done early in 1914, for at that time the faculty suggested to Scarborough that if he and the landscaper could not agree on plans for improving the campus, it would be better to follow the landscaper's proposals as closely as possible.[96] Scarborough also mentioned that about sixty residences were dotting the land adjacent to the campus.[97]

A much needed improvement had its beginning on March 21, 1911, when the trustees passed a resolution "to negotiate for a street car to the Seminary." This was very important. The seminary was located over a mile from the end of the city car line, and in wet weather it was practically impossible to walk through the fields. The only automobile on the campus belonged to Professor Scarborough and could be used only on official seminary business. Dean A. H. Newman had a buggy, and occasionally a student might have some sort of private transportation. On September 29, 1911, the trustees approved a resolution by which Scarborough would engage in a project to build a private streetcar line from the end of the city streetcar line on Hemphill to the seminary. On May 29, 1912, the trustees were notified that it was "impracticable to close up and consummate the construction of a street railway as was provided for and contemplated." Instead, the local trustees reported that they had secured a

> Motor Street Car Line from the South end of the Northern Texas Traction Company at the Bolt Works on Hemphill Street, South to Hammond Street and West on Hammond Street to Reeves Street, and South on Reeves Street

to Boyce Avenue; thence West on Boyce Avenue along the Southern
boundry [sic] of the Seminary Campus, passing the Southwest corner of
said Campus, and proceeding West to the Right-Of-Way to the G. C. & S. F.
Railway Company.

L. R. Scarborough, J. K. Winston, and H. C. McCart had formed a
corporation, titled "The Seminary Hill Street Railway Company," and
received a charter from the state to operate such line. The trustees
approved this action, and it seemed that the question of transportation
was settled. From the language of the contract with C. T. Hodge, which
was signed by Scarborough, it appears that this motor car required
standard gauge track upon which to run. The motor car had a seating
capacity of thirty-five people.[98]

However, this motor car did not provide dependable service. Often it
would not start, and it was rarely on schedule. It became familiarly
known as the "Doodle Bug." On December 22, 1913, the trustees
approved a contract with the Northern Texas Traction Company (which
operated the city streetcars) to take over this private line and connect it
officially with the city's lines. It became necessary to run a shuttle car
until the roadbed of the new line could be prepared. There was rejoicing
at the seminary in August, 1914, when the first city streetcar left the
courthouse and carried special guests all the way to the seminary. W. W.
Barnes recalled how quickly this better transportation to the city affected
the development of the seminary.

> New houses are being constructed along the old Seminary car line. People
> bought lots years ago and held them waiting for the car service to build
> homes. One of the city schools is now located south of what was the old
> Seminary car line and morning and afternoon children may be seen going to
> and fro to attend school where ten years ago there was open prairie and
> herds of milk cows were being grazed. The car line brings Seminary Hill
> and the business section of the city into closer contact. That means that
> more of the people living on Seminary Hill will go to Ft. Worth to trade. It
> also means that more of the people of Ft. Worth will attend the public
> services in the Chapel of the Seminary.[99]

Upon recommendation by the faculty, the trustees added new faculty
and staff between 1911 and 1914. In 1912, J. B. Gambrell was elected as a
half-time teacher in ecclesiology and denominational polity, and in the
following year he served as a full-time professor in this area. It will be
recalled that in the spring of 1911 Professor Jeff D. Ray had accepted a
pastorate in west Texas because of the illness of his wife. By 1913,
because of the great improvement experienced by his wife, Ray was able
to resign the church and return to the seminary to teach homiletics.[100]

When President Carroll dismissed A. H. Newman and J. J. Reeve in the spring of 1913, he turned to the seminary at Louisville to replace them. Two young men were offered the positions. William Wright Barnes, just graduating, accepted the chair of church history. He was a native of North Carolina, having received two degrees with distinction from Wake Forest College. In 1904, after receiving the second degree, he was appointed by the Home Mission Board of the Southern Baptist Convention to serve in Cuba as tutor of children in American families and as principal of the Cuban-American College in Havana. Because of his wife's health, he was forced to return to America in 1912. He enrolled in Southern Seminary and completed an additional degree in the field of church history. He began teaching in the fall of 1913.[101]

The other man chosen for the faculty was Jesse Burton Weatherspoon, another North Carolinian. He also had received two degrees from Wake Forest College and two degrees from Southern Seminary. At the time of his election to the faculty of Southwestern Seminary, he was pastor of the Oxford Baptist Church, Oxford, North Carolina.[102]

In addition to these changes in the regular faculty, a beginning was made in the teaching of instrumental and vocal music. Mrs. Herbert Haywood was named to teach choral music and basic culture in 1911. She must have been viewed as temporary, for her husband was a ministerial student in the seminary at that time, and when he graduated in 1912, she left the school.[103] She was not replaced during the following two years. On May 27, 1914, R. H. Cornelius was elected by the trustees as instructor in vocal music. This probably occurred when Miss Mary Tupper, who became superintendent of the Woman's Training School in the fall of 1913, convinced Professor Scarborough that the women needed someone to instruct them in vocal music.[104] Incidentally, she also suggested that Spanish might be offered for these women. Although not reflected in the minutes of the trustees or the faculty, the trustees reported to the state convention that Cornelius's wife would teach instrumental music.[105]

As mentioned, Miss Mary Tupper was named superintendent of the Woman's Training School in 1913-14, while Mrs. J. S. Cheek continued as matron of the boarding hall. On May 28, 1914, upon the recommendation of the Advisory Committee of the Baptist Women Mission Workers, the faculty voted that Mrs. Alma W. Lile be elected assistant to Miss Tupper in the training school. Upon the recommendation of the faculty, Conant M. King, a young Christian businessman, was named as bookkeeper and registrar on September 23, 1913. He later became manager of the boarding hall.[106]

During each of these years, the commencement was held in the chapel

on the second floor of the Fort Worth Hall. Various denominational
leaders were secured by the faculty to address the graduates. The
trustees approved the first six graduates from the Woman's Training
School in May, 1912. In addition, at this commencement twenty-seven
others were awarded degrees, including John W. Jent, Richard Peterson,
and Gustav T. Vickman with the Doctor of Theology. In 1913, the
seminary awarded thirty-two diplomas and degrees, including thirteen
from the Woman's Training School, and Alvin Swindell and J. R.
Saunders with the Doctor of Theology. In 1914, the seminary awarded
thirty-six diplomas and degrees, including eleven from the training
school and James S. Rogers with the Doctor of Theology.[107]

It is interesting to notice occasional variations in terminology. During
his last years, B. H. Carroll was sometimes elected president of the
faculty, rather than of the seminary, and he referred to himself as such.[108]

As indicated heretofore, the minutes of the faculty during these final
three years of Carroll's administration show that they were considerably
involved in administrative as well as academic matters. This probably
occurred because Carroll personally presided over the faculty when he
was well and felt free to handle administrative matters in the faculty as
he chose. After Carroll became ill, the faculty seemed to have continued
in this pattern. The faculty minutes often speak of "electing" faculty
members, although this authority actually rested with the trustees. The
faculty named C. B. Williams as dean after the resignation of A. H.
Newman[109] and named C. M. King as registrar and bookkeeper.[110]
Various adjunctive needs were handled by the faculty. It arranged for
what became a book store[111] and for a post office,[112] chose "recruiters" for
the school,[113] named the superintendent of Fort Worth Hall,[114] arranged
speakers for openings and commencements,[115] authorized the installation of sidewalks on the campus and landscaping of the grounds,[116] began
the observance of Mission Day,[117] prepared the catalogues and schedules,[118] arranged for staff and faculty additions,[119] combined staff
duties,[120] set the price for room and board of the students,[121] handled
student loans,[122] closed school for conventions,[123] increased staff salaries,[124] handled chapel,[125] assigned faculty to attend state conventions,[126] introduced classes in remedial English,[127] approved textbooks,[128] and handled scores of other similar details.

Evidently this widespread faculty involvement in administration
slowed after C. B. Williams replaced A. H. Newman as dean in May,
1913. Upon his election, Williams promptly inquired about the scope of
his duties. The faculty appointed a committee on May 30 to confer about
this with the president and board of trustees. The committee reported:

It is the intention of the president of the Seminary and the board of trustees that the dean shall have charge of the internal administration of the Seminary in the absence of the president and his assistant; or in the presence of the president and the absence of the assistant, which will probably be most of the time, all internal administration shall belong to the dean.[129]

In the early years, the faculty acted as a committee of the whole and often spent more of its time approving substitutions and exceptions for the students than it did for anything else. It was not unusual for the faculty to meet every day or two to discuss some ad hoc situation. By the end of the period, however, a regular time for faculty meeting was set for the first Thursday night of each month, and committees were appointed to handle many of the details which had heretofore occupied the time during the regular meetings.

The faculty handled strictly academic problems of many kinds. It continued efforts to build an adequate library for the school. On May 25, 1911, it named a library committee to purchase books. Professor Williams, the librarian, was its chairman, and Professors Newman, Conner, and Reeve constituted the committee. The trustees took the same action on the following day. On May 28, 1912, the faculty thanked W. E. James for donating his library to the school. On the same day, the faculty began a subscription to buy books for the library, and $275 was subscribed with the recommendation that if possible an additional $500 be provided from the emergency fund of the seminary for purchasing books. On May 30, 1913, the faculty recommended that $700 be appropriated from seminary current expense funds to buy books for the library for the following year. A committee was named to buy these books. On October 2 of the same year, the faculty asked Dean Williams to write the thanks of the school to J. M. Frost of the Sunday School Board and J. F. Love of the Home Mission Board for bound copies of the minutes of the Southern Baptist Convention which had been presented to the library. On May 28, 1914, the faculty recommended that $500 be appropriated to purchase books for the following year, and a committee was named to oversee this. The catalogue announcements for 1914 said that the library contained about five thousand volumes and appealed for someone to donate $1,000 or more to provide funds to purchase needed books.

The faculty recommended a change in degree terminology in 1912. Before 1912-13, a student completed the English diploma in two years. It required two or three years to earn the Th.B., at least three years for the Th.M., at least four years for the degree in English Bible, and one year's additional study beyond the Th.M. to receive the Th.D. On May 1, 1912, the faculty voted that the terminology of the English diploma be changed and that the student completing this study be awarded the degree Graduate in Theology (Th.G.). The curriculum was modified to require the same study as the Bachelor in Theology (Th.B.) without the Hebrew and Greek. The requirements for the Th. M. were changed to require one year's study beyond the Th.B. and the writing of a dissertation.[130] Another change involved the titles of degrees. In the early catalogues, the graduates were shown as Bachelor *of* Theology, Master *of* Theology, and Doctor *of* Theology.[131] By May, 1914, on the other hand, the catalogue showed the graduates as receiving the Bachelor *in* Theology, Master *in* Theology, and Doctor *in* Theology.[132] In later years, W. W. Barnes remarked that the *in* made it clear that a graduate had not mastered the entire field but had worked in the field. From the beginning, the faculty minutes had used the word *in*.

On February 18, 1914, the Curriculum Committee appointed by the faculty recommended several changes: first, that the regular session continue to be divided into four terms of nine weeks each, including terms in the fall, winter, spring, and summer; second, that all examinations at the end of each term be included in the time for recitation in each course of study; third, that the Th.B. degree be changed to a three-year degree not requiring Hebrew and Greek; fourth, that for the work in residence the Th.D. degree require eight courses (four hours a week for nine weeks constituted one course) distributed as follows—three courses in the major department, two courses each in what were termed "leading minors," and one course in a subordinate minor; fifth, that a course of one year be given to train pastors' assistants, evangelistic singers, and other Christian workers. This report was adopted by the faculty and put into effect.[133] To accomplish the first recommendation, the trustees approved the beginning of a summer quarter for 1914,[134] but this was not implemented until later.

A significant new program was begun during the last year of this period. On May 13, 1913, the faculty requested Professor Charles T. Ball to draw up a plan for an extension department. On December 18, 1913, and April 14, the faculty discussed his proposed plan and on the latter date elected Ball as secretary of the Seminary Extension Division. On May 27, 1914, the trustees authorized the development of this study, and the catalogue announcements for 1914 described the offerings of the Seminary Extension Division.

This division had three departments: a department of instruction by correspondence, a department of instruction by lecture courses, and a reading course. Degree credit would be given through the correspondence department; whether credit could be earned by enrollment in the lecture courses, which involved five to ten lectures by a member of the seminary faculty to a location approved by the school, was not indicated. The reading course involved the study of some theological topic chosen by the student, who would be assisted by outlines, books, and suggestions for study by a faculty member.[135]

Other innovative action by the faculty during this period included the organization of the student body,[136] the development of a special course for pastors,[137] the beginning of classes for Negroes,[138] the introduction of kindergarten and settlement (Good Will Center) work for the Woman's Training School, [139] and the offering of classes in music.[140]

The Beginning of the Norris Controversy

The most violent attacks on the seminary for the next generation would be made by J. Frank Norris, pastor of the First Baptist Church, Fort Worth. This rather sudden change of attitude seems strange, since Norris played a prominent role in bringing the seminary to Fort Worth. His animosity was restrained before the death of B. H. Carroll on November 11, 1914, but the groundwork for his attacks on the seminary was already being laid.

A word must be said about Norris's background in order to understand the vitriolic attacks he later made on the seminary. He was born on September 18, 1877, in Dadeville, Alabama, into the home of a godly and devoted mother but an alcoholic and ne'er-do-well father. The family moved to a farm near Hubbard, Texas, in 1888, where the boy grew up in poverty and, because of his father, in public scorn. His mother instilled in him a deep desire for fame and success. Although he was converted in a Methodist revival in 1890, he later came under the influence of Catlett Smith, pastor of the Hubbard Baptist Church, who baptized him. He felt a call to preach at the age of eighteen. In 1903, he took his first degree from Baylor, where he had come under the teaching of B. H. Carroll and other strong men of the faculty. On May 5, 1902, J. B. Gambrell united him in marriage with Lillian Gaddy, daughter of J. M. Gaddy, a veteran missionary of the Baptist General Convention of Texas. In October, 1903, he enrolled at The Southern Baptist Theological Seminary, Louisville, Kentucky, completing the course in two years and making a fine record as a student. Promptly after graduation, he accepted the pastorate of the McKinney Avenue Baptist Church, Dallas, Texas, where he quickly gained a reputation for being an able preacher. In April, 1907, Norris purchased a controlling interest in the *Baptist Standard*, published in Dallas, and in the following year became its editor. From this post, he vigorously fought the gambling interests in Texas, especially horse racing.

When the question of locating the seminary in Fort Worth arose, Norris supported it enthusiastically and opened his paper freely to its proponents. B. H. Carroll was favorably impressed with Norris, and when C. W. Daniel resigned as pastor of the First Baptist Church, Fort Worth, and preached his last sermon on June 17, 1909, Carroll urged the church to call Norris as pastor. With this high recommendation, Norris supplied the pulpit of the church on July 4, the following Sunday, and most of the Sundays thereafter until he accepted the call of the church about November 1, 1909. He had been preaching at the church on September 13 when the leadership of the Baptist churches of Fort Worth had a mass meeting there to hear B. H. Carroll present the claims of Southwestern Seminary. Norris preached on September 27 when the women of Tarrant County met to pledge $10,000 for the seminary. He was also preaching on October 11 when the church pledged $45,000 to help bring the seminary to Fort Worth.[141] He attended the several meetings that resulted in Fort Worth's pledging support for the seminary. He was a member of the board of trustees from 1909 until 1915, after B. H. Carroll's death, and there was never a suggestion in any of the trustee meetings that he had lost his appreciation for the seminary and its faculty. Indeed, as pastor of a wealthy and influential church, Norris seemed to have a position that would totally challenge a relatively young man. His first two years were rather quiet. Norris was the respected and refined leader in a successful pastorate and seemed destined to write his name large in Southern Baptist life.

However, in the summer of 1911 he experienced a dramatic personal change. While preaching at a revival meeting in Owensboro, Kentucky, he found himself "liberated" from the thin layer of sophistication that had been stifling him in his ministry at First Church. He said to his wife on the telephone:

> Wife, wife, we have had the biggest meeting you ever saw—more than half a hundred sinners have been saved, and they are shouting all over this country, and the biggest part of it is, wife, you have a new husband. He has been saved tonight, he is starting home and we are going to start life over again and lick the tar out of that crowd and build the biggest church in the world.[142]

Upon his return to Fort Worth, Norris began the sensational type of preaching for which he later became famous. As a matter of fact, no one has ever said that Norris was not an outstanding pulpit orator who could shower his congregation with stardust. After 1911, he determined to make his church "not a place of ease for respectable church members but a great soul-winning station in the heart of the city."[143] His church became primarily a preaching place. He all but eliminated Woman's Missionary Union, standing committees, and other organizations which might threaten his leadership.

He attacked sin at every point. The liquor traffic was a constant area of conflict. He used the most sensational methods in exposing various evils, and his church became too small for the crowds that tried to hear him. Some of the leaders of the church, thoroughly alarmed by his tactics, began moving their membership to other churches as early as 1911.

Things took a violent turn. Shots were fired at Norris in his study. Someone set fire to the church, causing damage to the amount of eight thousand dollars. Twice, attempts were made to burn the pastor's home. Then, on the night of February 4, 1912, the church building was entirely destroyed by fire. A grand jury brought an indictment against Norris for arson. He was acquitted and became even more sensational.[144] It is interesting that one of the seminary students at the time, Charles M. Smith of Yoakum, Texas, recalled almost forty years later his great admiration for Norris, although he said that most of the faculty of the seminary were not pleased with the sensational pastor.[145]

The trial brought a schism in the First Baptist Church, however. Many of the most influential members of the church moved their letters to other churches at this time. Typical of the consternation in the church was the response of deacon G. H. Connell, one of the bankers who had labored faithfully to bring the seminary to Fort Worth. He wrote B. H. Carroll on October 5, 1912:

> I have felt constrained to call you often since this awful calamity came on our church here, but I have put it off from time to time. Still the thought comes back to me that if any man in this country could help the situation it would be you. Remembering the letter that you wrote to me from Plainview or Amarillo some three years ago before this pastor was called here, which letter I feel sure was the cause of turning the tide towards calling him. In other words, had it not been for that recommendation he would never have been called here. I can recall the effect that it had upon me, and the hand that I had in the call, and I do not find any fault with you for writing that letter, but feel that you were honestly mistaken at the time, as we all are at many times in life; that you thought you were doing what was best for the church and the cause in this city, just as I did for quite a while thereafter, until it dawned upon me so clearly that I could not resist the change of view that came over me. I have never felt any malice in the whole matter. I have

sought God to take every vestige of malice and evil thoughts away from me
when considering it, and I have had an assurance that He has answered my
prayer in this respect. My course has been one that has been carefully
considered and prayed over until I thought I had the guiding of the Spirit,
and I know that I have had nothing but the best interest of the church and
the Cause of Jesus Christ at heart at any time during the whole controversy.
After patiently waiting upon God for His direction the conviction has
settled on me more and more that my position was pleasing in His sight. I
have wanted to take a different course at times from the one I have pursued,
but my conscience would not permit.

I am just informed this evening that the meeting of the brethren called
for tomorrow afternoon at four o'clock has been called off because it has
been learned that the pastor is preparing to submit a proposition that the
brethren could not under any circumstances entertain. I don't know what
it is, but in view of this, and the total disruption that I fear will follow, I
appeal to you to use your good offices and influence, if you can find it in
your heart to do so, to get the pastor to resign without further trouble.

There is quite a number of our best men who are well-nigh ruined
already for all Christian service, and it makes my heart sick to see it. I
have done my best to hold the thing together thus far, trusting and waiting
and hoping that God would hear the prayers of those who are really His
servants, and would cause something to relieve the situation. And I feel
now that you can do it if any man living can, by your influence with the
pastor.

Still trusting that the total disruption may be averted by your good offices
in the matter, I am, . . .[146]

President Carroll, despite the fact that he was undergoing much
physical suffering at this time, replied in a long letter to Connell on
October 19. He said that he had been giving the letter "the very gravest
consideration," but had been so crowded with work, so unwell, and so
pressed with matters connected with the opening of the new term that he
had been unable to get his reply prepared. He expressed his deep
personal esteem for Connell and said that for many months he had been
"profoundly stirred" over the situation. Privately, he continued, he had
tried to exercise a "healing and conservative influence over the situation," but because of his illness which prevented attendance at church
and also his desire that the seminary should not even seem to dominate
over any church of Jesus Christ, he had refrained from taking an active
part in trying to solve the problem. He confessed that "I am not wise
enough and have not hold enough upon the situation to suggest a solution
of the difficulty with any confidence." Carroll said that he had conferred
more than once with L. R. Scarborough, also a member of Norris's
church. He had also heard that efforts had been made by prominent
members of the church to induce the pastor to resign, and while making
no promise, Norris had indicated a purpose to resign by the end of the

year. Carroll suggested that nothing should be done until it was determined whether Norris would do so. He felt that it would have been well if Norris had resigned immediately upon his acquittal by the court. If Norris did not resign by late December, Carroll thought that a "respectful and fraternal" petition should be drawn up containing no accusation and carefully worded so that all appearance of partisanship would be eliminated.[147]

Not long after this exchange of correspondence between Carroll and Connell, members of the faculty began to leave the First Baptist Church. Carroll, J. D. Ray, Charles B. Williams, and Charles T. Ball moved their membership to Broadway Baptist Church. Many others, including W. W. Barnes and J. B. Weatherspoon, put their letters in College Avenue Baptist Church. J. W. Crowder joined Southside Baptist Church. L. R. Scarborough, hopeful of maintaining fellowship despite the bristling attitude of Norris, remained a member of First Church until September 23, 1917.[148]

The Death of B. H. Carroll

W. W. Barnes recalled the day that he first met the president of the seminary. He could observe from the gaunt frame and the hanging clothing that Carroll had lost from seventy-five to one hundred pounds of weight. After the meals each day, Carroll and Barnes visited at the table, mainly with Carroll talking and Barnes listening. Barnes learned to love this stricken giant, despite all he had heard about the Whitsitt controversy. Barnes recalled, "Dr. Carroll never once asked me what I believed about Baptist succession." Barnes also recalled with amazement how Carroll still possessed a remarkable memory of history, literature, and current events.

Students heard of a somewhat humorous experience of Mrs. Carroll during these difficult days. Carroll had always been known as a man who was powerful in prayer. On many occasions, Professor Scarborough would come to Carroll's home and say, "We just do not have enough money to pay the salaries of the faculty this month." Carroll would go into another room and engage in earnest prayer for this specific need. Emerging, he would say to his wife, "Hallie, it's all right. God will provide our financial needs." And God did. The humorous incident occurred when Carroll's medical doctor changed his medicine to ease his discomfort. The new prescription seemed to sedate Carroll, and he would murmur aloud as he lay on the bed. One day Mrs. Carroll heard him pray:

> O Lord, you know that I don't mind dying. I am ready to go. But I worry so much about Hallie and my family. What will they do after I am gone? I hate to go and leave them in this wicked world, so Lord, I pray that you will take Hallie and my family before I go, so that I can go in peace.

Knowing the many answered prayers of her husband in days gone by, Mrs. Carroll was understandably upset. She quickly asked the doctor to discontinue this medicine and prescribe something else.[149]

After many days in a coma, the venerable man of God died on November 11, 1914. His last words to L. R. Scarborough have been variously reported. W. W. Barnes, who sat by Carroll's bed during many of the last hours, recorded them as follows:

> Lee, keep the Seminary lashed to the cross. If heresy ever comes in the teaching, take it to the faculty. If they will not hear you and take prompt action, take it to the trustees of the Seminary. If they will not hear you, take it to the Convention that appoints the Board of Trustees, and if they will not hear you take it to the great common people of our churches. You will not fail to get a hearing then.[150]

Eulogies of B. H. Carroll came from everywhere. Memorial services were held in Fort Worth and in the First Baptist Church, Waco, where denominational leaders exhausted their vocabularies endeavoring to honor the great man who had fallen.[151] Perhaps the most poignant words came from leaders of the seminary as they endeavored to conceal their dismay and sorrow. Evidently written by L. R. Scarborough, the report to the Baptist General Convention of Texas in 1914, just a few days after Carroll's death, began:

> Out from the shadow of the death of our honored and beloved Founder and President, the Trustees of the Southwestern Baptist Theological Seminary make their annual report to the Convention.
>
> No greater sorrow could afflict, nor heavier loss be sustained by this Seminary than by the death of Dr. Carroll. He was at the genesis of the institution. He saw it in vision. He planned it, nurtured it, formed its ideals, set its standards, projected its endowment, and contributed most largely to its spirit. It was born in his loving heart, and has grown up to its present strength feeding on his heart's blood. It is his dearest spiritual offspring. It is the crowning work of his last years.
>
> He has stamped it with his matchless character. Through it his great soul will be projected during the remainder of time and all eternity. It is the last diadem which his deft hand formed for the crown of the Redeemer.
>
> Your board, feeling the almost unbearable sense of their loss, would here make record of their gratitude to God for his gift to us and the world of this great preacher, peerless teacher, and unmatched interpreter of God's Word.

The memory of his great loving spirit abides on us as a Heavenly benediction. His teachings, his sermons, his life, the work of his hands, will abide to bless many generations.

We are not dispirited, nor cast down. We believe God has led us thus far that He may lead us on. We trust in God, and go forward to the task left us by our honored leader. We herein commit ourselves to the ideals and standards set for this Seminary by its founder, and will do our best to build it along the lines laid out by him, under the direction of the Spirit of God.[152]

The trustees decided that in view of the grave and vital importance of the decision about a new president, they would defer electing a president until some days in the future, probably after the first of the next year.

This was a critical time for the young seminary. Despite the fact that he was seriously ill during the last years of his life, B. H. Carroll's great shadow over the institution had promoted confidence and brought stability. Now that he was gone, other hands must grasp the torch.

Notes

1. *Proceedings*, BGCT, 1907, pp. 45-46.

2. *Catalogue*, Southwestern Baptist Theological Seminary, Fort Worth, Texas, 1907-1908, p.2 (hereafter cited as Southwestern *Catalogue*). This list was pasted in the trustee minutes, p. i.

3. See *Appendix* for the complete charter.

4. B. H. Carroll, "Southwestern Baptist Theological Seminary," *Standard*, 26 March 1908, pp. 1 ff.

5. W. W. Barnes, "The Formative Years of Southwestern Seminary," Fleming Library, Southwestern Seminary. (Typewritten manuscript.)

6. Southwestern Baptist Theological Seminary (Fort Worth, Texas), Minutes of the Meetings of the Board of Trustees, meeting of 8 May 1908. These are on file at the seminary and will be referred to hereafter as Trustee Minutes.

7. A. J. Barton, "First Meeting of the Board of Trustees of Southwestern Theological Seminary," *Standard*, 11 June 1908, p .7

8. There were many articles concerning this in the *Standard*. See articles on 10 May 1906, p. 2; 8 November 1906, p. 10; 22 November 1906, p. 13; 6 December 1906, p. 4; and 17 January 1907, pp. 10 ff.

9. B. H. Carroll, "Southwestern Baptist Theological Seminary," *Standard*, 26 March 1908, pp. 1 ff.

10. Trustee Minutes, 8 May 1908. See also those of 12 November 1908, for corrections in graduates.

11. "Commencement Program," 24 June 1908, published in Southwestern *Catalogue*, 1908-1909, p. 46.

12. Scarborough, pp. 84-85.

13. Ibid., pp. 10-11. See also correspondence between Scarborough and Carroll in File 279, Carroll Papers.

14. *Encyclopedia*, II:1133-34.

15. President P. W. Crannell to B. H. Carroll, 13 July 1908, File 178, Carroll Papers.

16. L. R. Scarborough, "Our New Seminary and its Opening," *Standard*, 15 October 1908, pp. 4, 12.

17. Ibid., p. 12.

18. Different statistics are quoted by various persons about the enrollment each year. The figures used are those secured from the catalogues which were printed in the spring term of each year. These show the names of the individuals enrolled.

19. Trustee Minutes, 12 November 1908.

20. *Proceedings*, BGCT, 1908, p. 67.

21. B. H. Carroll to Mrs. Sue Alderman, 25 March 1909, File 178, Carroll Papers.

22. Letter from Lewis Holland, San Antonio, Texas, 10 March 1909, File 179, Carroll Papers. See also *Proceedings*, BGCT, 1909, pp. 60-61 and 1914, p. 17.

23. J. W. Jent to B. H. Carroll, 28 September 1908 and 15 October 1908, File 178, Carroll Papers.

24. "Commencement Program," 28 May 1909, published in Southwestern *Catalogue*, 1908-1909, p. 48.

25. *Proceedings*, BGCT, 1909, pp. 58-59.

26. Trustee Minutes, 1 June 1910.

27. *Proceedings*, BGCT, 1910, pp. 76-77.

28. *Encyclopedia*, I:310.

29. Trustee Minutes of the Executive Committee, 28 May 1909.

30. *Encyclopedia*, I:337-38.

31. W. K. Penrod, "A Plea for a Great Southwestern Seminary," *Standard*, 17 October 1907, p. 3. See also S. P. Brooks, "Baylor University and the Seminary," *Standard*, 23 January 1908, p. 3.

32. Penrod, ibid.

33. B. H. Carroll, "Southwestern Baptist Theological Seminary, Article 3," *Standard*, 2 April 1908, p. 8.

34. Prince E. Burroughs, "Fort Worth Launches a Campaign to Secure the Southwestern Baptist Theological Seminary," *Standard*, 9 April 1908, p. 1.

35. *Minutes of the Tarrant County Baptist Association* (Fort Worth, Texas) for 1908, p. 27 (hereafter cited as *Minutes*, Tarrant Association).

36. Prince E. Burroughs, "As Things Go in Fort Worth and Tarrant County," *Standard*, 3 September 1908, pp. 1, 5.

37. For this correspondence see Files 178 and 179, Carroll Papers. Also see Scarborough, p. 62.

38. Recollections of Professor Cal Guy of conversations with his parents, Southwestern Baptist Theological Seminary, Fort Worth, Texas, August 1981.

39. Scarborough, p. 65.

40. Trustee Minutes, 2 November 1909.

41. Scarborough, p. 64.

42. Ibid., pp. 64-65.

43. J. Frank Norris, "Seminary Goes to Fort Worth," *Standard*, 7 October 1909, p. 1.

44. Scarborough, p. 65.

45. Trustee Minutes, 2 November 1909.

46. Scarborough, p. 70.

47. J. Frank Norris, "Fort Worth Gives $200,000 for Seminary," *Standard*,

11 November 1909, p. 1. See also his editorial in the *Standard*, 7 October 1909.

48. For a popular pictorial account of the story of Fort Worth see Caleb Pirtle III, *Fort Worth—The Civilized West* (Tulsa: Continental Heritage Press, Inc., 1980).

49. Trustee Minutes, 15 November 1909.

50. *Proceedings*, BGCT, 1909, p. 57.

51. Ibid., pp. 58-60.

52. Ibid., 1910, p. 78.

53. Trustee Minutes, 1 June 1910.

54. *Proceedings*, BGCT, 1910, pp. 201-2.

55. L. R. Scarborough, "Missionary Training for Women," *Standard*, 14 July 1910, p. 6.

56. Southwestern *Catalogue*, 1909-10, pp. 53-60.

57. Scarborough, pp. 73-74.

58. *Proceedings*, BGCT, 1910, p. 77.

59. J. Frank Norris, "The Seminary Opening," *Standard*, 13 October 1910, p. 9.

60. *Proceedings*, BGCT, 1910, p. 76.

61. W. W. Barnes, unpublished personal memoirs, Fleming Library, Southwestern Baptist Theological Seminary, Fort Worth, Texas, n.p.

62. Scarborough, p. 73.

63. Taped interview entitled, "J. Howard Williams, Tape Recording by A. P. Smith and Brother about Southwestern Baptist Theological Seminary," evidently secured between 1953 and 1958 while Dr. Williams was president of the seminary. Fleming Library, Southwestern Baptist Theological Seminary, Fort Worth, Texas.

64. Recollections of Professor Cal Guy.

65. Georgia Miller Ray, *The Jeff D. Ray I Knew* (San Antonio: The Naylor Company, 1952), p. 136.

66. *Encyclopedia*, II:1280.

67. *Proceedings*, BGCT, 1914, p. 18.

68. Scarborough, p. 74.

69. Ibid., pp. 73-75.

70. *Encyclopedia*, II:1283-84.

71. "Accession Book," Fleming Library, Southwestern Baptist Theological Seminary, Fort Worth, Texas.

72. *Proceedings*, BGCT, 1910, p. 75.

73. Trustee Minutes, 26 May 1911.

74. *Encyclopedia*, I:105-6.

75. Georgia Miller Ray, pp. 143-44. See also reference to Dargan on 3 July 1911 in correspondence of B. H. Carroll, File 180, Carroll Papers.

76. Trustee Minutes, 26 May 1911.

77. *Proceedings*, BGCT, 1911, p. 22.

78. William M. Shamburger, "A History of Tarrant County Baptist Association 1886-1922" (Th.D. dissertation, Southwestern Baptist Theological Seminary, 1953), pp. 175-79.

79. Miss Bess Boone (Coldwater, Mississippi) to Robert A. Baker, 15 February 1981, describing her parents' experiences when they were students at that time. On file in Fleming Library, Southwestern Baptist Theological Seminary, Fort Worth, Texas.

80. Taped interview by A. P. Smith and brother. See also letters of B. H. Carroll describing this in 1912, File 181, Carroll Papers.

81. Recollections of Professor Cal Guy.

82. Southwestern Baptist Theological Seminary (Fort Worth, Texas), Minutes of the Meetings of the Faculty, meeting of 2 January 1912. These are on file at the seminary and will be referred to hereafter as Faculty Minutes.

83. A. H. Newman (Waco, Texas) to W. C. Taylor (Fort Worth, Texas), 8 June 1913. On file in Fleming Library, Southwestern Baptist Theological Seminary, Fort Worth, Texas.

84. Trustee Minutes, 29 May 1913.

85. Faculty Minutes, 30 May 1913.

86. *Proceedings*, BGCT, 1912, p. 17.

87. Ibid., 1913, pp. 25-26.

88. Ibid., 1914, pp. 19, 23.

89. *Minutes*, Tarrant Association, 1913, p. 17.

90. *Proceedings*, BGCT, 1914, p. 17.

91. Ibid., p. 20.

92. Ibid., 1913, p. 23.

93. *Minutes of Baptist Women Mission Workers*, 1910, bound with *Proceedings*, BGCT, 1910, pp. 201-202.

94. Ibid., p. 202.

95. *Proceedings*, BGCT, 1914, pp. 18-19.

96. Faculty Minutes, 13 January 1914.

97. *Proceedings*, BGCT, 1914, p. 16.

98. Trustee Minutes of the Executive Committee, 29 September 1911.

99. Barnes, unpublished personal memoirs, n.p.

100. Georgia Miller Ray, pp. 143-44.

101. *Encyclopedia*, III:1608.

102. Ibid., III:2044.

103. Faculty Minutes, 25 May 1911; Trustee Minutes, 26 May 1911.

104. Faculty Minutes, 2 October 1913.

105. *Proceedings*, BGCT, 1914, p. 16.

106. Faculty Minutes, 23 September 1913. See also *Proceedings*, BGCT, 1913, p. 22.

107. Trustee Minutes, passim.

108. Ibid., 26 May 1911 and 29 May 1913.

109. Faculty Minutes, 20 May 1913.

110. Ibid., 23 September 1913.

111. Ibid., 29 May 1912 and 22 April 1913.

112. Ibid., 3 September 1912, 22 April 1913, and 21 December 1913.

113. Ibid., 1 May 1912.

114. Ibid., 5 May 1911 and 20 May 1914.

115. Ibid., 23 September 1913, 13 February 1914, and 17 March 1914.

116. Ibid., 23 October 1913, 6 November 1913, and 13 January 1914.

117. Ibid., 3 October 1911.

118. Ibid., 21 March 1911.

119. Ibid., 23 September 1913 and 28 May 1914.

120. Ibid., 30 May 1913.

121. Ibid., 18 February 1914.

122. Ibid., 25 May 1911.

123. Ibid., 6 November 1912.

124. Ibid., 4 December 1913.

125. Ibid., 23 February 1913.

126. Ibid., 2 October 1913.

127. Ibid., 12 March 1913.

128. Ibid., 23 September 1913.

129. Ibid.

130. Southwestern *Catalogue*, 1911-12, pp. 18-19.

131. Ibid., p. 15.

132. Ibid., 1914-15, p. 15.

133. Faculty Minutes, 28 February 1914.

134. Trustee Minutes, 29 May 1913.

135. *Proceedings*, BGCT, 1914, p. 17.

136. Faculty Minutes, 25 May 1911, 3 October 1911, and 25 November 1911; and Trustee Minutes, 26 May 1911.

137. Faculty Minutes, 4 December 1913.

138. Ibid., 13 January 1914.

139. Ibid., 28 May 1914. See also Southwestern *Catalogue*, 1914-15, p. 62.

140. Faculty Minutes, 2 May 1914 and 20 May 1914.

141. For this see issues of *Standard*, 8 July 1909, p. 13; 9 September 1909, p. 13; 16 September 1909, p. 13; 30 September 1909, p. 13; 14 October 1909, p. 13; and 1 November 1909, p. 1.

142. J. Frank Norris, *Inside History of First Baptist Church, Fort Worth, and Temple Baptist Church, Detroit* (n.p.: n.p., © 1945), p. 127.

143. George W. Dollar, *A History of Fundamentalism in America* (Greenville, S.C.: Bob Jones University Press, 1973), p. 123.

144. J. B. Gambrell, "The Vindication of Pastor Norris," *Standard*, 2 May 1912, p. 1. See also *Standard*, 7 March 1912, p. 8.

145. Taped interview by A. P. Smith and brother.

146. G. H. Connell to B. H. Carroll, 5 October 1912, File 182, Carroll Papers.

147. B. H. Carroll to G. H. Connell, 19 October 1912, File 182, Carroll Papers.

148. For details of this story see Shamburger, passim, and Royce Measures, "Men and Movements Influenced by J. Frank Norris" (Th.D. dissertation, Southwestern Baptist Theological Seminary, 1976), passim. I am indebted to Mrs. Felix Gresham for researching the minutes of Gambrell Street Baptist Church, Fort Worth, to determine the date L. R. Scarborough put his membership there.

149. Recollections of Professor Cal Guy.

150. Barnes, p. 209. L. R. Scarborough also used this language. See Scarborough, p. 90.

151. Crowder published several of the funeral messages, pp. 89 ff.

152. *Proceedings*, BGCT, 1914, p. 14.

Lee R. Scarborough
President (1915-42)
Evangelism (1908-42)

Cowden Hall
Erected 1926

Mr. and Mrs. George E. Cowden

Robert A. Baker
Church History (1942-81)

William Barclay
Organ (1928-48)

Floy Barnard
Educational Arts (1933-60)
Dean (1944-60)

E. L. Carlson
Old Testament (1921-64)

E. L. Carnett
Music Theory (1920-33)
Dean (1945)

Baker James Cauthen
Missions (1935-39)

B. A. Copass
Old Testament (1918-42)

H. E. Dana
New Testament (1919-38)

Robert T. Daniel
Old Testament (1937-52)

N. R. Drummond
Principles of R. E.
(1920-31)

L. R. Elliott
Librarian (1919-57)

Vinnie Gammill
Records (1923-44)

Andrew Hemphill
Voice (1919-48)

W. L. House
Administration of R. E.
(1933-55)

Mrs. W. E. Kimbrough
Superintendent, Fort
Worth Hall (1922-45)

W. H. Knight
Missions (1919-23
and 1929-31)

T. B. Maston
Christian Ethics (1922-63)

B. B. McKinney
Music Theory (1919-31)

Edwin McNeely
Voice (1920-63)

Wayne McNeely
Piano (1919-56)

Frank K. Means
Missions (1939-46)

S. A. Newman
Philosophy (1936-52)

Jesse Northcutt
Preaching (1939-45
and 1950-)

J. M. Price
Principles of R. E.
and Dean (1915-56)

Georgia Miller Ray
Secretary (1915-38)

I. E. Reynolds
Music Theory and
Dean (1915-45)

Mrs. I. E. Reynolds
Piano (1919-21 and
1932-57)

Mamie Storrs
Secretary (1938-58)

Ray Summers
New Testament (1938-59)
Dean (1949-53)

D. A. Thornton
Cashier (1919-53)

Albert Venting
Philosophy (1921-37)

Mrs. F. H. Waldrop
Nursery (1922-62)

W. R. White
Missions (1923-27)

Mrs. W. L. Williams
Shrubs and Trees (1915-31)

Barnard Hall
Erected 1915

Faculty
About 1920

Faculty and Administration
1938

Faculty 1938

5

A Challenging Decade

The death of B. H. Carroll was the greatest crisis faced by the seminary in its early history. His towering figure and eloquent voice had captivated Texas Baptists for more than forty years. In his own lifetime, his gifts and achievements had become legendary, and his death magnified his greatness. Mankind has always tended to immortalize its departed heroes. Through oral recollections, writings, monuments, and other memorials, all races and nations in history have treasured the noble deeds of their forebears, usually glossing over any faults or weaknesses and gilding their exploits with an aura of extraordinary wisdom and strength. Whenever a Roman emperor came to die, for example, he knew that he would not only be given a place of honor but would actually be apotheosized. Emperor Vespasian (AD 69-79) even joked about it. As this phlegmatic professional soldier lay dying, he murmured with a wry smile, "I think that I am becoming a god."

So, the stature of Carroll made it difficult to find an acceptable person to succeed him as president of the seminary. Who could take the place of this colossus? Charles T. Alexander reflected this spirit in a poem written after Carroll's death, which began:

> How wearily the years have dragged, great friend,
> Since last we felt the clasp of thy warm hand,
> We've trod alone, we've roamed a lonesome land.
> You gone, the path seems lonely, yet we wend
> We stumble and we almost lose the way,
> We miss thy constant care, so true and kind,
> We falter oft until the path we find
> Wherein thy steps lead on to perfect day.[1]

But God had been preparing a man to become the new leader of the seminary. Lee Rutland Scarborough had already proved his mettle. In 1901, he had accepted the call of the church at Abilene, Texas, "when it was a mere handful, worshipping in a weather-beaten shack on a dusty corner, and left it a conquering church, one of the greatest in the Southwest, with provisions for its work and worship in a marvelously beautiful temple."[2] He had borne the burden of raising $100,000 in Fort Worth to provide the bonus for locating the seminary there and had

197

shouldered the responsibility of supervising the erection of the first
building on the campus. During the last two years of Carroll's presidency,
Scarborough had shared the task of raising funds for operating the
school. His gifts and spirit made him the logical successor to the beloved
Carroll. He was a warmhearted and effective teacher of evangelism in the
"Chair of Fire." On February 9, 1915, the trustees unanimously elected
him as the second president of the seminary. Jeff D. Ray wrote:

> Many feared that the institution would die with the death of the great
> man in whose heart and brain it seemed to have its life. But God had
> planned and ordered otherwise. Within a few months L. R. Scarborough,
> who had been professor of Evangelism from the second year of the
> Seminary's life and who had been Acting President during Dr. Carroll's long
> illness, was elected President. . . . The growth and efficiency, under his
> administration, has amply justified Dr. Carroll's oft-expressed wish that he
> should be chosen as the Seminary's second president.[3]

On February 11, two days after the election of L. R. Scarborough as
second president of the seminary, the faculty began to make arrangements for his inauguration. It was held on May 28, 1915, in conjunction
with the spring commencement. In his inaugural address, Scarborough
asserted that Southwestern Seminary, like Southern, had been built
"largely on the principles laid down by Dr. James P. Boyce in his
immortal address at Greenville, South Carolina, in 1858." Scarborough
described his own philosophy of seminary education in this outstanding
message. The biblical educational purpose, he said, was to train men to
be efficient preachers of the gospel. This was the dynamic that motivated
the founding of Baylor University, "out of the heart of which has grown
this Seminary." Scarborough stated that

> It was to supply this same demand of Christ's growing kingdom that led
> Boyce, Broadus, and their immortal co-laborers to toil, sacrifice, and build
> through the weary years the foundations and superstructure of our great
> Seminary at Louisville, Kentucky. It was a love for Christ's cause in
> supplying his churches with worthy and trained preachers that led the
> deathless Carroll to lay aside his great pastorate and devote himself without
> reserve to his dying day to the building of Southwestern Seminary.

The seminary, continued Scarborough, was built on a threefold foundation. First, it was denominationally anchored as a distinctively Baptist
institution. This character was guarded by the requirement that its
teachers be Baptist, by its Baptist confession of faith, and by its
organizational structure that made its trustees responsible to the Baptist
constituency. Second, its teachings were based upon the Word of God.

> Unitarianism and destructive criticism, with their schemes against Christ's
> deity, their plots against Paul's integrity, their denials of the Bible's

inspiration and their denunciations of the supernatural in Christianity, cannot receive even a faint smile of approval in any corner of the Seminary's theology. We are happy to take Christ as divine Lord, salvation through his blood, membership in his churches, orders from his commission and go forth in the power of his Spirit to save a lost world.

Third, following the pattern of James P. Boyce, this seminary magnified both scholarship and spiritual life and practical efficiency in church and kingdom service. "We believe in and encourage the highest reaches and profoundest depths of learning in college, university, and seminary. . . . We put a premium on broad and accurate scholarship." But also "we remember Amos, Simon Peter, and John the Baptist in God's lists of preachers and prophets, as well as Moses, Paul, and the cultured John." Scarborough continued,

Our great aim is to meet the needs of a suffering world in high places and low, with adaptable, efficient, evangelistic and Spirit-filled men. We confess that our aim is found in the subject of this address—kingdom efficiency through culture, scholarship, training, consecration, and the power of God.

Scarborough then discussed the five marks of the efficient minister of Jesus Christ: he should be Christian in character, sincere in spirituality, accurate and compassionate in scholarship, biblical in doctrinal convictions, and consistent in denominational sympathy and cooperation.[4]

The incoming president faced a new and difficult day. The technological advances during his lifetime can be illustrated by the fact that he never saw an automobile until he was almost grown, yet before his death the *Enola Gay* had dropped an atomic bomb on Hiroshima. During his administration, the world would be embroiled in two frightful world wars and would experience two serious depressions. More menacing from a religious point of view, the spirit of antisupernaturalism was spreading rapidly in the world. Charles Darwin had helped initiate this latest onslaught against faith in God by the publication of his *Origin of the Species* in 1859. His impressive biological research provided the base for his theory of evolution which asserted that man developed from a lower animal ancestry. As usual, a seminal work of this kind provided a watershed for many disciplines. German scholarship reflected Darwin's principles in the sphere of biblical literature, and higher criticism became popular. Southern Baptists like James P. Boyce, John A. Broadus, and B. H. Carroll struggled against this movement in the late nineteenth century. The Social Gospel thrust developed in part from the desire of liberal theologians to retain the social and ethical teachings of Jesus without reference to his essential deity. Many types of theological liberalism sprang from efforts to maintain both a scientific and a religious stance.

The reaction of American conservatives to this new theological liberalism developed rapidly after the opening of the twentieth century. One of the chief factors in precipitating a structured doctrinal response was the movement known as Fundamentalism. Lyman and Milton Stewart, two wealthy laymen, consulted with A. C. Dixon in 1909 relative to publishing a series of pamphlets on the fundamentals of the faith as held by conservatives. Dixon, pastor of the Moody Church in Chicago at this time, wrote B. H. Carroll on October 23, 1909, asking him to prepare an article or two on some doctrinal theme. Dixon said that the two laymen planned to spend $300,000 on the project, to publish the first pamphlet on January 1, 1910, send it unannounced to every Protestant preacher in the English-speaking world, and then mail another pamphlet each month during that year. Dixon urged that Carroll keep this letter confidential for the time being.[5] Carroll was deeply involved in locating the seminary at this time, and no reply to Dixon was found in his files. However, J. J. Reeve and C. B. Williams, two professors of the seminary, provided articles for these pamphlets. The twelve small publications appeared in 1910 under the title, *The Fundamentals: A Testimony of the Truth*. Approximately three million copies of these were circulated, two-thirds of them in the United States.[6] It is ironic from the perspective of the seminary that despite its consistently conservative stance, the Fundamentalists, led by J. Frank Norris of Fort Worth, were much more active in attempting to destroy Southwestern Seminary than were the liberals or antisupernaturalists.

A Good Beginning

During the first five years of Scarborough's administration (1915-19), the seminary made significant advances in spite of the hostile forces just described. It showed a substantial growth in every area, an improvement in the quality of work being done, and the development of better organizational structures for instruction and administration.

Substantial Growth

The number of resident students dropped in 1914-15 to 187, but by the session of 1918-19 the enrollment had increased to 361. In the latter session, almost half of this number were women in the training school. Students in correspondence study increased slightly from 70 at the beginning of the period to 77 at the close.

The number of graduates began to increase slowly, as follows:

1914-15	48
1915-16	37
1916-17	37
1917-18	43
1918-19	58

The faculty voted on April 7, 1916, that the graduates from the Woman's Missionary Training School would henceforth receive their diplomas at the same time as the remainder of the seminary. This was reflected in the catalogues, which no longer listed the training school graduates in a different section from other graduates of the seminary.

The following chart shows the financial growth of the seminary in its operating fund.

Session	Receipts	Disbursements
1914-15	$31,947.23	$31,947.23
1915-16	28,230.41	29,539.07
1916-17	31,520.17	41,323.42
1917-18	37,575.00	44,121.00
1918-19	43,395.33	44,014.17

The endowment of the school hovered around $400,000, but this fluctuated becuse some of it was in unpaid pledges.[7] In each of these five years, the trustees reported to the state convention that Scarborough was forced to spend much of his time raising from $20,000 to $40,000 in cash each year to keep the seminary operating.

The indebtedness of the seminary increased during these five years from approximately $125,000 in 1914 to $194,000 in 1919. Most of this debt accrued from the deficit in the building of Fort Worth Hall. The total bonus was not collected, and the cost of the building far exceeded the original estimates. Part of the debt came from the purchase in 1919 of the one-half interest of J. K. Winston and his sons in approximately 525 lots around the campus, for the sum of $35,000. This farsighted action provided the seminary with an adequate expansion area for the future.[8]

The action of the Baptist General Convention of Texas in 1918-19 altered this debt situation. In 1918 that body named a committee to study the debts of the schools in the correlated Texas Baptist system. L. R. Scarborough was its chairman and T. V. Neal, an expert in financial management, and R. E. Burt, an influential layman, worked with him. The seminary was not a part of the correlated system of Baptist schools in Texas, but "since it is so closely identified with and so largely helped by the Convention and people of Texas," it was made a part of the plan.

This committee made a thorough survey of Texas Baptist educational institutions and recommended a ten-year program, as follows: (1) that the convention seek to raise for educational purposes at least $300,000 in cash each year by statewide campaigns; (2) that it issue Loyalty Bonds in the amount of $1,000,000, which would be secured by deeding the physical property of the schools in trust to the Executive Board of the convention; (3) that these bonds be issued in amounts ranging from $50 to $10,000, bearing interest at 6 percent annually, and be sold to Texas Baptists as far as possible; (4) that $50,000 of the money raised from the campaigns be applied on the payment of bonds maturing each year, and approximately $210,000 be used each year to pay accrued interest on bonds and current school deficits in operating expenses and ministerial education; (5) that it provide a sinking fund for the last $500,000 of bonds; and (6) that it pay the salary and expenses of an educational secretary. Any balance left after these preferred items had been paid would be used for improving the properties of the schools, providing endowment, and similar matters. It was further recommended that an educational secretary be named to supervise the bond program and promote the campaigns each year. The Ways and Means Committee of the Executive Board made several additional recommendations involving the general plans for the handling of the bonds and the deeding of the property of the participating institutions to the board as security. It was hoped that this program would result in paying all the debts of the schools and reducing the amount of interest being charged the several institutions.

Pursuant to this plan, on March 14, 1919, the trustees of the seminary authorized the execution of a note for $250,000 to the Baptist General Convention of Texas, in consideration for which the convention would take over the indebtedness of the seminary in the amount of $192,442 through the issuance of Loyalty Bonds. Approximately $20,000 of this debt was paid off in the next five years.

In addition to this growth in enrollment and finances, the seminary faculty was significantly enlarged between 1914 and 1919. B. H. Carroll's assistant, J. W. Crowder, became the teacher in English Bible. This move retained the distinctive English Bible Department which had been so important to Carroll. John Milburn Price, a graduate of Baylor University, Brown University, and The Southern Baptist Theological Seminary, was elected in 1915 to teach Christian education.[9] He would provide notable leadership in this area for the next half century. Isham

Emmanuel Reynolds also was named to the faculty at this time. He had attended Mississippi College and Moody Bible Institute and had been well trained in voice, theory, and composition under private teachers.[10] Reynolds pioneered in the area of gospel music at Southwestern Seminary until his retirement in 1945.

With the resignation of Miss Mary C. Tupper in 1915, Mrs. Alma Wilson Lile was named superintendent of the Woman's Missionary Training School. At this time, Mrs. W. L. Williams was elected assistant superintendent of the training school. A longtime worker with Baptist women and former president of the Baptist Women Mission Workers, "Mother" Williams, as she was affectionately known, had moved to Seminary Hill and was assuming the voluntary task of beautifying the campus through the planting of shrubs and flowers. Mrs. Lile served until 1919, when she was replaced by Mrs. J. W. Byars as superintendent.[11]

J. B. Weatherspoon, professor of Hebrew and Old Testament, resigned from the faculty in 1918 to accept the pastorate of the First Baptist Church, Winston-Salem, North Carolina. To replace him the trustees elected Benjamin Andrew Copass, the scholarly associate secretary of the Executive Board of the Baptist General Convention of Texas. Copass was a graduate of Bethel College, Russellville, Kentucky, with two degrees and was a full graduate of The Southern Baptist Theological Seminary in 1894. He joined the faculty at the age of fifty-three, coming from a career as a successful pastor and denominational leader. His teaching and scholarly writing endeared him to a generation of Southwestern students.[12]

In 1919, when Charles T. Ball resigned from the faculty, the trustees elected William Henry Knight, an instructor in biblical languages, as assistant professor of missions. He was a graduate of Louisiana College and had just received his Master of Theology degree from Southwestern.[13]

Another excellent addition to the faculty was James Bruton Gambrell, who had previously taught from 1912 to 1914 while serving as editor of the Texas *Baptist Standard*. He had resigned from these positions when named the general secretary of the Baptist General Convention of Texas in 1914. He remained as secretary until 1917 when he was elected president of the Southern Baptist Convention. He returned to the seminary in that year to teach ecclesiology, missions, and denominational polity until his death on June 10, 1921.

The year 1919 was a momentous one for the seminary. A series of events was begun by the resignation of C. T. Ball to become secretary of the Baptist student missionary movement. Ball had been professor of missions and superintendent of the Extension (Correspondence) Department. As will be pointed out, the naming of J. W. Crowder to the Extension Department precipitated an important organizational revision in the seminary. W. H. Knight became professor of missions, and James Sterling Rogers returned to the campus to teach junior Greek and English New Testament. C. B. Williams, professor of Greek since 1905, resigned during the summer to accept the presidency of Howard College in Alabama.[14] Harvey Eugene Dana, a graduate of Mississippi College, began teaching in the Department of Hebrew and Old Testament but would soon turn to the Greek New Testament and begin a brilliant career in that field.[15]

In that same year, Baylus Benjamin McKinney joined the staff of the Department of Gospel Music. A graduate of Louisiana College and the seminary, he became an outstanding gospel songwriter.[16] Mrs. I. E. Reynolds began teaching piano in 1919; E. L. Carnett was asked to teach music theory in 1920; and to complete the permanent faculty, Leonidas M. Sipes, a graduate student, was named librarian while continuing to serve as pastor of the Seminary Hill Baptist Church.

The campus in 1915 had two buildings—Fort Worth Hall and the Woman's Missionary Training School. The latter had been completed during the summer of 1915, principally through the collection of funds by Mrs. R. F. Stokes of the Baptist Women Mission Workers. At the dedication of the building on September 23, 1915, L. R. Scarborough expressed his appreciation for the women who had initiated the project and had helped bring it to completion. He also thanked J. M. Frost of the Baptist Sunday School Board, Nashville, Tennessee, which had contributed ten thousand dollars to assist in the erection of this building. The women of Texas also agreed to give financial assistance for the operation of the training school each year.[17]

Increasing the Quality

In his inaugural address, President Scarborough had emphasized the need for both technical scholarship and practical efficiency in the ministry, and this principle was followed during these early years. As one glances through the pages of the *Southwestern Evangel*, the faculty journal at that time, he must be impressed with this dual emphasis. H. E. Dana, while editor of this journal, often wrote on the importance of good scholarship. The crucial problem, he said, was "to keep evangelism and scholarship in proper balance." To maintain this equilibrium between the two, it was necessary "to have the most possible of both."[18] The quotation credited to John S. Tanner was often repeated, "The Spirit of God seems to have an affinity for a trained mind."[19]

The makeup of the student body reflected the constantly rising standards of scholarship. A survey of one of the dormitories showed that 92 percent of the students there were college trained, either on the junior college level or as full college graduates. Some students had delayed coming to Southwestern in order to complete their college work, while others had dropped out in order to return to college for additional literary work.[20]

Factors reflecting this greater emphasis on scholarship included the strengthening of the curriculum, the sabbatical leave program for the faculty, the acquisition of able scholars to deliver the Holland Lectures, the encouragement of faculty writing, the developing strength of the library, and a creative interaction with outside Christian and denominational currents which enriched the background and increased the outreach of the faculty.

The minutes of the faculty and trustees reveal the important steps taken between 1914 and 1919 to strengthen the curriculum. Faculty minutes show a sensitivity to contemporary education currents and a constant reflection on the kind of training needed by the students to meet the demands of the world of that day. It will be recalled that while at Waco the seminary had utilized the services of Professor Frederick Eby from the Department of Education of Baylor University as a lecturer in pedagogy. The need for specific training in Sunday School methodology and other areas of religious education had been increasingly recognized by Southern Baptists for over half a century, and the organization of the second Baptist Sunday School Board in 1891 marked the aggressive reentrance of Southern Baptists into this field. At the opening of the twentieth century, almost half of the churches affiliated with the Southern Baptist Convention had no Sunday Schools; but the vision and activity of J. M. Frost, the first secretary of the infant board, brought a new day to Southern Baptists. One of his many projects was the effort to train young preachers in pedagogy and religious education. To that end, in 1901 he developed a plan by which an annual lecture was delivered each year to the students of The Southern Baptist Theological Seminary, Louisville, on the subject of the Sunday School. In 1906, the board began to provide support for a professorship at Louisville to teach Sunday School pedagogy. By 1916, it had invested sixty thousand dollars in this program at Louisville to help endow a chair in this discipline.[21]

After Southwestern Seminary moved to Fort Worth in 1910, only one course in this area of study was offered, which included psychology, pedagogy, organization, curriculum, and the history and administration of religious education. In 1913, C. B. Williams offered two courses, one dealing with the psychology and pedagogy of the Sunday School and the other with the history, organization, and administration of religious education. In the following year, W. W. Barnes, who had taken this training at the Louisville seminary, offered two courses in Sunday School pedagogy and one in Christian sociology. In the spring of 1915, upon the recommendation of the faculty, the trustees of Southwestern Seminary voted to establish the Department of Religious Education.[22] J. M. Price offered five hours of study in this field as a part of the theological curriculum in that year. In 1916 he developed a curriculum for a diploma in religious education, and by 1919 the faculty approved the offering of a Bachelor of Religious Education degree. Miss Lou Ella Austin was graduated in May, 1917, with the diploma in religious education, the first person anywhere to receive a diploma designated "Religious Education." Two others received this diploma in each of the following two years.[23] In 1919 two additional pioneering steps were taken. One was the structuring of age-group studies, including courses in elementary, adolescent, and adult religious education. The other, by vote of the faculty on March 21, 1919, was the admission of students in religious education to apply for the Doctor of Theology degree with a major in religious education.

Another important curiculum change came in 1915. It will be recalled that classes had been offered in vocal and instrumental music sporadically in previous years, mainly for the benefit of the students in the women's training school. In the spring of 1915, I. E. Reynolds came to the seminary to head the new Department of Gospel Music. Nine students were enrolled in the first year, including B. B. McKinney, who would later become one of the faculty of the school. The catalogue for 1915-16 described courses in sight-reading, harmony, composition, conducting, general chorus, male chorus, women's chorus, history of music, history of hymns and tunes, voice, and piano.[24]

The introduction of a full schedule in music created some problems relative to the time and place of practice. Evidently some of the students in Fort Worth Hall were attempting to practice instrumental music during class hours in that building, and the faculty was forced to develop rules for practice times.[25] A separate building for the music department was badly needed.

As indicated previously, the requests of the ladies in the training school brought the additions to the curriculum of such activities as music, settlement work, kindergarten, and expression.[26] At the faculty meetings during this period, the curriculum was gradually expanded to allow credit for these activities on the women's diplomas and degrees.[27]

It has been mentioned that a Seminary Extension Department under the leadership of Professor C. T. Ball was announced in 1914. The program was described in the catalogue of that year.[28] In the first year, the department enrolled seventy-five students in thirteen courses.[29] A significant advance was made in 1919 when J. W. Crowder was transferred from the Department of English Bible to the Extension Department. In that year the report showed 519 students enrolled in 110 courses.[30]

On May 27, 1915, another important curricular change was approved by the board of trustees, who passed a resolution authorizing President Scarborough to organize a field force of evangelists, their number and salaries to be determined by Scarborough. To the state convention on November 20, 1915, President Scarborough revealed his plan for this program, as follows:

> For some years the Seminary force has believed that there should be in connection with the Seminary a department of field evangelism, and through the years a number of evangelists have been employed to hold meetings under the auspices of the Seminary, and thus create sentiment, tie the gospel onto the work of educating the ministry, winning souls, and otherwise building the kingdom of God. At the May meeting of the Board of Trustees, on the recommendation of the President, a department of Evangelism was established, and Rev. F. M. McConnell was elected Superintendent of the department. He accepted, and began work the first of August. Since that time he has been engaged in meetings in the two cities of San Antonio and El Paso, and other places, and God has marvellously blessed his labors.

Scarborough said that two additional evangelists had been added to the seminary staff and that others were being sought for this work. He urged the pastors to use these men in revivals.

> Their work is to win souls, build souls, call out the called, secure students for our Seminary, make friends for our Seminary, help in all the educational, missionary, and benevolent work of this Convention, and otherwise co-operate in the financial support of the Seminary.[31]

During the remainder of this period, he reported that in 1915-16 there were five evangelists employed by the seminary, six in 1916-17, seven during 1917-18, and seven in 1918-19. Each year Scarborough reported the results of the soul-winning efforts by the evangelists, students, and faculty of the seminary, along with the amount of money the evangelists had raised for their own support. As Scarborough predicted, these evangelists always raised enough money to provide for their own salaries and therefore were not an expense to the seminary.

Finally, the curriculum during this first period of L. R. Scarborough's administration reflected a constant sensitivity to the needs of the constituency. Additional courses were added to provide instruction in specific areas. For example, in the catalogue for 1914 a course in "Problems of the Country Church" was offered by Professor Jeff D. Ray. This subject had been discussed in Baptist periodicals and at various conventions, and the faculty felt that the need was great enough to offer a course of this kind. In the following year, the Baptist General Convention of Texas named a committee to discuss the problems of rural churches.[32] In 1917, the seminary reported to the convention that it had a "country church department," although actually this referred to the course by Professor Ray on "Problems of the Country Church."[33]

In addition to enlarging the curriculum, the faculty also revised it during this period. Rarely was a faculty meeting convened that it did not make some type of revision in credit given for courses or introduce some new course into the schedule. A major revision in the Doctor of Theology program was developed by a faculty committee on March 23, 1917, and was announced in the catalogue for 1917-18. The new program emphasized that candidacy would be restricted to those "who not only excel in scholarship and have shown ability for original investigation, but possess as well such personal qualities as give promise of a successful career." To this end, the faculty would take the initiative in inviting students to enter this program, taking into consideration a student's university and seminary work, his use of ancient and modern foreign languages as instruments of research, and his intellectual, moral, and spiritual qualities for leadership.

Doctoral work was offered in four departments: Hebrew and Old Testament theology, Greek and New Testament theology, systematic theology, and church history. The applicant chose one of these departments as a major and, in addition, completed a minor in two of these departments or in missions, evangelism, homiletics, religious education, or English Bible. The chairmen of a student's major and minor departments formed a committee to supervise his work. Resident study of at least one full session of thirty-six weeks was required out of a total of at least eighteen months of study. An oral examination of ninety minutes over the student's major field and thirty minutes over each minor field was required. A dissertation of at least fifteen thousand words, the subject of which must be approved by the faculty, was to be submitted at least two months before the date of the proposed graduation.[34]

Year by year various changes were made in the requirements for the several degrees. The principal single revision was adopted by the faculty on January 2, 1918, when the curricula for all diplomas and degrees were altered to provide a better academic balance.

A second area of improving the quality of the instruction was the development of sabbatical leave and leave of absence programs. W. T. Conner was away for study in 1914, J. M. Price in 1916, and W. W. Barnes in 1918—simply by agreement of the faculty and the president. In connection with a sweeping administrative change made on March 14, 1919, however, the trustees approved the following recommendation by President Scarborough:

> That it be understood that each teacher must take one summer off, at least, out of three in study, and that in rotation each teacher be given a year off, one being away each year, with salary continued, in further study, looking to improvements in his or her department.

This program continued unchanged during the remainder of Scarborough's administration.

The Holland Lectures provided another opportunity for elevating the level of scholarship. As mentioned, George W. Truett delivered the first of these on "The Preacher." During this period, W. L. Poteat of Wake Forest College, North Carolina, spoke on "Christianity and Culture"; J. R. Sampey of The Southern Baptist Theological Seminary, Louisville, brought a series on "The Religion of the Bible, a Progressive Revelation"; and H. C. Mabie lectured on "A Kingdom Without a Tremor."

Another aspect of the increasing emphasis on scholarship was the effort to publish the manuscripts written by the faculty. After informally discussing the problem, the faculty named a committee on March 19, 1919, consisting of Scarborough, Williams, and Copass "to draw up regulations concerning the lending of money by the Seminary to members of the faculty for the purpose of publishing books." Two days later the committee made a long report. It began:

> Since it is quite necessary for the Faculty of the Southwestern Seminary to render their part in the publication and circulation of Baptist literature, and since there are a number of textbooks which are very greatly needed for our Baptist schools and seminaries, and since the members of the Faculty are not financially able to finance the publication of such books, we recommend that the Seminary loan to the members of the Faculty who write and desire to publish books, on the following terms and conditions.

The conditions were that the faculty member must submit a typewritten manuscript to a three-member faculty committee for approval; that the president of the seminary must approve any business arrangements with a publishing firm; that a promissory note for the necessary funds be signed by the faculty member for a time not over five years at the rate of 6 percent per annum, with the privilege of renewal; that all money received in the sale of the book should be applied on this note; that the author was responsible to pay the note and interest whether the book was a success or not; that after the payment of the note, the seminary would release all other profits or royalties to the author. The records do not show which of the faculty, if any, called upon the seminary for these loans.

Another writing venture involving most of the professors was begun during this time. There were two literary societies in the student body at this time: the B.H.C. and the Adelphian. These societies raised the question with the faculty about the publication of a seminary journal. This was mulled over in the faculty, and on December 1, 1916, a committee was appointed to study the matter. A week later, the faculty voted to begin the publication of a quarterly in April, 1917. C. B. Williams was elected managing editor, and it was planned to sell the journal for one dollar per year. W. W. Barnes was named the review editor, and J. B. Weatherspoon, the seminary editor. The books reviewed were to be placed in the seminary library. The name adopted was *The Southwestern Journal of Theology*. During the next few years, the faculty would have a running debate about whether or not to continue this publication. Despite having over five hundred subscribers, the *Journal* proved to be a financially burdensome child.

Still another factor in raising the level of scholarship during this period was the developing strength of the library. It will be recalled that the seminary used one of its faculty as the librarian during the early years. C. B. Williams held that post until 1915, when he was succeeded by W. W. Barnes, who in turn was replaced by W. T. Conner while Barnes was absent on sabbatical leave in 1918-19.[35] The last figure given in the catalogues for the number of volumes in the library was five thousand in 1919. This figure probably was not accurate, since the estimate was shown several years earlier, and it is known that many books had been added since that time.

Finally, the creative interaction of the faculty and administration with contemporary currents in Christian and denominational life provided another factor in enriching the faculty and its work. The outreach of the faculty and staff by 1919 was astounding. They served as pastors of churches, leaders in the associations, state bodies, and the Southern Baptist Convention, and pioneers in denominational movements. Random illustrations of these activities may be glimpsed in the work of W. T. Conner, C. T. Ball, and W. W. Barnes.

W. T. Conner became pastor of the Seminary Hill Baptist Church (now Gambrell Street Baptist Church) when it was organized on November 14, 1915. Many of the faculty had long desired to form a church on Seminary Hill because of the difficulty in obtaining transportation to other Baptist churches. Regular services had been held in the seminary chapel on Wednesday nights and Sundays for several years. A church council was called on November 14, 1915, consisting of C. T. Ball, W. W. Barnes, J. W. Crowder, Forrest Smith, C. V. Edwards, L. L. Whitley, and Z. C. O'Farrell, with L. R. Scarborough presiding. The Seminary Hill church was consitituted with fifty-two charter members, and W. W. Barnes preached the first sermon. Conner had been pastor of the Rio Vista church, but he accepted the call of the Seminary Hill church as her first pastor. For several years, the church met in the seminary chapel on the second floor of Fort Worth Hall. Before the church was two months old and was yet without a pastor, she began a mission on Hemphill Street and within another few months had established a second one; then, in a few years, a third one was organized across town. In 1919, an arrangement was made with President Scarborough by which the seminary would contribute one hundred dollars a month to the salary of the pastor, who would serve also as librarian of the seminary.[36] This typical experience of Conner and the seminary faculty in utilizing the scholarship of the classroom to interact with community needs enriched the quality of instruction and demonstrated the relevance of the curriculum.

Charles T. Ball was professor of comparative religion and missions in the seminary. He was one of the leaders of a movement among schoolmen in May, 1914, to provide a structure for enlisting Baptist students on the denominational campuses. In conferences at Nashville, Tennessee, and Waco, Texas, plans were developed to organize a denominational body to foster this work. At the third conference at Fort Worth, Texas, Ball led in the formation of the Baptist Student Missionary Movement of North America on November 16, 1914. The Southern Baptist Convention endorsed the movement in the following year.[37] The purpose and goals of this student organization were spelled out in a report to the Southern Baptist Convention on May 18, 1916.[38]

During the spring of 1915, Professor Ball was granted a leave of absence by Southwestern Seminary to spend six weeks in the promotion of this movement. On March 22-26, 1916, the first convention of the new movement assembled in Fort Worth, Texas, and in the following year met at Louisville, Kentucky. Over five hundred Baptist students attended a conference involving five days of study on the subject of missions.[39]

In January, 1917, Professor Ball and his staff published the first issue of the *Baptist Student,* which described the beginning and program of the Baptist Student Missionary Movement. Ball also utilized denominational periodicals to inform Southern Baptists about the progress of this work.[40] This movement continued an active program until 1920 when it evolved into a denominational structure which ultimately became the Baptist Student Union.[41]

W. W. Barnes is the other illustration of the outreach of the faculty. He served as an interim pastor of churches in Fort Worth during this period. Between 1914 and 1924 he served intermittently as moderator of the Tarrant County Baptist Association, presiding when J. Frank Norris was first denied a seat in 1922. Barnes's thorough training, wide culture, and profound spirituality enhanced the quality of the faculty and made him most useful in denominational activities.

Improved Organizational Patterns

During the period from 1914 to 1919, both the faculty and the trustees adopted new organizational patterns that provided more efficiency and better performance.

More and more, the faculty appointed committees to study and bring recommendations on various matters. On May 30, 1918, for example, the faculty named six permanent committees to serve during the year, as follows: Schedule and Curriculum, Classification and Graduation, Publication, Book, Public Exercises, and Mission Day Exercises. In the previous year, there had also been committees on the student fund, the library, and credentials.[42] Through these committees, the faculty was able to have the benefit of small-group study and recommendations before taking action on some matter.

The earliest structural change during this period was the initiating of the two new departments of religious education and gospel music, which has been mentioned already in connection with the curriculum revisions.

An important structural change occurred in the summer of 1916. For over a year, the faculty had been discussing the need for a summer term, which had been authorized earlier but had not been put into operation because of the lack of personnel. On June 5, 1915, the faculty voted not to attempt a summer term, but on December 1, 1916, they reversed this decision. Plans were made for a summer school in 1917. Professor J. B. Weatherspoon served as dean of this first summer session, and Professors Williams, Conner, Barnes, and Louis Entzminger were the teachers.[43]

From this time to the present, the summer term has been a regular part of the seminary program.

An unexpected structural change in 1919 was the elimination of the Department of English Bible, which had been established by B. H. Carroll. At the meeting of March 14, 1919, the trustees elected two young men to the faculty to teach English New Testament and English Old Testament in connection with their work in the departments of Greek and Hebrew. The former was James Sterling Rogers, a Th.D. graduate of Southwestern, who resigned as secretary of missions in Arkansas to accept the New Testament post. The other was H. E. Dana, who had just been approved to begin his Th.D. study. Dana had chosen to major in Greek and New Testament, but his minors included Hebrew and Old Testament. Following the pattern of previous years, the faculty chose Dana for the Old Testament teaching because of his ability. He had been an excellent student in all departments of the curriculum. Neither the faculty minutes nor the trustee minutes refer to the discussions that evidently took place before the important decision was made to dismantle the Department of English Bible. There were hurdles to clear before this action could take place. Professor J. W. Crowder had assisted B. H. Carroll in these English Bible classes during Carroll's last illness and had continued at this post after Carroll's death. Apparently it was the resignation of Charles T. Ball in 1919 to accept the position of secretary of the Baptist Student Union that triggered the sensitive change. Ball had been director of the Extension Department and professor of missions. W. H. Knight was named to succeed him in missions, and Crowder was prevailed upon to accept the extension work. In an editorial review of this change a few years later, H. E. Dana remarked that after the death of Carroll in 1914, the plan of having one man do all the teaching of the English Bible was followed for several years, J. W. Crowder being the teacher. He continued:

> When, however, Professor Crowder became head of the extension depart-
> ment, it was decided to separate the teaching of the Old and New Testament
> in English. The present plan is to have the head of the Old and New
> Testament departments to teach the classes in English exegesis. This gives
> the advantage of having all English exegetical work done by a man who is a
> specialist in the original language.[44]

The other hurdle involved the attitude of the trustees. Some of the men on the board had been close to B. H. Carroll and knew his fervent desire to maintain the Department of English Bible. When on March 14 President Scarborough recommended that the two new young men be elected and that the Department of English Bible be discontinued, there came one of the few split votes in the records of the trustees. A terse sentence in the trustee minutes touched upon the agony of spirit involved in this decision. It said:

> In the vote which involved the election of two teachers in the English Bible Department, thus dividing the department, Dr. Cranfill voted for the two men elected, but against dividing the English Bible Department.

Unfortunately, shortly after this action was taken, Professor C. B. Williams resigned as professor of Greek and New Testament in order to accept the presidency of Howard College (now Samford University) in Alabama. He went on later to an active teaching career in several schools but perhaps was best known for his *Translation of the New Testament* in which he reproduced the tenses of the Greek verbs, in particular, with unusual skill and accuracy. His departure left the New Testament Department of Southwestern Seminary with a shortage of teachers, but Professor Conner and others filled the gap.[45] Professor Rogers was forced to resign in the following year because of eye difficulties. His resignation resulted in the shifting of H. E. Dana to New Testament, securing J. R. Mantey to assist in elementary Greek, and naming E. Leslie Carlson to teach Hebrew and Old Testament.[46]

Another significant change in structure was voted by the trustees on March 14, 1919. Prior to this time the faculty of the seminary had been on salary for only nine months of the year. It was expected that they would supplement their income during the summer by preaching, singing, teaching, and similar activities. However, at the March meeting, upon the recommendation of President Scarborough it was resolved (1) that these professors and teachers be put on full year's salary to be paid by the month, except in cases of assistants and other teachers whose positions were not regarded as permanent; (2) that all of the time of the teachers belonged to the seminary, and any income they received from supply preaching and revival meetings be turned over to the seminary; and (3) that each male teacher who was also a preacher be expected to hold at least two revival meetings each year, the income from which was to be given to the seminary. All other teachers who were not engaged otherwise in the service of the seminary would be expected to spend their summers in further study, looking to the strengthening of their departments.

The long illness and absence of W. D. Harris, chairman of the trustees, doubtless led to the creation of the office of vice-president of the trustees on May 27, 1915. The new officer was clothed with authority to perform the duties of the president when that officer was absent or unable to act. O. S. Lattimore was named vice-president. After a long and faithful service to the seminary, Harris died in May of the following year, and Judge Lattimore became the new president of the board.[47]

On November 18, 1915, the trustees approved a change in the charter of the seminary so that it might reflect the contemporary situation. The words "and other Christian workers" were added to the second article, making it read, "and such other instruction as may be needful to equip preachers *and other Christian workers* for their life work." This recognized the work of the new departments of religious education and music and other related areas in Christian service.

During the years 1914 to 1919 several additional state bodies began supporting the seminary and electing trustees, so that in the latter year the following were represented on the board: Texas, Arkansas, Tennessee, Kentucky, Florida, Oklahoma, Mississippi, Louisiana, New Mexico, and Southern Illinois.[48]

Additional structural improvements took place in the Woman's Missionary Training School during this period. In 1914, the Baptist Women Mission Workers were invited by the trustees to appoint an Advisory Board to cooperate with the board "in the upbuilding and management of this Training School."[49] Mrs. R. F. Stokes, who had been the principal field worker to raise money for this training school since its opening in 1910, was retiring from that post at this session, and she paid tribute to many who had sacrificed to provide funds for the training school. In accordance with this invitation from the trustees, the first Advisory Board of the Woman's Missionary Training School from the Baptist Women Mission Workers was named in the seminary's catalogue for 1914-15, as follows: ex officio members were the three officers of the Baptist Women Mission Workers—Mrs. F. S. Davis, president; Mrs. A. F. Beddoe, correspondence secretary; and Mrs. Abell D. Hardin, recording secretary—Mrs. W. L. Williams, Mrs. E. G. Townsend, and Mrs. Thomas Van Tuyl for a three-year term; Mrs. J. Z. Wheat, Mrs. Alice Brooker, and Mrs. G. L. Paxton for a two-year term; and Mrs. W. M. Reeves, Mrs. T. H. Claypool, and Mrs. R. E. Burt for a one-year term.[50]

The trustees had also invited the women of other states which were cooperating with the seminary to name members to the Advisory Board of the training school.[51] By 1919, the women of two states had accepted this invitation—Louisiana and New Mexico.[52]

The Close of an Era

Thus, by 1919 the good beginning made by L. R. Scarborough in administering the affairs of the seminary after the death of B. H. Carroll had ended much of the foreboding over the future of the school. Developments between 1919 and 1925 would confirm this optimism. Scarborough's ability to share responsibility enabled him to bear unusual burdens in addition to his teaching, fund raising, and administrative duties between 1919 and 1925. During these last five years of Scarborough's first decade as president, four simultaneous movements took place. They must be described consecutively, but each of these movements impinged on the others, providing for Scarborough a most strenuous and often grievous situation. These movements were the involvement of the seminary in the Seventy-Five Million Campaign of the Southern Baptist Convention, the critical outbreak of the Norris controversy, the continuing internal development of the seminary, and the change in the ownership and control of the seminary from the Baptist General Convention of Texas to the Southern Baptist Convention.

The Seventy-Five Million Campaign

Although this was a movement by the Southern Baptist Convention, it played a very significant part in the history of the seminary. It developed from the context of the spectacular financial campaigns during World War I which brought millions of dollars to the Red Cross and other wartime benevolences. Denominational and interdenominational campaigns were being projected in a spirit of jubilant optimism after the winning of the war. Southern Baptists radiated this same spirit. Rufus W. Weaver called for Southern Baptists to subscribe $100,000,000 for Jesus in five years; the Education Commission of the Convention wanted a campaign for $15,000,000 for Christian education in five years; and the Relief and Annuity Board of the Convention urged that the Convention raise $5,000,000 for its work.

President J. B. Gambrell reflected this optimism in his opening address to the Southern Baptist Convention in 1919 and appointed a large and influential Committee on the Financial Aspect of the Enlarged Program. This committee recommended that the Convention undertake to raise $75,000,000 in five years. With some modifications, the Convention adopted this recommendation and appointed a Campaign Committee of Fifteen to work out the details with the Executive

Committee of the Convention and the secretaries of the general boards and the state conventions in the South.[53]

The combined committees so appointed met on June 5, 1919, at Atlanta, Georgia. George W. McDaniel of Virginia presented a paper on principles of procedure, and the group agreed that the Executive Committee would make the distribution of the $75,000,000 while the Campaign Committee would make plans and direct the campaign to secure the funds.[54] With J. B. Gambrell presiding for the Executive Committee and George W. Truett for the Campaign Committee, the proposed distribution was made,[55] and the proposed procedures for raising the money were set out.[56] President L. R. Scarborough of Southwestern Seminary was named general director for the campaign.[57] The distribution of the $75,000,000 allocated $20,000,000 for foreign missions, $12,000,000 for home missions, $3,000,000 for ministerial education, and $2,500,000 for ministerial relief. The remaining half of the $75,000,000 was reserved for state causes.

President Scarborough called a special faculty meeting at his home on June 7, 1919, and announced that he had been asked to lead the campaign to raise the $75,000,000 and told the faculty that "he felt that it was his duty to accept." After discussion, the following motion was passed unanimously.

> Although personally regretting to give up the personal presence and leadership of our honored president, yet we cheerfully accede to the request of the committee . . . that he become, in this way, the leader in the greatest campaign ever launched by Baptists.

During the next five years, Scarborough was away from the seminary for months at a time. He appointed some member of the faculty to serve as "Acting President" during these months. Nearly all the senior faculty members served in this position at one time or another.

The Campaign Committee made detailed plans for raising these funds. Goals were accepted by each of the state leaders in a meeting at Nashville on July 2-3, 1919, attended by members of the Executive Committee, the Campaign Committee, leaders of the Woman's Missionary Union, secretaries of the four general boards, secretaries of the state conventions, and editors of all the Baptist papers. Scarborough submitted a plan by which July would be used as preparation month; August, information; September, intercession; October, enlistment; November, stewardship; and from November 30 to December 7, victory week. After an unprecedented campaign during these months, the Campaign Committee reported that the grand sum of $92,630,923 had been pledged and that thousands of young people had committed themselves to vocational Christian service.[58] This emphasis on "calling out the called," a favorite expression of Scarborough, was a very important part of the campaign. When the combined committees met in Nashville on February 19, 1920, for their third meeting, the overall objectives of the campaign were set out as being (1) the enlistment of people in gospel service, (2) the collection of funds, (3) a continuing campaign for cash and subscriptions, and (4) the indoctrination of the people and the saving of souls. The mind-set of Scarborough can be glimpsed in these objectives.

An important decision for the seminaries was made when the Executive Committee met on April 22, 1920. The Southern Baptist Theological Seminary had been on the verge of inaugurating a campaign to erect much needed buildings on their new campus when the Seventy-Five Million Campaign was launched. That school had been promised by the Southern Baptist Convention on May 16, 1919, that the funds needed to erect these buildings would be included in the Seventy-Five Million Campaign.[59] Thus, at the April meeting the Executive Committee voted that the Louisville seminary should receive $1,000,000 for new buildings. Although the Convention had not specifically directed that the other seminaries should receive building funds, both Southwestern and the Baptist Bible Institute at New Orleans had requested these from the Executive Committee. On the basis of equity, the Executive Committee voted also that Southwestern and the New Orleans institute should receive $500,000 each for needed buildings.[60] These allocations were to be over and above the appropriation of $3,000,000 made for ministerial education. The knowledge that over $92,000,000 had been pledged caused the Executive Committee to take a further step. It recommended that these extra building fund amounts for the seminaries should come from gifts currently being received by the Foreign Mission Board, the Home Mission Board, and the Education Board, each providing a pro rata part of the $2,000,000 special building fund appropriation. It was emphasized that these special appropriations for the building needs of the three seminaries did not mean the diminution of the amounts appropriated for the three boards in the original allotment of funds, but that these boards would be reimbursed out of the first money collected beyond the $75,000,000.[61]

These developments in the Seventy-Five Million Campaign were reported to the next meeting of the Southern Baptist Convention on May 12-17, 1920, and with high enthusiasm all of the recommendations of the Executive Committee and the Campaign Committee were approved. The impact of these events on Southwestern Seminary was almost instantaneous. On April 8, 1920, the trustees approved making an addition to the Woman's Missionary Training School building at a cost of $125,000; building a temporary administration building east of Fort Worth Hall, which could be utilized for the chapel and five recitation rooms at a cost of $25,000; providing a central power plant, including a well and boiler, to cost $50,000; and remodeling the old chapel on the second floor of Fort Worth Hall to provide bedrooms for students at a cost of $50,000. An ebullient L. R. Scarborough reported to the state convention in November, 1920, that the last year "was in every way a most prosperous and heaven-blessed session" for the seminary. He reported borrowing $200,000 from various banks to pay for the capital improvements and said that this would be paid back from the collections of the Seventy-Five Million Campaign.[62] He reminded the convention that only about $20,000.00 of the $82,495.60 operating expenses of the last year had been provided by the endowment of the seminary and that the president had gone afield to secure the remainder.

In the following year (1921), Scarborough reported that the seminary had received $274,110.35 from the Seventy-Five Million Campaign. Of this, $130,000 had been provided from the Education Board, plus $8,850 in government bonds; $30,639 had come from the Foreign Mission Board; $21,157 had been received from the Home Mission Board; and the remainder had been contributed by the state board of the Baptist General Convention of Texas. These amounts from the three boards were the result of the decision by the Executive Committee to grant to the three seminaries the extra sums for building purposes, as described heretofore.[63] In 1922, the seminary received $133,365.32 from the Convention-wide boards through the Education Board.[64] In 1923, the seminary received $139,813.25 from the Seventy-Five Million Campaign, all but $56,096.90 being from the three Southwide boards.[65] By 1924, the total received by the seminary from the campaign rose to $672,299.50 and to $782,663.31 by 1925.[66] Of this final total from the campaign, $330,757.92 had come from Texas gifts, while the remainder had been provided by the three general boards.[67] In his report to the trustees on February 23, 1923, Scarborough said that since the beginning of his administration in February, 1915, the operating expenses for these eight years had totaled $563,192, all of which had been paid except about $3,000, which was more than balanced by interest due on endowment notes by three persons. This statement indicates the importance of the Seventy-Five Million Campaign in providing operating expenses.

In a final summary in his story of the seminary in 1939, Scarborough wrote:

The immense fund of more than three-fourths of a million dollars was expended by the Southwestern Seminary in the sound, constructive education of multitudes of young men and women and in sending them out trained, consecrated forces to carry on the work and to do the will of Jesus Christ. More students enrolled in the Southwestern Seminary during these five years than enrolled in any five years before or in any five years since. We count it a glorious section of the Seminary's growth and life.[68]

An Unexpected Adversary

At the same time President Scarborough was leading the Seventy-Five Million Campaign, he became embroiled in a bitter controversy with J. Frank Norris of Fort Worth. Because Norris became such an influential leader in a movement designed to undercut and destroy the seminary and because he continued his harsh attacks until his death several decades later, his initial relations with the seminary form an important part of its history.

After the death of B. H. Carroll in November, 1914, Norris began a slow process of alienation from the seminary. In some respects, this retrogression was surprising, since his support for the seminary in its early years seemed to be total and sincere. A series of events, however, turned him from being a friend of the school to becoming an implacable enemy by the close of this period in 1925. This deteriorating process began when some of the members of his church, including B. H. Carroll and others of the seminary faculty, withdrew from the First Baptist Church and placed their letters in other Baptist churches in Fort Worth because of the sensational preaching of Norris and his church fire. When Norris refused to grant letters to some of the members, they were received by statement by other pastors. Norris tried without success to persuade the Tarrant County Baptist Association to condemn this action. One of the state's witnesses against Norris in his arson trial in 1912 was his former financial secretary. After the trial she joined College Avenue Baptist Church, whose pastor was C. V. Edwards. Norris began to berate Edwards in the church paper and in one issue referred to him as a "long, lean, lank, yellow suck-egging dog." At the next meeting of the Pastors' Conference at Fort Worth in 1914, Norris was expelled from this body. Twice again Norris, after asserting his repentance and being forgiven, was ejected from this Pastors' Conference.[69]

Another development occurred in 1917. Norris became enamored with the program of Moody Bible Institute, where he had held a stirring revival meeting. Copying its interdenominational stance, he began to move toward an interdenominational Fundamentalism. Norris invited various non-Baptists to fill his pulpit and in 1917 had a two-month Bible conference in his church featuring non-Baptist speakers and emphases. His attitude may be illustrated by his statement in 1922 that if his pulpit were vacant, the best man to succeed him would be a nearby Methodist Fundamentalist pastor.

Another rift came in the following year (1918), during World War I. The Tarrant County Baptist Association began a ministry among the soldiers at Camp Bowie, inviting the First Baptist Church to participate. Instead, the church informed the association that she was unwilling to conform to the structures used by others outside the membership of the church, but that on the principle that each New Testament church must work out and meet the problems of her own field, the First Baptist Church would carry on her own program at the camp apart from that of the association.[70]

In 1919, the Seventy-Five Million Campaign was launched by the Southern Baptist Convention. Norris publicly and privately stated initially that his church would pledge $100,000 on this movement, but soon he not only repudiated the pledge but began a vigorous campaign to persuade other Baptist churches not to pay the amounts which they had subscribed.[71]

About this time Norris interspersed his scathing attacks on the "Baptist bishops" of the denomination with a declaration that he was unwilling to use any of the literature of the Sunday School Board and asserted that he would prepare any lesson helps that might be needed in his church. This was an ironical move, for through Louis Entzminger and Arthur Flake, Norris had contributed to the development of the structure and literature of the Sunday School Board.

Norris also was abandoning the pattern of Baptist churches by suppressing all internal organizations that might challenge his control of the church and by conferring on an inner circle of deacons all of the authority that belonged to the congregation. Typical of his high-handed attitude in controlling his church was his treatment of Charles E. Matthews. Matthews had been converted and called to preach under Norris's ministry but became disillusioned with Norris's continued attacks on the denomination and his autocratic leadership. While Norris was away, the church ordained Matthews to preach; but when Matthews entered Southwestern Seminary as a student, Norris forced the church to rescind Matthews's ordination and refuse to grant him or his family a church letter. Matthews had been supplying at the First Baptist Church, Breckenridge, Texas, and this church, learning what had happened, accepted him as a member and ordained him to the ministry.

The event that led directly to the open break of fellowship between Norris and the denomination occurred in the fall of 1921. Upon returning from a trip to Europe, Norris learned that a prominent Methodist professor nearby had written a book denying the truth of the Genesis account of creation. With L. R. Scarborough and others, Norris loudly denounced this book. Someone then called Norris's attention to the fact that "there were some rank infidels in Baylor University." Disregarding advice from "the Baptist fathers generally," he began an attack on Baylor. Professor Samuel Dow there, in a book which he had written, had made a statement which Norris believed to be completely evolutionary. After advertising widely that he would expose infidelity at Baylor, Norris stood before a huge gathering at his church in early November, removed his tie and collar, accused Dow of being an evolutionist, and attacked Baylor for its compromising spirit, its acceptance of evolutionary teachings, its complacency, and its infidelity.[72]

Convention leaders like George W. Truett and L. R. Scarborough promptly defended Baylor. The *Baptist Standard* quoted Dow as saying that he did not now believe, nor had he ever believed, that man came from any other species. During the remainder of 1921, Norris, with pungent and sarcastic language, assaulted Baylor and all who defended the school. The circulation of Norris's paper multiplied rapidly. He planned to debate the Baylor issue on the floor of the state convention. On December 1, 1921, when the convention gathered, there was a brief exchange of charges and countercharges. M. T. Andrews then presented a resolution, which was adopted, calling on all parties to cease their agitation on this matter until a committee could investigate the truth of the charges and make its report to the convention in the following year.[73]

Meanwhile, awaiting the meeting of the convention in 1921, Norris was active in the interdenominational Fundamentalist movement. He joined forces with the Fundamentalist leaders in the North, and at a preconvention caucus before the meeting of the Northern Baptist Convention in 1921, he helped develop a plan to make a concerted attack upon modernists in Canadian, Northern, and Southern Baptist struc- tured bodies.[74]

In the early fall, Norris published an oblique attack on Professor W. W. Barnes of the seminary, hinting that Barnes did not believe the story of creation in Genesis. At the next meeting of the Tarrant County Baptist Workers' Conference on November 21, 1921, L. R. Scarborough abruptly arose and, pointing his finger at Norris, said:

> Frank, you told me not more than three weeks ago in my office that if you
> saw or thought you saw anything wrong in the Seminary you would tell me

first and give me a chance to straighten out anything necessary. Now the
first I hear is this in your paper.

W. T. Conner, who attended this conference, said that Scarborough then,
for the first time, casting aside all restraint, thoroughly castigated Norris
before the group. On the following day, Scarborough met Barnes in the
hall at the seminary and said that Norris wanted Barnes to answer in
writing a number of questions that Norris would submit. Barnes replied:

> Before the questions come, in order that the nature or content of the
> questions may not be involved, let me say, I would not answer any question
> he asks me for two reasons: First, that he was not the inquisitor of my
> conscience; and in the second place, he would misuse anything that I wrote
> him. The next day I received a list of twelve questions from Norris, but I
> ignored them as I ignored some ten or twelve letters that he wrote me
> through the years. I never one time paid any attention to any letter he wrote
> me. [75]

Barnes later commented, "The fight between Dr. Scarborough and Norris
became so bitter that within thirty days I was forgotten and took no
further part in the controversy nor received any further attack."

Barnes was right. Norris was taking direct aim at Scarborough and
Truett, and Scarborough's correspondence of the next decade contains
much coarse (and occasionally obscene) language about them by Norris.
The rapid deterioration of relations between Scarborough and Norris can
be observed in a caustic letter addressed by Norris to the seminary
president less than a week after the Dallas convention. Norris accused
Scarborough and others of dishonesty, duplicity, and fraud; and he
demanded the right to examine the records of the seminary. Scarborough
replied:

> I notice that you wish access to the Seminary books, to see whether or
> not we have some twisted funds. Yes, come out and bring our mutual friend
> Mr. J. T. Pemberton, or some other reliable man with you and I will be glad
> to get you to help me find any twisted funds in the Seminary accounts. So
> far I have been unable to find them; but if you can help me in this matter,
> why we will do our best to straighten them out. . . .
>
> I notice also you say you have information concerning the matter of some
> private and personal transactions of mine with reference to a certain tract of
> land adjoining the Seminary. When you come out I will be glad to give you
> any information you may wish on this matter. The conduct of the Seminary
> and my own private concerns are, of course, open to review by anybody at
> any time and I will be glad to help throw any light on the subject if it is
> needed.
>
> You also ask if you may have access to my files and a copy of any letter
> pertaining to you or your work which I have written. You say you have some
> letters that I have written concerning you and your work. I do not object at
> all to you having any letter I have ever written concerning you or your work;

and if there are any of the letters that you think I have written, if you can furnish the name I will be very glad to furnish you a carbon copy of it. I have never said anything concerning you or your work to your back that I would not say to your face.

Of course, you will understand that giving you the privilege of going into the Seminary accounts and my personal and private business will carry with it the understanding that I will have the privilege with anybody whom I may select of going into the books and accounts of the First Baptist Church and your personal accounts; and if you insist in going into the private and personal matters in this controversy, why I will be very glad to side [sic] you in it. When you come out to investigate the Seminary and me we will also go into some matters which I have information on concerning you and your work there. I am perfectly willing for the light to be thrown on anything out here that is necessary; and if it becomes necessary you will find me throwing some light on things down there, too. Come out with all the information you have concerning the twisted funds and any crooked private concerns of mine and we will go into them and find the truth and if there is anything wrong that we can correct I will be glad to join you in correcting them.

We are trying to live in the open out here and let the light come. If you think you can help the situation in any way, turn the blaze on and let the light shine. It is a job two of us can work at.[76]

Scarborough, however, wanted to expose the falseness of the insinuations and accusations of Norris about the teaching at the seminary. Therefore, on November 23, 1921, just two days after the controversy with Norris at the Workers' Conference, the faculty met in a special session and adopted the following doctrinal statement:

In view of certain criticisms that have been made on Baptist schools and Baptist educators in Texas as to their orthodoxy and in view of an insinuation concerning an unnamed member of the Seminary Faculty published in the "Searchlight" of Nov. 18, 1921, we, the members of the Faculty and the assistants in the theological department of the Southwestern Baptist Theological Seminary, desire to make the following statement:
1. We affirm our belief in the Bible as the Word of God and as our infallible rule of faith and practice;
2. We repudiate the rationalistic method of dealing with the Bible and religious truth that has come into vogue in Europe and in many universities and seminaries in our own country in recent years, and the results thereof;
3. We repudiate the evolutionary theory that man has come by a process of development from any lower animals. We believe that he is a direct creation of God on both the physical and the mental or spiritual sides of his being;
4. We believe in the Genesis account of the origin of the world and of man. We believe that this is the only true and satisfactory account of the origin of the world and of man to be found in any literature;
5. We reaffirm our belief in the fundamentals of Christianity—the inspiration of the Bible, the sovereignty of God, the deity of Christ, the personality of the Spirit, the fallen condition of all mankind, Christ's death

and resurrection as man's only hope and the regenerating and sanctifying work of the Holy Spirit as the only power that can lift man out of his fallen condition;

6. We believe that the churches of Jesus Christ are independent and autonomous bodies ordained of Him to bring in the Kingdom of God on earth and together with their pastors are under moral obligation to work together under the leadership of the Spirit for the propagation of the Gospel and the carrying out of Christ's commission;

7. We reaffirm our allegiance to the doctrines of faith as adopted by the Trustees of this Seminary.

This statement was signed by all of the regular faculty and was read in chapel by the secretary of the faculty on November 25.

During the summer and fall of 1922, Norris added to his list of grievances against Texas Baptists a charge that state convention officials were misusing funds of the body and covering up the evidence of these crimes by doctoring the books. He offered no proof for this allegation, but the charge itself was galling to the leadership because it stirred up unfounded suspicions which could cause some to withhold their gifts.

A critical confrontation took place at the meeting of the Tarrant County Baptist Association on September 6, 1922. The venerable W. A. Pool had served for many years as moderator, but since he had almost lost both his sight and his hearing, he was elected moderator emeritus. W. W. Barnes was named moderator. On that afternoon Forrest Smith, pastor of the Broadway Baptist Church, Fort Worth, presented a challenge to the seating of messengers from the First Baptist Church. The principal allegation against the church involved the articles of faith and bylaws she had adopted on March 31, 1922, which gave to the deacons the final authority in all matters of discipline and admission of new members. Furthermore, no item could be presented to the church at a business meeting without the recommendation of the deacons, and, with a reference to the Seventy-Five Million Campaign, the church could never accept assessments or apportionments of any kind. After an extended discussion, the messengers of the First Baptist Church of Fort Worth were refused seats by a vote of 135 to 16.[77]

In this action, L. R. Scarborough was one of the leaders pressing for the unseating of Norris. He had left his membership in the First Baptist Church long after other faculty members had moved elsewhere, hopeful that he could retain Norris within the circle of seminary supporters; but in 1917 he put his letter into Gambrell Street Baptist Church, and the attack on Professor Barnes seems to have precipitated the final rupture between the two.

Two months later, the Baptist General Convention of Texas met at

Waco. The effect of Norris's attacks may be glimpsed in the context of the meetings of the convention. On the first afternoon, the trustees of Baylor University submitted their report. Included was a section condemning Darwinian evolutionary theories and asserting that any teacher not holding to the basic Baptist doctrines would be dismissed.[78] The convention followed this with a resolution affirming belief in the Genesis account of the creation of man.[79] Without calling Norris by name, a large committee of leaders of the convention presented "A Statement of Facts and Some Resolutions." This statement condemned Norris's attacks on the institutions and work of the convention, terming them "misrepresentations, insinuations, and reflecting upon the proper conduct in office of the appointed and trusted leaders of the Convention." The statement continued by asserting an "open denominational policy" which allowed every cooperating Baptist to investigate the books of every institution and board of the convention. It denied that the Seventy-Five Million Campaign had harmed the autonomy of the churches and condemned "open church membership" and

> that type of interdenominationalism that compromises our doctrines of theology and violates our teachings on ecclesiology and Scriptural order of the churches. We believe church government invested in a Diaconate, is as unscriptural and un-Baptistic as a church government invested in Presbyters.

Pointing specifically to the debate in the Tarrant County Association, this statement declared that there should be nonfellowship with any church that turned all matters of discipline, disbursing of church funds, and passing on the fitness or unfitness of applicants for membership to the deacons because this violated Baptist democracy. The resolutions then denounced "the wholesale method of the indiscriminate and destructive criticism of Baptist work and workers which has been waged against this Convention."[80] The Investigating Committee, appointed the previous year to look into heresy in the schools, reported that Baylor University and its faculty had denied that the evolutionary hypothesis and other unorthodox doctrines were held by its administration and staff, and the committee recommended support for this school.[81] A resolution was then adopted instructing the trustees of all institutions controlled by the convention not to employ a teacher who denied the deity of Christ, the inspiration of the Scriptures, or the Genesis account of creation.

Perhaps this rebuke to Norris caused him to relate even more closely to the interdenominational Fundamentalist bodies during 1923. He had been active in the World's Christian Fundamentalist Association, which had been organized in 1919 to unite the Fundamentalists of all denominations, and this body met in Fort Worth in 1923. Norris was prominent in its sessions. Perhaps he sensed that he could no longer affiliate with the existing Baptist structures.

An amusing incident in 1924 revealed the general attitude of hostility toward Norris by Tarrant County pastors. Most of the pastors had been critical of President Scarborough for remaining in the First Baptist Church until 1917, long after all of the other members of this church from the faculty had moved their letters elsewhere. After the Tarrant County Association had expelled Norris in 1922, he asked forgiveness and promised to change his church structure back to the pattern of congregational authority that existed in Baptist churches. The association, fearing that it might appear to be unforgiving if it refused to accept the promises of Norris, seated messengers from his church at the meeting of the association in September, 1924. Norris was invited to preach to the body. With obvious pleasure at his victory, Norris arose to speak, using as his text a portion of the Ten Commandments. In his introductory remarks, he noted with a flourish that Professor Jeff D. Ray, sitting on the front seat of the church, would have been able on this occasion to sweep the audience with his eloquence were he in the pulpit. This unconcealed attempt at flattery did not impress Ray; he remembered some of Norris's attacks on the faculty; he was in no mood to be flattered or cajoled. Slowly rising from his seat, as Norris stopped for breath, Ray pointed his finger at the preacher and cried out, "If I were up there preaching to you on a commandment, I would take the text, 'Thou shalt not *lie!*'" As W. W. Barnes reported this incident, he said that the congregation erupted in laughter and delight as Ray slowly sat down. Nonplussed, Norris made no more references to Ray.

When the Baptist General Convention of Texas met on November 15, 1923, the credentials of the messenger of the First Baptist Church, Fort Worth, were challenged. Allegations included the expelling of Norris from the Tarrant County Association, his opposition to the Seventy-Five Million Campaign and his continuing efforts to destroy that program, his efforts to lead Baptist people into inderdenominational movements seeking to divide the Baptist denomination, and his continuing attacks on the boards and institutions of the Baptist General Convention of Texas. These allegations were documented, and the sole representative from the First Church was denied a seat in the convention.[82]

Norris then "confessed" to the truth of these charges and promised that he would mend his ways. It appeared that he would keep his word for a brief period in 1924, but soon he returned to his scalding attacks on Baylor, the seminary, and prominent Baptist leaders. He was expelled again from the Tarrant County Baptist Association in September, 1925; already when the state convention had gathered in Dallas in November, 1924, all of the messengers from the First Baptist Church, Fort Worth, had been rejected.[83] Norris continued his assaults until his death in 1952, but now he was on the outside of Texas Baptist life. Scarborough wrote a tract, entitled "The Fruits of Norrisism," which greatly angered Norris, and his attacks on the seminary and Scarborough increased in intensity.[84]

Advance on All Fronts

Despite the furious onslaughts of Norris and the lengthy absences of President Scarborough from the campus as general director of the Seventy-Five Million Campaign, the seminary made good progress between 1919 and 1925. As Scarborough commented, the enrollment of students during the five years of the campaign reflected the emphasis on challenging young people to commit themselves to vocational Christian service. The number of students at Southwestern leaped from 361 in residence and 77 in correspondence study in 1918-19 to 587 in residence and 960 in correspondence study in 1924-25. Graduates increased from 58 in 1919 to 114 in 1925.

In retrospect, the lists of graduates for particular years call attention to the excellent quality of graduates. In the Master of Theology class of May, 1920, for example, the graduates included E. L. Carlson, E. D. Head, N. R. Drummond, Albert Venting, A. C. Gettys, and A. J. Holt— all of whom distinguished themselves as teachers, presidents of institutions, or outstanding pastors. In the class of May, 1922, such names as Charles L. Culpepper and J. Howard Williams stood out. The class in May, 1925 included W. R. White, T. B. Maston, L. R. Elliott, and Victor Koon. Maston was the first graduate of the School of Religious Education with the Doctor of Religious Education degree, the offering of which had been approved by the faculty on May 11, 1924. Of historical interest was the conferring of the first Doctor of Theology degree upon a woman by this seminary. Mrs. E. O. Thompson was awarded the degree on November 30, 1920.[85]

As one glances down the list of graduates during these years, he must be impressed by the number who were volunteers for the foreign mission fields. The interest in missions, both home and foreign, ran deep on the campus. *The Southwestern Evangel* for January, 1925, listed seventy-four missionaries from Southwestern serving at that time in China, Japan, Africa, Chile, Brazil, Puerto Rico, Spain, India, Mexico, and

Rumania.[86] Each graduating class carried unfamiliar names of young people who left the campus to carry out the purpose of God in their lives in some out-of-the-way place across the world. Lucille Reagan, for example, received the Bachelor of Missionary Training degree in 1921 and before the end of that year was serving in Africa under the auspices of the Foreign Mission Board. On her first furlough, she returned to the campus to lecture on missions at the Woman's Missionary Training School. But hers would be a still greater witness. In the summer of 1937, as she worked in Nigeria, the dreaded yellow fever struck West Africa. Missionaries had been spared during previous sporadic attacks, but in June, 1937, Leonard Long, Frances Carter Jones, and Kathleen Manly became ill with this fever. Miss Reagan heard about the illness of these missionaries, and on June 25 she voluntarily went to Ogbomosho to help care for the three who had been stricken. Long and Kathleen Manly recovered, but on June 26 Frances Carter Jones succumbed to the disease. On the following day George Green and Miss Reagan went to the European cemetery near Ogbomosho to find a cemetery plot for Miss Jones. They found room for just two more graves, and one of these was marked off for Miss Jones. Green remarked: "There is room now for only one more grave. I wonder whose it will be?" Doubtless bitten by infected mosquitoes in the old mission compound, Lucille Reagan became ill on July 6 and, after much suffering, died on July 12. She was the one who was laid beside Frances Carter Jones.[87] The names of these heroic missionaries were not as well known as those who performed outstanding service in the denomination at home, but each graduation list contained a few persons whose names were better known on some far-flung mission field than any of these denominational leaders at home.

The faculty minutes and *The Southwestern Evangel* give many glimpses of student life at this time. Discipline was swift and rigorous. To give or receive help on examinations, to infringe on strict regulations concerning conduct toward members of the opposite sex, to marry during the school year, to exhibit an unchristian spirit, and similar acts brought quick retribution. The student's lot, however, was not altogether grim. Social life, although viewed by the faculty with some suspicion, was structured through a committee of faculty and students, which made it possible for members of the opposite sex to engage in light conversation at the proper time and with adequate supervision. Students felt free to petition the faculty on any matter and often did so. It must be admitted that at times the rules became somewhat fuzzy. For example, on May 24, 1924, the faculty scribe wrote: "Voted to request the Social Committee to eliminate all social or other meetings on Monday night"; a week later the same hand gravely announced: "Voted to have a lawn social next Monday at 6:30 p.m. in charge of the Social Committee."[88] As a matter of fact, however, the social calendars of the students were quite full. The pages of the *Evangel* regularly outlined Sunday School socials, Baptist Young People's Union socials, school socials, musical recitals, conferences for young people, and the like. Even the more formal lectures provided an opportunity for fraternizing. Perhaps the scholarly Holland Lecture of E. C. Dargan on "The History of Homiletics" was not the greatest fare for social mingling, but those by Samuel Judson Porter on "The Gospel of Beauty" and W. J. McGlothlin on "The Growth of Faith in Jesus" doubtless attracted large numbers.

For students interested in athletics and recreation, a faculty committee was developed to plan this activity.[89] As a matter of fact, by 1924 two of the standing committees of the faculty were the Social Committee, composed of three professors and a student, and the Recreational Committee.[90]

The campus was becoming more attractive. The report of the Woman's Missionary Training School in 1918 praised the work of "Mother" (Mrs. W. L.) Williams, who had moved to Seminary Hill in 1915 and was voluntarily improving the appearance of the campus.

> Through fair weather and foul she has given unstinted labor and care in beautifying the grounds of the campus of the Seminary and Training School, in the planting of trees, laying out of walks and driveways, in the planting and nurturing of flowers, and even in the raising of vegetables for the students. In her quiet, patient, beautiful spirited care and loving interest for the young ladies of the Training School building and for the preachers and their wives and for the faculty and their families, she has contributed untold assistance and joy.[91]

The campus also had some new building taking place, as described heretofore, including a temporary administration building, an addition to the women's training school building, and other improvements.[92]

A chronic problem of the seminary was finally solved when the city of Fort Worth assumed operation of the streetcar line that provided transportation from the campus to downtown. At the faculty meeting of April 9, 1921, President Scarborough announced to the faculty that he was personally arranging a service to celebrate the completion of this agreement with the city. After almost a decade of costly adventures in the streetcar business, the seminary was now relieved of this burden.

It is probable that the most significant internal advance by the seminary during this period, however, was achieved in its organizational revisions. Four of these gave new direction to the development of the school.

Chronologically first was the formation of the Practical Work Department in 1921 with W. A. Hancock as its superintendent. This department evolved from the desire of students to carry the gospel to downtown Fort Worth. During the early years of President Scarborough's administration, in an effort to assist the students in this work, College Avenue Baptist Church provided a "Gospel Wagon" drawn by horses to take the students downtown for services. A Ford automobile was then used for a short time for this purpose. On October 2, 1918, a small group of seminary students met in Fort Worth Hall to discuss forming an organization to foster this work. President Scarborough encouraged this movement, and on October 24, 1918, he presented the matter to the students at chapel and said that the school would furnish a Ford truck for conveyance. The student body, aided by the seminary, pledged a salary of $150 per month to employ a superintendent for this work.[93]

The catalogue for 1919-20 announced the official establishment of this work as a part of the curriculum.

> The Seminary has this year established a Practical Work Department which will offer practical experience to students in any line of Christian service for which they may be preparing. Every student in the institution will be required to take an active part in at least four religious services each month. For next session Rev. W. A. Hancock, B. S., Th. B., will be General Superintendent. Rev. Wm. McMurray will be Superintendent of the Down-town Mission, and of Institutional work.[94]

In the following year, the catalogue outlined the areas of service in which all students must have a part: (1) city mission work—on the streets, in the downtown mission, in the jails, and in hospitals and other institutions; (2) settlement work, especially provided for the young ladies of the training school; (3) immigration work in the Russian and Mexican settlements of the city of Fort Worth; (4) extension work by the Schools of Gospel Music and of Religious Education and the Department of Missions; and (5) work done on local church fields as pastor or supply, or other worker.[95]

The second of these structural changes occurred in 1921. It is curious that there was little mention made of this important action in either the minutes of the trustees or those of the faculty. The catalogue published in April, 1921 (for 1920-21 with announcements for 1921-22) for the first time changed the titles to show that the former departments of religious education and gospel music had now become the *schools* of religious education and gospel music. Each of these new schools published a catalogue in 1920-21 as a part of the general school catalogue.[96] The School of Religious Education, headed by J. M. Price, was departmentalized in 1922 into six divisions: principles of religious education, administration of religious education, Christian sociology, adolescent religious education, elementary religious education, and kindergarten education. In the following year a Church Efficiency Department was added.[97] The School of Gospel Music was headed by I. E. Reynolds and was constituted into five departments: theory, voice, piano, orchestra and band, and practical work.[98]

With the adoption of this structure for these two schools, it was logical that the faculty would vote on February 9, 1923, that the theological curriculum would be given the title of School of Theology in order to unify the various departments not included in the other two schools. Perhaps the full impact of this title was not realized until the reorganization of 1925, for most of the historical references in the catalogues give the year 1925 for this change.

The third and fourth structural changes developed from a sweeping faculty revision in 1925. As a part of this revision, the faculty voted on January 16, 1925, "to create a Department of Philosophy of Religion. The courses to be taught in this department are to be specified after the return of Dr. Venting, the head of this department, next September." Venting was studying on sabbatical leave at this time.

The principal part of the faculty revision of 1925 involved the relationship among the faculties of the several schools within the seminary and the lines of authority between the general faculty and the individual school faculties. On January 9, 1925, the faculty appointed a committee to make a thorough study and prepare recommendations for the reorganization of the faculty. This committee, consisting of Professors Scarborough, Conner, Dana, Price, and Reynolds, made an extensive report on January 16. This report asserted that the unity of the seminary resided in the School of Theology but said that this did not disparage in any sense the equality of all other disciplines which had grown up around the original curriculum. It recommended: (1) that each of the three schools of the seminary have its own faculty, with the superintendent of the training school counted as a member of the faculty of the School of Theology since most of the teaching in the training school was done by the theological faculty; (2) that the faculty of none of the three schools have the right to pass on matters affecting the entire seminary, but that each faculty should deal only with those matters specifically touching its own school; (3) that the director of each school act as chairman of the faculty of that school under the supervision of the president of the seminary; and (4) that twice each year all the faculties meet together for counsel, information, and fellowship.

Central in the new plan was the formation of a Faculty Council to replace the general faculty. This council consisted of the following: four members of the faculty of theology, elected by that faculty; the superintendent of the training school; and the directors of the Schools of Religious Education and Gospel Music and one other member from each of these schools, elected by their faculties. This council received a copy of the minutes of the separate faculties, and any action taken by them was subject to review by the council. It was expected that each individual school faculty would "work in harmony and co-operation with each of the other faculties and departments and for the great fundamental purpose of the Seminary." This program was adopted by the general faculty.

Since some areas of authority were not clearly defined in this plan, the same committee was asked on September 16, 1925, to define further the powers and duties of the various faculties. On September 24, the supplementary recommendations were unanimously adopted by the general faculty. They provided that all matters involving the adjustments of the courses of study of an individual student would be handled by the faculty of the school in which he was enrolled; that matters of curricula, degrees, and graduation would be considered by each school and submitted with or without recommendations to the Faculty Council for action; that all discipline of students would be handled by the Faculty Council; that the Faculty Council would review and could reverse any decision by any of the separate faculties; and that all policies and plans of the seminary as a whole which came under faculty jurisdiction or which the administration desired to submit for advice and counsel would be decided by the Faculty Council, although each separate faculty might be consulted on matters involving their own school and might make suggestions on any matters of general interest.

A regular schedule for the meetings of the Faculty Council and the separate faculties was approved. An interesting entry in the faculty minutes of January 16, 1925, reads: "Voted to adopt the following division between administrative and teaching functions." The remainder of the page is blank. Either Secretary Elliott expected to write the material into the minutes later and forgot to do so, or perhaps he could not interpret whatever action was taken.

The catalogue for 1924-25 reflected these organizational changes. The Faculty Council consisted of the following: from the School of Theology—Professors Conner, Barnes, Copass, and Dana; from the School of Religious Education—Professors Price and Drummond; from the School of Gospel Music—Professors Reynolds and McKinney; and from the Woman's Missionary Training School—Mrs. W. B. McGarity. L. R. Elliott was shown as secretary of the council. This reorganization could be shown in the catalogue for 1924-25 since it was not published until the spring of 1925.

When the faculty of the School of Theology first met on March 25, 1925, under the provisions of this revision, Jeff D. Ray was elected as the first chairman of this faculty and E. L. Carlson as its first secretary.[99]

This extensive faculty reorganization came at a time when a number of changes were being made in the personnel of that faculty. It was mentioned that in 1919 a radical change in the curricular structure eliminated the Department of English Bible. The teaching of the Old Testament portion of this department was placed in the Department of Hebrew and Old Testament, while the New Testament interpretation was placed in the Department of Greek and New Testament. This required additional teachers in these departments. Unfortunately, C. B. Williams, J. S. Rogers, and J. R. Mantey, from the Greek and New Testament Department, resigned shortly after the opening of this new period, and prompt action was necessary to fill these vacancies. H. E. Dana was shifted from the Department of Hebrew and Old Testament to his major field of study—Greek and New Testament. W. H. Knight was moved from missions to New Testament, but in May, 1923, he also resigned; and W. T. Conner again assisted in the teaching of New Testament. Albert Venting, a gifted doctoral student, was asked to assist in systematic theology in courses which Conner had given up to help in New Testament. To replace Knight in missions, the seminary secured Robert T. Bryan, a veteran missionary on furlough in 1921-22. When Bryan returned to his field in 1923, William Richardson White, a doctoral student, replaced Bryan and also taught in New Testament. To replace Dana in Hebrew and Old Testament, E. Leslie Carlson, a doctoral student, began teaching in 1921-22. In 1925, when the faculty authorized a department in philosophy of religion, Albert Venting (after a sabbatical year for specialized study in this area) became the teacher in that field.

Other changes were made in the faculty of the School of Theology. J. B. Gambrell died on June 10, 1921. His distinguished life as pastor, editor of the *Baptist Record* (Mississippi) and the *Baptist Standard* (Texas), president of Mercer University (Georgia), superintendent of missions and later executive secretary of the consolidated board in Texas, and president of the Southern Baptist Convention had honed his extraordinary gifts and insights. Twice he had enriched the seminary faculty as a teacher—in 1912-14 and 1916-21.[100] Gambrell's work in ecclesiology and missions was taken up by Professors Conner and Mantey.

Another loss from the faculty occurred on September 10, 1922, when L. M. Sipes resigned as librarian. The man chosen to replace him was a serious young scholar named Leslie Robinson Elliott, a graduate of William Jewell College and a doctoral student at the seminary. Elliott had served as summer assistant librarian in 1922, and his election as the first full-time librarian of the seminary began a fruitful ministry at this post.[101]

Mrs. J. W. Byars resigned as superintendent of the Woman's Missionary Training School, and she was succeeded by Mrs. W. B. McGarity on September 1, 1925.[102]

There were other additions to the faculties in the schools of education and music during this period from 1919 to 1925. Norvell Robertson Drummond, a scholarly young graduate of the seminary in religious education, began teaching in the fall of 1920, as did Bertha Mitchell, a graduate of the training school. In 1922, Thomas Buford Maston began his teaching on the faculty of the School of Religious Education. This young layman would transfer to the School of Theology later and experience a remarkably fruitful career as one of the pioneers among Southern Baptists in the area of Christian ethics. In 1924, Lewis A. Myers was added to the faculty to teach religious publicity and journalism.

In the School of Gospel Music, the catalogue for 1919-20 showed Miss Wayne Walker as assistant teacher of piano. In the following year, with special permission of the faculty, she married a war veteran in the student body; and in the catalogue for 1921-22, her husband, Edwin M. McNeely, was shown as a student teacher in voice, while she taught piano.[103] In 1920 Ellis Lee Carnett began teaching voice.

New additions were made to the staff in this period. D. A. Thornton became the school's bookkeeper in 1919. Mrs. W. E. Kimbrough was engaged as superintendent of Fort Worth Hall, and Mrs. F. H. Waldrop began supervision of the nursery in 1922. Miss Vinnie Gammill was employed as secretary in 1923. These names were familiar to students for many decades.

When J. W. Crowder became superintendent of the Extension Department in 1919, it had 519 students enrolled and reported 110 courses completed. By 1924, the department showed an enrollment of 1,020 and 430 courses completed.[104]

The faculty continued its sabbatical leave program during this period. However, the changes in personnel and the lengthy absences by President Scarborough in the Seventy-Five Million Campaign made it difficult to arrange schedules for any faculty members to be away.

The Southwestern Journal of Theology experienced trying days. After the resignation of C. B. Williams, W. T. Conner was made its managing editor in the fall of 1919. On September 19, 1920, and September 21, 1922, the faculty debated whether or not to continue the *Journal*. On September 26, 1923, L. A. Myers, who had become publicity director in the fall of 1922, inquired if the faculty would approve a weekly promotional newspaper for the seminary. This was agreed to later, and when the *Journal* showed no improvement in its financial condition, the faculty voted on December 11 that it be combined with the weekly newspaper to provide a theological monthly. This was done in October, 1924.[105] The name of the new magazine was *The Southwestern Evangel*, and the editorial staff was H. E. Dana, editor; L. R. Elliott, book review editor; and L. A. Myers, business manager.[106]

The faculty also tightened the scholastic requirements during this period. On December 23, 1922, it was voted that a master's degree should be conferred only on those students who had earned a college baccalaureate or its equivalent; bachelor's degrees would be conferred only on students who were graduates of junior colleges. Those receiving a diploma from the seminary must have at least a high school diploma or its equivalent. A certificate showing the work done would be given to those who had none of these prerequisites.[107] These requirements were approved by the trustees on February 15, 1923.

The End of Texas Control

The seminary was owned and operated by the Baptist General Convention of Texas from the time of its founding in 1908 until 1925. In the latter year, it became the property of the Southern Baptist Convention. This change was effected over a period of several years. It was not a surprising development. For one thing, ten Baptist state conventions had joined Texas in the support and control of the seminary by the end of World War I. These were New Mexico, Louisiana, Oklahoma, Mississippi, Florida, Southern Illinois, Tennessee, Kentucky, Arkansas, and Missouri. Furthermore, when the Baptist Bible Institute was organized in

New Orleans in 1917, it developed with the approval of the Southern Baptist Convention. The Southern Seminary at Louisville, Kentucky, although basically organized on the society plan, had a loose relationship with the Convention in the nomination of trustees. It seemed apparent that the future direction of theological education would be under the auspices of the Southwide body rather than under state bodies, although there was no particular Baptist ecclesiological principle that so dictated. Finally, during the Seventy-Five Million Campaign, it became evident that some leaders were wondering about the principle of providing funds of the Southern Baptist Convention for institutions (like Southwestern Seminary) which were owned and operated by some other Baptist body. As early as 1918, the Convention appointed a Committee on Legal Status of the Boards, and in the several years that followed, this committee began to concern itself with the legal status of the Convention in relation to other Baptist institutions.[108]

President Scarborough was cognizant of these several factors. As early as 1917 he discussed with the faculty the question of tendering the seminary to the Southern Baptist Convention. They replied that it would be better if he delayed this action until the Convention had given some indication that it would want the seminary. When the response to inquiries made at this point by Scarborough were favorable, the faculty voted unanimously for this move.[109] On May 23, 1917, the matter was discussed at the meeting of the trustees, and they appointed a committee to study the question. On April 18, 1920, the trustees authorized Scarborough to negotiate with Southern Baptist Convention leaders about taking control of the seminary.[110]

On February 15, 1923, the trustees unanimously passed a resolution which offered the ownership of the seminary to the Southern Baptist Convention. President Scarborough had already discussed this with the leadership of the Baptist General Convention of Texas, and at the meeting of that body in November, 1923, it unanimously passed a resolution authorizing the trustees to amend the charter of the seminary to "vest its future patronage, control, and general direction in The Southern Baptist Convention."[111]

On May 17, 1923, President Scarborough appeared before the Southern Baptist Convention meeting at Kansas City, Missouri, and after reviewing the history of the seminary and describing its resources and program, he sketched the several reasons why this seminary should be owned and controlled by this Southwide body, as follows. (1) The seminary was now owned by the Baptist General Convention of Texas and controlled by a board of trustees appointed by the Texas convention and ten other state conventions cooperating with the Southern Baptist Convention. (2) The seminary drew students from every state in America and from many foreign lands. (3) The seminary shared in the contributions of the Seventy-Five Million Campaign, and by right of this contribution the Convention should have ownership and control of the school. (4) The Southern Baptist Convention in May, 1922, had adopted a committee report which said:

> Believing that all theological institutions which receive money from our South-wide educational funds should be under the direct legal control of the Southern Baptist Convention, we recommend that no trustee shall hold office for life, but that each trustee shall be elected for a term not exceeding five years, that whatever changes in the charters of our theological institutions may be necessary to transfer to the Southern Baptist Convention either the legal control of election or the legal control of the nomination of trustees serving for a definite term of years shall be made before the inauguration of the next campaign, and that each of these Southern Baptist institutions fostered and supported through the 75 Million Campaign shall report annually to this body, giving a full account of its work and its finances.[112]

Scarborough then formally offered the Southern Baptist Convention the ownership and control of Southwestern Baptist Theological Seminary. J. J. Hurt of North Carolina offered a resolution expressing the Convention's pleasure at this tender and calling for a committee of one from each state to work out the details of the transaction. It is interesting that A. J. Barton promptly moved that the same committee consider the relation of all Southwide institutions to the Convention.[113]

On May 15, 1924, George W. McDaniel, chairman of the committee to report on the tender of Southwestern Seminary, recommended the acceptance of the seminary and arranged for a committee to represent the Convention in the legal transfer.[114] On May 14, 1925, the Convention's committee made a lengthy report detailing the legal steps taken to transfer ownership and control of the seminary to the Convention. A copy of the amended charter of the seminary was included in this report.[115] The report of this committee was adopted.[116] President Scarborough then made the report of the new board of trustees of the seminary, as named by the Southern Baptist Convention, and informed the Convention that the formal transfer to the new board had been made on February 20, 1925.[117]

The acceptance of the seminary by the Southern Baptist Convention brought to a close a distinct era in the life of the school. It had made considerable progress during this first decade in the administration of President Scarborough under the auspices of the state body. During his first year, the enrollment reached only 187; in 1925, there were 587 in residence and 960 in correspondence study. The permanent faculty numbered fewer than ten in the first year; in 1925, it had more than doubled. The assets of the school in 1915 were approximately $900,000; by 1925, Scarborough reported to the Southern Baptist Convention that they amounted to $2,000,000.[118] Some outstanding trustees had fallen, including loyal supporters like W. D. Harris, George E. Cowden, J. B. Gambrell, and J. K. Winston; but new, strong leaders were stepping into their places. The reorganization of the faculty into three schools and the acquisition of scholarly young teachers augured well for the future. Overall, there was much to bring rejoicing in 1925, and the faculty recognized that.

On January 25, 1924, the faculty voted to plan for a special celebration in February, 1925, to commemorate the tenth anniversary of the presidency of L. R. Scarborough. They did not realize at that time that they would have much more to celebrate than this. Two large gifts cheered them. On May 14, 1924, the trustees were informed that George W. and Ida Bottoms of Texarkana, Arkansas, were giving the seminary one-half interest in a three-story brick building located at the corner of Jackson and Jefferson streets in Dallas. The principal amount of the gift was to be untouched, but the interest was to be used to endow a chair of missions in the seminary. This half interest was valued at about $75,000.[119] The endowed chair was later named after the donors. The other gift was made on February 10, 1925, by Mrs. George E. Cowden, the widow of a former trustee and close friend of Scarborough. She said that she would donate $150,000 to erect a building for the School of Gospel Music.[120]

By the fall of 1924, the faculty decided that the celebration would commemorate four significant achievements: the tenth anniversary of Scarborough, the completion of the Seventy-Five Million Campaign, the transfer of the seminary to the Southern Baptist Convention, and the transfer of the Woman's Missionary Training School to the Southwide Woman's Missionary Union.[121] This celebration was held on February 16-20, 1925. Distinguished visitors crowded the campus from all denominational agencies: the four boards, Baptist schools and seminaries, Woman's Missionary Union, the Laymen's Missionary Movement, the Southern Baptist Convention, state secretaries, the editors of the state papers, and many outstanding preachers. The mornings, afternoons, and evenings of the week were spent discussing some aspect of denominational activity. Faculty members found themselves without enough hours in the day to teach their classes, take some rest and eat lightly, and attend the numerous meetings. George W. Truett ended the long week with a message on evangelism.[122]

It was good that the seminary could have this brief time of rejoicing in 1925. Dark clouds were already appearing on the horizon. The Seventy-Five Million Campaign, while very successful in many ways, was severely crippled by the postwar rural depression of the early 1920s. Only $58,591,713.69 of the $75,000,000 goal was raised in the five years. The resulting debts on all of the agencies of the convention and the state bodies amounting to about $18,000,000, along with the most serious depression the nation had ever known, imperiled the very life of the seminary in the next decade. It would be many years before there would be another occasion for celebration.

Notes

1. Crowder, p. 188.

2. J. M. Dawson, "The Apostolate of L. R. Scarborough," *The Southwestern Evangel* 9 (January 1925):41.

3. Jeff D. Ray, "The Seminary's Marvellous Growth," *The Southwestern Evangel* 9 (January 1925):46-49. See also *Proceedings*, BGCT, 1915, p. 108.

4. Scarborough, pp. 164-85. Also in *Standard*, 3 June 1915, pp. 1, 13.

5. A. C. Dixon to B. H. Carroll, 23 October 1909, File 179, Carroll Papers.

6. Stewart G. Cole, *The History of Fundamentalism* (Westport, Conn.: Greenwood Press, 1931), pp. 52-64. Most of these twelve pamphlets are in Fleming Library, Southwestern Baptist Theological Seminary, Fort Worth, Texas.

7. Scarborough, pp. 107-8. For the endowment figures see report of trustees to state convention each year.

8. Trustee Minutes, 14 March 1919.

9. *Proceedings*, BGCT, 1915, p. 109. See also Trustee Minutes, 27 May 1915.

10. *Encyclopedia*, II:1164. Also Trustee Minutes, 27 May 1915.

11. *Proceedings*, BGCT, 1918, p. 56.

12. *Encyclopedia*, I:324.

13. Ibid., II:754.

14. Ibid., II:1501.

15. Ibid., I:346.

16. Ibid., II:842.

17. Faculty Minutes, 14 September 1915; *Proceedings*, BGCT, 1915, p. 110.

18. *The Southwestern Evangel* 9 (January 1925):51.

19. Ibid., p. 61.

20. Ibid., 8 (October 1924):8.

21. For this story see Baker, *Sunday School Board*, p. 82.

22. Trustee Minutes, 27 May 1915.

23. *The Southwestern Evangel* 9 (January 1925):66-67.

24. Southwestern *Catalogue*, 1915-16, pp. 55-57.

25. Faculty Minutes, 11 October 1917.

26. Ibid., 28 May 1914.

27. Ibid., 22 September 1914.

28. *Proceedings*, BGCT, 1914, p. 17; and Southwestern *Catalogue*, 1913-14, pp. 49-53.

29. *The Southwestern Evangel* 9 (January 1925):84.

30. Ibid.

31. *Proceedings*, BGCT, 1915, pp. 111-12.

32. Ibid., 1916, p. 88.

33. Southwestern *Catalogue*, 1917-18, p. 51.

34. Ibid., pp. 32-33.

35. *The Southwestern Evangel* 9 (January 1925):88.

36. W. W. Barnes, "Formal Opening, Gambrell Street Baptist Church," Fleming Library, Southwestern Seminary. (Typewritten pamphlet dated 6 February 1949.)

37. *Annual*, SBC, 1915, p. 45.

38. Ibid., 1916, pp. 36-37.

39. Barnes, pp. 192-93.

40. C. T. Ball, "The Baptist Student Missionary Movement," *Home and Foreign Fields*, November, 1917, p. 13.

41. Barnes, pp. 193-97.

42. Faculty Minutes, 25 May 1917.

43. Southwestern *Catalogue*, Summer 1917, p. 4.

44. *The Southwestern Evangel* 9 (January 1925):56-57.

45. Faculty Minutes, 20 September 1919.

46. Southwestern *Catalogue*, 1919-20, p. 9; and 1920-21, p. 27.

47. Trustee Minutes, 25 May 1916.

48. Southwestern *Catalogue*, 1918-19, p. 6.

49. *Minutes of Baptist Women Mission Workers*, 1914-15, bound with *Proceedings*, BGCT, 1915, pp. 249-50.

50. Southwestern *Catalogue*, 1914-15, p. 57.

51. Trustee Minutes, 16 November 1914.

52. Southwestern *Catalogue*, 1918-19, p. 58.

53. *Annual*, SBC, 1919, pp. 73-74, 82, and 122.

54. *Record and Minutes of Executive Committee*, Southern Baptist Convention, June 1919 through June 1928, Archival 182, p. 3 (hereafter cited as *Minutes of Executive Committee*, SBC). These are located in the archives of the Southern Baptist Convention, Nashville, Tennessee.

55. Ibid., p. 4.

56. Ibid., p. 6.

57. Ibid., p. 10.

58. *Annual*, SBC, 1920, pp. 48-59.

59. Ibid., 1919, p. 76.

60. *Minutes of Executive Committee*, SBC, 22 April 1920, p. 3.

61. Ibid., p. 4.

62. *Proceedings*, BGCT, 1920, pp. 108-9.

63. Ibid., 1921, pp. 83-88.

64. Ibid., 1922, pp. 137-42.

65. Ibid., 1923, p. 162.

66. Ibid., 1924, p. 111; and 1925, p. 64.

67. Scarborough, p. 110.

68. Ibid., pp. 111-12. For a detailed story of the campaign see L. R. Scarborough, *Marvels of Divine Leadership or The Story of the Southern Baptist 75 Million Campaign* (Nashville: Sunday School Board, 1920).

69. *Proceedings*, BGCT, 1923, p. 20.

70. *Minutes*, Tarrant Association, 1918, p. 47.

71. *Proceedings*, BGCT, 1923, p. 21.

72. J. Frank Norris, *The Searchlight* (Fort Worth, Texas), 11 November 1921, p. 1. On file in Fleming Library, Southwestern Baptist Theological Seminary, Fort Worth, Texas.

73. *Proceedings*, BGCT, 1921, p. 18. For a significant article see George W. Truett, "Some Frank Words with Texas Baptists," *Standard*, 19 October 1922, pp. 1-2.

74. Cole, pp. 282 ff.

75. W. W. Barnes, "L. R. Scarborough's Break with Norris," Fleming Library, Southwestern Seminary. (Typewritten manuscript.) For the twelve questions see also J. Frank Norris to L. R. Scarborough, 23 November 1921, L. R. Scarborough Collection, Fleming Library, Southwestern Baptist Theological Seminary, Fort Worth, Texas.

76. L. R. Scarborough to J. Frank Norris, 7 December 1921, Scarborough Collection.

77. *Minutes*, Tarrant Association, 1922, pp. 9, 43. See also J. Frank Norris to L. R. Scarborough, 12 January 1924; and Scarborough's reply, 21 January 1924; both in Scarborough Collection.

78. *Proceedings*, BGCT, 1922, pp. 31-32.

79. Ibid., p. 13.

80. Ibid., pp. 15-17.

81. Ibid., pp. 17-18.

82. Ibid., 1923, pp. 18-24.

83. Ibid., 1924, pp. 24-26.

84. Baker, *Source Book*, pp. 196-97. The best books on Norris are E. Ray Tatum, *Conquest or Failure: Biography of J. Frank Norris* (Dallas: Baptist Historical Foundation, 1966); and Roy E. Falls, *A Fascinating Biography of J. Frank Norris* (Euless, Texas: n.p., 1975).

85. Faculty Minutes, 30 November 1920; and Trustee Minutes, 12 May 1921.

86. *The Southwestern Evangel* 9 (January 1925):87.

87. Charles E. Maddry, *Day Dawn in Yoruba Land* (Nashville: Broadman Press, 1939), pp. 197-99.

88. Faculty Minutes, 3 June 1924.

89. Ibid., 21 September 1923 and 12 October 1923.

90. Ibid., 24 May 1924.

91. *Bulletin of the Southwestern Baptist Theological Seminary*, special issue dated November 1918, pp. 28-29, bound with other catalogues of the seminary.

92. Trustee Minutes, 8 April 1920. See also *Proceedings*, BGCT, 1920, pp. 108-9.

93. *The Southwestern Evangel* 9 (January 1925):83.

94. Southwestern *Catalogue*, 1919-20, p. 17.

95. Ibid., 1920-21, p. 47.

96. See *Proceedings*, BGCT, 1921, pp. 86-87.

97. *The Southwestern Evangel* 9 (January 1925):66-67.

98. Ibid., pp. 71-72.

99. Theological Faculty Minutes, 25 March 1925.

100. See *Encyclopedia*, I:523-24; also E. C. Routh, *The Life Story of Dr. J. B. Gambrell* (Dallas: Baptist Book Store, 1929).

101. See *Encyclopedia*, III:1687-88.

102. Southwestern *Catalogue*, 1925-26, p. 101.

103. Ibid., 1921-22, p. 69.

104. *The Southwestern Evangel* 9 (January 1925):84.

105. Faculty Minutes, 24 May 1924.

106. Ibid., 26 May 1924.

107. Ibid., 26 December 1922.

108. See *Annual*, SBC, 1918, pp. 33-34; 1919, p. 116; 1920, pp. 83-84; 1921, pp. 26-27; 1922, p. 71; 1923, p. 53; 1924, pp. 111-12; and 1925, pp. 65-66.

109. Scarborough, *Modern School*, p. 142.

110. Ibid., pp. 142-43. See also Trustee Minutes, 17 May 1918.

111. *Proceedings*, BGCT, 1923, p. 163.

112. *Annual*, SBC, 1923, pp. 38-41.

113. Ibid., pp. 40-41.

114. Ibid., 1924, pp. 45-46.

115. See *Appendix* for this amended charter.

116. *Annual*, SBC, 1925, pp. 53-61.

117. Ibid., p. 61.

118. Ibid., p. 62.

119. Scarborough, *Modern School*, pp. 121-22.

120. Trustee Minutes, 19 February 1925.

121. *The Southwestern Evangel* 9 (January 1925):10-11.

122. The entire issue of *The Southwestern Evangel* for January 1925 was devoted to this celebration.

6

Storm and Struggle

All Southern Baptists should cherish the inspiration of a high moment of dedication in the history of The Southern Baptist Theological Seminary, then located at Greenville, South Carolina. The school had suspended its classes in June, 1862, at the close of just its third session because of the Civil War. The four original faculty members, James P. Boyce, John A. Broadus, William Williams, and Basil Manly, Jr., met in the summer of 1865, after the war had ended, to determine whether or not the seminary could open. Fortunately, the institution had no debt, but South Carolina was prostrate from the battering it had received during the war. Finally, having faced their bleak prospects of survival, John A. Broadus arose from their time of prayer and said, "Suppose we quietly agree that the Seminary may die, but we'll die first."[1] Through dark days they survived—although at the first session after reopening, the school had only seven students, one of whom was blind.

Southwestern Seminary has a similar heroic saga. The heavy debts of state and Convention-wide agencies incurred during the Seventy-Five Million Campaign, the severe rural depression of the early 1920s and the plummeting of the national economy after the stock market crash of 1929, the huge deficit of the Home Mission Board of the Southern Baptist Convention after the defalcation of C. S. Carnes in 1928, and the rapid decline in giving to Convention-wide interests because of the critical needs in local and state bodies had their blighting effect on Southwestern Seminary, as they did on all agencies of the Convention. Not only did the seminary slash in half the salaries of faculty and staff in this period, but it was unable to pay even those reduced amounts. The number of salaried employees was pared to the very minimum. With grim courage and sacrifice, the remainder stood in their places. Some received calls to churches which could have paid them many times the amounts they were promised at the seminary, but they did not turn aside. The list of the faithful included L. R. Scarborough, C. M. King, Georgia Miller, Mrs. W. E. Kimbrough, Mrs. W. A. Johnson, D. A. Thornton, Vinnie Gammill, and Luther Adams of the administration; Jeff D. Ray, J. W. Crowder, W. T. Conner, W. W. Barnes, B. A. Copass, H. E. Dana, L. R. Elliott, E. L. Carlson, and Albert Venting of the School of Theology;

J. M. Price, T. B. Maston, W. L. Howse, and Floy Barnard of the School of Religious Education; and I. E. and Lura Mae Reynolds, Edwin M. and Wayne McNeely, E. L. Carnett, and William Barclay in the School of Gospel Music. There were others who served for a brief period during those difficult years, but they were not counted as part of the regular faculty and staff. President Scarborough recorded his bittersweet memories of those years as follow:

> The income on the Seminary's small endowment was greatly affected by the general depression. The rents on its buildings went down and many of the students were unable to pay their rent bills. It must be remembered that, though the Seminary greatly reduced the salaries (in some cases to the amount of 40 per cent) of its teachers and administrators, there was a limit to such reductions. The student body was still large. They kept coming in great numbers and making demands for proper instruction. We reduced the salaries to the minimum, even to the point of sacrifice; and we reduced the membership of the faculty to a point not below the minimum required for the efficiency of the Seminary. We trusted the denomination to take care of us in our effort to save the life of the institution, and this is our explanation for this large deficit.
>
> The figures show a glorious and tragic history of the Southwestern Seminary on its current fund support through the thirty years of its history. These facts have back of them prayer, faith, unremitting toil, constant heartache and nerve strain, and in some parts of it very great sacrifice, the period from 1929 to 1936 representing the period of the long and pressing depression. It can easily be stated that the Seminary employees gave back in these seven years of salaries they did not and never shall receive more than $300,000. This represents only a small part of their sacrifices. The Seminary had to discontinue some of its noble force in the interest of economy. Some men and women, as fine as we have ever had, had to go out, and in only a few cases by resignation; and those that did stay experienced sacrifices recorded only in heaven. I can say that not in my life of a wide experience have I ever known a braver, more uncomplaining, sacrificial group of men and women than those who have co-operated with me in the administration and teaching of the Seminary through these tragic years. After the salaries were thus greatly reduced, the income was insufficient to pay more than half salaries, and that went on for years, creating a large debt, which would be chargeable to the future.[2]

This example of heroic sacrifice provided the pattern for the history of Southwestern Seminary in the period from 1925 to 1942. During this time, the school began its new relationship with the Southern Baptist Convention, faced an unprecedented crisis in its financial support, affirmed its doctrinal stance in the midst of controversy, and devoted itself steadfastly to its task despite numerous hardships. These several facets of the seminary story during this period will be discussed briefly in the following pages.

The New Relationship

The shift in ownership and control of Southwestern Seminary in 1925 from the Baptist General Convention of Texas to the Southern Baptist Convention did not appear to be a radical one. Both bodies were structured on the associational or convention plan; that is, the trustees in each case were selected by a denominational body which was linked specifically to the churches in a multibenevolent ministry. Both the state body and the Southern Baptist Convention had retained some of the characteristics of the older society method, but by 1925 the state convention had eliminated most of these antidenominational society characteristics.

The Southern Baptist Convention, on the other hand, was just in the process of altering some long-standing society distinctives when Southwestern Seminary came under its control. These distinctives included the society concept of supporting benevolences by designated giving, with the result that the Convention itself was isolated from general financial support; the limited benevolent support both in the number of areas and in adequacy; the financial basis of representation at the Convention; the disjunctive relationship between the several benevolent agencies within the Convention because of the lack of unified control; and a haphazard methodology in the collection of benevolent funds.[3]

The historical effects of this ambivalence between the society and the associational methods of denominational work were displayed in the constant bickering over the structure of the Southern Baptist Convention between 1845 and 1917. A remarkable forward leap by the Convention occurred between 1917 and 1931. First, the beginning of an Executive Committee in 1917 marked the breakdown of the concept of the Southern Baptist Convention as an isolated annual gathering which had no functional existence between meetings. This Executive Committee was strengthened greatly in 1926 and 1927, and it became the fiduciary, fiscal, and executive agency of the Convention in all affairs not committed specifically to some other agency of the Convention.

The second important advance in the Convention structure took place in 1925. The carry-over of the society principle of designated giving into the structure of the Southern Baptist Convention had essentially stripped the Convention of the element of control over its own agencies. It did not have enough funds of its own even to print the minutes of the annual meeting but regularly borrowed money from the boards for this purpose. Whatever else was accomplished by the Seventy-Five Million Campaign from 1919 to 1924, it led directly to the inauguration of the Cooperative

Program in 1925. This was a plan by which the various state conventions could work with the Southern Baptist Convention to provide it with undesignated funds for allocation to the several benevolences it promoted.

> By this plan, each state became an active participant in both fostering appeals for benevolent objects promoted by the Convention and in the financial well-being of the Convention itself. This fusion between the state programs and the Convention's activities brought a new denominational unity to Southern Baptists.[4]

Two additional refinements of the Convention's structure were made in 1931. In a sweeping constitutional revision, the strictly financial basis of representation at the Convention was changed to permit each local congregation contributing to the work of the Convention to designate from one to ten messengers to the Convention, the number depending upon the size of the church and the amount contributed by the church. This significant change emphasized the important place of the local congregations and brought an increased denominational consciousness to them somewhat similar to the effect of the Cooperative Program on state conventions.

The other change in the constitutional revision of 1931 was the adoption of a bylaw which provided a supplementary structure for decision making by utilizing the principle of establishing state representation on the boards, commissions, and standing committees of the Convention. It is likely that 95 percent of all decisions made at the annual meetings of the Southern Baptist Convention follow the study and recommendations of the trustees of these various components of the Convention structure.[5]

These several changes, as can be seen, occurred at the very time Southwestern Seminary was moving into the orbit of the Convention. These changes affected all of the agencies of the Convention, including the seminary after 1925. As the Executive Committee, strengthened and enlarged in 1926-27, began to seek direction, it found that its hands were shackled by the immense indebtedness of over $6,500,000 which burdened most of the agencies of the Southern Baptist Convention. The revenues of the Convention itself also had been sharply curtailed by the similar paralyzing indebtedness of every Baptist state convention in the South. As one reads the minutes of the Executive Committee from 1925 to the 1940s, he must acknowledge that the conduct of the committee during these crucial years, while the subject of criticism by individuals and agencies who were struggling with their own problems, reflected splendid statesmanship and courageous Christian integrity which are unsurpassed in Southern Baptist history. The interplay between the Executive Committee and the seminary during these years will be discussed briefly in connection with the financial struggles of the school.

Financial Stringency

A critical part of the seminary story from 1925 to 1942 was the distressing financial paralysis which made it appear that the school would lose all of its property to creditors. The darkest years were from 1925 to 1933. A slight note of optimism slowly begins to appear in the reports of the school after 1933, perhaps because the Baptist Hundred Thousand Club had been formed to help pay the debts of the Convention and its agencies.

The Seminary Facing Bankruptcy

In 1926, the first year after the Southern Baptist Convention assumed control of the seminary, the prospects for the school were bleak. An unfortunate set of circumstances compounded the financial crisis. In 1925, Mrs. George E. Cowden had made a gift of $150,000 to the seminary for the erection of a building for sacred music on the campus as a memorial to her late husband. This was a sacrificial bequest by a devoted Christian woman at a time when the economy was in a perilous state. She would later say, as recalled by her grandson E. Cowden Henry, "If I should lose everything in this financial crisis, I still would have an asset on Seminary Hill that cannot be lost." President Scarborough was in a quandary. The seminary was badly in need of this building, not simply for sacred music but also to provide a place for administrative offices, faculty offices, classrooms, a chapel, and similar functional needs. Scarborough felt obligated to fulfill the conditions of the bequest, perhaps with the hope that additional gifts might be forthcoming. He knew, however, that the building would cost far more than the $150,000, that the seminary debt was already $196,580, that the new owners of the school were badly in debt because of the failure of the Seventy-Five Million Campaign's financial goals, and that the economic climate was not good. Finally, Scarborough and his trustees decided that this Cowden gift must be used for the purpose for which it was given, and the Cowden Music Hall was erected in 1926 at a cost of $335,000. Upon entering this building in 1926, the music school changed its name from the School of Gospel Music to the School of Sacred Music.

It was a hazardous time to embark on this building project, and President Scarborough was widely criticized for his decision. The debt of the seminary increased to more than $450,000, and the interest payments alone absorbed a substantial portion of the seminary's total income. Scarborough himself later said that the faculty had a large part in paying for this building with the money they lost in salaries during the following decade.[6]

In addition to this huge debt, the operating fund for 1925-26 showed a deficit of approximately $42,000. Similar reports of operating at a deficit and of being unable to pay anything on their bonded and unbonded indebtedness came from most of the other agencies of the Convention.

There was no improvement in the following year. Southwestern Seminary's report to the Convention in 1927 showed an operating deficit of $46,058.55, bringing the total debt to a whopping $452,997.56.[7] Scarborough said that he had studied every aspect of the seminary operation and believed that he would be able to cut around $35,000, "not in waste but in real vitalities," from the budget for the next year.[8]

The newly enlarged Executive Committee of the Southern Baptist Convention faced a staggering task. Neither it nor the Convention had ever known a situation like this before. The state and Convention-wide debts totaled about $18,000,000, of which the Convention-wide body owed about $6,500,000. These debts developed because the agencies of the Convention and the state bodies had quickly enlarged their programs on the basis of anticipated receipts from the Seventy-Five Million Campaign, but the severe economic crisis, especially in the rural South between 1920 and 1924, caused the Campaign to fall short of the amount pledged by about $34,000,000. The magnitude of this problem was one of the reasons the Convention clothed this committee with additional authority and assigned to it the promotional aspect of the Cooperative Program as a part of its fiscal responsibilities. The Executive Committee was reorganized at the June, 1927, meeting, and Austin Crouch was elected executive secretary. At this June meeting, the committee promptly began discussing how to end these increasing deficits by the Convention's agencies and where to find funds to pay the old debts left by the Seventy-Five Million Campaign. A Total Objectives Campaign Committee was appointed, of which President Scarborough was a member, to seek large gifts from individuals for paying the debts.[9]

On January 11-12, 1928, the Executive Committee discussed various other ways to meet the financial crisis. To stop the continuing large deficits reported each year by the agencies of the Convention, the committee voted that in making their budgets for 1928-29 and thereafter, all agencies having indebtedness must not exceed the total of their cash receipts for the previous year and that the first item of the budget must be for payment of interest.[10] After discussing a campaign to raise large sums beyond the regular gifts in order to pay some of the complaining creditors, the committee named a special group of twenty-five to make a study concerning the best way to meet the indebtedness of the boards and agencies of the Convention. President Scarborough was one of the subcommittee of five to prepare recommendations. Their report encompassed a wide-ranging effort to raise funds during the following year, including recommendations that Southern Baptists promote a thank offering at Christmas, 1928, to be applied to the principal of the debts of the agencies. The two-million-dollar goal would be divided on the same percentage as that prevailing for the Cooperative Program, less the first 5 percent to be reserved by the Executive Committee for unforeseen emergencies. Additional recommendations included special emphases on the Every-Member Canvass, the Cooperative Program, the biblical principles of stewardship and tithing, personal solicitation of large gifts from individuals, special days in Sunday School, and the like.[11]

President Scarborough reported to the Convention in 1928 that Southwestern Seminary had been able to pay $11,205.15 on the school's indebtedness, despite an operating loss of about $28,000.00 during the year, bringing the debt down to $441,047.11.[12] He said that he would be able to cut the operating expenses in the coming year about $15,000, principally by lowering the salaries of the teachers.[13]

The deepening of the financial depression in the nation was reflected in the report of Scarborough for 1929. The student body at Southwestern had pledged more than $10,000 on operating expenses, despite the fact that student fees for the year had been doubled. The decreasing faculty had pledged $3,000. Others had made smaller gifts. A proposal by Mr. and Mrs. T. W. Carter of Mercedes, Texas, was described. They had offered to give the school two hundred acres of citrus fruit land in the Rio Grande Valley on several conditions, one of which was that the seminary would set out and develop fruit trees on the land.[14] The trustees of the seminary had approved this transaction and, to provide funds for setting out the trees, had sold some of the securities in the endowment fund of the school.[15]

In the report to the Convention for 1928-29, Scarborough indicated that the seminary had paid $27,085.53 on interest and principal, but that the indebtedness had been reduced only $603.49. He then began a story that would be continued year by year—namely, that receipts from the Cooperative Program had dropped substantially. In the previous year, the seminary had received an allocation of 4.5 percent of undesignated Convention-wide receipts, which had amounted to $73,551.71. The percentage of allocation was the same in 1928-29, but the drop in Convention-wide receipts had caused the seminary to receive only $59,679.81, a loss of $13,871.90. The seminary had also received $18,863.79 in the previous year from a special Texas campaign, but in 1928-29 this amount had dropped to $2,605.70, which made a total of $30,129.99 less in receipts than the seminary had received the year before. Scarborough urgently appealed to the Convention to endow the seminary by at least $1,000,000 more.[16]

Whatever optimism Scarborough might have felt in making this report to the Convention was abruptly quenched when he learned about the theft from the Home Mission Board of almost a million dollars by C. S. Carnes, the treasurer of the board, during the fall of 1928. This left that board in a critical condition. The Executive Committee necessarily ignored pleas from other agencies and approved a special offering for the Home Mission Board on a Sunday designated as "Baptist Honor Day," when it hoped to raise approximately the amount embezzled by Carnes.[17]

At this same session of the Southern Baptist Convention in 1929, the Executive Committee recommended a new financial plan that would set the pattern for the future financial operation of all agencies controlled by the Southern Baptist Convention, including, of course, the seminaries. Essentially this plan curtailed the authority of the local trustees and administrations of all agencies by requiring that they submit to the Executive Committee each year a detailed itemized budget showing the estimated income from all sources other than the Cooperative Program anticipated by the agency, together with the estimated expenditures for the next calendar year, including operating expenses, proposed work for the year, interest on all debts, the amount of the principal of funded debts maturing, and how much would be paid on current debts. The Executive Committee would then prepare a total budget for the Convention which would not exceed the anticipated receipts for the next year. The committee recognized the right of donors to designate gifts to specific causes, stating, however, that no agency of the Convention could accept any gift that would incur an additional outlay of funds or expenses on the part of the agency without the consent of the Convention or the Executive Committee.

In this plan, the committee included a controversial item which asserted that if, before the end of the year, any agency should receive funds from the Cooperative Program, either designated or undesignated, which were equal to its total allocation, "then the treasurer of the Executive Committee shall make no further remittances from undesignated funds to such agency." Additional designated funds to the agency would be used preferably for payments on debts. Several other details of the financial plan were spelled out. Each agency would make a monthly detailed report to the Executive Committee of all other monies, designated or undesignated, received from any source; any special campaign by an agency should first receive the approval of the Convention or the Executive Committee; no agency could borrow more for seasonable needs than the amount of their budget allowance at the time; no agency could solicit gifts designated to its use, except as provided in this plan; and the states should leave the percentages of distribution of undesignated Convention-wide funds to the Convention, rather than set the percentages themselves.[18]

The item involving the cutting off of undesignated funds to an agency when its receipts equaled the total allocation made in that year became controversial because this practically nullified the motivation for making designated gifts. It was finally rescinded at the meeting of the Executive Committee on March 5, 1931.[19]

This was not the only part of the financial plan that raised problems. The basic reason for the new plan, as set out in the introductory paragraph of the Executive Committee's recommendation, was that

> the time has arrived when the Southern Baptist Convention should adopt a policy in its Cooperative Program of attempting to provide for the approved operating budgets of its various agencies by allocating specific sums instead of percentages as heretofore.[20]

This purpose was reflected in the request of the Baptist Bible Institute, New Orleans, in 1929, that their allocation of undesignated funds be raised to 5 percent. The Executive Committee replied that the "new financial plan . . . will make it possible to adjust the matter without changing the percentage of allocation."[21] This purpose was further indicated when the committee voted to publish only the amounts of the allocations to the agencies and not any percentages.[22]

When the Executive Committee reported the allocations for 1930, they were shown in amounts and not percentages. These amounts were apparently based upon the committee's examination of the proposed budgets and the needs of the several agencies rather than upon simply the allocation of a percentage to an agency. In this allocation, Southwestern Seminary would receive $152,000 in 1929-30 from the Cooperative Program, while Baptist Bible Institute was to receive $110,000, and Southern Seminary, $100,000. It is interesting that the Executive Committee's vote on these allocations divided over whether these sums should be the "guaranteed objective" or the "goals."[23]

Unfortunately, the reduced receipts of the Executive Committee made it impossible for any of these schools to receive the amounts shown. Southwestern received $59,987.40 in 1929-30, a $450.00 increase over the previous year. Designated gifts during that year had decreased from $48,924.58 in the previous year to $40,472.86, a loss of $8,451.72. The deficit in operating expenses was $4,294.00, and the total debt was increased by $15,445.78, leaving it at $455,889.40.

President Scarborough had high hopes that another substantial investment in the citrus fruit orchards in the Rio Grande Valley might provide a future endowment for the seminary. The trustees authorized him to trade the seminary's interest in the building in Dallas, given by Mr. and Mrs. George W. Bottoms, for one thousand additional acres of land, of which five hundred acres were to be set out in citrus fruit and the remainder sold.[24] The trustees also authorized the cutting of faculty salaries by approximately 10 percent. The teachers of voice and instruments in the music school were authorized to charge their pupils for lessons rather than receive a salary.[25]

At a meeting of the Executive Committee of the Convention on June 11, 1930, the financial crisis at Southwestern Seminary was discussed sympathetically. The committee met again on September 10, 1930, in Nashville. It must have been at one of these meetings that the experience related by Gaines S. Dobbins took place. Writing over thirty years later, he said:

> Few of this generation realize the distress of those depression years. Vividly I recall the meeting of the Executive Committee of the Convention in 1933 at Nashville. Report after report of the Convention's boards and agencies indicated practical bankruptcy. At length Dr. L. R. Scarborough, president of Southwestern Seminary, arose and choking with emotion said in effect, "Brethren, we are through at Southwestern. For two years we haven't paid faculty salaries. We have nothing with which to meet expenses. Our percentage of the allocation will not see us through another year. Here is my resignation and I turn over to you the seminary property. You'll have to sell it to pay our debts, and Southwestern will go out of existence."
>
> There was a stunned silence. We sat in tears. Then Dr. Sampey arose, drummed with his fingers on the table in characteristic fashion, and said in effect, "I may lose my job for what I am about to say. Southern Seminary has some income from endowment on which we can live. I move that Southern Seminary's apportionment be cut and the difference given to Southwestern."[26]

The date of 1933 for this event was incorrect. *The Christian Index* (Georgia) for June 8, 1933, described it as occurring "two or three years ago." It must have occurred before the Executive Committee meeting on December 8, 1931, for at that time President Sampey requested the Executive Committee to negate this extra allocation for Southwestern and equalize the allocation of Southern Seminary. It appears that the only meeting in 1930 at which all three of the men were present was on September 10, although the records are not always precise at that point.

No matter when it occurred, this was simply another example of the genuine graciousness (although he sometimes tried to conceal it) of the warmhearted John R. Sampey. In the previous year (1929), he had asked the Executive Committee to take four thousand dollars from the Southern Seminary allotment and add this amount for the American Baptist Theological Seminary.[27]

At the meeting of the committee on September 10, 1930, the allotment of the American Baptist Theological Seminary was raised from 2/5 percent to 1 percent. This may seem strange in view of the objectives of the new financial plan adopted in the previous year by the committee and the Convention, but doubtless it developed from the fact that the committee realized that it could not depend upon Cooperative Program receipts to provide the amounts budgeted for the agencies, so the only equitable manner of dividing the receipts would be on a percentage basis.

The kindness of President Sampey provided only a brief respite for Southwestern, however. On March 5, 1931, the Executive Committee approved a request that Southwestern Seminary be permitted to conduct a quiet campaign among the people to raise $100,000 as a special emergency offering. On March 26, the seminary's trustees authorized the president, with the assistance of J. W. Bruner, to conduct this campaign by asking three hundred people to pledge $100 a year for three years and supplement this with other gifts to raise $50,000 a year for the next three years.

Also at this March 26 meeting, the seminary's trustees prepared a letter of appreciation to the faculty for their loyalty to the institution under difficult circumstances and expressed the hope that their reduced salaries could be paid before long. The trustees pledged that at least one-half of the salaries of the teachers and staff would soon be paid, if at all possible. On May 13, 1931, the trustees named a committee to work with the Executive Committee to find some way to pay the seminary's debts. Faculty salaries were again reduced for the following year.

Another letter was sent to the faculty expressing appreciation for their sacrifices.

In the report to the Convention in 1931, President Scarborough noted that while the Convention had put $152,000.00 in its budget for this school, the seminary had received only $46,941.21. This was a drop of almost $13,000 from the previous year's receipts. By reducing salaries and "the cutting of blood," the operating expenses had been decreased about $30,000 for the year, but the indebtedness had increased by $4,725 to a total of $459,725. Of this amount, $226,460 had to be paid during the next convention year unless the entire debt of the seminary could be refinanced.[28] When the Executive Committee met on June 10, 1931, the financial condition of the seminary was again discussed. Apparently someone raised the question of whether the Executive Committee could endorse the notes of the agencies, and a resolution was promptly passed indicating that it could not do so.[29]

At the convening of the Executive Committee on June 10, 1931, permission was granted for Southwestern Seminary to refinance its debts. The minutes of the trustees during the remainder of this period record their efforts to do this. The last refinancing took place on January 29, 1941, shortly before the debts were erased. When the trustees met on January 6, 1931, a suggestion was received from the Faculty Council, in reply to an invitation by the trustees. The faculty urged the trustees to seek a moratorium by the seminary's creditors which would allow the school to pay the interest only for the next three years. This the trustees agreed to attempt, promising the faculty that they would "bring some financial relief to them soon." The continuing financial pinch made it necessary for the trustees to authorize President Scarborough on April 13, 1932, to sign notes for money to meet operating expenses. In attempting to secure a moratorium on some of the indebtedness, the trustees agreed to give liens on seminary property to those creditors who had unsecured notes of the school.

In his report to the Convention in 1932, President Scarborough mournfully recounted that in the last three years Southwestern had cut the salaries of the force by 50 percent and had not been able to pay half of that amount. The indebtedness had risen to $498,636.43, an increase of almost $39,000.00. The receipts from the Cooperative Program had been $45,608.43, a decrease of about $14,000.00 from the previous year. Donations had decreased by over $13,500. A slash in personnel had been made, and another reduction was planned for the next year. But, Scarborough said, "we cannot further reduce our teaching and administrative force without very considerable impairment to the work we must do, and to the very large overworking of our force."[30]

For the first time in many years, the 1933 report by the seminary's trustees and administration contained a cautious note of optimism about the future. There was not a great deal of foundation for this optimism. The indebtedness of the school had risen to $500,858; gifts from the Cooperative Program were down almost $10,000 from the previous year; donations from friends were down almost $1,500; and receipts from fees and administration were down over $6,000. The reason for the optimism lay in the fact that many of the faculty had agreed to accept some of the citrus fruit land in the Rio Grande Valley as payment on their back salaries. This exchange made it possible for the school to pay about $27,500 on the principal of its debt and, along with reductions in expenses, allowed the school to complete the year with a deficit of only $2,222. It had not been able to balance its budget, as the Convention and Executive Committee had instructed it to do, but promised to make every effort to do that in the following year.[31]

During these trying years as Scarborough struggled to keep the seminary alive, he was under constant attack by J. Frank Norris. As one reads the files in the Scarborough correspondence between 1925 and 1933, he is forced to conclude that the influence of Norris undoubtedly contributed to the lack of financial support for the seminary during these days. His blatant attacks on the school in his church paper, on his radio programs, and in his correspondence gleefully prophesied the downfall of "poor Truett and Scarborough," the chairman of the board and the president of the seminary. When the faculty was struggling along at half salary, and this not half paid, Norris taunted them by having a fruit basket delivered to them with his compliments. Equating financial solvency with God's favor, he constantly called attention to his own prosperity and the critical condition of the "bankrupt seminary."

The Baptist Hundred Thousand Club

After so many proposals for paying the debts of the Convention and its agencies had proved to be inadequate, it was not surprising that the suggestion of Frank Tripp to the Executive Committee on April 13 and the adoption of a detailed plan on May 18, 1933, to launch the Baptist Hundred Thousand Club were not viewed with universal enthusiasm at the time. This plan was approved by the Southern Baptist Convention on May 20, 1933. Its purpose was to liquidate all the debts on the agencies of the Convention by enlisting 100,000 Baptist church members to pledge one dollar per month over and above their regular subscriptions to the church budget. The campaign was thoroughly organized. The committee asked Frank Tripp, pastor of the First Baptist Church, Saint Joseph, Missouri, to lead it. His church agreed to give him a leave of absence, with salary, for this work, and the Sunday School Board paid all operating expenses, so that every dollar raised could be applied directly to the principal of the debts.

By the time the Convention met in 1934, the club reported thirty thousand members. Annual membership campaigns were conducted each January and February for the following decade. Between 1937 and 1943, the last seven years of the campaign, six states made an agreement with the Southern Baptist Convention to receive half of the receipts of the campaign and apply them on their debts. The results were extraordinary. The following table shows the amounts paid on Convention debts between 1933 and 1943:

Year	Amount
1933	$ 37,588.28
1934	160,565.96
1935	198,372.31
1936	191,296.88
1937	191,500.00
1938	161,726.07
1939	159,447.96
1940	158,279.43
1941	261,143.63
1942	377,277.82
1943	730,624.02[32]

In 1936, at Tripp's urgent request, the Convention, with profuse thanks, released him to return to his pastorate. On August 1, 1936, J. E. Dillard assumed the leadership task.

With the constantly increasing gifts from the Hundred Thousand Club and larger allocations from the Cooperative Program as the depression lessened, Southwestern Seminary was able to pay all of its debts shortly after the end of the presidency of L. R. Scarborough, as shown in the following chart:

Year	Receipts from Cooperative Program	Receipts from Hundred Thousand Club	Total Debt
1934	$ 48,646.79	$ 5,386.28	$499,479.78
1935	49,434.88	27,332.67	484,729.17
1936	51,008.58	27,687.53	454,412.08
1937	53,964.53	26,857.62	436,634.65

Year	Receipts from Cooperative Program	Receipts from Hundred Thousand Club	Total Debt
1938	56,397.06	34,544.98	401,153.03
1939	57,338.03	30,666.35	363,978.50
1940	60,554.49	32,508.91	336,486.93
1941	61,077.84	32,002.86	289,472.12
1942	70,234.78	49,482.38	240,284.39
1943	81,448.67	75,728.37	120,429.38
1944	108,265.00	152,331.70	None

A note-burning celebration was observed on November 12, 1943, commemorating the payment of the last of the old debts of Southwestern Seminary. Former President Scarborough and his wife returned to the campus to spearhead the festive occasion.

An interesting financial note in the report of the seminary to the Convention in 1937 said:

> From the first of January we have been able to pay for the first time since the beginning of the depression the full salaries of the teachers. This is on the basis of a reduction of 33⅓ per cent of salaries at the beginning of the depression.[33]

Another landmark was reported in 1940. A salary increase of 10 percent had been granted, the first upturn after the depression.

Doctrinal Controversy

Between 1925 and 1942, J. Frank Norris continued his efforts to undermine the seminary financially and to attack its orthodoxy. He had used the evolutionary hypothesis of Charles Darwin to mount his original attack on Baylor University; but after his expulsion from the Tarrant County Baptist Association and the Baptist General Convention of Texas in 1924, he entered into an aggressive personal vendetta against George W. Truett and L. R. Scarborough, who had played the largest role in unseating him. It is difficult to believe that even Norris would say some of the crude personal things that are found in the Scarborough correspondence. At first, Scarborough tried to answer him but then adopted the attitude of Truett and simply did not respond to the bitter attacks against him.

But Norris would not be ignored. Through his newspaper and radio, he constantly agitated his accusations against these men, as well as others in the "machine" of the Baptist General Convention of Texas. At every session of the state convention and the Southern Baptist Convention, he distributed recriminative literature and usually competed with the programs of the conventions by preaching in a building near the place where the convention was meeting. After Norris killed D. E. Chipps on July 17, 1926, there was a noticeable cooling of the relationship between him and the Northern Fundamentalists, although it is probably true that this withdrawal was due as much to Norris's desires as to those of the Northern group. By the following year, he had decided that he did not need the Northern movements and turned his efforts toward developing a strong Fundamentalist program built around himself. He had made thorough plans. Between 1919 and 1924, he erected a new church building with one of the largest auditoriums in America, an ideal place for large conferences and conventions. He installed a printing press in the building and changed the name of the church paper successively from the *Fence Rail* (1917), to the *Searchlight* (1922), to the *Fundamentalist* (1927). Its circulation reached fifty-five thousand in regular issues, not to speak of special editions for distribution at the meetings of the state conventions and the Southern Baptist Convention. The building also was equipped with a radio station.

Tragedy struck in 1929 when this building was ravaged by fire. However, with his insurance and ability to raise money, Norris was able to replace it, although not on the same ornate scale as the old one. A curious result of this fire was the scattering of some of the people of the church to form new independent Baptist churches after the Norris pattern in Fort Worth and its vicinity. These churches subsequently provided the foundation for the denominational movement which Norris led.

Coincident with Norris's break with the Northern Fundamentalists in both the World's Christian Fundamentalist Association and the Baptist Bible Union, he laid plans for the formation of the World Fundamental Baptist Mission Fellowship, formally organized in 1938, and the founding of the Fundamentalist Baptist Bible Institute, a Norrisite seminary to challenge Southwestern and other Convention schools. Perhaps reflecting his desire to associate himself with the golden memory of B. H. Carroll, Norris affixed a sign in huge neon lights across the front of his seminary stating, "The Only Seminary in the World Teaching the Entire English Bible." This, of course, was not true.

After 1924, Norris accelerated his attacks on the orthodoxy of the "machine-run" schools, particularly Baylor University, and the "machine leaders," George W. Truett and L. R. Scarborough. He challenged

Scarborough's use of Seventy-Five Million Campaign funds, his sale of lots around the seminary, and his personal character and integrity. Norris always referred in his correspondence about Southwestern Seminary to "that bankrupt Seminary." He vowed that he would "knock the halo" off Truett's head. He fought the evolutionary issue until his death.

Concomitant events brough Norris's attacks on evolution to the fore during the 1920s. It will be recalled that the Baptist General Convention of Texas was deeply involved in this controversy in 1923 and 1924 when Norris made his earliest attacks on Baylor University. Baylor, Southwestern Seminary (at that time owned and operated by the Texas convention), and the Baptist General Convention of Texas adopted statements denying that man was the evolutionary development of a lower animal. Norris, however, continued his attacks through his correspondence, newspaper, and radio and by preaching in competition with the programs of the state and Southern Baptist conventions. Paralleling his assaults and those of the national Fundamentalist groups, the state of Tennessee passed a statute on March 21, 1925, which forbade any educational institution supported by public funds in Tennessee "to teach the theory that denies the story of the divine creation of man as taught in the Bible." A biology teacher, John T. Scopes, provided a test case. His trial attracted world attention, and although he was convicted, his sentence was set aside by the Supreme Court on a technicality. It is not surprising that when the Southern Baptist Convention met in Memphis, Tennessee, at the very time this trial was taking place, the question of evolution was being discussed in every coffee shop. The Convention had spoken on this issue in 1922 and 1923, but the agitation was so great at the Memphis Convention of 1925 that it adopted the first confession of faith in its history, not as a confession binding on Southern Baptists but representing the consensus of the messengers at that particular session.[34] For several reasons, this confession did not distinctly and specifically deny the evolutionary hypothesis, despite efforts to have it do so.[35]

There was a clamor for the Southern Baptist Convention to adopt a clear statement on evolution, so at Houston in 1926 George W. McDaniel ended his presidential address to the Convention with the following words:

> This Convention accepts Genesis as teaching that man was the special creation of God, and rejects every theory, evolution or other, which teaches that man originated in, or came by way of, a lower animal ancestry.[36]

By previous arrangement, M. E. Dodd moved that the statement of the president on the subject of evolution and the origin of man be adopted as the sentiment of the Convention, "and that from this point on no further consideration be given to this subject, and that the Convention go forward with the consideration of the main kingdom causes to which God has set our hearts and hands." The vote was unanimous. However, the discussion was not ended. On that afternoon, President Scarborough, probably conscious that J. Frank Norris was watching, convened the trustees of Southwestern Seminary who, in addition to accepting the Articles of Faith adopted at Memphis the year before as the doctrinal statement of the seminary, voted to include the McDaniel statement as an addendum to the seminary's confession.[37]

On the fourth day of the Convention, Selsus E. Tull of Arkansas presented a resolution, the rules being suspended to allow its adoption. This Tull resolution read:

> Whereas, The Southern Baptist Convention in its Session May 12, 1926, by unanimous vote, declared that it "accepts Genesis as teaching that man was the special creation of God, and rejects every theory, evolution or other, which teaches that man originated in, or came by way of, a lower animal ancestry," and
>
> Whereas, our great school of the Prophets, the Southwestern Baptist Theological Seminary, through its Board of Trustees, on May 12th, accepted and incorporated the same action of the Convention in its "Statement of Faith" and through its Honored President, so announced to this Convention on May 13th, and said President further announced that this "Statement of Faith" would be made a test of all officers and teachers of said Seminary,
>
> Therefore, the Southern Baptist Convention does now resolve that it commends the Board of Trustees of the Southwestern Baptist Theological Seminary for its prompt and hearty acceptance of the Convention's action; and
>
> In order that no unfair comparisons or unjust accusations be brought against any of our Seminaries, Schools or other Convention agencies, be it further resolved that this Convention request all its institutions and Boards, and their missionary representatives, to give like assurance to the Convention and the Baptist Brotherhood in general, of a hearty and individual acceptance of the said action of this Convention to the end that the great cause of our present unrest and agitation over the Evolution question may be effectively and finally removed in the minds of the constituency of this Convention and all others concerned.[38]

It should be added that both The Southern Baptist Theological Seminary and Baptist Bible Institute also subsequently notified the Convention of their acceptance of the McDaniel statement.[39]

Long after this took place, Norris continued to berate L. R. Scarborough on the evolutionary issue in both his correspondence and his paper. It is amazing that Norris had the time and inclination to keep up these assaults while serving as pastor of two large churches—one at Detroit, Michigan, and the other at Fort Worth; developing his own denomination; organizing a seminary; and rebuilding his burned church structure in Fort Worth. Many times, in his correspondence, he would pause in his outrageous assaults to remark that he and his antagonists would later discuss these differences and smile at them when they were all together in heaven. He seemed to view these controversies as a game to be played and won while on earth and as the subject matter of amiable discussion in heaven later. When Scarborough lay dying in the hospital, Norris wrote to say they would meet in heaven.[40]

Staying by the Stuff

Amid the financial crisis and doctrinal attacks, the seminary steadily continued its instructional task. Every part of the school's program was affected by the financial dilemma: faculty members were dismissed or voluntarily resigned to enter other places of service; the curriculum was reduced because of the lack of personnel and students; and the operating structures were revised to meet changing conditions. On the other hand, neither the financial problems nor the doctrinal attacks weakened the inner vitality of the school. At the end of the period of 1942, the outbreak of World War II had shattered the depression cycle of the 1930s, presaging a brighter day for the school.

Losses of Faculty and Students

The loss of faculty personnel in all three schools during this period was critical. Some capable men and women left voluntarily to accept other posts of service. President Scarborough called it "cutting blood" when he was forced to release teachers because of the budget restrictions.

The School of Theology lost many able teachers. W. R. White resigned in May, 1927, to accept a pastorate. He went on to a distinguished career as pastor, editor with the Sunday School Board, and educator. He retired as president of Baylor University in 1961. On January 26, 1932, W. H. Knight accepted a pastorate in Atlanta, Georgia. He served as pastor of some of the oustanding churches in the South and as an evangelist. During the last decade of his life, he was executive secretary-treasurer of the Louisiana Baptist Convention.[41]

H. E. Dana, one of the foremost New Testament scholars among Southern Baptists, accepted the presidency of Central Baptist Theological Seminary, Kansas City, Kansas, on May 29, 1938. He was the author of fifteen scholarly books and numerous articles in various periodicals. His students at Southwestern Seminary never forgot his vivid historical re-creation of New Testament events. Two of his lectures were particularly memorable. Philemon became a living person as Dana utilized the known historical background and geography of the New Testament period to detail how Onesimus made the journey to Rome and returned to Philemon as a Christian brother. Dana's story of the conversion of James, the half brother of Jesus, closed with a picture of the unbelieving James working at the carpenter's bench where he and Jesus had labored side by side in earlier years. As James tarried, he heard the familiar voice of One who had risen from the dead, and he turned to fall at the feet of Jesus, now his Lord. Dana's death in 1945 was a severe loss to Southern Baptists and all New Testament scholars.[42]

A group of young teachers was added to the theological faculty as the depression declined. Baker James Cauthen, a graduate of Baylor and Southwestern, became missions professor in 1935. He resigned in 1939 to become a missionary to China during the Japanese war. Later he rendered distinguished service as executive secretary of the Foreign Mission Board. Stewart A. Newman, a graduate of Hardin-Simmons University and Southwestern, was added to the faculty in 1936 to teach philosophy of religion; and Robert T. Daniel, a graduate of Mercer University, Texas Christian University, and Southwestern, began his teaching in Old Testament in the following year. In 1937, T. B. Maston was shown as teaching in both the School of Religious Education and the School of Theology. He would transfer completely to the latter school in 1944. Ray Summers, a graduate of Baylor and Southwestern, began his teaching in 1938 in the field of New Testament. Jesse J. Northcutt, a graduate of Oklahoma Baptist University and Southwestern, began teaching in theology and New Testament in 1939; and Frank K. Means, trained in the same institutions, was added in that year to teach missions. In 1942, just at the end of this period, Robert A. Baker, a graduate of Baylor and Southwestern, began teaching in church history and Greek.

The faculty of the School of Religious Education also underwent changes in this period. J. M. Price gave a dismal résumé of the effect of the depression on the faculty and curriculum of the school. He wrote:

> During the depression it was necessary to reduce the staff and consequently the courses. At one time there were only two regular teachers, two part-time temporary teachers, and two student assistants. The Kindergarten Department was dropped, Elementary and Adolescent

Education combined with Administration, Journalism with Education Arts
(set up in 1927), and Student Work with Social Work. Departments were
reduced from seven to four, courses from 48 to 32, the enrollment to 92,
and only 17 were in the graduating class.[43]

William L. Howse, a gifted graduate of Union and Baylor universities
and Southwestern, began teaching in 1932 in the area of administration
of religious education. In the following year, Floy Barnard, a graduate of
Colorado College of Education and Southwestern, joined the faculty to
teach educational arts. Other teachers were used on a part-time basis or
for a short time because of the financial stringency. These included
W. Forbes Yarborough, Courts Redford, Nane Starnes, Vella Jane Burch,
Ivyloy Bishop, A. V. Washburn, Mrs. W. R. Lambert, Anne Laseter,
Mrs. T. B. Maston, Mary Ellen Caver, Marie Thurman, Floyd Hawkins,
Ruby Addison, Gracia Halsted, Mrs. H. R. Bumpas, Mrs. Harris Shinn,
Miller Mikell, Mrs. Ira Prosser, Mrs. W. L. Howse, Virginia Ely, Mrs.
Tillman Newton, Mrs. William Oakes, Mrs. Sue Wright, Hazel Moseley,
Bertha Mitchell, Mrs. Orabelle Jones, Mrs. Lake Pylant, and Lewis A.
Myers. Myers had served as publicity director for the seminary, in
addition to his class work, and when he resigned on April 2, 1930, the
publicity program of the school disappeared. *The Southwestern Evangel,*
which he helped edit, was discontinued in June, 1931. The faculty
arranged to publish their book reviews in the *Baptist Standard* of Texas.[44]

The School of Sacred Music sustained a substantial loss in the
resignation of B. B. McKinney on May 23, 1930. His outstanding career
thereafter led him from an extensive ministry in the churches to a
musical editorship at the Sunday School Board in 1935 and to the
headship of the new Department of Church Music at the board in 1941.
He was the author of the words and music for 149 gospel hymns and
songs and of the music alone for 114 texts by others.[45] In 1933, E. L.
Carnett resigned from the music faculty but returned in 1945, as will be
mentioned hereafter.

The lack of faculty personnel often necessitated the use of temporary
music faculty. The catalogues showed such service for short periods by
J. Frank Cheek, W. B. Moore, John Josey, Mrs. L. R. Elliott, Paul H.
Medsker, Mr. and Mrs. Carlyle Bennett, Ruth Mitchell, Lake Pylant,
Mrs. Thomas Patterson, Albert Luper, Carroll Gillis, Raymond Culp, Ira
Prosser, Wayne Dunlap, and Ruth Mulkey. W. W. Barnes from the School
of Theology taught hymnology in this school after 1938 when Albert
Venting resigned.

In the Woman's Missionary Training School, Mrs. W. B. McGarity was replaced in 1932 by Mrs. Minnie R. Shepherd, who served one year. Mrs. W. A. Johnson succeeded her in 1933 and after 1935 was a teacher in the School of Religious Education.

It was ironic that just at the time the new Cowden Hall was erected and classroom space was available, the enrollment began to decline because of the financial crisis. In 1926, the administration and faculty moved into the new facilities in Cowden Hall for classes, offices, chapel, and other functions. Dormitory students in Fort Worth Hall no longer chafed as music students practiced vocally or on their instruments in the building far across the campus. In 1926, the old frame chapel building which had been located just east of Fort Worth Hall was given to the Gambrell Street Baptist Church for her worship services.

The student enrollment decreased from an average of 643 in the 1920s to 466 in the 1930s. Graduates averaged 89 each year in the former decade and 58 in the latter. Despite this decrease, this school had a huge enrollment for a seminary. The two new buildings on the campus by no means swallowed up the smaller enrollment, but they served to relieve the problem of crowding and provided space for future growth. It was good that they did, for the seminary would not add to its facilities for two more decades.

The quality of the training received during the 1930s can be glimpsed by noting some of the leaders graduating during this decade, such as E. D. Head, Homer Lindsay, J. D. Brannon, W. D. Wyatt, Helen Bagby, Robert Ricketson, Frank W. Patterson, Ben M. David, Buford L. Nichols, Baker James Cauthen, W. Forbes Yarborough, W. J. Carswell, J. D. Grey, R. E. Naylor, T. W. Patterson, Nane Starnes, Carl A. Clark, G. Kearnie Keegan, Rogers M. Smith, Jesse Northcutt, Ray Summers, Lee Gallman, Frank K. Means, Franklin M. Segler, George Humphrey, S. A. Newman, and Robert Preston Taylor, to name but a few.

Revisions in Structure and Curriculum

In 1927, after a lengthy discussion, the faculty decided to phase out the Practical Work Department.[46] This was not done because there was a paucity of practical work being accomplished but, on the contrary, the widespread practical involvements of the students made it most difficult to administer this kind of program. The three schools endeavored to provide supervision separately after 1927, but on April 4, 1930, it was decided that all formal supervision of this work should be discontinued.[47]

Another important change became effective in the fall term of 1927. The school had operated on a quarterly basis from its beginning, but by faculty vote the school year was divided into two semesters and a summer term.[48]

In the spring of 1928, the Faculty Council was enlarged by including all members of the faculty holding the rank of professor or associate professor. The librarian was added later.[49]

A significant revision in the structure of the seminary occurred on November 27, 1934, when the Faculty Council voted to integrate the instruction and degree programs of the Woman's Missionary Training School into the regular seminary curriculum. Upon the suggestion of President Scarborough, the faculty made a thorough study of the matter and recommended to the Advisory Board of the Woman's Missionary Union of the South that the curriculum of the women's training school be absorbed principally into the Department of Administration of the School of Religious Education and that separate diplomas and degrees in missions be discontinued. One reason for this change was that these degrees in missions were not recognized by the educational institutions of the United States, while other seminary degrees were. It was felt that a new curriculum and a standard degree would be of much more value than an unrecognized missions degree.[50]

Other faculty recommendations to the Woman's Missionary Union suggested that the superintendent of the training school begin supervising all women in the seminary, that courses in domestic science and home nursing be discontinued, and that every woman enrolled in the seminary be required to take the two courses describing the history and operation of the Woman's Missionary Union. The Advisory Board of the union adopted these recommendations, and the training school curriculum was merged into that of the three schools.

Many additional revisions brought the internal organization of the school closer to its modern appearance. It will be possible here to include only a brief résumé of the activity reflected in the minutes of the faculty during this period. A stronger committee for advanced work was structured. On October 11, 1926, the Faculty Council voted to form a Graduate Committee consisting of three members of the theology faculty, two of the religious education faculty, and any professor under whom a graduate student was taking his work. A Graduate Council was formed on May 27, 1939, consisting of all professors and associate professors in those departments where Th.D. and D.R.E. students were enrolled, and all graduate matters were regularly referred to this council. It will be seen that this overlapped the work of the earlier Graduate Committee, resulting later in the organization by each individual school of its own Graduate Committee.

The nomenclature of diplomas and degrees was changed. In 1927, it was voted that the certificate, which had been awarded those without high school diplomas, would be discontinued and that diplomas would be given to those without the necessary educational background to work for degrees.[51] Theses for the Th.M. degree were discontinued in 1939.[52] A new department in the School of Theology known as Philosophy of Religion and Historical Theology was structured in 1939 to utilize the expertise of S. A. Newman.[53]

An effort was made to require all students to enter into a program of physical education to guard their health.[54] Serious consideration was given to offering a Ph.D. degree instead of the Th.D.[55] A permanent summer school curriculum was adopted.[56] T. B. Maston gradually moved from the School of Religious Education to the School of Theology, beginning about 1937, and his courses in social ethics were soon approved as a department of graduate work in theology.[57] On June 1, 1937, the office of registrar was separated from that of business manager, and L. R. Elliott became registrar. C. M. King remained as business manager.[58] Night classes and extension work were utilized as an adjunct to day classes.[59] A Christian Workers' Normal School began in February, 1927, but became a casualty of the depression. The Stella Ross awards for outstanding academic achievement were initiated in May, 1929.[60] The students petitioned the faculty to use caps and gowns at the graduation, but a split vote delayed this for a decade.[61] At the close of the period, the faculty was seeking ways to provide medical facilities and hospitalization insurance for the students, but this was postponed.[62]

Student organizations began to flourish as the depression slowly declined. In the fall of 1939, several student wives met to consider the need for an organization which would offer the opportunity for fellowship with other wives and for discussion of problems that were of major concern to wives of preachers, religious educators, and musicians. After the faculty approved the formation of this organization, the name "Metochai" was chosen by its members and Mrs. C. Murray (Willene Short) Fuquay was elected its first president.[63] For over forty years this organization has provided fellowship and information for student wives.

The Student Council was formally structured in this period. On September 17, 1940, the faculty approved the reorganization of this body. The purpose of the council was fourfold: to build a unified spirit among all the students, to give form to student opinion and serve as the official voice of the student body to the faculty in matters of general student interest, to promote the work of the Baptist Student Union on the campus, and to correlate all extracurricular activities. These activities included the developing of a student calendar of activities, fostering recreational and social programs, unifying mission activities and devotional services, and cooperating with the faculty in arranging occasional chapel programs.

The council included one elected representative from each of the three schools. A faculty representative selected by the Faculty Council served as an adviser. The presidents of the following organizations on the campus formed the Student Council: the Ministerial Alliance, the Volunteer Band, the Young Woman's Auxiliary, the Religious Education Club, the Music Club, Metochai, and the superintendent of the downtown mission work.[64]

The faculty minutes reflected the entrance of the United States into World War II on December 7, 1941. Numerous exceptions of various kinds to seminary regulations were made to allow young men who were leaving to join the armed forces as combatants or chaplains to make a hasty departure. Coming up for discussion on several occasions were resolutions asking for the deferral of young men who were vocational music and education ministers.[65]

When the Social Security system was being developed, the faculty discussed many aspects of how it would apply to ordained and unordained faculty members. A resolution was passed urging the Southern Baptist Convention to provide some form of denominational social security for unordained denominational workers in Southern Baptist life.[66]

The revived interest in combating the liquor traffic in the early 1940s led the faculty to encourage students to attend a prohibition rally for young people to be held in Austin on February 18, 1941.[67] Evidently some of the faculty also attended this rally, for the minutes stated that the regular faculty meeting of February 18 was not held because of the prohibition rally in Austin.

A small step was taken toward the admission of Negro preachers to seminary classes. For some years, the faculty had accepted diploma credit for work done at Bishop College, Dallas, a Baptist-oriented Negro school. Without giving a reason for the action, the faculty voted on May 6, 1941, that this program be discontinued and that night classes for Negro preachers be offered at the seminary instead.

Off and on during the decade of the 1930s, the faculty discussed the question of what to do with portraits of retired faculty members. This was probably triggered initially when A. H. Newman, who had taught at the seminary before its corporate beginning and continued until 1913, offered to donate his portrait to the school. The faculty cordially accepted the gift.[68] It was presented formally during the celebration of the twenty-fifth anniversary of the seminary in March, 1932. After occasional discussion, the faculty voted in 1939 that a teacher could have his portrait displayed at the school after he had served twenty-five years or more.[69] Two years later, it was voted to secure the portraits of J. B. Gambrell, Jeff D. Ray, B. A. Copass, and J. W. Crowder "for suitable preservation in the Seminary."[70]

Much of the faculty's time was spent during this period in providing numerous conferences and workshops—theological, educational, and musical—for the enrichment of the students, as well as inviting outstanding leaders for the chapel and lectures.[71] In 1927, faculty wives, women of the administration and faculty, and a few other ladies organized the Seminary Woman's Club. Mrs. L. R. Scarborough was its first president. It has flourished to the present, providing opportunities for fellowship, inspiration, information, and service for the talented faculty wives. A list of its presidents may be found in the Appendix.

Finally, in this period the faculty moved toward the accreditation of the School of Theology. President Scarborough had previously ignored the need for theological accreditation, but this was called forcibly to his attention when doctoral graduates of the seminary were told by Baptist universities that they could not be employed as teachers unless their degrees were accredited. Southwestern Seminary had neither the national accreditation offered by the American Association of Theological Schools nor the regional accreditation which provided the standards for schools and universities. The very practical mind of Scarborough quickly recognized the advantages of accreditation when this situation was called to his attention. On January 23, 1940, the faculty voted to investigate the question of membership in the national accrediting body. The process was lengthy. On March 12, 1940, the school applied for membership, and on February 25, 1941, the completed schedules were mailed to the association. In reply, the association named several problems, including the difficulty of attempting to accredit only the School of Theology when it was organically related to the other two schools which were not applying for accreditation; the need for the seminary to adopt degree nomenclatures similar to those in other seminaries; the large amount of correspondence work of the school; the teaching of both college and noncollege students in the same classes; the enrollment of more noncollege students than the percentage approved by the association; and the financial stability of the school. Undeterred by these difficult problems, the faculty voted on April 21, 1942, that an effort be made to solve the difficulties named by the associations so that accreditation could be granted.

Occasionally the minutes of the faculty meetings detail some minor event that must have been purposely included to provide an in-house note of humor. For example, one of the problems of the seminary classes before the 1940s was the lack of a cooling system. Windows in the basement of Cowden Hall, where most classes were held, were small; and almost every professor felt constrained to leave his classroom door open with the hope of receiving some cross ventilation from whatever breeze might be stirring. As a result, if one were to sit in the back of a class by a door, he could usually hear the professor across the hall or in the next classroom much more clearly than he could hear his own teacher. Professor E. L. Carlson had a high, penetrating voice, which he exercised with much enthusiasm in teaching Old Testament. It was a standing joke among the faculty that until he got the children of Israel away from Mount Sinai, the teachers in nearby classrooms might just as well mark time or close their doors. When the theological faculty met on October 7, 1941, long before Carlson was able to transport Israel beyond Mount Sinai, the secretary of the faculty gravely inscribed in the minutes: "Dr. Carlson reported that he was having difficulty in making himself heard in the large room in Cowden Hall." The scribe did not note the response of the faculty to this announcement, but it must have brightened what could have been a dull meeting.

Library Development

Under the leadership of L. R. Elliott, the library was beginning to make good progress. In almost every seminary catalogue during this period, he reported gifts to the collection. The library remained housed in a large room on the southeast wing of Fort Worth Hall until 1939, when it moved into more spacious quarters on the northwest wing of the women's training school building. At the end of this period in 1942, the collection numbered a few over twenty thousand volumes. There was no annual budget for the library and no regular appropriation for books. Because of the critical financial struggles during the 1930s, the principal accessions were book review copies provided by faculty members and gifts of pastors' libraries. In 1942, at the very close of this period, the first annual library budget was prepared, and the rapidly improving economic situation augured well for this important part of seminary life. [72]

The active mind of L. R. Elliott was reaching out into new directions beyond the procuring of books for the library. He desired to preserve the

records of history being made all around him. The Baptist General
Convention of Texas had on several occasions appointed committees to
preserve its history and had authorized J. M. Carroll to write the Texas
Baptist story. This was published in 1923, and his source materials were
deposited in the seminary's library. At the suggestion of George J.
Mason, treasurer of the state body, a committee of the state convention
was formed in 1933 to encourage the collection and preservation of Texas
Baptist history. Harlan J. Matthews chaired this committee, which
consisted of Alvin S. Swindell as secretary and W. W. Barnes, W. W.
Chancellor, and L. R. Elliott as other members. The library of the
seminary became the official repository for these records. In November,
1936, this history committee received an appropriation from the state
convention of three hundred dollars a year to be used in the collection
and preservation of the historical papers of the Executive Board. In that
year, Elliott edited a volume, published by the convention, commemorating the centennial of Texas independence, entitled *The Centennial Story
of Texas Baptists.* Elliott's reports to the state body year by year are found
in the convention's minutes.

Elliott was principally responsible for introducing Southern Baptists
to the use of microfilm in acquiring and preserving Baptist material.
Since Southwestern Seminary was not born until the opening years of the
twentieth century, it was impossible to purchase files of original Baptist
newspapers and other valuable material; so, Elliott determined to make
them available to library patrons by making microfilm copies. This
method also insured the preservation of older material which would
disintegrate from the ravages of time and use. As early as 1937, Elliott
had purchased a microfilm reader and was microfilming such old
newspapers as *The Texas Baptist* (1855-61), *The Texas Baptist Herald*
(1865-86), and *The Tennessee Baptist* (1847-62) and was arranging to
make copies of other older Baptist papers like the *Religious Herald* of
Virginia and the *Christian Index* of Georgia. These have been invaluable
as source material for many types of Baptist research, especially on the
graduate level. Elliott introduced this method of preserving Baptist
material to Norman W. Cox, the first executive secretary of the Southern
Baptist Convention's Historical Commission.[73]

Trustees and Administration

The board of trustees struggled constantly during this period to use its
best wisdom in the face of what seemed to be impossible financial odds.
Its personnel changed periodically, but the leadership was remarkably

stable. Five men had served as its president: J. B. Gambrell (1908-12), W. D. Harris (1912-16), O. S. Lattimore (1916-30), Forrest Smith (1930-31), and George W. Truett (1931-44). The board actively supported President Scarborough in his financial policies at a time when J. Frank Norris ridiculed every effort of the school to survive, especially poking fun at the citrus fruit investments in the Rio Grande Valley. Both trustees and administration sought funds for the school.

President Scarborough worked tirelessly to find donors for both the operating and endowment funds of the seminary. While he was engaged in a revival meeting during the early 1920s in Texarkana, Texas, J. K. Wadley, a Baptist deacon there, promised to make an annual gift of six thousand dollars to the operating expenses of the school and did so for the following decade.[74] Herbert Kokernot of San Antonio also provided three thousand dollars a year for several years.[75] Other smaller gifts were made for this purpose.

A large gift to the school came from Mr. and Mrs. W. J. Buhrman of Texarkana, Arkansas, who provided approximately $200,000 in their wills for use in the permanent endowment of the seminary.[76]

As mentioned earlier, one of the investments of endowment funds was the development of citrus fruit orchards in the Rio Grande Valley. It will be recalled that in 1929 Mr. and Mrs. T. W. Carter made a conditional gift of two hundred acres of this land. This was the beginning of a constantly enlarging investment by the seminary in developing these orchards and securing additional contiguous lands in the Valley. In 1924, George W. and Ida Bottoms had given the seminary one-half interest in some business property in Dallas. With the permission of the donors, the other half of this property was purchased by the seminary for $42,500. It was then exchanged for another thousand acres of land in the Valley.[77] It has been mentioned that part of this land was conveyed to the faculty in 1932-33 in lieu of their back salaries. President Scarborough wrote in 1938 that the seminary owned one thousand acres, most of which was in cultivation, and that the prospects for the future of this investment were bright.[78] At that time he hoped that the seminary could enlarge its holdings in this investment.

With this in mind, President Scarborough called a meeting of the local trustees in February 11, 1941, and informed them that for a good price the seminary could now purchase one hundred acres of additional land lying immediately south of the seminary orchards in the Rio Grande Valley. The trustees voted to purchase this land. On March 12, 1941, the local trustees again met on call. Scarborough said that the seminary could now buy 188 acres of land adjoining the seminary orchards on the north, and the trustees agreed to purchase this acreage also.

Despite the severe depression, the trustees began a retirement program for seminary employees in 1934. The Southern Baptist Convention had discussed this need in both the 1932 and 1933 sessions, advising that all of its agencies cooperate in arranging annuity contracts with the Southern Baptist Relief and Annuity Board, since no single agency had enough personnel to provide actuarial accuracy. On May 16, 1934, noting that the seminary had "never before faced this problem," the trustees approved a "Plan for Retirement for Teachers and Administratives," by which a teacher or member of the administrative force who had served fifteen years of consecutive service could retire at the age of seventy and must retire at age seventy-five, except by special vote of the trustees. The person so retiring would receive one-half of the salary being paid at the time of retirement. If an eligible person were to have a breakdown in health, even before reaching the age of seventy, he would also receive one-half of the salary paid at the time his health failed. In both cases, the person would be subject to increases or decreases in proportion to the other teachers in his salary class. A faculty widow would receive fifty dollars per month if she remained unmarried and had no income for reasonable support. With some alterations, this agreement was reapproved by the trustees on November 21, 1934, May 15, 1935, and May 13, 1936.

Retirement of Two Veterans

At the trustee meeting on May 14, 1942, B. A. Copass and L. R. Scarborough presented their resignations. Copass, after serving twenty-four years as head of the Department of Old Testament and Hebrew, found his waning strength inadequate to continue his teaching ministry. In his letter to the trustees, he remarked:

> This year I have stayed because your President requested me to try to finish the book on Isaiah. I have done the best I could to finish the book and it is now about ready for a publisher if I can find one.[79]

This beloved teacher did finish the book which was about his favorite prophet, Isaiah. With regret, the trustees voted to accept his retirement, and the Faculty Council honored him with a laudatory resolution and a gift. He died on January 2, 1950.

Exhausted by thirty-four years of service to the seminary, L. R. Scarborough also presented his resignation and made his farewell address to the trustees. His words had a patriarchal tone and were received with unbidden tears by his comrades of many years. He said:

In the present situation I regard it as profitable to cast eyes back over the period since, by the suggestion of Dr. Carroll and the election of the Board of Trustees and, I trust, by the will of God, I became president of the Southwestern Baptist Theological Seminary. That happened on the fifteenth of February, 1915.

I have been the Professor of Evangelism since June 1, 1908, thirty-four years. I was Acting President for a short time during the sickness of Dr. Carroll, and was associated with him in many matters touching the administration, the raising of funds, the building of Fort Worth Hall, and other matters. I have tried to handle this as a sacred trust from the Board and from the Lord for these more than twenty-seven years.

The enrollment of students in 1910, when we moved to Fort Worth, was 201. The number of the faculty was 6. The number of buildings was one. The endowment, in promissory notes from donors which proved to be good, was about $200,000.00. The annual cost of operation then was around $10,000.00 to $15,000.00. The ownership of the Seminary then was in the Texas Baptist Convention, later in ten other states among the Southern states, and in 1925 it was taken over by the Southern Baptist Convention. At that time the curriculum covered the subjects taught by a theological seminary. Later the curriculum was enlarged to include the Schools of Music and Religious Education.

Comparing the start with the present situation, we find evidences of continual favor and blessings from God and great enlargement in every direction. The enrollment now of resident students is 760, and including correspondence students is 937. We have enrolled and helped to train in these thirty-four years more than 8,000 students. The faculty now of professors, assistants, and part-time teachers is 27. The endowment now is $1,215,398.00, not including the amount we have in hand on the present endowment campaign. The prospects on the present campaign are very encouraging indeed, and the outlook for a larger endowment, through promises, wills, etc., gives us a fine state of optimism concerning the future of the Seminary. The operating expense for this past year, including all, was $132,690.00.

Concerning our noble force of teachers and administrators, I cannot say too much. Their scholarship, their love for the Seminary, their devotion to their tasks, their cooperation with me in helping to construct this great Seminary through the years, their sacrifices in times of financial depression, their loyalty to the fundamentals of faith, their wide influence in the practical things in building the Kingdom of God, their consecration of character, their spirit of constant unity and beautiful willingness to serve and sacrifice, make a romantic story that when known in detail, as I know it, reminds one of the Acts of the Apostles. They are independent, trained, thinking men and women. In all details we have not thought absolutely together, but we have always beautifully worked together, and present to you a force of scholarly teachers and experienced administrators of mighty power as the builders of your Seminary. I could tell you much of my devotion to and appreciation of them. I am turning them over to you with my most hearty recommendation, valuation and appreciation. They have been and are vital factors in making the Seminary you now have and will be greatly useful in making it greater and better.

I cannot tell you how great a wrench to my soul it has been and is to separate myself from this noble band. When the vital blood stream of one's soul flows into a great institution, with its operation, struggles and triumphs, it is no small task to turn the currents of that blood stream in another direction. Except for the necessity brought on by declining strength and age, a deep sense that the Seminary should have the highest service and the strongest vitalities of a strong leader, the hope of rendering further service in another direction for the dear Seminary, and for the consciousness that I am following the leadership of the Divine Spirit, I could not be strong enough to do what I am doing today.

I also wish to express my inexpressible gratitude and appreciation to this Board of Trustees for your long, tender support, prayers, and full-length cooperation in the work of trying to guide the Seminary to success. Your remarkable cooperation in unity and love has made possible the success that we have had. I hold it as one of the cherished memories of life. Through all these twenty-seven years of labors together we have been so guided to see alike that in all the plans and proposals for the guidance of the Seminary there has never been a contrary vote. I am indebted more than I can ever say to the presidents of this Board, and especially to the present president, Dr. George W. Truett, during his long period of service, for their love and cooperation, as I am to each and all the members, who have been so gracious and cooperative.

I congratulate my successor, whosoever he will be in the unfolding will of God, on having such a Board of Trustees and such a faculty and administrative force to stand by him and pray for him and love him into further great successes for this institution.

President Scarborough then enunciated the great principles upon which the seminary had been built: the lordship of Jesus Christ, the missionary spirit, the centrality of the churches, the freedom and competency of each soul, cooperation in the building of the kingdom of God, and warmhearted continuing evangelism. He closed:

> I now hand back to you the trust you gave me more than a quarter of a century ago. This institution will continue to be in my vital blood stream the rest of the days of this life and through eternity.[80]

At his request, the trustees voted that President Scarborough and his wife might live near the seminary's orchards in the Rio Grande Valley and, without salary, supervise the daily operations.

President Scarborough's work as an administrator was of a high quality despite unusual difficulties; as a teacher he was unsurpassed in inspiring his students to make personal soul-winning the center of their ministries. He set the example. Herschel H. Hobbs recalled an experience of Scarborough's earnest spirit.

One summer he preached a revival in a rural church out from Mineral Wells. During that time he sought to win a lost man to Christ, but with no visible results. The following winter about eleven o'clock one night he received a phone call from the man. He was under deep conviction, and he asked Dr. Scarborough if he would come immediately to his home. The roads were covered with snow and ice on a bitterly cold night.

Without a moment's hesitation Scarborough said that he would be there as soon as he could drive to his home. It was over a fifty-mile drive, part of it over country roads. When he arrived about 2:30 a.m. he found the man up and waiting for him. In a short time the man received Christ as his Savior.

Then the man said, "I suppose you have wondered why I would ask you to make this long drive at night in this weather and over such roads." Dr. Scarborough replied, "Yes, I have." Then the man said, "When you talked with me last summer, I wondered if you really cared about me and if what you were telling me was real. Had you told me you would come when the weather was warmer and the roads were clear, you could as well forget the whole thing. But when you came tonight, I knew that you really cared about me and that your words to me were real."

The perceptive Hobbs remarked: "I imagine that on his return drive to Fort Worth the weather was warm and the roads seemed clear—made so by the 'Chair of Fire.'"[81]

One of the last official acts of President Scarborough before his own retirement was to present to the school during a chapel program the portraits of Professors Jeff D. Ray, J. W. Crowder, B. A. Copass, and J. B. Gambrell on December 31, 1941. The first three, who were still living, responded to the tender words of Scarborough.[82]

At the May commencement in 1942, the portrait of President Scarborough was formally presented to the school in "a most touching and fitting service." He and his wife returned with rejoicing to the celebration in the chapel on November 12, 1943, when the last debt of the seminary was retired.

His death occurred on April 10, 1945, and Baptist leaders everywhere mourned his passing. Next to that of B. H. Carroll, his was the greatest contribution of any person to the life of Southwestern Baptist Theological Seminary.[83]

His faculty recognized his stature. Those who had worked most closely with him, often in trying times and unpleasant experiences, wrote about him:

As President of the Seminary, he was faithful and energetic. He carried the whole institution on his heart. He loved it in its entirety, and gave painstaking attention to the smallest detail. He could see the Seminary in its large significance to the Kingdom of God, as well as small matters of daily routine. He believed in its divine origin and its divine preservation.

His love for the Seminary was such that he was its father and big brother, as well as its President.

He had a clear vision of the importance of other agencies in the Kingdom of God. He loved all the work of his Baptist people, as well as the Seminary. His devotion to the work of the Tarrant County Association, the Baptist General Convention of Texas, the Southern Baptist Convention, and the Baptist World Alliance, was animated by the same love for the Kingdom of God as kindled his devotion to the Seminary. Because of this world view, his brethren in all of these four organizations called on him much and often for service in the Lord's work. He responded to any of these calls with holy enthusiasm and apostolic energy. None of us who knew him through the years of his activity can recall many times when he said "No" to such calls for service. He loved the Lord's work everywhere. His devotion to Christ is the explanation of his service in the larger denominational connections, and of his strong emphasis on Baptist cooperation. He believed in building the denomination because he believed that thereby the Saviorhood and Lordship of Jesus Christ would be extended among men.

He was a flaming evangelist and a compassionate soul-winner. It was not his habit to permit personal inconvenience to stand in the way when any opportunity for private soul winning or public evangelism presented itself. None of us can ever forget his lifetime emphasis on going with Christ after the lost. He believed that every disciple should be endued to win with power from on high.

As a part of this same consecration to the work of Christ he loved his preacher brethren and the Lord's people everywhere. He loved the uneducated and lowly brother as well as the brother of high degree. The memories of his colleagues are crowded with instances of this expression of his Christian devotion. For this reason the common people heard him gladly.

His life was intensely devoted to the service of Jesus Christ. He was not wont to hesitate at any sacrifice if he could serve his Lord. For nearly half a century he drove himself under this impelling motive with a mental abandon and an output of physical energy that was the constant wonder of his fellow laborers. Few men have expended more physical energy or shown more consecrated devotion of heart to the cause of Christ.[84]

Notes

1. Robertson, p. 214.

2. Scarborough, *Modern School*, pp. 113-14.

3. For a more extended discussion of this see Baker, *Southern Baptist Convention*, pp. 308-18.

4. Ibid., p. 404.

5. Ibid., pp. 400-409.

6. Scarborough, *Modern School*, p. 114.

7. *Annual*, SBC, 1927, p. 104.

8. Ibid., p. 101.

9. *Minutes of Executive Committee*, SBC, 1 June 1927, p. 5. See also *Annual*, SBC, 1927, pp. 42-43.

10. *Annual*, SBC, 1928, p. 30.

11. Ibid., pp. 40-41.

12. Ibid., pp. 59-60.

13. Trustee Minutes, 17 May 1928.

14. Ibid., 14 November 1928.

15. Ibid., 14 November 1928, 9 May 1929, and 25 May 1929.

16. *Annual*, SBC, 1929, p. 27.

17. Ibid., pp. 69-70.

18. Ibid., pp. 73-75.

19. *Minutes of Executive Committee*, SBC, 5 March 1931.

20. *Annual*, SBC, 1929, p. 73.

21. *Minutes of Executive Committee*, SBC, 5-6 March 1929, p. 65.

22. Ibid., p. 76.

23. Ibid., p. 75.

24. Trustee Minutes of the Executive Committee, 14 January 1930; and Trustee Minutes, 14 May 1930.

25. Trustee Minutes, 14 May 1930.

26. Gaines S. Dobbins, *Great Teachers Make a Difference* (Nashville: Broadman Press, 1965), p. 44.

27. *Minutes of Executive Committee*, SBC, 25 September 1929, p. 75.

28. *Annual*, SBC, 1931, p. 79.

29. *Minutes of Executive Committee*, SBC, 10 June 1931, pp. 124-25.

30. *Annual*, SBC, 1932, p. 114.

31. Ibid., 1933, pp. 81-82, see also p. 58.

32. Ibid., 1944, p. 38.

33. Ibid., 1937, p. 93.

34. Ibid., 1925, p. 76.

35. For a discussion of the background of this confession see James E. Carter, "The Southern Baptist Convention and Confessions of Faith 1845-1945" (Th.D. dissertation, Southwestern Baptist Theological Seminary, 1964), pp. 88-172.

36. *Annual*, SBC, 1926, p. 18.

37. Trustee Minutes, 12 May 1926.

38. *Annual*, SBC, 1926, p. 98.

39. Ibid., 1927, pp. 98 and 105.

40. Louis Entzminger, *The J. Frank Norris I Have Known for Thirty-Four Years* (n.p.: By the author, n.d.), pp. 180-82. See also letters of Norris, 1921-33, in Scarborough Collection.

41. See *Encyclopedia*, II:754 for his biography.

42. Ibid., I:346.

43. J. M. Price, "School of Religious Education," Price Collection, Fleming Library, Southwestern Baptist Theological Seminary, Fort Worth, Texas. (Typewritten manuscript.)

44. Faculty Minutes, 26 September 1930 and 30 December 1930.

45. See *Encyclopedia*, II:842-43 for his biography.

46. Faculty Minutes, 17 March 1927.

47. Ibid., 9 March 1928, 21 March 1928, and 4 April 1930.

48. Ibid., 25 March 1927. See also Southwestern *Catalogue*, 1926-27, p. 19.

49. Faculty Minutes, 24 February 1928 and 29 March 1939.

50. Ibid., 3 March 1932 and 11 March 1932.

51. Ibid., 9 April 1927.

52. Ibid., 29 March 1939.

53. Ibid., 27 January 1939.

54. Ibid., 24 February 1928.

55. Ibid., 28 January 1929.

56. Ibid., 24 January 1934 and 19 December 1939.

57. Ibid., 13 January 1937.

58. L. R. Elliott, "Current Events in the Life of the Southwestern Baptist Theological Seminary," I:47. This material consists of sixteen volumes of newspaper clippings and occasional notes kept by Elliott from 1932 to 1966 (hereafter cited as *Scrapbook*). Fleming Library, Southwestern Baptist Theological Seminary, Fort Worth, Texas.

59. Faculty Minutes, 12 March 1940 and 10 May 1940.

60. Ibid., 25 May 1929.

61. Ibid., 7 March 1930.

62. Ibid., 25 February 1941 and 20 January 1942.

63. Ibid., 9 April 1940. See also *Metochai Yearbook*, 1980-81, Fleming Library, Southwestern Baptist Theological Seminary, Fort Worth, Texas.

64. Faculty Minutes, 17 September 1940.

65. Ibid., 13 January 1942.

66. Ibid., 9 December 1941.

67. Ibid., 4 January 1941.

68. Ibid., 27 October 1931 and 18 December 1931.

69. Ibid., 29 March 1939 and 5 May 1939.

70. Ibid., 18 November 1941.

71. For example see ibid., 22 May 1931, 29 March 1939, 1 November 1940, and 18 February 1941.

72. Keith C. Wills, "Leslie Robinson Elliott, Librarian of Vision," *Southwestern Journal of Theology,* 2nd ser., 11 (Spring 1969):123-30. See also Mrs. Leslie R. Elliott, *From Faith to Fact* (n.p.: By the author, n.d. [probably 1968 at Fort Worth, Texas]).

73. Keith C. Wills, "Librarian L. R. Elliott and Baptist History," *Baptist History and Heritage* 6 (July 1971):156-63.

74. Scarborough, *Modern School*, p. 125.

75. Ibid.

76. Ibid., pp. 124-25.

77. Ibid., pp. 121 ff.

78. Ibid., pp. 122-23.

79. Trustee Minutes, 14 May 1942.

80. Ibid.

81. Herschel H. Hobbs to Robert A. Baker, 1 August 1981. On file in Fleming Library, Southwestern Baptist Theological Seminary, Fort Worth, Texas.

82. Elliott, *Scrapbook*, I:84-91.

83. See J. W. Bruner, "A Great Leader Called Home," *Standard*, 19 April 1945, pp. 1-2, and editorial, p. 3. Also see editorial in *Standard*, 26 April 1945, p. 1.

84. Faculty Minutes, 19 June 1945.

E. D. Head
President (1942-53)
Evangelism (1942-53)

B. H. Carroll Memorial Building
Erected 1949

J. M. Price Hall
Erected 1950

A. Donald Bell
Psychology (1951-60
and 1963-72)

Ann Bradford
Childhood Education
(1945-70)

H. C. Brown
Preaching (1947-73)

Ralph Churchill
Religious Journalism
(1944-70)

H. J. Davis
Maintenance
(1946-)

Gladys Day
Organ
(1952-78)

H. L. Drumwright, Jr.
New Testament
(1951-59; 1960-80)
Dean (1973-80)

R. Othal Feather
Educational
Administration
(1947-70)

Cal Guy
Missions (1946-82)

Joe Davis Heacock
Educational Adminis-
tration (1944-73)
Dean (1956-73)

W. Boyd Hunt
Theology (1944-
46 and 1953-)

Gracie Knowlton
Educational Arts
(1947-71)

J. W. MacGorman
New Testament
(1948-   )

James McKinney
Voice (1950-   )
Dean (1956-   )

Alpha Melton
Social Work
(1945-71)

John P. Newport
Philosophy (1952-76)
Vice-President
(1979-   )

Nannie Don Northcutt
Secretary (1947-81)

Katie Reed
Registrar
(1944-70)

Franklin Segler
Pastoral Ministry
(1951-72)

Ralph L. Smith
Old Testament
(1949-   )

Sara Thompson
Music Librarian
(1945-66)

Curtis Vaughan
New Testament
(1950-   )

Grace Wilson
Records
(1949-   )

7

A Shining New Day

The mantle of L. R. Scarborough fell upon Eldred Douglas Head, a deeply spiritual pastor, whose training and gifts made him a logical choice to be the third president of Southwestern Seminary. Born in a tiny Louisiana hamlet in Bienville Parish on November 15, 1892, he distinguished himself early as an excellent student and preacher. He earned two degrees from Baylor University and two from Southwestern Seminary. His doctoral dissertation at the seminary, a study in Greek papyri, marked him as a fine technical scholar. While yet a student at Baylor University, he taught in the academy section and from 1920 to 1932 was a professor in the Department of Bible there. He was a superb preacher, having held about a dozen pastorates before accepting the call of the First Baptist Church, Houston, Texas, in 1932. He was just completing a decade of service there when he was chosen as president of the seminary. The decision to leave the pastorate to accept this academic position was difficult for him. He was greatly loved by his people and was in constant demand as a speaker at revivals, conferences, and conventions.[1]

In many ways, the new seminary leader was of a different mold from that of Carroll and Scarborough. By nature and grace they had been aggressive, outspoken extroverts, more polemical than irenic. Head, on the other hand, while articulate and knowledgeable, was a gentle and unpretentious person who preferred to avoid noisy controveries. The world situation was also quite different when E. D. Head assumed the presidency of the seminary. The Japanese attack on Pearl Harbor on December 7, 1941, just a few months before Head accepted his new task, marked the beginning of a new era in world history. Along with many problems that war always brings to Christian institutions and the world, the sudden clamor for war supplies and manpower annihilated the economic depression of the 1930s and began a period of inflation and prosperity for America. The receipts of the seminary soon reflected this new affluence. Another distinct dissimilarity in the period of E. D. Head's presidency was the enormous increase in the size of the student body. This development was encouraging and challenging, but it strained to the limit the ability of the school to assimilate a large number of new students from widely divergent backgrounds and training.

These several factors—a new kind of leader, a more favorable economic climate, and the large influx of students unaware of the history and tradition of the school—posed a threat to the distinctive spirit which Southwestern Seminary had developed from its background. It is difficult to put a spirit into words, but from its leadership and history the seminary had developed a fourfold character. In the first place, the early financial struggles during the administrations of Presidents Carroll and Scarborough had forced the school to learn to live by faith. Southwestern Seminary had never known economic security. Carroll had begun the school on a shoestring, depending upon personal pledges of ten thousand dollars a year to operate the seminary for the first three years. Scarborough struggled with debts and deficits during every year of his presidency. A dependent faith in God in the midst of sacrifice became a way of life during these lean years.

Albert McClellen related a story told him by Ira C. Prosser, a student at the seminary during the depression days of the 1930s. Late one Saturday night, after working downtown, Ira returned to Fort Worth Hall.

> When he passed the president's office he heard someone talking, and realized that it was Dr. Scarborough at prayer. He paused to listen. Dr. Scarborough was telling the Lord, "You know these professors are yours, these students are yours. We are at the bottom of our resources. The teachers have not been paid and we are running out of food. Oh Lord, please move the hearts of the brethren to do something about our situation." Ira went on upstairs and to bed.
>
> In chapel one day the next week, the professors sat in their places with long faces, the students were quiet and Dr. Scarborough was late. Suddenly Ira heard something at the door of the little chapel. It was Dr. Scarborough coming down the aisle and talking, "Brethren, you can get your faces out of your laps. God has heard our prayers and moved the brethren. From Dallas and the Cooperative Program we have enough money to keep the seminary going. Let us sing the doxology."[2]

When Scarborough greeted new students with a friendly word during those years, he usually smiled and said, "You will have a happy hard time in the seminary." He meant all that the statement implied.

This severe financial struggle inculcated a second aspect of the Southwestern spirit. Students and faculty alike shared a common poverty. How could a student in patched clothing complain when he saw W. T. Conner lecturing in patched clothing? Perry Crouch, a graduate of the seminary in 1932, at the very depth of the financial depression, spoke at the seminary's Midwinter Conference in February, 1951, on the theme of the Southwestern spirit. He said:

> The students had no money, but neither did the faculty. Some of the most
> acute financial problems were among these consecrated, scholarly, God-
> fearing men and women of Southwestern, who without thought of quitting,
> carried on almost without salary during those difficult days. On one or two
> occasions, students took showers of food to hardship cases among students
> and faculty. We wore old clothes together. It did something for us that
> prosperity could not have done. . . . There is something about sacrifice and
> hardship that is redemptive.[3]

A part of that "something" was a deepened sense of camaraderie between
needy students and needy faculty. Each admired the other and shared a
fellowship far beyond the affection of the student for a teacher. This
became a part of the Southwestern spirit.

A third ingredient in the spirit of Southwestern was the concept of the
president and faculty concerning the nature of a theological seminary.
Carroll, Scarborough, and the faculty did not conceive of Southwestern
Seminary as an academic ivory tower in which to retire from the world for
study but saw it as a front-line bunker where students participated in the
contemporary spiritual battles. The weekly memorization of many
Scripture verses in the evangelism class of L. R. Scarborough was not an
academic exercise; it was the loading of the students' weapons for regular
use in winning people to Christ, after the example of their teacher. The
profound lectures of W. T. Conner became apologetic or polemical grist
for a student's mill. The sermon outlines submitted in the homiletics
classes were used in church or mission services in the following week.
The Sunday School principles enunciated by J. M. Price were practiced
almost before the ink had dried in the students' notebooks. Music
students made preparation for weekly services through their daily
classes in music.

The fourth component of the Southwestern spirit which had developed
by 1942 might be called a spiritual sensitivity. Evangelism and missions
were central in all of the classes. B. A. Copass seemed to prepare his
Old Testament lectures with the purpose of sending the students out for
effective service on the weekend. This was true about all the faculty.
Perry Crouch remarked:

> Many are the times I have left a class in evangelism taught by Dr.
> Scarborough, or New Testament taught by Dr. Dana, or a course in the
> atonement taught by Dr. Conner, wishing it were Saturday, so I could go to
> my church and preach the good news of the gospel of Christ. There were no
> compromises taught here. No substitutes, no uncertainties. We were taught
> that "there is no other name under heaven given among men whereby we
> must be saved."[4]

This spiritual sensitiveness to world needs by the teachers was transmitted into action. L. R. Scarborough often said in his evangelism class, "I can awaken in the middle of any night and weep over the souls of people without Christ." The students knew that this was true, for their teacher went from the classroom to practice personal soul-winning as well as to conduct sweeping revivals. After Baker James Cauthen lectured to his mission classes about the critical need for missionaries in China, he was moved to resign in 1939 from a promising career as a teacher and as the pastor of a strong church in Fort Worth to give himself to a dangerous ministry in the midst of warring China. Later, as executive secretary, he led the Foreign Mission Board to new heights in missions. This personal sensitivity permeated the student body. A large proportion of the missionaries on Southern Baptist foreign mission fields have come from Southwestern's campus because of this spirit.

But Carroll and Scarborough were gone. Gone also were the chilling winds of financial depression, and many new students were flocking to the campus. In this new atmosphere, would Southwestern still retain its spirit of a dependent faith, a warmhearted camaraderie, a zealous Christian activity, and a continuing sense of spiritual commitment?

President Head did his part well. He had been a student at Southwestern during its difficult days and had been shaped by its spirit. His first meeting with the faculty took place on July 3, 1942. Not a great deal was done, but L. R. Elliott, secretary of the faculty, added a handwritten word to the brief minutes of that meeting, which said:

> This was the first meeting of the Faculty Council over which the new president of the Seminary, Dr. E. D. Head, presided. His friendliness, humility, religious earnestness, skill in presiding and his vision won the hearts of all present. But this was only what we all expected as most of us already knew him and his qualities of heart and mind.[5]

The faculty prepared a formal inaugural program for October 13, 1942. The entire day was devoted to this service. W. W. Barnes, chairman of the theological faculty, presided, and the incomparable George W. Truett brought a powerful message to close an impressive morning service. Trustee J. B. Tidwell chaired the afternoon meeting, and President Pat M. Neff of Baylor University delivered the principal address on "Christian Citizenship." At the evening service, the new seminary president gave his inaugural address, followed by a reception in his honor. Head's message was titled "Scholarship in Leadership." It magnified the need for scholarship in leadership and described the qualities which should characterize that scholarship. These qualities he declared to be reverence, vision, compassion, and Christ centeredness.[6]

In his first message to the alumni through the *Southwestern News*,

President Head spoke of the glorious heritage of the school, the love shown by the alumni, the need for improved physical equipment, the worth of an "evangelistic and scholarly faculty," and the opportunities of the future.[7]

During his eleven years as president, E. D. Head led in some remarkable advances in the life of the seminary. For the first time in its history, the school broke the shackles of deficits and debts; it developed far-reaching organizational improvements in both the trustee and faculty structures; it courageously faced the growing needs of a new and challenging era; and it deepened and enriched the Southwestern spirit.

Breaking the Shackles

Perhaps the most significant development during this period of the seminary's history was the elimination of the great burden of debt that had inhibited its work from almost the very beginning of its life. All progress of the school had been hampered when the institution was shackled with a debt of about $500,000 and the Southern Baptist Convention owed about $6,500,000 in a decade when the nation was undergoing the most virulent financial depression in its history. Exercising a high quality of leadership and utilizing the Baptist Hundred Thousand Club and the Cooperative Program, Southern Baptists reversed the pattern of mounting deficits and debts in the 1930s, and by the time President Scarborough retired in 1942, the debt of the seminary had been slashed in half.

"Debt Free in '43"

With a strong financial surge in 1940 and 1941, the Southern Baptist Convention adopted a goal in 1942 of paying all the indebtedness of its agencies by 1943, and this was accomplished with a balance of $38,846.49.[8] It hardly seemed possible that the seminary could be freed from its remaining debt of over a quarter of a million dollars in a little more than a year after the coming of President Head, but the unusually large receipts from the Cooperative Program and the Baptist Hundred Thousand Club reduced the debt to $163,061.42 by January 1, 1942, and to $120,429.38 by the time the Convention met in May, 1943. On November 2, 1943, President Head notified the Faculty Council that the seminary had funds to pay off the remainder of its debts. A thanksgiving service was held on November 12. It was fitting that L. R. Scarborough could attend. The terrible strain of mortgaging all of the seminary's property during his feverish efforts to refinance the school's debts and the constant struggles to secure funds to keep the school operating had undoubtedly helped to undermine his strength. He was feeble when his trembling hands ignited the last note owed by the seminary, but how he must have rejoiced at the debt-free celebration as he saw his faith justified![9]

In the following spring, the trustees faced an unusual problem: How should the seminary invest the operating profit of more than $100,000 reported for that year? These funds were invested with the Texas Baptist Foundation, as were similar surplus funds in the following year. This pleasant problem did not persist, however, for a burgeoning student body, additional buildings for the campus, escalating inflation, and an enlarged and better-paid faculty and staff rapidly increased the budget, and the threats of operating losses began to appear.[10] On November 28, 1951, President Head reported to the trustees that the proposed budget for the next year showed a substantial deficit and said that it would be difficult to trim down the deficit without vitally affecting the work of the institution. From this time until the end of Head's administration, each year brought the problem of keeping the budget balanced. To do this, some of the peripheral programs of the seminary were trimmed, various plans for enlarging the endowment were developed, and appeals were made to the Executive Committee of the Southern Baptist Convention to increase the school's allocation for operating expenses. A particular point of appeal concerned the operation of the women's training school, which was not receiving an allocation from the Convention as was the training school at the Louisville seminary. The trustees urged the Executive Committee to work out some equitable formula for the distribution of funds based upon the size of the student bodies at the several seminaries.[11] It should be added, however, that by careful management the trustees were able to avoid operating deficits. In his last report to the Convention in 1953, President Head noted that there was an operating surplus for the year of $5,849.26.[12] Each year, the president expressed his gratitude to the women of Texas who provided over 90 percent of the gifts for the scholarship funds of the women's training school.[13]

Improving the Campus

The buildings, cottages, and apartments on and adjacent to the campus had long been neglected because of insufficient finances.

Beginning in 1945, a program was instituted to paint and repair these properties within and without. All available space in Fort Worth Hall was converted into bedrooms to care for students. The old dining room in Fort Worth Hall was renovated and made into a cafeteria in order to serve a larger number of students.[14] Through gifts from the Woman's Missionary Union of Texas, a number of needed improvements were made in the women's building. The nursery was provided with additional equipment, and plans were made to erect a permanent nursery building when funds were available.[15] New pianos were provided for Cowden Hall, and the organ was renovated.[16] The old water tower just to the south of Fort Worth Hall, a landmark to older students, was removed.[17] The street just north of Broadus was converted into one of the principal east-west thoroughfares, and its name was changed from Kellis to Seminary Drive.

Both the Southern Baptist Covention and the seminary named committees to study the building needs of the campus. The seminary committee reported on November 28, 1950, that two immediate priorities were the modernization of the older buildings at an estimated cost of $500,000 and the construction of additional student-housing units at an estimated cost of $500,000. Future needs were listed as a gymnasium, an infirmary, quarters for furloughed missionaries, and a nursery building. This report contained a recommendation that the seminary plan to attack the two immediate priorities—the modernization of the older buildings and the construction of additional student-housing units—as soon as adequate reserve funds were available and to establish the policy of trying to purchase any property immediately adjacent to the campus whenever it was for sale.[18] These proposals pointed to the direction the seminary would take in trying to meet its housing needs.

Additional committees were named to study the capital needs.[19] On June 17, 1952, William Fleming reported that the city of Fort Worth might consider selling to the seminary the vacant property just north of the campus between James Avenue and the Santa Fe Railroad.

The adoption of new bylaws provided for a standing committee on buildings and grounds. On March 11, 1953, this committee recommended that improvements be made in Fort Worth Hall, Cowden Hall, and the women's building and that an architect be employed to study the possibility of a major renovation of Fort Worth Hall. On May 7, 1953, the trustees approved the architect's proposed refurbishing of Fort Worth Hall at a cost not to exceed $250,000. Meanwhile, William Fleming reported that $33,173 had been spent in the repair of seventeen apartments and that about $5,000 more would be needed to improve three additional houses.[20]

Two Significant Buildings

In addition to the improvement of the property of the seminary, the trustees authorized the erection of the first two new buildings on the campus since Cowden Music Hall was completed in 1926. The new buildings were badly needed. It is difficult to conceive how over one thousand students, thirty-one full-time faculty members, about a dozen staff members of the administrative force, and many teaching fellows and secretaries from all three schools of the seminary could have been crammed into one floor of Fort Worth Hall and the basement and a part of the first floor of Cowden Hall for classrooms and offices, but this was the case in 1945.

The inspiration for the first of these buildings occurred in July, 1944. George W. Truett, a trustee of the seminary for over thirty years, distinguished world leader, and pastor of the First Baptist Church, Dallas, died in that month after a long illness. He was especially beloved by Southwestern Seminary, where he had delivered more sermons and lecture series than any other leader outside the seminary. As chairman of the seminary's board of trustees since May 13, 1931, he had lavished upon the school his love and leadership during a critical period. As G. Kearnie Keegan, president of the alumni of the seminary, sat at the funeral service and watched thousands of mourning friends file past the casket of this outstanding man, his soul was struck with the conviction that this great life should be memorialized on the campus of the school which he had loved so deeply. Sitting next to Keegan was Herschel H. Hobbs, to whom he whispered his vision of a memorial chapel at Southwestern to honor Truett. Hobbs agreed and urged Keegan, as president of Southwestern's alumni, to assume the leadership and promptly begin this worthy undertaking.[21]

The original plan called for the raising of $500,000 for this memorial.[22] However, William Fleming, a deacon in Broadway Baptist Church, Fort Worth, proposed to give $250,000 if other friends of the seminary would raise the $500,000.[23] The final plan of the building was enlarged to include a rotunda and an auditorium in the center as a memorial to George W. Truett, an administration wing on the west as a memorial to L. R. Scarborough, and a library wing on the east. This east wing was later named Fleming Library in recognition of the large gift of Fleming.

In the midst of the active campaign to raise funds for this building, word came of the death of Lee Rutland Scarborough on April 10, 1945. His funeral was held in the chapel of Cowden Hall, where he had so often taught huge classes in evangelism. From across the world came words of love and appreciation for the man who loomed so large in the story of Southwestern.[24]

By March 10, 1948, the Memorial Building Fund had reached $634,427.05 which, with allocations from the Southern Baptist Convention for capital needs, exceeded the campaign goal of $750,000.00.[25] Bids were taken on the proposed building, and on April 2 the trustees authorized the acceptance of the lowest bid. The contractors promptly set up offices and equipment on the grounds. Groundbreaking ceremonies were observed on May 7, immediately following the spring commencement, with Mrs. George W. Truett, Mrs. L. R. Scarborough, William Fleming, and President Head wielding the shovels.[26] The building was occupied in the fall of 1949. The new Truett Memorial Auditorium provided seating for approximately fifteen hundred students. Scarborough Hall, the west wing of the building, housed the registrar, business offices, the president's suite, offices for faculty members, and four classrooms. The library collection was moved from the cramped quarters in the women's building to the glistening three-story Fleming Library wing to the east of the Truett Memorial Auditorium.[27]

Simultaneous with the campaign for the Memorial Building was an effort, initiated by J. M. Price, the director of the School of Religious Education, to raise funds for a specialized building for the teaching of religious education. Price later wrote:

> The need had been felt for some time since the class in Religious Dramatics met in the basement of the Woman's Building, now Barnard Hall; the class in Recreation on the campus; and the Kindergarten off the campus.[28]

The first reference to this project was found in the correspondence of J. M. Price. Early in April, 1945, he and the religious education faculty had a conference with President Head; J. Howard Williams, chairman of the Executive Committee of the Southern Baptist Convention; W. R. White, chairman of the Special Gifts Committee for the Truett-Scarborough Memorial Building; and Mrs. B. A. Copass, president of the Woman's Missionary Union of Texas. There was unanimous agreement that an effort should be made to raise the funds for the religious education building promptly, not through an all-out campaign but by allotments and special gifts. On April 28, Price wrote T. L. Holcomb, secretary of the Sunday School Board, about the possibility that the board would provide a gift for this religious education building. After some consultation, the board made a gift of twenty-five thousand dollars to each of the four Southern Baptist seminaries for their building funds.[29]

Publicity for the proposed religious education building appeared first in the *Southwestern News* of November, 1945. In a brief article it was pointed out that President Scarborough had made plans for this building as early as 1927, but the onset of the depression had prevented any action. Price wrote that the Woman's Missionary Union of the South had agreed to provide $25,000 a year for two years; that the Southwestern Baptist Religious Education Association would attempt to raise $25,000; and that all churches should follow the example of several which had already placed substantial gifts in their budgets for this building.[30] Goals were set for state alumni organizations and other interested groups.

The earliest reference to this building in the minutes of the trustees appeared on February 27, 1946, when they approved the report about it to the Southern Baptist Convention. The fund slowly increased: $33,366.61 by March, 1947; $70,564.17 by March, 1948. On September 10, 1948, the trustees voted to let a contract for the building. The amount available was $184,281.28, consisting of $71,090.07 in cash, $17,540.27 in pledges, and $95,650.94 from the capital needs funds of the Southern Baptist Convention. A groundbreaking ceremony was held on October 6, 1948, with T. L. Holcomb, Mrs. B. A. Copass, President Head, and J. M. Price handling the shovels.[31] The new building was occupied for the spring term of 1950.

This was the first building of its kind to be constructed in the United States. Its two stories and basement were designed specifically for the teaching of all aspects of religious education. It contained, in addition to classrooms, faculty offices, a chapel, a charming demonstration kindergarten, a demonstration church library, and other facilities for specialized educational study and activities.[32] On March 9, 1949, upon the recommendation of the faculty, the trustees named this building J. M. Price Hall, a worthy memorial to a pioneer religious educator.

The financial campaigns in Fort Worth for these buildings aroused interest in the seminary in Fort Worth businessmen. They developed an organization called "Friends of the Seminary," which had as its objective the enlistment of others to become interested in the work and needs of the school.[33]

Increasing the Endowment

The elimination of the indebtedness of the school and the enlarging of its facilities turned the attention of the trustees to the vital need of increasing the seminary's endowment. During all of President Head's administration, this subject was repeatedly discussed. Various efforts were made to accomplish this goal.[34] Near the close of President

Scarborough's administration, a quiet endowment campaign had been begun; and William Fleming, the wealthy Fort Worth Baptist deacon, challenged the seminary to raise fifty thousand dollars with the promise that he would match this amount. The faculty, administrative staff, and students enthusiastically made substantial pledges to begin this campaign. By the time the Convention met in 1943, the sum of $114,000 had been added to the school's endowment.[35]

Many gifts were received to apply on endowment. A campaign of Texas Baptists to raise endowment for its state institutions in 1947 brought some funds to the seminary.[36] Two of the larger gifts for endowment were received in the wills of friends. T. G. Hendrick, Abilene, Texas, remembered the school with a $100,000 gift in 1947;[37] in the following year Mr. and Mrs. A. L. Wasson, Big Spring, Texas, included the seminary in their wills for approximately $200,000.[38]

It will be recalled that part of the endowment of the seminary was invested in citrus fruit orchards in the Rio Grande Valley. Many had been critical of this investment by President Scarborough, especially J. Frank Norris. On September 3, 1943, the trustees were informed that sixty-one additional acres of this land lying immediately to the east of the seminary's orchards could be purchased from Luther Adams at a good price and that L. R. Scarborough, who was living near the seminary's orchards, had recommended that the school purchase these additional acres. The purchase was approved.

At the request of the trustees, on March 16, 1944, C. M. King, business manager of the seminary, presented a detailed statement of the investment of the school in the Valley and the return on the investment made by the seminary. His report showed that the seminary owned 1,662 acres of Rio Grande Valley land. The investment in this land during the fourteen-year period after the first acreage was received amounted to $223,113 by 1944. The average annual profit over this period was $6,820, or a total of $95,500. This average annual profit amounted to 4½ percent per year for the fourteen years, which was almost twice the amount of interest received on bank loans in 1942-43. In addition, the property had doubled in value since the school had acquired it, showing an appreciation of about $200,000. Returns on the investment had increased rapidly during the previous four years, totaling $72,689 in 1943.[39] The trustees discussed the wisdom of selling the seminary's holdings in the Valley and investing these funds in the Baptist Foundation, but it was decided that in view of the prospects of a good return, the land should not be sold at that time.

However, flooding conditions in the Valley during the summer of 1944 led the trustees to vote to dispose of all of the Valley property as soon as possible.[40] On November 11, 1944, the Executive Board of the trustees entered into a contract to sell this property for $630,000. On May 9, 1945, the full board confirmed the sale. The faith of L. R. Scarborough that this property would provide good endowment for the seminary was fulfilled. The endowment fund of the seminary in 1942 was $1,201,957.53; by 1953, this had increased to $1,807,139.82.

Enhancing of Faculty and Staff Benefits

With the rapid lifting of the financial depression after the outbreak of World War II, the trustees and administration promptly began the process of restoring faculty and staff salaries to their earlier level. As inflationary trends increased, President Head made this an item of trustee discussion almost each year. A uniform salary scale was adopted; the salaries of teachers in all three schools were equalized; and the salaries of women were adjusted upward.[41]

A plan was developed with the Southern Baptist Relief and Annuity Board to provide retirement benefits for faculty and staff,[42] and a Widow's Supplementary Annuity Plan was adopted.[43] Some of the older faculty members were dismayed by the small pension of the widow's plan. The seminary undertook to pay the members' retirement dues;[44] but on November 28, 1951, in a salary adjustment, the individual members again became responsible for paying these. The policy of a regular Christmas bonus was begun and maintained during all of this period.

President Head's thinking regarding the importance of providing adequate salaries and benefits for faculty and staff can be glimpsed in a statement that he made in his report to the trustees and to the Southern Baptist Convention in 1949. Rejoicing in the imminent completion of the memorial and religious education buildings, President Head wrote:

> But whatever the achievements and successes, trials or defeats, may this institution never lose sight of him whose providence made it possible and whose hand now guides its destinies. With all our building, may the buildings never become bigger than the professors or the students. May we never go up on masonry and down on manhood or true intellectuality and spirituality.[45]

Further encouragement was given to the faculty with the inauguration on May 15, 1952, of a "Sabbatical Year Assistance" program by the alumni. As finally developed, this program planned to make financial awards to faculty members on leave so that they could have additional funds for writing, study, or whatever their project might be during their sabbatical absence. Yearly grants would be made on the basis of receipts for the prior year to avoid the possibility of debt.[46] These extra funds, while not large in amount, would provide much needed assistance to some of the faculty.

Improving the Structure

As one reads in a single sitting the minutes of the trustees and faculty for the years between 1942 and 1953, one immediately becomes aware of an unusual development. The quiet, deeply spiritual president of the school, perhaps without realizing the full implications of his actions, put his orderly and logical mind to the task of improving the efficiency of the institution which he headed. L. R. Scarborough had continued B. H. Carroll's practice of mingling the functions of the administration and those of the faculty. Each of these presidents, in his dual role as an administrative officer and a member of the faculty, often introduced administrative affairs into the discussion of the faculty. The presidents made their own decisions, but they were influenced considerably by their faculty. Too, President Scarborough was away from the seminary so often and for such long periods in revival meetings, denominational service (such as the Seventy-Five Million Campaign), and fund raising for the seminary, that he left many administrative matters and all academic affairs in the hands of the faculty and an "Acting President" from among them.

This situation changed with the coming of President Head. He slowly began the orderly transition from the somewhat informal administration of the school to the development of a well-structured body of trustees and a more efficiently organized faculty. The records of both groups document this change.

Modernizing the Trustee Structure

The personnel of the board of trustees underwent substantial changes during this period. George W. Truett, who had chaired the body since May 13, 1931, died on July 7, 1944, after a protracted illness. On May 9, 1945, C. E. Matthews, pastor of Travis Avenue Baptist Church, Fort Worth, replaced him as chairman. Matthews was forced to resign on March 12, 1947, because he was leaving the state to become superintendent of evangelism for the Home Mission Board in Georgia. A. J. Holt was elected chairman at that meeting and continued his service during the remainder of this period. C. M. King continued as secretary of the trustees until November 28, 1951, when he resigned because of his impending retirement. The trustees voted their high appreciation for his many years of faithful and efficient service. The seminary honored him with a retirement dinner on April 30, 1951, recalling his thirty-eight years of service as business manager.[47] He was replaced as secretary of the trustees and business manager by D. A. Thornton. The trustee body was composed of many strong, progressive leaders like E. C. Brown (Arkansas), E. L. Carnett (Texas), William Fleming (Texas), A. D. Foreman (Tennessee), Sam S. Hill (Kentucky), A. J. Holt (Texas), Robert E. Naylor (South Carolina), J. E. Rains (Missouri), Loyed R. Simmons (Texas), Scott L. Tatum (Louisiana), and W. D. Wyatt (New Mexico).

At the beginning of this period much of the work of the trustees consisted of approving the acts of the local Executive Committee, certifying the graduates, electing the faculty for the following year, and acting as a Committee of the Whole in deliberating about mattters on the agenda. Gradually, under President Head, the trustees increased the use of ad hoc committees to study such things as the salary scale,[48] faculty load,[49] the possibility of securing an FM radio station,[50] surveying building needs,[51] and the like.

But several steps were taken toward providing a more efficient plan of organization and operation. At the meeting on March 12, 1947, it was arranged that

> committees be appointed to work on any problems which may arise during the year, meeting the afternoon of the day before the Board meeting so that such matters as may need the consideration of the Board can come with recommendations from such committee.

This initiated the valuable program of providing time for deliberation by committees appointed for various matters.

On March 9, 1949, the chairman of the Committee on Committees noted that the trustees had only three standing committees—the Executive Committee, the Finance Committee, and the Auditing Committee. The trustees approved his four recommendations: (1) that the bylaws be amended to show President Head as an ex officio member of all committees, including the Executive Committee; (2) that each member of the board of trustees be placed on some committee or committees; (3) that three new standing committees be provided—one on instruction, one on buildings and grounds, and one on curriculum; and (4) that the chairman of the trustees be authorized to appoint such additional committees as might seem advisable and necessary. This clearly moved toward the pattern of referring most matters to the appropriate standing committee for recommendation.

Another advance toward the modern structure of the trustees was made on November 28, 1950. The Committee on Committees recommended that the board utilize five standing committees (combining instruction and curriculum), and the duties of these committees were described in some detail. The Curriculum Committee, in particular, provided trustee control of all courses offered by the seminary. This structure, along with including each trustee on some standing committee and having each committee meet on the day before the entire board gathered, was approved.

On November 28, 1951, a further step was taken that continued the modernization process of the board of trustees. By motion a committee was appointed to study the bylaws of the seminary, and on November 25, 1952, the proposed bylaws were discussed seriatim and approved. As adopted, these new bylaws gathered up all of the structural advances of the previous decade, particularly in the development of committees for study and recommendation. Three types of committees were named: the Executive Committee, the standing committees, and the special committees. The duties of the Executive Committee were continued as before, consisting principally of taking charge of the institution between meetings of the full board of trustees and transacting all matters which could not be deferred until the regular board meeting. Major policy and important financial decisions would be made by the entire board, and all actions taken by the Executive Committee were to be approved by the full board when it next met.

Five standing committees were named. They were Finance, Faculty and Curriculum, Building and Grounds, Real Estate, and Endowment. Each committee was to be composed of two members from the Executive Committee and three from members of the board at large. On any necessary minor emergency involving the work of any of these standing committees, the two members from the Executive Committee, together with the presidents of the seminary and the board, were authorized to take action; major matters required the calling of the entire committee for deliberation. Special committees would be named from time to time as the board authorized them and the circumstances required them. The president of the seminary served in an advisory capacity to both the entire board and each committee.

In the discussion of the functions of the faculty, the new bylaws drew exact boundaries between the responsibilities of the faculty and those of the administration for the first time in the school's history. A faculty member's responsibility was to teach his or her classes; any task beyond that was to be performed only "by the request or upon the authority of the President and Board of Trustees."

Thus, by November 25, 1952, the board of trustees had developed an efficient and comprehensive committee system of operation, had instituted procedures for committee deliberation in preparation for recommendations to the entire board of trustees, and had marked out precise lines of authority in governance.

Faculty Reorganization

The orderly mind of President Head may also be observed in the modernizing of the faculty during the period from 1942 to 1953. At the earliest meeting of the Faculty Council in the fall of 1942, the new president began a careful study of the operation of all facets of the faculty structure and procedure.[52] He suggested that the faculty observe more carefully the laws of parliamentary procedure.[53] In a significant move on December 8, 1942, President Head requested that a Plans and Policies Committee be named "to study and recommend relative to matters presented to the Council." Head named the committee and became its chairman. This committee immediately became the channel for initiating action in almost every area of seminary life. It fixed times for faculty meetings, developed a medium for alumni contact, and named the registrar;[54] it supervised the quality of student work and named the advisor to Fort Worth Hall;[55] it scheduled the registration of students and fixed student loans;[56] it determined that the school would have no midwinter graduation and led in revising faculty rules and regulations;[57] and it modified Student Council representation.[58] This committee also changed committee assignments and named the speakers for all occasions;[59] it disciplined students[60] and set holidays;[61] it decided in favor of the use of caps and gowns at graduation;[62] it made recommendations about the operation of the book store;[63] it established fees and waived faculty rules.[64] The recommendations of this committee were never questioned or voted down, since they were recognized as policies of the administration.

Another important structural development of the faculty in this period was the appointment by the trustees of a director of the School of Theology. On March 9, 1949, Professor Ray Summers was named to this post by the trustees. This was a logical organizational move. The religious education and music schools had been headed by such a director since 1921. President Scarborough had felt no necessity for such a director in the School of Theology because he counted himself to be both president of the school and chairman of a faculty which centered in the theological disciplines from the beginning of his administration. In his absence, he appointed an "Acting President" from the faculty. After the resignation of Charles B. Williams in 1919, he saw no need for a dean.

When the faculty of the School of Theology first met on March 25, 1925, as a distinct entity, Jeff D. Ray was elected chairman "in the absence of Dr. Scarborough." W. W. Barnes became chairman of the theology faculty on December 10, 1926, and he retained that position until the election of Director Summers in 1949. Thereafter, the directors of the three schools met regularly with the president for the purpose of bringing recommendations to the faculty, somewhat after the fashion of the old Plans and Policies Committee.

Still another organizational revision of the faculty structure took place. It will be recalled that the extensive faculty revision of 1925 had eliminated the meeting of the entire faculty and introduced an elitist Faculty Council, evidently because of the temporary status of many of the young teachers and the need to expedite the handling of many academic and administrative affairs. The full faculty met only occasionally during the remainder of President Scarborough's administration, mainly at the opening of the school year for announcements and at special times to discuss college visitation. In a major faculty restructuring, on December 5, 1950, Director Summers presented a recommendation to the Faculty Council from the president and school directors which said, "We recommend that the faculty council be replaced by a joint meeting of the regular faculties of the three schools as elected by the trustees, together with the Registrar and Librarians." After discussion, a substitute motion was made to refer the matter back to the president and directors for additional details on how such revision would affect the decision-making process.

Evidently there was some resistance from the faculty to these several structural revisions, for at the next meeting of the Faculty Council on January 2, 1951, even before the revised report from the directors was made, President Head "suggested a need and desire for a faculty prayer meeting." It was agreed to meet each Tuesday morning at 7:30 AM to pray for thirty minutes before classes began. On January 17, Director Summers presented the report on "Future Policy of Faculty Action," which spelled out the details of the elimination of the Faculty Council. The joint faculty meeting hereafter would be authorized to admit students, work out schedules, publish the catalogue, and receive student petitions not directly relating to a particular school. These were clearly academic functions only. For each of their own schools, the three separate faculties were to approve textbooks and new courses, direct graduate work, and approve their curricula. The president and directors of the schools were to direct all publicity, approve the curriculum and any new courses, administer all matters involving the seminary as a whole, serve as a program committee to nominate speakers for conferences and commencements, and work out the school calendar. The first full faculty meeting was held on February 20, 1951, under the new structure.

The abolishing of the Faculty Council replaced a small and rather powerful faculty group with a large general faculty representation. One of the first developments following this change was reflected in the appointment of the standing committees of the faculty. All teachers and some administrative employees were included in the nineteen committees for 1951-52. Hereafter the work of the general faculty consisted mainly of approving committee reports of various kinds.

It is not surprising that this inevitable process of organizational modernization was greeted less than enthusiastically by some of the more mature members of the theological faculty. Just a few years earlier, they had been a part of the small Faculty Council who sat in a circle around the desk in President Scarborough's office and dialogued with him about almost every administrative and academic decision. Now, without any warning, one of their younger colleagues had been elected by the trustees to supervise their work, and they no longer had a part in any administrative decisions. It should be added that the new director was as surprised as anyone about his appointment. He had made no effort to secure this post.

President Head shortly reported to the trustees that he had conferred with some individuals and several groups of the faculty "to discuss problems relative to the welfare of the School of Theology." On March 7, 1951, he and Director Summers met with representatives from the School of Theology. This meeting resulted in two recommendations to the faculty of the School of Theology: (1) that the board of trustees be requested to make the appointment of the director of the School of Theology a three-year term and (2) that the faculty of the School of Theology be permitted to nominate the director to the trustees. The faculty of the School of Theology approved these recommendations on March 8. However, at the July 22, 1951, meeting, the trustees declined these requests. Polarities developed, and it is likely that these events were important factors in the decisions of several faculty members to accept challenging tasks in other institutions; although, of course, in every instance the leadership of the Holy Spirit was diligently sought and found. In retrospect, after thirty years have passed, it appears that the principal cause of this imbroglio was the modernization of the trustee and faculty structures which eliminated the older overlap in governance. The response of the trustees and the adoption of new, precisely worded bylaws made it unlikely that such a situation would arise again. Jesse J. Northcutt was elected director of the School of Theology by the trustees on May 7, 1953.[65]

Revising the Extension Program

A third rather substantial change in structure developed during this period in the extension and correspondence program of the school. It will be recalled that J. W. Crowder accepted leadership in this area in 1919. Upon his retirement on June 1, 1943, a committee of the faculty recommended that the amount of correspondence study for seminary credit be limited and that a separate Home Study Department be formed to provide correspondence-type study without credit.[66] Frank K. Means was asked to direct this work. Growing out of interseminary discussions, the faculty agreed to work out a program by which all three of the Southern Baptist seminaries would jointly offer this type of study.[67] On January 17, 1951, Ralph D. Churchill, who had become director of the Extension Department after the resignation of Frank K. Means, recommended the elimination of the Extension Department effective June 1, 1951, so that the seminary could cooperate with the new Seminary Extension Department organized jointly by the three Southern Baptist seminaries, and this was done. Lee Gallman of Jackson, Mississippi, was the new head of this Convention-wide program and was viewed as a faculty member of each of the three seminaries. Credit for this work would be allowed on the diploma level.[68] The trustees approved this action.[69]

Meeting the Growing Needs

Between 1942 and 1953, the seminary made strenuous efforts to prepare its students for the troubled world in which they would be ministering. These efforts included strengthening the faculty, revising the curriculum, grappling with the problems of a burgeoning student body, and building an adequate library to support the classroom instruction.

Strengthening the Faculty

There was a considerable turnover in the seminary's faculty between 1942 and 1953. Four of the pioneer teachers retired in these years, and some of the veterans already retired completed their earthly course. Many other changes took place. The best method of observing these events is by individual schools.

Four of the stalwarts of the School of Theology retired during this period. The first was J. W. Crowder, who had been the protégé of B. H. Carroll. Crowder taught English Bible from 1909 until 1919, when he accepted the Correspondence and Extension Department. He was responsible for collecting Carroll's sermons and lectures on the English Bible and editing them for publication. During the final fifteen years of his teaching, he worked to beautify the campus by supervising the landscaping and planting of trees and flowers. When he retired in the spring of 1943, the faculty saluted his faithful service with words of high appreciation. He died on July 20, 1954.[70]

Jeff D. Ray, a member of the first faculty of Southwestern, taught homiletics for thirty-seven years before his retirement in 1944. He wrote extensively for denominational periodicals. For many years, he prepared the weekly Sunday School lesson for the *Fort Worth Star-Telegram*. His biography of B. H. Carroll is the best known of his seven books. Never did any man emphasize more the proper manner in which to read the Scriptures, and he exemplified his teaching. Greatly beloved and full-of-years, he died on June 18, 1951.[71]

W. T. Conner, who had begun his teaching in the year the seminary moved to Fort Worth, suffered a severe stroke on April 9, 1949, forcing him to retire from the classroom. He had taught systematic theology for thirty-nine years and often took temporary assignments in Greek, New Testament, ecclesiology, and related subjects when help was required in these disciplines. In addition to fifteen significant books, he wrote scores of articles for denominational periodicals and was constantly sought as a lecturer. When he died on May 26, 1952, tributes came from across the world. Some, not Southwesterners, called him the South's greatest theologian.[72] The entire issue of the *Southwestern News* in November, 1952, was devoted to him and his work. G. Kearnie Keegan enjoyed telling his favorite story about this profound theologian. He wrote:

"Dr. Conner has the reputation of being the intellectual flower of the Seminary faculty," quipped the brilliant H. E. Dana in one of his immortal chapel talks, "but the Lord didn't give him much of a vase to put it in." The student body laughed, and a shy grin appeared on the homely face of Dr. Conner. He knew his day would come and it did. With that devastating droll, so familiar to the ears of his students, he gave a monotonic reply which brought gales of laughter from his listeners and a hearty "head to toe" laugh from Dr. Dana.

Keegan remarked further:

Dr. Conner's ability to illustrate with simplicity the most profound theological truth was a gift from God. He opened to me mines of great spiritual treasure which I did not know existed. With a few well chosen phrases, punctuated by a pointed right index finger, this humble man of God would deftly illustrate perplexing, seeming paradoxes so that even I understood. He was a genius. [73]

"Connerisms" were constantly repeated around the campus. His students could hardly forget such pungent remarks as: "It doesn't matter how high you jump when you are converted. The important thing is how straight you walk when you come down." "Our main need is not the power to speak in tongues but the grace of the Lord to use the tongue that we have." "Let's get over being so grateful when a scientist tells us we can believe in God and immortality." [74]

The fourth pioneer faculty member retiring during this period was William W. Barnes, who had taught church history (and other courses when necessary) for forty years after joining the faculty in 1913. He was the dean of Southern Baptist historians, having prepared the first official history of the Southern Baptist Convention. As chairman of the faculty of the School of Theology from 1926 to 1949, he, along with W. T. Conner, exercised much influence in the life of the seminary. He was well known for "chasing rabbits" in his classes, a phrase describing his use of numerous stories as examples of the principles of history. He possessed a broad culture and a remarkable memory of historical details. He had the reputation of giving difficult tests. Professor L. Jack Gray recalled a humorous note about an event which occurred when he was a student. He said:

We were in Dr. W. W. Barnes' Church History class. The professor, famous for his all-encompassing exams, was writing such an exam on the blackboard. The telephone range across the hall. Virginia Smith, manager of the Baptist Book Store nearby, answered the phone and came to our classroom door just as Dr. Barnes stepped back from the board and the large class read the difficult survey-type questions. "Is Paul Aiken in here?" she asked. To which some wag replied, "Sister, everybody is achin' in here." The tension was broken and we dug into the impossible exam. [75]

When this distinguished scholar and cultured leader died on April 6, 1960, expressions of condolence came from every part of the world.[76]

Two retired veterans joined the company of the redeemed made perfect. L. R. Scarborough died on April 10, 1945. The entire issue of the *Southwestern News* for May, 1945, memorialized him. President Head preached an eloquent funeral message.[77] The other worthy was B. A. Copass, who died on January 2, 1950. His outstanding twenty-four-year service with the school has already been described.[78]

Two of the faculty resigned during this period but later returned. Jesse J. Northcutt, who had taught in theology, New Testament, and preaching since 1939, resigned on March 1, 1948, to become pastor of the First Baptist Church, Abilene, Texas. He returned to the faculty on January 1, 1950. W. Boyd Hunt, who had begun teaching in systematic theology in 1944, resigned on September 1, 1946, to accept the pastorate of the First Baptist Church, Houston, Texas. He returned to the faculty on January 12, 1953.

Six of the theology faculty resigned and did not return. Frank K. Means, professor of missions since 1939, left in May, 1947, to join the staff of the Foreign Mission Board. Stewart A. Newman, who had taught in philosophy since 1936, and Robert T. Daniel, Old Testament professor since 1937, resigned in May, 1952, to join the staff of the new Southeastern Baptist Theological Seminary, Wake Forest, North Carolina. Each of these three men had held important positions in the faculty. John A. Barry joined the faculty in 1946 in the Department of Preaching but resigned on September 1, 1949, to accept a professorship in Furman University, Greenville, South Carolina. G. Earl Guinn taught preaching from June, 1948, to July, 1951, when he resigned to accept the presidency of Louisiana College, Pineville, Louisiana. Charles A. Trentham taught theology from 1947 to January 15, 1953, when he accepted the pastorate of the First Baptist Church, Knoxville, Tennessee.

Eleven new faculty members were added in the School of Theology and continued teaching during the remainder of this period. They were Cal Guy in missions (1946), John W. MacGorman in New Testament (1948), Ralph A. Phelps, Jr., in Christian Ethics (1948), James Leo Garrett, Jr., in theology (1949), Ralph Lee Smith in Old Testament (1949), H. C. Brown, Jr., in preaching (1949), William Curtis Vaughan in New Testament (1950), Huber L. Drumwright, Jr., in New Testament (1951), Franklin M. Segler in pastoral ministry (1951), John P. Newport in philosophy of religion (1952), and Thomas M. Bennett, Jr., in Old

Testament (1952). It can be seen that the number of teachers added to the faculty of theology did not exceed the number resigning or retiring, and the resulting problem of large classes became bothersome at times.

The faculty of the School of Religious Education also experienced several changes during this period. One of their number, Mrs. W. A. Johnson, who had served as superintendent of the Woman's Missionary Training School since 1933, retired at the close of the summer term in 1944. She had taught on the faculty since 1935.[79] Floy Barnard, greatly beloved teacher of educational arts, was elected dean of women to succeed Mrs. Johnson in 1944.[80]

The School of Religious Education faculty added eight teachers during the remainder of this period. They were greatly needed, not only because of the increasing student body and enlarging curriculum, but because T. B. Maston had transferred to the School of Theology completely by 1944 and Floy Barnard was forced to drop some of her courses to assume the deanship of the women's training school. Joe Davis Heacock (1944) began teaching in the field of principles of religious education; Ralph Churchill (1944), in religious publicity and journalism; Ann Bradford (1945), in elementary education and kindergarten; Mrs. Alpha Melton (1945), in social work; R. Othal Feather (1947), in clinical training; Gracie Knowlton (1947), in secretarial service; Philip Harris (1949), in adolescent education; A. Donald Bell (1951), in psychology and counseling; and James Daniel (1953), in elementary education and administration.[81]

The School of Sacred Music had several significant faculty changes. I. E. Reynolds, the pioneer in this field, retired from the faculty on September 1, 1945. When he began his service in 1915, there were but nine students and one other teacher. Under his leadership, the faculty had grown to fifteen, and the number of students had averaged about one hundred for several years. He had helped sketch plans for Cowden Music Hall. For over twenty-five years, he directed the annual presentation of Handel's *Messiah*. He was a composer of gospel songs, anthems, and other musical forms and prepared textbooks on church music. When he died on May 10, 1949, the funeral services were held in Cowden Hall where he had served for so many years. On November 28, 1950, the trustees voted that the new pipe organ for Truett Auditorium should bear the name the I. E. Reynolds Memorial Organ.[82]

To succeed Reynolds as director of the School of Sacred Music in 1945, the trustees elected E. L. Carnett, a former member of the music faculty, but he resigned after one year to accept the pulpit of the Travis

Avenue Baptist Church, Fort Worth, Texas. J. Campbell Wray, who had come to the music faculty in the area of choral music in 1943, was then made the director.[83]

Other faculty additions in this school were Sara V. Thompson (1945) in theory and music history, Charles Flint (1947) in theory, William Hargrave (1947) in voice and speech, Cecil Bolton (1948) in piano, Arthur King (1948) in organ, Evelyn (Marney) Phillips (1948) in church music education, Forrest Heeren (1949) in voice, Woodrow W. Wall (1949) in voice and choral music, James C. McKinney (1950) in theory, Gladys Day (1952) in organ and keyboard harmony, and L. Sarle Brown (1952) in voice. Resigning from the regular faculty were William Barclay (1948), who had taught organ since 1928, one of the survivors of the critical depression years; Mrs. Carlyle Bennett (1946), who had taught theory since 1936; Cecil Bolton (1950); William Hargrave (1951); and Forrest Heeren (1952) to head the music faculty at The Southern Baptist Theological Seminary.

The library made a significant addition on October 1, 1947, when Charles P. Johnson was named assistant librarian to L. R. Elliott.

In 1948-49 the *Southwestern News* carried a series of brief vignettes of six of the administrative staff who had served long and well. Many older alumni will recognize these persons as having played an important part in the operation of the school. C. M. King served as business manager from 1913 to his retirement in 1951.[84] Mrs. F. H. Waldrop had supervised the nursery since 1922.[85] D. A. Thornton had been bookkeeper in the business office since 1919.[86] F. A. Hilliker began as an assistant to R. C. Spurlock in the upkeep of the campus in 1930.[87] Robert Parr was employed in 1936 to assist J. W. Crowder as superintendent of the campus, and upon Crowder's retirement in 1943 he took over this responsibility.[88] Mamie Storrs began serving L. R. Scarborough as secretary in 1938 and performed a like service for President Head.[89] Head personally prepared these articles on little publicized people on the campus, reflecting the kind of gracious and thoughtful spirit that characterized him.

Staff changes included the retirement of Miss Vinnie Gammill as assistant registrar in 1944 and the employment of Miss Katie Reed for this task.[90] In 1950, she was named registrar, replacing S. A. Newman.[91] In September, 1944, John A. McIver was employed to direct student employment and missionary extension.[92]

In an effort to solve the problem of huge classes, during this period the teaching load was increased from a minimum of eight to ten hours a week.[93] Also, specific limitations were made in the sabbatical leave program.[94]

Curriculum Revisions

The faculty of the School of Theology made more extensive revisions in the curriculum than either of the other two schools of the seminary. With the retirement of J. W. Crowder from the Extension Department, the faculty agreed to limit the number of credit correspondence courses that might be taken and arranged for these courses to be revised and updated. The new Home Study Department, headed by Frank K. Means, was inaugurated on January 1, 1944.[95] It later was absorbed into the Convention-wide Seminary Extension Department, as previously mentioned.

The School of Theology made a thorough study of its entire curriculum in the opening years of this period, partly as the result of its application for accreditation to the American Association of Theological Schools and partly because of contemporary trends in educational circles toward more elective work. On May 27, 1943, this faculty named a small committee to study Southwestern's degree structure in the School of Theology, to examine the curricula of other seminaries accredited by the association, and to make recommendations about elective work. Each theological faculty meeting during the remainder of the year brought extensive discussion of proposed revisions. After this faculty had examined the proposals of the committee seriatim on November 23 and 28 and December 10, 1943, a radically revised curriculum was approved by the Faculty Council on January 4, 1944. New curricula were provided for noncollege students, one which would lead to a Certificate of Christian Training; for those with two years of college, one which would lead to a Diploma in Theology; and for those with a full college degree, one which would lead either to a Bachelor of Theology or Master of Theology degree. The bachelor's degree was awarded to those whose curriculum did not include the study of Hebrew and Greek.

For both degree programs, a total of ninety-six hours was required, of which forty-eight were basic designated courses, eighteen were in a category called "required-electives," while the remaining thirty hours were free electives. The "required-electives" were required in the sense that they had to be distributed among the four major fields—biblical, historical, theological-philosophical, and practical.[96] On September 26, 1944, the theological faculty voted to combine the certificate and diploma programs into the Diploma in Theology, and on February 12, 1945, they voted to designate the three-year degree course as the Bachelor of Divinity, permitting students to substitute electives for Hebrew and Greek.[97] The languages were required as prerequisite for advanced study. The Master of Theology became an advanced degree based upon one year's additional work beyond the Bachelor of Divinity. These changes were approved by the Faculty Council.[98]

A second extensive curriculum revision was made in the School of Theology in 1951. The purpose was "to keep step with current trends in theological education and to fill specific needs which faculty and alumni felt existed." Questionnaires were sent to large groups of Southwestern alumni to determine their evaluation of their training in terms of the ministry in which they were then engaged. All contemporary literature concerning curriculum was digested, and catalogues of other seminaries were examined. As a result of this study, in 1951 the Faculty Council approved the formation of two new departments in the School of Theology. A Department of Biblical Introduction was structured, providing instruction in geography, formation of the canon, social custom, and archaeology. A Department of Pastoral Ministry was formed "to give more specific preparation for the ministry of the pastor," including such courses as pastoral leadership, parliamentary procedure, pastoral duties, ministerial ethics, and pastoral counseling. In this curricular revision, the number and scope of free electives were reduced, and the category of "required-electives" was eliminated.[99]

Some of these curriculum changes developed from the interaction between the school and the American Association of Theological Schools. After the coming of President Head, the faculty continued its efforts to gain accreditation.[100] A representative of the accrediting body visited the campus on April 18, 1944, and at the December, 1944, meeting of the Accreditation Committee of the association, the seminary was granted full accreditation.

Several changes were also made in the areas of specialization by different members of the theological faculty. Jesse J. Northcutt moved from theology into preaching; W. Boyd Hunt replaced him in theology. Robert A. Baker turned from Greek to church history, and T. B. Matson moved totally into the School of Theology from the School of Religious Education. After Frank Means accepted the position with the Foreign Mission Board, Cal Guy headed the Department of Missions. When the new Department of Pastoral Ministry was formed in 1951, Franklin M. Segler resigned a strong pastorate to lead it. On March 10, 1948, President Head, who had been teaching evangelism since September,

1942, requested the trustees to secure a professor for this course since his numerous administrative duties made it difficult for him to continue teaching it. Different members of the faculty, particularly Ray Summers, assisted in supplying this instruction until a permanent professor could be found. On February 27, 1946, President Head broached the question of appointing W. W. Barnes as research professor in Baptist history, and the trustees approved this action.[101] Barnes was at this time preparing the official history of the Southern Baptist Convention, and this appointment promised him the opportunity of using four hours of his teaching load in the area of research, if this could be arranged.

The School of Religious Education made several alterations in its curriculum in the period from 1942 to 1953, but in the main it retained the basic pattern initiated by J. M. Price. This pattern had been mutilated by the financial depression of the 1920s and 1930s. A professorship in Baptist Student Union work and clinical training was begun in September, 1947, and R. Othal Feather, a graduate of Oklahoma Baptist University and Southwestern Seminary, was assigned to this department. The content of the work in clinical training was changed in 1951, and it became the Supervised Field Work Department of the School of Religious Education.[102] Church library training, formerly included as a part of another study, became a separate course in 1948.[103] Religious journalism was reestablished as a department in 1950, and Ralph D. Churchill became its head.[104]

This was a period when the needs of the child were being emphasized. It will be recalled that in 1922 the Department of Elementary Religious Education had been formed, but the depression stunted all of the seminary's curriculum. In 1945, Ann Bradford was brought to the religious education faculty to reorganize the work of this department, including the kindergarten work. Seven courses were offered, and in 1948 a doctoral student could take a minor in childhood religious education.

An important recognition came to the School of Religious Education in 1951. The American Association of Schools of Religious Education had been organized in Chicago in 1936, and at its fifteenth session on December 27-28, 1951, after developing national standards for schools of religious education through an Accreditation Commission, this body named Southwestern's School of Religious Education as one of its first seven accredited institutions. This certified the quality of the school's curriculum for its master's and doctor's degrees.[105]

The curriculum of the School of Sacred Music remained substantially the same during the years 1942 to 1953, although new emphasis was given to some areas of musical discipline and some organizational nomenclatures were altered. In 1942, the catalogue showed a new Division of Choir and Choral Music with the coming of J. Campbell Wray. In 1949, the title "Church Music Education" was adopted. In 1950, what had been called "Specific Church Music" was changed to "Music in Evangelism." At the end of the period, the four principal divisions of the school were applied music (both voice and instrumental), church music education, composition and theory, and music in evangelism. As in the case of both the School of Theology and the School of Religious Education, the School of Sacred Music occasionally utilized student or adjunct teachers for a year or two. Among such teachers were Don Gillis, Mrs. Ruth Mulkey Lyon, Wayne Dunlap, William J. Reynolds, and others.

Adjunctive to the several curricula of the seminary, all three schools increased their programs of conferences, lectureships, workshops, drama presentations, musical recitals, and the beautiful choral presentations at special seasons and on festive occasions. Distinguished chapel speakers enlarged the world of the students. The annual Midwinter Conference, formally begun in 1939, included the Holland Foundation Lectures, the Founder's Day address, the quarterly Mission Day address, and a special series of sermons by an outstanding pastor. Conferences and workshops were held regularly to share the expertise of leaders in specialized fields such as the rural church, visual aids, Good Will Centers and social work, student secretaries, and music. Dramatic and musical presentations were numerous and of high quality.

A Burgeoning Student Body

Providing both a problem and a challenge, the enrollment of the seminary accelerated rapidly between the years 1942 and 1953. In the former year, the number of students was 760; by 1953, it had reached 2,160, including 1,354 in the School of Theology, 749 in the School of Religious Education, and 124 in the School of Sacred Music (with 67 duplicates). Before the acquisition of the two new buildings on the campus, President Head reported to the Southern Baptist Convention that the teachers were lecturing to "congregations," not classes. Even with the addition of the space for teaching, the rapid growth of the student body far outstripped the size of the faculty. The number of faculty grew from 23 full-time teachers in 1942 to 42 in 1953, an increase of almost 83 percent, but the student body increased by over 184 percent during the same period.[106]

In a period sensitive to discrimination against minorities, the seminary had no problem, of course, relative to the training of women. From
the very beginning of the school, women were admitted to all classes and
degree programs, including the doctorate in theology.[107] A large step was
taken by Southwestern, however, toward eliminating racial discrimination. During the early years of this period, the seminary provided night
classes and extension work for Negroes on the diploma level only. These
were then graduated in a special evening service. Extension courses
continued to be offered for Negroes in various cities until the end of this
period. Additional Negro extension classes were organized in Austin,
Waco, Beaumont, Mexia, Mission, and Dallas.[108] However, the seminary
was forced to face the question of admitting qualified Negroes to the
degree programs in the regular day classes. Upon the recommendation of
the faculty, on November 28, 1950, the trustees unanimously passed a
motion to

> approve the admission of negro graduates of senior colleges, who have
> received definite calls from the Lord to definite religious work, as regular
> students in Southwestern Baptist Theological Seminary, and that we notify
> our sister seminaries of such action and invite them to consider such matter
> and inform them that we desire to defer official announcement of our action
> until they have had time to consider, that all seminaries may move together
> if possible.

Other racial groups had already been admitted to classes of the
seminary, so this action, subsequently modified to eliminate all remnants
of segregation, developed a more nearly Christian stance at this point.

The student body played an active part in the programs of the school.
As a result of their petitions, caps and gowns were used at the time of
graduation.[109] A student newspaper, called the *Scroll*, began publication
in 1946.[110] The trustees were constantly seeking ways to provide
additional housing for the students. An active athletic program was
fostered by the school with intramural sports like touch football in the
fall, basketball during the winter, and softball in the spring. In 1944-45,
the seminary entered a basketball team in the Industrial League and the
Major City League, winning the championship in both. A biennial
"Faculty Take-Off" provided much amusement. The Student Council was
active, and state clubs began to be formed. The three schools, as well as
the training school, had their individual student organizations, the
theological students reorganizing in 1949. The first student *Handbook*
was published also in that year.[111] *The Southwestern Evangel* had been
discontinued in June, 1931, because of the depression. A small quarterly
called the *Southwestern News* was begun early in 1943, with T. B. Maston

as editor. In October, 1947, it was expanded and published monthly under the editorship of Ralph Churchill.[112]

The United States was involved in World War II from December 7, 1941, until peace was declared on August 15, 1945. The seminary contributed in every way to support the nation in this crisis. Periodically the Faculty Council endorsed War Chest pledges throughout the school. Students and graduates entered all branches of the service, principally as chaplains. Southwestern was the only Southern Baptist seminary qualifying for the V-12 program of theological training for Navy chaplains.[113] The faculty authorized the preparation of a plaque in recognition of Southwestern students and alumni who had participated in the conflict. A total of 557 men and women from Southwestern served in the armed forces in World War II, 434 of whom were chaplains.[114] Special recognition was given to nine men who were killed in action. They were Somers E. Barnett, Morris E. Day, William Dawson, Roy A. Griffin, Percy E. Haley, Edwin U. Monroe, Thomas H. Reagan, A. E. Teem, and Andrew Thigpen.[115] Many Southwestern graduates were cited for heroic conduct, especially Chaplain Robert Preston Taylor, who survived the tragic Bataan march. Others not in the armed forces were victims of the hostilities. Reflecting the suffering of scores of Southwestern missionaries whose lives were assaulted by the world conflagration was a single sentence in the *Southwestern News* for November, 1945, which announced that the speakers for the first Mission Day on October 17, 1945, were Southwesterners Cleo Morrison and Fern Harrington, who had been interned and held in Japanese prison camps for over three years. Who can ever forget the matter-of-fact recital of the terrible suffering in these internment camps related in a hushed chapel service by Charles L. Culpepper, Sr.?

During the war and in the Korean "incident" developing later, the faculty joined with other theological schools in attempting to protect vocational Christian students from the effects of the draft. On June 26, 1944, after thorough discussion in the previous week's meeting, the Faculty Council detailed the program to be followed by pretheological students in the universities as they prepared for enrollment in the seminary. The theological faculty, in particular, in concert with other Southern Baptist seminaries, made repeated efforts to secure the recognition of vocational education and music students as having the same status in the draft classification as students of the School of Theology.[116] Special programs of study were planned for those returning to school from the armed services. A course for those preparing for the military chaplaincy was developed.[117] High-ranking military chaplains regularly visited the school, and a reserve training unit of the chaplaincy was formed on the campus.

A significant student project not officially related to the seminary was the publication of a religious monthly for the blind. One of the students of the School of Religious Education was Edwin Wilson, who was almost totally blind. In October, 1947, under the sponsorship of several Texas Baptist leaders, including seminary professors, he launched the first monthly publication of *The Braille Evangel*, a succinct summary of sermons, devotional helps, religious news, special Bible teachings, and stories to enrich the lives of those without sight. This publication was continued after Edwin Wilson completed his seminary work, and editions in Spanish were issued.[118]

Building an Adequate Library

This was a time of rapid expansion for the library of the seminary. On September 21, 1943, Librarian Elliott secured approval of the Faculty Council to enter into a program of obtaining microfilm copies of valuable out-of-print books, and by 1951 the library owned two microfilm and one microcard readers. Much emphasis was being given to the acquisition of scholarly works in other languages.[119] In the spring of 1947, the men's Sunday School class at Broadway Baptist Church, Fort Worth, which Librarian L. R. Elliott had taught for twenty-five years, surprised him with a gift of twenty-five thousand dollars to be used in purchasing important books for the library over and above the regular seminary appropriation for this purpose. On two occasions Elliott went to Great Britain in search of books, returning each time with valuable collections for the library. On March 12, 1947, the trustees gave full faculty status to the librarian and his assistants.

The library had been moved often. From its original location on the first floor of Fort Worth Hall, it had been transferred in 1939 to the first floor of the Woman's Missionary Training School building, where it remained for a decade. During this time in the women's building, the increase in holdings and the enlarged student body demanded more space. There were only 125 seats in the reading room to serve over 1,000 students in 1947. The shelving capacity had almost reached the saturation point.

A new era was begun in the fall of 1949 when the library entered the east wing of the new Memorial Building. Because of his significant contribution for the construction of the building, this wing was named Fleming Library after William Fleming, a trustee of the seminary and wealthy oil man of Fort Worth. This three-story wing had a shelf capacity for 125,000 books and a seating capacity of 300.[120] By March, 1951, Elliott reported the purchase of the fifty-thousandth volume of the library, a staff of three professional librarians, and a large number of student assistants.[121] By the close of this period, the holdings of the library included over sixty thousand volumes.[122]

An innovation in library service occurred in the spring of 1951. Working with Director J. Campbell Wray of the School of Sacred Music, L. R. Elliott removed the music books not used extensively by the other two schools from Fleming Library to a room on the lower floor of Cowden Music Hall. Sara Thompson, one of the music faculty, was appointed as music librarian and was provided seven student assistants. The books were grouped into a reference section, collected works, hymnals and gospel songbooks, and a magazine rack of current periodicals. An earphone listening system was purchased to utilize the recorded music. The music faculty and the librarian felt that this relocation would greatly assist music students in utilizing the musical resources of the library better than if the materials were located in another building.[123]

During this period L. R. Elliott became one of the outstanding library authorities in the nation. He was active in the formation of the American Theological Library Association and served as its first president from 1947 to 1949. He also initiated the preparation of the first *Baptist Union List of Serials*, a significant reference tool.[124]

The Deepening Spirit of Southwestern

Despite the dissimilarity between the personality of E. D. Head and his presidential predecessors, the changed economic conditions of the seminary, and the enormous enlargement of the student body, the traditional spirit of Southwestern was not diminished nor diluted during the administration of President Head. Instead, it was deepened and broadened.

E. D. Head was very conscious of history and heritage. His first addresses at the seminary looked back before they looked forward. His reports to the Southern Baptist Convention between 1943 and 1953 could well have been prefaced, "Look to the rock from which ye have been digged." In particular, his summaries in 1946, 1947, and 1948, just prior to the fortieth anniversary of the seminary, pointed to the voices and spirit of Carroll and Scarborough in relation to the needs of the seminary.[125]

The continuation of the older spirit of an importunate faith became evident in the face of new distresses caused by the rapid growth of the student body, the need for long-delayed capital improvements, the multiplication of operating expenses because of inflation, and the additional pressures from World War II and the Korean incident. There is an echo of the appeals of L. R. Scarborough in the reports of President Head to the Southern Baptist Convention concerning the "imperative, clamant, inescapable" needs of the seminary.

> We have one thousand students more than we had seven years ago. We are glad they came to Southwestern and we hope still more will come. But their coming does mean that we are literally "bursting at the seams." We have been able—and are immeasurably grateful for it—to provide classrooms, library, and auditorium which are still adequate to care for our 2,074 students. But we have not been able to provide any new dormitories, or apartment houses, or even one single cottage, in the last twenty-five years—since our enrollment was 627.[126]

President Head pointed out that 64 percent of the students were forced to live off the campus because of lack of housing; student fees provided almost half of the seminary's income; and the teacher-student ratio was one to fifty. There were still "happy hard times" on the Hill.

The tradition of comradeship between students and faculty, first fostered by their common financial poverty, continued during this period, despite financial inflation, because of the presence of surviving veterans of the faculty as they blended with the young teachers who had known as students the rigors of depression days. This spirit was "caught," not taught.

The Carroll-Scarborough concept of the seminary as an active participant in contemporary Christian struggles was also the spirit of President Head. His reports to the Southern Baptist Convention regularly recited the activity of students and faculty in the day-by-day work of the Kingdom.[127]

The dominant themes of evangelism and missions also were a major passion of E. D. Head. Every report to the Convention during his presidency called attention to the evangelistic and missionary outreach of the school. As teacher of evangelism during most of his presidency, he inculcated in his students the spirit of the "Chair of Fire" after the pattern of Carroll and Scarborough. Typical of his regular emphasis on missions was his word to the Convention in 1951. He wrote:

> The spirit of missions continues to move with great power through the life of the Seminary. The scheduled mission days have proved to be peaks of inspiration and dedication for all who came under their sway, particularly

for those who responded to the call of the Lord to special fields of service. Fifty-eight have been appointed for mission service so far this school year: 41 foreign missionaries and 17 home missionaries. During the years of the full history of the Seminary 422 missionaries have gone out to foreign fields, while 298 have gone to home fields. The number of volunteers for mission service in the current student body has reached 416, which is one-fourth of the enrollment.[128]

One reason for this enthusiastic report was the inauguration of student mission conferences on the campus of Southwestern. In 1949, several missionary candidates and others vitally concerned with missions engaged in discussions with faculty members about the need for a workshop type of conference which would encourage and instruct young mission volunteers on college campuses, who usually had little contact with the foreign and home mission boards until almost the very time of their appointment. Students like Giles Fort, Ernest Gregory, Ann Alexander, and Roy McGlamery, among others, conferred with several of the faculty about the possibility of an annual conference on Southwestern's campus where college mission volunteers might meet veteran missionaries and catch the inspiration of mingling with people with similar commitments. Encouraged in this project by W. F. Howard, Baptist Student Union leader in Texas, leaders organized the initial conference, held in 1951 under the guidance of Cal Guy, professor of missions. The movement was so enthusiastically received by the students both in Texas and beyond that it became necessary to establish limits on the number who could attend. This problem of size was relieved, however, as other seminaries initiated these mission conferences for college and university students, resulting in a widespread thrust in behalf of missions.[129]

President Head made his own contribution to the spirit of the school. His quiet dedication and excellent scholarship deepened these aspects of campus life. These qualities were not new to the Southwestern campus, but they were incarnated so fully in E. D. Head that all who knew him were moved to imitate him. From the eleven years of his presidency came many outstanding leaders on the mission field and in denominational life on the home field.

Retirement of E. D. Head

The strenuous schedule of President Head can be found in the monthly reports of his activities in the *Southwestern News*. The entire year 1951 was one of constant engagements and little relaxation. At the invitation of the Foreign Mission Board, he flew to Japan on September 17 for a preaching mission. His schedule there was arduous and his strength severely tested. On January 6, 1952, shortly after his return to the campus, he suffered a heart attack. The trustees authorized their vice-president, E. L. Carnett, to act as president during Head's illness.[130]

President Head returned to his task in early March, presiding at the Founder's Day services for his first public appearance. In a gracious letter of appreciation to students, faculty, trustees, and others, he said that if his health continued to show improvement he would go on as president of the school.[131] However, on March 11, 1953, he submitted a letter of resignation to the trustees with the statement that although he was feeling "as good as new" physically, he had come to the conviction by an "irresistible and mandatory" impression that he should resign as president of Southwestern. With expressions of regret from every side, he completed his work on August 1, 1953.[132]

Accomplishments during his presidency had been impressive. The debt of almost $200,000 had been paid. Two new buildings costing about $2,000,000 had been erected without any indebtedness. Both the School of Theology and the School of Religious Education had been accredited. The music library had been established. New driveways had been completed and the old buildings refurbished. Enrollment had increased from 734 in 1942 to 2,160 in 1953. The number of teachers had increased from 23 to 42. Permanent employees had increased from 40 to 87. The monthly payroll had grown from over $7,700 a month to approximately $29,000. Faculty and administrative salaries had doubled. The Reynolds Memorial Organ for Truett Auditorium had been purchased for $59,617. The School of Sacred Music had been provided with new pianos, and its old organ had been renovated. Endowment had increased over $600,000. The faculty and trustee organizational structures had been modernized. And the spirit of missions and evangelism pervaded the campus.[133]

Notes

1. See *Encyclopedia*, III:1753-54 for his biography.

2. Albert McClellan (Nashville, Tennessee) to Robert A. Baker, undated but approximately 24 January 1981, Fleming Library, Southwestern Baptist Theological Seminary, Fort Worth, Texas.

3. *Southwestern News*, May 1951, p. 3. For a portion of Conner's diary describing how the students brought food to him see Stewart A. Newman, *W. T. Conner, Theologian of the Southwest* (Nashville: Broadman Press, 1964), p. 67.

4. *Southwestern News*, May 1951, p. 3.

5. Faculty Minutes, 3 July 1941.

6. See *Southwestern News*, undated but probably published in January 1943, p. 2.

7. E. D. Head, "Our Alluring Future," *Southwestern News*, May 1943, pp. 1-2.

8. *Annual*, SBC, 1944, p. 37.

9. Ibid., p. 104. See also *Southwestern News*, January 1944, p. 3.

10. Trustee Minutes, 12 March 1947.

11. Ibid., 25 November 1952 and 11 March 1953.

12. *Annual*, SBC, 1953, p. 385. See also *Southwestern News*, October 1952, p. 4, relative to operating needs.

13. Trustee Minutes, 22 March 1944; and *Annual*, SBC, 1944, p. 107; 1945, p. 78; 1947, p. 251; 1948, p. 298; and elsewhere.

14. Trustee Minutes, 27 February 1946.

15. Ibid., 9 March 1949.

16. *Southwestern News*, February 1951, p. 1.

17. Ibid., December 1950, p. 1.

18. Trustee Minutes, 28 November 1950.

19. Ibid., 15 May 1952; and Trustee Minutes of the Executive Committee, 17 June 1952.

20. Trustee Minutes, 11 March 1953.

21. *Southwestern News*, October 1944, p. 2. In confirmation of an oral statement see Herschel H. Hobbs to Robert A. Baker, 3 August 1981, Fleming Library, Southwestern Baptist Theological Seminary, Fort Worth, Texas. See also Leon McBeth, "George W. Truett and Southwestern Seminary," Founder's Day Address, 16 March 1971, on file in Fleming Library.

22. *Southwestern News*, October 1944, p. 1.

23. Ibid., January 1945, pp. 2-3.

24. Ibid., May 1945, entire issue.

25. Trustee Minutes, 10 March 1948.

26. *Southwestern News*, June 1948, p. 1.

27. Ibid., October 1949, p. 2.

28. J. M. Price, "School of Religious Education," p. 8, Price Collection.

29. *Annual*, SBC, 1946, p. 356.

30. *Southwestern News*, November 1945, pp. 2, 4.

31. Ibid., October 1948, p. 1.

32. Ibid.

33. *Annual*, SBC, 1947, p. 253.

34. Trustee Minutes, 22 March 1944, 12 March 1947, 10 March 1948, 9 March 1949, 25 November 1952, and elsewhere.

35. Ibid., 6 May 1943; and *Annual*, SBC, 1943, p. 85.

36. Trustee Minutes, 22 March 1944.

37. Ibid., 12 March 1947.

38. Ibid., 12 March 1947.

39. Trustee Minutes of the Executive Committee, 21 March 1944.

40. Ibid., 19 September 1944.

41. Ibid., 10 June 1943, 10 December 1945, 21 December 1950, 16 January 1951,

and 27 November 1951. See also Trustee Minutes of the Finance Committee, 10 December 1948; and Trustee Minutes, 6 May 1943, 9 May 1945, 27 February 1946, and 29 November 1949.

42. Ibid., 6 May 1943 and 9 May 1945. See also Trustee Minutes of the Executive Committee, 21 March 1944; and Trustee Minutes of the Finance Committee, 24 July 1944.

43. See Trustee Minutes, 9 March 1949 and 10 May 1950. Also see Trustee Minutes of the Finance Committee, 24 July 1944.

44. Trustee Minutes, 12 March 1947.

45. Ibid., 9 March 1949.

46. *Southwestern News*, October 1952, p. 2.

47. Ibid., June 1951, p. 1. This issue was dedicated to C. M. King.

48. Trustee Minutes of the Executive Committee, 10 December 1945.

49. Ibid.

50. Trustee Minutes, 12 March 1947.

51. Trustee Minutes of the Executive Committee, 16 March 1950.

52. Faculty Minutes, 4 September 1942, 8 September 1942, 22 September 1942, 6 October 1942, and elsewhere.

53. Ibid., 3 December 1942.

54. Ibid., 12 December 1942.

55. Ibid., 19 January 1943.

56. Ibid., 23 February 1943.

57. Ibid., 9 March 1943.

58. Ibid., 8 May 1943.

59. Ibid., 10 May 1943.

60. Ibid., 3 September 1943.

61. Ibid., 16 November 1943.

62. Ibid., 4 January 1944.

63. Ibid., 3 March 1944.

64. Ibid., 28 March 1944.

65. *Southwestern News*, June 1953, p. 1.

66. Ibid., May 1943, p. 3.

67. Faculty Minutes, 19 February 1946, 6 January 1947, 16 March 1948, 6 April 1948, 20 April 1948, 21 March 1950, and 17 January 1951.

68. Ibid., 8 September 1951.

69. Trustee Minutes, 10 May 1950 and 7 May 1953.

70. Faculty Minutes, 25 May 1943. See also *Southwestern News*, May 1943, p. 3. His biography may be found in *Encyclopedia*, I:337-38.

71. His biography may be found in *Encyclopedia*, II:1133-34, and also in Georgia Miller Ray's story.

72. *Southwestern News*, December 1947, p. 1.

73. Ibid., November 1952, p. 2.

74. S. A. Newman has a number of these "Connerisms" at the close of his book. See *Encyclopedia*, I:310, for his biography.

75. L. Jack Gray to Robert A. Baker, 8 April 1981, Fleming Library, Southwestern Baptist Theological Seminary, Fort Worth, Texas.

76. *Southwestern News*, April 1953, p. 4; and May 1960, p. 8. Also see *Encyclopedia*, III:1608, for his biography.

77. For his biography see H. E. Dana, *Lee Rutland Scarborough, A Life of Service*

(Nashville: Broadman Press, 1942), and *Encyclopedia*, II:1186-87. Also see *Southwestern News*, April 1954, pp. 1-2.

78. *Southwestern News*, February 1950, p. 1. Also see *Encyclopedia*, I:324, for his biography.

79. Faculty Minutes, 4 May 1944 and 30 June 1944; also *Southwestern News*, May 1944, p. 4.

80. *Southwestern News*, November 1944, p. 5.

81. Pictures of these and other new faculty members and brief articles about them are found in the *Southwestern News* at the time they became a part of the faculty.

82. *Southwestern News*, November 1951, p. 4.

83. Trustee Minutes, 12 March 1947; also *Southwestern News*, November 1946, p. 3.

84. *Southwestern News*, November 1948, p. 2; and June 1951, p. 1.

85. Ibid., December 1948, p. 2.

86. Ibid., January 1949, p. 2; and December 1953, p. 1.

87. Ibid., March 1949, p. 2.

88. Ibid., May 1949, p. 2.

89. Ibid., June 1949, p. 2.

90. Ibid., November 1944, p. 4.

91. Ibid., June 1949, p. 2. See also Southwestern *Catalogue*, 1950-51, p. 7.

92. *Annual*, SBC, 1945, p. 78.

93. Trustee Minutes, 11 March 1953.

94. Ibid.

95. Faculty Minutes, 23 February 1943 and 3 September 1943. See also *Southwestern News*, May 1943, p. 3; and November 1943, pp. 3-4.

96. W. W. Barnes, "Curriculum for the School of Theology, Revised," *Southwestern News*, January 1944, p. 1.

97. This was approved by the trustees on 9 May 1945.

98. Faculty Minutes, 13 February 1945.

99. See *Southwestern News*, March 1951, pp. 1-2; and Southwestern *Catalogue*, 1951-52, pp. 42 ff.

100. Faculty Minutes, 20 October 1942, 17 November 1942, 24 November 1942, and 14 December 1943.

101. *Southwestern News*, March 1946, p. 3.

102. Southwestern *Catalogue*, 1951-52, pp. 86-87.

103. Ibid., 1948-49, pp. 46, 61.

104. Ibid., 1950-51, pp. 73-74.

105. *Southwestern News*, February 1949, p. 2; and February 1952, pp. 1-2.

106. Ibid., March 1953, p. 2.

107. Ibid., November 1949, p. 4.

108. Ibid., March 1953, p. 2.

109. Faculty Minutes, 8 June 1943 and 4 January 1944.

110. Ibid., 25 September 1945. See also *Southwestern News*, March 1946, p. 5.

111. *Southwestern News*, September 1949, p. 1.

112. Ibid., October 1947, p. 1.

113. Ibid., January 1948, p. 1.

114. Ibid.

115. Ibid., December 1945, p. 6.

116. Faculty Minutes, 2 January 1945, 6 January 1947, and 17 April 1951.

117. Ibid., 19 February 1952. See also *Southwestern News*, May 1952, p. 1.

118. *Southwestern News,* March 1947, p. 4; February 1948, p. 3; and November 1951, p. 3.

119. Ibid., May 1947, p. 2.

120. Ibid., June 1949, p. 8; and November 1949, p. 1.

121. Ibid., March 1951, pp. 1, 3.

122. Ibid., June 1952, p. 4; and March 1953, p. 2.

123. Ibid., March 1951, p. 2; and December 1951, p. 3.

124. Ibid., January 1947, p. 3; September 1949, p. 2; and January 1951, p. 4.

125. *Annual,* SBC, 1943, p. 86; 1944, p. 106; 1945, p. 77; 1946, p. 100; 1947, pp. 253-54; and 1948, p. 298.

126. Ibid., 1952, pp. 368-69.

127. Ibid., 1944, p. 107; 1950, p. 327; and 1951, p. 354.

128. Ibid., 1951, p. 354.

129. Cal Guy to Robert A. Baker, 20 October 1981, Fleming Library, Southwestern Baptist Theological Seminary, Fort Worth, Texas.

130. Trustee Minutes, 16 January 1952.

131. *Southwestern News,* April 1952, p. 1.

132. Ibid., April 1953, p. 2.

133. Ibid., December 1952, p. 2; and March 1953, p. 2.

J. Howard Williams
President (1953-58)

J. Howard Williams Student Village
Begun 1958

Faculty
About 1957

T. M. Bennett
Old Testament (1953-76)

C. W. Brister
Pastoral Ministry (1957-   )

Robert L. Burton
Conducting (1956-   )

Robert S. Douglass
Musicology (1954-   )

John W. Drakeford
Psychology (1956-   )

William R. Estep
Church History (1954-   )

Wayne Evans
Vice-President (1954-   )

Virtus E. Gideon
New Testament (1957-   )

L. Jack Gray
Missions (1956-   )

Felix Gresham
Seminary Chaplain
(1955-　)

James Leitch
Director of Properties
(1953-　)

Leon Marsh
Foundations of Education
(1956-　)

Dorothy Pulley
Secretary (1957-　)

C. W. Scudder
Christian Ethics (1954-75)

Frank D. Stovall, III
Voice (1957-　)

S. Charles Williamson
Voice (1955-　)

Floreid Wills
Catalog Librarian (1954-75)

8

Five Golden Years

On June 2, 1953, E. L. Carnett, chairman of the committee of the trustees to recommend a new president, reported to them as follows:

> We have had four meetings. We had the names of a number of fine men and carefully considered each name in the light of the needs of the seminary. We are united in our choice. After much prayer we bring you the name of Dr. J. Howard Williams, executive secretary of Texas Baptists, as the one for president of Southwestern Seminary, a great leader and administrator who is second to none.

It required a great deal of earnest praying before J. Howard Williams even considered becoming the fourth president of the school. As early as 1945, while he was visiting with retired President L. R. Scarborough, that venerable soul-winner startled Williams by saying that he believed God would one day call the gifted young preacher to be president of Southwestern Seminary. Williams replied promptly, "Dr. Scarborough, I am not a school man. I am hardly qualified for that work." Scarborough responded, "Howard, do not limit God!" Although he did not say it at that time, Scarborough could have said to Williams what he often expressed to others:

> Howard, I was not a school man either, but I leaned heavily upon my faculty—men like Barnes, Conner, Copass, Dana, Price, Ray, and others—and they helped me in school matters while I administered the school in such a way as to use their resources to the fullest.

William Fleming, a member of the committee, later described how the committee had approached Williams after they were firmly convinced that he was "the most able man in our Southern Baptist Convention for president." At first Williams "felt sure that God could not be calling him to the presidency of the seminary." Despite this rebuff, the committee refused to consider anyone else until Williams had time to "think and pray and let God speak to his heart." Mrs. Williams was reluctant for her husband to assume the burden of seminary leadership since he had experienced a severe heart attack about five years earlier. William Fleming described how the decision was finally reached.

> One morning about 10:00 a. m. Dr. Williams called me on the telephone and said, "Deacon, Mrs. Williams and I want to have a season of prayer

329

with you and Mrs. Fleming. Could we meet at your home about 1:30 p. m.?"
When we were seated in our living room, he asked if the committee were
still waiting on him. I told him that the name of no other person had been
mentioned. Dr. Williams said, "The Lord has been keeping this before me
day and night. We want you to join us in prayer that God will help us to a
decision."

We prayed and talked for three hours. . . . I feel that God helped Dr.
Williams to decide in an hour, but not Mrs. Williams. She seemed to be
holding back, not saying all she was thinking. She could understand that
Dr. Williams was ready to accept the call. Mrs. Williams, who was sitting
on the sofa, moved to her knees and leaned on the sofa and prayed a
sobbing prayer of surrender to God. She said, "Lord, I give Howard to you
to use as you will. If it means he gives his life in the work—and you want
him—take him." Dr. Williams knelt by her and together they agreed to his
being recommended by the committee to the Board of Trustees as the fourth
president of Southwestern Baptist Theological Seminary. Mrs. Williams
seemed to believe it would end just as it did, but I have never heard her
complain. She was and is a great Christian woman.[1]

When approached for this task, J. Howard Williams was a mature and
experienced leader at the age of fifty-nine. He was accounted to be one of
the finest denominational executives among Southern Baptists. Born on
July 3, 1894, at Dallas, Texas, the third of twelve children, he was reared
in a devout Christian home and called to preach at the age of sixteen.
Obtaining an education was a struggle, but he was awarded his
baccalaureate from Baylor University in 1918 and his Master of Theology
from Southwestern Seminary in 1922. He completed his resident
doctoral study at The Southern Baptist Theological Seminary in 1923.
He did not write his dissertation and take the degree because he felt
God's leadership to accept the call to become pastor of the First Baptist
Church, Sulphur Springs, Texas. Baylor University conferred an honor-
ary doctorate on him in 1932. He served as a chaplain in Europe in
World War I. Later he was pastor of some of the strongest churches in the
Southern Baptist Convention, including the First Baptist Church of
Amarillo, Texas, and the First Baptist Church of Oklahoma City,
Oklahoma. He had been president of the Baptist General Convention of
Texas, president of the Board of Trustees of Oklahoma Baptist University,
president of Texas Alcohol-Narcotics Education, Inc., and a member of
the Executive Committee of the Baptist World Alliance. Twice he was
executive secretary of the Baptist General Convention of Texas. In all of
these places of service he had displayed exceptional administrative
skills, unusual versatility, remarkable vision, and complete dedication to
the work of Jesus Christ.[2] He had been well prepared for his last
responsibility as president of Southwestern Seminary.

"Hoops of Steel"

J. Howard Williams possessed a spiritual gift which overshadowed even his many talents as a leader and his considerable ability as an administrator. This unfailing boon was his graciousness. He elicited the best from his co-workers without any suggestion of arrogance or domination. Those who counted themselves his antagonists, he uniformly viewed with a warmhearted attitude of rational goodwill. Not long after moving to Seminary Hill, he wrote an article for the *Southwestern News* which revealed this spirit. He had visited a number of churches and was commenting on "the common denominator" among them. The early churches, he wrote, were "primarily fellowships" with little or no organization, but they were bound together "as with hoops of steel." He concluded by saying, "Organization is indispensable to the most effective service. It should never be permitted, however, to get in the way of fellowship." Although writing about churches, it was evident that President Williams was thinking about the primacy of fellowship in the seminary.[3]

Not without reason, many of his friends described him as the "apostle of good fellowship." When about a dozen men were asked to provide one chapter each in recounting the life of Williams, almost without exception each one, without the knowledge of the others, emphasized this wholesome and contagious spirit of friendliness and goodwill as one of the most excellent spiritual gifts of J. Howard Williams.

At the time the committee of the trustees was seeking permission to present his name for the presidency, some of Williams's denominational associates warned him that there had been friction and misunderstanding between the faculty and the administration of the seminary and counseled him not to get involved in the situation. But his spirit was such that from the moment he stepped on the campus until the time of his death, there was never a hint that any such problem had ever existed. For several years before his move to the seminary, the theological faculty had been conducting an informal preterm retreat, partly to make final preparations for the fall term of the seminary and partly for fellowship and relaxation. The new president accepted the invitation to attend this retreat, and his common touch and transparent honesty immediately won the wholehearted allegiance of every faculty member there. Because of this experience, he encouraged the development of a regular retreat for all of the faculty before the beginning of the fall term each year.[4]

There are numerous examples of how this warmhearted man used this spiritual gift as a means of Christian fellowship and witness.[5] One of these examples illustrates the pattern of his entire life. In the mid-1950s a comity meeting between Baptists in the North and the South assembled at Washington, DC, and President Williams and one of his faculty represented Southwestern Seminary. Shortly after the plane became airborne, Williams introduced himself to the stewardess and learned that he had baptized her father and mother and that she was a member of a church where he had formerly been a pastor. At the rear of the craft where a table was provided, he took from his briefcase a well-worn set of dominoes. Before long a game was underway, in which a colonel from the United States Air Force and a businessman from New York took part. Before the plane landed near Washington, Williams had won the colonel to Christ and had created a wholesome Christian atmosphere among all of the passengers around him.

This winsome spirit of President Williams was contagious. In each report to the trustees he spoke of the excellent spirit among the faculty and the entire seminary family.[6] In the spring of his first year, the trustees invited any of the faculty who chose to do so to attend the meetings of the trustees.[7]

In his first greetings to the students and alumni of the school, President Williams wrote:

> Surely, there is no one who has spent any time on the Hill who does not love *Southwestern*. The shape of things has changed considerably since I was here first in 1919. . . .
>
> The spirit of *Southwestern*, however, is the same. The founding fathers plowed deep furrows and the main currents of the life of this Seminary are not easily diverted. I am glad to report that even in these brief days of my stay here I have felt something of the surge of the older days, when as a student here my life was so blessed and my vision enlarged.[8]

"The Long Look"

The new president was superbly equipped for his new administrative task by his two successful periods of service as the executive secretary of Texas Baptists. He knew the motivational value of setting challenging goals and possessed the administrative skills required to achieve them. He said:

> Sometimes problems cannot be met because we are smothered with the sense of the immediate. To solve present problems with greatest wisdom one needs always to have the proper perspective. The long look is an essential ingredient in the proper solution of present problems.[9]

With this long look, he came to his first trustee meeting on November 24,

1953, which was held rather early in the morning before the beginning of the crowded inaugural schedule of that day. After lunch the trustees continued to transact their numerous items of business. They faced many problems. Additional faculty were required; capital needs were numerous; operational expenses threatened a deficit in the budget; additional endowment was imperative. The trustees must have been amazed at the manner in which Williams grasped the entire situation and took the long look to solve the problems.

In his inaugural address on that evening, President Williams emphasized the spiritual needs of the world and the important place of the theological seminary in meeting this challenge.[10] At the close of this message, in a startling postscript to his address, Williams called for an advance program to raise $10,000,000 during the next five years for Southwestern Seminary. Half of this amount, he said, should be added to the endowment. He specified how the other $5,000,000 should be expended. "Above all," he said, "we must have a larger faculty. We must do away with our present packhorse method of teaching," where some professors had as many as 180 students in a class. The school badly needed some new buildings, he continued. These included a student union center, a gymnasium, and a nursery. "There are 900 wives of ministerial students now unable to attend classes and prepare themselves to work side by side with their husbands because they have no place to leave their children." Another ciritcal need, he remarked, was for 500 housing units for students, for "1,100 student families are now paying exorbitant rents for sub-standard housing off the campus." At least $500,000 was needed to repair existing structures, and the same amount for building a wing to house the School of Theology "which is badly overcrowded and has to borrow space in other buildings."[11] The large audience, including faculty and students, was stunned by this bold program, which had been approved by the trustees on that day. They had indeed been "smothered with the sense of the immediate," and this surprising challenge provided a new climate for facing their problems.

Hatching His Dreams

In all of his previous places of pastoral and denominational service, J. Howard Williams had always projected what appeared to be unattainable challenges, then, with a wisdom and vigor which caused his associates to marvel, he accomplished them. In a summary chapter in the biography of Williams, describing him as a superb denominational executive,

R. A. Springer, the treasurer of the Baptist General Convention of Texas for many years, remarked that through many years of dreaming impossible dreams, Williams had failed to reach the objective in very few cases. His achievements in breaking new ground for denominational service while executive secretary of Texas Baptists were significant.[12]

Those who had known him and his ability as a leader may have been astonished at the bold program he set for the seminary after his first few weeks as president, but none doubted that he would follow his normal pattern: visualize impossible dreams and then achieve them. Mrs. J. Howard Williams said about him, "I always knew when he was 'hatching' a dream. It spilled over and ran all over the place. He would say to a guest in the home, 'Get in the car. I want to show you something.'"[13] He would then take the guest to the spot on or near the campus where he had by faith seen in his mind the building that was needed there. His enthusiasm was usually converted into promises of assistance.

Despite his sudden death in less than five years, it is surprising how near he came to accomplishing all of his dreams for the seminary. He was well on his way toward his objectives when he ran out of time. His principal goals, as expressed in his inaugural address, were (1) faculty enlargement and support, (2) increased allocations from the Southern Baptist Convention for seminary operations, (3) more teaching space, (4) a campaign for funds, (5) student housing, (6) campus renovation, (7) added endowment, and (8) other student facilities like a gymnasium and a kindergarten-nursery building.[14] Most of these overlapping goals were attacked simultaneously, but they will be described singly to reveal to what extent they were accomplished.

Faculty Enlargement and Support

President Williams had deep convictions about the centrality of a strong and stable faculty. In February, 1955, he put into written form the spirit that he so often expressed orally to his faculty. He wrote:

> Now that I am well into my second year with *Southwestern*, I can say that my admiration of and affection for the faculty have increased with the passing months. I like them as men and women who are agreeable to work with. I like them as a team cooperating in a united effort. I admire them as Christian men and women who are dedicated to the high calling of teaching. Their dedication is evidenced by the preparation they have made for the task. Numbers of them have the native ability, the academic training, the earned degrees, and the necessary experience to enable them to teach anywhere in the fields of their studies. Some of them could well be members of the faculties at Harvard, Yale, Oxford, Cambridge, or any

other institution of higher learning whether theological or academic.

The dedication of the faculty to the Lord, to *Southwestern*, and to the high calling of teaching is further evidenced by the fact that many of them stay here even though they are sought for in other fields of service. Frankly, their financial income would be markedly enhanced if they should leave. . . .

At a recent faculty meeting I took occasion to commend them that, so far as I know, none of them has "itching feet." I reminded them again that no seminary can render a greater service than that made possible by the faculty and that no faculty can do its best work where there is a lack of stability, uneasiness, or the wistful looking of its members for greener pastures. So far as I know, such does not characterize any member of the faculty at *Southwestern*. . . .

The primary function of administration is to enable the faculty to deliver its fullest potential impact on the student body. The school, of course, exists for the student, and the primary help to the student must come from the faculty. It is easy to be fond of our faculty as individuals, but it is far more important to so conduct the affairs of this Seminary that these devoted friends may be able, as servants of the Lord, to give their best to this all-important work, "that the man of God may be perfect, thoroughly furnished unto all good works."[15]

With President Williams holding this point of view, it is not surprising that efforts were promptly made by the trustees to add new faculty members and to provide adequate support in the face of growing inflationary trends in the economy. Some of the familiar names added to the faculty of the School of Theology during this period were Carl A. Clark in pastoral ministry, W. R. Estep in church history, William H. Rossell in Old Testament, and C. W. Scudder in Christian ethics (1954); Gordon Clinard in preaching, C. E. Autrey in evangelism, and Jeremiah Vardaman in archaeology (1955); Milton Ferguson in philosophy of religion and L. Jack Gray in missions (1956); and C. W. Brister in pastoral ministry and Virtus E. Gideon in New Testament (1957). In the School of Religious Education new faculty were John Drakeford in psychology and James H. Daniel in childhood education (1954); Lee H. McCoy in church administration and Miss Monte McMahon in church administration (1955); Leon Marsh in principles of education (1956); and Harvey Hatcher in educational arts (1958). The School of Sacred Music added Robert S. Douglass in music history (1954); S. Charles Williamson in voice (1955); Robert L. Burton in church music education, Paul Green in conducting, Talmadge W. Dean in theory, and Jo Ann Shelton in voice (1956); and Frank D. Stovall in voice and John E. Woods in piano (1957).[16]

There were several losses from the faculty. The retirement of L. R. Elliott, who served as occasional teacher in the School of Theology but whose principal contribution was made in the library, will be mentioned later. Ralph Phelps resigned in 1953 to become president of Ouachita Baptist University, Arkadelphia, Arkansas. The School of Religious Education sustained two severe faculty losses in this period. On July 1, 1954, W. L. Howse, professor of administration of religious education, accepted the post of director of the new Educational Division of the Southern Baptist Sunday School Board, Nashville, Tennessee. He had taught at Southwestern since 1932 and had served numerous large churches as educational director. He was a superb teacher and author and an excellent leader. Resolutions of appreciation for him came from trustees, faculty, and students.[17] After a distinguished service with the Sunday School Board, he died on December 27, 1977.

The other major loss of this school was the retirement of J. M. Price on July 31, 1956. He had been one of the earliest religious education specialists in the nation and, despite opposition from many sides, had pioneered in numerous aspects of the field. In the year of his retirement the seminary catalogue listed a number of "firsts" initiated by Price in the School of Religious Education.

1. It was the first school among Baptists to offer vocational training for workers in religious education (1915).
2. It was also the first institution in America to confer religious-educational diplomas and degrees (1917).
3. It was the first school among Baptists to offer a doctor's degree with a major in religious education (1919).
4. It led Baptists in requiring supervised field work (observation, practice, and clinical work) as a requirement for graduation (1920).
5. It initiated the first Sunday School Superintendent's Conference (forerunner of state Sunday School Conventions) in the South (1920).
6. It held the first vocational conference on religious education (1921), now the Southwestern Religious Education Association.
7. It originated the first church demonstration and practice kindergarten in a Southern Baptist seminary (1921).
8. The movement among Southern Baptist seminaries for requiring academic prerequisites for Seminary degrees originated in this school (1922).
9. The provision for separate special courses for Seminary students without college training likewise originated in this school (1922).
10. It sponsored the first Vacation Bible School west of the Mississippi and the oldest existing one in the South among Southern Baptists (1922).
11. It has America's first building designed exclusively for teaching and practice of all activities of religious education (1950).
12. It was the first School of Religious Education among Southern Baptists to be accredited (1951).
13. The school offered the first complete credit courses among Baptists in Age-Group Work (1919), Recreational Leadership (1921), Vacation

and Weekday Schools (1921), Secretarial Training (1922), Religious Publicity (1922), Church Finances (1923), Baptist Student Union Work (1923), Arts and Crafts (1923), Religious Dramatics (1924), Visual Aids (1926), Religious Counseling (1933), and Church Library Work (1948).

14. It sponsored the first Workshop for Ministers of Education in the Southern Baptist Convention (1957).[18]

Many of these "firsts" could not have been achieved without the alert and tenacious mind of J. M. Price. His teaching was methodical and thorough, enlivened by a keen sense of humor. When he learned that some of the students had called him "Dusty Price" because they considered his teaching dry, he often began his new classes with this story on himself.

At the May commencement, 1956, this outstanding educator and author was honored for his achievements. Words of appreciation came from his grateful students in many parts of the world. His ministry continued after his retirement, and he was the recipient of many additional honors before his death on January 12, 1976.[19]

There were three major losses from the School of Sacred Music. Mrs. I. E. Reynolds, who had been teaching in this school since 1915, retired in June, 1956. Her dedication and spirit had endeared her to the seminary family. On February 5, 1957, the recital auditorium in Cowden Hall was dedicated to her and her husband and became "The Reynolds Recital Hall." She died on March 30, 1971.

On April 16, 1957, the talented and gracious Mrs. Edwin McNeely died after a long illness. She had taught since 1920. Knowing her love for the piano, the school dedicated a new concert grand piano to her memory.[20]

The third loss from the School of Sacred Music was that of J. Campbell Wray. He had served well since 1943, and after 1947 he had provided excellent leadership as director of the school. His resignation effective July, 1956, was received with regret.[21]

With the retirement of J. M. Price and the resignation of J. Campbell Wray, the seminary had lost two of the three directors of its schools. To replace Price the trustees named Joe Davis Heacock to head the School of Religious Education effective August 1, 1956.[22] Succeeding J. Campbell Wray as head of the School of Sacred Music was James C. McKinney.[23] Jesse Northcutt remained the head of the School of Theology. On February 26, 1957, the trustees voted to change the title of *director* for these men to that of *dean*.

In the report of the trustees to the Southern Baptist Convention in May,

1958, after the death of President Williams, it was noted in summary that during the administration of Williams the faculty of the School of Theology had been increased by eighteen, the School of Religious Education by eight, and the School of Sacred Music by eleven, for a total of thirty-seven.[24] In addition, each year the seminary increased its use of contract teachers and teaching fellows, who could be employed by the administration as need arose.[25] President Williams often wrote about the need for "doubling" the size of the faculty, but his dreams at this point were limited by the allocations from the Convention for operating funds.

It should be added that not only was it the dream of President Williams to increase the number of the faculty, but he also made a determined effort to bring their remuneration and other benefits to a scale comparable with those of other Southern Baptist seminaries. Consonant with the availability of funds, salaries were slowly increased. Other benefits were provided. On November 24, 1953, the trustees voted to allow each faculty member the sum of one hundred dollars as expense to attend either the Southern Baptist Convention or a professional meeting each year. A retirement plan was introduced on March 2, 1954, by which faculty and staff members who were not covered by the contract with the Relief and Annuity Board would pay 2 percent of their salaries and the seminary would provide the other 3 percent to secure this coverage. Young teachers were assisted in buying their homes through a program in which the seminary would indemnify the bank loans to them of not more than three thousand dollars for a five-year period.[26] Over a dozen teachers took advantage of this. Faculty members beyond forty-five years of age were encouraged to enter into writing projects by a program which allowed them to reduce their teaching load by two or four semester hours for one year and which promised secretarial help and assistance in finding a publisher.[27]

Perhaps one of the offshoots of this encouragement to do additional writing was the move by the faculty of the School of Theology to reestablish the *Southwestern Journal of Theology*, which had been published as a quarterly by the faculty from 1919 to 1924. In 1958, James Leo Garrett became its managing editor, and the first issue was published in October of that year. The new journal was designed to inform pastors, teachers, denominational workers, and others concerning theological trends from the perspective of a constructive Baptist evangelicalism. Its format included a homiletical section for pastors, articles by the faculty and others, book reviews, and, later on, a special annual issue devoted to particular bibilical emphases of the Southern Baptist Convention, such as the January Bible Study.[28]

The sabbatical leave program for the faculty received considerable impetus from the alumni during this period. At the annual breakfast of the Convention-wide alumni in May, 1952, a plan was adopted to provide funds for pro rata allocation to faculty members taking sabbatical leave. For several years this program was actively promoted by Stanley E. Wilkes, Convention-wide alumni president, and about a dozen faculty members benefited from it.[29] In addition, to encourage faculty members to use this time for study, the trustees voted on February 26, 1957, to allow full salary for one year when faculty members used their sabbatical leave to study for an additional doctorate. Previously, the faculty member had been allowed full salary for a one-semester leave and half salary for an entire year's leave.

In his last two trustee meetings before his death, President Williams called attention to some additional benefits for the faculty and staff which he and the Finance Committee had included in the budget for 1958-59. These included the assumption by the school of retirement dues in the amount of 8 percent of the individual's salary on a four-thousand-dollar base, the payment of hospitalization coverage, and an equalization of salaries of ordained men who had waived their exemption under the Social Security law.[30] It should be added that the trustees had constantly kept abreast of the developing Social Security system in order that they might provide the best protection for the faculty and staff consonant with Baptist principles.[31] In his final trustee meeting, President Williams approved the participation of Southwestern in the uniform retirement plan known as the Southern Baptist Protection Plan.[32] He also favored the deduction of housing allowances for ordained faculty as provided by the law.[33]

Increasing Operating Allocations

To enable the administration to provide additional faculty and adequate support for them, it became necessary to seek a larger allocation of funds from the Southern Baptist Convention. Often this effort involved a rivalry with other agencies, particularly seminaries, for available funds. This competitive spirit was so completely alien to President Williams that he always returned to the campus from these Executive Committee meetings with frustration and total exhaustion. Those closest to him felt that this burden was probably the heaviest that he encountered during his presidency. After the meeting in Nashville in early 1954, where he had strenuously contended for an increased allocation, he reported to the trustees on March 2, 1954, that Southwestern was receiving the lowest per student allocation by far of any of the seminaries, due to the fact that the current method of making the allocation did not take into account the huge student body. He noted that in the allocation for 1954 Southern Seminary and Southwestern each had received 3.51 percent of the total Convention budget for operating funds, New Orleans Seminary (formerly Baptist Bible Institute) had received 3.83 percent, Southeastern Seminary had received 2.91 percent, and Golden Gate Seminary had received 2.27 percent. These percentages were arrived at by the Executive Committee on the basis of the forceful presentation by the president of each school concerning the needs of his own institution. The reason for President Williams's distress may be glimpsed by the fact that from these allocations Southwestern was training 2,375 students; Southern, 1,633 students; New Orleans, 947 students; Southeastern, 394 students; and Golden Gate, 277 students. Since 1945, Southwestern had trained over 46 percent of all students in the Southern Baptist seminaries but had received less than 28 percent of the operating allocations. Or, in another comparison, Southwestern had trained approximately the same number of students as both Southern and New Orleans seminaries put together and was allocated less than 28 percent of the distributable funds, while these two schools had together received allocations during the same period of over 51 percent of the distributable funds.

The trustees strongly supported President Williams's call for a formula that would redress this inequity. In 1955 and 1956 no such formula was developed. In the latter year, however, the Executive Committee of the Convention, acting upon the recommendation of the Committee to Study the Total Southern Baptist Program, began a careful review of the allocations for theological education and, after some revisions, proposed a formula for the allocations of 1958. Unfortunately, however, the allocation for 1958-59 for Southwestern was more than $100,000 below the amount projected by the proposed operating budget adopted by the trustees in the fall of 1957.

The problem was constantly being exacerbated by the inflationary economy. Appropriations through the Cooperative Program increased from $652,183.80 in 1954 to $739,366.71 in 1958; but the critical need for enlarging the number of the faculty and providing the facilities for teaching the huge student body, which had grown so rapidly during the administration of President Head, demanded more funds than were being provided. On February 28, 1958, at the last trustee meeting before the death of President Williams, the trustees carefully scrutinized the proposed budget for 1958-59 which was almost $105,000 more than the proposed allocation from the Convention. By cutting it at every point they could, they were able to reduce it by $37,224.24, leaving an anticipated deficit of $67,337.49 for the year. The minutes said:

> It was noted that no further reductions could be made without seriously impairing the ministry of the Seminary, and that the deficit would completely consume the Seminary's unappropriated current fund surplus of $63,992.61, which constitutes its sole reserve for operations.[34]

The last paragraph of President Williams's last report to the Southern Baptist Convention, however, reflected his optimism and gracious spirit:

> The Cooperative Program is the life-line for our seminary, as it is for all other phases of our work. Increasing support has been granted to the seminaries in recent years. Though deeply grateful for this added support, fairness compels us to report that it is not adequate. We are grateful that many leaders of our Convention are aware of this, and ways are being sought by which Southern Baptists can make possible the adequate training of those who in the days ahead are to have much of the responsibility for the ongoing of our great denomination.
>
> We hereby register our gratitude to Southern Baptists for their support of Southwestern and in the best way we know how voice our praise for the provisions of Providence so evident to us now as we look back over fifty years of history of this "School of the Prophets," whose birth we believe was inspired of the Spirit and whose life and ministry have been sustained by the presence and power of God.[35]

More Teaching Space

The third of President Williams's dreams visualized the acquiring of more teaching space, an imperative need if new teachers were added and if smaller classes were to be achieved. After carefully studying the entire problem, Williams concluded that the best method of accomplishing this goal was to add a wing to the Memorial Building for use by the School of Theology, which was facing a critical shortage of space for teaching and faculty offices. The architectural firm which had been engaged to assist in long-range planning of the campus made the suggestion that not only should a wing be built to the west side of the Memorial Building but that a similar wing, to provide balance for the entire structure, be added to the east side of the building for the expansion of the overcrowded library. On June 3, 1954, the trustees approved the addition to the Memorial Building for the School of Theology. On November 22, 1954, the Buildings and Grounds Committee approved preliminary plans for both the theology wing and a library wing. On the following day the trustee board confirmed this action and began the move to construct the two wings to the Memorial Building.

On January 27, 1955, Director Jesse Northcutt of the School of Theology and Librarian L. R. Elliott met with the Executive Committee and the Buildings and Grounds Committee to provide input on the plans. The architect was then asked to prepare final plans and specifications for bids on these two wings as soon as possible. Groundbreaking took place on April 15, 1955. The two wings were occupied in the summer of 1956.[36] The theology wing provided ten standard classrooms and three specialized rooms that could serve for classes. On the ground floor was a large visual-aid center equipped for all types of visual presentation. Also on this floor was a chapel seating several hundred students. Adjoining it was a studio equipped with facilities for remote radio broadcasting, recording, and closed-circuit televising from the chapel, for use in teaching preaching and communication classes. The first floor housed the president's suite and classrooms, while the second floor provided faculty offices and a faculty room.

The library addition was planned to care for pressing student needs. The entire first floor and part of the ground floor provided reading rooms for students. The remainder of the ground floor and most of the second floor were equipped as stack space for books and special collections, together with over a hundred carrels for graduate students and twenty-seven study rooms for faculty and visiting scholars.

A curious incident provided an additional large classroom for teaching. On May 18, 1955, President Williams reported to the trustees that William Fleming had purchased a life-size replica in wax of Leonardo da Vinci's famous painting "The Last Supper" and wanted to make a gift of this to the seminary. The matter was delayed because there was no suitable place to house this large display. When this was considered on June 1, 1955, Fleming offered to make a further gift of an addition to one of the present structures on the campus to house this art exhibit. On June 7, 1955, the local trustees and the chairman of the Buildings and Grounds Committee voted to accept the gift and house it in a one-story structure added to the west side of Truett Memorial Auditorium. Although the trustee minutes do not reflect it, there was opposition by some to displaying the art exhibit at the seminary lest the life-size images might be interpreted as favoring the use of icons in Baptist worship, and the gift was finally declined. Since the addition to the auditorium had already been completed, this left the question of what to do with the large room. The matter was considered again on November 22, 1955, and on January 17, 1956, President Williams indicated that its best use might be for a missions-history classroom and museum. The basement was left unfinished for the time.[37]

The completion of these new facilities provided classrooms and office space for the increasing faculty. Even so, the allocated operating funds for the school did not bring the desired lowering of the teacher-student ratio, particularly in the School of Theology. To meet this problem, as has been mentioned, the trustees authorized the utilization of additional teaching fellows, contract teachers, and guest teachers. The number of the first two of these categories, particularly, was increased substantially. Their duties, remuneration, and status were approved by the trustees.[38] President Williams was able to say in his last report to the Southern Baptist Convention that the teacher-student ratio had been decreased by one-third during his administration. Smaller classes and the improvement of library facilities brought an improved climate for learning.

Golden Jubilee Expansion Campaign

The fourth dream of J. Howard Williams expressed in his inaugural address was the raising of ten million dollars for needed buildings and endowment. Half of this, he felt, should be used for buildings and half for endowment.

At this first meeting with the trustees on November 24, 1953, President Williams spoke briefly of his dreams, saying that his recommendations would be brought through the various committees. Later in this meeting, at the request of William Fleming, he discussed in more detail the capital needs of the seminary. Evidently this was the occasion when he first challenged them with a goal of ten million dollars for capital needs and endowment. During the year, the president worked with the Buildings and Grounds and the Finance committees to plan the total building program.[39] While the seminary was already engaged in the adding of two wings to the Memorial Building, he expressed his concern for student housing. As a result, plans were laid for a Golden Jubilee Expansion Campaign, aimed principally at Fort Worth but including efforts in all of the major cities of Texas.

The campaign proper probably was initiated in the summer of 1955 when J. Howard Williams prepared an editorial for the May issue of the *Southwestern News* in which he introduced L. B. Reavis as the new director for endowment of the school, saying:

> We now have a great expansion program. It is drastically needed NOW. It calls for $5,000,000 for buildings and a like amount for added endowment. Such amounts are not easy to raise but are clearly in the bounds of our

ability. When people know what our blessed Seminary has done, is doing
and is destined to do, they will gladly support it with extra gifts.[40]

However, the campaign was delayed until the spring of 1956 in order that
the trustees might complete proposed land purchases, secure major
individual gifts prior to the general campaign, and make careful plans
for the concentrated effort.[41]

On June 1, 1955, President Williams reported that approval had been
given by the Solicitations Committee of the city of Fort Worth for the
seminary to conduct a financial campaign during February, March, and
April, 1956. To fix the amount needed in the campaign, the trustees
noted that the Southern Baptist Convention had promised capital needs
allocations estimated at $242,466.67 a year from 1955 to 1957, or a total
of $727,400.01 from this source. Other sources of capital needs income
were available to bring the estimated total amount to be counted on the
campaign to $1,132,761.31. On June 20, 1955, the local trustees voted to
employ a professional firm to assist in the campaign, and Homer Covey, a
deacon in Broadway Baptist Church, Fort Worth, was elected permanent
campaign chairman. Members of the campaign committee included
Chairman Covey, Cochairman T. J. Harrell, William Fleming, Robert E.
Naylor, J. T. Luther, J. H. Steger, President Williams, Endowment
Secretary L. B. Reavis, and Business Manager Wayne Evans.

Beginning with July, 1955, each issue of the *Southwestern News*
trumpeted the story of the Golden Jubilee effort. Much of this material
was prepared by L. B. Reavis, endowment secretary.[42] He and President
Williams visited prospective donors across the state and received cordial
acceptance.[43] Alumni in strategic cities of the state pledged their
cooperation. On January 5, 1956, W. A. Criswell addressed the students
in chapel, mentioning to them that the faculty and administration had
pledged $20,000, and within sixty minutes the student body had
pledged $60,000 to be paid over a three-year period after graduation. On
the same evening, leaders of the campaign met with approximately two
hundred leading citizens of Fort Worth to provide a formal kickoff of the
campaign for $1,500,000 in Fort Worth.[44]

Homer Covey met often with the trustees to describe the progress of
the campaign. The first official tabulation of the results came at the
trustee meeting of May 20, 1956. William Fleming reported that
$922,720.67 had been pledged at that time. Expenses for the campaign
had totaled $67,319.05. Although falling short of the $1,500,000 goal
for Fort Worth, this amount provided funds for the expansion already
taking place. Funds slowly continued to come in, long after the campaign
had ended.

Student Housing

Another of the dreams articulated by President Williams was the provision for student housing. In the early discussions of this project, Williams secured the aid of J. T. Luther, an expert in the field of planning and building in Fort Worth, and this was the beginning of a long and fruitful relationship between this man, later a trustee, and the seminary.[45] On June 3, 1954, the trustees requested the Buildings and Grounds Committee to work with the president in the preparation of recommendations for building priorities. When the Executive Committee of the trustees met on August 23, 1954, President Williams pointed to the great need for student housing and said that he had conferred with the Park Board of the city of Fort Worth concerning the possibility of purchasing the large tract of unimproved land across Seminary Drive just north of the campus as a site for building student apartments. The trustees

> gave enthusiastic support to the arrangement which Dr. Williams felt would be the probable outcome of the purchase of approximately twenty-eight acres of land immediately north of Seminary Drive at the north side of the present campus, at a price of $1,500 per acre plus removal of present civil defense towers.[46]

After the discussion of this site for proposed student housing, the trustees requested their committees to bring recommendations in the March meeting. The Buildings and Grounds Committee together with the Executive Committee met with President Williams on January 27, 1955, when he informed them that surveys were being made and that further plans would have to be delayed until the city had completed its in-house discussions. Williams also reported that a 9.3-acre tract immediately west of the city land would be necessary for the adequate completion of the project. This property belonged to the Santa Fe Railway, and efforts were being made to determine if the seminary could obtain it. On May 13, 1955, the local trustees and the chairman of the Buildings and Grounds Committee studied preliminary sketches of the proposed student village, which had been prepared with the aid of J. T. Luther.

The project was delayed, however, by the failure of efforts to secure the Santa Fe Railway land. President Williams reported on May 18, 1955, that the seminary had purchased the 30.6 acres of land from the city. Proposed layouts of the streets, student apartments, parking areas, and perhaps faculty apartments, were mulled over by committees and the full board of trustees awaiting the outcome of negotiations with the railroad.[47] On August 26, 1955, learning that the city of Fort Worth was planning to widen Seminary Drive from McCart Street to South Adams Street, the trustees voted additional footage to the city for street approaches to the proposed student village and approved the construction of a pedestrian underpass beneath Seminary Drive to connect the campus with the student-housing area.[48] Further plans were delayed to await talks with the Santa Fe officials about the 9.3 acres needed by the seminary.[49]

This final roadblock was removed in the fall of 1956. On August 3, 1956, the Executive Committee of the trustees approved a proposition from the railway officials to exchange the 9.3 acres for 28 lots belonging to the school if a "restricted light industrial" classification could be obtained for these lots. This condition was met, and the exchange was made.[50] From this time the project moved rapidly. The construction of the first 16 buildings, providing 128 units, was approved on August 3, 1956. The cost was estimated at $800,000, which was approximately the amount of the pledges in the financial campaign then being conducted by the seminary. Immediate financing was a problem, but after several alternatives had been explored, the Executive Committee of the Southern Baptist Convention authorized the seminary to borrow $400,000 to initiate the project.[51] Plans and specifications were let out for bids, but on February 26, 1957, the trustees rejected the best bid because it was substantially higher than the architect's estimate.[52] In his remarks to the trustees at this time, President Williams expressed the fervent hope that an acceptable bid could be secured so that groundbreaking exercises for the student village might take place on Founder's Day, March 14, 1957. Perhaps he had a premonition that he would not be able to witness the beginning of this project, which was close to his heart, if there were many more delays.

Finally, on May 9, 1957, contracts were approved for erecting and servicing the first contingent of buildings. However, because of increased costs, it was voted to erect only twelve buildings instead of sixteen, as first planned.[53] Work began promptly. President Williams lived to see these buildings almost completed and to visualize the appearance of the whole project. On February 27, 1959, the trustees voted to memorialize President Williams by naming this project the J. Howard Williams Student Village.

Renovation of the Campus

President Williams also emphasized the need for campus renovation in his inaugural address. This program had already begun. On May 7,

1953, before Williams had assumed the leadership of the seminary, the trustees approved the renovation of Fort Worth Hall at a cost not to exceed $250,000. This was badly needed after forty-three years of hard service. The Buildings and Grounds Committee employed a professional architect to assist in planning this renovation. On November 24, 1955, the trustees were informed that the renovation of Fort Worth Hall had been completed for approximately $172,000 and that the renovation had substantially improved the functions and appearance of the building.[54]

In the fall of 1954, James R. Leitch became superintendent of buildings and grounds, and his many skills were promptly evident. On January 27, 1955, he reported to the trustees that the women's building needed a number of repairs, which he estimated would cost approximately $36,000. He believed that the seminary maintenance staff could make most of these repairs. The work was completed shortly after the opening of the fall term in September.[55]

On November 24, 1953, the trustees approved the installation of air conditioning in the Memorial Building. On April 24, 1954, a bid was accepted, and on November 23, 1954, President Williams reported that the work had been completed. The renovation and air conditioning of Cowden Hall were approved on November 26, 1957. On February 28, 1958, at the last trustee meeting of President Williams, it was reported that an architect for this project had been secured. Price Hall also underwent repairs and renovation. The concrete slab under the south half of the building had cracked and was beginning to sag.[56] On August 3, 1956, the trustees were advised that cement was being pumped under the slab in an attempt to raise floors and corridors and close cracks in the walls. This was successfully done.

On November 26, 1957, the trustees approved the construction of a duplex at 1901-1903 Seminary Drive to provide two three-bedroom quarters for missionary families. On February 28, 1958, it was reported that this project was almost completed.

On March 2, 1954, the Buildings and Grounds Committee recommended that a trailer park for students with trailer homes be developed adjacent to the campus. Plans for this were approved on June 3, 1954, and on November 23, 1954, President Williams advised the trustees that this park, located just south of the campus, had been completed. The park became so popular that on November 22, 1955, the trustees voted to add twenty-six spaces to it. Street improvements were made in the area of the park, and on November 26, 1957, it was enlarged to fifty-two spaces.[57]

One of the significant decisions of the trustees during this period was to beautify the campus. Grass began to be watered throughout the summer, and trees and shrubs were planted; parking lots were hard topped; overall beautification plans for the campus were discussed by committees and the full board; and lights were provided to illumine the buildings by night.[58]

Before J. Howard Williams came to the presidency, the trustees had purchased the home of Mrs. Perry Evans, located on the site of B. H. Carroll's residence in 1910.[59] This became the new president's home. It was later enlarged to provide additional space for seminary functions.[60]

On September 13, 1955, President Williams called the attention of the Executive Committee of the trustees to the need for a maintenance warehouse. This was approved and the warehouse constructed.[61]

The provision of space for a student center and an infirmary required considerable renovation. On November 22, 1955, the trustees approved a committee recommendation that preliminary sketches for these two facilities be prepared. At first the Buildings and Grounds Committee looked toward locating these in a separate student union building. On February 28, 1956, a tentative floor plan and a sketch of the proposed building were presented to the trustees. The idea was that perhaps some prospective donor could be interested in providing this facility as a memorial. However, on July 12, 1956, President Williams met with local trustees and introduced Weldon Dennis, who had been secured to head a department which included food service, the student center, and the infirmary. Out of the recommendations of this group, the trustees on August 3, 1956, approved President Williams's suggestion that a student center be inaugurated on the ground floor of Scarborough Hall. The trustees also approved a recommendation that an infirmary be located on the ground floor of the new mission center building which had been erected on the west side of the Memorial Building through the gift of William Fleming and his wife. A medical fee of two dollars per student was suggested, with the opportunity of including a wife and family for an additional two-dollar fee. On February 26, 1957, the trustees were told that the infirmary and student center had completed a successful year of operation under Weldon Dennis, superintendent of food and health services.[62]

Increasing the Endowment

The efforts to enlarge the endowment had been a constant concern of the trustees since the school was founded. President Williams took up the cry in his inaugural address, urging that at least five million dollars should be the goal for new endowment. This became another of the high priorities of Williams's administration. J. W. Bruner was named endowment secretary effective September 1, 1953. It was agreed at the time that he would occupy this position only until a permanent secretary could be found, since he had already made a commitment for his future service. On November 23, 1954, after fourteen months at this post, Bruner requested that he be released effective December 31, 1954, to meet his other assignment.[63]

On March 1, 1955, the trustees approved the recommendation of the Endowment Committee that L. B. Reavis, pastor of the First Baptist Church, Denton, Texas, be elected halftime endowment secretary from April 1, 1955, until May 1, 1955, when he would be able to give his full time to the task. In almost every report of the trustees during the remainder of this period, the work of Secretary Reavis was praised.[64] In his first statement to the trustees on September 13, 1955, he reported that since beginning his service five months earlier he had received $15,425.00 in pledges, $21,411.85 in cash, and approximately $800,000.00 for the seminary in wills to be probated in years ahead. He presented a long report on his involvement in the Golden Jubilee Expansion Campaign for buildings and endowment and outlined a program for future endowment activities. In 1956, his title was changed to Director of Endowment and Promotion.[65]

Early in his administration, President Williams had requested the trustees to establish an Advisory Council which would have no executive powers but would function as a body of friends of the seminary. Williams constantly made reference to the helpfulness of this council and the benefits for the seminary from it, not only in goodwill and added interest in the school, but also in substantial gifts.[66] On February 26, 1957, Reavis reported to the trustees that this council consisted of "men in strategic places" who would be of invaluable service to the seminary. A rare picture of this group appeared in the *Southwestern News* of November, 1957. Those present at this meeting were W. A. Barker, Denton; Vergal Bourland, Fort Worth; John Crain, Paris; Ted Ferguson, Amarillo; Marshall Formby, Plainview; Cullum Greene, Fort Worth; Walter Hamilton, Fort Worth; T. E. Hunt, Sr., Paris; A. A. Jackson, Fort Worth; Gordon Maddox, Denton; Hulin Means, Albuquerque, New Mexico; Freland Murphy, Houston; and Jim Whittenberg, Amarillo.

As Reavis pointed out, the gracious spirit of J. Howard Williams in his contacts with these men and others played a large role in adding to the endowment funds of the seminary. Two of the larger gifts during this period, for example, were from William Fleming and his wife and Ted L.

Ferguson and his wife. The Williamses and the Flemings had been close friends for many years when the former became president of the seminary.[67] The Flemings deposited $250,000 with the Baptist Foundation of Texas, the interest from which would endow the Department of Evangelism and provide for the expenses of an annual revival meeting at the seminary. The school was also authorized to borrow from this fund for a reasonable time at low interest rates for the purpose of purchasing or constructing student housing.[68] The Fergusons transferred ownership of their 640-acre farm near Hereford, Texas, to the Baptist Foundation of Texas for the endowment of the seminary. It was valued at approximately $150,000 at that time. These two splendid gifts were made in the context of the close friendship of Williams and the two families.[69]

In 1956, in connection with his efforts to raise endowment for the school, L. B. Reavis sponsored the production of a color film, entitled "By My Spirit," which described the meeting of two young people on the campus of the seminary, their marriage, and how they prepared together for the foreign mission field.[70]

The dream of J. Howard Williams of raising ten million dollars for Southwestern's buildings and endowment was not realized before his death early in 1958. In his last report to the Southern Baptist Convention he wrote that "nearly six million dollars of this amount has been pledged or paid in."[71] He noted that $864,551.76 for new endowment had been secured; he did not say that he had set in motion a spirit that would cause friends of Southwestern to make gifts, leave bequests in wills and trusts, and use other means that would ultimately bring Southwestern much more than his original goals.

Other Student Facilities

The minutes of the trustees reveal that they explored the possibility of providing other buildings for the benefit of the students. Financial limitations delayed construction of these. For the time being, as noted, the student center and infirmary were provided in the limited space available. On May 18, 1954, President Williams called attention to the need for a nursery and kindergarten building and a gymnasium. Preliminary sketches were drawn for the former.[72] Beginning on February 28, 1954, the trustees regularly discussed the possibility of investing in the Carroll Park Apartments, located about one mile north of the campus on McCart Street, for the purpose of providing additional student housing.[73] These dreams remained on the drawing board for fulfillment in the future.

The Central Power Plant

In his inaugural address J. Howard Williams quoted a statement by John Foster Dulles which described theological seminaries as "central power plants." This was the concept of his administration. In monitoring the in-house programs of the school, Williams constantly stressed the vital nature of what the seminary was doing. He viewed the student as the principal product of this power plant. With trustees, staff, and faculty, he endeavored to provide facilities, teachers, and curriculum that would contribute most to student development.

The student body increased regularly during the administration of J. Howard Williams. Between 1953 and 1958 the enrollment grew from 2,160 to 2,471. However, there had been 1,711 new students added between 1942 and 1958, almost doubling the enrollment, and this increase had not yet been absorbed by the facilities and staff of the school. The needs of the students were many. A brief survey of the improvements in the curriculum and student services shows other student benefits in addition to smaller classes, student housing, a student center, and the infirmary.

There were few substantial changes in the curriculum during Williams's administration. A new emphasis was given to rural pastoral training. On June 3, 1954, upon the president's recommendation, the trustees approved the employment of a professor to offer courses in the Department of Pastoral Ministry which would provide instruction for students expecting to minister to rural churches. The Baptist General Convention of Texas had offered to pay one-half of the expense for this professorship, since so many of the churches of Texas (and the Southern Baptist Convention, for that matter) were rural churches. This professor was to teach a minimum of six hours, advise and assist student pastors of rural churches, be available for conferences and other denominational meetings sponsored by the Texas state convention, and assist rural churches in locating prospective pastors. Carl A. Clark was appointed to this position, effective September 1, 1954.[74] A rural church fellowship was formed by those interested in this field. Further, in the School of Theology the program leading to the Doctor of Theology degree was substantially strengthened.[75]

The most significant curriculum change was made in the School of Sacred Music. On February 26, 1957, the trustees changed its name to the School of Church Music and the titles of its degree offerings to Diploma of Church Music, Bachelor of Church Music, and Master of Church Music. The school was authorized to develop a curriculum leading to the degree Doctor of Church Music. The structure was modified to provide eight departments of study: church music education; conducting and choral activities; ministry of music; music history and literature; theory and composition; organ; piano; and voice. At this same meeting, the trustees discussed a new combination music-education program to replace the one approved on March 2, 1954, but no action was taken. At the very close of the period, the trustees were making a careful study of the entire curriculum of the seminary.[76]

In addition to these improvements in the curriculum, the faculty continued its practice of hosting conferences, workshops, exhibits, formal lectures, and similar adjunctive teaching situations. Annually such meetings involving church secretaries, chaplains, musicians, public relations, radio and television, arts and crafts, architecture, and church recreation were held. Religious dramas, musical dramatic productions, and such lectures as the Holland Foundation series were provided for student participation. Of particular interest was the first workshop for Southern Baptist ministers of education on February 28–March 1, 1957, and the first annual Southwestern pastors' conference on June 10–14, 1957.[77]

An added incentive for thorough study was provided when the W. T. Conner Memorial Award in Theology was instituted in the spring of 1954. Its first annual presentation was made at the seminary commencement on May 7, 1954.

Another boon for the student was the matching of the splendid new library wing with a substantial increase in the number and quality of books and other library collections. The personal libraries of George W. Truett, Jeff D. Ray, J. W. Crowder, and many others were given to the seminary. L. R. Elliott secured additional microfilm and libraries from Great Britain.[78]

On February 28, 1956, because of the initiation of the separate music library in Cowden Hall and other proposed collections, the title of the librarian was changed to Director of Libraries. L. R. Elliott retired on August 1, 1957. He had been the first full-time librarian of the seminary and had served since 1922. Under his leadership, the library had grown from a few thousand volumes to a total of over 136,500 items. Of these, 118,558 were books and 13,597 were periodical volumes. The remainder consisted of 4,137 slides, 70 filmstrips, and 331 tape recordings. During Elliott's last year, the circulation was 351,012 books, an average of about 1,000 books a day, reflecting the substantial way in which the library was being utilized as a teaching tool. With the new library addition, the seating space had been increased to 840, and the book capacity to 250,000.[79]

In the retirement of L. R. Elliott the seminary lost one of the most distinguished library leaders in the nation. He was honored by his peers as one of the founders of the American Theological Library Association and its first president. For over twenty-five years he was curator of the Texas Baptist Historical Collection and was often in demand as a consultant to universities and seminaries in the building of libraries. A gifted exegete of the Greek language, he taught and published materials in this area. Most of all he was a scholarly and gifted man—eager to serve, personable in mien, and a wise counselor. At his death on May 2, 1965, students, friends, and distinguished leaders expressed their condolences.

Upon Elliott's retirement he was succeeded by Charles P. Johnson, the well-trained and experienced reference librarian, and Keith C. Wills replaced Johnson as reference librarian.[80] Vella Jane Burch, who had served with faculty status as catalogue librarian since 1948, resigned in 1954 to accept a foreign mission appointment, and Floreid Wills replaced her.

The question of student hospitalization insurance had been discussed by both faculty and trustees since the time of L. R. Scarborough's presidency. On November 23, 1954, the trustees voted to provide a small subsidy for student hospitalization insurance if such a plan could be arranged. Business Manager Wayne Evans studied the matter and reported his findings to the trustees on March 1, 1955. No further action was taken at that time. It had been thought that the opening of the seminary infirmary in the fall of 1956 might meet the needs of the students at this point; but on February 26, 1957, President Williams informed the trustees that in view of some recent student emergencies, it might be well to consider requiring adequate accident and hospitalization insurance for all students. This was referred to the Executive Committee of the trustees for study and at the end of the period was still under consideration.

Almost the last institutional remnant of racial discrimination was erased during this period. It will be recalled that qualified Negro students had been admitted to regular classes in 1950. In the spring commencement of 1955, the first two Negro graduates of Southwestern received their degrees. They were Leon F. Hardee, awarded the Bachelor of Divinity degree, and Marvin C. Griffin, the Master of Religious Education.[81] However, the dormitories of the school continued to be segregated. The trustees discussed this matter on November 23, 1954, and again on May 20, 1956. At the latter meeting President Williams said that the request to admit all students to the boarding facilities of the school came from the Student Council. The faculty also, under the quiet leadership of T. B. Maston, strongly favored this action by the trustees. As a result, this vestige of racial discrimination was eliminated from all boarding facilities of the seminary.

Of special concern to President Williams was the training of the wives of religious workers. In a long editorial in the *Southwestern News* of June, 1955, he appealed to the wives of students to make every effort to secure training along with their husbands. A reduced matriculation fee for them and more attractive offerings in night school, he said, should make it possible for every wife to get some additional training.

As indicated, the voice of the students in the affairs of the seminary was heard by the administration. New student organizations were formed during this period, and these were represented in the Student Council.

A significant step toward providing assistance to students came on November 23, 1954, when the trustees authorized the president of the seminary to select a dean of students. Felix M. Gresham was approved for this office on March 1, 1955. His duties were many, principally involving assisting students and coordinating the activities of various committees dealing with student relations and different areas of need among the student body. This included admissions, student functions, student loans, foreign students, adviser for veterans and dormitory men, and the like.

There was no diminution of the emphasis on missions and evangelism during the administration of President Williams. Practically every issue of the *Southwestern News* contained reports of inspiring Mission Day services, sacrificial offerings for mission causes by the students, and the appointment of Southwestern students to the mission fields. Typical of the personal interest of President Williams in the spirit of missions on Southwestern's campus was a suggestion which he made to the trustees at the first official meeting that he attended on November 24, 1953. When the discussion took place of the renovation of the old president's home to make it available as missionary apartments, he urged that these facilities be named the Lucille Reagan Apartments. This was agreed, and on May 27, 1954, students and faculty assembled on the front lawn at 2000 Broadus where President Williams dedicated the apartments to the memory of the courageous alumna of Southwestern who gave her life on the foreign mission field.[82]

At an unusual service in chapel on July 2, 1954, a large map of the world was presented to the president celebrating his sixtieth birthday. Surrounding this map were the names of 393 Southwesterners serving on the foreign fields, constituting 42 percent of all missionaries serving under the Foreign Mission Board at that time. President Williams spoke on this occasion of his burning zeal for missions and his deep appreciation for this gift to remind him of the need for worldwide prayer. Another occasion of joy to him was the official recognition of Josephine Skaggs, one of Southwestern's graduates, "for her selfless services to the river people" on the Orashi River in the Joinkrama area of West Africa. Queen Elizabeth II presented her the award, *Member of the British Empire,* in a colorful ceremony at Enugu, Nigeria, on February 7, 1956, mentioning her seventeen years of service to the Nigerian people.[83]

The annual spring mission conference for college and university students, begun in 1951, continued to thrive during this period. In several of his brief annual reports to the Southern Baptist Convention, President Williams spoke feelingly of the large number of Southwestern students on campus who were mission volunteers. In 1956, he noted that 388 mission volunteers were in the student body.[84] His interest in missions was reflected by an invitation from the Foreign Mission Board to be a part of a preaching group in Japan. He spent the latter part of November, 1956, in a fruitful campaign there.[85]

This missionary zeal was shared, of course, by the faculty. Finlay M. Graham, a missionary for the Middle East, returned on his furloughs to work on his doctorate at Southwestern. He recalled the dedication of the faculty to world missions.

> I learned that the invitation does not necessarily end with the benediction at the close of a Mission Day program in chapel. On one memorable Mission Day, my Greek class met immediately after chapel. The Spirit of God was still moving in our hearts, and our sensitive professor, Dr. Jack MacGorman, suggested that we continue in the attitude and spirit of prayer. After some time, another invitation was given. Several responded who had not done so in the chapel program, and at least three of these are now serving as missionaries. That is Southwestern.[86]

The evangelistic thrust of Southwestern also was a part of J. Howard Williams's heartbeat. On January 27, 1955, he expressed his concern to the trustees that "emphasis be increased in evangelism and that by the time of the spring meeting of the Trustees a recommendation for the Chair of Evangelism might be made." On May 20, 1955, C. E. Autrey was named professor of evangelism.[87] After Autrey resigned to head the Home Mission Board's Department of Evangelism on May 22, 1958, Kenneth Chafin was elected to this post. The Chair of Evangelism was endowed by a gift of William and Bessie Fleming on February 26, 1957.[88] The trustees also worked with the Flemings to promote their interest in evangelism and theological training in the northwestern section of the nation.[89]

The Effective Trustees

A student of Southwestern Seminary's history cannot fail to be aware of the additional activity of the trustees of the school since the extensive development of committees and the precise definition of areas of governance initiated in the administration of E. D. Head. One of the first statements of President Williams to the trustees was that he would work through individual trustee committees to bring his recommendations to the entire body. As a well-trained executive, Williams was familiar with this kind of orderly administration. At no point did the trustees inhibit his dreams or refrain from supporting him faithfully—not because they were dominated by him or suppressed their own judgment, but because they had confidence in his leadership as an executive and loved him as a person. The great strides taken during the five years of his administration could not have been taken without this trustee input and support.

A new and vigorous trustee president was elected on November 23, 1954. A. J. Holt had served for eight years as president of the trustees and felt that he must step down because of declining health. This decision was accepted, and words of high appreciation for him and his service to the seminary were spread on the minutes. Robert E. Naylor, longtime veteran of the board, was elected president, and William Fleming accepted the office of vice-president. Wayne Evans was elected secretary of the trustees on March 2, 1954, after the death of D. A. Thornton on November 29, 1953. Evans had become the new business manager of the seminary on February 15, 1954, moving from the post of educational director, University Baptist Church, Abilene, Texas. He had already achieved a distinguished career as a deacon, farmer-rancher, and businessman of Hereford, Texas.[90]

During the five years of Williams's administration, the trustees and their committees met often to approve and implement his numerous dreams. The Executive, Finance, Buildings and Grounds, Faculty and Curriculum, and Endowment committees especially were busy. While the trustees were seeking financing, erecting buildings, beautifying the campus, and electing faculty, they also approved a program of determining the rank and promotion of the faculty,[91] adopted principles involving course descriptions in the catalogues,[92] changed the charter of the school to add at-large members to the board,[93] and updated their bylaws.[94]

The trustees also developed some new staff positions during these years. A director of publicity had been utilized since 1944 in connection with the publishing of the *Southwestern News.* Ralph D. Churchill had served in this position until 1957, when he moved totally into the faculty of the School of Religious Education. He was replaced by Archibald McMillan, who was succeeded after one year by David K. Morris as director of news and information.[95] L. B. Reavis became director of endowment and promotion, which involved some of the duties formerly assigned to the Publicity Department. It will be seen that all of these functions will subsequently be assumed under a single administrative office.

Falling in Battle

Early in the spring of 1954, during his first year as president, J. Howard Williams mentioned to the trustees that the year 1958 would commemorate the fiftieth anniversary of the seminary and that plans should be underway promptly to observe this occasion in a fitting manner. His first editorial in 1958 magnified the inspiration that comes from looking to the founders of the institution and emulating their faith and courage. He closed this editorial by writing:

> We have much over which to rejoice and for which to celebrate. We can say without any reservation that in our best moments we attribute it all to the blessings of our Lord and the leadership of His Spirit, working in and through His people.[96]

Each of the three schools of the seminary set aside a full week to celebrate the fiftieth anniversary. The School of Religious Education chose February 17-21; the School of Theology, March 17-21; and the School of Church Music, April 14-18, 1958. Distinguished scholars and leaders gathered during each of these weeks to speak of the contributions and challenges of Southwestern Seminary.[97] In the last editorial before his death, President Williams looked forward to the climax of celebrating this half-century of service by Southwestern at the meeting of the Southern Baptist Convention on May 22.[98]

Before that time came, however, he was called up higher. Ten years earlier he had experienced a severe heart attack, and he had lived with the knowledge that his days were limited. He did not let this impair the effectiveness of his service. Indeed, as the *Southwestern News* published his increasingly heavy schedule month after month between 1953 and 1958, his friends urged him to lighten his load and reduce his activity. If he did so, it was not evident. His last full day of life found him at the Gatesville State School for Boys, where he helped dedicate a new chapel and mingled with the boys. On the following day he was stricken. As he was rushed to the hospital in an ambulance, he shared with Wayne Evans his dreams for the school. He died on April 20, 1958. It was fitting that this man should fall in full battle uniform as he was fighting the good fight for Christ to the very end of his day. Like the athlete crowned in the midst of his race or the scholar pillowing his head among his books as his pen was stilled, J. Howard Williams was translated quickly from active service into the presence of the Captain of his salvation.

One of the members of the seminary's Advisory Council, Walter R. Humphrey, editor of the *Fort Worth Press*, could not forget this man of great dreams and great achievements. Four years later, when a new section of the student village was being dedicated, Humphrey wrote:

> The dreams of a man so often live long, long after him.
> If they were good dreams, dreams which involved the progress and welfare of his fellow man, others usually are there to take the torch and bring the dreams to fulfillment.
> So the good dreams never die.
> This was impressed on me Friday when a new section of the J. Howard Williams Student Village was dedicated.
> Mrs. Williams was there to share the happiness of this occasion and to tell how much the dream of this village meant to Dr. Williams.
> It was his dream and he carried it in his heart for a long time. Long before he died, Dr. Williams saw the beginning of fulfillment.
> Now, this center is something very special for students of the seminary. It will carry to all who live there a message of confidence and hope from the Dreamer—through all the years ahead.
> The memory of the great president of the seminary is preserved in many places of this fine institution, but nowhere is it more alive than in the student village.
> This is the nice thing about a good dream. Others are swept into it, also, and become a part of it.
> On each unit in the village is the name of a donor . . . in one case of a community, Amarillo . . . and in all these units are preserved the names and memories of men and women who shared another man's dream.
> They have brought it to fulfillment.[99]

Notes

1. H. C. Brown, Jr., and Charles P. Johnson, comps. and eds., *J. Howard Williams, Prophet of God and Friend of Man* (San Antonio: The Naylor Company, 1963), pp. 119-20.

2. Ibid., pp. 144-45. See also *Encyclopedia*, III:2051.

3. *Southwestern News*, February 1954, p. 2.

4. Ibid., October 1954, p. 3.

5. Brown-Johnson, pp. 108-43.

6. For example, see Trustee Minutes, 1 March 1955, 15 September 1956, and elsewhere; also *Southwestern News*, October 1954, p. 2 and February 1955, p. 2.

7. Trustee Minutes, 3 June 1954.

8. *Southwestern News*, October 1953, p. 2.

9. Ibid., November 1955, p. 2.

10. See ibid., January 1954, pp. 5-6 for the text of this address.

11. See report in *Fort Worth Star-Telegram*, 25 November 1953, pp. 1,4, found in Elliott, *Scrapbook* V:39-40.

12. Brown-Johnson, pp. 73-84.

13. Ibid., p. 94.

14. *Annual*, SBC, 1954, p. 353; and 1955, p. 287.

15. *Southwestern News*, February 1955, p. 2.

16. Biographical articles and pictures of these faculty additions may be found in the *Southwestern News* shortly after they were employed.

17. Trustee Minutes, 3 June 1954. See also *Southwestern News*, July 1954, p. 2; October 1954, p. 6; and December 1954, p. 3.

18. Bulletin of the School of Religious Education, 1957-58, back cover.

19. Trustee Minutes, 22 November 1955; *Southwestern News*, May 1956, pp. 4-5; and *Fort Worth Star-Telegram*, 24 July 1956, p. 24. See *Southwestern News*, June 1956, p. 7 for retirement program.

20. Trustee Minutes, 29 May 1957, and *Southwestern News*, May 1957, p. 7.

21. Trustee Minutes, 28 February 1956. See also *Southwestern News*, April 1956, p. 2.

22. Trustee Minutes, 22 November 1955, and Trustee Minutes of the Executive Committee, 17 January 1956. See also *Southwestern News*, December 1955, p. 1.

23. Trustee Minutes, 28 February 1956 and 26 February 1957.

24. *Annual*, SBC, 1958, p. 355.

25. Trustee Minutes of the Executive Committee, 1 June 1955, and Trustee Minutes, 28 February 1956 and 26 February 1957. See also *Annual*, SBC, 1957, pp. 328-29.

26. Trustee Minutes of the Executive Committee, 13 September 1955 and 3 August 1956, and Trustee Minutes, 28 February 1956, 25 February 1957, and elsewhere.

27. Trustee Minutes, 26 November 1957 and 28 February 1958.

28. See *Southwestern News*, April 1958, p. 7, and October 1958, p. 4.

29. Ibid., September 1953, p. 3; July 1954, p. 5; November 1954, p. 5; May 1955, p. 3; and May 1956, p. 7.

30. Trustee Minutes, 26 November 1957.

31. Ibid., 24 November 1953, 23 November 1954, 1 March 1955, 26 November 1957, and Trustee Minutes of the Executive Committee and the Buildings and Grounds Committee, 27 January 1955.

32. Trustee Minutes, 28 February 1958, see also 22 May 1958.

33. Trustee Minutes of the Executive Committee and the Buildings and Grounds Committee, 27 January 1955, and Trustee Minutes, 26 November 1957 and 28 February 1958.

34. Trustee Minutes, 28 February 1958.

35. *Annual*, SBC, 1958, p. 356.

36. *Southwestern News*, May 1955, p. 1; January 1956, p. 8, and March 1956, p. 1. The issues of March and April 1955 carried the floor plans for the two wings.

37. Trustee Minutes, 28 February 1956.

38. Trustee Minutes of the Executive Committee, 1 June 1955, and Trustee Minutes, 28 February 1956 and 26 February 1957. See also *Southwestern News*, February 1954, p. 2.

39. Trustee Minutes, 3 June 1954 and 23 November 1954.

40. *Southwestern News*, May 1955, p. 2.

41. Trustee Minutes, 23 November 1954; and Trustee Minutes of the Executive Committee and the Buildings and Grounds Committee, 27 January 1955.

42. *Southwestern News*, July 1955, pp. 4-5; October 1955, pp. 4-5; November 1955, pp. 4-5; December 1955, pp. 4-5; January 1956, pp. 1,4-5; February 1956, pp. 1-5; March 1956, pp. 1,3-5; April 1956, p. 1; May 1956, pp. 1,4-5; June 1956, pp. 4-5; and July 1956, p. 1.

43. Trustee Minutes, 28 February 1956.

44. *Southwestern News*, February 1956, pp. 4-5.

45. See Trustee Minutes of the Executive Committee and the Buildings and Grounds Committee, 18 May 1954.

46. Trustee Minutes, 23 November 1954 showed revised wording.

47. Trustee Minutes of the Executive Committee and the Buildings and Grounds Committee, 7 June 1955; Trustee Minutes of several committee members, 15 June 1955, and Trustee Minutes of the Executive Committee 20 June 1955.

48. See *Southwestern News*, November 1955, p. 1.

49. Trustee Minutes of the Executive Committee, 13 September 1955 and 17 January 1956, and Trustee Minutes, 22 November 1955 and 28 February 1956.

50. Trustee Minutes of the Executive Committee, 3 August 1956, and Trustee Minutes, 26 February 1957.

51. Trustee Minutes of the Executive Committee, 11 January 1957.

52. Ibid., 11 October 1956 and 11 January 1957, and Trustee Minutes, 26 February 1957.

53. Trustee Minutes, 29 May 1957.

54. *Annual*, SBC, 1954, p. 353. See also *Southwestern News*, February 1954, p. 7.

55. Trustee Minutes of the Executive Committee, 26 August 1955.

56. Trustee Minutes of several committee members, 12 July 1956.

57. Trustee Minutes, 28 February 1956; and Trustee Minutes of the Executive Committee, 31 January 1958. See also *Southwestern News*, November 1954, p. 8.

58. For these improvements see Trustee Minutes, 2 March 1954, 3 June 1954, 23 November 1954, 1 March 1955, 22 November 1955; Trustee Minutes of the Executive Committee and the Buildings and Grounds Committee, 18 May 1954; Trustee Minutes of the Finance Committee, 28 February 1955; and Trustee Minutes of the Executive Committee, 26 August 1955.

59. Trustee Minutes, called meeting 7 May 1953, and 24 November 1953.

60. Ibid., 1 March 1955; and Trustee Minutes of the Executive Committee and the Buildings and Grounds Committee, 7 June 1955.

61. Trustee Minutes, 22 November 1955.

62. Ibid., 26 November 1957. See also *Southwestern News*, July 1956, p. 2.

63. Trustee Minutes, 23 November 1954.

64. Trustee Minutes of the Executive Committee, 26 August 1955 and 13 September 1955, and Trustee Minutes, 22 November 1955, 28 February 1956, and 28 February 1958.

65. Trustee Minutes, 22 November 1955, 28 February 1956, and 30 May 1956.

66. Ibid., 24 November 1953, 2 March 1954, 26 February 1957, 26 November 1957, and Trustee Minutes of the Executive Committee, 29 October 1956.

67. Brown-Johnson, pp. 117-19.

68. Trustee Minutes, 26 November 1957. Also see *Southwestern News*, December 1957, pp. 3-4.

69. *Southwestern News*, December 1957, pp. 3-4.

70. Ibid., November 1956, p. 3, and November 1957, p. 4.

71. *Annual*, SBC, 1958, p. 355.

72. Trustee Minutes, 22 November 1955, 28 February 1956, and 25 February 1957.

73. Trustee Minutes of the Executive Committee, 17 January 1956 and 3 August 1956, and Trustee Minutes, 28 February 1956.

74. *Southwestern News*, October 1954, p. 6.

75. Ibid., November 1953, p. 1; and February 1954, p. 8.

76. Trustee Minutes, 28 February 1958.

77. See *Southwestern News*, December 1956, p. 3, and May 1957, p. 3 for announcements of these two meetings.

78. Ibid., October 1955, p. 1, and December 1955, p. 6.

79. Ibid., November 1957, p. 5. See *Encyclopedia*, III:1687-88 for his biography.

80. *Southwestern News*, October 1957, p. 7, and November 1957, p. 5. See also Trustee Minutes, 25 February 1957, and Trustee Minutes of the Executive Committee, 1 August 1957.

81. *Southwestern News*, June 1955, p. 2; and December 1955, p. 3.

82. Ibid., July 1954, p. 8.

83. Ibid., April 1956, p. 1, and May 1956, p. 2.

84. *Annual*, SBC, 1956, p. 296.

85. Trustee Minutes, 1 March 1955, and Trustee Minutes of the Executive Committee, 3 August 1956. See also *Southwestern News*, January 1957, p. 2, and February 1957, p. 2.

86. Finlay M. Graham (Nicosia, Cyprus) to Robert A. Baker, 10 February 1981, Fleming Library, Southwestern Baptist Theological Seminary, Fort Worth, Texas.

87. *Southwestern News*, July 1955, p. 1; and October 1955, p. 8.

88. Trustee Minutes, 26 November 1957. The legal instrument by which the Flemings made an additional gift to the "Fleming Church Loan Trust" for this purpose follows these minutes.

89. Ibid., 28 February 1956 and 25 February 1957.

90. Ibid., 23 November 1954, and Trustee Minutes of the Executive Committee and the Buildings and Grounds Committee, 27 January 1955. See *Southwestern News*, March 1954, pp. 1,8.

91. Trustee Minutes, 3 June 1954.

92. Ibid., 23 November 1954.

93. Ibid., 23 November 1954 and 1 March 1955, and Trustee Minutes of the Executive Committee and the Buildings and Grounds Committee, 27 January 1955.

94. Trustee Minutes, 28 February 1956.

95. *Southwestern News*, May 1957, p. 2. Also see the issue of November 1944, p. 5.

96. Ibid., January 1958, p. 3.

97. Ibid. This entire issue was devoted to the Golden Jubilee celebration. See also the issues of February 1958, p. 3; March 1958, p. 3; and April 1958, p. 3.

98. Ibid., May 1958, p. 2.

99. Brown-Johnson, pp. 113-14.

Robert E. Naylor
President (1958-78)

The Goldia and Robert E. Naylor Children's Building
Erected 1973

Myra K. and J. Roy Slover Recreation/Aerobics Center
Erected 1979

President's Home
Erected 1971

J. Roy Slover
Donor

Myra K. Slover
Donor

F. Howard and Mary D. Walsh
Donors

Robert E. Naylor Student Center
Erected 1965

Walsh Medical Center
Erected 1968

Faculty
1958

Faculty
1969

Jeroline Baker
Preschool Education (1964-)

Trozy Barker
Dean of Men (1963-)

Jack H. Coldiron
Voice (1963-)

Robert O. Coleman
Biblical Backgrounds
(1958-79)

Harold Dill
Field Education
(1959-)

D. David Garland
Old Testament
(1959-)

W. L. Hendricks
Theology (1958-78)

T. W. Hunt
Piano and Organ (1963-)

H. Leon McBeth
Church History (1962-)

Mrs. Elizabeth McKinney
Piano (1967-   )

Wesley Meyers
Plant Maintenance (1959-   )

G. Lacoste Munn
New Testament (1959-   )

Evelyn Phillips
Church Music Education
(1948-52 and 1967-   )

Cecil M. Roper
Church Music (1960-   )

Barbara Jean Russell
Catalog Librarian
(1960-   )

John Earl Seelig
Vice-President (1960-   )

Mrs. Virginia Seelig
Voice (1958-   )

Sara Stovall
Cashier (1964-   )

Thomas C. Urrey
New Testament (1963-)

James D. Williams
Adult Education (1964-)

William and Bessie Fleming
Donors

George W. Truett
Trustee (1908-44)

9
Unprecedented Growth

The sudden death of President Williams shocked the Baptist community, although it was known that he had not been well. The Search Committee for his successor turned without delay to the chairman of the trustee body—Robert Ernest Naylor. J. Thurmond George, a member of the Search Committee, wrote:

> In our search all paths seemed to lead to Robert Naylor, the Chairman of our Trustees and Pastor of Travis Avenue Baptist Church of Fort Worth. . . . Perhaps I would never have thought of Bob Naylor as President of the Seminary except for the fact that he had shown such ability as Chairman of Trustees. All of us on the Committee felt led to Bob Naylor. It was a unanimous feeling after much prayer and thought.[1]

With this unanimous feeling, on June 20, 1958, the Search Committee recommended that Robert E. Naylor become the fifth president of Southwestern Seminary, and on June 22, convinced that this was "the will of God," Naylor accepted the post.[2]

The new president was born on January 24, 1909, at Hartshorne, Oklahoma. Reared in the home of a courageous Baptist preacher who had ministered in Indian Territory before it became a state, young Naylor attended East Central State College in Oklahoma, showing his precocity by graduating at the age of nineteen. In his senior year at college, he surrendered to preach. When he attempted to enroll in Southwestern Seminary in the fall of 1928, he learned that the minimum age for entrance was twenty. Special permission from President Scarborough was required in order for the nineteen-year-old lad to matriculate. He soon was called to be pastor of the Oak Avenue Baptist Church, Ada, Oklahoma. This demanded a 360-mile round-trip train ride from Fort Worth each weekend. Despite his crowded schedule of studying, traveling, and preaching each week, young Naylor found time to keep company with a charming young student, Goldia Geneva Dalton, from Virginia. Curiously, she also had been too young to enroll without special permission. The two were married on August 29, 1930. Their three children became outstanding in their own fields. At the present time, Robert Ernest, Jr., is a scientist with the DuPont Corporation; Richard Dalton has settled at Pecos, Texas, to practice law; and Rebekah, after excellent medical training, accepted an appointment by the Foreign Mission Board of the Southern Baptist Convention and is serving as a surgeon and chief-of-staff in the Baptist hospital at Bangalore, India.

At the very depth of the depression in 1932, following his graduation from the seminary with the Master of Theology degree, the young minister accepted the call of the First Baptist Church of Nashville, Arkansas. He later received honorary doctorates from Ouachita Baptist University, Arkadelphia, Arkansas, and Texas Christian University, Fort Worth, Texas. During the next fifteen years, he served successively as pastor at Nashville, Malvern, and Arkadelphia, Arkansas, and Enid, Oklahoma. From 1947 to 1952, he was pastor of the historic First Baptist Church, Columbia, South Carolina. In 1952 he accepted the pulpit of the Travis Avenue Baptist Church, Fort Worth, Texas, where he was serving when called to the presidency of the seminary in 1958.

Robert E. Naylor was well prepared to shoulder the responsibilities the seminary would place upon him during the next twenty years. His zeal for missions and evangelism was intense. From his inaugural address to his last word to the trustees, he magnified the gospel of Jesus Christ and the need to take it to every person. What better testimony could there be to show the depth of his feeling about missions than that his own daughter left kin and country to serve as a foreign medical missionary at a hospital in faraway India?[3]

His background and training deepened his convictions about the integrity of the gospel, and his devotion to "the Book" as the inspired revelation of God was a constant theme of his ministry. His chapel talks and editorials in the *Southwestern News* were almost totally pastoral in their tone and constantly emphasized the verities of the gospel and the duty of witnessing. So widely known were his personal convictions that those who later raised questions about the doctrinal integrity of the leadership of the seminaries never once pointed an accusing finger at him.

Of great value to the new president also was his total knowledge of the intricacies of Southern Baptist ecclesiology. He had been a trustee of colleges and hospitals in several states; had been active on committees of associations, state conventions, and the Southern Baptist Convention; and had been a leader of many civic and benevolent groups in various cities. In his immediate relations with the seminary, he had been trustee from 1941 to 1958, serving as chairman of the board from 1955 to 1958. He was well known to Southern Baptist leadership as an eloquent speaker in large groups and as a persuasive logician in small meetings.

Articulate, knowledgeable, and confident that he was in God's will, he worked tirelessly at his task and expected his colleagues to keep pace.

It was good that President Naylor possessed these distinctive gifts and a strong sense of divine leadership, for he served the seminary during a difficult period in its history. The agonies of the Vietnam War and its aftermath, the cold war, the struggles against environmental pollution and its dangers, political assassinations and scandals, exacerbated racial tensions, student revolts in what became known as "the decade of Me," denominational doctrinal controversies, and the inability of the nation to control the stubborn inflationary economic spiral were some of the factors impacting the seminary during these twenty years of President Naylor's regime. The uncontrolled inflation was already becoming disastrous. There was hardly a meeting of the trustees between 1958 and 1978 that they did not find it necessary to deal with the problem. Consumer prices, which had not reached the index level of 80 in all previous American history, broke over that mark in the year President Naylor began his period of leadership and had passed 100 by 1960, 150 by 1972, and reached 200 by 1978.[4] Such an economic climate was inimical to stable growth and planning.

The extraordinary amount of activity in many different areas during the twenty years of President Naylor's administration makes it difficult to tell the story in a brief and intelligible form. Perhaps he himself provided the best framework for discussing his administration. In an editorial he wrote for the *Southwestern News* during his first months as president of Southwestern, he emphasized one of his favorite themes—the "must-ness" of man's obligation to be a good steward in whatever function God calls upon him to perform. He wrote:

> Trusteeship describes our total Seminary responsibility better than any single word. To get an understanding of all the things committed to all of us in Southwestern's task is a glimpse of a new world that is breathtaking.
>
> To the Trustee is committed the largest dimension in that they are responsible for a *Direction*, for a commission. It is their sole responsibility to establish the line of march and to keep the institution central in the will of God.
>
> To the President and administration is committed a *Function* and a fellowship. This is the executive responsibility. His task is to keep the forces marching together in the direction that has been indicated.
>
> To the Faculty there is committed the trust of the *Message* and the ministers of that message. The very life of the institution passes directly through their hands.
>
> To the Student there is committed the responsibility of a divine call and theirs is the *Trust of a Dedication*.

TELL THE GENERATIONS FOLLOWING

To the Alumni there is committed the responsibility for a *Fruitage* that proves the vitality of the vine. To the denomination, to the friends and supporters of the institution there is committed the privilege of a *Continuing Witness* through Southwestern's ministry.[5]

This brief summary of the responsibilities committed to different persons touches each part of the seminary's history during this period—the trustees to give direction, the administration to lead, the faculty to teach, the students to learn, the alumni to be fruitful, and the friends of the institution to give support. Although this outline involves some overlapping, it will be used to discuss the story of the seminary in these significant years.

"We Must Give Direction"

The seminary was blessed with an unusually strong board of trustees during this period, developing, in part, from the action of the Southern Baptist Convention in 1959. By an addition to what was then Bylaw Seven, the Convention required that all boards of trustees of its agencies must include both ordained and lay persons as members, not over two-thirds of the board to be from either category. This brought some fine lay persons to the Southwestern board. Between 1958 and 1978 the board had twenty-two nonordained persons in its membership. Included were such gifted people as Kendall Berry, Howard E. Butt, Jr., David C. Casey, Oswin Chrisman, William Fleming, Jenkins Garrett, Raymond Gary, Louis E. Gibson, Ray Graham, Jay Heflin, Luman W. Holman, Gladys Lewis, J. T. Luther, Ralph W. Pulley, Robert H. Spiro, J. H. Steger, F. Howard Walsh, and other faithful lay persons. Elected in 1974, Gladys Lewis was the first woman to serve on the board of Southwestern Seminary.[6] She was elected vice-chairman in 1977. The addition of these lay persons to the trustees added immeasurably to the effectiveness of the board. The principal creative activity of the trustees developed from the work of the committees. It can be seen how the quality of the deliberations of the Finance Committee, for example, was enriched when it was chaired by a successful and concerned business leader; or how the counsel of an experienced teacher and administrator helped the Faculty and Curriculum Committee; or how the expertise of the Buildings and Grounds Committee increased when a dedicated and experienced land developer helped to guide its decisions. The quality of this kind of lay leadership may often be glimpsed by reading the knowledgeable and sometimes complex recommendations of the various committees in the minutes of the trustees. Along with these lay persons, the board claimed some of the outstanding ministers and other ordained people among Southern Baptists.

Officers of the Trustees

When Robert E. Naylor, the president of the trustees in 1958, was elected president of the seminary, William Fleming was named acting president of the trustees on June 20 and full president on November 24, 1958. At the latter meeting, Scott L. Tatum was elected vice-president of the body, and Wayne Evans continued as secretary. The three were reelected in 1959 and 1960. Fleming continued to head the trustees until his death in 1963. Serving with him from 1961 to 1963 as vice-president and secretary were J. H. Steger and Wayne Evans, respectively.

The death of William Fleming on May 4, 1963, was a great loss to the Christian cause and the seminary. He had been a trustee of Southwestern in 1936-37 and continuously from 1950 until his death, serving as vice-president from 1954 to 1958 and president from 1958 to 1963. His experience as an oil man and a business leader was constantly used in behalf of the seminary. His personal gifts to the school for endowment, operating funds, and capital needs were "vast and impossible to enumerate." He was equally generous in assisting other institutions with financial gifts and took special joy in funding missionary and evangelistic efforts. One of his business associates estimated that Fleming's gifts for Christian work had totaled about twenty million dollars. At his memorial service, however, the several speakers emphasized that even more significant than these financial gifts was Fleming's constant display of Christian character and his witness in his everyday living.[7]

After the death of William Fleming, some changes were made in nomenclature and tenure of the leadership of the trustees. Upon the recommendation of the Executive Committee, the trustees voted that the bylaws be amended to change the name of the executive officer of the trustees from "president" to "chairman" and the vice-president's title to "vice-chairman." Also approved was the recommendation that the tenure of consecutive service of the chairman and vice-chairman be limited to two years for each office.[8] By common consent it was later agreed that a trustee may be elected again as chairman or vice-chairman after a year or more has elapsed following the maximum period of two years' consecutive service in the same office.[9]

Under these new rules, the officers of the trustees during the remainder of the period were:

Years	Chairman	Vice-Chairman	Secretary
1963-65	J. H. Steger	W. M. Shamburger	Wayne Evans
1965-67	W. M. Shamburger	James S. Riley	Wayne Evans
1967-69	James E. Coggin	Ralph M. Smith	Wayne Evans
1969-70	J. T. Luther	James W. Taylor	Wayne Evans
1970-71	J. T. Luther	Louis E. Gibson	Wayne Evans
1971-73	Ralph M. Smith	Louis E. Gibson	Wayne Evans
1973-75	Louis E. Gibson	Oswin Chrisman	Wayne Evans
1975-77	Oswin Chrisman	T. Earl Ogg	Wayne Evans
1977-78	Ray L. Graham, Sr.	Gladys Lewis	Wayne Evans

Jenkins Garrett was elected seminary legal counsel in 1968.[10]

An Effective Service

The trustee body performed well during the twenty-year period of President Naylor's administration. It would be impossible even to summarize in brief compass their many achievements. Their effectiveness was enhanced by a constant monitoring of their organizational structure. Before President Naylor began his service there had been only one major change in the bylaws since the administration of President Scarborough. This had come on November 25, 1952, partly because of the imbroglio over governance during the 1940s and early 1950s, although the trustees had been pushing for a revision before this situation became critical. This change transformed the simple and brief set of bylaws of 1942 into a document with extensive and precise definitions of structures and duties. It provided for the functions of the Executive Committee and five standing committees—Finance, Faculty and Curriculum, Buildings and Grounds, Real Estate, and Endowment.

In President Naylor's administration the trustees made many revisions of the bylaws. In 1959 they were amended to show the retirement age for employees.[11] Faculty tenure was involved in the revision of 1962.[12] On November 21, 1967, a special committee on bylaws and charter was appointed. Among other things, it recommended changes to show the nature of the faculty (instructors or contract teachers, elected faculty without tenure, elected faculty with tenure, and special appointees); discussed academic freedom; outlined the responsibilities of faculty members; and set out principles for the election, promotion, and termination of faculty. An Investment Committee to assist the administration in placing funds *ad interim* was named on November 21, 1967, and reactivated on November 23, 1971, at the suggestion of President Naylor. The bylaw alterations on February 25, 1969, included changes in the number of trustees and in nomenclature, as well as a more precise wording of several articles and an editorial revision of the charter. On November 21, 1971, the retirement age of employees was revised.

The significant modification in the organizational structure of the administration in 1973 brought about a change in the organization of the committees of the trustees. After the accreditation study and recommendations by the Southern Association of Colleges and Schools, a committee of the trustees was appointed on November 20, 1972, to work with President Naylor to study a possible restructuring of the administration.[13] This resulted in dividing the administrative functions of the seminary into four major areas, each headed by a vice-president and all responsible to the president. The trustees approved this change and named John Earl Seelig as vice-president for administrative affairs (to include development, public relations, and alumni activities), Jesse J. Northcutt as vice-president for academic affairs, and Wayne Evans as vice-president for business affairs. A vice-president for student affairs was not elected at this time.[14] On November 20, 1973, and in succeeding meetings, the trustees thoroughly discussed the altering of their bylaws to reflect these and other changes. Consonant with the administrative changes, the trustees named four standing committees: for academic affairs, for business affairs, for administrative affairs, and for student affairs.[15] Felix Gresham, who had been director of admissions since 1955, became dean of students, effective June 1, 1974.[16]

The trustee board had been an efficient vehicle for the governance of the seminary even before the substantial organizational restructuring of the administration in 1973. All of the numerous activities of the school between 1958 and 1973 originating with the administrative staff and the trustees were channeled through the five standing committees of the board. The renovation of the older buildings, the erection of new facilities, the election of faculty and supervision of their performance, the approval of the curriculum and degree nomenclature, the efforts to raise endowment for the school—indeed, all of the vast programs of the school were painstakingly planned and accomplished through the efficiency of the board under the old committee structure. A description of how one of the several new buildings was planned and erected will illustrate how these committees, singly and in cooperation, accomplished the task smoothly and efficiently. The Buildings and Grounds Committee would establish the priority of a particular facility and prepare plans for it; the Finance Committee would include the necessary funding for it in the seminary's capital needs request to the Executive

Committee of the Convention; the Real Estate Committee would secure the land, if necessary, for the edifice; the Endowment Committee would attempt to find private funds to assist in the financing of the building; and the Executive Committee would unify the work of all the committees between the two annual meetings of the full board and help bring the project to a conclusion.

Supplementing the work of the Real Estate Committee, a separate corporation was formed by the seminary in 1960 as a subordinate holding company for acquiring and disposing of seminary property. The formation of this type of corporation had been suggested as early as May 18, 1954, by J. T. Luther, a friend of President Williams, to assist the seminary in its expansion program; but nothing was done at that time. On July 14, 1960, with the approval of the Southern Baptist Convention and the legal aid of Jenkins Garrett, the Southwestern Baptist Seminary Development Foundation, Incorporated, was chartered to acquire and dispose of property for the use of the seminary.[17] Other Southern Baptist seminaries had similar holding corporations.

Named by the trustees as directors of this foundation were William Fleming, J. T. Luther, J. H. Steger, and Jenkins Garrett from the trustees; H. B. Fuqua, T. J. Harrell, and J. Loyd Parker as nontrustee members. At their initial meeting on August 3, 1960, after incorporation, the directors elected William Fleming as president of the corporation, J. Loyd Parker as vice-president, and Wayne Evans as secretary.[18] Each year thereafter the trustees of the seminary elected seven directors for this foundation, four from the trustees and three who were nonmembers of that body.[19] These directors reported their operations and holdings to the seminary trustees each year.[20]

Most of the advancements of the period were made under this older type of structure before 1973 since it operated from 1958 to 1973 in President Naylor's regime. After 1973, the board continued its effective operation under the new administrative structure which President Naylor reported had brought increased efficiency.[21]

In all of this period the trustees dealt sympathetically with the financial needs of the faculty and staff. Each semiannual meeting seemed to have faculty and staff salaries as an item of business.[22] Bonuses were provided.[23] Expenses to the Southern Baptist Convention or to a professional society meeting were paid in part.[24] A policy on disability insurance was developed.[25] The seminary increased from 2 percent to 6 percent its contribution to match a voluntary supplement by the employee for retirement.[26] Hospitalization insurance,[27] group life insurance,[28] and travel insurance were provided.[29] A plan to give special recognition to longtime employees was inaugurated in 1975.[30]

The proper committees studied the functioning of every part of the seminary operation at each semiannual meeting and made detailed reports based upon their consultation with administrative officers for each function of the school. Significant innovations were developed in many areas. Long-range planning had been carried on for many years, but a trustee committee in 1973 suggested a more extensive study, which resulted in *IMPACT: 2000,* as will be discussed later.[31]

Campus expansion had been discussed during several administrations, but it became a reality in this period.[32] On March 1, 1960, J. T. Luther urged the seminary to hold all real estate from the Santa Fe Railroad on the west side of the campus, to Bolt Street on the north, James Avenue on the east, and Southcrest Street on the south. Approximately 93 percent of the land in this area had been secured by 1977.[33]

The trustees approved the purchase of a computer in May, 1971.[34] It quickly became an efficient tool for many activities of the seminary, and by 1976 it became necessary to install a larger type.[35] It contributed meaningfully to the areas of student registration and schedules, business office records, library acquisitions, alumni records, and long-range planning.

The trustees became involved in a landmark court suit during this period. On November 20, 1972, they were informed that the United States Equal Employment Opportunity Commission had demanded that all six of the Southern Baptist seminaries must follow its guidelines in filing Form EEO-6 which showed demographic information on all seminary personnel. Upon the advice of Jenkins Garrett, the seminary declined to acknowledge the right of the federal government to require a religious institution to make such reports on the ground that it constituted a violation of the First Amendment involving the separation of church and state. After consultation with the other five Southern Baptist seminaries, Southwestern agreed to become a part of a test case for all six seminaries. The commission filed suit in 1977 to require the seminary to file the proper forms. The suit was still pending at the close of this period.[36]

In an attempt to evaluate the faculty, the trustees in 1971 introduced standard university procedures by which students evaluated their teachers.[37] This practice continued during the remainder of this period. In addition, in 1976 the trustees employed R. Orin Cornett to act as consultant for the seminary in developing the formula for allocations from the Southern Baptist Convention. As a part of developing a proposed salary scale, Cornett recommended methods of evaluating employees to determine who deserved increased remuneration and tenure. One of these was the use of the system known as "Management by Objectives." For a faculty member, this meant that he would prepare a list of objectives each year and later would report on the number of these objectives he had been able to accomplish during the year. This program was instituted in 1976 and became a part of administrative and faculty procedures.[38] The trustees were also concerned about the disproportionate number of Southwestern's faculty who were tenured and those who had attained the rank of full professors.[39]

In 1977 in another important action, the trustees began making plans for the establishment of a World Mission/Church Growth Center on the campus.[40]

During this period, the trustees voted to establish several endowed chairs and an endowed professorship. The seminary had already named two chairs. One was the L. R. Scarborough Chair of Evangelism (the Chair of Fire), which had been endowed partly from gifts of individuals before the death of President Scarborough and totally by the income from a trust by William Fleming, as mentioned heretofore. In 1924, Mrs. George W. Bottoms made a gift of $100,000 to endow a chair in missions, to which Cal Guy was named in 1948.[41]

No other endowed chairs or professorships were established until the administration of President Naylor. On November 23, 1965, the trustees voted to approve the J. Wesley Harrison Chair of New Testament in recognition of the generous gift of the one so honored. In 1976, the trustees voted to initiate the George W. Truett Chair of Ministry when A. Webb Roberts of Dallas contributed $150,000 for this purpose on the condition that the seminary raise an additional $600,000 before December 31, 1977. This condition was met, and the chair was established.[42] The fourth chair resulted from an offer of the Sunday School Board of the Southern Baptist Convention early in 1977 to fund a chair for teaching the principles set out by that board. This was approved by the trustees on November 22, 1977, and Charles A. Tidwell was named to the chair.[43] The E. Hermond Westmoreland Professorship in Preaching was inaugurated in 1977 by a gift of $100,000 from the South Main Baptist Church, Houston, Texas.[44]

As one reads the minutes of the trustees during this period, he gains the impression that the spirit of the group was always harmonious. They worked well in their committees and in the general meetings. They were quick to express appreciation. Conscious of the dedication of President Naylor, they provided for him a trip to South America in 1960, to the

Orient in 1963, to Africa in 1966, to Australia and related areas in 1968, to Sweden and on to India in 1975, and a round-the-world trip on his retirement in 1978. He was lauded on the occasion of his tenth anniversary in 1968.[45] On March 1, 1960, they voted to present certificates of appreciation to trustees completing their terms of service on the board. They often thanked John E. Seelig; expressed gratitude to Wayne Evans on his fifteenth year of service; and regularly complimented James Leitch, the superintendent of the physical plant, for the quality of his work. J. M. Price and J. K. Winston, Jr., the latter one of the pioneer benefactors of the seminary, were remembered with appreciation.[46] When illness or death visited any member of the trustees or employee of the seminary, they were quick to engage in special prayer before transacting any business. This kind of spirit displayed Southwestern Seminary at its best.

"We Must Lead"

Although President Naylor differentiated between the stewardship of the trustees and that of the seminary's president, it is evident that he and the trustees worked together very closely and harmoniously in providing direction and leadership between 1958 and 1978. The school had many crucial needs when he began his work. Death had interrupted the dreams of President Williams to provide adequate personnel and facilities for training the large student body at Southwestern. The new president, totally conversant with the needs of the school because of his long service as a trustee and as recent chairman of that body, threw himself wholeheartedly into a program which obtained more funds from the Southern Baptist Convention for both operations and capital needs, increased and strengthened the faculty and staff, renovated the older buildings and updated the appearance and utility of the campus, provided new facilities, increased administrative efficiency, enlisted more financial support from private sources, and faced the doctrinal controversies which would develop in the two decades of his presidency.

Obtaining More Funds from the Southern Baptist Convention

It goes without saying that increased financial support from the Convention was a high priority. Since over half of the seminary's budget was provided by the Cooperative Program, it was logical to look to the Convention for an increased allocation for Southwestern.[47] However, it appeared that additional funding from this source would be difficult to secure. Both President Scarborough in the depression decade and Presidents Head and Williams in the more prosperous years had made these appeals without success. Still, the situation had altered in many ways by 1958 which gave promise of better results from these requests. For one thing, the Convention was receiving more funds from its constituents through the Cooperative Program than ever before. In 1958, for example, the budget of the Convention was \$24,808,919.58.[48] By 1978 this had ballooned to \$105,330,123.23.[49] Part of the reason for this increase in the budget was the Convention's effort to deepen the stewardship consciousness of its people by promoting what was called the "Forward Program of Church Finance of Southern Baptists." In the fall of 1956 this plan was tested on a select group of forty-four churches, and in 1957 it was presented to all the churches related to the Convention. A survey of the representative churches which had introduced this plan to their members showed that Cooperative Program gifts, as well as other gifts to these churches, had increased approximately 50 percent in one year.[50] Implemented by the Stewardship Commission formed in 1960, this Forward Program was an important factor in providing additional funds for both operating and capital needs of the seminaries. The resultant increases in the budgets of the Convention year by year brought some additional funds for the seminaries, but it was obvious that the percentage of additional funding for theological education was not keeping pace with the rate of growth in the Convention's receipts. The percentage of the total budget being appropriated for theological education had been dropping.

A second favorable factor was the increased sensitivity of the Convention to its own structure and functions. After all of the debts of the Convention and its agencies had been paid by 1943, the Convention immediately began an intensive self-study in the light of the critical decade it had just experienced. With particular reference to theological education, a committee was named on May 7, 1944, to study this field and bring recommendations.[51] As a result, the Southern Baptist Convention assumed operation of the Golden Gate Baptist Theological Seminary in California in May, 1950, with the hope that large enrollments of other Southern Baptist seminaries would be diminished.[52] This was followed in September, 1951, with the opening of a new seminary at Wake Forest, North Carolina, called the Southeastern Baptist Theological Seminary. In 1955, still faced with the problem of climbing enrollments in the seminaries, the Convention appointed another committee to study the needs of theological education. This resulted in the founding of the

Midwestern Baptist Theological Seminary at Kansas City, Missouri, in September, 1958.[53] This activity by the Convention revealed its concern with the problems of the large enrollments in its seminaries.

While not directed specifically toward theological education, another action by the Convention greatly affected Southwestern Seminary. In 1956, the Convention appointed a committee to study the total program of the Southern Baptist Convention. With the aid of the professional consulting firm of Booz, Allen and Hamilton, this committee made a series of widespread recommendations at the 1958 meeting of the Convention. Concerning the seminaries, it recommended that "immediate steps should be taken to provide the seminaries with the funds required to provide quality education." To implement this the committee urged that "allocations of Cooperative Program funds should be related more directly to the number of students the seminaries are expected to train." This, of course, had been the focal point of the requests of the trustees of Southwestern for a decade. This study committee pointed out that Southern Baptist seminaries had averaged a cost of between $300 and $400 per year for each full-time student, while other seminaries had averaged a cost of $527 annually per student. The Convention's study committee went on to recommend that the seminary presidents adopt a revised formula for distribution of Cooperative Program funds which would (1) allocate funds more directly in proportion to enrollment; (2) assure that the allocation would afford all seminary students the same quality of training; (3) consider the differences in costs of educating students in different fields and on different levels; (4) allow a sufficient base amount for operating costs to assure that essential operation of all seminaries would be provided for even if they had small enrollments; and (5) take endowments into consideration in the formula for distribution of funds.[54] These recommendations proved to be the direction the Convention would take in the future.

Another structural modification in the Southern Baptist Convention affected the new efforts of Southwestern Seminary to obtain increased allocations from the Convention. In 1958, the Inter-Agency Council was reorganized and enlarged to assist the Convention in coordinating its work. This provided a forum where denominational leaders from different agencies (including the seminaries) could establish better communication. It will be seen that this council and adjunctive conferences by the executives of all of the seminaries helped provide a new day in cooperation and understanding among the seminaries of the Convention.[55]

One of the most significant structural modifications in the functioning of the Southern Baptist Convention was made in 1958. The committee studying the total Convention program felt that there was a need to define better the specific objectives of each agency in the functions assigned to it by the Convention and to utilize this methodology to develop long-range planning to meet these objectives. As a result, between 1959 and 1966 all of the agencies of the Convention prepared careful statements of their objectives and eliminated overlapping and duplication of functions as far as possible. This completed, the Executive Committee utilized the Inter-Agency Council to initiate and develop long-range planning procedures, urging the agencies to follow this course. The allocation of funds thereafter was predicated on these long-range planning procedures as all Convention agencies projected their future capital needs and priorities through program planning, program budgeting, and program evaluation.[56]

Furthermore, "the most extensive study of higher education by Southern Baptists," known as the Baptist Education Study Task (BEST), was made by the Education Commission of the Convention in 1966-67. Some of the findings of this study were utilized by Southwestern Seminary.[57]

Another favorable factor in the requests of Southwestern Seminary for larger allocations from the Convention has been suggested briefly already but demands specific notice. That was the employment of external professional firms and individuals to provide a better perspective in evaluating the needs of the seminaries of the Convention. President Naylor and the other seminary executives utilized the findings of Booz, Allen and Hamilton to press their requests for additional funds;[58] and later President Naylor employed R. Orin Cornett, former head of the Education Commission, to assist in securing a better hearing for both the appropriation and the distribution of Cooperative Program funds for theological education.[59]

Finally, a new tack was taken in attempting to procure much-needed funds for Southwestern Seminary. Mention has been made of the unintentional rivalry that developed between seminary presidents as they appeared before a subcommittee of the Executive Committee to appeal for more funds for their individual schools. During President Naylor's regime this rivalry diminished greatly because all of the seminaries began to work together to secure a larger total appropriation from the Convention for theological education. In fact, it became the practice for only one seminary president to appear before the committee on appropriations to speak for all the seminaries and the need for a larger appropriation to be distributed among them.[60] President Naylor explained how this new sense of cooperation developed among the seminaries.

> At the first of these twenty years, the relationship between the six [seminaries] were [sic] greatly strained. Being required by the Executive Committee to divide among themselves an appropriation that was inadequate was in itself a tremendous strain to the men well-motivated and yet struggling for the survival of their institutions. Rivalries between the institutions were often keen. There were those who were involved in recruiting practices for students that were not healthy. It was the proposal of your president, having been present in such crisis with his president [President Williams], that all of the six presidents should meet together without agenda to talk about the common problems and personal relationships and seek to achieve a frankness and honesty that made brotherhood possible. The first of these meetings was in 1958.
>
> For twenty years, step by step, the institutions have grown closer together. Soon, total openness had been achieved though not without struggle. There came about a willingness to share salary schedules, internal information, admission policies and all the rest. There already existed the rubric of an Inter-Seminary Conference. This became a real channel for doing things in relatively the same way and presenting a common front in our response to the stewardship that had been given us by the Southern Baptist Convention. Nothing said here would be adequate to describe what this means in the long look for theological education in Southern Baptist life.[61]

The development of a formula for allocating operating funds became almost a regular item on the agenda of the six seminary presidents during the remainder of this period. The size of the seminary enrollments and the amount of the Convention's appropriation for theological education were variable items that demanded constant attention.[62]

The energetic activities of President Naylor and the more favorable response from the Southern Baptist Convention brought an unprecedented amount of funds to Southwestern Seminary from the Convention during this twenty-year period. To illustrate the dimensions of the increase in operating funds of Southwestern between 1958 and 1978, it can be observed that Southwestern received a total of $1,839,467.34 in operating funds during the entire five years of President Williams's administration, but in the last year alone of President Naylor's administration, the seminary received $3,456,658.00 for operations. The total amount received for operating funds during President Naylor's administration was $29,484,843, or an average of $1,474,242 for each of his twenty years, compared with an annual average of $367,893 during the five-year stint of President Williams.

The allocations for capital needs had followed a different pattern. As early as 1945, the Executive Committee made a thorough study of the capital needs of each of its agencies and made allocations based upon this survey. Again in 1951 a similar survey was begun to determine the capital needs of each agency, and multiyear appropriations were made on the basis of this information.[63] The Executive Committee requested each agency desiring capital funds to include these requests along with its operating budget. It is interesting that in 1952 Southwestern Seminary reported that it had not yet decided how to use the $300,000 which had been allocated to the school for capital needs.[64] The proposed $1,095,800 capital needs funding for three years beginning in 1953 also brought no indication of how this money would be used.[65] J. Howard Williams must have shocked the Executive Committee when he presented his first request for capital funds in 1954. He listed the need of $3,500,000 for student housing, $500,000 for a wing to the Memorial Building, $700,000 for repairs and renovations to all of the buildings on the campus, $500,000 for a student union building and a nursery, and $5,000,000 for additional endowment. He very well knew how to use $10,200,000.[66]

President Naylor utilized this long-range planning system to good advantage in requesting capital funds. In his first proposed budget presented to the Executive Committee, he noted that the seminary had a debt of $398,000 on its student-housing project.[67] By effectively presenting the long-range capital needs to the Executive Committee, he was able during his twenty-year period of service to secure a total of $4,700,250 for renovation and building.[68]

Thus, for operating expenses and capital needs during the twenty-year period from 1958 to 1978, Southwestern Seminary received a total of $34,246,350 from the Southern Baptist Convention. It will be noted shortly that there was also a large increase in bequests and gifts from financial campaigns during the latter years of President Naylor's administration. This infusion of large sums of money into the program of Southwestern Seminary is reflected by the following chart which shows the rapid rise in the budget of the school year by year.

Year	Total Budget
1958-59	$1,349,846
1959-60	1,374,820
1960-61	1,471,882
1961-62	1,489,238
1962-63	1,508,146
1963-64	1,577,821
1964-65	1,598,363
1965-66	1,696,908

Year	Total Budget
1966-67	1,886,470
1967-68	2,025,499
1968-69	2,246,848
1969-70	2,387,307
1970-71	2,529,310
1971-72	2,516,637
1972-73	3,266,743
1973-74	3,744,428
1974-75	4,400,723
1975-76	5,234,357
1976-77	6,238,549
1977-78	6,396,434

Strengthening Faculty and Staff

The increased operating funds from the Convention were promptly utilized to meet the most critical need of the school. As a longtime trustee, President Naylor knew the problem of huge classes where teachers lectured to congregations more often than they taught normal-sized groups of students. When he assumed his task in 1958, there were 2,395 students enrolled in the classes of 53 teachers. This represented a teacher-student ratio of approximately 1:45, a totally unacceptable format for effective teaching. In 1960, President Naylor was elected to membership on the Executive Committee of the Association of Theological Schools, the accrediting agency for all theological institutions in America and Canada.[69] In this position he took a leading part in revising the constitution and bylaws of the body, meanwhile increasing his own sensitivity to the high standards of the best theological schools. This deepened his urgency to provide additional faculty at Southwestern to improve the distressing teacher-student ratio which was so incompatible with the standards of accreditation. Slowly at first but consistently he began adding faculty members. By the time of his retirement in 1978, the faculty numbered 125 men and women serving as professors, teaching assistants, adjunct teachers, and guest professors. The teacher-student ratio had been lowered to approximately 1:28.

Another glaring deficiency was the disparity between the salaries being paid by other accredited seminaries (and even other Southern Baptist institutions) and those at Southwestern. The president and trustees began a program of increasing faculty and staff salaries and other benefits as rapidly as possible.[70] A breakthrough occurred in 1967.

At that time President Naylor reported to the Southern Baptist Convention:

> On the basis of a completed study of seminary faculty compensation by
> the Southern Baptist Theological Seminary, a first step was taken toward
> the improvement of faculty compensation scales and benefits. Reflected in
> the reports made to the Convention are improvements in salary scales
> introduced into the year's budget and of increased benefits in a total amount
> of $103,000. This will be only the first step and reflects the determination
> of the trustees to bring the level of compensation to the average scale in the
> accredited seminaries in America and comparable with our Baptist
> universities and colleges.[71]

As mentioned in connection with the work of the trustees, President
Naylor and the board discussed salary needs at almost every regular
semiannual meeting during the following decade. As a result, the
salaries of the faculty and staff quadrupled by the end of the Naylor era.
The many fringe benefits already described were added year by year, so
that by the end of the period President Naylor could affirm that the
salaries and fringe benefits at Southwestern were equal to those of any
other Southern Baptist seminary.

Perhaps the involvement of President Naylor with the Association of
Theological Schools, which he fully supported and often interpreted to
others,[72] brought him into contact with the regional accrediting agencies
(which set the standards for the best universities and colleges in the
United States); so when he learned that New Orleans Baptist Theological
Seminary had obtained accreditation from one of these bodies, he
promptly urged similar action by Southwestern.[73] Application was made
to the Southern Association of Colleges and Schools,[74] and on November
24, 1970, Naylor reported to the trustees that all three schools of
Southwestern were accredited by both the Association of Theological
Schools and the Southern Association.[75] A faculty manual was developed
in 1976, growing out of a recommendation by these agencies. During this
same period, as will be discussed in connection with the School of
Church Music, that school met the rigid accreditation standards of the
National Association of Schools of Music and in 1966 became the first
music school of a seminary of any denomination to achieve full
accreditation from that body.[76]

There were many changes in the staff during President Naylor's
administration. Several of the longtime staff members from previous
administrations continued their services to the seminary when President
Naylor began. These included Floy M. Barnard, dean of women and
teacher since 1933; Katie Reed, the registrar since 1944; Harlan J.

Davis, who had been named to the maintenance staff on October 28, 1946; Nannie Don Beaty, who had served as secretary to L. R. Elliott and Jesse J. Northcutt since July 19, 1947; Mrs. Grace Wilson, who had begun her service in the registrar's office on May 1, 1949; James R. Leitch, who had headed the Maintenance Department since September 11, 1953; Wayne Evans, who had been business manager and vice-president for business affairs since he joined the staff on February 17, 1954; Floreid Wills, catalogue librarian since 1954; Felix M. Gresham, who had served as director of admissions since February 14, 1955; L. B. Reavis, the director of endowment since 1955; and Dorothy Pulley, secretary to the dean of the School of Religious Education since September 3, 1957.

President Naylor added some key staff members. On March 1, 1960, John Earl Seelig became the assistant to the president responsible for public relations, news and information, student recruitment, alumni affairs, student placement, and printing-photography, plus numerous other responsible tasks assigned by the president.[77] His achievements in these areas were often praised by President Naylor and the trustees. He succeeded Bill Moyers as editor of the *Southwestern News.*[78] As supervisor of all seminary publications, Seelig won awards every year for the quality of his work. For seven consecutive years, for example, he received the highest awards of the Baptist Public Relations Association, as well as many other such awards each year.[79] When the administrative reorganization was effected in 1973, he was named vice-president for administrative affairs with the added responsibilities of planning and supervising the raising of funds from sources other than the Convention. Other outstanding additions to this developmental area of seminary life were Robert Preston Taylor on January 1, 1967, Clayton E. Day on January 1, 1971, and W. Edwin Crawford on September 1, 1974.

After the resignation of Floy Barnard as dean of women on June 1, 1960, she was succeeded by Mrs. Andrew Q. Allen, who resigned in 1966. Mrs. Doris Norton West served in this capacity until 1969 when Neta Stewart was named dean of women and director of student activities. The first full-time dean of men and superintendent of Fort Worth Hall was Trozy R. Barker, appointed on July 15, 1963. His wife, Emma Jean, was the secretary to President Naylor for a decade before his retirement.[80]

Other valuable personnel who served for a substantial time in this period were Aubrey Liverman, who retired in 1971 after sixteen years as seminary accountant; Sara Stovall, who became cashier on September 30, 1964; and Hubert R. Martin, named director of purchasing and matériel on January 1, 1975. Gordon Maddox began his service as seminary physician in the fall of 1963, retiring in 1976. His death on September 13, 1977, removed a dedicated Christian and benefactor of the seminary.[81] Wallace Shamburger was named seminary physician early in 1978.[82] Jack Gordon served as seminary dentist from 1969 to 1976. Barbara Jean Russell began her service in the library on September 5, 1960, while Keith C. Wills was named director of libraries on February 1, 1966. L. L. Collins, became registrar on March 1, 1974.

Renovating the Older Buildings and Campus

As has been mentioned, the long-range planning program of the Southern Baptist Convention caused all of its agencies and institutions to make their reports on this pattern. Allocations of capital funds for campus improvements were based on specific planning and evidence of need. At his first fall trustee meeting after assuming office in 1958, President Naylor suggested that long-range capital needs be made a special order for the spring meeting of 1959.[83] This marked the beginning of a regular review each year of capital improvement needs and the establishment of priorities by the trustees so that these might be included as a part of the presentation to the Executive Committee of the Convention.[84] From these various studies by their committees, the trustees developed an active program of renovating the older buildings of the campus, erecting new ones to meet the needs of the school, purchasing additional property and housing for students, enlarging the campus by purchasing property to the south and east, and improving the parking and street facilities adjacent to the campus.

The removal of offices and classrooms of the School of Theology from Cowden Hall to the Memorial Building made it imperative that the first priority be given to renovating Cowden Hall for use by the School of Church Music.[85] The seminary was authorized to borrow funds to get this project started promptly. By 1961 the renovation had been completed.[86] Additional improvements were made in 1964, 1970, and 1971.[87]

Price Hall also required attention. A new roof was provided in 1960.[88] When the children's building was completed in 1974, the removal of kindergarten facilities from Price Hall triggered the extensive remodeling of this building at a cost of approximately $500,000.[89]

The women's dormitory was listed as the next priority for renovation. In 1965, James Leitch, maintenance superintendent, reported the need for major repairs, for which he could use his staff.[90] This work was completed for the fall term of 1965 at a cost of $340,000, substantially less than the original estimate.[91] The trustees again praised Leitch for his excellent work in this project and on many occasions expressed their appreciation for his efficient use of the seminary maintenance staff. When the children's building was completed in 1974, the trustees authorized the renovation of this area in the women's building formerly occupied by the nursery. The conversion of this area into additional dormitory space provided room for twenty-four more students.[92]

Fort Worth Hall, the oldest building on the campus, was badly in need of repairs and remodeling. Because of its age, however, extensive tests were first made by professional engineers to determine if the footings and walls of this building would justify the cost of a major remodeling.[93] After the removal of the cafeteria from Fort Worth Hall to the new student center, a major remodeling of this building took place in 1965-66 at a cost of $486,266.[94]

The Memorial Building underwent several repairs and improvements during this period. In 1967, the air-conditioning system of Scarborough Hall was renovated. In that same year, the basement of Scarborough Hall was reconstructed when space became available with the removal of the student snack area and the book store. At a cost of approximately sixty thousand dollars three classrooms, a language laboratory, a research center, an archaeological museum, and a missions museum were constructed.[95] In 1969, the exterior of the building was cleaned.[96] Other repairs were made to Truett Auditorium between 1970 and 1972, including a renovation of the organ.[97]

In addition to these major renovations, the seminary revamped the units in the Carroll Park Apartments after they were purchased in 1965.[98] The original buildings of the J. Howard Williams Student Village also were repaired and renewed.[99] Attention was given to beautifying the campus, to retopping with asphalt the streets contiguous to it, and to providing student and faculty parking.[100]

Providing New Facilities

The extensive renovation of the older buildings and caring for the needs of the campus were just the beginning of an unprecedented building program. The first contingent of buildings in the student village had been completed a few weeks after the death of President Williams,[101] and, as mentioned, the trustees voted to name this the J. Howard Williams Student Village. Adding to the facilities in this village became a high priority during the Naylor regime.[102] Seminary personnel were utilized on much of the construction of later units. By the end of this period, there were thirty-five buildings in this village, providing approximately three hundred family units.

A student center was the next priority in new facilities. This had been discussed for many years by the trustees. They were hopeful that private funds might be found to construct this building,[103] and some substantial gifts were received from these sources.[104] After much planning, a contract was let on February 25, 1965, and the facility was completed in that year. On February 27, 1968, the trustees voted to name this the Robert E. Naylor Student Center.[105]

The third building to be erected was the medical center. It will be recalled that this service had been housed in the basement of the Memorial Building addition. After extensive committee studies by the trustees concerning the type and location of the new structure, ground was broken early in 1968, and the building was completed in that year.[106] The facility was named in honor of F. Howard Walsh, a generous donor and trustee, and a plaque was placed in the waiting room memorializing Gordon Maddox, the seminary physician from 1963 to 1976.[107] It was dedicated on August 25, 1969.

The official home for the president was the fourth major new structure. Preliminary studies were made in early 1968, and the older houses and apartments on the selected location were moved or dismantled in the fall of that year.[108] After much discussion by the trustees and others, the plans for the house were approved in the spring of 1971.[109] It was completed in the late fall of that year.

A building for the care and instruction of children had been a high priority of the trustees for many years.[110] The Executive Committee of the Southern Baptist Convention had made an allocation for this building; but on November 22, 1971, the trustees were informed that Mrs. William (Bessie) Fleming, one of God's gracious noblewomen, wished to make an anonymous gift in the form of the interest on a $750,000 trust fund so that the building might be erected and endowed. She requested that it be named the Goldia and Robert E. Naylor Children's Building.[111] It was dedicated in the spring of 1974.

The last of the major building projects during this period was the physical fitness center, which had also been a high priority project for many years. As early as 1963 the trustees had discussed the possibility of providing this center, and it was brought up again in both trustee meetings of 1971.[112] The trustees were pleased that Kenneth Cooper, the well-known aerobic exercise authority, had agreed to assist in the planning of a first-class facility.[113] The formal groundbreaking took place on March 25, 1977, and construction was completed shortly after the retirement of President Naylor. The trustees voted to name the gymnasium the W. Marvin Watson Gymnasium, honoring Watson for his many contributions to the project; the baseball field adjacent to the new center was named Berry Field, honoring the Kendall Berry family of Arkansas and Alvan Berry of Tennessee.[114]

In addition to erecting these facilities, the school acquired additional married student housing in another way. On October 14, 1965, the trustees approved the purchase of the Carroll Park Apartments, located on McCart Street a few blocks from the campus, which could house 184 student families.[115] Almost a decade later the Rosemont Apartments, consisting of 54 family units near the campus, were purchased for additional student housing.[116] New facilities were also provided as missionary quarters,[117] and the mobile home park was enlarged in the fall of 1968 to add nine additional spaces.[118]

The erection of these major buildings changed the appearance of the campus. Differing from the Memorial Building, the new student center faced the south side of the original campus, while the president's residence and the physical fitness center were located across the street to the south from the old campus. These arrangements gave credence to the plans of the trustees to extend the campus to the south.

Increasing Administrative Efficiency

At the suggestion of President Naylor, the trustees appointed a committee on November 20, 1972, to study the possibility of restructuring the administrative organization of the school. As has been mentioned, this committee recommended on March 2, 1973, that the trustees name four vice-presidents: for administrative affairs, for academic affairs, for business affairs, and for student affairs. The selection of a vice-president for student affairs was postponed at this time, as pointed out, but on March 25, 1977, Felix Gresham was elected to this position. He had served as dean of students since June 1, 1974.

Under the new structure, the vice-president for administrative affairs supervised the work of development, public relations, and alumni activities. The vice-president for academic affairs was charged with overseeing the academic program of the school, including the work of the three deans, the director of admissions and registrar, the director of libraries, and the director of the continuing education program. The office of vice-president for business affairs involved leadership in the work of the business manager, the controller, the director of computer services, and the director of medical services. The function of the vice-president for student affairs included giving direction to the chaplain and the director of student aid, the dean of men and director of missionary housing, the dean of women and director of student activities, and the director of recreation and the physical fitness center.[119]

President Naylor was pleased with the results of this administrative overhaul.[120] In the trustee body the reports submitted by the several vice-presidents, already carefully scrutinized by the parallel committees of the trustees, made it possible to identify problems quickly in any area. In addition, the long-range planning program known as *IMPACT: 2000*, which will be discussed in connection with the work of Vice-President Seelig, provided guidelines for possible developments in all aspects of the seminary's work during the remainder of the twentieth century and assisted the trustees in making short-term plans in relation to long-term objectives.

Enlisting More Financial Support from Private Sources

President Naylor recognized that the gifts from the Southern Baptist Convention alone would not meet all of the needs of Southwestern Seminary. He often mentioned hearing President Scarborough's constant plea that the seminary must be endowed. In order to follow the outline proposed earlier, the efforts of President Naylor to seek additional funds from private sources will be discussed in a separate section a little later. It is enough to say here that the seminary had never received as much financial support from the private sector as it did during these years of President Naylor's administration.

Facing Doctrinal Controversies

During almost all of these two decades, the Southern Baptist Convention was engaged in doctrinal controversy. In 1961 Broadman Press published *The Message of Genesis*, written by Professor Ralph H. Elliott of Midwestern Baptist Theological Seminary, Kansas City, Missouri. Some Southern Baptist pastors criticized the doctrinal interpretations of the book as being liberal and subversive to Southern Baptist views on the inspiration of the Scriptures.[121] President Naylor made a statement condemning theological liberalism at the fall meeting of the trustees in 1961 and affirmed that Southwestern Seminary and its teachers were totally conservative.[122] The session of the Convention in 1962 was marked by a debate over the book of Elliott. After a stormy discussion, two resolutions were adopted. One affirmed faith "in the entire Bible as the authoritative, authentic, infallible Word of God"; the other condemned theological views which undermined the Bible's historical accuracy and doctrinal integrity, and it requested the trustees and administrative officers of Southern Baptist institutions and agencies to see that the Southern Baptist historic position on these matters be affirmed.[123] The administration and faculty at Southwestern had been flooded with inquiries about its doctrinal position from almost the beginning of the controversy. At the spring meeting of the trustees in 1962, President Naylor referred to this matter and stressed that Southwestern Seminary held to a "Bible centered scholarship and the authority of the Scriptures."[124] At the November meeting of the trustees, he presented to each of them a copy of the resolutions adopted by the Convention at San Francisco and indicated his support of these views.[125] The trustees agreed to investigate every instance where any of Southwestern's employees appeared to hold a different position from that of the Convention statement.[126]

As a result of this uproar, the Convention authorized a committee to develop a confession of faith which would reflect the views of the body in doctrinal matters. In 1963 the Convention adopted this confession, which consisted basically of the Memphis Articles of 1925 with a few revisions, making it clear that this statement of faith represented simply the consensus of the messengers at that particular meeting and was not binding on any Southern Baptist.[127] On November 23, 1965, the trustees formally adopted this confession as the official statement of faith of Southwestern Seminary.

This debate was renewed in October, 1969, when the first volume of the *Broadman Bible Commentary* was published. The interpretations of the events of Genesis in this book came under attack on the ground that they impugned the doctrine of the inspiration of the Scriptures. In 1970 the Convention asked the board to withdraw this volume and have it rewritten from a conservative viewpoint.[128] In response to many inquiries about Southwestern's stance in this discussion, the administration and faculty affirmed their adherence to the 1963 confession as expressing their doctrinal views.[129] When additional agitation over the inspiration of the Scriptures arose near the end of President Naylor's administration, he suggested that the 1963 confession adequately reflected Southwestern's position.[130]

"We Must Teach"

More than once President Naylor emphasized that the center of the whole seminary enterprise was the imparting of the message to the student by the teacher. In this sense, all administrative functions which provided classrooms, housing, supplies, and other physical necessities were intended to be supportive of this principle stewardship: to teach the student the gospel message and the most effective methods of communicating it to others as a lifelong vocation.

Leadership Changes

For the men and women making up the faculty of Southwestern, the two decades of the Naylor administration were busy years. Two of the three schools of the seminary experienced a change in leadership. Two events occurring almost simultaneously brought this shift. The first was the administrative restructuring in 1973 which added several new vice-presidents to the organizational chart of the school. To fill one of these, Dean Jesse J. Northcutt of the School of Theology was named vice-president for academic affairs. To replace him as dean of the School of Theology, on March 2, 1973, the trustees appointed Huber L. Drumwright, a veteran of twenty-one years on the faculty. The second event that brought new leadership was the retirement of Joe Davis Heacock, dean of the School of Religious Education, on July 31, 1973. Heacock had played an important role in bridging a difficult gap and providing continuing leadership when J. M. Price, the founder of the School of Religious Education, retired in 1956. In his relations with his faculty and the other two schools of the seminary, Dean Heacock fostered a new unity that reflected his gracious ministry. As will be noted, he broke new ground in building on the foundations laid by J. M. Price. He had the ability to seek out creative men and women for his faculty and utilize their talents completely. He was popular as administrator, teacher, writer, and speaker before his retirement and has continued to be effective in these areas since that time. Honored by the trustees and faculties of the three schools when he retired, he was named by the trustees to be dean emeritus of the School of Religious Education on November 22, 1977. To replace Dean Heacock, effective August 1, 1973, the trustees elected

Jack D. Terry, Jr., who had joined the faculty in 1969. James McKinney continued as dean of the School of Church Music during this period.

Changes in Faculty Personnel

Along with these leadership shifts, there were many modifications in the makeup of the faculty during these twenty years. For clarity these changes will be listed by schools.

School of Theology.—Dated according to their official election to the faculty, the following teachers were added to this school: Robert O. Coleman in biblical backgrounds (1958); William L. Hendricks in theology (1958); Kenneth Chafin in evangelism (1959); G. Lacoste Munn in New Testament (1959); Milton U. Ferguson in philosophy of religion (1959); D. David Garland in Old Testament (1959); Huber L. Drumwright in New Testament (1951-59 and after 1960); Harry Leon McBeth in church history (1962); Thomas C. Urrey in New Testament (1963); William M. Pinson, Jr., in Christian ethics (1963); Roy J. Fish in evangelism (1965); F. B. Huey in Old Testament (1965); Clyde J. Fant in preaching (1966); William B. Tolar in biblical backgrounds (1967); Larry L. Walker in Old Testament (1967); John J. Kiwiet in theology (1968); Gerald E. Marsh in pastoral ministry (1969); Farrar Patterson in preaching (1969); David F. D'Amico in church history (1970); Douglas Ezell in New Testament (1970); Bert B. Dominy in theology (1970); J. N. Boo Heflin in Old Testament (1972); Jimmie L. Nelson in field education (1972); Yandall C. Woodfin in philosophy of religion (1960-67 and since 1973); James W. Eaves in evangelism (1973); J. David Fite in pastoral ministry and continuing education (1973); Justice C. Anderson in missions (1974); Harold Freeman in preaching (1974); W. Oscar Thompson in evangelism (1974); Ebbie C. Smith in Christian ethics and missions (1975); Scott L. Tatum in preaching (1975); L. Russ Bush in philosophy of religion (1975); Al Fasol in preaching (1975); Lorin L. Cranford in New Testament (1976); Bobby E. Adams in Christian ethics (1976); James A. Brooks in New Testament (1976); Harry B. Hunt, Jr., in Old Testament (1976); R. Bruce Corley in New Testament (1976); and Tom Nettles in church history (1976).

Retirement and death claimed some of the veteran teachers as well as some of the younger faculty. E. Leslie Carlson, who had taught biblical backgrounds, archaeology, Old Testament, and the Semitic languages since 1921, retired on August 1, 1964. He died on December 12, 1967, after a full life and fruitful ministry. He had written or collaborated on five scholarly books, prepared the text and a critical study of Micah for the *Wycliffe Bible Commentary*, and was a frequent contributor to Southern Baptist publications,[131]

William H. Rossell, who had taught Semitics and Old Testament since 1954, unexpectedly died on August 12, 1964. He was recognized as an accomplished scholar in his field. Albert Venting, who had taught from 1921 to 1934 in the School of Theology and from 1923 to 1934 in the School of Church Music, died on June 13, 1965. He was well known as a pastor, author, and writer for Baptist periodicals.[132]

After struggling for many years with a damaged heart caused by an attack of rheumatic fever when he was only ten years of age, H. C. Brown succumbed on June 10, 1973. He had served as professor of preaching since 1949, during which time he had either authored or contributed to twenty-seven books. He was sorely missed by his colleagues and students.[133] His close friend, Gordon Clinard, who had been professor of preaching from 1955 to 1966, died in an automobile accident on December 4, 1973. This gifted preacher had resigned from his seminary post in 1966 to become pastor of the First Baptist Church, San Angelo, Texas, and had taught one year at The Southern Baptist Theological Seminary in 1971 before accepting a professorship at Hardin-Simmons University. He was president of the Baptist General Convention of Texas from 1967 to 1969. He was also an author and widely sought speaker.[134]

Four outstanding members of the theological faculty retired during this period. One of the stalwarts of the difficult depression days, Thomas B. Maston, professor of Christian ethics since 1922, announced his retirement on May 31, 1963. He was honored at a faculty-staff-student banquet on May 2; a T. B. Maston Scholarship Fund was begun by his students in June, 1963; he was named "Distinguished Alumnus" of Southwestern Seminary in June, 1965; and he was presented with the Distinguished Service Award of the Southern Baptist Christian Life Commission in 1966, given

> in recognition of unique and outstanding contributions to Southern Baptists and to the kingdom of God through inspired teaching, insightful writing, and prophetic proclamation of the ethical imperatives of the Christian gospel.[135]

He has been one of the leaders among Southern Baptists in the area of Christian ethics, and students from his classes have attained significant posts of leadership where they have reflected his teachings and spirit. In retiring five years before it was mandatory to do so, Maston said that he would miss the classroom: "I'd rather teach than eat. I've never taught a class that I didn't enjoy." He was retiring, however, so that he could "do more writing."[136] This was no idle statement. By July, 1971, when he and his beloved wife were feted on their fiftieth anniversary, he had not only traveled extensively for speaking engagements but had also written for numerous Baptist periodicals and was completing the writing of his fourteenth book.[137] By October, 1977, he had published ten more books since retiring fourteen years earlier, had taught at five of the six Southern Baptist seminaries as guest professor, and had lectured in Israel, Mexico, and many other countries of the world. His books have been translated into Chinese, Arabic, Spanish, Portuguese, and German.[138] He continues to inspire his colleagues by his spirit and example.

On July 31, 1970, Carl A. Clark retired from his post in pastoral ministry after teaching faithfully for sixteen years. As he remarked at the banquet honoring him, he really was not retiring; he was just "changing my base of income."[139]

On July 31, 1972, Franklin M. Segler, professor of pastoral ministry, retired from the faculty after twenty-one years in the classroom. He was promptly secured by Broadway Baptist Church, Fort Worth, Texas, as minister of pastoral care. He had distinguished himself as a preacher, author, and denominational leader during his years of service at the seminary.[140]

Retiring on July 31, 1976, was Thomas M. Bennett, professor of Old Testament since 1953. Beyond his teaching duties during these twenty-three years, Bennett served effectively in faculty leadership. He authored a book on Micah and was one of the writers for the *Broadman Bible Commentary*.[141]

One of the veterans of the school moved to another part of God's vineyard. Ray Summers, professor of New Testament for twenty-one years, resigned effective May 31, 1959, to join the faculty at The Southern Baptist Theological Seminary. At that time he had written three major books and scores of articles for various scholarly publications. He was popular as a preacher, lecturer, and inspirational speaker. He said:

> My going does not mean less love for nor loyalty to Southwestern. It means that I am following the principle that I have tried to teach, that is, "the field is the world; it matters little into what corner of the field the seed is planted just so it is that part desired by the Lord of the Harvest."[142]

Another loss was the resignation of James Leo Garrett, professor of theology, on June 30, 1959. He also accepted a post at Southern Seminary.[143] He had served at Southwestern since 1949 and would return again in the next period.

The theological faculty was diminished also by the resignation of several other able faculty members. Kenneth Chafin had taught evangelism at Southwestern since 1960, but resigned on June 1, 1965, to accept a similar position at Southern Seminary.[144] Milton U. Ferguson resigned as professor of philosophy of religion on February 1, 1973, to become president of Midwestern Baptist Theological Seminary, Kansas City, Missouri,[145] He had been an outstanding teacher and leader among the faculty.

Clyde Fant, Jr., professor of preaching from 1966 to 1974, resigned to accept the pastorate of the First Baptist Church, Richardson, Texas, on January 1, 1975. In 1982 he accepted the presidency of the European Baptist Theological Seminary, Ruschlikon, Switzerland. He has written several scholarly works and contributed to many Baptist periodicals.[146] C. W. Scudder, professor of Christian ethics since 1954, resigned on September 1, 1975, after over two decades of effective service on the faculty, to become assistant to the president of Midwestern Seminary. His contributions in leadership and effective teaching were numerous.[147] Another loss from Southwestern's Christian ethics faculty was William M. Pinson, who had taught at Southwestern since 1963. He resigned on December 19, 1975, to accept the pulpit of the First Baptist Church, Wichita Falls, Texas. He has authored more than a dozen books and contributed to many others. He became president of Golden Gate Baptist Theological Seminary, Mill Valley, California, in 1977.[148] David D'Amico, teaching in the field of church history since 1970, also resigned on December 19, 1975, to become minister of international work for the South Main Baptist Church, Houston, Texas.

John P. Newport, professor of philosophy of religion since 1952, resigned on July 1, 1976, to accept a professorship at Rice University, Houston, Texas. He returned to the seminary in the next period to become vice-president for academic affairs. Another loss to the theological faculty was the resignation on July 31, 1978, of William L. Hendricks, professor of theology since 1958, to become professor of theology and Christian philosophy at Golden Gate Baptist Theological Seminary. Author of four books and numerous articles in denominational and scholarly journals, Hendricks had rendered distinguished service as a teacher and faculty leader.[149]

School of Religious Education.—The School of Religious Education also experienced many faculty changes during this period. Additions included the following: Harvey B. Hatcher in communication arts (1958); Harold T. Dill in youth education (1959); A. Donald Bell in psychology and human relations (1951-60, returning in 1963); James D. Williams in adult education (1964); Jeroline Baker in childhood education (1964); Charles A. Tidwell in church administration (1965); LeRoy

Ford in foundations of education (1966); Jack D. Terry, Jr., in philosophy and history of education (1969); Phillip H. Briggs in youth education (1971); Hazel M. Morris in childhood education (1971); Clark Dean in social work (1973); Theodore H. Dowell in psychology and human relations (1973); Alva G. Parks in education administration (1973); George R. Wilson, Jr., in education administration (1973); Derrel R. Watkins in social work (1974); William G. Caldwell in education administration (1976); Tommy L. Bridges in education administration (1977); and Charles W. Ashby in foundations of education (1978).

This faculty also suffered losses during this period from death and retirement. The death on July 5, 1965, of Lee H. McCoy, who had taught in the field of church administration, removed an effective and beloved teacher and author after ten years of fruitful service.[150]

Nine of the faculty retired. Floy Barnard, who had served as professor of missionary education and educational arts since 1933 and dean of women since 1942, retired to other tasks after spring graduation in 1960. Her gracious spirit and total dedication had so endeared her to the women's Advisory Board and the education faculty that they requested that the women's dormitory be named Floy Barnard Hall, and the trustees concurred. Author of several books and inspirational speaker at many conventions in America and around the world, she found her greatest joy in serving the young ladies in Barnard Hall.

> The girls have contributed more to me than I ever have to them. They have such high ideals and so many plans. The other night they went to the Rescue Mission and made a contribution to help organize a women's mission. They gave the offering in honor of me. . . . And they are always in some type of work—in Mexican churches, at the Goodwill Center, and in the large Fort Worth churches working as though they were going to stay there forever. I would say that positively they are the most wonderful girls in the world.[151]

R. Othal Feather, professor of education administration since 1947, retired after the spring term in 1970. He also simply changed his base of income, for he has been active in teaching, writing, lecturing and leading clinics, and in other Christian ministries since his official retirement.[152] At this time Ann Bradford, who had led and taught effectively in the area of childhood education since 1945, and Ralph D. Churchill, who had taught religious journalism since 1944 and served well as editor of the *Southwestern News* for several years, retired also.[153] In 1971, Alpha Melton retired after an effective service in social work since 1945, and at the same time Gracie Knowlton retired from her splendid teaching in educational arts since 1947. A. Donald Bell, professor of psychology and human relations, took early retirement on August 1, 1972. He had begun his seminary teaching in 1950, and after a stint as executive vice-president of Howard Payne University from 1960 to 1963, he had returned to the faculty to continue his seminary ministry. Author of almost a dozen books and numerous scholarly articles, he felt that he could give more time to writing by taking early retirement, although he confessed that he would miss the classroom.[154]

A major administrative change in the School of Religious Education was triggered with the retirement on July 31, 1973, of Joe Davis Heacock, dean of the school. He had been teaching at the seminary since 1944 and had succeeded J. M. Price as dean in 1956. His wise leadership prevented a potential crisis that the retirement of the founder of this school might have caused. His comrades in all three of the faculties recalled his significant achievements and spoke their appreciation at a banquet in his honor.[155]

Harvey B. Hatcher, known as a "friend of students," retired on July 31, 1974. A member of the faculty since 1958 and gifted in drama, music, and creative communication, he has continued to use his talents in Christian ministry.[156]

School of Church Music.—This school added several faculty members during this period. These were David P. Appleby in piano (1960); Cecil M. Roper in church music (1960); David L. Conley in music theory (1961); Jack H. Coldiron in voice (1963); T. W. Hunt in piano and organ (1963); Scotty W. Gray in church music (1966); Evelyn M. Phillips in church music education (1948-52 and since 1967); Phillip W. Sims in music bibliography and librarian (1967); Virginia Seelig in voice (1969, after eleven years as resident teacher); William W. Colson in music theory and composition (1971); A. Joseph King in church music education (1976); Claude L. Bass in music theory and composition (1977); and Albert L. Travis in organ (1977).

Retirement took four of the music faculty. One of the colorful faculty members to retire was Edwin McNeely, who had taught at Southwestern Seminary from 1921 to 1961. For twenty-five years he had been the bass soloist in the *Messiah* productions; for the same number of years he had served as minister of music at Evans Avenue Baptist Church in Fort Worth; and during all of his teaching years he had spent every extra moment in revivals, evangelism crusades, music conferences, and workshops. He was both a musician and poet. His song entitled "New Life for You" was chosen as the theme song for the 1959 evangelism crusade by Southern Baptists. He was greatly beloved by his colleagues and the students.[157] L. Sarle Brown, professor of voice since 1952, retired in 1964. At a faculty banquet honoring him, he expressed his appreciation for the fellowship of these twelve challenging years.[158]

Sara Thompson retired on July 31, 1966, after twenty-one years as teacher in music bibliography and as the first seminary music librarian in America. She had taught theory and music history for six years before turning to the library task. The music faculty recognized the need for a centralized library for music students, for the stock of music books was in Fleming Library and musical scores and records were in the dean's office. In 1951, after taking graduate work in library science, Miss Thompson helped to develop the first separately housed church music school library. At the time of her retirement in 1966, it contained more than 9,000 volumes of books and collected editions, over 8,800 catalogued scores, and more than 5,000 records, many of them with accompanying scores. Approximately 15,000 different anthem titles in sheet music and 500 tapes of campus productions completed the collection.[159]

Another veteran from the music school retired on July 30, 1978. Gladys Day, teacher of organ at Southwestern since 1952, not only was a competent teacher, but her performance skills amazed those who watched her accompany the seminary choirs year by year as they sang the *Messiah* and other oratorios.[160]

Resigning from the music faculty to take responsible positions elsewhere were R. Paul Green (1956-60); Charles M. Sego (1957-63); T. W. Dean (1956-65); and David Appleby (1960-65).

William A. Barclay, who had headed the organ department of the seminary from 1928 to 1948, died on January 18, 1969. He was active in Fort Worth music circles before and after his retirement in 1948.[161]

It may be seen, then, that all three of the schools of the seminary experienced substantial changes in their faculties. In addition to the regular faculty, the seminary also employed a number of guest professors, teaching fellows, and adjunct teachers in order to lower the teacher-student ratio. For the 1977-78 session, for example, the trustees approved one guest professor, thirteen Ph.D. teaching fellows and tutors, five teaching fellows who had completed their Ph.D. teaching requirements, seven adjunct teachers in the School of Theology, and seven adjunct teachers in the School of Religious Education.[162] In 1978 President Naylor could report a total of 125 professors, teaching assistants, adjunct teachers, and guest professors compared with the 55 full-time faculty members reported in 1958 when he assumed his task.

Curricular Modifications

The three schools made significant changes in their curricula during the Naylor years. Perhaps these can be summarized best by noting several common characteristics of the curricular activities of all three schools. These included an intensive self-study, strengthened curricula and the offering of new degrees, and an increased student-oriented program.

Intensive Self-Study.—Several factors led the faculty to engage in detailed studies of their objectives, organizational structures, and functions. One was the several self-studies involved in the accreditation procedures of the seminary. Twice the Association of Theological Schools and the Southern Association of Colleges and Schools sent visitation teams to the campus for accreditation inspections. Each visit by an accreditation team required the usual detailed self-study in order that these agencies might be able to evaluate every part of seminary life. A second reason for such self-examination was the constant advance in theological, educational, and musical circles in response to the changes in the surrounding culture and philosophy. Better methodology and specific training were required to keep pace. Still another reason was the reflection of the needs of the seminary's constituency. Churches began instituting new activities to meet the needs of the people. These new activities required trained persons in areas which had not been emphasized in seminary curricula.

For these and other reasons this period was characterized by careful attention to the seminary's curricula in all three of its schools. This study took two forms: a continuing process of adding or revising individual courses to meet current needs and the initiation of major curricular studies designed to accomplish specific objectives. This constant preoccupation with the curriculum reflected the concern of the faculty that the substance of what they were teaching would be relevant to the ministry of the students and would utilize the highest principles of communication and good pedagogy. This task was time-consuming and exhausting. As President Naylor remarked to the trustees on March 10, 1972, these curricular revisions, along with their regular duties, their writing, and their service to the churches, kept the faculty quite busy.

Strengthened Curricula and New Degrees.—Because of their distinctive areas of function, the three schools will be discussed separately in their curricular and degree modifications.

The School of Theology made substantial changes in many areas.[163] The format of the Diploma in Theology program was examined on several occasions, and the requirements for this diploma, awarded to those who had not earned a degree from an accredited four-year college, was modified to give the very best training possible to this small group in the seminary.[164] The Bachelor of Theology degree program was discontinued in May, 1962.[165]

The Bachelor of Divinity curriculum was the subject of constant study during this period. Free electives were increased.[166] Field education was given academic credit in 1961.[167] In the spring of 1964, biblical backgrounds became a part of the curriculum offerings.[168] Perhaps the most substantial alteration of this degree program developed in 1966-67. The Association of Theological Schools had noted that most standard seminaries were providing a master's degree to show the advanced nature of their training over the college baccalaureate. In addition, many of Southwestern's theological faculty had not been comfortable with the divided nature of the Bachelor of Divinity degree in the curriculum. Since 1945, the requirements for this degree had permitted a student to choose either the curriculum which included the biblical languages of Hebrew and Greek or to substitute other courses for the languages with the understanding that no additional advanced degree study at Southwestern could be undertaken unless the student had acquired the use of the biblical languages. A careful restudy of this degree program resulted in the change of the nomenclature of this degree to Master of Divinity in 1966 and the elimination of any degree program in the School of Theology which did not require the biblical languages.[169]

A new professional doctoral program was adopted during this period. The Association of Theological Schools had been discussing the need for this degree since the early 1960s.[170] Southwestern's theological faculty studied the proposed programs intermittently between 1966 and 1970.[171] In December, 1971, this faculty recommended to the trustees that this degree be offered in an effort to correlate studies in the basic preparation of the pastor with the classical theological disciplines to develop skills in "doing ministry."[172] A Committee for Professional Studies was named by the president, and enrollment was begun in the fall of 1972.[173] W. Boyd Hunt was the first chairman of this committee.[174] He was succeeded by D. David Garland in 1974, who was followed in 1977 by Jimmie Nelson.[175] The name of the committee supervising this program was changed on November 25, 1975, to the Committee for the Doctor of Ministry Degree. The School of Religious Education was represented on this committee, and one of the areas of functional concentration was church and education, which attracted some vocational ministers of education to this degree.

In the early years this Doctor of Ministry program was conceived in terms of in-sequence training rather than in-ministry; that is, the main thrust was toward enrolling the student immediately after he completed his first degree. However, in 1975 the faculty provided a better balance by approving a program for both in-sequence and in-ministry training (for those already serving in churches or institutions away from the campus).[176]

The older advanced study programs of the School of Theology also underwent substantial changes during this period. In the opening months of President Naylor's administration, the Committee on Advanced Studies was engaged already in a major study of the two advanced degrees the school was offering—the Master of Theology and the Doctor of Theology. The former degree, less attractive with the introduction of the Master of Divinity degree, was revised to make it a major evaluative program for those who desired to apply for doctoral study. However, with the introduction of the Doctor of Ministry degree in 1972, it was voted to phase out the Master of Theology program.[177]

The doctorate in theology also underwent radical alterations. There had been little major revision of this degree program since the school began in 1908. On February 9, 1959, upon the recommendation of the Committee on Advanced Studies, the theological faculty met by fields to organize the curriculum for the theological doctorate after the pattern suggested by the Association of Theological Schools. On March 10, 1959, the curriculum for doctoral studies was divided into four fields— biblical, historical, theological or systematic, and practical—and each field elected a chairman. A core curriculum was developed, including interrelated disciplines, electives, and a working knowledge of two modern foreign languages.[178]

Another large step was taken in 1973. After a lengthy study of the trends in theological education, the introduction of the professional doctorate, and the needs of the students, the theological faculty voted on October 9, 1973, to change the nomenclature of the Doctor of Theology degree to Doctor of Philosophy. This was approved by the Board of Trustees on November 20, 1973. Workshops for the faculty were held on February 4 and November 4, 1974, to discuss all phases of this program. Distinctive elements in the new program were the introduction of a seminar on research and teaching, the requirement that each Ph.D. student demonstrate his skill in tutoring or teaching seminary classes for at least one semester, and the completion of at least four semester hours of supportive work in the student's major field to be taken in the doctoral program of an accredited university.[179]

The School of Religious Education also made substantial changes in its curriculum. The fact that in these twenty years this school added 143 new courses, 62 of which were doctoral seminars, gives some idea of how busy it kept its Curriculum Committee. This extensive amount of curricular activity may be accounted for by the fact that many new faculty members were added, and their expertise opened new areas of study; that the faculty carefully defined their objectives and functions, resulting in the publication of a book describing each course in their curriculum; and that substantial revisions of their programs were made. It becomes difficult to select those areas of most significant advance because this faculty continuously studied and revised their programs during most of President Naylor's administration. Perhaps, as in the case of the theological school, the results of this school's study and revisions may be briefly summarized in terms of the modifications in its diploma and degree programs.

The program known as the Associate in Religious Education was changed in 1962 to become the Diploma in Religious Education.[180] The Master of Religious Education degree was substantially strengthened.[181] When Joe Davis Heacock, former dean, was asked to reflect on the principal curricular developments of the period, he identified them in terms of the addition of competent faculty who provided enrichment for the curriculum. This was noted in educational communication and all age-group studies. The social work program was expanded in 1964, making it possible for students to do major work in this area and receive seminary credit on Master of Social Work degree study in nearby universities.[182] New personnnel increased the effectiveness of studies in church administration and instructional technology. Discussions with the Convention-wide mission boards brought agreement on the training of missionaries. Unusual progress was made in the program for children with the completion of the Goldia and Robert E. Naylor Children's Building in 1974. Ann Bradford, Jeroline Baker, and Hazel Morris from the faculty helped in the planning of this building. The erection of the physical fitness center at the end of the period promised an enlarged program in the recreation area. Field education was greatly strengthened during this period.[183]

The new degree, Graduate Specialist in Religious Education, was developed in 1961 for those desiring to specialize in some specific area.[184] The Bachelor of Religious Education degree was phased out in 1962.[185]

An outstanding achievement in 1965 was the replacing of the older Doctor of Religious Education degree with an improved format for a new degree—the Doctor of Education. Leon Marsh, director of the doctoral program, aided by Dean Heacock, made a thorough study in 1964-65 of the direction advanced study in religious education was taking in other schools plus the needs of Southwestern Seminary, and he sought the counsel of distinguished educational leaders. From these studies the Doctor of Education degree was instituted to replace that of the Doctor of Religious Education.[186] The requirements for the new degree were drastically upgraded. Entrance examinations, including portions of the Graduate Record Examination, were required; a grade point average of A − on the Master of Religious Education degree became a prerequisite; and the prospective student was required to give evidence of his professional competence. Interviews and entrance examinations were begun. The curriculum was increased from eight to twenty courses, including the requirement of research and statistics as a part of each student's work. An oral examination and a defended dissertation were also required.[187]

The naming of Charles A. Tidwell to the new Chair of Denominational Relations, funded by the Sunday School Board, provided additional instruction in the programs fostered by that board.[188]

One of the important curricular workshops held by the School of Religious Education must be mentioned. After much preparation, this workshop was held on April 6-8, 1970. Religious educators from across the nation met with the faculty and selected students to discuss the importance of a performance-oriented curriculum. Out of this conference came additional study committees and a major change in curriculum design, bringing new flexibility. The number of electives in the basic course was doubled.[189] The Department of Principles and Philosophy of Education was renamed Foundations of Education.[190] New areas of study concentration were developed.[191]

The School of Church Music, as well, was engaged in curricular studies during almost the entire period. The music faculty, led by its Curriculum Committee, spent much time examining all aspects of its functions and degrees. Its minutes reveal that serious studies were being made at the opening of this period concerning the need of offering a doctorate in music.[192] On November 22, 1960, the trustees approved the degree, Doctor of Church Music, which was to be granted upon completion of a strong curriculum outlined by the music faculty. The title of this doctorate was changed in 1967. From conversations with the National Association of Schools of Music, the music faculty recommended and the trustees approved the new nomenclature of Doctor of Musical Arts (with a major in church music).[193] The curriculum included a minor in either the School of Theology or the School of Religious Education.

A major revision took place in 1973. The old Master of Church Music curriculum was divided into two degree programs: a Master of Church Music and a Master of Music. The former degree was designed to equip students for music ministry in local churches and similar services, while the new Master of Music degree aimed to provide students with advanced levels of performance and scholarship needed for college and seminary teaching. The latter degree also was preparatory for entry into the Doctor of Musical Arts program.[194] At this time, the Bachelor of Church Music program was phased out.

Near the close of this period, the music school was working with the other two schools to provide combination degrees of Master of Religious Education with a minor in music and Master of Divinity and Doctor of Ministry degrees with minors in music.[195]

The School of Church Music received recognition during this period for its excellence in scholarship, curriculum, performance, and facilities. Both the Association of Theological Schools and the Southern Association of Colleges and Schools granted accreditation to this school along with the other two schools of the seminary.[196] More significant than this was the achievement of full accreditation from the National Association of Schools of Music. As previously suggested, Southwestern's School of Church Music was the first seminary of any denomination to be so accredited by this body.[197]

In addition to changes in curricula and degrees, the School of Church Music made careful studies of its organization. Departments were combined and individual courses were shifted to comport with logical grouping, while other areas, such as the Ministry of Music program designed for nonmusicians, were developed into cohesive units.[198]

An Increased Student-Oriented Program.—In a sense, all curricular revision looks to benefiting the student. Gone are the days when some outstanding scholar spent his time writing ponderous tomes for publishing that were not relevant to the students' needs and reading this material to his classes as a substitute for teaching. The modern curriculum is carefully constructed in terms of clear objectives which speak to student needs, and it provides a cohesive plan of instruction and training. The curricula of all three schools of Southwestern displayed this. The School of Religious Education, in particular, had developed its curriculum to provide much elective study, had organized its faculty to give maximum counseling for the student, and had published in 1979, under the editorship of Phillip Briggs, an excellent guide to its curriculum entitled *Course Description for the Master of Religious Education Degree*. All three of the schools included representatives from the student body and alumni in their curricular studies. Many alumni have expressed approval of the new curricula and the new facilities which have made it possible to provide better teaching.

New Thrusts

It would be palpably impossible to describe all of the innovative areas of ministry developed by the seminary faculty during this twenty-year period. Some of these will be mentioned briefly.

In 1959, under the leadership of John Drakeford of the School of Religious Education, a Marriage and Family Counseling Center was instituted. Its need was quickly demonstrated. During that first year 229 students, local residents, and others attended the center for 362 counseling sessions. Most of the sessions were devoted to marriage problems, many to personal problems, some for premarital counseling, and some for meeting parent-child difficulties, grief reactions, and vocational problems. This important program continued during the remainder of the period.[199]

An increased effort to help in the training of the wives of students was made during this period. The School of Religious Education developed a cooperative arrangement with Dallas Baptist College which would permit a student wife to take class work at both institutions and secure a teacher's certification with her diploma.[200] This was a boon to bivocational workers, especially, who might find it necessary to support themselves and their families while doing Christian work in a pioneer area. An Institute of Theology was developed in 1969 to provide instruction during the summer for college students. Qualified persons were given tuition scholarships and attended regular seminary classes.[201]

An important aid to the curricula was the development of the Continuing Education Department. On June 11, 1971, President Naylor discussed this program with the trustees, and on July 1, 1971, J. David Fite became its director.[202] It was directed toward alumni, staff persons, and others who desired to continue their learning experience. Educational opportunities in many types of study were offered for seminary credit through this program. For example, the numerous course offerings of the Seminary Extension Department, Nashville, Tennessee, could provide sixteen hours of seminary credit on the diploma level for students completing selected courses. Fleming Library developed a Continuing Education Program which, for a small fee, provided off-campus students with a monthly list of new book titles acquired by the library and permitted them to borrow books, cassette tapes, and sermon material. Among the other offerings of the Continuing Education Department in a typical year were such numerous and diverse activities as small church conferences, preacher training conferences, a seminar in the January Bible Study series, a workshop for furloughing mission-aries, a marriage enrichment conference, a writers' conference, a couples' communication workshop, a Spanish workshop on family ministry and counseling, a senior adult leaders' conference, a preaching enrichment seminar, a church music workshop, a workshop on church planning, a management skills workshop for directors of missions, a marriage enrichment leadership training workshop, a week's workshop for invited doctoral graduates, a chaplains' conference, a workshop on the pastor as a staff leader, a Baptist Student Union directors' con-ference, a couples' communication leadership training workshop, a workshop for church secretaries, a conference each spring on an emphasis of the School of Religious Education (the child, the family, etc.), a workshop on church publicity, a youth ministers' laboratory, an archaeological expedition or study tour, a summer institute for lan-guages, a workshop on new missions/church development, an annual pastors' conference (with a separate program for the pastor's wife beginning in 1971), and an on-the-field preaching enrichment seminar. It may be seen that this program of continuing education, the format of which was altered year by year to meet the needs of the constituency, provided the opportunity for almost anyone to utilize seminary resources for study in almost any field of interest or vocational need.[203]

An earlier aspect of this continuing educational emphasis was the initiation of an off-campus week of study without credit for those who could not attend on-campus conferences. This was known as the Continuing Theological Studies program.[204] Under this plan, two or three faculty members, representing several disciplines, would spend a week lecturing to small groups who had requested this type of refresher study. Such conferences were held in Colorado, Ohio, Illinois, Michigan, at an army post in Ford Hood, Texas, and elsewhere.[205]

An additional step was taken in 1975, perhaps influenced by some of these antecedents. A number of interested pastors in and around Houston, Texas, broached the question of whether or not the seminary could open a branch center in their area where those desiring to do so could study with credit toward a basic degree from one of the three schools of the seminary. A format was developed by which several associations united to sponsor this, and a center was opened on the campus of Houston Baptist University in the fall of 1975.[206] These classes continue to be taught each Monday by faculty members from the seminary.

A second off-campus center was opened in 1976 in the classrooms of Oklahoma Baptist University, Shawnee, Oklahoma.[207] This center was sponsored by the Baptist General Convention of Oklahoma and Oklahoma Baptist University. Another off-campus center was begun on the campus of the Mexican Baptist Bible Institute in San Antonio, Texas, in the fall of 1977.[208]

Differing somewhat from these centers, an additional off-campus program was begun in 1977 with the initiation of a Doctor of Ministry study center at Memphis, Tennessee, under the joint sponsorship of Southern, Southwestern, New Orleans, and Midwestern seminaries.[209]

Many other important new programs were developed. Limitation of space forbids discussion of these, but they included such activities as tying into the programs of the Council of Southwestern Theological Seminaries, an interdenominational organization of accredited seminaries in the Southwest;[210] active cooperation with the association, the state body, and the Southern Baptist Convention's agencies in various programs;[211] better correlation with the curricula of the colleges and universities;[212] the increasing use of Fleming Library as a teaching tool; the rapid acceleration of the Pioneer Penetration program in which students hold revivals, organize churches, and teach the Bible in the pioneer areas;[213] the development of a Learning Center on the campus;[214] the inauguration of night classes on the campus by Dallas Baptist College for college credit;[215] the initiation of plans for a World Mission/Church Growth Center at Southwestern;[216] and many other activities.

As will be noted in the discussion of student life on the campus, each year the seminary sponsored distinguished Christian scholars for lectures, workshops, conferences, and chapel messages. Mrs. Edwin M. Reardon, III, provided funds for a series of annual scholarly messages, which were begun in 1965, and in 1976 the Northcutt Lectures were initiated in honor of Fannie and Jesse J. Northcutt.[217] The celebration of the fiftieth anniversary of the schools of education and music in 1965 also brought outstanding leaders to the campus.[218]

Faculty Writing and Service Activities

During this period the faculty made substantial contributions through publications and service to churches and other groups. They published over 150 books, prepared scores of Sunday School lessons to be taught in approximately 35,000 Southern Baptist churches, and wrote articles for scholarly journals, denominational literature, and Baptist papers too numerous to count. The faculty publication, the *Southwestern Journal of Theology*, had members of all three faculties on its staff.

Quite impressive also were the service activities of the faculty during this period. The music faculty made appearances as guest performing artists in all parts of the country. Their music on campus, vocal and instrumental, either as soloists or in groups, received high praise from critics. They were in demand for music workshops, as guest lecturers in conferences, as guest or interim musicians in many churches, and as soloists in sacred concerts or oratorios. Members of the religious education faculty were also active in the churches, workshops, conferences, lectureships, and made numerous appearances on Convention programs in the areas of their expertise. Professors in the School of Theology rendered similar services. Usually each theological professor had his calendar crammed with engagements for supply preaching, interim pastorates, January Bible studies, workshops, conferences, conventions, and other types of service.

To catch a glimpse of the vast amount of writing and service by the seminary faculty, one needs only to leaf through one year of the *Southwestern News*. Sometimes an entire issue was practically filled with reports on the writing and service activities of the faculty members.

Perhaps a single illustration of the domino effect that developed from the ministry of one of the faculty may suggest the significance of this widespread activity. LeRoy Ford of the School of Religious Education happened to have car trouble while near the campus of the National Autonomous University of Mexico in Mexico City in the summer of 1971. While waiting for repairs, he visited the Center of Didactics to observe what they were doing in teacher training, since he taught instructional technology involving programmed instruction. He conversed with Inge Alphonso Bernal Sahagun at the center, who became so interested in Ford's work that they talked for two hours, and the American teacher promised that he would return to assist the faculty in Mexico in mastering the principles they had discussed. On his first sabbatical leave thereafter, Ford returned to Mexico City to fulfill his promise. He was asked by the university to develop a system of teacher training for use by its faculty. Feeling that he could do this for the university while devising a system for helping Sunday School teachers of Southern Baptists to improve their instruction, Ford returned to the seminary to work on this project. Using some of his Southwestern students as a control group to validate the tests, Ford devised a program to increase the effectiveness of teachers by "hitching their teaching to a goal."[219] Professors at the National University of Mexico were so impressed by the thoroughness and effectiveness of the program that a group of their teachers, mainly scientists, were sponsored by the Mexican government to make a visit to Southwestern's campus in 1973 to study the teaching techniques involved in this program. This group returned in succeeding years. Accompanying representatives of the National University of Mexico for this conference in 1974, for example, were professors from the University of Oaxaca, University of Ieretaro, University of San Luis Potasi, University of Morelia, University of Colima, and the University of Chihuahua. The director of the San Antonio branch of the National University of Mexico also was a part of the group.[220] At the invitation of the Mexican universities, some of Southwestern's faculty later visited the National University in Mexico City. This exciting international fellowship of scholars has been fruitful. Professor Ford has had more than seventy conferences outside of the United States involving his area of expertise.[221]

An Added Faculty Unity

President Scarborough had emphasized often that the division of the seminary curriculum into three schools to provide functional efficiency did not mean that the seminary was not one in spirit and fundamental objectives. During President Naylor's administration the unity of the three schools was also a matter of concern. It was fostered by many things. The self-studies required by the accreditation bodies brought the faculties of the three schools into single committees, which provided better communication and understanding through dialogue and reflection. The common accreditation of all three schools by the Association of Theological Schools and the Southern Association of Colleges and Schools brought a wider perspective to the individual faculties. Combination degree programs utilizing the competencies of all three schools helped coordinate the entire faculty. Standing committees of the general faculty, such as the Curriculum Council and the Advanced Studies Council, brought more integrating radials. The preschool retreat of the theological faculty was modified to include the entire faculty, and the programs at these retreats were widened to appeal to the interests and concerns of all the seminary faculty. The new administrative structure of 1973 provided another unifying factor in that the vice-president for academic affairs and the deans of the three schools worked closely together in leading all three faculties.

Fleming Library

Functioning as a part of the teaching process, the library advanced substantially in all areas during this twenty-year period. Charles P. Johnson was librarian in 1958 and provided outstanding leadership until his death in 1965. As president-elect of the American Theological Library Association in 1964, he was requested by that body to make a consultant visitation and tour of theological schools in India for two months during the summer of 1964 in an effort to improve the methodology in the administration of India's theological libraries.[222] Unfortunately, during the tour he was found to have a serious physical disease. He died on May 22, 1965.[223] During his eight years as director of libraries at Southwestern, its holdings increased from 114,000 to over 335,000.[224] His work was characterized by a gracious spirit, quiet efficiency, and total commitment to his task.

After a brief interim, Keith C. Wills, a trained theological librarian, was named the new director of libraries in February, 1966. Under his direction the library continued its growth. Additional services were developed. A media center had existed during several years of limited operations due to lack of space. This center endeavored to meet the instructional media and audiovisual needs of the classroom and campus, which included acquiring materials and operating the equipment for their presentation. The principal thrust was for the classroom, but assistance was also given to students seeking to present materials in their churches. Slides, slide sets, overhead transparencies, tape recordings, and many types of filmstrips and movies were made available.[225] By 1974, however, the audiovisual needs had far outgrown the facilities. A faculty committee studied the possibility of restructuring the center for greater usefulness. As a result, a major learning center was opened in Price Hall in January, 1975. Not only did this center provide resources and assistance for audiovisual presentations, but it made possible the setting up of sophisticated self-study units for the students to enable them to hear and see taped lectures, locate additional reading resources, and even test their own progress. With this center the teacher was provided with a wide range of teaching methodologies, and the student could utilize the extensive collection to increase his knowledge in a particular field of interest.[226]

Additional impetus was given to the library's collection of Texas Baptist history. It will be recalled that when the Texas Baptist Historical Committee was formed in 1933, the library at Southwestern was designated as the official depository for its historical materials. In 1971, after an extensive study, the Texas Baptist Historical Committee, an auxiliary of the Baptist General Convention of Texas, confirmed and continued Fleming Library as the official depository for Texas Baptists; and a continuing flow of valuable material has enriched the collection year by year.[227]

With the cooperation of the faculty, the library staff published in 1972 a bibliography entitled *Essential Books for Christian Ministry: Basic Reading for Pastors, Church Staff Leaders, and Laymen.*[228] This was developed primarily in order to give guidance to students in all three schools of the seminary in the building of balanced and selective libraries for their later use.

Still another service of the library was the extension of library privileges to those away from the campus. Through the years, the alumni of the school made individual arrangements for checking out library books which were not available to them on their fields of service. This activity slowly increased and resulted in the inauguration of what became known as the Continuing Education Program of Fleming Library. In 1972, the library was servicing 187 patrons from a 32-state area, and by 1978 the records showed over 3,000 mailings to more than 1,000 patrons of the program.[229]

Finally, the affiliation of Fleming Library with the AMIGOS Library Network in 1976 enlisted the aid of computer technology to expand the resources of the library. Sponsored by the AMIGOS Bibliographic Council, the network computer system provided information instantly on the holdings of seventy libraries with over four million books. The system was particularly beneficial in the areas of interlibrary loans, cataloging, and ordering.[230]

By the close of this period in 1978, Fleming Library showed holdings numbering 453,176, which included books and pamphlets, periodicals, catalogues, items in the music library and learning center, church minutes, manuscript collections, historical artifacts, anid other typical library items. Book circulation in 1977-78 numbered 229,220; interlibrary loans, 610; mail service for the Continuing Education Program, 3,044; audiovisual materials, 43,545; music materials, 53,009; periodicals and other serials, 33,269; and vertical file materials, 757. Total circulation was 363,452 for this year.[231]

"We Must Learn"

In the categories of stewardship developed by President Naylor, the student's responsibility was to be faithful to God's call and dedicate himself to the best preparation possible for his service. It is rather curious that the number of students enrolling in Southwestern Seminary showed an unexpected decline in the first fourteen years of this period. This decline in enrollment was not confined to Southwestern. Practically all seminaries, including other Southern Baptist seminaries, had the same experience. The reports of the Southern Baptist Education Commission to the Convention prior to this decline had been optimistic about the prospects for rising enrollments.[232] However, beginning in 1958 the enrollment in Southern Baptist seminaries began to show a drop almost each year. Baptist colleges and universities also reported a regular decline in the number of students preparing for vocational Christian service. Doubtless economic and social factors were in part responsible for this. Whatever the reason, the annual cumulative enrollment of Southwestern Seminary did not regain the 1958-59 figure of 2,395 until the 1972-73 session when 2,406 enrolled. The low point was reached in 1966-67, when 1,859 enrolled. It is interesting to observe that this decline was more marked in the schools of theology and religious education than it was in the area of music.

However, with the record enrollment in 1972-73 the trend was reversed, and new enrollment records were set as each year showed substantial gains. The average increase in students each year between 1972-73 and 1977-78 was 346, or over 14 percent. By the close of the period in 1978 the cumulative enrollment at Southwestern Seminary had reached the astounding figure of 4,136 students in the three schools. The makeup of this enrollment was as follows:[233]

Category	Total
Men	3,460
Women	676
School of Theology	2,420
School of Religious Education	1,345
School of Church Music	366
Master of Divinity program	2,030
Master of Religious Education program	1,209
Graduate Specialist in Religious Education program	14
Master of Church Music program	236

Category	Total
Master of Music program	90
Doctor of Philosophy program	71
Doctor of Theology program	9
Doctor of Ministry program	131
Doctor of Education program	57
Doctor of Musical Arts program	30
Diploma programs of the three schools	269

The facilities for the students were the best the school had ever known. Student housing, while not adequate to provide for all of the burgeoning enrollment, was available for many; a new student center contained a book store and cafeteria, and reception, social, and conference areas; an increase in the number of the faculty had reduced the teacher-student ratio to approximately 1:28; health services had been improved with the construction of a medical facility; a children's building made it possible to provide for more practical service to students with families and to utilize this service for training kindergarten specialists; and a physical fitness center was under construction. The long lines of students waiting to register, a familiar sight in the past, were now disappearing. Computer registration provided a much more efficient operation.[234] Scholars in every field of student interest and training were brought to the campus in workshops, conferences, lecture series, chapel, and as guest professors.

Student organizations on campus provided the opportunity for many students to participate in campus affairs. The Student Council was the integrating body. Its membership included representatives from the student body at large; from the various state clubs; from Barnard and Fort Worth Hall dormitories; from the Theological Fellowship, which included all students enrolled in the School of Theology; from the Student Religious Education Association, made up of all students enrolled in the School of Religious Education; from Zimrah, the campus organization for students in the School of Church Music; from the National Baptist Fellowship, composed of Black students related to this fellowship; and from other student organizations, such as the Intercessory Prayer Ministry, the Student Missions Fellowship, and the International Fellowship. Mention has been made earlier of Metochai, an organization for wives of students in all three schools of the seminary. The School of Church Music, in addition to the Zimrah Club, provided opportunity for musicians to participate in five other organizations: the Consort Singers, consisting of ten singers chosen by audition, who presented sacred and secular madrigals, ancient and modern motets, and a wide variety of other music in concert, on tour, and at other functions representing the seminary; the Men's Chorus, open to interested students in all three schools; the Oratorio Chorus, which presented an oratorio of major proportion each semester and was open to all who wished to sing in it; the Seminary Choir, composed of seminarians who were unable to enroll in other musical organizations; and the Southwestern Singers, an *a cappella* choir of trained voices, which was the official touring choir of the seminary.[235]

A chronological reading of the *Southwestern News* from 1958 to 1978 reveals an increasing amount of student participation month by month in numerous ministries near and beyond the campus. Over eight hundred students were employed regularly as pastors, educational directors, and musicians by the churches during the 1977-78 session.[236] Retreats were begun in 1973 for those interested in serving as evangelists.[237] Senior Preaching Week was begun in 1964 and was repeated annually. This involved four senior students preaching in chapel, four other seniors from the School of Religious Education reading the Scriptures and leading in prayer, and four others providing special music.[238] Inspirational retreats were held for students with different vocational goals.[239] Preaching on the streets, at rescue missions, and in the jail services was carried on regularly. In addition, students in social work assisted in Well Baby Clinics, served as "block shepherds" in some of the lower economic areas of Fort Worth, and witnessed on a one-to-one basis on the streets.[240] Jail ministry by women students to women inmates was begun.[241] A tutoring program to aid students in a nearby public middle school was initiated.[242] A pilot project in which several students served in Georgia in specialized ministries was undertaken.[243] Field trips to the state capital brought a better perspective to the student's work.[244]

Most of the extracurricular activities centered in evangelism or missions. All three schools shared in these projects.[245] The Journeyman Program thrived,[246] as did the summer mission program in the Bahamas.[247] The student mission conference was held regularly on the campus each spring, and US-2 missions were fostered.[248] As mentioned, a very active program involving several hundred students was the revival movement known as Pioneer Penetration, which had been begun in 1958 by the departments of evangelism and missions and was regularly promoted thereafter.[249] The *Southwestern News* consistently published the names and photographs of Southwestern's mission volunteers who were constantly being appointed by the two boards to serve on mission fields at home and around the world. It was a special occasion on April 11, 1978, when the Foreign Mission Board held a commissioning service before over seven thousand Tarrant County Baptists in Forth Worth. This was the first such service in Forth Worth since 1968. At this time Secretary Baker James Cauthen challenged thirty new missionaries, twenty-six of them from Southwestern, to be faithful in their testimony.[250] Almost one-fourth of the student body at Southwestern were mission volunteers.

The increasing upward spiral that marked the economic inflationary pattern during the 1960s and 1970s threatened to make theological education too expensive for the average young person who had received a call to ministry. Recognizing this, the seminary and the Southern Baptist Convention adopted the principle of keeping the expenses of the students as low as possible while at the same time providing the finest quality of theological education.[251] The administration and trustees endeavored to do this on the one hand by seeking more adequate funding from the Southern Baptist Convention and from private gifts of individuals to the school and, on the other hand, by a constant study of how to improve the quality of training provided for the student. It is true that the student had always been the focal point of every administration at Southwestern Seminary, but when the administration and trustees were reorganized in 1973 a significant advocate within the board of trustees was provided to monitor the needs of the students. This Student Affairs Committee of the trustees regularly secured input from not only the administrative personnel working with students but also involved student leadership in administrative decisions. Felix Gresham, dean of students, working with the trustee chairman of the Student Affairs Committee reported at each meeting of the board concerning the needs of students and how provision could be made for them.

The financial needs of the students represented one aspect of this concern. As Dean Gresham remarked, "Student aid is a vital expression of love and concern which is generated toward the student body of Southwestern Seminary."[252] Student aid increased during a portion of this period in a dimension never before experienced. Between 1965 and 1975 the amount of funds available for student aid skyrocketed. Even the casual reader of the *Southwestern News* during that decade had to be aware that almost every issue contained the report of new gifts and scholarships that were established for the benefit of the students.[253] These funds were of three types. The major category was the Invested Principal Fund. Gifts made to this fund were invested and the interest used to aid students. The Expendable Principal Fund was made up of short-term gifts, in which the principal sum was used for student aid over a certain period of time until the funds were exhausted. In 1975, these two funds yielded about $30,000 in student aid. The third type of student aid was the Designated Fund. Many gifts to the seminary were designated for students who met certain requirements which were determined by the donor. Some funds, for example, were for music students only, some for students from certain states only, some for the children of employees of certain corporations providing the funds, and so on. From these three types of funds—invested, expendable, and designated—grants to students totaled approximately $188,000 in 1975.

Another aspect of the student aid program was the Student Loan Fund. These loans were made possible by scores of loan funds established by individuals or groups, often as memorial funds. These funds were loaned to the students without interest for use toward seminary-related expenses. In 1975-76 the Student Loan Fund was utilized by 882 students, totaling $127,913.17.[254] The amount of financial aid, including scholarship grants and student loans, totaled $389,107.16 in 1975-76; $507,554.98 in 1976-77, and $551,095.47 in 1977-78.[255] Dean Gresham remarked:

> There are many graduates of this seminary who are now serving in church positions who would not have been able to complete their training had it not been for these funds. We would hope no student would let financial need interfere with his seminary career.

Other student services developed during the period. Like a watchdog, the Student Affairs Committee of the trustees continued to focus specifically on those student needs that could be understood only by those close to the student body. Personal counseling by a professional psychiatrist was made available for students with severe emotional problems;[256] loan limits for students were raised;[257] a better method of assisting students to find secular and church employment was sought, and search was begun for a student-church liaison person to meet this need.[258] Students were included in the important committees of the seminary, both standing and special committees when relevant, such as the Presidential Search Committee, the Self-Study Committee for the accrediting agencies, and the Long-Range Planning Committee.

"We Must Give"

One of the spectacular achievements of the Naylor regime was the remarkable increase in gifts to the seminary from donors other than the Southern Baptist Convention. As mentioned before, the seed had been planted for a vigorous developmental fund-raising program during

President Williams's administration when J. W. Bruner was named head of the Endowment Department on September 1, 1953. Bruner reported to the trustees after his first year:

> For some years preceding the establishment of the Endowment Department there had been very little information going to prospective donors and because of this interest was at a low ebb. It has been necessary to try to revive the interest of the people. It has been a slow process, but we are glad to report progress.[259]

When L. B. Reavis was named endowment secretary on March 1, 1955, he promptly outlined a vigorous program to inform and cultivate possible donors, to utilize the potential resources of the Advisory Council, and to insure future benefits to the seminary by appealing to its friends to remember the institution in their wills. In pursuing this three-pronged effort, Reavis published an article in almost every issue of the *Southwestern News* from September, 1963, until his retirement in 1969. These articles pointed to the heritage of the seminary, its effective service to the cause of Christ and the denomination, and its need for assistance. Particularly significant was his long-running series of articles, "Among Our Friends," in which he described individuals who had given funds to the school, some from their poverty and some from their abundance. Usually the same amount of space was given to expressing appreciation for the small gifts of a few dollars as for the large ones amounting to hundreds of thousands of dollars.[260] Reavis magnified the importance of the Advisory Council, whose activities were regularly described in the *Southwestern News.*[261] Many members of this council made substantial gifts to the seminary.[262]

Evidently the effectiveness of Reavis triggered the decision by the trustees to seek additional personnel to cultivate possible donors.[263] In 1966, Robert Preston Taylor, who was retiring as a chaplain (General) from the armed forces, joined Reavis in the Endowment Department.[264] The organizational structure of the department changed somewhat. Reavis had first been employed as director of endowment and promotion. When John E. Seelig was named assistant to the president in 1960, he was assigned the promotional aspect of the program, and Reavis was made director of development. When Taylor was added in 1966, he became director of institutional resources. After fifteen years of devoted service, Reavis retired in 1969 with many expressions of appreciation by the trustees and administration.[265] Taylor then became director of development on January 1, 1970. In that year Clayton E. Day, a retired chaplain (Colonel) also, was elected as director of institutional resources.[266] On December 31, 1973, Robert Preston Taylor retired, and the functions of the Development Department were assigned to John E. Seelig as the new vice-president for administrative affairs under the revised administrative structure.

Coincident with the adoption of the new administrative structure in 1973, a new direction was taken which involved a significant forward step in seeking private funds for capital needs and endowment of the seminary. This new direction developed partly from the intensive self-study of 1971-73 for accreditation by the Southern Association of Colleges and Schools and partly from the recommendation of the Executive Committee of the Southern Baptist Convention to the effect that an "orderly, systematic process should be initiated to include the fundamental steps prerequisite to coping with the basic problem of financing seminary education." On June 22, 1973, the Executive Committee of the trustees appointed a special committee to study the feasibility of a capital funds campaign. This committee was supplemented by a study committee of the Advisory Council, and the combined group met with the faculty on November 2. It became apparent that a fund-raising campaign would require a thorough study of the seminary's objectives and prospects for the years just ahead, so this committee recommended to the trustees on November 20, 1973, that the trustees name a Long-Range Planning Commission. This was approved, and the steering committee included trustees, faculty, laymen, ministers, students, alumni, and administration. Seven study subcommittees were named; and their combined reports included chapters on the purpose and objectives of the seminary, along with possible developments and goals for the next twenty-five years in terms of educational programs, human resources, physical resources, financial resources, the organizational structure, and world outreach.[267] The results and recommendations of this study were entitled *IMPACT: 2000*. On February 28, 1975, Vice-President Seelig presented to the trustees the report of this extensive study. A principal recommendation urged that the trustees initiate a fund-raising campaign between 1975 and 1980 to raise $8,000,000 for capital needs and endowment of the seminary. With their approval a campaign slogan of "Eight-by-Eighty" (to raise $8,000,000 by 1980) was adopted, and Vice-President Seelig outlined the plans to reach this goal.[268] The Executive Committee of the Convention approved this campaign on September 3, 1975.

At a communitywide dinner on February 23, 1976, the first phase of the campaign officially began.[269] The Fort Worth thrust was already underway. Additional campaigns were held in Dallas, Houston, San Antonio, Austin, and nationwide—the first time the seminary had ever

conducted such a widespread campaign.[270] Vice-President Seelig kept
the trustees informed about this project at each meeting.[271] Major
publicity was given in almost every issue of the *Southwestern News*
between September, 1975, and February, 1978.[272]

The results of the campaign were impressive. A total of $9,441,666
was pledged, the principal amounts being raised in Forth Worth
($2,713,764), Houston ($2,694,284), and Dallas ($1,354,695). Alumni
pledged over $1,000,000.[273]

In his report to the trustees at the beginning of the Eight-by-Eighty
Campaign, Vice-President Seelig pointed out that this sort of vigorous
campaign for funds, composed of a connected series of systematic efforts
designed to secure gifts, must always be complemented by developmental fund raising or a continuous effort to motivate gift money from
every known source by the most effective and proper method. The Eight-
by-Eighty Campaign was assisted by the less spectacular but continuous
effort to interest possible donors in the welfare of Southwestern. Almost
every issue of the *Southwestern News* during this period reported gifts
from many persons, some of them entirely unknown to seminary leaders.
Evidently these were people who had been touched in some way by their
seminary in earlier days and wanted to make some contribution to its
ministry.[274]

Thus, with the huge increase in Cooperative Program receipts,
substantial allocations for capital funds, and the funds raised from
private sources by both campaign fund raising and the developmental
fund-raising methods, it is not surprising that the assets and endowment
of the seminary showed gains year by year. The following tables show this
advance:

Assets of the School 1958-1978

Year	Amount
1958-59	$12,186,243
1959-60	12,919,009
1960-61	13,613,465
1961-62	14,593,368
1962-63	15,228,064
1963-64	15,864,029
1964-65	16,487,322
1965-66	17,483,514
1966-67	18,451,154
1967-68	18,964,541
1968-69	19,729,475
1969-70	20,430,193

Assets of the School 1958-1978

Year	Amount
1970-71	21,670,349
1971-72	23,761,991
1972-73	24,821,643
1973-74	27,280,986
1974-75	28,897,364
1975-76	30,849,769
1976-77	33,136,393
1977-78	37,700,714

Endowment Funds of the School 1958-78

Year	Amount
1958-59	$ 3,752,120
1959-60	4,273,789
1960-61	4,420,329
1961-62	4,845,896
1962-63	4,911,706
1963-64	5,078,159
1964-65	5,031,246
1965-66	5,337,929
1966-67	5,903,128
1967-68	6,337,591
1968-69	6,551,731
1969-70	6,717,155
1970-71	7,397,272
1971-72	7,620,240
1972-73	7,996,783
1973-74	8,966,577
1974-75	9,545,525
1975-76	10,342,078
1976-77	11,182,971
1977-78	12,081,335

"We Must Be Fruitful"

It boggles one's mind to try to visualize the vast areas of fruitful service of Southwestern's alumni. During all of this period in a column entitled

"Around the World with Southwesterners," the *Southwestern News* carried personal items about missionaries, pastors, educational workers, musicians, and others who were former students. Marriages, births, and deaths were recorded, and special articles were prepared to spotlight some worker in a small country church or some graduate who had achieved national prominence.[275] For many years each issue also had a column entitled "Among Our Chaplains" in which the activities of this particular group were reported. Several of the national presidents of the Southwestern Alumni Association wrote articles for each issue of the *Southwestern News* for a long period. State presidents of the alumni were invited to return to the campus each year beginning in 1972. A "homecoming" celebration was initiated in 1974 to welcome alumni back to the campus.[276] A careful record, kept up-to-date by the alumni information office, made it possible to circulate campus news and information regularly among former students. All of these activities reflected the love and concern of Southwestern for its alumni.

Another program Southwestern developed for its alumni sought to encourage them to write books and articles and to keep the school informed of their progress in Christian work. It would be most difficult to determine the number of books and articles which have been prepared by Southwestern's alumni. Many hold places of service which demand that they write. Doctoral graduates are professors in Southern Baptist seminaries and universities and in other schools; many are editors of Baptist papers; many are denominational executives. For example, in 1978, at the end of this period, four of the six presidents of Southern Baptist seminaries were alumni of Southwestern, as were the heads of both mission boards and the Annuity Board. Many of the editors and executives of the state conventions graduated from this school. The *Southwestern News* shamelessly publicized the achievements of its sons and daughters in the work of the Kingdom.[277]

The alumni also were involved in the financial campaigns of the school. During the Eight-by Eighty Campaign, the alumni association took an active part in promoting and supporting the financial drive. They were particularly interested in providing the physical fitness center, and all of their undesignated funds in the campaign went for that purpose.[278]

Finally, a plan to bestow what has been termed the *Distinguished Alumni Award* was developed. It was recognized that awards of this kind could not always acknowledge the most worthy ministries performed by the alumni, but it was the desire of the alumni association to provide this tangible evidence of appreciation for some whose contributions had been notable. The Executive Committee of the alumni association met in Fort

Worth in February, 1964, and inaugurated the plan of conferring this award each year upon a small number of men and women. The Award Committee consisted of the president of the alumni association and the three former presidents of that body.[279] The first such awards were presented on May 20, 1964, to Baker James Cauthen, executive secretary of the Foreign Mission Board since January 1, 1954; J. D. Grey, pastor of the First Baptist Church, New Orleans, Louisiana, since 1937 and former president of the Southern Baptist Convention; W. L. Howse, director of the Education Division of the Baptist Sunday School Board and professor at the seminary for twenty-two years; Robert E. Naylor, president of Southwestern Seminary since 1958; Courts Redford, executive secretary-treasurer of the Home Mission Board; and W. R. White, president emeritus of Baylor University—all of whom were distinguished denominational leaders for many years.[280]

Like the mother of the Gracchi in early Roman history, Southwestern counts its children to be its jewels and greatest ornaments.

Retirement of Robert E. Naylor

On November 22, 1976, President Naylor informed the trustees that he would retire on August 1, 1978. The trustees had desired to retain him as long as possible, so they voted year by year to continue his services after he had reached retirement age.[281] A committee was appointed to honor the retiring president and make provision for his needs after retirement.[282]

From this brief summary of the twenty-year administration of Robert E. Naylor, it is apparent that the seminary experienced unprecedented growth during this period. By securing additional funding from the Southern Baptist Convention and because of private gifts and bequests, President Naylor achieved a substantial strengthening of the faculty. He encouraged the recognition of the quality of their teaching by accrediting agencies. In the needed renovation of the older buildings and the erection of new facilities on and around the campus, he made it possible to provide housing and classroom space for a greatly enlarged student enrollment. A major administrative restructuring brought more efficiency in operation. By his known doctrinal conservatism, he was a stabilizing factor in the controversies of the 1960s and 1970s. His gracious wife played a large part in the overall effectiveness of his service during these twenty years of unprecedented growth. In his last message to the trustees, he said:

At the outset of this last twenty years, I made a fresh commitment to my Lord and to the Trustees of this seminary that we would faithfully follow Him and that we would adhere to the authoritative revelation of God in Christ Jesus set forth in the One Book. It is on this commitment that I stand, that I ask under God that the years be measured, and that I ask only of Him that I be found faithful.[283]

He was indeed faithful.

Notes

1. J. Thurmond George (Gilroy, California) to Robert A. Baker, received 26 June 1981, Fleming Library, Southwestern Baptist Theological Seminary, Fort Worth, Texas.

2. *Southwestern News*, July 1958, p. 3.

3. See, for example, Trustee Minutes, 21 November 1967. He made many trips to the mission fields.

4. John A. Garraty, *The American Nation*, 4th ed. (New York: Harper and Row, 1979), pp. 762-63.

5. *Southwestern News*, December 1958, p. 2.

6. Trustee Minutes, 25 November 1974. See also *Southwestern News*, July 1974, p. 3.

7. Trustee Minutes, 26 November 1963. See also *Standard*, 15 May 1963, p. 14. His will left $100,000 to the seminary. See Trustee Minutes of the Executive Committee, 1 March 1973.

8. Trustee Minutes, 26 November 1963.

9. Ibid., 25 February 1964.

10. Trustee Minutes of the Executive Committee, 18 July 1968.

11. Trustee Minutes, 27 February 1959.

12. Ibid., 27 February 1962.

13. Trustee Minutes of the Executive Committee, 20 November 1972 and 22 June 1973.

14. Trustee Minutes, 2 March 1973. See *Southwestern News*, March 1973, pp. 1,3.

15. Trustee Minutes, 1 March 1974 and 26 November 1974.

16. Ibid., 20 November 1973.

17. Trustee Minutes of the Executive Committee, 23 November 1959; and Trustee Minutes, 1 March 1960.

18. *Minute Book*, Southwestern Baptist Seminary Development Foundation, Inc., p. 1. This book is kept in the vault of the Business Office of the seminary.

19. *Southwestern News*, October 1960, p. 5.

20. See, for example, Trustee Minutes, 22 November 1960, 28 February 1961, 25 February 1964, 28 February 1967, and 21 November 1967.

21. Ibid., 28 February 1975.

22. See, for example, ibid., 24 November 1958, 27 February 1959, 24 November 1959, 27 November 1962, 26 February 1963, 26 November 1974, and elsewhere.

23. Ibid., 24 November 1958, 26 February 1963, 25 February 1964; and Trustee Minutes of the Executive Committee, 24 September 1974 and elsewhere.

24. Trustee Minutes, 28 November 1961, 10 March 1972, and elsewhere.

25. Trustee Minutes of the Executive Committee, 24 February 1969.

26. Trustee Minutes, 26 November 1974.

27. Ibid., 20 June 1958, 26 February 1963, 1 March 1966, and 22 November 1976.

28. Ibid., 27 February 1968, 24 November 1970, 23 November 1971; and Trustee Minutes of the Executive Committee, 23 May 1967.

29. Trustee Minutes, 27 February 1968.

30. Trustee Minutes of the Executive Committee, 27 February 1975.

31. Trustee Minutes, 26 November 1974. See also *Southwestern News,* December 1973, pp. 1,3; February 1973, p. 3; March 1974, p. 3; and December 1974, p. 1.

32. See, for example, Trustee Minutes, 28 November 1950 for earlier discussions.

33. Ibid., 27 February 1968, 25 February 1969, 3 March 1970, 24 November 1970, and 25 March 1977.

34. Ibid., 24 November 1970, 23 November 1971, 21 November 1972, and 20 November 1973; also *Southwestern News,* December 1970, p. 4.

35. Trustee Minutes, 23 November 1976 and 25 March 1977.

36. See Trustee Minutes of the Executive Committee, 20 November 1972, 1 March 1973, 24 March 1977, and 26 January 1978. See also Trustee Minutes, called meeting 15 June 1977.

37. Trustee Minutes, 21 November 1972.

38. Trustee Minutes of the Executive Committee, 28 May 1976 and 8 July 1976.

39. Trustee Minutes, 25 November 1974; and Trustee Minutes of the Committee on Business Affairs, 27 April 1976.

40. Trustee Minutes, 25 March 1977 and 22 November 1977.

41. L. R. Scarborough mentioned the donation of several gifts for the Chair of Evangelism; see Scarborough, *Modern School,* p. 126. He also made several references to the Bottoms gift; see ibid., pp. 121-22,126.

42. Trustee Minutes of the Executive Committee, 8 July 1976; also Trustee Minutes, 25 March 1977 and 22 November 1977.

43. Trustee Minutes, 25 March 1977.

44. Ibid., 22 November 1977.

45. See *Southwestern News,* February 1968, p. 2; and March 1968, p. 5. Also see Trustee Minutes of the Executive Committee, 25 March 1977 and 9 September 1977.

46. Trustee Minutes, 24 February 1976.

47. Ibid., 26 November 1974. See also *Southwestern News,* February 1975, p. 1.

48. *Annual,* SBC, 1959, p. 116.

49. Ibid., 1979, p. 221.

50. Ibid., 1958, p. 94.

51. Ibid., 1944, p. 17.

52. Ibid., 1951, p. 371.

53. Ibid., 1957, pp. 399-417.

54. Ibid., 1958, p. 444.

55. See *Encyclopedia,* III: 1780-81, 1918-23 for this story. Also see *Annual,* SBC, 1959, pp. 127,447-48; and Trustee Minutes, 28 November 1961.

56. See Baker, *Southern Baptist Convention,* pp. 423-25.

57. For the final report of this commission see *Annual,* SBC, 1968, p. 234.

58. See Trustee Minutes, 1 March 1966, 28 February 1967, 27 February 1968, and 26 November 1968. See also Trustee Minutes of the Executive Committee, 23 January 1968.

59. See Trustee Minutes, 24 February 1976; also *Southwestern News,* December 1976, p. 2.

60. Trustee Minutes, 2 March 1971.

61. Ibid., 26 November 1968; also *Southwestern News,* May 1978, p. 8.

62. See, for example, Trustee Minutes, 27 February 1962, 27 November 1962, 2 March 1965, 28 February 1967, 26 November 1968, and elsewhere. Practically every meeting of the Executive Committee of the trustees discussed this. See, for example, their minutes of 20 November 1972, 25 November 1975, 26 January 1978. Also see *Southwestern News,* February 1977, p. 1; October 1977, p. 5; and June 1978, p. 1.

63. *Annual,* SBC, 1951, p. 67.

64. Ibid., 1952, p. 82.

65. Ibid., 1953, p. 84.

66. Ibid., 1954, p. 91.

67. Ibid., 1959, p. 107.

68. See, for example, Trustee Minutes, 25 February 1964, 24 November 1964, 28 February 1967, 21 November 1972, 20 November 1973, 1 March 1974, 24 February 1976, and elsewhere. The amounts of the capital needs funding from the convention were secured from Vice-President Wayne Evans. There is some discrepancy in the exact figures in the *Annuals* of the Southern Baptist Convention each year because of a difference in fiscal years used by the seminary and the convention.

69. See *Southwestern News,* July 1960, p. 2; and September 1960, p. 3. See also Trustee Minutes, 22 November 1960.

70. Trustee Minutes, 24 November 1958, 27 February 1959, 22 November 1960, 27 November 1962, 24 November 1964, 2 March 1965, and 1 March 1966. The trustees' Executive Committee and Finance Committee regularly discussed this matter.

71. *Annual,* SBC, 1967, p. 275.

72. Trustee Minutes, 28 November 1961 and 24 November 1964.

73. Ibid., 21 November 1967.

74. Ibid., 27 February 1968.

75. See ibid., 23 November 1965, for application of all three schools for accreditation in the Association of Theological Schools. Also see minutes of 25 November 1969.

76. Ibid., 22 November 1966 and 24 November 1970.

77. Ibid., 1 March 1960.

78. See *Appendix* for a list of the editors of *Southwestern News.* For Moyers see *Southwestern News,* January 1966, p. 3; May 1973, p. 6; July 1973, p. 1; and March 1975, p. 1.

79. See, for example, *Southwestern News,* February 1966, p. 2; June 1966, p. 3; February 1967, p. 4; April 1967, p. 13; April 1968, p. 4; February 1980, p. 7; and elsewhere.

80. Ibid., June 1978, p. 8.

81. Ibid., October 1977, p. 9.

82. Trustee Minutes of the Executive Committee, 26 January 1978.

83. Trustee Minutes, 24 November 1958.

84. See, for example, ibid., 22 November 1960, 28 February 1961, 28 November 1961, 27 February 1962, 26 November 1963, 25 February 1964, 2 March 1965, and regularly until the end of this period.

85. Ibid., 27 February 1959.

86. Ibid., 24 November 1959, 22 November 1960, and 28 February 1961.

87. Ibid., 25 February 1964, 24 November 1964, 3 March 1970, and 2 March 1971.

88. Ibid., 24 November 1959, 1 March 1960, and 22 November 1960.

89. *Annual*, SBC, 1975, p. 188.

90. Trustee Minutes, 2 March 1965 and called meeting 31 May 1965.

91. Ibid., called meeting 31 May 1965 and 23 November 1965.

92. Ibid., 1 March 1974. See also *Annual*, SBC, 1975, p. 188 and 1978, p. 174.

93. Trustee Minutes, 25 February 1964.

94. Ibid., 1 March 1966 and 22 November 1966.

95. Ibid., 21 November 1967; also *Annual*, SBC, 1967, p. 277.

96. Trustee Minutes, 25 February 1969 and 25 November 1969.

97. Ibid., 25 November 1969, 3 March 1970, and 21 November 1972.

98. Ibid., 22 November 1966.

99. Ibid., 1 March 1974; see also 26 November 1969.

100. Ibid., 26 February 1963 and 25 November 1969.

101. Ibid., 20 June 1958.

102. For example, see ibid., 20 June 1958, 24 November 1959, 22 November 1960, 28 February 1961, 28 November 1961, 26 February 1963, called meeting 31 May 1965, 23 November 1965, 24 November 1970, 2 March 1971, 23 November 1971, 10 March 1972, and intermittently until the end of the period.

103. Ibid., 24 November 1959.

104. Ibid., 27 November 1962.

105. See *Southwestern News*, April 1968, p.1. Also see Trustee Minutes, 1 March 1960, 26 November 1963, and 25 February 1964.

106. Trustee Minutes, 26 November 1968, 25 February 1969, and 25 November 1969.

107. See Trustee Minutes of the Executive Committee, 23 January 1968, 16 July 1968, and 28 May 1976. Also see *Southwestern News*, October 1967, p. 3; January 1968, p. 2; April 1968, p. 1; December 1968, p. 1; and January 1969, p. 9.

108. Trustee Minutes, 26 November 1968 and 25 November 1969.

109. Ibid., 25 February 1969, 3 March 1970, 24 November 1970, 2 March 1971, and 23 November 1971.

110. Ibid., 1 March 1966, 22 November 1966, and 28 February 1967.

111. See also *Southwestern News*, December 1971, p. 1; and February 1973, pp. 1-2.

112. Trustee Minutes, 26 February 1963, 2 March 1971, and 23 November 1971.

113. Trustee Minutes of the Executive Committee, 28 May 1976.

114. See *Southwestern News*, April 1977, p. 1; September 1977, p. 1; and July 1978, p. 1. See also Trustee Minutes, 22 November 1977.

115. Trustee Minutes, 23 November 1965. See also *Southwestern News*, March 1966, p. 1.

116. See Trustee Minutes of the Executive Committee, 24 September 1974, also 25 November 1974.

117. Trustee Minutes, 24 November 1958 and 27 February 1959.

118. Trustee Minutes of the Executive Committee, 18 July 1968.

119. See articles discussing the functions of each of these officers in *Southwestern News*, March 1975, p. 4 for academic affairs; April 1975, p. 4 for administrative affairs; and May 1975, p. 4 for business affairs.

120. Trustee Minutes, 28 February 1975.

121. For this story see *Encyclopedia*, II:1841-42, "Midwestern Baptist Theological Seminary," by C. Hugh Wamble.

122. Trustee Minutes, 28 November 1961.

123. *Annual*, SBC, 1962, pp. 65, 68.

124. Trustee Minutes, 27 February 1962; also see 28 November 1961.

125. Ibid., 26 November 1962.

126. For one such instance see ibid., 27 February 1962, 26 November 1962, and 26 February 1963.

127. For this confession see Baker, *Source Book*, pp. 205-11.

128. *Annual*, SBC, 1970, pp. 77-78.

129. Trustee Minutes, 1 March 1971.

130. Ibid., called meeting 15 June 1977.

131. For this biography see *Encyclopedia*, III:1638. Also see *Southwestern News*, May 1964, p. 5; and January 1968, p. 3.

132. *Southwestern News*, September 1964, p. 4; and July 1965, p.7.

133. Ibid., July 1973, p. 5.

134. Ibid., January 1974, p. 6.

135. Ibid., April 1966, p. 7.

136. Ibid., April 1963, p. 4.

137. Ibid., July 1971, p. 6.

138. Ibid., October 1977, p. 6.

139. Ibid., May 1970, p. 5; and June 1970, p. 4.

140. Ibid., April 1972, p. 16.

141. Ibid., July 1976, p. 5.

142. Ibid., May 1959, p. 3.

143. Ibid., June 1959, p. 3.

144. Ibid., May 1965, p. 7.

145. *Annual*, SBC, 1973, p. 185.

146. *Southwestern News*, November 1974, p. 3.

147. Ibid., September 1975, p. 3.

148. Ibid., September 1977, p. 3.

149. Ibid., January 1978, p. 3.

150. Ibid., September 1965, p. 2.

151. Ibid., May 1960, p. 3; also see April 1960, p. 5.

152. Ibid., May 1970, p. 5; and June 1970, p. 4.

153. Ibid.

154. Ibid., May 1960, p. 5; and April 1972, p. 16.

155. Ibid., May 1973, p. 1.

156. Ibid., June 1974, p. 5.

157. Ibid., June 1961, p. 6.

158. Ibid., April 1963, p. 4.

159. Ibid., June 1967, p. 6.

160. Ibid., May 1978, p. 3.

161. Ibid., March 1969, p. 2.

162. Trustee Minutes, 24 March 1977.

163. See Theological Faculty Minutes, 23 June 1959, 13 October 1959, 30 October 1962, 21 September 1965, 6 September 1966, 6 February 1968, 25 March 1968, 8 April 1969, 1 May 1973, 23 April 1974, 8 April 1975, 17 June 1975, and many other places.

164. Ibid., 30 October 1962; also *Southwestern News*, December 1973, p. 1.

165. Trustee Minutes, 28 November 1961.

166. Ibid., 25 February 1969.

167. Ibid., 28 February 1961; and Theological Faculty Minutes, 23 June 1959, 25 October 1960, and 3 January 1961.

168. Theological Faculty Minutes, 26 February 1963, 25 February 1964, and 1 March 1966; and Trustee Minutes, 24 November 1964.

169. Theological Faculty Minutes, 1 November 1966, 21 December 1966, 28 February 1967; and Southwestern *Catalogue*, 1967-68, p. 55. See also Trustee Minutes, 22 November 1966, 28 February 1967, and 21 November 1967.

170. For example, Theological Faculty Minutes, 21 September 1965.

171. Ibid., 1 March 1966, 28 October 1969, and 24 November 1970.

172. Ibid., 7 December 1971; Trustee Minutes, 23 November 1971 and 10 March 1972; also *Southwestern News*, March 1972, pp. 1 ff.

173. Southwestern *Catalogue*, 1972-73, p. 63. Also see *Southwestern News*, March 1972, p. 1; and April 1972, pp. 1-2.

174. Trustee Minutes, 21 November 1972.

175. Ibid., 1 March 1974 and 24 March 1977.

176. Theological Faculty Minutes, 8 April 1975, 17 June 1975, and 9 September 1975.

177. Trustee Minutes, 10 March 1972. See also Southwestern *Catalogue*, 1972-73, p. 57.

178. Theological Faculty Minutes, 22 September 1959, 13 October 1959, and 27 October 1959. For a description of the new program see Southwestern *Catalogue*, 1960-61, pp. 73-82; and *Southwestern News*, December 1973, p. 3.

179. Trustee Minutes, 20 November 1973. Also see Southwestern *Catalogue*, 1974-75, pp. 56-61; and *Southwestern News*, December 1973, p. 3.

180. Religious Education Faculty Minutes, 6 November 1962; and Trustee Minutes, 27 November 1962 and 24 November 1970.

181. Trustee Minutes, 21 November 1972.

182. Ibid., 26 November 1963, 25 February 1964, and 27 February 1968. See also *Southwestern News*, February 1964, p. 5; and July 1971, p. 8.

183. *Southwestern News*, September 1974, p. 1.

184. Trustee Minutes, 28 February 1961 and 27 November 1962.

185. Ibid., 28 November 1961.

186. Ibid., 2 March 1965.

187. Ibid., 22 November 1966. See also Southwestern *Catalogue*, 1965-66, pp. 111-116; and *Southwestern News*, April 1965, p. 4.

188. Trustee Minutes, 25 March 1977 and 22 November 1977.

189. Ibid., 21 November 1972.

190. Ibid. See also Religious Education Faculty Minutes, 16 October 1972.

191. See, for example, Religious Education Faculty Minutes, 11 November 1974.

192. Music Faculty Minutes, 27 October 1959; and Trustee Minutes, 24 November 1959.

193. Trustee Minutes, 21 November 1967 and 27 February 1968. Also Music Faculty Minutes, 26 August 1967, 10 October 1967, and 8 November 1967.

194. Music Faculty Minutes, 5 February 1973. See also *Southwestern News*, March 1973, pp 1,4.

195. Music Faculty Minutes, 3 November 1975, 11 October 1976, 4 April 1977,

2 May 1977, 9 September 1977, and 17 October 1977.

196. Ibid., 28 November 1961; and Trustee Minutes, 23 November 1965.

197. Music Faculty Minutes, 4 September 1963, 17 September 1963, 8 September 1964, 1 December 1964, 22 March 1966, 26 April 1966, and 29 November 1966. Also see Trustee Minutes, 1 March 1966 and 22 November 1966; and *Southwestern News*, January 1965, p. 2; and December 1966, p.1.

198. Trustee Minutes, 28 February 1961.

199. Ibid., 27 February 1962. See *Southwestern News*, November 1960, p. 2; February 1962, p. 3; November 1970, p. 11; and February 1978, p. 5.

200. Trustee Minutes, 20 November 1973.

201. *Southwestern News*, March 1969, p. 1; and May 1970, p. 1.

202. Trustee Minutes, 2 March 1971; and Trustee Minutes of the Executive Committee, 11 June 1971 and 23 November 1971. See also *Southwestern News*, July 1971, p. 1; January 1973, p. 4; and many other references.

203. Trustee Minutes, 2 March 1965.

204. Ibid.

205. See *Southwestern News*, November 1964, p. 2; November 1965, p. 1; May 1968, p. 1; January 1970, p. 7; and April 1972, p. 13.

206. Trustee Minutes of the Executive Committee, 17 June 1975. Also see Trustee Minutes, 25 November 1975.

207. Trustee Minutes, 28 May 1976; and *Southwestern News*, July 1976, p. 1.

208. Trustee Minutes, 24 March 1977; and *Southwestern News*, June 1977, p. 1.

209. Trustee Minutes, 24 March 1977; and Theological Faculty Minutes, 8 February 1977. Also see *Southwestern News*, January 1978, p. 1.

210. Theological Faculty Minutes, 8 October 1957, 4 October 1958, and elsewhere.

211. Trustee Minutes of the Executive Committee, 4 October 1958 and 2 March 1970. Also see *Southwestern News*, February 1971, p. 7, and elsewhere.

212. See, for example, Theological Faculty Minutes, 28 March 1961, and elsewhere.

213. For example, see the reference to 128 students being involved in 19 states in this program in the spring of 1977 in *Southwestern News*, May 1977, p. 5.

214. Theological Faculty Minutes, 23 April 1974; and *Southwestern News*, September 1975, p 3.

215. Trustee Minutes, 25 March 1977.

216. Ibid., 25 March 1977 and 22 November 1977.

217. Ibid., 24 February 1976. See also *Southwestern News*, March 1976, p. 4.

218. *Southwestern News*, January 1965, pp. 8 ff; March 1965, pp. 3-4; and May 1965, p. 7.

219. Ibid., March 1976, p. 3.

220. Ibid., November 1974, p. 7.

221. Interview with LeRoy Ford, Southwestern Baptist Theological Seminary, Fort Worth, Texas, 23 March 1982.

222. *Southwestern News*, April 1964, p. 6.

223. Ibid., June 1965, p. 2.

224. From records of Fleming Library, 1965, secured from Keith Wills, director of libraries.

225. *Southwestern News*, January 1972, p. 7.

226. Ibid., September 1975, p. 3.

227. Ibid., January 1972, p. 11.

228. *Essential Books for Christian Ministry: Basic Reading for Pastors, Church Staff Leaders, and Laymen* (Fort Worth: Southwestern Baptist Theological Seminary, 1972).

229. *Southwestern News*, January 1972, p. 12, and circulation records of Fleming Library 1977-78, secured from Keith Wills.

230. *Southwestern News*, January 1977, p. 4.

231. From records of Fleming Library, 1978, secured from Keith Wills.

232. *Annual*, SBC, 1957, p. 415 shows projections.

233. Ibid., 1978, p. 173.

234. *Southwestern News*, May 1971, p. 6, and September 1971, p. 1.

235. Ibid., December 1970, p. 8.

236. Trustee Minutes, 22 November 1977.

237. *Southwestern News*, October 1974, p. 3.

238. Ibid., February 1970, p. 17, and April 1971, p. 11.

239. Ibid., January 1970, p. 7.

240. Ibid., January 1976, p. 4.

241. Ibid., January 1973, p. 3.

242. Ibid., May 1974, p. 7.

243. Ibid., October 1974, p. 8, and June 1975, p. 3.

244. Ibid., April 1975, p. 8.

245. Trustee Minutes, 27 February 1959.

246. *Southwestern News*, October 1966, p. 1; November 1969, p. 7; and May 1970, p. 6.

247. Ibid., October 1968, p. 8; June 1972, p. 4; and December 1972, p. 3.

248. Ibid., November 1968, p. 11.

249. Each spring the *Southwestern News* promoted this activity between January and March.

250. Ibid., April 1978, p. 7.

251. Trustee Minutes, 2 March 1973 and 22 November 1976.

252. *Southwestern News*, November 1975, p. 1.

253. For typical examples see ibid., June 1970, p. 3; February 1971, p. 12; May 1971, p. 7; June 1972, p. 3; February 1974, p. 4; May 1974, p. 7; May 1975, pp. 1,7; November 1975, p. 1; March 1976, p. 7; and elsewhere.

254. Ibid., November 1975, p. 1.

255. See *Institutional Self-Study 1979-80*, p. VIII/32, on file in Fleming Library, Southwestern Baptist Theological Seminary, Fort Worth, Texas.

256. Trustee Minutes, 28 February 1975 and 24 February 1976.

257. Ibid., 28 February 1975. See also Trustee Minutes of the Executive Committee, 30 September 1975.

258. Trustee Minutes, 24 November 1958 and 22 November 1977.

259. Ibid., 23 November 1954.

260. See, for example, *Southwestern News*, September 1963, p. 5; October 1963, p. 6; November 1963, p. 6; January 1964, p. 6; February 1964, p. 6; etc.

261. For example, see ibid., January 1967, p. 2; March 1967, p. 15; March 1968, p. 15; May 1968, p. 3; etc. After Reavis's retirement see ibid., January 1975, p. 3; January 1976, p. 5; November 1976, p. 5; December 1976, p. 4; January 1977, p. 5; November 1977, p. 4; and December 1977, p. 6.

262. Trustee Minutes, 3 March 1970 and 10 March 1972.

263. Ibid., called meeting 31 May 1965.

264. Ibid., 22 November 1966.

265. Ibid., 27 February 1968 and 25 February 1969. See also *Southwestern News*, December 1969, p. 5.

266. Trustee Minutes of the Executive Committee, 5 May 1970; and Trustee Minutes, 24 November 1970.

267. Trustee Minutes of the Executive Committee, 5 February 1974, 2 July 1974, and 24 September 1974.

268. Ibid., 17 June 1975.

269. *Southwestern News*, March 1976, pp. 1,3.

270. Ibid., November 1976, p. 1; January 1977, p. 1; January 1978, p. 4; and July 1978, p. 5.

271. Trustee Minutes, 25 November 1975, 22 November 1976, 24 March 1977, and 22 November 1977. Also see Trustee Minutes of the Executive Committee, 30 September 1975, 10 February 1976, and 8 July 1976.

272. For example, see *Southwestern News*, October 1975, p. 1; January 1976, pp. 1-2; February 1976, pp. 1,3; March 1976, pp. 1,3; May 1976, p. 1; etc.

273. These figures were secured from W. Edwin Crawford, endowment secretary of the seminary.

274. See remarks of President Naylor in *Southwestern News*, June 1978, p. 2.

275. See, for example, article on a country pastor, ibid., June 1964, p. 1; and many articles on Bill Moyers as mentioned heretofore in n. 78 above.

276. Ibid., February 1974, p. 4.

277. Ibid., November 1969, p. 8.

278. Ibid., September 1973, p. 3; February 1974, p. 6; July 1974, p. 1; February 1975, pp. 7,15; and June 1976, p. 1.

279. John Earl Seelig to Rheubin South (North Little Rock, Arkansas), 22 April 1965, Public Affairs Office, Southwestern Baptist Theological Seminary, Fort Worth, Texas.

280. *Southwestern News*, March 1964, p. 3, and June 1964, p. 8. A list of the recipients of this award is included in the *Appendix*.

281. Trustee Minutes, 20 November 1973 and 1 March 1974.

282. Trustee Minutes of the Executive Committee, 9 September 1977, and Trustee Minutes, 22 November 1977 and 17 March 1978.

283. *Southwestern News*, June 1978, p. 7.

Russell H. Dilday, Jr.
President (1978-)

A. Webb Roberts Library

A. Webb Roberts
Donor

Directors of Libraries

L. R. Elliott
(1919-57)

Charles P. Johnson
(1957-1965)

Keith C. Wills
(1966-)

Faculty of School of Theology
1981

Faculty of School of Religious Education
1981

Faculty of School of Church Music
1981

Officers of the seminary
1981

Administrative staff of the seminary
1981

Deans and Former Deans

Mrs. Andrew Allen
Women (1960-66)

Trozy Barker
Men (1963-)

E. L. Carnett
Music (1945)

Huber L. Drumwright, Jr.
Theology (1973-80)

Felix M. Gresham
Students (1974-79)

J. D. Heacock
Rel. Ed. (1956-73)

J. C. McKinney
Music (1956-)

Jesse J. Northcutt
Theology (1953-73)

J. M. Price
Rel. Ed. (1915-56)

I. E. Reynolds
Music (1915-45)

Neta Stewart
Women (1969-)

Ray Summers
Theology (1949-53)

Jack D. Terry
Rel. Ed. (1973-)

William B. Tolar
Theology (1981)

Doris Norton West
Women (1966-69)

J. Campbell Wray
Music (1947-56)

Support staff of the seminary
1981

Southern Baptist Convention Presidents

James T. Draper (1982-)

Bailey E. Smith (1980-82)

J. D. Grey (1952-54)

Ramsey Pollard (1960-62)

Jimmy Allen is shown under Convention executives.

Seminary Presidents

Milton U. Ferguson
Midwestern Baptist
Theological Seminary,
Kansas City, Missouri

W. Randall Lolley
Southeastern Baptist
Theological Seminary
Wake Forest, North Carolina

William M. Pinson, Jr.
Golden Gate Baptist
Theological Seminary
Mill Valley, California

Southern Baptist Convention Board Executives

R. Keith Parks
Foreign Mission Board
Richmond, Virginia

William G. Tanner
Home Mission Board
Atlanta, Georgia

Darold H. Morgan
Annuity Board
Dallas, Texas

Southern Baptist Convention Commission Executives

Jimmy R. Allen
Radio and Television
Commission, Fort Worth,
Texas. President SBC
(1978-80)

Foy Valentine
Christian Life Commission
Nashville, Tennessee

A. R. Fagan
Stewardship Commission
Nashville, Tennessee

10
The Vision Will Not Tarry

It has been true with every president of Southwestern Seminary: God has chosen a man for the place who has had the unique background to fit the precise needs of the seminary at the time he began his task. The physical and intellectual giant B. H. Carroll was superbly equipped to found the seminary; the "hot-hearted" L. R. Scarborough was needed for the trying pioneer years; the scholarly E. D. Head added a dimension that strengthened the school; the administrator par excellence J. Howard Williams challenged the seminary with the magnitude of his dreams; and the dynamic and effective Robert E. Naylor brought many of those dreams into reality. A nominating committee of the trustees sought for many months to find the man whose background and stature had prepared him to take up the task of leading the seminary in a challenging era.[1] On November 22, 1977, James E. Carter, chairman of this committee, brought to the trustees the committee's recommendation that Russell H. Dilday, Jr., pastor of the Second-Ponce de Leon Baptist Church, Atlanta, Georgia, be named as the sixth president of the seminary.

The man recommended by the committee was born on September 30, 1930, at Amarillo, Texas. His father was an outstanding religious educator and later a denominational leader of Texas Baptists. Trained at Baylor University and Southwestern Seminary, with degrees which included the Doctor of Philosophy from the latter, he served churches at Antelope and Clifton, Texas, before accepting the Tallowood Baptist Church, Houston, Texas, in 1959. After ten fruitful years there he moved to the Atlanta church. Here he continued his active denominational service. He was a member of the Georgia Baptist Convention's Executive Committee (1970-75), moderator of the Atlanta Baptist Association (1973-74), president of the Atlanta Baptist Association's Pastors' Conference (1974-75), and second vice-president of the Southern Baptist Convention (1970-71). He had authored two books and written extensively for various periodicals. For three years he had served on the faculty of Baylor University and later was a trustee of Baylor and San Marcos Academy in Texas and of Pace Academy in Georgia. He had been president of the trustees of the Convention's Home Mission Board from 1974 to 1976; and, as if it were a preparation for his task as president of the seminary, he had been named as a member of the Convention's Mission Challenge Committee to recommend a seventy-five-year mission plan for Southern Baptists. His three children, Robert, Nancy, and Ellen, were already attending Baylor University in Texas, so for the new president and his wife Betty the move to Seminary Hill was like a homecoming.

Strong, capable, articulate, and personable, he was the incarnation of the spirit of Southwestern. He had a far-reaching vision for the school which had nurtured him. More than once he referred to the prophetic words of Habakkuk 2:3, "The vision is yet for an appointed time . . . though it tarry, wait for it; because it will surely come, it will not tarry."[2]

After his unanimous election on November 22, 1977, the trustees greeted the new president with a standing ovation. His first words to them spoke of his vision for Southwestern—for its spirit, its academic excellence, its mission, its prophetic role, its assurance to its graduates, and its financial undergirding. He closed his brief message by saying,

> As a denominational leader, pastor, and now as seminary president, I want to be a model through my stewardship, tithe and personal witnessing. And I think our faculty should be models. How we teach is as important as what we teach.[3]

It was not long before newcomers on Seminary Hill would hear a knock on their door and be greeted by these words, "I'm Russell Dilday visiting from Gambrell Street Baptist Church. We would like very much for you to attend our services, and if God leads, to make this your church home."

An Ideal Transition

The trustees praised President Naylor for giving them advanced notice on November 22, 1976, that he would retire two years hence. This early announcement, remarked one of them, would provide a better opportunity for finding a new leader and "for having continuity without conditions of emergency." This proved to be true. When the trustees named Russell H. Dilday, Jr., as the sixth president of the seminary on November 22, 1977, they voted that he would become president-elect on January 1, 1978. During January and February he participated in the American Management Association Executive Development Program for thorough grounding in management and finance and moved his family to

Fort Worth. From March through May he engaged in conferences with President Naylor and the faculty members. On June 1 the transition in leadership began, with the new president fully responsible from this date. On August 1, 1978, President Naylor assumed the title President Emeritus, and the transition was complete.

At the first meeting with the trustees as the new president on October 24, 1978, President Dilday expressed his appreciation to them, the faculty and staff, and especially to President Naylor "for facilitating a positive transition of leadership." Wayne Evans, vice-president for business affairs who had served with two previous presidents, expressed his appreciation for what many had termed "one of the smoothest transitions in Baptist history."[4] The new president was inaugurated in impressive ceremonies on October 25, 1978, and for the first time in seminary history he wore about his neck a medallion signifying the presidential office. The entire issue of the *Southwestern News* for November, 1978, described the inaugural, giving a cordial welcome to Betty Dilday and the Dilday family.

Sharing the Vision

Ofttimes the man with a vision does not possess the gift of translating his dreams into reality because he cannot take the very practical steps necessary to implement the changes required to realize that vision. Authentic visions must begin with reality, just as reality rests upon heritage. The patient and sometimes painful process of bringing those visions into existence demands additional gifts of a high order. At his first meeting with the Executive Committee of the trustees on August 10, 1978, President Dilday briefly sketched the outlines of his vision for the seminary; but he and the trustees knew well that the critical test would be to develop practical plans to transform this vision into reality. Some of the trustees knew that President Dilday was already assembling a staff to provide administrative support for an enlarged program and was in the process of developing plans that would challenge the faith of the trustee body.

Assembling the Staff

After full discussions with the leadership of the board of trustees, the faculty, and the persons involved, President Dilday, at his first full meeting with the trustees on October 24, 1978, made specific recommendations relative to the staff that would provide administrative support.

Beginning with the existing staff of four vice-presidents, he made several recommendations. (1) No change was needed in the function or the leadership of the vice-president for business affairs. (2) The title "Vice-President for Administrative Affairs" did not accurately describe the functions of John E. Seelig and should be changed to "Vice-President for Public Affairs." (3) A major long-range study needed to be made in the area of student affairs. President Dilday recommended the creation of a new position entitled "Seminary Chaplain and Director of Student Aid" and that Felix Gresham, who had been serving as vice-president for student affairs, be elected to this new position. It was hoped that by the time of the next trustee meeting the president might have a recommendation for a person to fill the vacated position of vice-president for student affairs. (4) President Dilday recommended that with the retirement of Jesse J. Northcutt as vice-president for academic affairs on July 31, 1979, he be named the "E. Hermond Westmoreland Distinguished Professor of Preaching." Recommended for the position of vice-president for academic affairs was John P. Newport, who would return from Rice University to the teaching faculty on January 1, 1979, and assume the vice-presidency on August 1. (5) President Dilday also recommended that a fifth leadership position be created entitled "Executive Vice-President," to be filled by Lloyd Elder, who was then serving as assistant to the executive secretary of Texas Baptists.

Along with these recommendations, President Dilday presented a position or job description for the vice-presidents and the newly named seminary chaplain and director of student aid. The descriptions were thorough and precise. Wayne Evans, the vice-president for business affairs, was responsible for the reception, custody, disbursement, and investment of funds; the development and maintenance of an adequate and useful system of accounting records and information reporting procedures; the procurement, conservation, and servicing of the physical plant equipment and supplies; provision of computer service where needed; operation and maintenance of the physical plant; assistance to the president in the development and control of operating budgets and capital projects; supervision of auxiliary enterprises and contract services, including student housing, medical center, postal service, food service, and campus book store; the employment of nonacademic personnel and employee benefits for all personnel; the acquisition and development of real estate for campus expansion; supervision of seminary risk protection; availability to students, faculty, and staff in business matters; service as secretary-treasurer for the Southwestern Baptist Seminary Development Foundation, Inc.; service as corporate secretary and registered agent for the seminary; and service in other areas as requested by the president.

John E. Seelig, vice-president for public affairs, was given the responsibility of maintaining effective communication with all the various persons who support, benefit, or participate in the program of the seminary; improving public understanding and support of the mission of the seminary; developing and implementing a quality internal public relations program; organizing a program of fund raising among alumni, friends, businesses, foundations, and corporations to increase the annual financial support of the seminary; directing a program of alumni activity to involve former students of the seminary; designing and implementing a placement service for former students; providing professional help in the production of all seminary publications; informing prospective students about the seminary's programs and facilities through a planned program of student recruitment; supervising the printing and photography auxiliary service which included printing, xeroxing, photography, and central mailing; implementing and expediting all meetings of the seminary's board of trustees and advisory council and any other general meetings on campus in concert with the president; serving as official host for seminary functions; and attending other tasks as requested by the president.

Vice-President-Elect John Newport's responsibilities were to supervise the work of the deans of the theology, religious education, and church music schools, the director of libraries, the director of admissions, and the director of continuing education; to work with the president and the three deans in the process of replacing and adding faculty members in the three schools and evaluating faculty and other personnel in the division; to work with the president and the three deans in the process of maintaining the necessary curriculum to meet the seminary's educational mission and channeling all curriculum recommendations to the president and trustees; to preside at faculty meetings as requested by the president; to serve as chairman of the Curriculum Council and the Advanced Studies Council; to direct all areas of academic research; to appoint all faculty committees in consultation with the president and to serve as ex officio member of such committees; to supervise all accreditation procedures; to assist the president in projecting and implementing new programs that would enhance the seminary's effectiveness in its primary mission; to represent the seminary as requested by the president at academic functions and other conferences and programs related to theological education; and to serve in other areas as requested by the president.

The new position of executive vice-president carried the responsibility of assisting the president in the general operation of the seminary in coordination with the other vice-presidents; representing the seminary as requested by the president in denominational relations—the Southern Baptist Convention and its agencies, state conventions, associations, and churches; guiding in the long-range planning process in order to establish and implement the purpose, objectives, and goals of the seminary; coordinating the development and presentation of the annual budget based on the long-range planning and priorities of the institution; providing a sound base of research and statistics for planning and decision making; serving as a resource person for internal management development and practice; teaching periodically in the area of practical theology; and serving in other areas as requested by the president.

Felix Gresham's new position as seminary chaplain and director of student aid carried the responsibility of initiating and administering programs to contribute to spiritual growth on the part of students and faculty; coordinating programs of spiritual growth on campus such as prayer groups, discipleship development groups, and the like; working with the faculty committee in preparation for and direction of seminary revivals; working with the faculty committee to plan and promote chapel worship services; presiding in chapel in the absence of the president; providing personal counseling for students, particularly in spiritual crises; administering student loans, aid, and scholarship funds; administering the program of secular employment for students; and serving in other areas as requested by the president.

During the remainder of this period, additional personnel were secured for key positions. As developed by divisions, the staff presented the following appearance. Supportive of Vice-President Newport in academic affairs were the academic deans of the three schools—James McKinney, Jack D. Terry, Huber L. Drumwright, Jr., and William B. Tolar (1981); Jeter Basden, registrar and director of admissions (1981); Keith C. Wills, director of libraries; J. David Fite, director of continuing education; Justice Anderson, director of the World Missions/Church Growth Center; David C. White, supervisor of the Children's Center; and Darrel Baergen, director of the Center for Christian Communication Studies (1981).

The staff of Vice-President John E. Seelig in public affairs included Philip Poole, director of communications (1978); Edwin Crawford, director of development; James R. Holcomb, director of *VISION/85* (1981); Stanton H. Nash, director of planned giving (1981); and Phillip T. Copeland, director of printing and photography.

The executive staff of Vice-President Wayne Evans was composed of Hubert R. Martin, Jr., business manager; James R. Leitch, director of physical plant; Gary D. Skeen, controller (1981); Sara Stovall, director of personnel services; Joan Eakin, cashier (1981); Terry L. Bratton, director of computer services (1979); Wallace H. Shamburger, director of medical services (1978); and Sarah Bentley, housing director.

On the supportive staff for student affairs were Felix Gresham, seminary chaplain and director of student aid; Trozy R. Barker, dean of men and director of missionary housing; Neta Stewart, dean of women and director of student activities; Grady W. Lowery, director of the recreation/aerobics center (1978); and Edwin A. Seale, director of placement information (1982).

Vice-President Elder had W. Truett Myers, communications consultant (1979), assigned to his staff.

The only loss of the key administrative personnel came on May 31, 1981, when James D. Haynes, controller since 1973, submitted his resignation.

The Supportive Trustees

The new president had no difficulty in catching step with the trustees. He viewed them as responsible, knowledgeable, and committed leaders to whom the Convention had entrusted the supervision of the seminary. It was unfortunate that just at this time some of the caustic critics of the seminaries were asserting that the trustees of the agencies and institutions of the Convention were "not knowledgeable, not Bible centered, not Christ honoring but rather people who 'sit there like a bunch of dummies and rubber-stamp everything that is presented to them.'" President Dilday wrote in the *Southwestern News* that he knew and had worked closely with the men and women of Southwestern's board and that this "caricature and villification of dedicated and involved seminary trustees should be recognized and deplored by all responsible pastors and lay leaders who have elected them through the years."[5] From the beginning of his administration President Dilday had a close empathy with the trustees, and they in turn were committed to his leadership.

The trustees were conscious of the heritage of the seminary. On October 24, 1978, they voted to place a plaque in Fort Worth Hall honoring J. K. Winston, a pioneer benefactor of the seminary and a trustee. In 1982, the B. H. Carroll Founders Award was initiated to recognize men and women who had made a significant contribution in their civic, denominational, and seminary activities. The first recipients of this distinguished award were Mr. and Mrs. Ted Ferguson, Mr. and Mrs. J. T. Luther, and Mr. and Mrs. F. Howard Walsh. In another action, on March 24, 1982, the trustees voted to name the Memorial Building the B. H. Carroll Memorial Building. The center section would remain the George W. Truett Auditorium, the east wing would remain L. R. Scarborough Hall, and the west wing (then used as the library) would be named Fleming Hall in honor of William and Bessie Fleming. Mrs. Fleming died on December 25, 1981, eight years after her noble husband had gone to his reward. These two were the largest donors in the history of the school at that time, and they blessed the world with their lives and benefactions.[6]

The trustees were sensitive to the challenges of the times through which they were guiding the seminary. They wrestled with the problems involved in the legal litigation of the school with the Equal Employment Opportunity Commission. It will be recalled that this government agency filed suit against the seminary on May 24, 1977, to require the seminary to file Form EEO-6 which provided information on the sex, racial makeup, and salaries of seven categories of seminary employees. The school had declined to do so on the grounds that this would violate the first amendment of the constitution.[7] In February, 1980, the trustees were pleased to learn that the United States District Court had ruled in favor of the seminary on this matter, but the commission appealed the case to the Fifth Circuit Court of Appeals in New Orleans. On March 18, 1980, the trustees passed a resolution of appreciation to Jenkins Garrett, who had served as the seminary's legal counsel in this case. The arguments were heard in New Orleans on March 16, 1981. On July 17, this court rendered a mixed decision on the case. It held that "the character and purpose of the seminary are wholly sectarian" and that the school was entitled to the status of "church." However, it said that any employees performing tasks "which are not totally ecclesiastical or religious" were not entitled to protection under the first amendment to the constitution because they were not functioning as ministers.[8] The seminary appealed for a hearing on this matter, but the Court of Appeals declined this request.

After consultation with the presidents of the other five Southern Baptist seminaries, the seminary's attorneys filed an appeal with the United States Supreme Court. On March 29, 1982, the Supreme Court, without comment, declined to intervene in the decision of the Court of

Appeals. The position of the seminary was that if this decision stands, "every church congregation and its wholly religious mission and activities with 15 or more employees will be brought under the surveillance and monitoring of the EEOC."[9]

Another issue facing the trustees was the renewed doctrinal controversy over the inspiration of the Scriptures. This debate was more critical than the earlier ones, however, because a concerted move was made by one of the factions to gain control of the Convention's agencies and institutions through electing leaders from their own ranks to name the members of the trustees for the various boards, commissions, institutions, and committees. A part of this controversy involved an attack upon the teachers in the colleges and seminaries of the Convention.[10] At a called meeting on June 13, 1979, the trustees made a formal statement to the effect that the faculty and administration of Southwestern had signed the confession of faith adopted by the Convention in 1963.[11] Taking cognizance of some of the harsh language used against theological teachers in general, the trustees used the occasion

> to reaffirm our faith in the integrity and the commitment of the faculty and administrative staff and to express appreciation for their service in the Kingdom of God through theological education under the leadership of the Holy Spirit and under the Lordship of Jesus Christ.

A similar expression of "love, appreciation, admiration and prayers for them [the faculty] that they will continue their teaching responsibilities with the same kind of courage and dedication that they have demonstrated in the past" was unanimously voted later.[12] Another resolution of confidence in both faculty and administration unanimously passed at the fall meeting of the trustees in 1980.[13]

It should not be surprising that men and women of this caliber responded enthusiastically to the vision which President Dilday had for Southwestern Seminary. They promptly approved his staff recommendations and altered their bylaws to parallel his administrative changes.[14] Their officers during this period before the celebration of the seventy-fifth anniversary in 1983 were as follows:

Years	Chairman	Vice-Chairman	Secretary
1978-79	Ray L. Graham, Sr.	Gladys S. Lewis	James E. Carter
1979-80	Kenneth Chafin	J. Dan Cooper	James E. Carter
1980-81	Kenneth Chafin	Shad Medlin	James E. Carter
1981-82	James E. Coggin	Ralph Pulley	James E. Carter

It is interesting to notice that the minutes of the first meeting of the trustees under President Dilday reflected the personality of the new leader. As usual, the president made his report to the trustees at the opening of the meeting. Then, in a distinct move that emphasized the total unity of the administrative officers, he told the trustees that the several vice-presidents would "continue the president's report." This was emphasized several times during the following years.[15] Usually the vice-president for a specific area in the administration would report along with the chairman of the parallel trustee committee. The two reports always complemented one another, showing that the trustee committee meetings of the previous day had utilized the administrative staff's expertise to prepare their own reports.

In addition to approving the major staff changes, the trustees initiated another innovation in the fall of 1978. Wayne Evans had been secretary of the trustee body since 1954, but at the meeting of the Executive Committee of the trustees on August 10, 1978, in order that his duties might not overlap with his responsibilities as an administrative officer of the seminary, it was recommended to the full board that he be replaced by James E. Carter. Wayne Evans had served well as secretary during these twenty-four years, and his minutes were a model of reporting trustee activity.

The first full meeting of the trustees with the new president in the fall of 1978 provided substantial evidence that the vision of Russell H. Dilday for the seminary would be built on a foundation of careful preparation and thorough organization. Starting with the actual situation of the seminary, he utilized his new staff to prepare building blocks for translating his vision into specific objectives for the advancement of the seminary.

Implementing the Vision

Between the meeting of the trustees in the fall of 1978 and the spring meeting in March, the new president and his staff prepared an extensive program to translate the vision into specific objectives. This program was based upon thorough research, numerous conferences, and considerable reflection under the leadership of Vice-President Elder. Twelve specific objectives to be accomplished by 1985 were presented and approved by the trustees in this meeting and the one in the fall of 1979, as follows: (1) to provide for an average annual enrollment of 4,000 students; (2) to provide degrees and courses of study to produce an annual average of 750 graduates; (3) to support, develop, and enlarge the faculty in order to maintain academic excellence with an average teaching ratio of one teacher for every 20 full-time equivalent students; (4) to expand the continuing education program to meet the personal and functional growth needs for about 40,000 former students and more than 18,000 ministers who had no formal seminary training; (5) to establish a World Mission/Church Growth Center, the object of which was to prepare ministers for world missions, evangelism, and the church growth efforts of Southern Baptists; (6) to restructure and enlarge the Student Affairs Division to facilitate the total development of students; (7) to provide an expanded and coordinated placement service for seminary students, graduates, and former students, focusing on the ministry needs of the churches and denomination as well as the calling, gifts, and skills of ministers; (8) to construct a new library building as a resource and research center for the entire seminary program; (9) to renovate the present library facility when the new library building was completed; (10) to update the campus master plan which was adopted in the long-range plan, *IMPACT: 2000*; (11) to seek to generate, allocate, and manage the financial resources needed to support these objectives and the ongoing operation of the seminary; and (12) to continue to focus on achieving the purpose of Southwestern as other objectives and strategies emerged.

This program of major objectives was entitled *VISION/85*. It was adopted as a catalyst for growth and development through 1985. Since these objectives touch the principal areas of activity of the seminary during the first years of President Dilday's administration, they will be used to measure the progress of the school before the celebration of the seventy-fifth anniversary of the seminary in 1983.

Reaching Toward the Vision

The achievement of these twelve objectives would not constitute the full vision of President Dilday, of course, but this was the only method of beginning that process which would lead to the fulfillment of his dreams for the school. In many instances these objectives were completed quickly, providing a new plateau for additional objectives. In some cases they could never be totally completed. A review will be made of what was done before 1983 in each of the areas involved in these objectives.

Student Enrollment

This first objective concerned the size of the enrollment. Its wording indicates that it looked to the balancing of the size of the enrollment with

the resources and facilities of the seminary for training the students.
There were some signs that the seminary enrollment might begin leveling
off with the advent of the 1980s, but this did not occur. The enrollment in
1978-79 was 4,154 students, of whom 3,461 were men and 693 were
women. In 1979-80 the figure was 4,336, of whom 3,587 were men and
749 were women. Another increase in 1980-81 showed 4,412 enrolled, of
whom 3,642 were men and 770 women. In 1981-82 the enrollment
reached 4,605, of whom 3,792 were men and 813 were women. The
following chart shows the enrollment in off-campus centers.

Center	1978-79	1979-80	1980-81	1981-82
Houston, Texas	149	161	159	167
San Antonio, Texas	47	57	53	63
Shawnee, Oklahoma	55	67	63	94

One of the factors involved in this objective was the possibility of
limiting the enrollment to 4,000 each year until the seminary was able to
increase its resources to provide adequate training.

Seminary Graduates

As in the case of the enrollment, the number of graduates of the
seminary already exceeded the objective of 750. Those receiving
diplomas and degrees in 1978-79 numbered 769; in 1979-80, 863; in
1980-81, 880; and in 1981-82, 875. If the enrollment were limited, the
number of graduates would soon show a decrease also and bring the total
nearer the objective of 750 graduates each year.

Academic Instruction

Prompt attention was given to the third objective to support, develop,
and enlarge the faculty and lower the teacher-student ratio. Even though
the formal program on faculty enlargement planning was not adopted by
the trustees until March 24, 1981, the effort to locate qualified teachers
was begun during the early weeks of President Dilday's administration.
The stated objective of attaining a teacher-student ratio of 1:20 by 1985
seemed to be within reach. The following chart shows the reduction of
the ratio despite the increasing number of students enrolling between
1978 and 1982:

	1978-79	1979-80	1980-81	1981-82
Total Faculty (full-time equivalent)	114.77	119.72	127.20	131.78

	1978-79	**1979-80**	**1980-81**	**1981-82**
Permanent	79.00	84.00	88.00	92.40
Supplementary	28.77	27.72	30.20	30.38
Other	7.00	8.00	9.00	9.00
Enrollment (full-time equivalent)	2,978	3,101	3,204	3,317
Teacher-Student Ratio (involving full-time equivalent students)	1:26	1:26	1:25.2	1:25.2

Faculty Additions and Losses.—Shortly after assuming his post, President Dilday began the search for new faculty for all three schools of the seminary.

In the School of Theology, fifteen faculty members were elected between 1979 and 1982, as follows: James Leo Garrett in theology (1949-59 and since 1979); George H. Gaston in pastoral ministry (1979); Thomas D. Lea in New Testament (1979); Thomas V. Brisco in biblical backgrounds (1980); Guy Greenfield in Christian ethics (1980); George L. Kelm in biblical backgrounds and archaeology (1980); Dan G. Kent in Old Testament (1980); William David Kirkpatrick in theology (1980); Robert B. Sloan, Jr., in theology (1980); Bill Bellinger in Old Testament (1981); William M. Tillman, Jr., in Christian ethics (1981); Joel C. Gregory in preaching (1982); Malcolm McDow in evangelism (1982); Doyle L. Young in church history (1982); and Earl R. Martin in missions and world religions (1982).

Several retired from this faculty. Robert O. Coleman, who had joined the faculty in 1958, retired on December 31, 1979. He had worked tirelessly in season and out of season in forwarding his archaeological interests, conducting excavations in Palestine and in many areas of the Southwest. Robert A. Baker retired on July 31, 1981, after thirty-nine years on the faculty, during most of which time he served as chairman of the academic doctoral program of the School of Theology and, since 1953, as chairman of the Department of Church History. He was replaced as associate dean for the Ph.D. degree by James Leo Garrett in 1981. Another veteran of the faculty, Cal Guy, distinguished professor in the Bottoms Chair of Missions, retired on July 31, 1982, having taught since 1946. His great interest in, and zeal for, missions carried him to many mission fields at home and abroad through the years. His name became synonymous with missions. He retired to move into another phase of the mission task.

Four faculty members resigned during these years. Larry Walker, who had taught Old Testament and cognate languages since 1965, resigned on July 31, 1980; Doug Ezell, who had taught New Testament and Christian ethics since 1968, resigned on August 31, 1980; and Tom Nettles, who had taught church history since 1975, resigned on July 31, 1982. A change of leadership came in the School of Theology when Huber Drumwright, Jr., resigned as dean effective September 1, 1980, to accept the position of executive director of the Arkansas Baptist Convention.[16] He had given nearly thirty years of his life to the seminary and was recognized as a distinguished scholar, outstanding preacher and teacher, and an excellent administrator. Because he was popular as an author and speaker and beloved as a man of unsurpassed spirit and compassion, his resignation was a sore loss to the seminary. When word came of his unexpected death on November 1, 1981, a special memorial service was held in Truett Auditorium. The entire seminary family gathered in sorrow and love to mark the passing of one of its own.[17] The trustees named William Tolar as the new dean for the School of Theology effective January 1, 1981.[18]

Death took another young professor. Oscar Thompson, professor of evangelism, had been ill with cancer for several years but continued his teaching until almost the time of his death. He passed away on December 28, 1980, after serving for six years on the faculty. He was greatly loved by his colleagues and was a constant source of inspiration to his students.[19]

The School of Religious Education added five to its faculty, as follows: Bob W. Brackney in social work (1979); B. A. "Pat" Clendinning, Jr., in psychology and counseling (1979); William A. "Budd" Smith in foundations of education (1979); Jerry Privette in education administration (1980); and Robert P. Raus in church recreation (1980).

There were also five additions to the faculty of the School of Church Music. William Mac Davis, Jr., was elected in the field of music theory and composition (1979); Sue Biggs King in voice (resident teacher 1965-79, elected to the faculty in 1979); Elizabeth R. McKinney in piano (resident teacher 1967-79, elected to the faculty in 1979); C. David Keith in conducting (1980); and William J. Reynolds in church music (1981). David L. Conley, who had taught effectively since 1961 in music theory and composition, resigned on December 31, 1978.

Structural Changes.—On March 18, 1980, the trustees established a new faculty rank entitled "Distinguished Professor." Special criteria for appointment to this rank included peer approval; membership on the faculty for twenty-five years; attainment of the age of sixty-three (two academic years before normal retirement); and outstanding service in the classroom, in publication, or in some other area. On June 11, 1980, the trustees named John Drakeford, Cal Guy, and Boyd Hunt to the rank of distinguished professor. Before these criteria had been established, the trustees had already named Jesse J. Northcutt as the E. Hermond Westmoreland Distinguished Professor of Preaching on October 24, 1978.

In another structural change, the trustees voted to appoint rotating chairmen of the faculty divisions and departments, and the president appointed these effective August 1, 1980.[20]

Several changes were made in faculty titles. On March 25, 1981, the trustees voted to rename the two chairmen supervising doctoral study in the School of Theology. The title of Robert A. Baker was changed from "Chairman of the Committee for the Doctor of Philosophy Degree" to "Associate Dean for the Doctor of Philosophy Degree," and that of Jimmie Nelson from "Chairman of the Committee for the Doctor of Ministry Degree" to "Associate Dean for the Doctor of Ministry Degree." On June 10, 1981, the title of James Williams was changed from "Chairman of the Committee for Advanced Studies in Religious Education" to "Associate Dean for Advanced Studies in Religious Education." At the spring meeting of the trustees in 1982, the title of Robert S. Douglass was changed from "Chairman, Advanced Studies Committee in the School of Church Music" to "Associate Dean for Advanced Studies in the School of Church Music." At the same time, the title of Scotty W. Gray was changed from "Chairman, Academic Division of the School of Church Music" to "Assistant Dean, Academic Division, School of Church Music," while C. David Keith's title was changed from "Chairman, Performance Division, School of Church Music" to "Assistant Dean, Performance Division, School of Church Music."[21]

On October 22, 1980, the trustees adopted new principles for funding chairs, professorships, lectureships, and guest professors. To endow a chair required a gift of $500,000; for a professorship, $100,000; for a lectureship, $50,000; and for a guest professor, $35,000.

The endowed chairs and professorships pertaining to the School of Theology were filled. As mentioned, on October 24, 1978, Jesse J. Northcutt was named to the Westmoreland distinguished professorship. Another endowed professorship was in the offing for this school. In 1980, Mrs. Vernon Davidson made provision to fund a living trust to endow the Vernon D. and Jeannette Davidson Professorship of Missions.[22] On June 10, 1981, Roy Fish was named as the first professor to fill the George W. Truett Chair of Ministry for 1981-82. This was a revolving chair, and on March 24, 1982, James Eaves was elected to the Truett Chair for 1982-83. On October 20, 1981, J. W. MacGorman was appointed as the first professor to fill the J. Wesley Harrison Chair of New Testament. Justice C. Anderson was named by the trustees on March 24, 1982, to the Bottoms Chair of Missions upon the retirement of Cal Guy.

The School of Religious Education will be the recipient of an endowed chair to study "the role assessment of family relationships in the ministry." In February, 1981, Earl L. and Vivian Gray Shoemake announced the funding of the Chair of Personal Growth and Ministry by a living trust.[23]

The education school also made internal changes. Early in the period the trustees recorded with regret the retirement of Leon Marsh from the chairmanship of the Graduate Committee of the School of Religious Education, passing a resolution of appreciation for his valuable contributions during his long service at this post. James Williams was named as his replacement.[24]

One of the longtime service programs of the School of Religious Education changed hands on March 25, 1981. It will be recalled that John Drakeford had initiated the Marriage and Family Counseling Center in 1959 to provide assistance in these areas and to train students for this type of ministry. In the spring of 1981, the trustees authorized the transfer of supervision of this center to Theodore H. Dowell, effective August 1, 1981.[25]

In internal shifts for the School of Church Music, T. W. Hunt, professor of piano and organ, was made professor of church music effective August 1, 1981; while A. Joseph King, who had initially taught church music education, became associate professor of conducting at the same time.[26]

During this period, the entire faculty and staff also were provided additional financial and other fringe benefits. Regular pay hikes were approved by the trustees and administration; faculty members were given more generous allowances to attend their professional meetings or the Southern Baptist Convention;[27] a "fast track" salary plan to benefit faculty members financially during their period of greatest need was provided;[28] improved retirement and medical policies for both faculty and retirees were developed by the trustees;[29] and policies for faculty tenure and faculty sabbatical programs were approved.[30]

Curricular and Degree Changes.—There were many changes in the curricula of the three schools during this period, partly because of the introduction of new degrees and the establishment of new departments, and partly because of the extensive self-study in 1979-80 for the decennial inspection of the three schools by the Association of Theological Schools and the Southern Association of Colleges and Schools on

November 16-19, 1980. Professor Robert Douglass was the general chairman for this self-study, and his 555-page summary utilized the talents of most of the faculty, administration, and some of the students. The three schools of the seminary were reaccredited following this inspection.[31]

In the fall of 1978, the faculties of the three schools engaged in a project called "Readiness for Ministry," which was an effort to assess a student's preparation as measured by the expectations of Southern Baptists. Approximately three hundred entering students from the three schools participated in this evaluation.

In a concerted study by the three faculties, it was agreed that each school should retitle its diploma program. These were offered for students without university degrees. At a called meeting on June 10, 1981, the trustees voted to replace the diploma nomenclature with the three new degrees: the Associate of Divinity, the Associate in Religious Education, and the Associate in Church Music. Arrangements were made to permit those who held the diplomas from the three schools to exchange them for the new degrees.[32]

All three of the faculties were involved in the initiation of the World Mission/Church Growth Center and the Center for Christian Communication Studies, which will be discussed later.

The School of Theology made several curricular changes during these first years of President Dilday's administration. The trustees approved forty-nine new courses, mainly because of the initiation of the World Mission/Church Growth Center and the new curricula developed in cooperation with the other schools. On March 20, 1979, the trustees approved a curriculum for the Master of Divinity degree with a major in religious education. On the same date a curriculum was developed for a Master of Divinity degree with a music major. On October 13, 1981, the theological faculty approved a curriculum for the Master of Divinity degree with a concentration in Christian communications. The trustees approved this on March 24, 1982.

Under the leadership of Professor George Kelm, an archaeological expedition to the biblical town of Timnah was begun in the summer of 1981, making it possible to earn eight hours of seminary credit for excavations, lectures, and training sessions.[33]

The School of Religious Education added twenty-three new courses during this period, mainly in the areas of recreation and communications.[34] The faculty voted to approve a concentration in recreation for the Master of Religious Education degree, noting the increasing calls from the churches for this type of training.[35] This faculty also approved a curriculum for offering the Master of Religious Education degree with a concentration in theology and one with a concentration in communication arts.[36] A similar program with a minor in church music was also developed.[37] On March 20, 1979, the trustees agreed to establish a Doctor of Education study center at the Sunday School Board in Nashville, Tennessee, where seminars would be offered in conjunction with a staff development program of the board.[38]

Another curricular move was made in 1980. Under the leadership of W. F. Howard, adjunct teacher in adult education and retired director of student work for the Baptist General Convention of Texas, a program was developed to permit twelve semester hours of credit at the seminary for Baptist Student Union workers serving in a supervised internship for two semesters in an established center. To be eligible for this internship the student must have completed a minimum of thirty hours of seminary study on the Master of Religious Education or Master of Divinity degree.[39]

Another of the many "firsts" for this school occurred in the spring of 1981. One of the important emphases in the School of Religious Education was the offering of courses to train church business administrators. From May 25 to June 19, 1981, the National Association of Church Business Administrators, in conjunction with the Church Administration Department of the Baptist Sunday School Board and Southwestern Seminary, provided a certification program in church business administration. This was the first Baptist school to host this type of certification seminar.[40]

Still another significant innovative project was the joint launching of a new gerontology program by Southwestern Seminary and Baylor University on January 1, 1982. The curriculum included courses on death and dying, religion and the aging, physical fitness and the older adult, and current problems of the aging. A certificate in gerontology was offered under any degree program at the seminary, and a Master of Science in gerontology was available for completing forty-two hours of study beyond the Master of Religious Education degree.[41]

In 1981 and early 1982 the faculty of this school was engaged in a comprehensive revalidation of the Master of Religious Education curriculum design, which was expected to be completed by the fall of 1982.

The School of Church Music added approximately ten new courses during this period, principally in connection with the two new degree programs which were initiated and the development of an instrumental concentration in the curriculum. Under a new curriculum provided in

1979, a student could enroll for the Master of Church Music degree with a minor in religious education.[42] In 1981, growing out of the founding of the World Mission/Church Growth Center, the school initiated a Master of Church Music degree with a minor in missions.[43] At this same time, the trustees approved a new concentration in instrumental or orchestral music in the Master of Music curriculum. In 1982 this faculty began formulating a Master of Church Music degree with a minor in communication arts and was studying the scope and content of the Ministry of Music courses.

Continuing Education

The Continuing Education Division had made extraordinary progress since its initiation in 1971 and the naming of J. David Fite as its director. The wide variety of its activities was briefly described under the administration of President Naylor. The objective of expanding this program by 1985 developed from a recognition of the many needs of almost 40,000 former students of the school and over 18,000 Southern Baptist ministers without seminary training. As a part of the preparation for this thrust, Director Fite used his sabbatical leave in 1979-80, under a grant from the American Theological Society, to study and evaluate models of continuing education elsewhere.[44]

A measure of the significant ministry of this division is revealed in the number of persons involved in its programs during the early years of President Dilday's administration, as shown by the following chart:

Year	Number Involved in Programs
1978-79	1,917
1979-80	2,192
1980-81	2,896

In 1979 Director Fite completed a five-year study designed to identify areas where graduates of the seminary needed assistance in their ministry. A group of twelve couples was chosen randomly from the 1974 graduating class, nine from the Master of Divinity program, two from the Master of Religious Education program, and one from the Master of Church Music program. Through correspondence and three retreats (in 1974, 1976, and 1979), the specific needs of these couples were charted and monitored. Some trends discovered in this study included stress because of removal to new church fields; crises developing from loss of friends, family, and illness; conflicts in the job setting; and difficulties in finding family time on the church field. High on the list of important needs were help in refining the direction of vocational calls, personal counseling, and continuing education.[45]

Another forward step came with the approval of plans for a guest center located near the campus, which would provide the opportunity for those involved in continuing education to have quarters nearby when they returned to the campus for study.[46]

A significant new thrust occurred in the spring of 1981 when the Continuing Education Division along with the Church Services Division of the Baptist General Convention of Texas offered for the first time a bilingual workshop for couple communications. The group represented nine Spanish-speaking countries—Argentina, Mexico, Ecuador, Guatemala, Uruguay, Peru, Puerto Rico, and Cuba—as well as representatives from Texas, Louisiana, and New Mexico. The purpose of this workshop was to train local church and denominational ministers to lead interpersonal communication seminars which presented a biblical view of life and marriage.[47]

Another aspect of continuing education which offered much promise was the establishment on May 1, 1981, of the Seminary External Education Division (SEED) by the action of the six seminary presidents. The Southern Baptist Convention had discussed at length the possibility of opening a seventh seminary; but it was decided in the spring of 1981 that instead of moving in this direction, the six seminaries would be asked to provide seminary-level courses in different areas of the country, particularly in the pioneer areas of the Convention. The organization of SEED provided a new Seminary Satellite Department to work with the existing Seminary Extension Department. Raymond M. Rigdon, executive director of the Seminary Extension Department since 1969, was given the responsibility of developing this new division along with his extension program.[48] At Southwestern this project became a part of the seminary's continuing education program.

Meeting a need that had been apparent, the seminary established an Institute of Christian Studies to begin in September, 1981. The curriculum was directed toward lay persons in the Fort Worth area who desired to expand their knowledge and skills for spiritual growth and church service. It included Bible classes, music, financial planning, marriage and family relationships, and religious education. The faculty consisted of experienced teaching fellows who were doctoral students at Southwestern; however, their work was supervised by members of the regular seminary faculty. Classes met each Monday evening and continued for twelve weeks.[49]

A cursory reading of the *Southwestern News* discloses the wide range of the continuing education program of the seminary. Month by month this division called attention to numerous opportunities for lay persons, wives, alumni, and regular students to enrich their resources for ministry through some aspect of this program. For example, in the July, 1981, issue of the *Southwestern News* a brief article announced that twenty-eight workshops were scheduled for the 1981-82 academic year, offering diverse studies ranging from couple communication workshops to writers' conferences. This was typical of the wide extent of the growing ministry of this division.

World Mission/Church Growth Center

The fifth objective looked to the establishment of a World Mission/Church Growth Center. Interest in this project had begun in 1973 when the members of the Missions Department had discussed the matter with the administration. In the following year the importance of implementing the continuing zeal of Southwestern Seminary for missions and evangelism by a structured program was discussed by a committee from the three faculties, and by 1975 the trustees and other faculty were included in the planning. In 1978 and 1979 a trustee committee discussed this project with the mission boards and with Cal Guy, Jack Gray, Justice Anderson, Ebbie Smith, Roy Fish, Oscar Thompson, James Eaves, LeRoy Ford, and T. W. Hunt of the seminary faculty. The thinking behind the formation of this center was

> to help fulfill the purpose of Southwestern Baptist Theological Seminary by preparing students and practitioners for the world mission, evangelism and church growth efforts of Southern Baptists through philosophical study, vocational training, technical research and promotional activity.

In May, 1980, President Dilday announced that he had appointed Cal Guy, professor of missions, as the founding director of the center and that the center would be launched in the fall.[50] This took place on October 6-24, 1980, when a three-week conference was held on the campus, cosponsored by the seminary and the First Baptist Church, Wichita Falls, Texas. Donald A. McGavran, noted professor of missions at Fuller Theological Seminary in California and recognized as one of the outstanding world mission leaders, lectured during each of the three weeks. The first week was directed toward the pastor in partnership with the Foreign Mission Board of the Southern Baptist Convention; the second, the role of the pastor and staff in church growth and world missions; and the third, the pastor in partnership with the Home Mission Board. Leaders of both Convention mission boards and outstanding missionary pastors delivered addresses during the conference.[51]

A six-fold objective for the center was developed, as follows: (1) to provide study programs for mission volunteers through "Missions-Evangelism Concentrations" in all three schools of the seminary; (2) to develop conference and institute training for those seeking to increase effectiveness as practitioners; (3) to engage in extensive research into the philosophy, methods, and strategies of missions conducted by the Southern Baptist Convention and others; (4) to design ways to test and evaluate new models of strategies, resources, and structures; (5) to organize and encourage reflection, problem solving, evaluation, and consultation related to the corporate missionary enterprise of the Southern Baptist Convention; and (6) to publish research, evaluations, and scholarly findings and coordinate resources with other Southern Baptist Convention agencies.[52]

Justice C. Anderson was named director of this center effective August 1, 1981. A steering committee, representing the missions and evangelism departments and others of the faculty and administration, assisted the director in providing internal guidance; while an advisory committee composed of representatives from the mission boards of the Southern Baptist Convention and the state and associational bodies met periodically to provide coordination, guidance, and communication.[53] The director arranged to use a missionary couple in residence to forward the program, together with guest professors and outstanding Christian nationals from other countries to advise, teach, and work with interested students. When Fleming Hall was renovated, the center located its office in that area.[54]

This program has already attained some of its objectives. Missions concentrations in the Master of Divinity, the Master of Religious Education, and the Master of Church Music curricula were approved by the trustees. Three significant conferences were held in the spring of 1982. In conjunction with the Home Mission Board's Division of Church Extension and the state conventions of Arkansas, New Mexico, Oklahoma, and Texas, the center hosted and coordinated a conference on February 1-4, 1982, on planting churches in a changing, pluralistic urban society. Over 125 directors of missions from 6 states attended this meeting, plus 35 program personnel. A special day for student participation drew 130 students on February 2 for this conference. The second conference on management skills for missionaries was held conjointly with the Home Mission Board on February 8-10, 1982, where twenty-four practitioners from eight states and one foreign country attended. The third conference was a workshop on prison chaplaincy opportunities, hosted by the seminary on February 17. Twenty representatives from the Home Mission Board, state prisons, and other chaplaincy programs attended. Many additional exciting plans were made toward reaching the goals of this significant center.[55]

Student Affairs Division

The sixth objective looked to the restructuring and enlarging of the Student Affairs Division in order to facilitate the total development of the students. The key functions of this division were named as (1) orientation of students and wives; (2) spiritual formation and guidance; (3) counseling and guidance; (4) student activities and organizations; (5) recreation and physical fitness; (6) student aid, loans, and employment; and (7) coordination of other student services.[56]

Pending the election of a vice-president for student affairs, Executive Vice-President Lloyd Elder was temporarily placed in charge of the student division. On March 30, 1979, the president appointed a large committee to study the needs of the students and to recommend objectives for this division. On this committee were one member from each of the three faculties, three trustees, and two students, with seven additional faculty members to serve as resource persons. Vice-President Elder was chairman of this committee. On June 11, 1980, Lawrence R. Klempnauer was elected vice-president for student affairs effective August 18, 1980. His responsibilities were outlined at that time.[57] These were: to give administrative leadership to all areas of student affairs, including research, program planning and budget planning and control; to make a direct program response to the needs of spiritual formation and ministry placement; to provide supervision for the student affairs staff members as they perform their specific assignments and programs; to provide for coordination of student services managed within other divisions of the seminary; to direct student activities and the work of the Student Council; to direct the student orientation program of the seminary; to relate to the churches and the denomination concerning student affairs; to provide staff assistance to the Student Affairs Committee of the trustees; and to discharge other duties as requested by the president.

In addition to supervising the numerous student organizations and activities, which were described in some detail in the previous chapter, the new vice-president began a systematic effort to attain all of the objectives for student work. One of the immediate needs was the reorganization of the structure used in the orientation and advising of new students. On March 24, 1981, the trustees adopted his proposed structure for a pre-registration orientation plan. This was put into operation in the 1981-82 session, and the trustees were enthusiastic about the success of the program.[58]

Perhaps the numerous achievements of this division might be summarized by showing the continuing advances made by only one of the regular student activities, by noting the rapid development in the program of the new Recreation/Aerobics Center, and by charting the increase in the use of the student loan and aid funds.

One of the activities of the students illustrating the strong spirit of evangelism and missions among them was the Pioneer Penetration program, in which they voluntarily used their spring break each year to go into the pioneer areas of the Convention to preach, hold Bible schools, conduct revivals, and perform similar activities. In the spring of 1979 a total of 144 students volunteered and served in this capacity; in 1980, 120; in 1981, 140; and in 1982, 241. This was but one aspect of the widespread activities by students in voluntary service or through their organizations, which were described in more detail in the previous chapter.

Recreation/Aerobics Center Director Grady W. Lowery reported that the average weekly attendance from September 1981 to March 1982 was 4,435 students. The average annual attendance for the three years following the opening of the center was 182,412. During this three-year period the facility was used 547,200 times.

The growth of the participation in the student loan and aid funds may be glimpsed from the following charts:

Year	Number of Loans	Amount of Loans
1978-79	1,051	$201,152.36
1979-80	1,105	228,793.77
1980-81	1,296	275,947.04

Year	Number of Students Securing Aid	Amount of Aid
1978-79	1,265	$407,529.95
1979-80	1,350	480,248.35
1980-81	1,520	529,529.29

Certainly large strides were made in attaining the objective in this area in the first few years following the election of Vice-President Klempnauer, and bright days appear to be ahead.

Expanded Vocational Placement

One of the problems of Baptist ecclesiology has been the proper manner for a church to seek a pastor or other minister and how an individual's name should become known to the church for consideration. After long conferences with many of the denomination's leaders, the Texas directors of associational missions, and the church-staff relations directors, as well as with other Southern Baptist seminaries, the vice-president for student affairs reviewed with the trustees on March 24, 1981, the various methods pursued in assisting a church to find God's man. It was agreed that all of the seminary's efforts to accomplish this could be improved by naming a director of placement information. On March 24, 1982, the trustees approved the naming of Edwin A. Seale to this post.

New Library Building

The eighth objective sought to meet a crucial need. The old library quarters were badly overcrowded. Some idea of the growth of the library may be glimpsed in the following table showing the increases during the opening years of President Dilday's administration:

	1978-79	1979-80	1980-81
Holdings	465,255	475,773	484,466
Circulation	333,692	354,261	420,264
Budget	$601,445	$702,399	$791,145

The staff of the library continued to move toward a career corps status. By August 1, 1982, the following were so named: Keith C. Wills, director of libraries; Robert Phillips, assistant librarian for public services; Barbara Russell, catalogue librarian; Kenette Harder, assistant catalogue librarian; Carol Bastien, acquisitions librarian; Benjamin Rogers, archivist; Robert Trimble, audiovisuals librarian; Steven C. Storie, audiovisuals coordinator; Myrta Ann Garrett, serials librarian; and Phillip Sims, music librarian. The only loss from the library staff was Cecil White, who resigned as assistant librarian for public services effective June 30, 1980.

At the first meeting of President Dilday with the trustees on October 24, 1978, general plans for the new library building were approved. On March 20 and October 24, 1979, the trustees discussed additional plans. It became necessary to revise the original plans, however, and on June 11 and October 22, 1980, the new plans and specifications were approved by the trustees. At the June meeting a number of details were finalized, such as the location of the music library, the learning center, the audiovisual services, and the archaeological museum. Bids were obtained and a contract was signed on February 20, 1981, and on March 24, 1981, groundbreaking ceremonies were held. Construction was begun immediately.

While awaiting completion of the new facility, library and administrative personnel made specific plans for the functioning and furnishings of the new library. The new facility was computerized in its operations. This meant eliminating the public card catalogue as such and using public computer terminals for access to the catalogue records. The AMIGOS network was adapted for direct input into the seminary computer. A checkpoint electronic surveillance system provided security for the library holdings.

Two other matters should be mentioned. First, during the school year 1981-82 the Serials Department was involved in a complete inventory project, which included disposing of many titles received as gifts that were not useful for a theological library. These were offered as periodical exchanges with other libraries or were discarded. Books in storage also were sorted to dispose of those that had little or no value for a theological collection, and the excess books were sold to library patrons or sent to theological seminaries in foreign countries and elsewhere. The other significant item was administrative authorization to expend $25,000 each year for three years for scholarly works to undergird the Ph.D. program, looking chiefly to acquire additional foreign language titles in all theological disciplines. With the numerous titles already held in foreign languages, this should provide the seminary with an unusually strong collection for scholarly research.

Renovating the Old Library Space

The removal of the library collection to its new quarters in the summer and fall of 1982 released a substantial amount of space for classrooms, offices, and auxiliary services. On October 24, 1979, the trustees voted to employ professional assistance to renovate the released space. This was begun shortly after the library collection was moved to its new quarters.

Updating the Campus Master Plan

The long-range studies which resulted in the development of *IMPACT: 2000* in 1975 called attention to the need for revising these plans at regular intervals. For the period 1980-85, the trustees approved several goals for improving the master plan of the campus.[59] The first looked to a continuous program of increasing permanent parking space. This was implemented by adding 360 new parking spaces in 1980-81. A second goal was to continue the practice of acquiring land and property contiguous to the present campus in order to develop an attractive, enclosed campus. This pattern of purchasing adjacent land was continued during President Dilday's administration. The third goal was to add housing units for student families. This was discussed in the first meeting of President Dilday with the Executive Committee of the trustees on August 10, 1978, and forty-four additional units have been constructed in the J. Howard Williams Student Village since that time.[60] Much progress was made in the plans to construct a Southwestern guest facility in support of such seminary programs as continuing education, the World Missions/Church Growth Center, recruitment, placement, development, trustees, and committee meetings. Plans for this building were made and funds donated toward the completion of this project.

Another goal for the campus master plan was the building of a new Baptist book store in cooperation with the Sunday School Board of the Convention. The trustees approved this in 1979, and in early 1982 construction was begun on this facility across Stanley Avenue to the east of Barnard Hall.[61] Upon completion of the new book store building in the summer of 1982, renovation was begun to utilize the space it had occupied in the student center to provide additional room for food services.

With the completion of the Recreation/Aerobics Center in 1978, the way was clear to provide additional recreational areas for outdoor athletic and "parklike" family facilities.[62]

In 1980, a new central cooling tower was erected between Fleming Library and Barnard Hall to meet the needs of the seminary following the completion of the new library center.[63]

In addition to these changes in the face of the campus, the trustees named several other campus priorities for the immediate future. One was the enlargement of Cowden Hall to provide more space for the School of Church Music.[64] Another was the plan to move the physical plant building and enlarge the facility.[65] A boon for local student pastors will be the erecting of a new headquarters for the Tarrant County Baptist Association on seminary land just north of the new book store.[66] This will make it convenient for students to counsel with the leadership of the associational office concerning many aspects of church life and activity, and also it will give associational leaders the opportunity of working with

the faculty and administration of the seminary in carrying out denominational objectives.

Preventive maintenance and the beautification of the campus were two
emphases of President Dilday.[67] By the former was meant the planning of
regular maintenance of the buildings and equipment of the seminary
without waiting for emergency breakdowns. In this connection, both Fort
Worth Hall and Barnard Hall underwent renovation, the latter principally for the purpose of energy conservation.[68] The other emphasis of
the president was the beautification of the campus. Fortunately, the
seminary acquired the expertise of Carl Norton, retired senior consultant
for Norton of Texas, a horticultural firm of Midland, Texas. Disdaining
any payment despite the fact that there were other calls for his service,
Norton gave himself for a year to the task of the removal of diseased trees
and shrubs, insect control, soil chemistry, cast cavity work, and
numerous plantings during the year 1980.[69] With gifts from Noel G. Shaw
in memory of his sister, Lou Ellen Shaw Calloway, and from Mr. and Mrs.
Wash Storm, a memorial garden and seven heritage live oaks were
provided in the space between Price Hall and Scarborough Hall.[70]

Financial Resources

When President Dilday addressed the first full meeting of the trustees
on October 24, 1978, he noted that the seminary was in a healthy
condition. The objective of improving the financial situation was
difficult, for President Naylor, as pointed out, had made great strides in
securing funds for the seminary for both operating and capital needs
from the Southern Baptist Convention and by gifts and bequests of many
kinds from the private sector. The school was just in the midst of the
Eight-by-Eighty Campaign when the new administration took control.
Under the leadership of Vice-President John E. Seelig, the campaign
was vigorously pursued during 1978-79. Regular progress reports were
made to the trustees and the public.[71] At the October, 1979, meeting of
the trustees, Vice-President Seelig announced that the goal had already
been reached. The final amount pledged was $9,441,666.

Because of the imperative need for the library building and additional
endowment, a new campaign was launched promptly after the completion of the Eight-by-Eighty drive. On October 24, 1979, the trustees
voted to request the Southern Baptist Convention to permit the seminary
to initiate a new campaign, which was given the name *VISION/85*.
During the summer of 1980, this campaign was launched by a series of
luncheons in selected cities of Texas.[72] James Holcomb was secured as

director of *VISION/85*.[73] On December 1, 1981, Stanton H. Nash joined the seminary staff as director of planned giving.[74] The Advisory Council was active in the new campaign.[75] A President's Club was formed on January 1, 1979, to provide an opportunity for regular giving each year. By a gift of one thousand dollars to the seminary anyone could join the club for that year.[76] The *VISION/85* Campaign continues to progress well under the leadership of Vice-President John Seelig.

The Southern Baptist Convention increased the amount of its funding for operating expenses each year during the early part of President Dilday's administration. This was made necessary by the regular growth of the student body and by the continuing inflationary spiral. The following chart shows the amounts provided by the Cooperative Program and the annual budgets of the seminary during this period.

Year	Cooperative Program for Operating Funds	Annual Budget
1978-79	$3,768,063	$ 7,395,287
1979-80	4,117,316	8,452,508
1980-81	4,545,901	9,648,724
1981-82	5,143,654	11,867,360

Capital funds for the seminary from 1980 to 1984 totaled $2,000,000.

The trustees set a goal on October 24, 1979, of acquiring $25,000,000 for endowment by 1985. The following chart showing the growth in endowment funds and in total assets of the seminary is impressive.

Year	Total Endowment	Total Assets
1978-79	$16,638,958	$42,184,665
1979-80	19,375,421	47,372,036
1980-81	21,645,682	52,541,620

In appreciation for substantial gifts, the trustees voted that the new stress testing facility in the Recreation/Aerobics Center be named the Ben Williams Fitness Assessment Laboratory and that the next street developed by the student village be named Slover Drive, in honor of Roy and Myra Slover.[77] Further, the trustees approved the naming of the Recreation/Aerobics Center as the Myra K. and J. Roy Slover Recreation/Aerobics Center in recognition of their gift of one million dollars, which at that time was the largest single gift ever made to the school.[78] The new library building was named the A. Webb Roberts Library in honor of the man providing a large contribution toward erecting it.

Other Objectives and Strategies

The final objective adopted by the trustees on March 24, 1979, represented an effort to identify all other possible seminary projects as they might develop from additional planning or general operations of the seminary. It was thought that the decennial self-study for the Association of Theological Schools and the Southern Association of Colleges and Schools during 1979-80 might develop new objectives. For the most part, their recommendations were acted upon through the structure and objectives already adopted. The need for a new faculty manual was noted during this study, and in May, 1982, the new booklet was distributed.

Three significant new projects provided new objectives for the seminary. The first was initiated at the spring meeting of the trustees in 1981 when leaders of the Mexican Baptist Bible Institute, San Antonio, Texas, proposed to seminary trustees that the institute become a San Antonio branch campus of Southwestern Seminary with the primary focus of training Hispanic leadership for the Christian ministry. This proposal was discussed by J. T. Luther, chairman of the State Missions Commission of the Baptist General Convention of Texas; Daniel Rivera, president of the Mexican Baptist Bible Institute; and Charles McLaughlin of the State Missions Commission of the Texas convention. Earlier discussion had taken place between Executive Director James H. Landes of the Texas convention and officers of the seminary, and a conference had been held by leaders from both institutions. It was the desire of the institute and Texas Baptist leaders to make better use of the many resources of the institute—its faculty and administration; a student body with close relationship to Hispanic congregations; an adequate campus; financial support from the Texas convention, churches, friends, and mission boards; and its language and cultural expertise. If this school could be accredited through Southwestern Seminary and could benefit from the seminary's experience and leadership in theological education, it would open the door to a challenging educational and missionary opportunity. The trustees authorized the president to explore the various legal and accreditation problems such a union might bring.[79] On June 10, 1981, President Dilday appointed a committee of three from the seminary (Wayne Evans, John Newport, and Lloyd Elder) to serve on a nine-member study committee. This committee, consisting of three members from the Mexican Baptist Bible Institute, three from the State Missions Commission of the Baptist General Convention of Texas, and the three seminary representatives, met on June 25, 1981, and agreed on the following proposal. The new institution would maintain its identity but merge with, and become an integral part of, Southwestern Baptist Theological Seminary. It would assume the name the Hispanic Baptist Theological Seminary, San Antonio, Texas, a component institution of Southwestern Baptist Theological Seminary, Fort Worth, Texas. It would continue to provide programs of study leading to a diploma or certificate in ministry, which would not require a high school diploma. It would develop and offer an accredited associate degree in theology, religious education, and church music, which would require a high school diploma prior to graduation. It would provide general studies to prepare Hispanic students to proceed to a college baccalaureate and master's degree from the seminary. It would develop continuing education opportunities for Hispanic ministers and lay leadership. It would continue to cooperate with the seminary in the master's degree programs on the San Antonio campus. It would provide resources to enrich Southwestern's total efforts to prepare Hispanic leadership.

The ownership of the Hispanic Baptist Theological Seminary would pass to Southwestern Seminary, including property, other assets, and liabilities. The trustees of Southwestern Seminary would become trustees of the Hispanic Seminary with final authority in all matters. An Executive Council, representing the trustees of Southwestern, the San Antonio region, the Baptist General Convention of Texas, and the Home Mission Board of the Southern Baptist Convention (including Hispanic leadership), would constitute the governing body. The chief administrative officer of the Hispanic Seminary would be the president, who would be elected by the trustees of Southwestern Seminary upon proper recommendation. The faculty members teaching in the accredited associate degree programs would be named Southwestern Seminary adjunct teachers. This new relationship could be discontinued if the Hispanic Baptist Theological Seminary developed to a degree of independence.[80] On March 24, 1982, the trustees elected a Nominating Committee to name a transitional Executive Council for the proposed Hispanic Seminary, but further steps awaited the approval of this merger by the Baptist General Convention of Texas meeting in the fall of 1982.

The second of the new objectives was adopted by the trustees on March 25, 1981. A proposal had been received by them on October 22, 1980, that the seminary and the Radio and Television Commission of the Southern Baptist Convention explore and develop a "Center for Christian Communication Studies." The trustees agreed that President Dilday and officers of the seminary should meet with President Jimmy Allen and officers of the commission to initiate planning procedures and funding for such a project. On March 25, 1981, the seminary's trustees approved a joint program agreement between the seminary and the commission that this center be established with the objective of providing "functional, professional and graduate education for men and women preparing for Christian ministry in the specialized fields of communication." The center was to be controlled by a steering committee of the seminary and the commission which was responsible to the presidents of the two agencies. In all academic matters the center would function as an integral part of the seminary. All faculty members, courses, and degrees would be supervised by the seminary's trustees.

Darrel Baergen became director of this program, and the center began operation on April 27, 1981. During the following year the three schools of the seminary provided curricula to offer concentrations in communications arts. A Communications Committee from the three schools was named to provide internal consultation on curriculum and degree matters.[81]

The trustees also responded positively to a report made by President Dilday on October 20, 1981, that a feasibility study was underway for a possible joint venture in arranging for an educational television station in the metroplex under the supervision of the Radio and Television Commission of the Convention, Baylor University, and the seminary. From an educational standpoint, this would be advantageous to the seminary "to provide direct hands-on experience for students as a part of their training" and to offer telecourses "taught by our faculty through the low-power ACTS network and satellite transmission to provide credit courses for distant locations now being served by off-campus programs." From a developmental standpoint, this activity could give Southwestern a greater public visibility and a clearer identity before the immediate broadcast market and nationwide through the network and cable systems; and it would provide an opportunity to telecast music, drama, chapel speakers, and other programs "to let the public know what God is doing at this seminary." Friend-raising and fund-raising potential would also be enhanced.[82] After full discussion of this project, including the estimated costs, the trustees authorized the administration to cooperate in this enterprise, which probably will be operative by the fall of 1984.

The Vision Beckons

It is difficult to close this story in celebration of the seventy-fifth anniversary of the seminary, for the school is in midstream. Many of the objectives for 1985 have already been achieved, and President Dilday will doubtless soon challenge the trustees with additional objectives to translate his vision for Southwestern into reality. The dominant theme of evangelism and missions has not waned in these last years but has deepened. Billy Graham remarked, "I don't know of any other seminary quite like it in the world."[83] Baker James Cauthen wrote:

> Our love for Southwestern is very deep and we rejoice in the way God has blessed this institution and has brought to it such growth, spiritual strength, and excellence of scholarship as teachers and students have sought to bring glory to the name of our Lord. It has been a great joy to see the large number of Southwestern alumni who have been appointed as missionaries for service throughout the world. We have always been aware that the cause of missions has had a deep place in the love and prayers of all on seminary hill.[84]

God continues to bless the faith and faithfulness of the noble men and women who established this school through sacrifice and struggle. In the very week these words were written, another evidence of God's blessings took place. A. Webb Roberts, who gave a challenge gift to bring into being the George W. Truett Chair of Ministry, felt led of God to provide a million-dollar living trust and the promise of another similar gift to permit the seminary to establish a program of applied ethics in its curriculum. Not only so, but he made the seminary a residual beneficiary of a family trust, which means that another generation of Southwestern Seminary leaders will have additional resources for sharing the gospel story.

The psalmist calls his people to "tell the generations following" (see Ps. 48:13-14).

B. H. Carroll, what would be your message to the generations following?

> Tell them to be faithful to the heavenly vision. Despite my many infirmities and the nearness of my death, I found that following God's vision brought the most fruitful years of my life.

L. R. Scarborough, what would be your message to the generations following?

> Tell them that lost people at home and around the world wait for their message of the saving grace of Jesus Christ. Let the fires of evangelism and missions constantly burn in their hearts.

E. D. Head, what would be your message to the generations following?

> Tell them to cultivate the deep inner spirituality and devotion to God that will authenticate their witness and enable them to endure hardships as a good soldier of Jesus Christ.

J. Howard Williams, what would be your message to the generations following?

Tell them never to forget the spirit of Southwestern as they minister: the spirit of compassion, love, dedication, and comradeship.

Robert E. Naylor, what would be your message to the generations following?

Tell them that God gives to each of them a stewardship to perform and that the highest meaning of life comes from finding and doing God's will.

Russell H. Dilday, Jr., what would be your message to the generations following?

Tell them not to be disobedient to the heavenly vision; that in the midst of evil days, God gives us the opportunity to redeem the time through doing our very best for Christ in our day.

Notes

1. Trustee Minutes, 24 March 1977, called meeting 15 June 1977, and 22 November 1977; also Trustee Minutes of the Executive Committee, 10 February 1977.
2. *Southwestern News*, April 1981, p. 2.
3. Ibid., December 1977, p. 4.
4. Ibid., September 1978, p. 1.
5. Ibid., October 1980, p. 2.
6. Ibid., February 1982, p. 3.
7. Ibid., May 1979, p. 7.
8. Trustee Minutes, 20 October 1981.
9. *Fort Worth Star-Telegram*, 30 March 1982, pp. 1-2.
10. *Southwestern News*, July 1979, p. 2; September 1979, p. 7; December 1979, p. 3; April 1980, p. 1; and November 1980, p. 1.
11. See Trustee Minutes, 24 October 1979.
12. Ibid., called meeting 11 June 1980.
13. Ibid., 21 October 1980.
14. See ibid., 24 October 1978, 20 March 1979, 19 March 1980, 21 October 1980, 25 March 1981, and 24 March 1982.
15. Ibid., 21 October 1980, for example.
16. *Southwestern News*, July 1980, p. 5.
17. Trustee Minutes, called meeting 11 June 1980 and also 22 October 1980. Also see *Southwestern News*, December 1981, p. 3.
18. Trustee Minutes, 22 October 1980. See also *Southwestern News*, November 1980, p. 1; February 1981, p. 3; and April 1981, p. 3.
19. *Southwestern News*, January 1981, p. 3.
20. Trustee Minutes, 19 March 1980 and called meeting 11 June 1980.
21. Ibid., 24 March 1982.
22. Ibid., 19 March 1980. See also *Southwestern News*, July 1981, p. 3.

23. *Southwestern News*, February 1981, p. 7.

24. Trustee Minutes, 24 October 1978.

25. *Southwestern News*, September 1981, p. 3.

26. Trustee Minutes, 25 March 1981.

27. Ibid., 24 October 1978.

28. Ibid., 20 March 1979.

29. Ibid., 20 March 1979, 24 October 1979, 19 March 1980, and 21 October 1981.

30. Ibid., 24 March 1981.

31. Ibid., 24 October 1979, 19 March 1980, and 22 October 1980.

32. See ibid., 23 March 1982.

33. *Southwestern News*, January 1981, p. 1.

34. Trustee Minutes, 24 October 1979, 19 March 1980, and 24 March 1982.

35. See *Southwestern News*, June 1980, p. 1; and April 1981, p. 7.

36. See *Report of Academic Affairs Committee* to trustees, 22 March 1982, p. AA-19. This is on file in the Academic Affairs Office of the seminary.

37. Trustee Minutes, 20 March 1979.

38. See also ibid., 22 October 1980.

39. *Southwestern News*, November 1980, p. 23.

40. Ibid., March 1981, p. 4.

41. Ibid., November 1981, p. 23. See also May 1981 issue, p. 4.

42. Trustee Minutes, 20 March 1979.

43. Ibid., 25 March 1981.

44. *Southwestern News*, April 1979, p. 7.

45. Ibid., June 1979, p. 3.

46. Trustee Minutes, 24 October 1979.

47. *Southwestern News*, June 1981, p. 4.

48. Ibid., May 1981, p. 2.

49. Ibid., September 1981, p. 1.

50. Ibid., May 1980, p. 2.

51. Ibid., July 1980, pp. 1, 8.

52. See *Registration Bulletin—1981*. This is on file in the World Mission/Church Growth Center on the seminary campus.

53. *Southwestern News*, November 1979, p. 21.

54. Ibid., February 1982, p. 7.

55. See *Report of Academic Affairs Committee* to trustees, 22 March 1982, pp. AA-34-37, Academic Affairs Office of the seminary.

56. Trustee Minutes, 23 October 1979.

57. Ibid., called meeting 11 June 1980. Also see *Southwestern News*, July 1980, p. 8.

58. Trustee Minutes, 24 March 1982.

59. Ibid., 24 October 1979.

60. Trustee Minutes of the Executive Committee, 10 August 1978; and Trustee Minutes, 20 March 1979 and 24 March 1981.

61. Trustee Minutes, 20 March 1979, 18 March 1980, and 24 March 1981.

62. Trustee Minutes of the Executive Committee, 10 August 1978.

63. *Southwestern News*, October 1981, p. 1.

64. Trustee Minutes, called meeting 10 June 1981.

65. Ibid.

66. Ibid., called meeting 10 June 1981 and also 23 March 1982.

67. Ibid., 20 March 1979.

68. Ibid. See also *Southwestern News*, October 1978, p. 1.

69. *Southwestern News*, February 1980, pp. 4-5.

70. Ibid., May 1980, p. 7. Also see Trustee Minutes, 19 March 1980.

71. Trustee Minutes, 24 October 1978, 20 March 1979, 24 October 1979, and 19 March 1980. See also *Southwestern News*, February 1979, p. 1; March 1979, p. 3; and July 1979, p. 1.

72. *Southwestern News*, September 1980, p. 4, and April 1981, p. 3.

73. Trustee Minutes, 24 March 1981.

74. *Southwestern News*, October 1981, p. 1, and February 1982, p. 8.

75. Ibid., December 1977, p. 8; December 1978, p. 3; February 1979, p. 5; January 1980, p. 2; February 1980, p. 1; January 1981, p. 3; and March 1981, p. 3.

76. Ibid., February 1979, p. 8, and December 1979, p. 3. See also Trustee Minutes, 24 October 1979.

77. Trustee Minutes, 24 March 1981.

78. Ibid., 24 March 1982.

79. Ibid., 24 March 1981.

80. For this document, see addendum to ibid., 21 October 1981.

81. Ibid., 22 October 1980, 25 March 1981, and 24 March 1982. See also *Southwestern News*, November 1980, p. 1; and January 1981, p. 2.

82. Trustee Minutes, 24 March 1982.

83. *Southwestern News*, May 1976, p. 1.

84. Baker James Cauthen to Robert A. Baker, 10 August 1981, Fleming Library, Southwestern Baptist Theological Seminary, Fort Worth, Texas.

Appendix

1. Articles of Faith of the seminary.

2. Original charter of 1908.

3. Charter of 1925 transferring ownership to the Southern Baptist Convention.

4. Officers of the trustees, 1908-82.

5. Trustees, 1908-82.

6. Advisory Council, 1956-82.

7. Faculty, 1908-82.

8. Reference and Assistant Librarians, 1944-82.

9. Editors of the *Southwestern News* and Managing Editors of the *Southwestern Journal of Theology*.

10. Presidents, Convention-wide alumni association.

11. Distinguished alumni awards.

12. Resident enrollment and graduates, 1908-82.

13. Presidents of Seminary Woman's Club, 1927-1982.

14. Index.

The Articles of Faith
of
Southwestern Baptist
Theological Seminary

I. The Scriptures

The Holy Bible was written by men divinely inspired and is the record of God's revelation of Himself to man. It is a perfect treasure of divine instruction. It has God for its author, salvation for its end, and truth, without any mixture of error, for its matter. It reveals the principles by which God judges us; and therefore is, and will remain to the end of the world, the true center of Christian union, and the supreme standard by which all human conduct, creeds, and religious opinions should be tried. The criterion by which the Bible is to be interpreted is Jesus Christ.

II. God

There is one and only one living and true God. He is an intelligent, spiritual, and personal Being, the Creator, Redeemer, Preserver, and Ruler of the universe. God is infinite in holiness and all other perfections. To Him we owe the highest love, reverence, and obedience. The eternal God reveals Himself to us as Father, Son, and Holy Spirit, with distinct personal attributes, but without division of nature, essence, or being.

A. God the Father God as Father reigns with providential care over His Universe, His creatures, and the flow of the stream of human history according to the purpose of His grace. He is all powerful, all loving, and all wise. God is Father in truth to those who become children of God through faith in Jesus Christ. He is fatherly in His attitude toward all men.

B. God the Son Christ is the eternal Son of God. In His incarnation as Jesus Christ He was conceived of the Holy Spirit and born of the virgin Mary. Jesus perfectly revealed and did the will of God, taking upon Himself the demands and necessities of human nature and identifying Himself completely with mankind yet without sin. He honored the divine law by His personal obedience, and in His death on the cross He made provision for the redemption of men from sin. He was raised from the dead with a glorified body and appeared to His disciples as the person who was with them before His crucifixion. He ascended into heaven and is now exalted at the right hand of God where He is the One Mediator, partaking of the nature of God and of man, and in whose Person is effected the reconciliation between God and man. He will return in power and glory to judge the world and to consummate His redemptive mission. He now dwells in all believers as the living and ever present Lord.

C. God the Holy Spirit The Holy Spirit is the Spirit of God. He inspired holy men of old to write the Scriptures. Through illumination He enables men to understand truth. He exalts Christ. He convicts of sin, of righteousness and of judgment. He calls men to the Saviour, and effects regeneration. He cultivates Christian character, comforts believers, and bestows the spiritual gifts by which they serve God through His church. He seals the believer unto the day of final redemption. His presence in the Christian is the assurance of God to bring the believer into the fulness of the stature of Christ. He enlightens and empowers the believer and the church in worship, evangelism, and service.

III. Man

Man was created by the special act of God, in His own image, and is the crowning work of His creation. In the beginning man was innocent of sin and was endowed by His Creator with freedom of choice. By his free choice man sinned against God and brought sin into the human race. Through the temptation of Satan man transgressed the command of God, and fell from his original innocence; whereby his posterity inherit a nature and an environment inclined toward sin, and as soon as they are capable of moral action become transgressors and are under condemnation. Only the grace of God can bring man into His holy fellowship and enable man to fulfill the creative purpose of God. The sacredness of human personality is evident in that God created man in His own image, and in that Christ died for man; therefore every man possesses dignity and is worthy of respect and Christian love.

IV. Salvation

Salvation involves the redemption of the whole man, and is offered freely to all who accept Jesus Christ as Lord and Saviour, who by His own blood obtained eternal redemption for the believer. In its broadest sense salvation includes regeneration, sanctification, and glorification.

A. Regeneration, or the new birth, is a work of God's grace whereby believers become new creatures in Christ Jesus. It is a change of heart wrought by the Holy Spirit through conviction toward God and faith in the Lord Jesus Christ.

Repentance and faith are inseparable experiences of grace. Repentance is a genuine turning from sin toward God. Faith is the acceptance of Jesus Christ and commitment of the entire personality to Him as Lord and Saviour. Justification is God's gracious and full acquittal upon principles of His righteousness of all sinners who repent and believe in Christ. Justification brings the believer into a relationship of peace and favor with God.

B. Sanctification is the experience, beginning in regeneration, by which the believer is set apart to God's purposes, and is enabled to progress toward moral and spiritual perfection through the presence and power of the Holy Spirit dwelling in him. Growth in grace should continue throughut the regenerate person's life.

C. Glorification is the culmination of salvation and is the final blessed and abiding state of the redeemed.

V. God's Purpose of Grace

Election is the gracious purpose of God, according to which He regenerates, sanctifies, and glorifies sinners. It is consistent with the free agency of man, and comprehends all the means in connection with the end. It is a glorious display of God's sovereign goodness, and is infinitely wise, holy, and unchangeable. It excludes boasting and promotes humility.

All true believers endure to the end. Those whom God has accepted in Christ, and sanctified by His Spirit, will never fall away from the state of grace, but shall persevere to the end. Believers may fall into sin through neglect and temptation, whereby they grieve the Spirit, impair their graces and comforts, bring reproach on the cause of Christ, and temporal judgments on themselves, yet they shall be kept by the power of God through faith unto salvation.

VI. The Church
A New Testament church of the Lord Jesus Christ is a local body of baptized believers who are associated by covenant in the faith and fellowship of the gospel, observing the two ordinances of Christ, committed to His teachings, exercising the gifts, rights, and privileges invested in them by His Word, and seeking to extend the gospel to the ends of the earth.

This church is an autonomous body, operating through democratic processes under the Lordship of Jesus Christ. In such a congregation members are equally responsible. Its Scriptural officers are pastors and deacons.

The New Testament speaks also of the church as the body of Christ which includes all of the redeemed of all the ages.

VII. Baptism and the Lord's Supper
Christian baptism is the immersion of a believer in water in the name of the Father, the Son, and the Holy Spirit. It is an act of obedience symbolizing the believer's faith in a crucified, buried, and risen Saviour, the believer's death to sin, the burial of the old life, and the resurrection to walk in newness of life in Christ Jesus. It is a testimony to his faith in the final resurrection of the dead. Being a church ordinance, it is prerequisite to the privileges of church membership and to the Lord's Supper.

The Lord's Supper is a symbolic act of obedience whereby members of the church, through partaking of the bread and the fruit of the vine, memorialize the death of the Redeemer and anticipate His second coming.

VIII. The Lord's Day
The first day of the week is the Lord's Day. It is a Christian institution for regular observance. It commemorates the resurrection of Christ from the dead and should be employed in exercises of worship and spiritual devotion, both public and private, and by refraining from worldly amusements, and resting from secular employments, work of necessity and mercy only being excepted.

IX. The Kingdom
The Kingdom of God includes both His general sovereignty over the universe and His particular kingship over men who willfully acknowledge Him as King. Particularly the Kingdom is the realm of salvation into which men enter by trustful, childlike commitment to Jesus Christ. Christians ought to pray and to labor that the Kingdom may come and God's will be done on earth. The full consummation of the Kingdom awaits the return of Jesus Christ and the end of this age.

X. Last Things
God, in His own time and in His own way, will bring the world to its appropriate end. According to His promise, Jesus Christ will return personally and visibly in glory to the earth; the dead will be raised; and Christ will judge all men in righteousness. The

unrighteous will be consigned to Hell, the place of everlasting punishment. The righteous in their resurrected and glorified bodies will receive their reward and will dwell forever in Heaven with the Lord.

XI. Evangelism and Missions

It is the duty and privilege of every follower of Christ and of every church of the Lord Jesus Christ to endeavor to make disciples of all nations. The new birth of man's spirit by God's Holy Spirit means the birth of love for others. Missionary effort on the part of all rests thus upon a spiritual necessity of the regenerate life, and is expressly and repeatedly commanded in the teachings of Christ. It is the duty of every child of God to seek constantly to win the lost to Christ by personal effort and by all other methods in harmony with the gospel of Christ.

XII. Education

The cause of education in the Kingdom of Christ is coordinate with the causes of missions and general benevolence, and should receive along with these the liberal support of the churches. An adequate system of Christian schools is necessary to a complete spiritual program for Christ's people.

In Christian education there should be a proper balance between academic freedom and academic responsibility. Freedom in an orderly relationship of human life is always limited and never absolute. The freedom of a teacher in a Christian school, college, or seminary is limited by the pre-eminence of Jesus Christ, by the authoritative nature of the Scriptures, and by the distinct purpose for which the school exists.

XIII. Stewardship

God is the source of all blessings, temporal and spiritual; all that we have and are we owe to Him. Christians have a spiritual debtorship to the whole world, a holy trusteeship in the gospel, and a binding stewardship in their possessions. They are therefore under obligation to serve Him with their time, talents, and material possessions; and should recognize all these as entrusted to them to use for the glory of God and for helping others. According to the Scriptures, Christians should contribute of their means, cheerfully, regularly, systematically, proportionately, and liberally for the advancement of the Redeemer's cause on earth.

XIV. Cooperation

Christ's people should, as occasion requires, organize such associations and conventions as may best secure cooperation for the great objects of the Kingdom of God. Such organizations have no authority over one another or over the churches. They are voluntary and advisory bodies designed to elicit, combine, and direct the energies of our people in the most effective manner. Members of New Testament churches should cooperate with one another in carrying forward the missionary, educational, and benevolent ministries for the extension of Christ's Kingdom. Christian unity in the New Testament sense is spiritual harmony and voluntary cooperation for common ends by various groups of Christ's people. Cooperation is desirable between the various Christian denominations, when the end to be attained is itself justified, and when such cooperation involves no violation of conscience or compromise of loyalty to Christ and His Word as revealed in the New Testament.

XV. The Christian and the Social Order

Every Christian is under obligation to seek to make the will of Christ supreme in his own life and in human society. Means and methods used for the improvement of society and the establishment of righteousness among men can be truly and permanently helpful only when they are rooted in the regeneration of the individual by the saving grace of God in Christ Jesus. The Christian should oppose in the spirit of Christ every form of greed, selfishness, and vice. He should work to provide for the orphaned, the needy, the aged, the helpless, and the sick. Every Christian should seek to bring industry, government, and society as a whole under the sway of the principles of righteousness, truth, and brotherly love. In order to promote these ends Christians should be ready to work with all men of good will in any good cause, always being careful to act in the spirit of love without compromising their loyalty to Christ and His truth.

XVI. Peace and War

It is the duty of Christians to seek peace with all men on principles of righteousness. In accordance with the spirit and teachings of Christ they should do all in their power to put an end to war.

The true remedy of the war spirit is the gospel of our Lord. The supreme need of the world is the acceptance of His teachings in all the affairs of men and nations, and the practical application of His law of love.

XVII. Religious Liberty

God alone is Lord of the conscience, and He has left it free from the doctrines and commandments of men which are contrary to His Word or not contained in it. Church and state should be separate. The state owes to every church protection and full freedom in the pursuit of its spiritual ends. In providing for such freedom no ecclesiastical group or denomination should be favored by the state more than others. Civil government being ordained of God, it is the duty of Christians to render loyal obedience thereto in all things not contrary to the revealed will of God. The church should not resort to the civil power to carry on its work. The gospel of Christ contemplates spiritual means alone for the pursuit of its ends. The state has no right to impose penalties for religious opinions of any kind. The state has no right to impose taxes for the support of any form of religion. A free church in a free state is the Christian ideal, and this implies the right of free and unhindered access to God on the part of all men, and the right to form and propagate opinions in the sphere of religion without interference by the civil power.

Original Charter of 1908

First.—Whereas, the Baptist General Convention of Texas, at its last session in San Antonio, held November 7th to 9th, 1907, appointed the twenty-five persons hereinafter named as Trustees for the Southwestern Baptist Theological Seminary and instructed them to procure a charter for the same.

Therefore, we, J. B. Gambrell, A. J. Barton and D. I. Smyth, all citizens of the State of Texas, by this our act of voluntary association, had in conformity with Title XXI of the Revised Statutes of the State of Texas and the acts of the Legislature in said State amendatory thereof, do hereby create a private corporation to be known, called, and named The Southwestern Baptist Theological Seminary.

Second.—The purpose of said corporation is hereby declared to be mainly for the promotion of theological education, but to include the instruction of a Woman's Training School for special Christian service, and such other instruction as may be needful to equip preachers for their life work.

Third.—Said corporation shall have its domicile and place of business at Waco, in McLennan County, Texas, and the Educational Institution for the support of which this corporation is organized shall be established and maintained in said City of Waco.

Fourth.—Said corporation shall have corporate existence for fifty years.

Fifth.—Said corporation shall have twenty-five Trustees.

Sixth.—Said corporation shall have such rights, powers and duties as appertain to corporations under the general laws of this State, or which are inherent in like corporations. And said corporation shall have the power by its Board of Trustees, and upon the recommendation of its Faculty, to confer upon any pupils of said Seminary, or upon any other persons, any of the degrees usually conferred by Theological Seminaries, or other degrees arising from its curriculum.

Seventh.—Said corporation has no capital stock, but the estimated value of its goods, chattels, and lands owned by it amount to about Seventy-five Thousand Dollars.

Eighth.—Said corporation shall have the right to acquire and hold lands and personal property for all purposes for which the same may be required, and shall have the right and power to acquire, hold, and dispose of the lands, chattels, and credits for the purpose of its maintenance.

Ninth.—Said corporation shall be under the patronage and general direction of the Baptist Denomination in the State of Texas as represented by the Baptist General Convention of Texas, which Convention shall ordain and establish the Articles of Faith and permanent laws for the operation, management and control of said Seminary; provided, that such laws shall be consistent with its charter and the Constitution and Laws of this State; and provided, further, that when said rules and laws are promulgated they shall not thereafter be altered, annulled, or abridged by said Convention except by the following procedure, viz: A resolution providing for such alteration, annulment, or abrogation, shall be presented to said Convention at a regular session, signed by at least five accredited messengers to such body, which resolution, without other action, shall be printed in the minutes of said Convention, and shall not be acted on until the next session of that body. Said Convention may retire annually not more than six of the Trustees of said corporation, and shall fill the vacancies so caused by the citizens of this State, unless in the judgment of said Convention it would be to the advantage of said Seminary to have Trustees from other States, then same may be appointed, by similar Baptist bodies of other States, which may desire to co-operate in maintaining said institution, in such proportion and on such terms as may be satisfactory to the Texas Convention on the recommendation of the Seminary Board of Trustees.

In testimony whereof, we, the undersigned, all citizens of the State of Texas, do hereby subscribe our names to this charter with acknowledgment made as required by law, this the 5th day of March, A.D. 1908.

J. B. GAMBRELL,
D. I. SMYTH,
A. J. BARTON.

Amended Charter of 1925

First

The name and official designation of the corporation shall be "The Southwestern Baptist Theological Seminary."

Second

The purpose of said corporation is hereby declared to be mainly for the promotion of theological education, but to include the instruction of Women's Training School for the special Christian service, and such other instruction as is needful to equip preachers and other Christian workers for their life work.

Third

Said corporation shall have its domicile and place of business at Fort Worth, Tarrant County, Texas, and the Educational Institution for the support of which this corporation is organized shall be established and maintained in said city of Fort Worth.

Fourth

Said corporation shall have corporate existence for fifty years.

Fifth

Said corporation shall have twenty-five Trustees.

The Southern Baptist Convention shall appoint successors of such outgoing class and fill any vacancies that may otherwise occur each year, provided that, if for any cause said Convention shall fail to fill vacancies at its next annual session after the said vacancies occur, then the Board of Trustees shall fill such vacancies. And it is hereby made the duty of the Trustees to notify the said Southern Baptist Convention of any vacancies to be filled.

Provided that in all cases, Trustees appointed shall be citizens of the States composing the Southern Baptist Convention, and shall be members of regular Baptist Churches in co-operation with the appointing body.

Sixth

Said corporation shall have such rights, powers, and duties as appertain to similar corporations under the general laws of this State, or which are inherent in like corporations. And said corporation shall have the power by its Board of Trustees and upon the recommendation of its faculty, to confer upon any pupil of said Seminary or upon any other person any of the degrees usually conferred by Theological Seminaries, or other degrees arising from its curriculum.

Seventh

Said corporation is not organized for pecuniary profit, and has no capital stock, but the estimated value of the goods, chattels and lands owned by it amounts to Five Hundred Thousand Dollars.

Eighth

Said corporation shall have the right to acquire, hold and dispose of funds, lands and personal property for all the purposes and objects of the corporation; provided that the principal of funds, or lands or property given for permanent endowment shall never be applied to current expenses or equipment, or in any other way diverted from the purpose for which they were given, which, however, does not preclude any necessary or expedient change in the form of investment.

Ninth

Said corporation shall be under the patronage, general direction and control of the Baptist denomination of the South as represented by the Southern Baptist Convention, which Convention may establish articles of faith and permanent laws for said Seminary, provided that such permanent laws shall be consistent with its charter and the Constitution and laws of this State, and provided further that when said permanent laws are promulgated, they shall not thereafter be altered, annulled or abrogated by said Convention except by the following procedure, viz.: a resolution providing for such alteration, annullment, or abrogation shall be presented to said Convention at a regular session, signed by at least five accredited messengers to such body, which resolution, without other action, shall be printed in the minutes of said Convention, and shall not be acted on until the next session of said body. In all matters not included in the Articles of Faith and Permanent Laws, as set out in this clause, the corporation shall be subject to the rules and regulations of the Southern Baptist Convention, both general and specific, as these may be promulgated from time to time, and made a matter of record in the Minutes of said Convention.

Tenth

The primary right of appointing Trustees of said Seminary as hereinbefore vested in the Southern Baptist Convention shall so remain exclusively.

Eleventh

Amendments to this Charter shall be made only with the advice and consent of the Southern Baptist Convention, said action being duly recorded upon the Minutes of said Convention.

Endorsed: Filed in the office of the Secretary of State this 27th day of February, 1925.

Officers of the Trustees

1908-1982

Shad Medlin	1980-1981
Ralph Pulley	1981-1983

Secretaries

A. J. Barton	1907-1909
P. E. Burroughs	1909-1910
J. K. Winston	1910-1921
C. M. King	1921-1951
D. A. Thornton	1951-1954
Wayne Evans	1954-1978
James E. Carter	1978-1982

Bragg, B. Finney	Maryland	1953-1959
Breithaupt, Frank E.	Missouri	1970-1975
Brown, Archie E.	Illinois	1952-1965
Brown, E. C.	Arkansas	1949-1955
	At Large (Okla.)	1955-1957
Brown, F. F.	Tennessee	1921-1923 (Spr.)
Brown, George F.	Georgia	1938-1946
Bruner, J. W.	New Mexico	1918-1922
	Oklahoma	1926-1927
Bryant, James R.	Virginia	1941-1951
Bryant, James W.	Texas	1982-
Buchanan, John H.	Alabama	1955-1956
Bullard, G. W.	North Carolina	1952-1957
Burke, J. L.	New Mexico	1965-1976
Burnette, Joe E.	North Carolina	1967-1977
Burns, W. A.	Florida	1917-1920 (Spr.)
Burroughs, P. E.	Texas	1907-1910
Burt, R. E.	Texas	1920-1924
Burts, C. E.	Georgia	1926-1934
Butler, E. G.	Oklahoma	1923 (Spr.)-1923
Butt, Howard E., Jr.	At Large (Texas)	1955-1968
Byrd, J. E.	Mississippi	1919-1924
		1932-1938 (Spr.)
Campbell, R. C.	Texas	1933-1941
Campbell, S. H.	Arkansas	1916-1917
Carleton, J. Paul	Illinois	1947-1952
Carleton, W. A.	Oklahoma	1944-1948
Carnett, Ellis L.	Texas	1948-1956
	At Large (Texas)	1956-1958
Carpenter, William Carl, Jr.	Oregon-Washington	1973-1983
Carroll, J. M.	Texas	1907-1909
Carter, James E.	Louisiana-Texas	1973-1982
Casey, David	At Large (Texas)	1960-1970
Chaffin, Floyd	Texas	1947-1950
Chafin, Kenneth L.	Texas	1975-1980
		1981-1985
Chancellor, W. W.	Oklahoma	1911-1912
Chrisman, Oswin	At Large (Texas)	1971-1981
Clayton, Lynn P.	Kansas	1972-1979
Coggin, James E.	Texas	1966-1976
		1978-1983
Coleman, C. C.	South Carolina	1924-1926
Collier, J. P.	New Mexico	1909-1915
Compere, J. S.	Arkansas	1919-1924
Connell, G. H.	Texas	1909-1915
Cooper, Davis L.	Colorado	1978-1983
Cooper, J. Dan	Oklahoma	1971-1983
Covey, Homer	At Large (Texas)	1955-1957 (July)
Covington, W. E.	Kentucky	1917-1924

Cowden, George E.	Texas	1910-1921 (July)
Cowden, George E., Jr.	Texas	1921-1924
Cowden, J. M.	Texas	1907-1909
Cox, Norman	Georgia	1924-1927
Craig, Earl H., Jr.	Georgia	1972-1977
Craig, W. Marshall	Virginia	1924-1927
Cranfill, J. B.	Texas	1907-1934 (Sept.)-1942
Crawford, W. Edwin	Texas	1967-1977
Crotts, William P.	Arizona	1981-1983
Crouch, Austin	Tennessee	1917-1919
Crouch, J. P.	Texas	1907-1920
Crowley, A. F.	Texas	1909-1914
Crutcher, G. H.	Florida	1929-1932 (May)
Cumbie, William J.	Virginia	1971-1981
Cunningham, Milton	Texas	1976-1986
Daniel, J. P.	Maryland	1937-1944
Daniels, C. W.	Texas	1907-1909
Davidson, R. L.	Oklahoma	1923 (Spr.)-1923
Dawson, J. M.	Texas	1915 (Feb.)-1915
Day, James S., Jr.	Florida	1944-1948
Dickinson, Herbert	Colorado	1972-1978
Divers, Frank	New Mexico	1909-1915
Dodd, M. E.	Louisiana	1912-1927
		1933-1951
Dorian, Gordon	Kansas	1962-1972
Dunlap, E. D.	Texas	1941-1949
Durham, J. H.	Kentucky	1919 (Spr.)-1919
Ecton, T. C.	Kentucky	1935-1941
Edwards, C. V.	Texas	1921-1931
Elrod, Ben M.	Kentucky	1979-1986
Entzminger, Louis	Florida	1920 (Spr.)-1920
Estes, W. O.	Maryland	1944-1948
Eure, Otho A.	District of Columbia	1935-1936
Evans, Ellis B.	Alabama	1955-1956
Evenson, Darrell	Arizona	1971-1973
Farrar, Charles William	South Carolina	1982-
Faulkner, Melvin G.	Tennessee	1974-1980
Feezor, Forrest C.	Texas	1943-1944
Field, Glenn	Colorado	1963-1973
Fleming, William	Texas	1936-1937
		1950-1955
	At Large (Texas)	1955-1965
Flowers, Joseph B.	Virginia	1951-1961
Foreman, A. D., Jr.	Tennessee	1949-1960
Frazier, S. H.	Texas	1933-1937
	Illinois	1946-1947
Freeman, C. Wade, Jr.	District of Columbia	1974-1984
Fuqua, W. H.	Texas	1907-1915

Gambrell, J. B.	Texas	1907-1912
Gardner, David M.	Florida	1932-1945
	Texas	1945-1948
Garrett, Jenkins	At Large (Texas)	1958-1968
Gary, Raymond	Oklahoma	1965-1974
George, J. Thurmond	Oklahoma	1948-1956
	At Large (Okla.)	1956-1959
	California	1964-1974
Gibson, Finley	Arkansas	1911-1916
	Kentucky	1919-1924
Gibson, Louis E.	Texas	1968-1978
Gillon, R. L.	Mississippi	1915-1919
Graham, R. L.	Texas	1970-1980
Gregory, A. P.	Illinois	1915-1917
Grigg, Arthur	Illinois	1965-1975
Gunnells, Drew	Alabama	1980-1985
Guy, Daniel W.	South Carolina	1978-1984
Guy, R. E.	Tennessee	1940-1950
Hacker, J. D.	Oklahoma	1919-1921 (Spr.)
Haldeman, John H.	Florida	1948-1958
Hall, Gerald A.	Arizona	1950-1958
Hamblin, Robert L.	Missouri	1978-1983
Hamlett, W. A.	Oklahoma	1912-1913
Hand, Stanley I.	Florida	1978-1983
Hargrove, H. H.	Texas	1949-1954
Harmon, P. T.	Missouri	1921-1923
Harris, W. D.	Texas	1907-1916 (Spr.)
Harrison, W. B.	Texas	1910-1914
Harvell, Calvin T.	Indiana	1982-
Harvey, T. F.	New Mexico	1924-1926
Hawkins, Earl E.	Kansas-Nebraska	1978-1984
Hebard, Roger D.	At Large (Okla.)	1957-1960
Heflin, James L.	Mississippi	1981-1983
Heflin, Jay	Arkansas	1968-1976
Hening, B. C.	Tennessee	1919-1921
Herndon, T. V.	Louisiana	1927-1933 (May)
Hicks, J. E.	Maryland	1924-1933
Hicks, R. H.	Texas	1907-1910
Hill, Sam S., Jr.	Kentucky	1946-1954
Hite, Jesse R.	Virginia	1934-1941
Holman, Luman W.	At Large (Texas)	1958-1971
Holt, A. J.	Texas	1946-1957
Howard, James A.	South Carolina	1953-1964
Hudgins, W. Douglas	Texas	1937-1946
Hultgren, Warren C.	Oklahoma	1958-1968
Hulton, H. H.	Oklahoma	1912-1916
		1917 (Spr.)-1918 (Spr.)
Huyck, A. Warren	Georgia	1952-1953

Hyman, George	Florida	1920 (Spr)-1924
Inlow, R. N.	Tennessee	1917-1920
Jackson, B. M.	Texas	1931-1936
Jackson, E. Hilton	District of Columbia	1924-1926
Jenkins, R. F.	New Mexico	1916-1918
Jent, J. W.	Oklahoma	1924-1926
Jester, J. R.	North Carolina	1924-1927
Johnson, F. W.	Texas	1907-1911
Johnson, J. L.	Mississippi	1919-1932 (Spr.)
Joiner, T. D.	Texas	1907-1909
Jones, Carter Helm	Oklahoma	1911-1912
Jones, George W.	Indiana	1972-1982
Jones, Phillip A.	Ohio	1982-
Keith, James	Mississippi	1982-
Kirkpatrick, Jerry A.	Arizona	1975-1983
Knight, W. H.	Georgia	1934-1938
Kokernot, H. L.	Texas	1907-1909
Kunce, George H.	Illinois	1975-1985
Lattimore, O. S.	Texas	1910-1931 (Dec.)
Lawrence, J. B.	Louisiana	1911-1912
Lester, Melvin A.	New Mexico	1976-1986
Lewis, Gladys	Oklahoma	1974-1984
Lilly, Kenneth E.	At Large (Ark.)	1981-1986
Lindquist, Hugo T.	Oklahoma	1981-1983
Lindsay, Homer H., Jr.	Florida	1958-1968
Littleton, D. W.	Maryland	1931-1937
Long, A. J.	Texas	1910-1916
Luther, J. T., Jr.	At Large (Texas)	1955-1978
McBride, Jerold R.	Oklahoma	1968-1973
McCall, George W.	Texas	1909-1910
McConnell, F. C.	Texas	1912-1915 (Feb.)
McConnell, F. M.	Texas	1914-1915
McCoy, J. H.	Tennessee	1921-1924
McDonald, Lewis N.	Maryland	1979-1984
McGlamery, Harold P.	Oklahoma	1948-1958
	At Large (Okla.)	1959-1964
McGriff, E. A.	District of Columbia	1956-1957
McKay, John	Texas	1982-
McNaughton, John N.	At Large (Texas)	1980-1985
McRay, James W.	Georgia	1967
Maddox, A. L.	New Mexico	1922-1923 (Spr.)
		1927-1931
Mahon, R. P.	Louisiana	1914-1919
Martin, Fred A.	Texas	1923-1931 (Oct.)
Mason, Harry W., Jr.	Maryland	1959-1964
Masters, F. M.	Oklahoma	1913-1917 (Spr.)
Matthews, C. E.	Texas	1931-1947 (Mar.)
Means, G. Z.	Texas	1907-1909
Medlin, T. Shad	Arkansas	1976-1986

Miller, Carey	Colorado	1974-1978
Miller, R. C.	Oklahoma	1917-1921 (Spr.)
Millican, L. R.	Texas	1907-1909
Mitchell, Walter A.	District of Columbia	1954-1956
Moore, N. A.	New Mexico	1926-1927
Moore, Walter L.	Georgia	1946-1952
Morris, R. A.	Mississippi	1939-1948
Morrison, B. Ross	District of Columbia	1957-1974
Mulkey, S. M.	Ohio	1962-1972
Naney, Rupert F.	Oklahoma	1927-1934
Nardin, Michael W.	Michigan	1975-1985
Naylor, Robert E.	Arkansas	1941-1944
	Oklahoma	1944-1948
	South Carolina	1949-1953
	Texas	1954-1956
	At Large (Texas)	1956-1958
Nelson, T. W.	Missouri	1960-1970
Nichols, Holmes	Oklahoma	1916-1919
Norris, J. Frank	Texas	1909-1915
Ogg, T. Earl	Texas	1972-1982
O'Neal, Norman E.	Mississippi	1958-1968
Orr, Robert L.	Tennessee	1962-1970
Palmer, Wallace Blake	Louisiana	1982-
Payne, C. Royce	New Mexico	1919-1921 (Spr.)
Pemberton, J. T.	Texas	1915-1923 (Spr.)
Penick, I. N.	Tennessee	1924-1939
Penrod, W. K.	Texas	1907-1911
Pittman, C. Frank	South Carolina	1928-1929
		1936-1949
Pool, W. A.	Texas	1907-1914
Porter, J. W.	Kentucky	1917-1919 (Spr.)
Porter, S. J.	District of Columbia	1926-1935 (Spr.)
Portwood, W. P.	Texas	1915-(May) 1917
Posey, S. G.	Texas	1942-1948
Potts, Robert J.	Georgia	1975-1982
Prior, Loyal	Virginia	1961-1971
Pulley, Ralph W., Jr.	Texas	1974-1982
Quinn, Eugene F.	Kentucky	1966-1976
Ragland, George	Kentucky	1924-1926
Rains, J. E.	Missouri	1946-1960
Ray, Samuel Clemens	North Carolina	1957-1967
Ridgeway, Elmer	Oklahoma	1921 (Spr.)-
		1923 (Spr.)
		1938-1944
Riley, James S.	Texas	1957-1967
Robertson, B. P.	District of Columbia	1936-1944
Rodgers, James	District of Columbia	1944-1949
Rogers, J. S.	Arkansas	1915-1919
Sandifer, J. D.	Texas	1914-1924

Scott, D. J.	Missouri	1923-1924
Shamburger, W. M.	At Large (Texas)	1959-1972
		1974-1984
Sherwood, Arthur M.	At Large (Texas)	1978-1983
Shivers, E. B., Jr.	Georgia	1953-1967
Simmons, Lloyd B.	Texas	1948-1953
Simpson, Leon	Kentucky	1976-1981
Singletary, Donald J.	Texas	1967-1972
Sipes, L. M.	Arkansas	1917-1920 (Spr.)
		1924-1941
Skinner, T. Claggett	Virginia	1927-1934 (Sept.)
Slaughter, C. C.	Texas	1907-1911
Smith, Forrest	Texas	1923 (Spr.)-
		1931 (Feb.)
Smith, H. Marshall	Texas	1950-1956
	At Large (Texas)	1956-1964
Smith, Ralph	Texas	1964-1974
Smith, T. B.	Michigan	1965-1975
Smith, W. J., Jr.	North Carolina	1977-1982
Smythe, D. I.	Texas	1907-1917
Solomon, E. D.	Mississippi	1915-1919
Sparks, Buren	New Mexico	1921 (Spr.)-1922
Spencer, Harry Lee	Texas	1936-1949
Spencer, J. W.	Texas	1916
Spiller, E. A.	New Mexico	1931-1934
Spiro, Robert H.	Florida	1968-1978
Stallings, Harry L.	Ohio	1972-1982
Steele, Harry W.	Indiana	1962-1972
Steger, J. H.	At Large (Texas)	1955-1966
Stephens, A. P.	North Carolina	1927-1952
Stephens, Bunyan	Florida	1921 (Spr.)-1929
Strickland, Floyd W.	California	1974-1984
Stringer, Dan C.	Arizona	1965-1973
Stuckey, John R.	Washington, D.C.	1969-1974
Stumph, C. W.	New Mexico	1923 (Spr.)-1924
Tatum, Scott L.	Louisiana	1952-1962
Taylor, James W.	Louisiana	1962-1972
Thomas, A. Wade	Oregon-Washington	1963-1973
Throgmorton, W. P.	Illinois	1916 (Spr.)-
		1929 (Sept.)
Tidwell, J. B.	Texas	1907-1942
Todd, Byron F.	California	1954-1964
Tripp, Frank	Missouri	1930-1935
Truett, George W.	Texas	1907-1944 (July)
Turner, Boyd A.	South Carolina	1964-1974
Turner, R. L.	Florida	1917-1920 (Spr.)
Van Arsdale, A. B.	Alabama	1958-1970
Vermillion, H. F.	New Mexico	1915-1916
Wadley, J. K.	Texas	1924-1933

Walker, Crumpton	Kentucky	1926-1935
Walker, L. M.	New Mexico	1944-1950
Wall, Broadus	South Carolina	1929-1936
Walsh, F. Howard	Texas	1963-1975
Ward, J. L.	Texas	1914-1917
Warr, C. Michael	District of Columbia	1949-1954
Wasson, C. M.	Illinois	1917-1945 (May)
Watson, E. L.	Oklahoma	1921 (Spr.)-
		1923 (Spr.)
Watterson, Don	Alabama	1970-1980
Wauford, C. E.	Tennessee	1921 (Spr.)-1921
Wells, Onous J., Jr.	Mississippi	1968-1978
White, G. L.	Texas	1907-1911
White, W. R.	Texas	1931 (Dec.)-1936
	Oklahoma	1937-1938
Whiteside, Russell B.	Missouri	1921-1930 (Spr.)
Widemann, Donald	Missouri	1975-1980
Widick, Clyde R.	Kentucky	1941-1956
Wigger, W. M.	Missouri	1935-1946
Wilder, Jack B.	Virginia	1982-1986
Williams, H. G.	Alabama	1934-1950
Wilkes, E. Stanley	Tennessee	1960-1965
Wilkins, James R.	Maryland	1964-1969
Wilson, Lloyd T.	Tennessee	1923 (Spr.)-1924

Members of the Advisory Council

1956-1982

Name	Address When Serving	Years of Service
Abercrombie, E. F.	Clifton, Texas	1979-1985
Abernathy, James K.	Richardson, Texas	1976-1982
Allen, Bill G.	Burleson, Texas	1966-1977
Allison, J. R.	Hereford, Texas	1968-1977
Austin, T. L.	Dallas, Texas	1969-1975
Bagwell, John M.D.	Dallas, Texas	1971-1972
Barker, W. A.	Denton, Texas	Life Member
Barr, William	Fort Worth, Texas	1976-1982
Bass, Roy	Lubbock, Texas	1977-1978
Beebe, Eldon	Austin, Texas	1980-1983
Bell, Griffin B.	Atlanta, Georgia	1980-1983
Berry, Alan	Franklin, Tennessee	1976-1982
Blankenship, William T.	Kingwood, Texas	1978-1984
Bollinger, John	Brookshire, Texas	1973-1979
Bolton, Jim M.	Dallas, Texas	1981-1984
Bourland, Vergal	Fort Worth, Texas	1956
Bowles, Donald E., Sr.	Dallas, Texas	1978-1984
Box, J. N.	Grapevine, Texas	1980-1983
Brantley, Leonard H.	Fort Worth, Texas	1972-1978
Brentham, Jerry	Belton, Texas	1981-1984
Bright, Sam	Tyler, Texas	Life Member
Brinkley, Charles	Fort Worth, Texas	1976-1982
Bryan, Travis B.	Bryan, Texas	1968-1975
Burg, Kenneth E.	Dallas, Texas	1979-1985
Buske, G. B.	Friona, Texas	1968-1975
Cadwallader, Ralph	San Antonio, Texas	1956-1967
Cantrell, James C.	Dallas, Texas	1977-1983
Carden, Weldon G.	Fort Worth, Texas	1973-1983
Carter, B. A.	Corpus Christi, Texas	1956
Casey, D. C.	Lubbock, Texas	1956
Cates, Paul	Lubbock, Texas	1959-1960
Chabysek, Herb	Houston, Texas	1981-1984
Chavanne, Harry J.	Houston, Texas	1982-1985
Cooper, Kenneth H.	Dallas, Texas	1977-1983
Cotulla, W. Paul	Cotulla, Texas	1970-1984
Cowden, George M.	Austin, Texas	1979-1982
Crain, John J.	Paris, Texas	1957-1972
Cummings, Clifton H.	Lubbock, Texas	1982-1985
Cummins, Elmer C.	Fort Worth, Texas	1965-1985
Day, J. Warren	Fort Worth, Texas	1966-1980
Dickey, F. B.	Fort Worth, Texas	1956

Edwards, John Milton, Jr.	Seymour, Texas	1971-1983
England, Ed	Fort Smith, Arkansas	1982-1985
Ferguson, Ted	Amarillo, Texas	Life Member
Ferguson, Travis W.	Albuquerque, New Mexico	1981-1984
Finney, Jack	Greenville, Texas	1956-1965
Floyd, David R.	Dallas, Texas	1978-1984
Formby, Marshall	Plainview, Texas	Life Member
Garrett, Jenkins	Fort Worth, Texas	Life Member
Gibson, Louis	Corsicana, Texas	1981-1984
Glasscock, Mrs. Lucille	Corpus Christi, Texas	1980-1983
Glaze, Robert E.	Dallas, Texas	1974-1985
Godfrey, Berl E.	Fort Worth, Texas	1956-1984
Gooch, Thomas C., Jr.	Harlingen, Texas	1970-1975
Goodson, Frank T.	Jacksonville, Texas	1977-1983
Gould, Robert J.	Fort Worth, Texas	1977-1983
Graham, Ray L., Sr.	Franklin, Texas	Life Member
Greene, Cullum	Fort Worth, Texas	1956-1957
Grubbs, Bill G.	Dallas, Texas	1979-1985
Hale, Fred M.	Henderson, Texas	1967-1978
Hamilton, Walter B.	Fort Worth, Texas	1956
Hanks, Billie, Sr.	San Angelo, Texas	1969-1977
Harrell, T. J.	Fort Worth, Texas	1956-1965
Hathaway, Drury P.	Ballinger, Texas	1972-1983
Hawks, George W.	Arlington, Texas	1968-1980
Heflin, Jay L.	Little Rock, Arkansas	Life Member
Hughes, Glen D.	Marble Falls, Texas	1968-1973
Hughes, Vester T., Jr.	Dallas, Texas	1982-1985
Humphrey, C. J.	Amarillo, Texas	1968-1975
Humphrey, Walter	Fort Worth, Texas	1956-1970
Hunt, Dr. T. E., Sr.	Paris, Texas	1956-1957
Hurt, John J.	Dallas, Texas	1968-1975
Isom, George	Dallas, Texas	1974-1980
Jackson, A. A. "Gus"	Fort Worth, Texas	1956-1978
Jackson, F. R.	Longview, Texas	1956
Jackson, Homer	Dallas, Texas	Life Member
Jeffrey, James N.	Overland Park, Kansas	1982-1985
Johnson, J. Lee, Jr.	Fort Worth, Texas	1956
Jones, Archie L.	Haskell, Texas	1982-1985
Jones, Coy D.	Longview, Texas	1982-1985
Jones, Leo, Sr.	Tyler, Texas	1980-1983
Joseph, Thomas R., Jr.	Hamilton, Texas	1965-1983
Kennelly, Clyde B.	Rosenburg, Texas	1979-1985
Ladd, J. C.	Devers, Texas	1973-1979
Lansford, Robert M.	Fort Worth, Texas	1982-1985
Lee, Ralph B.	Houston, Texas	1977-1980
Lenamon, Joe T.	Fort Worth, Texas	1977-1983
Lilly, Ken E.	Fort Smith, Arkansas	1979-1982
Linebery, Mrs. Evelyn	Midland, Texas	1981-1984
Lovvorn, Martin C.	Dallas, Texas	1979-1985

Luther, J. T., Jr.	Fort Worth, Texas	Life Member
Maddox, Dr. W. Gordon	Denton, Texas	Life Member
Marsh, Glenn	Lexington, Kentucky	1980-1983
Martin, Paul E.	Houston, Texas	1978-1984
Martin, William L.	Dallas, Texas	1966-1977
Mason, Paul	Fort Worth, Texas	1976-1979
Mason, Richard A.	Brownwood, Texas	1978-1984
McCormick, James	Dallas, Texas	1966-1983
McCracken, Jarrell	Waco, Texas	1976-1982
McCullough, Robert D.	Tulsa, Oklahoma	1976-1981
McNaughton, John P.	Fort Worth, Texas	1979-1981
McNew, George J.	Fort Worth, Texas	1956-1977
McQueen, George F.	Fort Worth, Texas	1956
McVay, Minor B.	Eden, Texas	1965-1975
Mead, Bill O.	Dallas, Texas	1976-1979
Meadows, Mrs. Lucille L.	Dallas, Texas	1981-1984
Means, Huling	Albuquerque, New Mexico	1956-1965
Merrill, Wayne	Fort Stockton, Texas	1972-1978
Mora, A. R.	Kaufman, Texas	1979-1985
Motheral, Foist	Fort Worth, Texas	1980-1983
Murphy, Freland	Houston, Texas	1956-1965
Murray, Doyle	Fort Worth, Texas	1980-1983
Needham, Oran	Fort Worth, Texas	1976-1982
Oler, Stanley	Fort Worth, Texas	1977-1983
Parker, I. C.	Fort Worth, Texas	1968-1975
Parker, J. Lloyd	Fort Worth, Texas	1959-1961
Perkins, T. Ray	Olney, Texas	Life Member
Perry, Edgar H., III	Austin, Texas	1956-1972
Ponder, P. Ed	Sweetwater, Texas	1970-1974
Porter, William A.	Terrell, Texas	1979-1985
Presley, W. Dewey	Dallas, Texas	1967-1975
Pruitt, Warren D.	Vernon, Texas	1972-1983
Riley, Harold E.	Cameron, Texas	1978-1981
Roach, Frederick E.	Dallas, Texas	1979-1985
Roberts, A. Webb	Dallas, Texas	Life Member
Robinson, Lon	Fort Worth, Texas	1971-1975
Sams, Ross	Waco, Texas	1956-1965
Sarsgard, William R.	Fort Worth, Texas	1969-1984
Scarborough, Warren	Fort Worth, Texas	1956
Schmid, W. A., Jr.	Fort Worth, Texas	1956-1965
Sewell, Stewart	Jacksboro, Texas	1968-1975
Shackelford, O. D.	Fort Worth, Texas	1980-1983
Shearin, George L.	Dallas, Texas	1979-1985
Shinn, George	Raleigh, North Carolina	1977-1980
Simon, Peter	Fort Worth, Texas	1978-1984
Singletary, Donald J.	Fort Worth, Texas	1966
Skinner, Walter	Paris, Texas	1956
Slater, Norvell E.	Dallas, Texas	1968-1983
Sloan, Joe M.	Tulsa, Oklahoma	1982-1985

Slover, J. Roy	Liberty, Texas	Life Member
Smart, Kenneth	Kilgore, Texas	1976-1979
Smith, Harold	Amarillo, Texas	1981-1984
Smith, Herman	Hurst, Texas	1968-1984
Southerland, J. K.	Batesville, Arkansas	1967-1975
Stevenson, O. Roy	Fort Worth, Texas	1976
Stout, Carson	High Point, North Carolina	1965-1970
Stovall, David	Fort Worth, Texas	1976-1982
Stripling, W. C.	Fort Worth, Texas	1956
Tatum, James L.	Jacksonville, Florida	1981-1984
Taylor, J. Ray	Fort Worth, Texas	1976-1982
Thames, William D., Jr.	Lufkin, Texas	1976-1985
Vance, Estil	Fort Worth, Texas	1956
Vandervoort, H. C.	Fort Worth, Texas	1956
Von Netzer, Randy	Oklahoma City, Oklahoma	1982-1985
Walker, John R.	Fort Worth, Texas	1977-1983
Walker, William J.	Little Rock, Arkansas	1976
Walsh, F. Howard	Fort Worth, Texas	1956
Ward, John	North Little Rock, Arkansas	1980-1983
Watson, W. Marvin	Dallas, Texas	1974-1981
Wayman, L. Arch	Fort Worth, Texas	1980-1983
White, Mark W., Jr.	Austin, Texas	1977-1983
Whittenberg, Jim	Amarillo, Texas	1956-1957
Wilkins, Glenn	Fort Worth, Texas	1976-1982
Willcoxon, L. E.	Fort Worth, Texas	1979-1985
Williams, Fieldon E.	Fort Worth, Texas	1979-1985
Williams, J. Howard, Jr.	Houston, Texas	1966-1975
Wood, Cecil W.	Scottsdale, Arizona	1980-1983
Woodson, C. B.	Corpus Christi, Texas	1956
Yarborough, Donald V.	Dallas, Texas	1973-1983
Yates, Edmund R.	Dallas, Texas	1977-1983

Dates later than 1982 refer to terms of election rather than necessarily to years served.

Faculty

Southwestern Baptist Theological Seminary

(1908-1982)

Name	Years	Name	Years
Abernathy, Bettie	1930-1932	Brooks, Paula	1977-1979
Adams, Bobby E.	1976-	Brown, H. C., Jr.	1947-1973
Anderson, Justice C.	1974-	Brown, Lewis Sarle	1952-1964
Appleby, David P.	1960-1965	Bryan, Robert Thomas	1922-1923
Ashby, Charles W.	1978-	Burch, Vella Jane	1948-1954
Autrey, Cassius Elijah	1955-1960	Burton, Robert L.	1956-
Baergen, J. Darrel	1981-	Bush, L. Russell	1975-
Baker, Jeroline	1964-	Buster, Helen	1925-1927
Baker, Nathan Larry	1973-1975	Byars, Mrs. J. W.	1918-1925
Baker, Robert A.	1942-1981	Caldwell, William G.	1976-
Ball, Charles Thomas	1911-1919	Carlson, Ernest Leslie	1921-1964
Barclay, William A.	1928-1948	Carnett, Ellis Lee	1920-1933
Barksdale, Sue	1945-1946	Carroll, B. H.	1908-1914
Barnard, Floy M.	1933-1960	Cassidy, Mrs. J. H.	1927-1928
Barnes, William Wright	1913-1953	Cauthen, Baker James	1935-1939
Barnhill, Myrtle Fait	1929-1931	Chafin, Kenneth L.	1959-1965
Barrett, Mary Lois	1923-1934	Cheek, J. Frank	1922-1928
Barry, John Andral, Jr.	1946-1948	Cheek, Minnie Wells	1920-1923
Bass, Claude L.	1977-	Cheek, Mrs. M. O.	1920-1921
Baxter, Laura F.	1914-1915	Churchill, Ralph Dees	1944-1970
Bell, Arthur Donald	1951-60; 1963-72	Clark, Carl Anderson	1954-1970
Bennett, Carlyle D.	1936-1939	Clendinning, B. A. (Pat), Jr.	1979-
Bennett, Mrs. Carlyle	1936-1945	Clinard, Harold Gordon	1955-1966
Bennett, Thomas M. Jr.	1953-1976	Coldiron, Jack H.	1963-
Benson, Alan	1956-1957	Cole, Mrs. Katharine	1922-1924 1926-1927
Bobo, Bessie	1919-1920		
Bolton, Cecil	1949-1950	Coleman, Robert O.	1958-1979
Brackney, Bob W.	1979-	Colson, William	1971-
Bradford, Anna Laura	1945-1970	Conley, David L.	1959-1978
Bratton, Mrs. W. A.	1948-1949	Conner, Blanche Ray	1942-1944
Bridges, Tommy L.	1977-	Conner, Walter Thomas	1910-1949
Briggs, Philip H.	1971-	Copass, Benjamin A.	1918-1942
Brisco, Thomas V.	1980-	Corley, R. Bruce	1976-
Brister, C. W.	1957-	Cornelius, Mrs. R. H.	1915-1916
Brooks, James A.	1976-	Cossey, Mrs. J. I.	1919-1920

Cowan, Willie	1921-1925	Freeman, Harold V.	1974-
Cowsert, Mrs. J. J.	1919-1920	Fullerton, Maude	1923-1925
Cranford, Lorin L.	1976-	Gambrell, J. B.	1912-1914
Crowder, Joseph W.	1910-1943		1917-1921
Culp, Raymond	1934-1935	Gardner, Thurman C.	1921
Dalton, Dessie	1928-1931	Garland, D. David	1959-
D'Amico, David F.	1968-1975	Garrett, James Leo, Jr.	1949-1959
Dana, Harvey Eugene	1919-1938		1979-
Dance, Mrs. J. C.	1923-1925	Gaston, George H.	1979-
Daniel, James H.	1955-1962	Gideon, Virtus E.	1957-
Daniel, Robert Thomas	1937-1952	Gillis, Carroll O.	1933-1934
Dansby, Cisco	1926-1927	Gillis, Don	1935-1940
Davis, William Mac, Jr.	1979-	Goodspeed, Calvin	1908-1910
Day, Gladys	1952-1978	Gosney, Cora	1917-1918
Dean, Clark	1972-1976	Gray, L. Jack	1956-
Dean, Talmadge (Jack)	1956-1965	Gray, Scotty W.	1966-
DeSteiguer, Maudames	1919-1920	Green, Raymond Paul	1956-1960
Dill, Harold T.	1959-	Greenfield, Guy	1980-
Dobson, Pearl	1922-1923	Greenlee, William P.	1959-1965
Dockery, Myrtle	1914-1918	Gregory, Joel C.	1982-
Dominy, Bert B.	1970-	Grounds, Chester E.	1977-1978
Douglass, Robert S.	1954-	Guinn, George Earl	1948-1951
Dowell, Theodore H.	1973-	Guy, R. Calvin	1946-1982
Drakeford, John W.	1956-	Hall, Mrs. F. L.	1923-1927
Drummond, N. R.	1920-1931	Hargrave, William	1947-1950
Drumwright, Huber L., Jr.	1951-1959	Harris, Philip Brown	1949-1959
	1960-1980	Hatcher, Harvey B.	1958-1974
Dunlap, Wayne	1940-1942	Haveman, Edith	1934-1935
Eaves, James F.	1973-	Hawkins, Flora Floy	1926-1927
Edwards, Ernestine	1930-1931	Heacock, Joe Davis	1944-1973
Elliott, Mrs. Leslie	1919-1929	Head, Eldred Douglas	1942-1953
Elliott, Leslie R.	1919-1957	Heeren, Forrest	1950-1953
Ely, Virginia	1936-1938	Heflin, Jay N. Boo	1972-
Estep, William R., Jr.	1954-	Hemphill, Andrew	1919-1948
Evans, Elizabeth	1924-1927	Hendricks, William L.	1958-1978
Evans, Perry F.	1920-1921	Hepburn, Donald S.	1972-1978
Ezell, M. Douglas	1970-1980	Hobbs, Christine	1932-1934
Fait, Myrtle A.	1925-1927	Howse, William Lewis, Jr.	1933-1955
Fant, Clyde E., Jr.	1966-1974	Howse, Mrs. William L.	1935-1936
Farr, T. H.	1920-1922	Huey, F. B., Jr.	1966-
Fasol, Albert D.	1975-	Hunt, Harry B., Jr.	1976-
Feather, R. Othal	1947-1970	Hunt, W. Boyd	1944-1946
Ferguson, Milton U.	1959-1973		1953-
Fish, Roy J.	1965-	Hunt, T. W.	1963-
Fite, J. David	1973-	Jeffers, Clairbel	1927-1929
Fitzgerald, Ara	1918-1920	Johnson, Charles Price	1957-1965
Flint, Charles	1947-1955	Johnson, Ruth	1927-1928
Ford, LeRoy	1966-	Johnson, Mrs. W. A.	1935-1945
Fox, Mary Agnes	1924-1925	Johnston, Shelton D.	1946-1948

Jones, Mrs. Orabelle C.   1926-1932
Josey, John   1925-1927
Keith, C. David   1980-
Kelm, George L.   1980-
Kent, Dan G.   1980-
King, Adoniram Joseph   1976-
King, Arthur   1949-1953
King, Mrs. Sue Biggs   1965-
Kirkpatrick, W. David   1980-
Kiwiet, John J.   1968-
Knight, William H.   1919-1923
                             1929-1931
Knight, Mrs. W. H.   1920-1921
Knowlton, Gracie   1947-1971
Lamb, L. R.   1922-1924
Lambert, Mrs. W. R.   1915-1920
Larsen, Esther   1922-1926
Laseter, Ann   1922-1924
Lea, Thomas D.   1979-
Lile, Mrs. Alma   1915-1919
Lockler, W. E.   1921-1922
Luck, James T.   1953-1956
Luper, Albert   1932-1935
Lyon, Ruth Mulkey   1942-1946
Lytton, Nona   1920-1922
McBeth, H. Leon   1962-
McCoy, Lee H.   1955-1965
McGarity, Mrs. William   1926-1933
MacGorman, J. W.   1948-
McIver, Mrs. John A.   1921-1922
McKinney, B. B.   1919-1931
McKinney, Elizabeth R.   1967-
McKinney, James C.   1950-
McMahan, Monte Lee   1955-1957
McMillon, J. O.   1926-1927
McNeely, Edwin M.   1920-1963
McNeely, Wayne   1919-1956
McNew, George Jefferson   1910-1912
                             1915-1916
Malek, Michael Paul   1977-1979
Mantey, Julius R.   1920-1922
Marsh, Gerald E.   1969-
Marsh, James Leon   1956-
Maston, Mrs. Essie M.   1925-1926
Maston, T. B.   1922-1963
Means, Frank Kester   1939-1946
Medsker, P. H.   1923-1931
Melton, Alpha W. M.   1945-1971
Miller, Helen   1931-1934

Miller, May   1927-1930
Mitchell, Bertha   1920-1926
Mitchell, Ruth   1929-1932
Moore, W. B.   1921-1930
Morris, Hazel M.   1971-
Moseley, Hazel   1946-1948
Munn, G. Lacoste   1959-
Murphree, C. W.   1920-1921
Myers, Lewis A.   1924-1932
Nelson, Jimmie L.   1972-
Nettles, Thomas J.   1976-
Newman, Albert H.   1908-1913
Newman, Mrs. Mary A.   1910
Newman, Stewart A.   1936-1952
Newport, John P.   1952-1976
                             1979-
Newton, Tillman T.   1940-1942
Northcutt, Jesse J.   1939-1945
                             1950-
Oaks, Mrs. W. H.   1944-1945
Parks, Alva G.   1973-
Patterson, Farrar   1969-
Pearce, Mrs. Ora Belle   1949-1950
Penick, I. N.   1919-1922
Phelps, Ralph Arloe   1948-1953
Phillips, Evelyn M.   1948-1952
                             1967-
Phillips, Robert   1980-
Pinson, Williams M., Jr.   1963-1975
Potts, Donald   1959-1960
Pratt, Eugene T.   1962-1965
Price, John M., Sr.   1915-1956
Privette, Jerry   1980-
Prosser, Ira C.   1934-1936
Pruett, Ammie   1938-1940
Pylant, Agnes D.   1928-
Pylant, Lake   1931-1932
Raus, Robert P.   1980-
Ray, Jefferson Davis   1908-1944
Reaves, Mrs. A. W.   1920-1921
Redford, S. Courts   1926-1927
Reeve, James J.   1908-1913
Reynolds,
   Isham Emmanuel   1915-1945
Reynolds, Mrs. Isham E.   1919-1921
                             1932-1957
Reynolds, William J.   1981-
Riggs, R. S.   1920-1921
Rogers, James S., Sr.   1919-1921

Rogers, Velna	1921-1922	Wall, Woodrow W.	1950-1955
Roper, Cecil M.	1960-	Watkins, Derrel R.	1974-
Rossell, William H.	1954-1964	Weatherspoon, Jesse B.	1913-1918
Rowan, Eileen	1921-1922	Webb, Lottie	1925-1926
Scarborough, Lee R.	1908-1942	White, Mrs. Bessie	1920-1921
Scudder, Cleo Wayne	1954-1975	White, Cecil Ray	1970-1979
Seelig, Virginia G.	1958-	White, William R.	1923-27
Segler, Franklin M.	1951-1972	Williams, Charles B.	1908-1919
Sego, Charles M.	1957-1963	Williams, James D.	1964-
Shelton, Jo Ann	1956-1965	Williamson, S. Charles	1955-
Sheppard, Mrs. Minnie R.	1933-1934	Wilson, George R., Jr.	1973-1978
Shinn, Mrs. Harris	1947-1949	Wood, Rose	1934-1935
Sibley, Zula	1924-1925	Woodall, Sulu	1920-1924
Sims, Phillip Weir	1967-	Woodfin, Yandall C.	1960-1967
Singleton, Dovie	1920-1922		1973-
Sipes, Leonidus M.	1919-1921	Woods, John E.	1957-1967
Slawson, Colonel	1921-1923	Work, W. James	1921-1922
Sloan, Robert B.	1980-	Wray, J. Campbell	1944-1956
Smith, Ebbie C.	1975-	Yarborough, W. F., Jr.	1922-1926
Smith, Lucille	1923-1924	Yount, William R.	1981-
Smith, Marjorie	1923-1924		
Smith, Ralph L.	1949-		
Smith, William A.	1979-		
Sowell, Janie	1927-1929		
Starnes, Nane	1931-1932		
Starr, Jewell	1934-1935		
Stovall, Frank D., III	1957-		
Summers, Ray	1938-1959		
Tatum, Mattie Lou	1922-1924		
Tatum, Scott L.	1975-		
Taylor, William C.	1913-1916		
Terry, Jack D., Jr.	1969-		
Thompson, Sara V.	1945-1966		
Thompson, W. Oscar	1976-1980		
Tidwell, Charles A.	1965-		
Tillman, William M., Jr.	1981-		
Tolar, William B.	1967-		
Travis, Albert L.	1977-		
Trentham, Charles A.	1947-1952		
Tupper, Mary C.	1914-1915		
Turner, Leota	1915-1919		
Turner, Wilmer L.	1976-1978		
Urrey, Thomas C.	1963-		
Vardaman, Ephraim J.	1955-1960		
Vaughan, W. Curtis	1950-		
Venting, Albert	1921-1937		
Walker, Larry L.	1967-1980		
Walker, Ruby	1914-1915		
Walker, Wayne	1920-1921		

Reference and Assistant Librarians

(1944-1982)

Rowena R. Strickland	1944-1948
Charles P. Johnson	1947-1957
Keith C. Wills	1957-1958
Lewis Wingo	1958-1960
William P. Greenlee	1960-1966
Richard E. Traylor	1966-1967 (acting)
M. Douglas Ezell	1967-1968
Cecil R. White	1968-1970 (acting) 1970-1980
Robert L. Phillips	1980-

Editors of the *Southwestern News*

T. B. Maston	March 1943-September 1947
Ralph Churchill	October 1947-September 1956
Arch McMillan	October 1956-April 1957
David K. Morris	May 1957-September 1958
William Moyers	October 1958-February 1960
John Seelig	March 1960-present

Managing Editors of the *Southwestern Journal of Theology*

Charles B. Williams	1917-1919
W. T. Conner	1919-1923
H. E. Dana	1923-1924
(Not published 1924-1958)	
James Leo Garrett, Jr.	1958-1959
Gordon Clinard	1960-1963
W. R. Estep, Jr.	1963-1967
William L. Hendricks	1967-1971
Leon McBeth	1971-1975
F. B. Huey, Jr.	1975-1977
Bert B. Dominy	1978-1980
James A. Brooks	1980-1983

Presidents of the Convention-wide Alumni Association Beginning with 1940

Ralph R. Moore (Th.D., '39) 1940
Kearnie Keegan (Th.M., '33) 1942
W. R. White (Th.M., '22; Th.D., '25) 1946
J. D. Grey (Th.M., '32) 1948
W. Perry Crouch (Th.M., '32) 1951
James A. Howard (Ex, '30) 1952
Stanley E. Wilkies (Th.M., '38) 1953
Brooks H. Wester (Th.M., '41) 1956
J. C. Segler (Th.B., '44) 1958
Enoch C. Brown (Ex, '35) 1960
Homer G. Lindsay, Sr. (Th.M., '30) 1962
Rheubin L. South (B.D., '50; M.Div., '73) 1964
Hugh Bumpas (Th.M., '33) 1965
James S. Riley (Th.M., '47; Th.D., '55) 1966
Joseph B. Flowers (Th.M., '33) 1967
Warren C. Hultgren (B.D., '50) 1968
Gerald Martin (B.D., '49) 1969
Olan Runnels (B.D., '56; Th.D., '62) 1970
Ramsey Pollard (Ex, '38) 1971
Jesse Fletcher (B.D., '56; Th.D., '58;
    M.Div., '73; Ph.D., '75) 1972
Joe Burnette (M.R.E., '46) 1973
James G. Harris (M.R.E., '39; Th.M., '39) 1974
R. H. Dilday (B.D., '55; Th.D., '60) 1975
Lavonn Brown (B.D., '58; Th.D., '64) 1976
Cecil Sherman (B.D., '53; Th.D., '60) 1977
Frank Pollard (B.D., '59) 1978
Richard Jackson (B.D., '63) 1979
D. L. Lowrie (B.D., '62) 1980
Charles Fuller (B.D., '57) 1981
Robert O. Feather (M.R.E., '53) 1982

Distinguished Alumni Awards

1964

Baker James Cauthen
J. D. Grey
W. L. Howse
Robert E. Naylor
S. Courts Redford
W. R. White

1965

James H. Landes
T. B. Maston
Albert McClellan
Ralph A. Phelps, Jr.
Paul M. Stevens
Robert P. Taylor

1966

E. Leslie Carlson
Charles C. Culpepper, Sr.
L. R. Elliott
William Ramsey Pollard

1967

Floy M. Barnard
Edwin McNeely
Thomas A. Patterson

1968

Robert A. Baker
Arthur B. Rutledge
Ray L. Summers

1969

A. D. Foreman, Jr.
Roland P. Hood
Jesse J. Northcutt

1970

Foy Valentine
Frank W. Patterson
Homer Lindsay, Sr.

1971

Joe Davis Heacock
Agnes D. Pylant
Frank K. Means

1972

Enoch C. Brown
Herbert Caudill
Buford L. Nichols

1973

James E. Coggin
C. Wade Freeman
Darold Morgan

1974

Shervert H. Frazier
Warren Hultgren
W. Fred Swank

1975

Milton U. Ferguson
Bill D. Moyers
William J. Reynolds

1976

Perry Crouch
William G. Tanner
M. E. Williamson

1977

A. Donald Bell
Philip B. Harris
Mrs. Robert E. Naylor

1978

Jesse C. Fletcher
Helen Bagby Harrison
Cecil Ray

1979

Russell H. Dilday, Jr.
W. Randall Lolley
William Pinson

1980

Jimmy Allen
S. M. Lockridge
R. Keith Parks

1981

W. Curtis Vaughan
Jaroy Weber
Eula Mae Henderson

1982

Huber L. Drumwright, Jr.
Lucille Freeman Glasscock
Boyd Hunt
Clyde Merrill Maguire
Lucille Loyd Meadows

Resident Enrollment
and Graduates

1908-1982

The following table, taken from the records of the Registrar, shows the number of men and women enrolled for the entire period. The three separate schools were developed in 1920-21, and since that time the statistics show the enrollment in each. However, the total number of students will not equal the total of the three schools in the years from 1921 to 1955 because some students enrolled in more than one school at a time. Beginning with 1956 these duplications were allocated to one of the three schools, so the total number of students shown since that time will equal the sum of the enrollments in the three schools. The Missionary Training School was merged into the three schools in 1935, so there are no separate enrollment statistics for this unit after that year.

Year	Men	Women	Miss. Tr. School	School of Theology	School of Rel. Ed.	School of Music	Total Enrol.	Graduates
1908	189	26	26	189			215	21
1909	148	33	33	148			181	9
1910	171	30	30	171			201	15
1911	91	35	35	91			126	18
1912	114	51	51	114			165	33
1913	127	60	60	127			187	32
1914	133	75	75	133			208	36
1915	120	67	64	123			187	49
1916	169	112	112	169			281	39
1917	202	135	135	202			337	38
1918	212	138	138	212			350	43
1919	181	180	180	181			361	58
1920	285	250	250	285			535	61
1921	357	334	185	255	88	163	691	86
1922	406	390	159	301	138	228	796	99
1923	378	397	156	289	157	186	775	101
1924	333	316	84	278	137	156	649	125
1925	320	267	66	282	109	122	587	114
1926	367	301	81	276	122	170	668	86
1927	327	291	61	246	150	182	618	79
1928	305	234	40	201	131	166	539	61
1929	309	230	35	215	142	161	539	78
1930	293	235	40	224	143	135	528	76
1931	239	176	38	197	116	70	415	61
1932	194	159	30	170	99	61	353	61
1933	189	152	32	167	93	63	341	66
1934	214	162	30	151	109	64	376	36
1935	207	165	35	194	109	51	372	53

Year	Men	Women	Miss. Tr. School	School of Theology	School of Rel. Ed.	School of Music	Total Enrol.	Graduates
1936	252	188		237	148	80	440	45
1937	339	222		323	192	95	561	53
1938	376	240		313	213	100	616	63
1939	388	269		353	278	77	657	68
1940	437	328		394	344	90	765	133
1941	460	327		407	334,	114	787	130
1942	468	292		418	307	108	760	131
1943	442	292		447	252	80	734	90
1944	570	363		560	335	79	933	120
1945	632	442		641	393	85	1074	182
1946	730	465		685	486	111	1195	190
1947	853	523		694	607	201	1376	253
1948	902	540		695	665	210	1442	292
1949	971	484		750	617	201	1455	323
1950	1146	557		914	701	177	1703	314
1951	1376	520		1082	744	163	1896	367
1952	1562	512		1276	731	137	2074	374
1953	1649	511		1354	749	124	2160	469
1954	1721	583		1399	853	104	2304	481
1955	1826	549		1448	821	106	2375	471
1956	1878	536		1461	834	119	2414	490
1957	1849	562		1451	848	112	2411	482
1958	1956	515		1492	845	134	2471	461
1959	1900	495		1432	810	153	2395	427
1960	1925	469		1427	810	157	2394	439
1961	1878	402		1361	772	147	2280	488
1962	1735	332		1270	646	151	2067	460
1963	1716	340		1266	643	147	2056	447
1964	1711	320		1249	634	148	2031	426
1965	1638	326		1196	620	148	1964	417
1966	1595	316		1181	566	164	1911	402
1967	1546	313		1159	549	151	1859	350
1968	1622	304		1193	564	169	1926	381
1969	1708	328		1236	610	190	2036	383
1970	1823	273		1314	570	212	2096	405
1971	1883	288		1384	577	210	2171	416
1972	1970	325		1473	590	232	2295	455
1973	2054	352		1510	643	253	2406	489
1974	2235	387		1592	746	284	2622	543
1975	2432	426		1709	817	332	2858	562
1976	2968	502		2049	1049	372	3470	615
1977	3233	618		2246	1221	384	3851	688
1978	3460	676		2425	1345	366	4136	795
1979	3461	693		2374	1402	378	4154	769
1980	3587	749		2436	1501	399	4336	863
1981	3642	770		2467	1535	410	4412	880
1982	3792	813		2610	1588	407	4605	873

Presidents of
Seminary Woman's Club

1927-82

Scarborough, Mrs. L. R.	1927-1928	Guy, Mrs. R. Cal	1955-1956
Elliott, Mrs. L. R.	1928-1929	Heacock, Mrs. Joe Davis	1956-1957
Reynolds, Mrs. I. E.	1929-1930	Johnson, Mrs. Charles	1957-1958
Hancock, Mrs. W. A.	1930-1931	Harris, Mrs. Philip	1958
McNeely, Mrs. Edwin	1931-1932	McCoy, Mrs. Lee	1958-1959
Scarborough, Mrs. Lawrence	1932-1933	McKinney, Mrs. James	1959-1960
Miller, Miss Georgia	1933-1935	Evans, Mrs. Wayne	1960-1961
Ray, Mrs. H. C.	1935-1936	Gray, Mrs. L. Jack	1961-1962
Crowder, Mrs. J. W.	1936-1937	Drumwright, Mrs. Huber	1962-1963
Gammill, Miss Vinnie	1937-1938	Woodfin, Mrs. Yandall	1963-1964
Bruner, Mrs. J. W.	1938-1939	Roper, Mrs. Cecil	1964-1965
Carlson, Mrs. E. L.	1939-1940	Vaughan, Mrs. Curtis	1965-1966
Daniel, Mrs. R. T.	1940-1941	Hunt, Mrs. T. W.	1966-1967
Elliott, Mrs. L. R.	1941-1942	Pinson, Mrs. William	1967-1968
Newman, Mrs. S. A.	1942-1943	Tolar, Mrs. William	1968-1969
Waldrop, Mrs. F. H.	1943-1944	Gresham, Mrs. Felix	1969-1970
Maston, Mrs. T. B.	1944-1945	Huey, Mrs. F. B.	1970-1971
Head, Mrs. E. D.	1945-1946	Gray, Mrs. Scotty W.	1971-1972
Strickland, Miss Rowena	1946-1947	Terry, Mrs. Jack D.	1972-1973
Summers, Mrs. Ray	1947-1948	Guy, Mrs. R. Cal	1973-1974
Thompson, Miss Sara	1948-1949	Hunt, Mrs. Boyd	1974-1975
Thornton, Mrs. D. A.	1949-1950	Williams, Mrs. James	1975-1976
Ray, Mrs. Jeff D. (Georgia		Munn, Mrs. Lacoste	1976-1977
Miller)	1950-1951	Fasol, Mrs. Al	1977-1978
McNeely, Mrs. Edwin	1951-1952	Anderson, Mrs. Justice	1978-1979
Brown, Mrs. H. C.	1952-1953	Freeman, Mrs. Harold	1979-1980
Baker, Mrs. Robert A.	1953-1954	Dominy, Mrs. Bert B.	1980-1981
Feather, Mrs. R. Othal	1954-1955	Tidwell, Mrs. Charles	1981-1982
Segler, Mrs. Franklin	1955	Brister, Mrs. C. W.	1982-1983

Index

A

Accreditation, 270, 309-11, 377, 387-88
Adams, Bobby E., 397
Adams, Luther, 245
Advisory Council, 349-50, 502-505
Alexander, C. T., 197, 494
Allbright, W. T. 63
Alldredge, E. P., 494
Allen, Mrs. Andrew Q., 389
Allen, Jimmy, 475, 514
Allen, J. S., 63
Allen, Lyman Smith, 494
Alumni activities, 425-27
Alumni Convention-wide presidents, 512
American Baptist Home Mission Society, 27-29, 84-86
American Baptist Publication Society, 86-87
Anderson, Cecil O., 494
Anderson, Justice C., 397, 460, 466
Anderson, Mrs. Justice C., 517
Andrews, M. T., 222
Andrews, Reddin, 49
Andrews, S. P., 33
Appleby, David P., 402-3
Arnold, Major R. A., 152
Articles of Faith, 483-87
Ashcraft, Charles H., 494
Ashley, Charles W., 401
Atwood, E. B., 494
Aulick, A. L., 494
Ausmus, Charles, 494
Austin, Lou Ella, 206
Autrey, C. E., 335, 355

B

Baergen, Darrel, 450, 476
Baggott, Robert T., Jr., 494
Bailey, J. W., 95, 116-17, 124
Baines, George W., 40-41, 131, 136

Baker, Don, 494
Baker, Fredona M., xvi, 517
Baker, Jeroline, 400, 407
Baker, J. W., 494
Baker, Robert A., 264, 310, 457, 459, 513
Ball, Charles T., 164, 176, 181, 203-4, 207, 211-13
Baptist Bible Institute, 236, 262
Baptist Book Store, 471
Baptist Education Study Task, 384
Baptist General Association of Texas, 48, 78-79
Baptist General Convention of Texas, 79, 91, 111, 124, 130-31, 135, 168, 201-2, 225-26, 227-28, 247, 272, 351
Baptist Hundred Thousand Club, 257-59, 289
Baptist Religious Society of Charleston, 28
Baptist Student Missionary movement, 211-12
Baptist Women Mission Workers of Texas (later Woman's Missionary Union of Texas), 170-71
Baptist Young People's Union, Auxiliary to Southern Baptist Convention, 87
Baptist Young People's Union of America, 87
Barclay, William, 246, 308, 403
Barker, Emma Jean, 389
Barker, R. O., 494
Barker, Trozy, 389
Barnard, Floy M., 246, 265, 307, 401, 513
Barnes, William Wright, 137, 160, 173, 181-82, 206, 209-12, 222-23, 245, 265, 301, 305-6, 311
Barnett, Somers, 314

Barrett, Robert N., 116, 118
Barrick, C. R., 494
Barry, John A., 306
Barton, A. J., 67, 73, 131-32, 135, 136-37, 148, 150, 154
Basden, Jeter, 450
Bass, Claude L., 402
Bass, H. C., 494
Bastion, Carol, 496
Baten, A. E., 135-36
Bayless, O. L., 494
Baylor Female College, 103, 112
Baylor, R. E. B., 27, 29, 31-33, 42-43
Baylor Theological Seminary, 119-33, 139
Baylor University at Independence, 34-37, 39-46, 48, 57-8, 79, 111-33
Baylor University at Waco, 48-49, 259-62
Bays, Joseph, 27
Beasley, Pat Neff, 494
Beddoe, Mrs. A. F., 215
Bell, A. Donald, 307, 400, 402, 514
Bell, Ellen, 64
Bell, Jean, xvi
Bellinger, William H., Jr., 457
Bennett, Mr. and Mrs. Carlyle, 265
Bennett, S. H., 494
Bennett, Thomas Miles, 306, 399
Bentley, Sarah, 451
Berry, Don, 494
Berry Field, 393
Berry, Kendall, 393
Bible Department at Baylor University, 104-5, 114
Bickerstaff, Mina, xvi
Bigbee, Jess, xvi
Bishop, Ivyloy, 265
Blake, Amanda, 153
Blanton, Matt, 151

Bledsoe, Joseph, 29
Bolton, Cecil, 308
Boone, Bess, xvi
Boone, George H., 165
Boone, J. P., Jr., 131
Boone, Joseph, 494
Bottoms Chair of Missions, 460
Bottoms, George and Ida, 239, 254
Bowers, R. G., 494
Bowles, Ed Brooks, 494
Boyce, James P., 96, 133, 155, 198-99
Brackney, Bob W., 458
Bradford, Ann Laura, 307, 401, 407
Bragg, B. F., 495
Brann, W. C., 99-100
Bratton, Terry L., 451
Breithaupt, Frank E., 495
Brice, J. W., 131
Bridges, Tommy L., 401
Briggs, Philip H., 401
Brisco, Thomas V., 457
Brister, C. W., 335
Brister, Mrs. C. W., 517
Broadman Bible Commentary, The, 395
Broadus, John A., 96, 124, 133, 155, 199
Brooker, Alice, 215
Brooks, James A., 397, 511
Brooks, S. P., 73, 75, 117-18, 121, 127-35
Brown, Archie E., 495
Brown, E. C., 495, 512-13
Brown, F. F., 495
Brown, George F., 495
Brown, H. C., Jr., 306, 398
Brown, Mrs. H. C. Jr., 517
Brown, Lavon, 512
Brown, L. Sarle, 403
Brown University, 28
Bruner, J. W., 255, 349
Bruner, Mrs. J. W., 517
Bryan, Robert T., 234
Bryant, James R., 395
Bryant, James W., 395
Buck, W. C., 48
Buchanan, John H., 495
Buckner Orphans Home, 78
Buckner, R. C., 127, 131, 138
Buhrman, Mr. and Mrs. W. J., 273
Bullard, G. W., 495
Bumpas, Hugh, 512

Bumpas, Mrs. H. R., 265
Burch, Vella Jane, 265, 363
Burke, J. L., 395
Burleson College, 112
Burleson, Rufus C., 35, 38-40, 47, 57, 64, 66-67, 78, 97-98, 117
Burnette, Joe E., 495, 512
Burns, W. A., 495
Burroughs, Prince E., 136, 146-48, 150, 154
Burrows, Lansing, 84
Burt, R. E., 215
Burt, Mrs. R. E., 215
Burton, R. L., 335
Burts, C. E., 495
Bush, L. Russ, 397
Butler, E. G., 495
Butt, Howard E., Jr., 374, 495
Byars, N. T., 33
Byars, Mrs. J. W., 203, 235
Byrd, J. E., 495

C

Caldwell, William G., 401
Campbellism, 31-32
Campbell, R. C., 495
Campbell, S. H., 495
Carleton, J. Paul, 495
Carleton, W. A., 495
Carlson, E. L., 214, 234, 245, 357-58, 513
Carlson, Mrs. E. L., 517
Carnes, C. S., 245, 252
Carnett, Ellis L., 204, 235, 246, 265, 307-8, 329
Carpenter, William Carl, Jr., 495
Carroll, Andrew Fuller, 58-59
Carroll, B. H., 23-25, 48-49, 53-183, 197-200, 220, 277, 477
Carroll, B. H., Founders Award, 452
Carroll, B. H., Memorial Building, 452
Carroll, George, 113
Carroll, James M., 37, 55, 58-59, 63, 103-5, 111-13, 131, 135, 136, 272
Carroll, Laben, 59-60
Carroll Park Apartments, 391, 393
Carter, James E., 445, 453-4
Carter, Mr. and Mrs. T. W., 251, 273
Casey, David C., 374

Cassidy, "Butch," 153
Caudill, Herbert, 513
Cauthen, Baker James, xvi, 264, 477, 513
Caver, Mary Ellen, 265
Center for Christian Communication Studies, 475-76
Chaffin, Floyd, 495
Chafin, Kenneth, 355, 397, 399, 453, 495
Chancellor, W. W., 495
Cheek, J. Frank, 265
Cheek, Mrs. J. S., 164, 173
Chrisman, Oswin, 374, 376, 395
Christian, John T., 87
Christian Workers Manual School, 268
Churchill, Ralph D., 303, 307, 311, 314, 401, 511
Clark, Carl A., xvi, 335, 351, 399
Clark, George, 163
Clark, Horace, 39-40
Clark, J. Kenneth, xvi
Clayton, Lynn P., 495
Claypool, Mrs. R. H., 215
Clendinning, B. A. "Pat," Jr., 458
Clinard, Gordon, 335, 398
Coggin, James E., 376, 453
Coke, Richard, 65, 72
Coldiron, Jack, xv, 402
Cole, M., 63
Coleman, C. C., 495
Coleman, Robert O., 397, 457
Collier, J. P., 495
Collins, L. L., 390
Colson, William W., 402
Committee on Southwestern history, xv
Compere, J. S., 495
Conley, David L., 402, 458
Connell, G. H., 148, 154, 179-80
Conner, Walter Thomas, 139, 145, 209-11, 223, 234, 236, 245, 286-87, 304-5
Conner, Walter Thomas, Award, 352
Continuing Education, 410-12, 463-65
Cooper, Davis L., 495
Cooper, J. Dan, 495
Cooper, Kenneth H., 392-93

Cooper, Oscar H., 102, 115
Cooperative Program, 247-48,
251-52, 289, 339-41, 383 ff,
424
Copass, B. A., 203, 245,
274, 287, 306
Copeland, Phillip T., 451
Corley, R. Bruce, 397
Cornelius, R. H., 173
Cornett, R. Orin, 379
Correlated Texas Baptist
school system, 201-2
Covey, Homer, 344, 495
Covington, W. E., 495
Cowden, G. E., 148, 239,
249, 496
Cowden, G. E., Jr., 496
Cowden, Mrs. G. E., 249
Cowden, J. M., 496
Cowden, W. H., 113
Cox, Norman W., 496
Cox, T. W., 31-32
Craig, Earl H., Jr., 496
Craig, W. Marshall, 496
Crane, William Carey, 41, 79
Cranfill, J. B., 58, 90, 111,
113, 136, 150, 158, 214,
496
Cranford, Lorin L., 397
Crawford, T. P., 81-82
Crawford, W. Edwin, xvi,
389, 496
Creath, J. W. D., 36
Crittenden, T. K., 56
Crotts, William P., 496
Crouch, Austin, 250, 496
Crouch, H. H., 121
Crouch, J. P., 136, 150, 496
Crouch, Perry, 286-7, 512-13
Crowder, J. W., 74, 111,
144-45, 165, 181, 202,
204, 207, 211, 213, 235-6,
245, 304, 352
Crowder, Mrs. J. W., 517
Crowley, A. F., 496
Crutcher, G. H., 496
Culp, Raymond, 205
Cumbie, W. J., 496
Cunningham, Milton, 496
Curtis, Richard, 26
Culpepper, Charles C., Sr.,
513

D
D'Amico, David F., 397, 400
Dana, Harvey Eugene, 204,
213-14, 234, 236, 245,
263-64
Dancer, Asael, 31
Daniel, C. W., 131, 135, 136,
178
Daniel, J. P., 496
Daniel, James, 307, 335
Daniel, Robert T., 264, 306
Dargan, E. C., 164
Darwin, Charles, 199
Davidson, R. L., 496
Davidson, Vernon and
Jeanette Professorship of
Missions, 459
Davis, Harlan, 389
Davis, Mrs. F. S., 215
Davis, William Mac, 458
Dawson, J. M., 115, 132, 496
Dawson, William, 314
Day, Clayton E., 389
Day, Gladys, 403
Day, James S., 496
Day, Morris E., 314
Dean, Clark, 401
Dean, T. W., 335, 403
Decatur College, 111-12
DeMent, B. H., 118
Dennis, Weldon, 348
Denson, W. B., 131
Department of English Bible
discontinued, 213, 234
Dickinson, Herbert, 496
Dilday, Russell H., xiv, xvi,
445-78, 512, 513
Dill, Harold T., 400
Distinguished Alumni
Awards, 426, 513-14
Distinguished Professor
Rank, 458-59
Divers, Frank, 496
Dixon, A. C., 200
Dobbins, Gaines S., 254-55
Dodd, M. E., 496
Dominy, Bert B., 397, 510
Dominy, Mrs. Bert B., 517
Doolan, L. W., 118, 127
Dorian, Gordon, 496
Douglass, Robert S., 335,
459
Dow, Samuel, 222
Dowell, Theodore, H., 401,
460
Drakeford, John W., 335,
410, 460
Drummond, N. R., 235
Drumwright, Huber L., Jr.,
306, 396-97, 458, 514
Drumwright, Mrs. Huber L.,

Jr., 517
Dunlap, E. D., 496
Durham, J. H., 496

E
Eakins, Joan, 451
Eaton, T. T., 88 ff, 94
Eaves, James, 397, 459
Eby, Frederick, 33, 97, 125,
205
Ecton, T. C., 496
Edwards, C. V., 211, 220
Edwards, F. M., 139
Eight-by-Eighty Campaign,
423-24, 472
Elder, Lloyd, 448, 451, 454,
467
Elliott, Leslie R., 235-36,
245, 268, 271-2, 288,
315-16, 335-36, 353
Elliott, Mrs. Leslie R., 265,
517
Elliott, Ralph, 394
Ellis, Richard, 33, 35
Elrod, Ben, 496
Ely, Virginia, 265
End of Texas Baptist seminary
control, 236 ff
Endowed chairs and
professorships, 380
Enrollment, 1908-82, 515-16
Entzminger, Louis, 496
Estep, William R., Jr., 335
Estes, W. O., 496
Eure, Otho A., 496
Evans, Ellis B., 496
Evans, Mrs. Perry, 348
Evans, Wayne, xv, xvi, 356,
375-78, 381, 447-49, 454
Evans, Mrs. Wayne, 517
Evenson, Darrell, 496
Executive Committee,
Southern Baptist
Convention, 247-49,
250-59, 290, 383-86
Ezell, Douglas, 397, 458, 510

F
Faculty benefits, 209, 296,
338-9, 378, 387-88, 460
Faculty Council, 233-34,
301-2
Faculty portraits, 269-70, 277
Faculty members since 1908,
506-509
Fant, Clyde J., 397, 400
Farquhar, J. L., 33, 36

Farrar, Charles William, 496
Fasol, Al, 397
Fasol, Mrs. Al, 517
Faulkner, Melvin G., 496
Feather, R. Othal, 307, 311,
  401
Feather, Mrs. R. Othal, 517
Feather, Robert O., 512
Feezor, Forrest, 496
Ferguson, Milton U., 335,
  397, 400, 513
Ferguson, Mr. and Mrs. Ted
  L., 349-50, 452
Field, Glenn, 496
Fiftieth anniversary of
  seminary, 357
First Baptist association in
  Texas, 32
First Baptist Church, Dallas,
  78
First Baptist Church, Waco,
  67-70, 71-75, 105
First Great Awakening, 25-30
Fish, Roy J., 397, 459
Fite, J. David, 397, 410-12,
  463-65
Fleming Hall, 452
Fleming Library, 315-16,
  341-42, 352-53, 415-16
Fleming, William, 291-2,
  295, 315-16, 329, 349,
  356, 374-75, 378, 496
Fleming, Mrs. Bessie
  (William), 356, 392
Fletcher, Jesse, 512, 514
Flint, Charles, 308
Flowers, J. B., 496, 512
Ford, LeRoy, 401, 413-14
Foreman, A. D., 496
Formula for seminary support
  by Southern Baptist
  Convention, 339-41,
  383-86
Forward Program of Church
  Finances, 382
Frazier, S. H., 513
Freeman, C. Wade, 513
Freeman, Harold V., 397
Freeman, Mrs. Harold V., 517
Friends of the Seminary, 294
Frost, J. M., 175, 204, 205
Fuqua, W. H., 496
Furman, Richard, 28

G
Gaddy, J. M., 177
Gage ———, 63

Gambrell, J. B., 102, 119,
  126, 128, 131, 135-37, 139,
  154, 158, 172, 203,
  216-27, 234-35, 272
Gambrell Street Baptist
  Church, 211, 225, 266
Gammill, Vinnie, 235, 245,
  308
Gardner, David M., 497
Garland, D. David, 397, 405
Garrett, Hosea, 33
Garrett, James Leo, xv, 306,
  338, 399, 457
Garrett, Jenkins, 374, 378
Garrett, Myrta Ann, xvi, 469,
  517
Gary, Raymond, 374
Gaston, George H., 457
Gates, I. E., 132, 142
General Missionary
  Convention of the Baptist
  Denomination, 27
George, J. Thurmond, 371
Gibson, Louis, 374, 376
Gideon, Virtus E., 335
Gill, George, 27
Gillis, Carroll, 265
Gillis, Don, 312
Gillon, R. L., 497
Glisson, Jerry L., xvi
Golden Gate Baptist
  Theological Seminary, 382
Golden Jubilee Expansion
  Campaign, 343-44
Goodspeed, Calvin, 123,
  144-45
Gordon, Jack, 390
Gospel Mission movement,
  81-82
Gospel Music School, 212,
  231-32
Graham, Billy, 477
Graham, Finley M., 355
Graham, Ray L., 374, 376,
  453
Graves, Henry L., 35, 38
Graves, J. R., 79-83, 88, 95
Gray, L. Jack, xvi, 305, 335
Gray, Scotty W., 402, 459
Gray, Mrs. Scotty W., 517
Green, Paul, 335, 403
Greenfield, Guy, 457
Greenlee, William P., 510
Gregory, A. P., 497
Gregory, Joel C., 457
Gresham, Felix, 377, 393,
  448, 450

Gresham, Mrs. Felix, 517
Grey, J. D., 512, 513
Griffin, Marvin C., 353
Griffin, Roy, 314
Grigg, Arthur, 497
Groner, Frank S., 162
Gross, J. L., 131
Guinn, G. Earl, 306
Guy, Cal, xvi, 306, 310, 457
Guy, Daniel W., 497
Guy, R. E., 160, 497

H
Hacker, J. D., 497
Haldeman, John H., 497
Haley, P. E., 314
Hall, Gerald A., 497
Halsted, Gracia, 265
Hamblin, Robert L., 497
Hamlett, W. A., 497
Hancock, Mrs. W. A., 517
Hand, Stanley I., 497
Hankins, Floyd, 265
Hardee, Leon, 353
Harder, Kenneth, 469
Hardin, Mrs. A. D., 215
Hardshell Baptists, 30-32
Hargrave, William, 308
Hargrove, H. H., 497
Harmon, P. T., 497
Harrington, Fern, 314
Harris, James G., 512
Harris, Philip, 307, 514
Harris, Mrs. Philip, 517
Harris, Pinckney, 58
Harris, W. D., 136, 146, 148,
  150, 154, 156, 214-15, 273
Harris, W. M., 131
Harris, W. W., "Spurgeon,"
  58, 63
Harrison, General James, 66
Harrison, Helen Bagby, 514
Harrison, J. Wesley, Chair of
  New Testament, 380, 460
Harrison, W. B., 497
Hart, Oliver, 28
Hart, Travis, xvi
Harvell, Calvin T., 497
Hatcher, Harvey, 400, 402
Hatcher, W. E., 94
Hawkins, Earl E., 497
Hayden, S. A., 82-3, 90
Haydenism, 82
Haynes, A. G., 36
Haynes, James D., 451
Haywood, Mrs. Herbert, 164
Heacock, Joe Davis, xvi, 307,

521

337, 346, 402, 407, 513
Heacock, Mrs. Joe Davis, 517
Head, E. D., 285-319, 477
Head, Mrs. E. D., 517
Hebard, Roger, 497
Heeren, Forrest, 308
Heflin, J. L., 497
Heflin, Jay, 497
Heflin, J. N. Boo, 397
Henderson, Eula Mae, 514
Hendrick, T. G., 295
Hendricks, William L., 397, 400
Hening, B. C., 497
Henry, E. Cowden, 249
Herndon, T. V., 497
Hickman, William, 26
Hicks, J. E., 497
Hicks, R. H., 497
Hill, James C., xvi
Hill, Sam S., Jr., 497
Hilliker, F. A., 308
Hispanic Baptist Theological Seminary, 474-75
Hite, Jesse R., 497
Hobbs, Herschel H., xvi, 276-77, 292
Holcomb, James R., 451
Holcomb, T. L., 293
Holland, John, 131
Holland Lectures, 143, 209, 230
Holman, Luman W., 374, 497
Holt, A. J., 297, 356, 497
Holt, J. B., 139
Hood, Roland P., 513
Houston, Sam, 58
Howard, James A., 497, 512
Howard-Payne College, 111-12
Howard, W. F., 462
Howse, W. L., Jr., 246, 265, 336, 513
Howse, Mrs. W. L., 265
Huckins, James, 28-35, 46
Hudgins, W. Douglas, 497
Huey, F. B., 397, 511
Huey, Mrs. F. B., 517
Hultgren, Warren C., 512, 513
Hulton, H. H., 497
Humphrey, Walter, 358
Hunt, Boyd, xvi, 306, 310, 405, 514
Hunt, Mrs. Boyd, 517
Hunt, Harry B., Jr., 397
Hunt, T. W., 402, 460
Hunt, Mrs. T. W., 517

Hurt ———, 68
Huyck, A. Warren, 497

I
Impact:2000, 379, 394, 423, 470-71
Inlow, R. W., 498
Inter-Agency Council, 383-85

J
Jackson, B. M., 498
Jackson, E. Hilton, 498
Jackson, Richard, 512
James, W. E., 175
Jenkins, J. R., 38
Jenkins, R. F., 498
Jenkins, R. J., 150
Jenkins, W. H., 69, 121, 131
Jent, J. W., 143-44, 498
Jester, J. R., 498
Johnson, Charles P., 308, 353, 415, 510
Johnson, Mrs. Charles P., 517
Johnson, F. W., 136, 498
Johnson, J. L., 498
Johnson, Mrs. W. A., 245, 266, 307
Joiner, T. D., 136, 498
Jones, Carter Helm, 498
Jones, George W., 498
Jones, Mrs. Orabelle, 265
Jones, Phillip A., 498
Josey, John, 265

K
Keegan, G. Kearney, 292, 512
Keith, C. David, 458-59
Keith, Jones, 498
Kelm, George L., 457, 461
Kendall, W. B., 131
Kent, Dan G., 457
Kerfoot, F. H., 89, 95
Kimbrough, Mrs. W. E., 235, 245
King, C. M., 173, 245, 268, 295, 298, 308
King, A. Joseph, 402, 460
King, Sue Biggs, 458
Kirkpatrick, Jerry A., 498
Kirkpatrick, W. David, 457
Kiwiet, John J., 397
Klempnauer, Lawrence R., 467
Knight, W. H., 203-4, 213, 263, 498
Knowlton, Gracie, 307, 401-2
Kokernot, Herbert L., 113,

136, 273, 498
Kunce, George H., 498

L
Lambert, Mrs. W. R., 265
Landes, James H., 313
Landmarkism, 79-83
Lane, Tidence, 26
Laseter, Anne, 265
Lattimore, O. S., 148, 150, 215, 273, 498
Lattimore, Mrs. O. S., 148
Lattimore, W. C., 131
Lawrence, J. B., 498
Lea, Thomas D., 457
Leitch, James R., 347, 381, 391
Lewis, Gladys S., 374, 376, 453
Library, 163, 210, 315-16
Library, reference librarians and assistants since 1944, 510
Lile, Mrs. Alma W., 173, 203
Lilly, Kenneth E., 498
Lundquist, Hugo T., 498
Lindsay, Homer H. Jr., 498
Linebery, Evelyn, xvi
Literary societies at seminary, 210
Littleton, D. W., 498
Liverman, Aubrey, 389
Lockridge, S. M., 514
Lolley, W. Randall, 514
Long, A. J., 148, 498
Lovelace, Sandra, xvi
Lowery, Grady W., 451, 468
Lowrie, D. D., 512
Luper, Albert, 265
Luther, J. H., 98
Luther, J. T., 345, 374, 376, 378, 452, 498
Lyon, Mrs. Ruth Mulkey, 312

M
MacGorman, John W., 306, 459-60
Maddox, A. L., 498
Maddox, W. Gordon, 390, 392
Maguire, Clyde M., 514
Mahon, R. P., 498
Mantey, J. R., 214
Marriage and Family Counselling Center, 410, 460
Marsh, Gerald E., 397

Marsh, Leon, xv, xvi, 335, 408, 460
Marshall, Daniel, 26
Martin, Earl R., 457
Martin, Fred A., 498
Martin, Gerald, 512
Martin, Herbert R., 389, 451
Martin, M. T., 77
Mason, George J., 272
Mason, Henry W., Jr., 498
Masters, F. M., 498
Maston, T. B., 228, 235, 246, 264, 307, 310, 354, 398-99
Maston, Mrs. T. B., 265, 517
Matthews, C. E., 221, 297, 498
Matthews, Harlan J., 139
Maxcy, J. M., 36
McBeth, Harry Leon, 397, 511
McBride, Jerold R., 498
McCall, G. W., 154
McCart, Clara, xvi
McCart, H. C., 151, 172
McClellan, Albert, xvi, 286, 513
McConnell, F. C., 498
McConnell, F. M., 67, 70, 207, 498
McCoy, J. H., 498
McCoy, Lee, 335, 401
McCoy, Mrs. Lee, 517
McDaniel, George W., 67, 73, 76, 99, 238
McDonald, Louis N., 498
McDow, Malcolm, 457
McGarity, Mrs. W. B., 235, 265
McGavran, Donald A., 465-66
McGlamery, Harold P., 498
McGriff, E. A., 498
McIver, John A., 308
McKay, John, 498
McKinney, B. B., 204, 206, 265
McKinney, James C., 308, 337
McKinney, Mrs. James C., 458, 517
McMahon, Monte, 335
McMillan, Arch, 511
McNaughton, John N., 498
McNeely, Edwin M., 235, 246, 402-3, 513
McNeely, Mrs. Edwin, 235,

246, 337, 517
McRay, James W., 498
Meadows, Mrs. Lucille L., 514
Means, Frank K., 264, 303, 306, 309
Means, G. Z., 136, 498
Medlin, T. Shad, 498
Medsker, Paul H., 265
Melton, Mrs. Alpha, 307, 401
Memorial Building wings, 341-43
Mercer, Jesse, 28
Mercer, Silas, 28
Metochai, 268
Mexican Baptist Bible Institute, 474-75
Midwestern Baptist Theological Seminary, 383
Mikell, Miller, 268
Miller, Carey, 499
Miller, Georgia, 245, 517
Miller, R. C., 499
Millican, L. R., 136, 499
Mills, Roger Q., 72
Missions Conference for College Students, 318, 355
Mitchell, Bertha, 235, 265
Mitchell, Ruth, 265
Mitchell, Walter A., 499
Monroe, E. U., 314
Moore, N. A., 499
Moore, Ralph C., 512
Moore, W. B., 265
Moore, Walter L., 499
Morgan, Darold, 513
Morgan, Kate Durham P., xvi
Morgan, Nancy, xvi
Morrell, Z. N., 27, 29, 31-33, 42-43, 45
Morrill, D. B., 38, 46
Morris, David K., 511
Morris, Hazel M., 401, 407
Morrison, B. Ross, 499
Morrison, Cleo, 314
Moseley, Hazel, 265
Moyers, Bill D., 389, 511, 513
Mulkey, Ruth, 265
Mulkey, S. M., 499
Mullins, E. Y., 155
Munn, G. Lacoste, 397
Munn, Mrs. G. Lacoste, 517
Murray, Lois Russell, 33
Music library, 316
Musick, Thomas R., 27
Myers, Lewis A., 235-36,

265
Myers, Truett W., 451

N
Naney, Rupert E., 499
Nardin, Michael W., 499
Nash, D. R., 121
Nash, Stanton H., 451, 473
Naylor, Goldia and Robert E. Children's Building, 392
Naylor, Robert E., 356, 371-428, 446-47, 478, 513
Naylor, Robert E. Naylor Student Center, 392
Naylor, Mrs. Robert E., 371, 514
Neff, Pat M., 121
Negro students, 269, 313, 353-54
Nelson, Jimmie L., 397, 405, 459
Nelson, T. W., 499
Nettles, Thomas, 397, 458
New administrative structure, 377 ff, 393-94, 448-51
New Hope Baptist Church, 66-67
New Orleans Baptist Theological Seminary, 218
Newman, Albert Henry, 115-16, 141-42, 165-67, 171
Newman, Stewart A., 264, 306
Newman, Mrs. Stewart A., 517
Newport, John P., xvi, 306, 400, 448-50
Newton, Mrs. Tillman, 265
Nichols, Buford L., 513
Nichols, Holmes, 499
Norris, J. Frank, 144, 149-52, 154, 158, 177-81, 201, 212, 220-28, 257, 259-62, 273
Northcutt, Jesse J., xv, xvi, 264, 303, 306, 337, 377, 396, 448, 459, 513
Northcutt, Nannie Don Beaty, xvi, 389
Northen, W. J., 92

O
Oakes, Mrs. William, 265
O'Farrell, Z. C., 211
Ogg, T. Earl, 376, 499
O'Neal, Norman E., 499
Orr, Robert L., 499
Other states supporting

Southwestern before 1925, 215

Ousley, Clarence N., 147-48

P

Palmer, Wallace Blake, 499
Parker, Daniel, 30
Parker, J. Loyd, 378
Parks, Alva G., 401
Parks, R. Keith, 514
Parr, Robert, 308
Patterson, Farrar, 397
Patterson, Frank W., 513
Patterson, Thomas A., 513
Patterson, Mrs. Thomas A., 265
Paxton, Mrs. G. L., 215
Payne, C. Royce, 499
Pemberton, J. T., 223, 499
Penn, Major W. E., 68-69
Penick, I. N., 499
Penrod, W. K., 129-30, 136, 148, 150
Phelps, Ralph A., 306, 336, 513
Phillips, Evelyn Marney, 308, 402
Phillips, Robert L., 469, 510
Pilgrim Predestinarian Baptist Church, 30
Pilgrim, Thomas J., 27
Pioneer Penetration program, 468
Pinson, William M., Jr., 397, 400, 514
Pinson, Mrs. William M., 517
Pittman, C. Frank, 499
Pollard, Frank, 512
Pollard, William Ramsay, 512, 513
Pool, W. A., 499
Poole, Philip, xvi, 450
Porter, J. W., 499
Porter, S. J., 499
Posey, S. G., 499
Potts, Robert J., 499
Practical Work Department, 231
President's Club, 473
Price, John Milburn, 202, 206, 209, 245, 264, 336-37, 381
Price Hall, 293-4
Primitive Baptists, 30-32
Prior, Loyal, 499
Privette, Jerry, 458
Prosser, Ira, 265, 286

Prosser, Mrs. Ira, 265
Pulley, Dorothy, 389
Pulley, Ralph W., 374, 453
Pylant, Lake, 265
Pylant, Mrs. Lake, 265, 513

Q

Quinn, Eugene F., 499

R

Radio and Television Commission, 475-76
Ragland, George, 499
Rainey, Sue, xvi
Rains, J. E., 499
Raus, Robert P., 458
Ray, Cecil, 514
Ray, Mrs. H. C., 517
Ray, Jeff D., 53, 67, 68, 70, 82, 84-5, 99, 111, 121, 131, 139-41, 148, 150, 164, 169, 172, 181, 198, 208, 227, 234, 245, 301, 304, 352
Ray, Mrs. Jeff D. (Georgia Miller), 517
Ray, S. C., 499
Readiness for Ministry, 461
Reagan, Lucille, 229
Reagan, T. H., 314
Reavis, L. B., 343-4, 349-50, 422
Redford, Courts S., 265, 513
Reeve, J. J., 141-42, 165-67, 200
Reeves, William, 148
Reeves, Mrs. William, 148, 215
Regular Baptists, 26
Republic of Texas, 27
Reynolds, I. E., 202-3, 206, 246, 307
Reynolds, Mrs. I. E., 204, 246, 337, 517
Reynolds, W. D., 151
Reynolds, William J., 312, 458, 513
Ridgeway, Elmer, 499
Riley, James S., 499, 512
Roberts, A. Webb, 380, 477
Roberts Library, 469-70, 473
Robertson, A. T., 88-89
Robertson, B. P., 499
Rockefeller, John D., 113
Rodgers, James, 499
Rogers, Ben, xvi, 469
Rogers, James A., 204, 213-14, 499

Roper, Cecil M., 402
Roper, Mrs. Cecil M., 517
Ross, Gov. L. S., 72
Rossell, W. H., 335, 398
Rouse, William T., 144
Rowe, J. F., 121
Rusk Academy, 112
Runnels, Olan, 512
Russell, Barbara, 390, 469
Rutledge, Arthur B., 513

S

Sampey, John R., 89-90, 124, 254-55
Sandifer, J. D., 499
Scarborough, Mrs. Lawrence, 517
Scarborough, Lee Rutland, 25, 126, 139-41, 143, 145, 148-83, 197-240, 245-78, 292-3, 306, 329, 477
Scarborough, Mrs. L. R., 517
Scarborough Hall, 452
Scroll, 313
Scopes, John T., 261
Scott, D. J., 500
Scudder, C. W., 335, 400
Second Great Awakening, 25-27, 28, 30
Seale, Edwin A., 451
Seale, N. A., 131, 469
Seelig, John E., xv, xvi, 377, 381, 448-49, 472-73, 511
Seelig, Mrs. John E., 402, 422-24
Segler, Franklin M., 306, 310, 399
Segler, Mrs. Franklin M., 517
Segler, J. C., 512
Sego, Charles M., 403
Seminary charters of 1908 and 1925, 488-91
Seminary Extension Department, 207, 303
Seminary graduates, 1908-82, 515-16
Seminary Woman's Club, 270; presidents, 517
Separate Baptists, 26-28
Seventy-Five Million Campaign, 216-20, 250-58
Shamburger, Wallace, 390
Shamburger, William, 376, 500
Shelton, Jo Ann, 335
Shepherd, Minnie R., 266
Sherman, Cecil, 512

Sherwood, Arthur M., 500
Shinn, Mrs. Harris, 265
Shivers, E. B., Jr., 500
Shoemake, Earl L. and Vivian
  Gray, 460
Shurden, Walter, xvi
Simmons, Lloyd B., 500
Simpson, Leon, 500
Sims, Phillip W., xvi, 402,
  469
Singletary, Donald J., 500
Sipes, L. M., 204, 235, 500
Skaggs, Josephine, 355
Skeen, Gary D., xvi, 451
Skinner, T. Claggett, 500
Slaughter, C. C., 103, 136,
  500
Slaughter, T. Claggett, 500
Sloan, Robert B., Jr., 457
Slover, Myra K., and J. Roy,
  473
Slover Recreation/Aerobic
  Center, 473
Smalley, Freeman, 27
Smith, Abner, 31
Smith, C. M., 160, 165, 179
Smith, Ebbie C., 397
Smith, Evelyn R., xvi
Smith, Forrest, 211, 225,
  273, 500
Smith, H. Marshall, 500
Smith, J. L., 113
Smith, Ralph L., 306
Smith, Ralph M., 376, 500
Smith, Robert Carl, 458
Smith, T. B., 500
Smith, William A. "Budd,"
  458
Smith, W. J., Jr., 500
Smyth, D. I., 131, 135-36,
  148, 150, 500
Social Gospel, 199
Social Security system, 269
Solomon, E. D., 500
South, Rheubin L., 512
Southeastern Baptist
  Theological Seminary, 382
Southern Baptist Convention,
  39, 71, 77, 80-85, 87-8,
  91, 114, 216, 237-40,
  247-49, 251-63, 290-91,
  294, 337-38, 381-86, 473
Southern Baptist Theological
  Seminary, The, xvi, 23, 39,
  45, 87-96, 114, 120, 133,
  198, 205, 218, 245, 262,
  388

Southwestern Baptist
  Seminary Development
  Foundation, 378
Southwestern Evangel, The
  313
Southwestern Journal of
  Theology, 210, 236, 338;
  managing editors from
  1917-24 and 1958-82, 511
Southwestern News, 313-14;
  editors since 1943, 511
Sparks, Buren, 500
Spencer, Harry Lee, 500
Spencer, J. H., 88
Spencer, J. W., 148, 500
Spiller, E. A., 500
Spiro, Robert, 374, 500
Spirit of Southwestern,
  286-88, 316-18
Spurgeon, Charles H., 96-97,
  133, 137
Spurlock, R. C., 308
Stallings, Harry L., 500
Standifer, M. H., 121
Starnes, Nane, 265
Stearns, Shubal, 26-27
Steele, Harry W., 500
Steger, J. H., 374-76, 500
Stella Ross Awards, 268
Stephens, A. P., 500
Stephens, Bunyan, 500
Stevens, Paul M., 513
Stewart, Lyman and Milton,
  200
Stewart, Neta, 389
Stokes, Mrs. R. F., 204, 215
Storie, Steven C., 469
Storrs, Mamie, 308
Stovall, Frank D., 335
Stovall, Sara, xvi, 389, 451
Stribling, James H., 43, 46
Strickland, Floyd W., 500
Stringer, Dan C., 500
Stuckey, John R., 500
Student Affairs Division
  restructured, 462-68
Student Council, 268
Student Handbook, 313
Student organizations, 418-19
Student wives, 354, 410
Stumph, C. W., 500

T
Tandy, G. E., 151
Tanner, John S., 100-102,
  114-16, 205
Tanner, William G., 513

Tarrant County Baptist
  Association, 146-47, 164,
  220-23, 225, 227, 471
Tatum, Scott, 375, 397, 500
Taylor, J. H., 131
Taylor, James W., 376
Taylor, General Robert
  Preston, 314, 389, 422,
  513
Teem, A. E., 314
Terry, Jack D., Jr., xvi, 397
Terry, Mrs. Jack D., 517
Texas Baptist Educational
  Union, 78
Texas Baptist Education
  Commission, 103, 105,
  111-13
Texas Baptist Education
  Society, 32-33, 35-37, 42,
  44
Texas Baptist Historical
  Collection, 272, 353, 416
Texas Baptist State
  Convention, 35-36, 39, 80
Texeira, Antonio, 99-100
Theological Department at
  Baylor, 38-39, 41-42, 102,
  113-19
Thigpen, Andrew, 314
Thomas, A. Wade, 500
Thompson, Mrs. E. O., 228
Thompson, Sara, 308, 403,
  517
Thompson, W. Oscar, 397,
  458
Thornton, D. A., 235, 245,
  298, 308
Thornton, Mrs. D. A., 517
Throgmorton, W. P., 500
Thurman, Marie, 265
Tichenor, I. T., 85
Tidwell, Charles A., 380,
  400, 408
Tidwell, Mrs. Charles A., 517
Tidwell, J. B., 136, 288, 500
Tillman, William M., Jr., 457
Tinsley, Thomas, 26
Todd, Byron F., 500
Tolar, William B., 397, 458
Tolar, Mrs. William B., 517
Townsend, Mrs. E. G., 215
Toy, C. H., 96
Travis, Albert L., 402
Traylor, Richard E., 510
Trentham, Charles A., 306
Trimble, Robert, 469
Tripp, Frank, 257-59, 500

525

Truett, George W., 67, 69, 82, 98, 103, 126, 131, 135-36, 144, 150-1, 217, 240, 260, 273, 288, 292, 352
Truett Auditorium, 292-93, 452
Truett Chair of Ministry, 380, 459
Trustees, 272-73, 297-300, 356-7, 374-81, 451-55; list since 1908, 494-501
Trustee Officers, 1908-82, 492-93
Tryon, William M., 29, 32-33, 35
Tull Resolution, 262
Turner, Boyd A., 500
Turner, R. A., 500
Tupper, Mary, 173, 203

U
Unification of Texas Baptists, 78-79
Union Baptist Association, 32, 35, 49
United States Equal Opportunity Commission suit, 379, 452-53
Urrey, Thomas C., 397

V
Valentine, Foy, 513
Van Arsdale, A. B., 500
Vardaman, Jeremiah, 335
Vaughan, William Curtis, 306, 514
Vaughan, Mrs. William Curtis, 517
Venting, Albert, 234, 245, 265, 398
Vermillion, H. F., 500
Vision/85, 451, 455, 472-73

W
Waco Baptist Association, 42, 76-78
Waco University, 40-42, 47-48, 53, 72, 78-79
Wadley, J. K., 273
Waldrop, Mrs. F. H., 235, 308, 517
Walker, Crumpton, 501
Walker, J. A., 113

Walker, Larry L., 397, 457-58
Walker, L. M., 501
Wall, Broadus, 501
Wall, Woodrow W., 308
Walsh, F. Howard, 374, 392, 452, 501
Ward, J. L., 501
Warr, C. Michael, 501
Washburn, A. V., 265
Wasson, Mr. and Mrs. A. L., 295
Wasson, C. M., 501
Watkins, Derrel, 401
Watson, E. L., 501
Watson, W. Marvin, 393
Watterson, Don, 501
Wauford, C. E., 501
Wayland, Francis, 133
Weatherspoon, J. B., 173, 181, 203
Wells, Homer, 121
Wells, Onous J., Jr., 501
West, Doris Norton, 389
West, John, 60
Wester, Brooks H., 512
Western Baptist Theological Institute, 38-39
Westmoreland, E. Hermond, Professorship in Preaching, 380
Wheat, Mrs. J. Z., 215
White, Cecil R., 469, 510
White, David C., 450
White, G. L., 136, 150
White, Joe, 95
White, W. R., 234, 263, 501, 513
Whitefield, George, 26
Whiteside, Russell B., 501
Whitley, L. L. 211
Whitsitt controversy, 87-95, 117-18
Whitsitt, W. H., 81, 87-95
Widemann, Donald, 501
Widick, Clyde R., 501
Wigger, W. M., 501
Wilder, Jack B., 501
Wilkes, Stanley E., 339, 512
Williams, Ben, Fitness Assessment Laboratory, 473
Williams, Charles B., 123,

141, 166, 174-75, 181, 200, 204-6, 210, 214, 236, 511
Williams, H. G., 500
Williams, James D., 400, 459, 460
Williams, Mrs. James D., 517
Williams J. Howard, 329-58, 386, 478
Williams, Roger, 90
Williams Student Village, 345-46, 391-92, 471
Williams, Tallie, xvi
Williams Mrs. W. L. "Mother," 203, 215, 230
Williamson, M. E., 513
Williamson, S. Charles, 335
Wills, Floreid, 353
Wills, Keith C., xvi, 353, 390, 415-16, 469, 510
Wilson, Edwin, 315
Wilson, George W., Jr., 401
Wilson, Grace, xvi, 389
Wilson, Lloyd T., 501
Wingo, Lewis, 510
Winston, J. K., 151, 154, 172, 201, 381, 451
Woman's Advisory Board, 215
Woman's Missionary Training School, Dallas, 138, 157, 201
Woman's Missionary Training School, Fort Worth, 137, 138, 157, 215, 267
Woman's Missionary Union, Southern Baptist Convention, 267
Woman's Missionary Union of Texas, 291
Woodfin, Yandall, 397
Woodfin, Mrs. Yandall, 517
Woods, John E., 335
World Mission/Church Growth Center, 380, 461, 465-67
World War II, 314-15
Worth, General W. J., 152
Wray, J. Campbell, 308, 312, 337
Wright, J. T., 151
Wright, Mrs. Sue, 265

Y
Yarborough, W. Forbes, 265
Young, Doyle L., 457

526

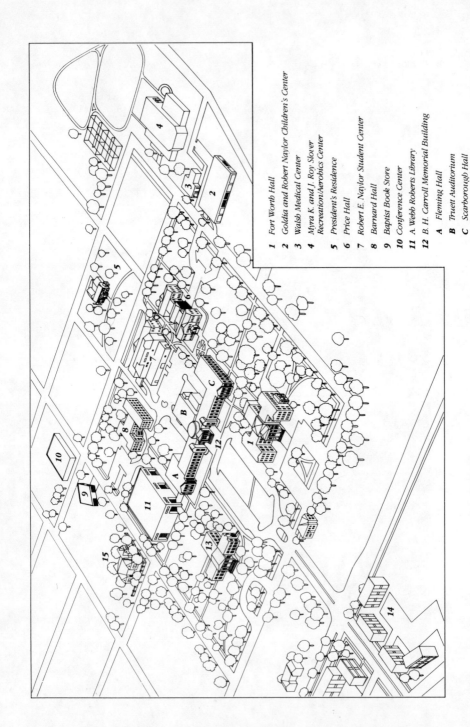

1 Fort Worth Hall
2 Goldia and Robert Naylor Children's Center
3 Walsh Medical Center
4 Myra K. and J. Roy Slover
   Recreation/Aerobics Center
5 President's Residence
6 Price Hall
7 Robert E. Naylor Student Center
8 Barnard Hall
9 Baptist Book Store
10 Conference Center
11 A. Webb Roberts Library
12 B. H. Carroll Memorial Building

A Fleming Hall
B Truett Auditorium
C Scarborough Hall

13 Cowden Hall
14 J. Howard Williams Memorial Student Village
15 Administrative Annex

Campus Guide
Southwestern Baptist Theological Seminary